MASTERWORKS
OF
CHILDREN'S
LITERATURE

MASTERWORKS OF CHILDREN'S LITERATURE

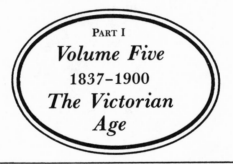

PART I
Volume Five
1837–1900
The Victorian Age

EDITED BY *Robert Lee Wolff*

GENERAL EDITOR: *Jonathan Cott*

THE STONEHILL PUBLISHING COMPANY
IN ASSOCIATION WITH
CHELSEA HOUSE PUBLISHERS
NEW YORK

GENERAL EDITOR: Jonathan Cott
ADVISORY EDITOR: Robert G. Miner, Jr.
VOLUME EDITOR: Robert Lee Wolff
PROJECT DIRECTOR: Esther Mitgang
DESIGNER: Paul Bacon
EDITORIAL STAFF: Joy Johannessen, Philip Minges III, Claire Bottler
PRODUCTION: Coco Dupuy, Heather White, Sandra Su, Susan Lusk,
   Christopher Newton, Carol McDougall

First Printing
Printed and Bound in the United States of America
ISBN: 0-87754-379-8
LC: 79-89986

Chelsea House Publishers
   Harold Steinberg, Chairman and Publisher
   Andrew E. Norman, President
   Susan Lusk, Vice President
A Division of Chelsea House Educational Communications, Inc.
133 Christopher Street, New York, NY 10014

Dedicated to the Memory of
Jeffrey Joshua Steinberg
Founder and President of
Stonehill Communications, Inc.

Contents

Robert Lee Wolff was Coolidge Professor of History at Harvard University at the time of his death in 1980. An avid collector of Victorian fiction, he taught a yearly course on the Victorian novel in addition to his history courses. Among his books are *Strange Stories: Explorations in Victorian Fiction, The Golden Key: A Study of the Fiction of George MacDonald,* and, as editor, numerous anthologies of Victorian literature.

Children's Literature: The Victorian Age

By Robert Lee Wolff

As THE VICTORIAN AGE opened in 1837, the trickle of books written for children swelled into a stream, and before long the stream became a positive torrent. The serious "quarterlies" seldom paid any attention to the subject, but an anonymous reviewer in the *London Review* for January 1860, who devoted a remarkable thirty-page article to children's literature, already fully realized what had happened. Looking over the "formidable and ever-lengthening catalogues of new books," he noted that books "professing" to be for children were "increasing at a higher ratio than any other class of literature," and that children's books commanded "the surest sale." It was a big business in itself, and he only wished that the growth in numbers of books meant that "children were better understood than formerly and that their mental and moral needs had been more accurately gauged." Not so, he maintained; there were all too many books written for children, but "a real child's book" was still a rarity. Much children's literature, he declared bluntly, was inferior stuff, "commonplace anecdotes, and diluted history, and sham science," all temptingly got up in gilt bindings with handsome illustrations.

In making a selection of Victorian literature for these volumes, then—a formidable job in itself—the first huge category to be rejected was simply that of trash. We want only "real" children's books here.

Next to go was the category of books by foreign authors, many of them highly cherished by English children. Grimm's and Andersen's *Fairy Tales* were first made available in the 1820s and 1840s respectively. A surprising number of American books attained great popularity, notably Susan Warner's lachrymose *The Wide, Wide World* (1850) and *Queechy* (1852), both published under the pseudonym "Elizabeth Wetherell," the name of her grandmother. Louisa May Alcott's *Little Women* (1868) and its second portion (published in England in 1869 as *Good Wives*) were sensational successes, outselling all children's books by English authors, and are still as widely read in England as in this country. The instructive "Peter Parley" books, launched by Samuel Goodrich

(1793–1860) in America, sold so well in England that a number of English imitators began to write under his name. And from France and Germany came such favorite books as the fairy stories of Madame de Genlis (1746–1830) and the romances of the Prussian Baron F. H. K. de La Motte-Fouqué (1777–1843), notably *Undine* and *Sintram*. Fredrika Bremer's tales of Swedish life were translated by Mary Howitt (1799–1888) in the 1840s. By then, there were three different translations of Manzoni's *I Promessi Sposi* (1825–1827). Later on, Jules Verne's stories were as popular in England as in America. Yet it seemed essential to limit our choices here to books by British authors.

Victorian English children also read and enjoyed many books not primarily written for them. From the beginning, Sir Walter Scott's Waverley Novels, especially perhaps *Guy Mannering* (1815), had their young devotees. Even in households that frowned on novel-reading, Scott was often an exception. As late as 1898, when a London newspaper, *The Pall Mall Gazette*, invited young readers to name their favorite books, one precocious little girl named *all* the Waverly Novels as a group. Children read Bulwer-Lytton's *Last Days of Pompeii* (1834) and his other historical novels, as well as his occult romances. They read Harrison Ainsworth's historical tales, among them *The Tower of London* (1840) and *Old St. Paul's* (1841). They read Thackeray's *Esmond* (1852), much of Dickens, the adult writings of Charles Kingsley (1819–1875), such as *Westward Ho!* (1855), as well as his other books written primarily for children. Similarly with Captain Frederick Marryat (1792–1848): children read his rollicking and faintly Rabelaisian sea stories for adults, such as *Peter Simple* (1834) and *Mr. Midshipman Easy* (1836), as eagerly as the stories he wrote directly for them: *Masterman Ready* (1841–1842), *The Settlers in Canada* (1844), and *The Children of the New Forest* (1847).

By the eighties, with the early writings of Robert Louis Stevenson (1850–1894) and H. Rider Haggard (1856–1925), stories for adults and those for young people had often become almost indistinguishable. While *Treasure Island* (1883) and *The Black Arrow* (1888) were surely books for boys, boys read the adult *Master of Ballantrae* (1889) just as eagerly. Were *King Solomon's Mines* (1885) and *She* (1887) books for grown-ups? Yes and no. And with Conan Doyle (1859–1930) soon afterwards, the same question arises: how about the Sherlock Holmes stories or his historical novels, like *Micah Clarke* (1889) and *The White Company* (1891)? Is Kipling's *Kim* (1901) a children's book? It has certainly puzzled several generations of children. So there were two additional large categories for elimination: adult books that children adopted, and books written without regard to the age of their potential readers.

These sweeping decisions, though perhaps arbitrary, seemed reasonable. But they only began to clear the decks. They helped establish categories for rejection, but how about categories for inclusion? What should an anthology of this kind attempt to do? It would, of course, be possible to select on the basis of past and present popularity. Old favorites would delight most readers: *Tom Brown's School Days* (1857), the *Alice* books (1865, 1871), *Just-So Stories* (1902, only one year post-Victorian), and others equally beloved and familiar. But obviously, any selection made wholly on such grounds would be *too* familiar: many readers would have already read all the books; most readers would have read most of them. There might be little new to say about sacred texts like these; or, perhaps better, little new to say that would be acceptable. For addicts (whose minds with respect to their cherished childhood reading would quite properly be made up), further commentary would be an intrusion. And such books are easily available elsewhere.

Yet old favorites could not be automatically thrown out. There should be an occasional favorite, but not too many, and it should suggest some comments that would enable a reader to see it in a fresh light, against the social and intellectual background of its author and of its initial public, as part of the age that gave it birth. It would not be enough for the reader merely to appreciate it all over again and indulge his nostalgia, all too commonly the only force at work among readers of Victorian children's books.

Certain positive criteria for inclusion having manifested themselves, it was time to think once again in terms of subject matter. Like books for adults, children's books can be divided into fiction and non-fiction, and it became obvious at once that non-fiction had no place in these pages. History, geography, mathematics, and science were often taught to children through books fictionalized to make such subjects palatable. They would be a highly interesting special field for students of psychology, education, and religion; yet even the best of such educational books seldom reached the level of literature. So there will be no *Parables from Nature* or *Stories from Roman History* here. That leaves fiction. And children's fiction subdivides itself at once into stories of real life and fantastic stories, although certain books combine, often quite remarkably, features of both. Here, then, was our first positive decision. These two divisions have been retained for Volumes 5 (in two parts) and 6.

II

Stories of real life include, of course, stories of the past. And, once Scott had blazed the trail and made the novel respectable, historical tales written specifically for children proliferated almost from the very beginning of the age. That remarkable bluestocking Harriet Martineau (1802–1876), who in the 1830s explained to a huge adult public the laws of "political economy" in a series of brilliant little fictional "Illustrations" propounding the iron doctrines of Malthus and the laissez-faire economists, published in 1841 four small square volumes for children collectively called *The Playfellow*. The first two were historical: *Settlers at Home*, set in the novelist's favorite period of the English Civil War, and full of exciting details of fenland adventure during floodtime; and *The Peasant and the Prince*, in which Martineau (simultaneously anti-Royalist and anti-Revolutionary) passed on her principles to her young readers in two linked stories of the French Revolution. Charlotte M. Yonge (1823–1901) ranged widely over past centuries, from eleventh-century Normandy in *The Little Duke* (1854) to the St. Bartholomew's-day massacre in Paris in 1572 (*The Chaplet of Pearls*, 1868) to the (imaginary) daughter of Mary, Queen of Scots (*Unknown to History*, 1882).

Yonge wrote a mere thirty-odd historical stories among her more than one hundred fifty books, but George Alfred Henty (1832–1902) wrote more than eighty, all for boys. Having served in the Crimea in the fifties, and having covered campaigns as a war correspondent in Austria, Ethiopia, Italy, France, Spain, West Africa, and the Balkans, Henty began his extraordinarily influential career as a full-time author of boys' books only in the early eighties. From then on, he never looked back, turning out three or four books a year, of uniformly high interest, until the end of his life. Henty wrote about ancient Egypt (*The Cat of Bubastes*, 1888) and about the Boer War (*With Roberts to Pretoria*, 1902), and he also wrote about almost everything that had happened in between. Most of his stories concerned the adventures of an English boy in some historic struggle: from the early Britons through the Saxons and Danes to the Normans and the wars of the barons, all the way down to the Boxer Rebellion. Often the hero went overseas—to Italy, to Russia, to "Greek Waters," to Africa, to India, to Burma, to Malaysia, to America for the Revolution, for the Civil War, for adventures in the Rockies. Each time, Henty "boned up" conscientiously on the best available account of the place and period; and each time, addressing "My dear Lads" in his preface, he told his readers where to go for more information. The English principles of fair play always triumphed. Apart from their backgrounds, one must concede, the stories are much alike. The young hero is always unbelievably stainless, and always returns to marry his childhood sweetheart. For a Henty buff, however, Henty has an integrity and a splendor all his own. If it had been possible to reproduce one of his books here, it would have been *The Lion of the North*, all about the Thirty Years' War and Gustavus Adolphus. But Henty and all other historical fiction had to go. However vivid such a Victorian historical novel may be, and however dear it remains to its admirers, essentially it reflects characteristic Victorian attitudes (toward pagans, toward Catholics, toward Frenchmen, toward women) only indirectly, from behind a historical screen. Better to remove the screen and study the attitudes directly.

Similarly with the entire category of adventure stories for boys, another large subbranch of stories of real life. Here too, it hurts to leave out some famous and delightful books, many of them "pretty books with plenty of killing," of the kind that Charlotte Yonge wholeheartedly recommended for boys. The Victorians expected boys to be rowdy at suitable times and to take strong vicarious interest in the rowdiness of their fictional counterparts. Captain Mayne Reid, R. M. Ballantyne, W. H. G. Kingston, and George Manville Fenn, four of the most assiduous and distinguished writers in this field, were all omitted with regret.

Thomas Mayne Reid (1818–1883; he never used the first name), of Irish Presbyterian stock, went off to New Orleans in 1840 and moved from job to job in the Deep South and Southwest, trading with the Indians, and fighting in the Mexican War as an officer in the U.S. Army while covering the campaigns for several newspapers. Wounded, he retired with the rank of captain and returned to England to raise volunteers for the Hungarian Revolution of 1848 against the Hapsburg Empire. But the Magyar cause collapsed before Mayne Reid could get his forces organized. His first two books, *The Rifle Rangers* (1850) and *The Scalp Hunters* (1851), both Mexican stories written for adults, won him a juvenile audience he never lost, even when he was not writing specifically for them. When he was, his stories took his readers to the Wild West (*The Boy Hunters*, 1852) or Canada (*The Young Voyageurs*, 1853) or Peru (*The Forest Exiles*, 1854) or South Africa (*The Bush Boys*, 1856) or the Himalayas (*The Cliff Climbers*, 1865), and often back to Mexico or Texas. Efforts to launch boys' periodicals both in England and in New York failed, and Reid died in London, having written more than seventy books. Rapid-moving and careless, as he himself recognized, and steeped in blood, they reflected his own impatient and active spirit. His wife, who married him in 1855 when she was only fifteen, adored him. He wrote a novel called *The Child Wife* (1868), and she wrote his biography after his death. Perhaps *The Headless Horseman: A Strange Tale of Texas* (1866) would have been the best choice to republish here, if there had been an opportunity, but perhaps Reid is best left to the antiquarians and those few survivors who once read him as children.

Ballantyne (1825–1894) and Kingston (1814–1880) were paired by Stevenson in the prefatory verses to *Treasure Island*, which he wrote in affectionate memory of their books: if *they* still had the power to charm boys, he felt, his own characters would thrive; if not, his efforts were doomed to failure. Of course, Long John Silver, Pew, Ben Gunn, Jim Hawkins, and the rest have lived longer than any personages created by the two men Stevenson invoked. But he was an excellent judge of boys' books, and Ballantyne and Kingston do not deserve oblivion.

Like Mayne Reid, Ballantyne began his career with books based on his own experiences: he had spent six years in the service of the Hudson's Bay Company as a fur trader. *Snow-Flakes and Sunbeams* (1856) and *Ungava* (1857) were both set in the frozen north. He followed them with his most famous book, *The Coral Island* (1858), a "Robinsonade" after the well-tried formula of *Robinson Crusoe* and, like *The Swiss Family Robinson*, involving children. But the three boys in *The Coral Island* had neither grown-up direction nor a wreck to return to for seemingly endless supplies: alone with an axe and a telescope—and Christian piety of Ballantyne's own Presbyterian variety—they faced starvation and solitude. In *The Coral Island* Ballantyne made a trivial but famous slip about a cocoanut and decided thereafter to do his own research before writing each book. This resolution took him to a lifeboat and a lighthouse, to temporary jobs on fire engines and railway trains, to the tin mines of Cornwall, to Brazil, to Iceland, as he cranked out more than eighty books. *The Coral Island*, despite its inadequate cocoanut, would be the obvious choice for revival.

Kingston began his professional life as a wine merchant in Portugal. He wrote novels for adults, including one about Pombal, the eighteenth-century Portuguese premier and enlightened despot. He launched his long career as a boys' author with *Peter the Whaler* (1851). Eventually Kingston turned out more than a hundred books. Four of the most popular, appearing at intervals in later years, told the linked stories of three friends who rose in the Royal Navy from midshipmen to admirals. Like Ballantyne, Kingston edited magazines for boys. George Manville Fenn (1831–1909), friend and biographer of Henty, was the most prolific of all. Few libraries—not even that of the British Museum— offer the leisured specialist a chance to read all his books. *Bunyip Land*, an Australian yarn, would be a characteristically readable choice. Still, it would be a finely tuned instrument that could tell a randomly chosen work of any of these three writers from a similarly chosen work of any other. Perhaps this salute to their memory may compensate for the failure to select one or more of their books for inclusion here.

III

Once historical tales and tales of adventure abroad had been eliminated, there remained the true core of Victorian children's fiction of real life: the stories of home and school. Whereas adventure stories were written mostly for boys, these were often written for both sexes impartially. Stripped of the glamor provided by alien settings such as ancient Carthage, a medieval tournament, the Russian steppes, or a tropical forest, the story of homelife, to be successful, had to appeal to parent and child by truly reflecting the life they knew: the life of the nursery, the lessons in the schoolroom, the domestic fireside, religious observance, the holiday by the seaside, the picnic on a grand excursion to see a ruined abbey, the changing of the seasons, the delights of Christmas, the contact with the poor in the rural cottage or the city slum, the affection for dogs and horses, the dramatic changes of fortune that came if papa suddenly proved to be the heir to the peerage and the great house or if he suddenly lost his money and the family had to adjust to poverty, the terrors and tragedy of a death in the family—and, above all, the *meaning* of all these experiences for growing up, for acceptance of what seemed like cruel blows, for due recognition of a child's relationship to God and God's universe.

What was it like for the eighteen-year-old daughter of a good family to find herself reduced to the role of governess in somebody else's household? What should one do if a ragged child asked for alms? What did it mean when one's beloved little brother died in agony after a lingering illness? And why did one family forbid its children to play on Sunday and another family encourage it—after church, of course? How should one spend one's savings, and what should one do with a gold piece given by a kind uncle? These and countless other aspects of daily existence in all social stations and in all corners of England and Scotland and Ireland, in castle and in hovel, at all ages from babyhood to adulthood, were the very stuff and substance of daily life, and of the children's fiction of daily life.

Similarly, the tale of life at school reflected experiences only a little less universal than the tale of life at home, except that life at school away from home was, in the earlier period at least, almost exclusively restricted to boys. The delighted anticipation or the fearful apprehension at leaving home, the encounter with bullying, with kind or unkind, gentle or brutal schoolmasters, the indoctrination in the eternal system of schoolboy ethics, the temptations to be lazy, to cheat, to smoke, to drink, to indulge in "worse evil," the shock of combat on the rugger field, the leisurely glories of a cricket match, the unattainable majesty shrouding the upper forms and the leaders of the school, the dreadful malaise of homesickness, the first real friendships: all this in the pages of a myriad of children's books reflected the truths of every day with greater or less skill and veracity. The stories appealed almost as much to the sisters left at home as to the brothers privileged—or condemned—to enjoy life at school in person.

In the stories of life at home and life at school, then, the modern reader will find himself—as in no other form of literature for children—brought face to face with Victorian codes of behavior. Here is the mirror to be held up to the society. If one understands what one sees in it, one has the clues that make it possible to understand not only the reasons for the success enjoyed by the best Victorian children's books but the nature of the Victorian world itself. But the reflections in the mirror are not always easy to read.

Apparently so near to us in time, the Victorians are often light-years away in attitudes. Writing for their own children, they did not need to spell out such matters in detail. A Victorian child brought up in an Evangelical household did not need to have the doctrines of regeneration or justification by faith or even imputed righteousness ex-plained to him: they were the stuff of every day. A modern reader, for example, will often miss the point—sometimes even the main point—of a Victorian children's story if he fails to note or cannot understand the apparently casual conversations about religion in its pages. In fact, he may make the mistake of skipping them. To most of us, Christian piety is Christian piety, and we fail to draw the distinctions between its nineteenth-century English varieties, absolutely fundamental to the understanding of an age of fierce religious contention and warring sects. It is fun to read the books written for the children of such an age: but it requires work to understand them.

That is why each of the stories in these volumes is provided with its own editor's headnote, which attempts to place the book in the life of its author and in its own social framework, and to single out for comment any points that might otherwise be missed. Although it seemed best to call these commentaries headnotes, they can of course be read *after* the book in question. Each one indicates reasonably fully the reasons why the book was chosen for inclusion here. The selections in Volumes 5 and 6 are arranged chronologically, in order to show more easily some of the changes in attitudes that marked the advancing decades of the Victorian age. The headnotes to the later selections often refer to matters mentioned in the headnotes to the earlier ones, and it is assumed that the reader will read the volumes consecutively.

IV

Inevitably, some splendid books had to be omitted. Of the four tales in Harriet Martineau's *Playfellow* (1841), the two historical ones had already been eliminated: the third, *Feats on the Fiord*, since it is set in Norway and owes its undoubted charm largely to its exoticism, also had to go. But it was a temptation to include the fourth, *The Crofton Boys*, a very early tale of Victorian schoolboy life. At Crofton, Hugh Proctor discovers the injustices against which there is no use complaining. He learns so thoroughly the lesson that one does not tell on a fellow schoolmate, that when his leg has to be amputated as the result of a roughhouse, he wins eternal respect by never revealing the name of the boy who was responsible. Yet Hugh is no superman in his self-denial. Like any boy, he feels bitterly the anguish of having to give up his active life.

The Crofton Boys gains in power from its very simplicity. Unlike so many of her contemporaries, Harriet Martineau was no Evangelical; when she wrote the book, she was still a Unitarian, although she later became a notable agnostic, and so the story lacks much of the religiosity that often seems forced to modern readers. But, though highly popular and often reprinted, it never reached the enormous public of two somewhat later schoolboy stories, *Tom Brown's School Days* (1857) and *Eric; or, Little by Little* (1858), which form so notable a contrast to one another. These two provided an irresistible opportunity for a comparison of their educational and religious ideas. Since neither of them could be omitted, there was, unfortunately, no room for *The Crofton Boys*.

Other stories of real life that might have been selected, and that other editors might have preferred, would surely include *The Steadfast Gabriel* (1848), probably the best children's story by the prolific Mary Howitt (1799–1888), the energetic Quaker woman who translated so many of Hans Christian Andersen's *Fairy Tales* from the Danish for the first time, as well as Fredrika Bremer's Swedish domestic stories. The fact that *The Steadfast Gabriel* is set in a remote part of rural England at the turn of the seventeenth century does not prevent it from portraying in simple, dramatic, and moving fashion the lasting ideals—shown through three generations—of the true English yeomanry: loyalty, hard work, courage, love of animals, and simple decency. Almost forgotten today, *The Steadfast Gabriel* should be rediscovered.

Elizabeth Missing Sewell (1815–1906), a devout High Church Anglican spinster, wrote a series of remarkable books mostly intended for, and mostly read by, older girls, of which *Margaret Percival* (1847), with its warning against the dangerous attractions of Catholicism, and *The Experience of Life* (1852), with its deep psychological insight into the tensions of predestined spinsterhood, would have been excellent choices. Jean Ingelow (1820–1897), the popular poetess who was nominated unsuccessfully for the laureateship at Tennyson's death, wrote some remarkable long short stories for children, originally published in *A Sister's Bye-Hours* (1868) and *Studies for Stories* (1870). But these had to yield to the superior claims of Harriet Mozley and Charlotte Yonge.

Mrs. Molesworth, a favorite of a notable modern authority on Victorian children's books, Roger Lancelyn Green, who wrote her biography in 1961, narrowly missed inclusion either with *Carrots* (1876, under the pen name "Ennis Graham") or with Mr. Green's own favorite, *The Carved Lions* (1895), in which it is a young girl who experiences the unhappiness of boarding school and separation from parents. Yet, however typical Mrs. Molesworth may be, her dozens and dozens of children's stories, *pace* Mr. Green, seem to lack any special quality that distinguishes them sufficiently to warrant their inclusion here. In any case the availability of Mr. Green's study renders it unnecessary to "revive" her again. And *The Carved Lions* includes one dream episode in which two carved lions in a shop take the unhappy child to South America to see her mother, a journey that takes the book out of the real-life category and puts it into that of fantasy, where many readers may believe that Mrs. Molesworth after all did her best work.

Objections of many sorts might be raised to Frances Hodgson Burnett's *Little Lord Fauntleroy* (1886): chiefly, perhaps, its overpowering sentimentality and the clear superiority of her *Secret Garden* (1911), whose late date puts it far beyond the Victorian period. Florence Montgomery's *Misunderstood* (1869), often regarded as a children's book, was in fact written to warn adults against misunderstanding children, and the lesson was laid on with a trowel. Children's deathbeds and the sentimental must not be overlooked, and will be found among the selections here included. In the high Victorian age they served a social and an educational purpose, while in the work of Florence Montgomery and her followers they degenerated into mere goo: tears for tears' sake we repudiate. So, on balance, the present selection, if necessarily a personal one, is at least explicable and defensible.

V

Children's stories of real life at home and at school have almost as many varieties as the English household itself, but no critic held them objectionable as such for children's reading. Fairy stories and tales of fantasy, on the other hand, were the subject of a long-standing debate, and many Victorians thought that they should be altogether banned. In the first place, such stories were manifestly *untrue* and would make their young readers insensitive to the difference between what was true and what was not—and therefore, perhaps, prone to tell lies, a major sin to the whole of the nineteenth century. Secondly, fantasy was a waste of time when the young might be so much better engaged in learning the facts of some subject or other. And thirdly, one could not introduce Christian principles into fairy tales as motives of action, and this rendered them useless. Not all opponents of fantasy based their opposition on all three grounds or on all three equally, but for these and other reasons there was a strong undercurrent of disapproval.

The debate was old before the Victorian age had begun. Coleridge in *Biographia Literaria* (1817) declared that his own childhood reading of fairy tales had "habituated" him "to the vast," instead of limiting him to the things he could test by his senses. He knew, he said, all the arguments against "romances and stories of giants, magicians, and genii," but he insisted that the arguments were wrong:

> I know of no other way of giving the mind a love of the great and the *whole*. Those who have been led to the same truths, step by step, by the constant testimony of their senses, seem to want a sense which I possess. They contemplate nothing but parts, and all parts are necessarily little, and the universe to them is but a mass of little things.

Perhaps fairy tales might make children credulous and even superstitious. But it was a better form of credulity than that induced in the practical man, the experimentalist, who trusted his senses alone. The debate continued, however, and a writer in 1831 declared that "the days of *Jack the Giant-Killer, Little Red Riding-Hood*, and such trashy productions are gone by, and the infant mind is now nourished by more able and efficient food." But of course, it was not so. Grimm, in Edgar Taylor's translation and with Cruikshank's illustrations, came to English children in the 1820s; and in the late 1830s English writers began to experiment with their own tales of fantasy.

It is interesting to note, however, that long after these excellent homegrown products had begun to appear, the issue lingered. The same reviewer in the *London Review* for January 1860 whom we found deploring the prevalence of shoddy children's books also warmly espoused Coleridge's position and came out vigorously for the fairy tale. It was the poetry of childhood, he argued, filling children "with images of nobleness and beauty." Or, when it did not, as when it disgusted them with the cruelty of Bluebeard or the greed of an ogre, it was still better than a story of real life about cruelty, which would make children congratulate themselves for being so much better than the cruel person in the story. The very remoteness of the personages of a fairy tale made it more effective as the teacher of such a lesson. Citing Dickens's *Hard Times*, and agreeing with his attack on an educational system in which all wonder at the universe and all imagination had been eliminated and pure fact substituted, the reviewer emphasized that "childhood is the time of enjoyment." The purpose of books should be "to make the little ones *happy*. . . . Let us respect the happiness of children; let us acquiesce without grumbling in the decision of a child who prefers *Jack and the Bean Stalk* or the *Ugly Duck* to a book on the properties of matter or the classification of animals."

Of the two examples he cited, *Jack and the Bean Stalk* is what the German folklorists and critics of the late eighteenth century called a *Volksmärchen*, a "folk fairy tale," going far back in time, and passed on from generation to generation by word of mouth long before the first scholar heard it, recorded it, and published it. *The Ugly Duck*, a story by Hans Andersen, is, on the other hand, what the same Germans christened a *Kunstmärchen*, literally an "art fairy tale," invented and written by a single author in modern times. Grimm, of course, was a collector and publisher of *Volksmärchen*; Andersen, like Goethe, Novalis, E. T. A. Hoffmann, and a great many other Germans before him, was a writer of *Kunstmärchen*. Despite the wide popularity of folk fairy tales in Victorian England, this book will include none. We deal only with *Kunstmärchen*, and only with those by English authors.

Since English authors about 1840 had begun to write and publish fairy tales of their own and children were enjoying them, it is obvious that opponents of the fairy tale had lost the battle. Nonetheless, in a strange way they had won the war. Modern students of Victorian children's literature repeatedly proclaim that a given *Kunstmärchen*—such as the "Nonsensical Story about Giants and Fairies" in Catherine Sinclair's *Holiday House* (1839) or Frances Browne's *Granny's Wonderful Chair* (1857)—was *not* written to point a moral. But, we submit, such modern students are wrong. These stories, both of which are reproduced in these volumes, emphatically *do* point a moral. This issue is discussed in the headnote to each, while the proof lies ready to hand. Similarly each of the home-grown English fairy tales here reproduced, except for Thackeray's *Rose and the Ring* (1855), has its moral. If one reexamines now the words of the 1860 reviewer, ostensibly championing the fairy tale, one finds him using the moral argument himself. When he argued that a fairy tale *taught lessons* better than a tale of real life because of its very remoteness from real life, he gave his show away at least in part. Because the fairy tale was the subject of so much controversy, it seemed well to include with the fiction two brief critical statements on the subject, one by Dickens and the other by Ruskin. Each is republished in its chronological place.

VI

Like the tale of everyday life, the Victorian children's tale of fantasy can be divided into several categories. Perhaps enough has already been said here about the *Kunstmärchen*. And much—perhaps even too much—has been said by others about pure fantasy, verging on nonsense. For success, this kind of fantasy requires the controlled gifts of a Lewis Carroll, together with some overall general theme—a game of cards, a game of chess—to give its disparate elements underlying unity. The many imitators of *Alice* often allowed their wild imaginations to surge out of control. Their productions can have amused few except themselves when they were published, and can amuse nobody now. One such imitation of *Alice*, Henry Kingsley's *Boy in Grey* (1871), is included here, partly as a demonstration of the way in which fantasy can go astray, partly because it is nonetheless a very interesting document by a very interesting author. Included for very different reasons is George MacDonald's *At the Back of the North Wind* (1871). Dream narratives emerge naturally from the tale of fantasy and, in the hands of a genius like MacDonald, become successful allegory as well, seeming to conceal a new layer of mystery and implied meaning beneath each such layer that yields to examination and permits decipherment.

Many notable examples of these popular genres of fantasy had to be omitted. Francis Edward Paget, writing as "William Churne of Staffordshire," published in 1845 his *Hope of the Katzekopfs; or, The Sorrows of Selfishness*, an early *Kunstmärchen*, following those of Catherine Sinclair and Ruskin, and preceding that of Mark Lemon, all included here. A vigorous propagandist in fiction for young and old of the High Church (Tractarian) position in the contemporary passionate debates over religion, Paget was writing a far more moral tale than either Ruskin or Lemon, as may be inferred from his subtitle. Still close to the Germans, like the other two, he set his scene in Germany and gave some of his characters German names that revealed their characteristics and their problems. So the prince is called *Eigenwillig*, literally "Self-willed" or "Selfish," and one of his three instructors in curbing this natural tendency is the imp *Selbst* ("Self"), while another is the elderly sage named, in English, "Discipline." Almost as heavy-handed as Catherine Sinclair and lacking her importance as a pioneer, Paget, unlike Ruskin and Lemon, allowed his didacticism to get in the way of his fairy story. The author of the *London Review* article of 1860—already praised so often—warned that writers for children were "apt to think it the highest triumph of art" if they could lead up to a moral, but they failed to realize that "the child seldom or never receives the moral at all in the form in which it is given." It must be "latent, or held in solution" before it will sink in *with the story*, and may later "unconsciously" influence the child's conduct. Most of the best Victorian writers of children's literature failed to grasp this point fully. But apparently it never occurred at all to the Reverend Francis Paget.

Among the allegorical tales that might have been included here, Norman MacLeod's *The Gold Thread* (1861) is a good example. Virtually forgotten now, it remains a simple, rather endearing story of a young prince, lost in the forest, who wins through to safety by keeping fast hold of a mysterious magic thread. Safety is his father's house—i.e., heaven—and the thread is clearly faith or obedience to the divine command. A pious Scot, MacLeod was Presbyterian chaplain to the Queen, and editor of *Good Words*, a popular magazine of the sixties. Its children's subsidiary was *Good Words for the Young*, which George MacDonald edited for a time, and in which he first published both *At the Back of the North Wind* and *The Princess and the Goblin*. Of course he knew MacLeod and *The Gold Thread*, and he quietly appropriated the idea of the thread that leads a child out of danger, and made it an unforgettable part of his "Princess" books. So the chief interest of MacLeod's *Gold Thread* remains the contribution it made to the writing of a far greater man.

Charles Kingsley's *Water-Babies; A Fairy Tale for a Land Baby* (1863) is one of the most important Victorian children's books. Kingsley (1819–1875), a major figure in the religious, literary, and intellectual worlds (he is discussed briefly in the headnote to *Tom Brown's School Days*), seethed with a mass of strong and sometimes contradictory opinions. Repudiating the stern doctrines of eternal damnation held by the Low Church, Evangelical wing of the Church of England, he was equally hostile to anything that smacked of Catholicism—notably clerical celibacy or the confessional—characteristic of the High Church wing. A dedicated naturalist, he was particularly interested in the study of marine biology, then carried on by enthusiasts in the tidal pools around the English coasts, and wrote a book for children about it, *Glaucus; or, the Wonders of the Shore* (1855). He was a parson and a stern moralist, himself haunted by feelings of guilt, and he deeply sympathized with the socially oppressed classes of both the countryside and the city in early Victorian England.

The Water-Babies reflects most of these characteristic views. Written for his five-year-old son, Grenville, it tells the allegorical story of a chimney sweep, Tom, a member of one of the most wretchedly underpaid classes of child worker, the only human beings small enough to go up chimney flues, who often fell victim to cancer of the genitals induced by repeated exposure to the accumulations of soot. Dirty, of course (and Kingsley had an almost pathological horror of dirt), Tom leaves behind the hopeless wretchedness of his life on land by shedding his blackened body and taking to the sea, becoming literally a "water-baby." Kingsley used the transformation to teach his young readers a good deal about his favorite marvels of the deep, all with deep overtones of piety. Much of this is still charming and often movingly written.

But the eternal moralizing of Mrs. Bedonebyasyoudid—who is in charge of Tom's education, and who punishes her victims on strict Old Testament principles—can hardly have edified young Grenville Kingsley or the other Victorian children who read *Water-Babies*. Her behavior and the ideals it represents are now chiefly of interest to Freudian students of Kingsley himself. Rarely does the modern reader get a clearer view of obsessions unconsciously revealed, of cruel urges satisfied on the printed page. At least the punishment always fits the crime, although it is sometimes disgusting. Mr. Grimes, the employer of chimney sweeps, must himself suffer imprisonment in a flue. Ghastly medicines are poured down the throats of incompetent doctors. In its view of education, *Water-Babies* reveals Kingsley's dislike of intellectuals: children who study systematically become all brains, mere vegetables who have never learned how to stretch their muscles in proper boyhood and manhood pursuits, such as sports and games. Kingsley's friend Thomas Hughes made this point abundantly in *Tom Brown*, where readers of these volumes will find it. For us, *Water-Babies* is redundant.

All of *Water-Babies* is an allegory of the spiritual preparation of Tom's soul for salvation, including that staple element in allegorical fantasy, an imaginary voyage. By his shedding of his chimney sweep's body at the very beginning of the story, Tom may be said to have died; and all his subsequent adventures are a sort of *post mortem* preparation for heaven. Though it is unquestionably a major Victorian document, and long popular with children, *The Water-Babies* today is difficult to read, even for the Victorian addict. In 1869, Charlotte Yonge, who loved it, finding it "more attractive than even the exquisite bits of fun in 'Alice,' " admitted that its "latent" meanings were "not always consistent." Today, alas, it seems a muddle. If its young readers got from it what Kingsley hoped they would get, then we (and the reviewer of 1860) are wrong about children's literature.

VII

Two of the editor's own childhood favorites—both still well known, and admired by students of the subject—proved when reexamined to be disappointments. The first— *The Little Lame Prince and His Travelling Cloak: A Parable for Young and Old* (1874–1875) by Dinah Maria Mulock (1826–1887), who became Mrs. Craik in 1865 when she married a successful publisher—as indicated by its subtitle, is an allegory designed to teach a lesson. The lame prince, Dolor (the name itself means "pain"), learns to overcome anguish, loneliness, and injustice by courage and by the development of his own intellectual and spiritual resources. The magic cloak that the good fairy gives him, and that takes him on enchanted journeys, may be made to stand for faith or for the imagination or even for the willingness to divert one's mind through books or pictures. As in most good allegories, the meaning can be debated. Dolor is comparable with George MacDonald's Diamond in *At the Back of the North Wind*, reprinted here; but Mulock's invention seems far more feeble, her message much more simple. Her *Adventures of a Brownie* (1871–1872), a less pretentious effort, in which a brownie plays delightful pranks on a family of children, now seems better than *The Little Lame Prince*. But to read Mulock at her very best, the modern reader will turn to her novel for adults, still famous, *John Halifax, Gentleman* (1856).

Mrs. Molesworth's *The Cuckoo Clock* (1877, as "Ennis Graham") remains in the mind because of its delightful initial scene, in which a little girl—in her dreams, of course—enters the door of a cuckoo clock and finds herself in the cuckoo's snug red-velvet-upholstered sitting room. But the promise held out by this enchanting idea is not entirely fulfilled, and some of the little girl's subsequent journeyings with the cuckoo now seem flat and sentimental. Other editors would surely have included, and would have made an excellent defense for, Jean Ingelow's *Mopsa the Fairy* (1869) or Dickens's own late fairy story "The Magic Fishbone" (1868).

One type of story notably absent from this collection—largely by accident—is the story with disagreeable, horrifying, or pathologically nasty elements. In the headnote to *At the Back of the North Wind*, there is a brief reference to this aspect of MacDonald's *Princess and Curdie*; but it should be emphasized here how often Victorian authors, perhaps subconsciously, included it. E. H. Knatchbull-Hugessen (1829–1893) in "The Pig-Faced Ladies," for example (printed in the collection *Queer Folk*, 1874), vented his hatred for feminism and perhaps his fear of it by imagining a country ruled by trousered women with porcine faces, who were brutal to men and ate from gold and silver troughs. Lucy Clifford (d. 1929), a charming and literate woman, early left a widow by the brilliantly original mathematician W. K. Clifford, wrote in order to support her two beloved daughters. In "The New Mother" (in *Anyhow Stories*, 1882) she produced a tale full of true brutality. Through no fault of their own, two little girls are deprived of their real mother and given a grotesquely frightening and horrible substitute. Even more astonishing, one of the two children is nicknamed "Turkey," which was the pet name for Mrs. Clifford's own elder daughter. Only if one supposes that this sophisticated woman of the world, friend of Henry James, and center of a circle of admiring friends, somehow found relief in imagining what it might be like if she—like their father—were taken away from her children, can one even begin to find an explanation for the thorough nastiness of the story. Our selection of stories of fantasy ends even earlier in the Victorian period than that of stories of real life, in part because these two stories of the seventies and eighties have been omitted.

Though much admired, the original fairy tales of Andrew Lang, appearing in the late eighties and nineties, count for less in the history of children's literature than the *Volksmärchen* he assiduously collected in the many volumes of different-colored *Fairy-Books* he published. His own *Kunstmärchen—Prince Prigio* (1889), *Prince Ricardo of Pantouflia* (1893), and others—are admiring and conscientious but feeble imitations of Thackeray's *Rose and the Ring*. (Lang's *The Princess Nobody*, after the fairyland illustrations of Richard Doyle, is reprinted in Volume 7, *Victorian Color Picture Books*.)

It seems astonishing, when one examines the table of contents of Volumes 5 and 6—selected, the editor stoutly maintains, with real rigor and all attention to literary quality—that of the nine authors whose stories of real life appear in Volume 5, Parts I and II, only two are men, while of the eight authors whose stories of fantasy (or comments upon them) appear in Volume 6, only one is a woman. Were women really so much better at stories of real life, and men at stories of the imagination? And why, of the nine authors in Volume 5, are Thomas Hughes and Charlotte Yonge the most eminent, while Dickens, Thackeray, Ruskin (twice), and George MacDonald all appear in Volume 6? Had *Alice* and *Water-Babies* been included, the distortion would have been even more pronounced. I can think of no explanation for these phenomena.

Holiday House

A Series of Tales

By CATHERINE SINCLAIR

HOLIDAY HOUSE:

A SERIES OF TALES.

BY

CATHERINE SINCLAIR,

AUTHORESS OF "MODERN ACCOMPLISHMENTS," "MODERN SOCIETY,"
"CHARLIE SEYMOUR," "HILL AND VALLEY," ETC. ETC.

"Young heads are giddy, and young hearts are warm,
And make mistakes for manhood to reform."—Cowper.

NEW YORK:
ROBERT CARTER & BROTHERS,
No. 530 BROADWAY.
1864.

S IR JOHN SINCLAIR, Baronet, of Edinburgh, and Lady Sinclair had "thirty-six feet of daughters": six girls, each of whom grew to be six feet tall. The fourth, Catherine (1800–1864), at the age of fourteen became secretary to her father, an active politician who was the first president of the Board of Agriculture, and served him until his death in 1835, Sir John's biographer in the *Dictionary of National Biography* describes him as humorless and of "unbounded conceit"; so probably his daughter's task was sometimes a trying one. As soon as it was ended, she became a successful novelist: *Modern Accomplishments; or, the March of Intellect* (1836) and its sequel, *Modern Society* (1837), sold well. The most notorious of her novels for adults, however, was surely *Beatrice; or, The Unknown Relatives* (1852), a virulently anti-Catholic tale complete with a money-grubbing, slinking Jesuit who conspires to establish Roman idolatry and submission to the Pope in proper Protestant Britain. Catherine Sinclair was also a philanthropist who provided her native Edinburgh with public drinking fountains and benches. She died a spinster and would be virtually forgotten today had she not published in 1839 a book that by common consent is a landmark in the history of children's literature: *Holiday House*.

Her inspiration, she tells us, came from a remark made to her many years earlier by Sir Walter Scott, who had deplored the prevailing fashion among writers for children of setting down "a mere dry record of facts," ignoring the imaginative. If this were to go on, the great man had lamented, there would be no poets, wits, or orators in the next generation. So Catherine Sinclair wrote *Holiday House* to portray "that species of noisy, frolicsome, mischievous children, which is now almost extinct, [and] to preserve a sort of fabulous remembrance of days long past, when young people were like wild horses on the prairies, rather than like well-broken hacks on the road." All later students of children's literature have duly noticed these words but have perhaps not fully grasped their meaning.

For, although *Holiday House* is a Victorian book—indeed, the first notable Victorian children's book—the children in it are not Victorian children. They were drawn as "a fabulous remembrance of days long past." And the chapter of *Holiday House* entitled "The Illumination" provides precise evidence: here, every house in Edinburgh is illuminated in honor of a great British victory, and the children see transparencies of Mars showering down laurel wreaths upon the Duke of Wellington. Since Wellington's last triumph was Waterloo, we can be sure that most of *Holiday House* takes place before 1815. The children are growing up late in the reign of George III. Moreover, they are not English children but Scotch children, living in an Edinburgh whose Calvinist atmosphere provided the proper environment for Sinclair's pronounced Evangelical views to blossom.

Harry and Laura Graham, who grow into their teens in the course of the linked stories that make up *Holiday House*, have lost their mother. Her death has so distressed their father that he has gone abroad, and remains off-stage until the final scene. The children's kind grandmother, Lady Harriet, and their jolly bachelor uncle, Major David Graham, share real responsibility for them and for their somewhat older brother, Frank, who is already at school. Mrs. Crabtree, the harsh nursery governess, has direct charge of Harry and Laura. Convinced that if you punish promptly you need not punish again, she finds herself nonetheless compelled to beat the children daily, and to shut them up in darkened closets and locked rooms. Lady Harriet and Major Graham are fully aware of her cruelty but are convinced that she loves the children deeply.

All Harry and Laura's toys are broken. They must begin each meal by eating anything they have failed to eat at a previous one. Though well-intentioned, they are thoughtless, disobedient, and destructive, breaking the china, the ornaments, and the clocks, inviting all their friends to tea without warning, constantly getting into scrapes. Laura cuts off her hair, which Crabtree has kept in tight and painful curlers; Harry plays with candles and sets the house afire; buckets of water ruin the nursery. This behavior, contrasting so greatly with that of the little angels thirsty for learning who inhabited most of the contemporary books for the young, has always aroused the comments of critics. As early as 1869, Charlotte Yonge wrote that "the quaint naughtiness of the children, and their unrivalled power of getting into scrapes is delightful, and the conversation as amusing as it is improbable." Ever since, others have echoed these views. "Catherine Sinclair," said Harvey Darton in 1932, "was the first to rollick," and in 1963 M. F. Thwaite declared that *Holiday House* shows "that the long domination of the moral tale was at an end." Yet to a modern reader there remains something hysterical or manic about the compulsive mischievousness and destructiveness of Harry and Laura; they no longer seem like the real children that their author intended to draw. And far from marking the end of the moral tale, *Holiday House* is an exceedingly moral tale indeed.

The children's elder brother, Frank Graham, reads his Bible assiduously, and everybody prophesies that he will "grow up to be a good and useful man; especially when it became evident that, by the blessing of God, he had been early turned away from the broad road that leadeth to destruction, in which every living person would naturally walk, and led into the narrow path that leadeth to eternal life." As a child, Frank had already experienced the "conversion" that Evangelical Anglicans, along with Dissenters, believed essential for spiritual rebirth and eventual salvation from eternal hellfire. Kind and affectionate to his younger brother and sister, Frank wins all the prizes at school, and when he embarks early on his naval career he severely criticizes the great Admiral Nelson for having said on his deathbed, "I have not been a great sinner." Like all other men, Frank sententiously points out, Nelson had greatly sinned. After two years at sea, Frank is a favorite in the mess because of his delight in Holy Scripture: surely Miss Sinclair took a highly personal view of the Royal Navy. And it is Frank's long-protracted last illness and edifying death that in the end brings sudden maturity to Harry and Laura, and leaves them, too, regenerate:

> All was changed within and around them,—sorrow had filled their hearts, and no longer merry, thoughtless young creatures, believing the world one scene of frolicsome enjoyment and careless ease; they had now witnessed its realities,—they had felt its trials,—they had experienced the importance of religion,—they had learned the frailty of all earthly joy,—and they had received, amidst tears and sorrow, the last injunction of a dying brother, to "call upon the Lord while He is near, and to seek Him while He may yet be found."

And Laura declares that Mrs. Crabtree had sought to lead them aright by severity, Uncle David and Grandmama by kindness, "but nothing was effectual till now, when God Himself has laid His hand upon us." *Holiday House* not a moral tale? Ridiculous.

Moreover, despite their persistent naughtiness, Harry and Laura do not quarrel with each other, commit mean actions, or fail to say their prayers and read their Bibles. They are "heedless, lively romps, who would not for twenty worlds have told a lie or done a shabby thing, or taken what did not belong to them." This accounts for Major Graham's tolerance of their destructiveness. Lying and stealing were the two most heinous crimes; Catherine Sinclair deplored the contemporary children's tale that, by dwelling on them, taught its readers how to commit them and get away with it. By carefully limiting the young Grahams' bad actions to "thoughtless" and "forgetful" deeds that only got them into "scrapes," Catherine Sinclair was teaching her young readers the difference between the venial and the unforgivable.

Harry thinks it absurd to learn to read and write: all grown-up people know how to do so; when he is grown-up, he will know too, and that will be time enough. He does not approve of Frank's "mooning about" with a book. Grandmama has to impress upon Laura the usefulness of lessons: if one pays attention as a child, one will not later make foolish and embarrassing mistakes in geography or arithmetic. Music has its own importance, and "no teaching can have greater influence in leading people to think and act aright, than the incidental remarks of an enlightened Christian." So edifying conversation too looms large in a proper education. Parents are "appointed by God to govern their children as He governs us."

But the seeming anti-intellectualism of *Holiday House* does not go very deep, since learning is so bound up with moral behavior. Amongst the episodes of every day that make up the larger portion of the book, there is embodied a single fairy tale, told to the children by Uncle David, a "nonsensical story about giants and fairies." This has been described as "the earliest example of nonsense-literature, and a direct precursor" of Lewis Carroll. Two fairies, Do-nothing and Teach-all, invite the greedy, lazy little boy No-book to visit them. He naturally accepts the invitation of Do-nothing, whose guests wallow in luxury, gluttony, and ease. Yet they are bored with their inactivity, and they are a tempting prey for the giant Snap-'em-up, who catches the fat, lazy little boys and hangs them up on meat hooks preparatory to slaughtering and devouring them. From his meat hook, No-book can see the happy, active guests of Teach-all, who eventually kills the giant and rescues No-book. Liberated, No-book reforms: he now loves his lessons, hates his holidays, stops overeating, joins a Temperance Society (!), and becomes Sir Timothy Bluestocking, who thrashes lazy boys with his stick. While there is an element of nonsense in Uncle David's story, it is nonetheless a moral tale designed directly for the edification of Harry, a "No-book" child. Moreover, it contains a strong element of horror and cruelty. Lewis Carroll would not have liked it at all.

Indeed, Catherine Sinclair's humor, though it has delighted many readers, and though it provided a welcome contrast to the humorless children's tales of her predecessors and contemporaries, seems forced and sometimes macabre. She relies on the piling-up of naughtinesses: broken toys are funny, a lame boy's failure to outrun a fat housekeeper is funny; a hairbreadth escape from a mad bull is funny; eating spiders, flies, and mice is funny. Bursts of loud laughter from her characters are funny in themselves. We do not laugh at these, as earlier readers did.

And though she was a philanthropist, Catherine Sinclair's attitude toward the poor seems primitive. When the children, driving in a coach, have finished their lunch, they throw the remains out of the window, and are "delighted to see the surprise and joy" of the poor roadside laborers who pick it up. When a poor boy, turned away from the Grahams' door by servants, signals outside a window and Harry wants to give him money, Uncle David warns that he will only get drunk, and Grandmama says it is cruel to encourage beggars who can work. The boy, however, is intent only upon returning intact Uncle David's pocketbook full of gold, which he has found. He is following the instructions of his dying and almost starving mother, who will never eat the bread of idleness and will not accept a reward. The virtuous youth is rewarded with a job as under-gardener, and Harry and Laura have been edified once more.

It is, then, as a pioneering effort in liveliness and realism that *Holiday House* still holds our attention. It stands at the beginning of a new period of development in writing for children. Yet behind the playfulness lurks the Evangelical moral. The ease is only apparent; the tensions and the strains are glaring.

The text of Holiday House *is reprinted from an American edition (New York: Robert Carter and Brothers, 1864).*

PREFACE

"Of all the paper I have blotted, I have written nothing without the intention of some
good. Whether I have succeeded or not, is for others to judge."
SIR WILLIAM TEMPLE

THE MINDS of young people are now manufactured like webs of linen, all alike, and
nothing left to nature. From the hour when children can speak, till they come to years of
discretion or of indiscretion, they are carefully prompted what to say, and what to think,
and what to look, and how to feel; while in most schoolrooms nature has been turned
out of doors with obloquy, and art has entirely supplanted her.

When a quarrel takes place, both parties are generally in some degree to blame;
therefore if Art and Nature could yet be made to go hand in hand towards the formation
of character and principles, a graceful and beautiful superstructure might be reared, on
the solid foundation of Christian faith and sound morality; so that while many natural
weeds would be eradicated and many wild flowers pruned and carefully trained, some
lovely blossoms that spring spontaneously in the uncultivated soil, might still be cherished into strength and beauty, far excelling what can be planted or reared by art.

Every infant is probably born with a character as peculiar to himself as the features in
his countenance, if his faults and good qualities were permitted to expand according to
their original tendency; but education, which formerly did too little in teaching the
"young idea how to shoot," seems now in danger of overshooting the mark altogether, by
not allowing the young ideas to exist at all. In this age of wonderful mechanical inventions,
the very mind of youth seems in danger of becoming a machine; and while every effort
is used to stuff the memory, like a cricket-ball, with well-known facts and ready-made
opinions, no room is left for the vigour of natural feeling, the glow of natural genius,
and the ardour of natural enthusiasm. It was a remark of Sir Walter Scott's many years ago,
to the author herself, that in the rising generation there would be no poets, wits, or
orators, because all play of the imagination is now carefully discouraged, and books
written for young persons are generally a mere dry record of facts, unenlivened by any
appeal to the heart, or any excitement to the fancy. The catalogue of a child's library
would contain Conversations on Natural Philosophy,—on Chemistry,—on Botany,—on
Arts and Sciences,—Chronological Records of History, and travels as dry as a road-
book; but nothing on the habits or ways of thinking, natural and suitable to the taste of
children; therefore, while such works are delightful to the parents and teachers who
select them, the younger community are fed with strong meat instead of milk, and the
reading which might be a relaxation from study becomes a study in itself.

In these pages the author has endeavoured to paint that species of noisy, frolicsome,
mischievous children, which is now almost extinct, wishing to preserve a sort of fabulous
remembrance of days long past, when young people were like wild horses on the
prairies, rather than like well-broken hacks on the road; and when, amidst many faults
and eccentricities, there was still some individuality of character and feeling allowed to
remain. In short, as Lord Byron described "the last man," the object of this volume is to
describe "the last boy." It may be useful, she thinks, to show, that amidst much requiring
to be judiciously curbed and corrected, there may be the germs of high and generous

feeling, and of steady, right principle, which should be the chief objects of culture and encouragement. Plodding industry is in the present day at a very high premium in education; but it requires the leaven of mental energy and genius to make it work well, while it has been remarked by one whose experience in education is deep and practical, that "those boys whose names appear most frequently in the black-book of transgression, would sometimes deserve to be also most commonly recorded, if a book were kept for warm affections and generous actions."

The most formidable person to meet in society at present, is the mother of a promising boy, about nine or ten years old; because there is no possible escape from a volume of anecdotes, and a complete system of education on the newest principles. The young gentleman has probably asked leave to bring his books to the breakfast-room— can scarcely be torn away from his studies at the dinner hour—discards all toys—abhors a holiday—propounds questions of marvellous depth in politics or mineralogy—and seems, in short, more fitted to enjoy the learned meeting at Newcastle, than the exhilarating exercise of the cricket-ground; but, if the axiom be true, that "a little learning is a dangerous thing," it has also been proved by frequent, and sometimes by very melancholy experience, that, for minds not yet expanded to maturity, a great deal of learning is more dangerous still,—and that in those school-rooms where there has been a society for the suppression of amusement, the mental energies have suffered as well as the health.

A prejudice has naturally arisen against giving works of fiction to children, because their chief interest too often rests on the detection and punishment of such mean vices as lying and stealing—which are so frequently and elaborately described, that the way to commit those crimes is made obvious, while a clever boy thinks he could easily avoid the oversights by which another has been discovered, and that if he does not yield to similar temptations, he is a model of virtue and good conduct.

In writing for any class of readers, and especially in occupying the leisure moments of such peculiarly fortunate young persons as have leisure moments at all, the author feels conscious of a deep responsibility, for it is at their early age that the seed can best be sown which shall bear fruit unto eternal life; therefore it is hoped this volume may be found to inculcate a pleasing and permanent consciousness, that religion is the best resource in happier hours, and the only refuge in hours of affliction.

Those who wish to be remembered for ever in the world—and it is a very common object of ambition—will find no monument more permanent than the affectionate remembrance of any children they have treated with kindness; for we may often observe, in the reminiscences of old age, a tender recollection surviving all others, of friends in early days who enlivened the hours of childhood by presents of playthings and comfits. But, above all, we never forget those who good-humouredly complied with the constantly recurring petition of all young people, in every generation and in every house—"Will you tell me a story?"

In answer to such a request, often and importunately repeated, the author has from year to year delighted in seeing herself surrounded by a circle of joyous, eager faces, listening with awe to the terrors of Mrs. Crabtree, or smiling at the frolics of Harry and Laura. The stories, originally, were so short, that some friends, aware of their popularity, and conscious of their harmless tendency, took the trouble of copying them in manu-script for their own young friends; but the tales have since grown and expanded, during frequent verbal repetitions, till, with various fanciful additions and new characters, they have enlarged into their present form,—or rather, so far beyond it that several chapters are omitted, to keep the volume within moderate compass.

Paley remarks, that "any amusement which is innocent, is better than none; as the writing of a book, the building of a house, the laying out of a garden, the digging of a fish-pond—even the raising of a cucumber;" and it is hoped that, while the author herself has found much interesting occupation in recording those often repeated stories, the time of herself and her young readers may be employed with some degree of profit, or she will certainly regret that it was not better occupied in the rearing of cucumbers.

It may add something to the interest, and yet more to the usefulness of those scenes and circumstances relative to the return from abroad and premature death of Frank Graham, to mention that they are not fictitious; and the author is deeply touched by the consciousness that some tears of juvenile sympathy have fallen from eyes that never saw him, for the early fate of a brother so loved and so lamented. With every endearing and admirable quality of head and heart, few ever held out a brighter promise of excellence, than he who, dying, resigned himself without a murmur to the will of God, and has long slumbered in a premature grave, his name being thus commemorated on a tomb-stone in the churchyard of Hackney:

In Memory

OF

LIEUTENANT JAMES SINCLAIR,

AGED 20,

WHO WAS ARRESTED BY THE HAND OF DEATH

ON HIS WAY HOME,

AFTER AN ABSENCE OF SOME YEARS, DURING WHICH HE LOST HIS HEALTH

ON SERVICE AGAINST THE BURMESE,

20th June, 1826.

"It is the Lord, let him do what seemeth him good."
"For I know that my Redeemer liveth."

CHIT CHAT

A school-boy, a dog, and a walnut tree,
The more you strike 'em, the better they be.

LAURA AND HARRY GRAHAM could scarcely feel sure that they ever had a mama, because she died while they were yet very young indeed; but Frank, who was some years older, recollected perfectly well what pretty playthings she used to give him, and missed his kind, good mama so extremely, that he one day asked if he might "go to a shop and buy a new mama?" Frank often afterwards thought of the time also, when he kneeled beside her bed to say his prayers, or when he sat upon her knee to hear her funny stories about good boys and bad boys—all very interesting, and all told on purpose to show how much happier obedient children are, than those who waste their time in idleness and folly. Boys and girls all think they know the road to happiness without any mistake, and choose that which looks gayest and pleasantest first, though older people, who have travelled that road already, can tell them that a very difficult path is the only one which ends agreeably; and those who begin to walk in it when they are young, will really find that "wisdom's ways are ways of pleasantness, and all her paths are peace." It was truly remarked by Solomon, that "even a child is known by his doings, whether his work be pure, and whether it be right." Therefore, though Frank was yet but a little boy, his friends, who observed how carefully he attended to his mama's instructions, how frequently he studied his Bible, and how diligently he learned his lessons, all prophesied that this merry, lively child, with laughing eyes, and dimpled cheeks, would yet grow up to be a good and useful man; especially when it became evident that, by the blessing of God, he had been early turned away from the broad road that leadeth to destruction, in which every living person would naturally walk, and led into the narrow path that leadeth to eternal life.

When his mama, Lady Graham, after a long and painful illness, was at last taken away to the better world, for which she had been many years preparing, her only sorrow and anxiety seemed to be that she left behind her three such very dear children, who were now to be entirely under the care of their papa, Sir Edward Graham; and it was with many prayers and tears that she tried to make her mind more easy about their future education, and future happiness.

Sir Edward felt such extreme grief on the death of Lady Graham, that instead of being able to remain at home with his young family, and to interest his mind as he would wish to have done, by attending to them, he was ordered by Dr. Bell to set off immediately for Paris, Rome, and Naples, where it was hoped he might leave his distresses behind him while he travelled, or, at all events, forget them.

Luckily the children had a very good, kind uncle, Major David Graham, and their grandmama, Lady Harriet Graham, who were both exceedingly happy to take charge of them, observing that no house could be cheerful without a few little people being there, and that now they would have constant amusement in trying to make Frank, Harry, and Laura, as happy as possible, and even still happier.

"That is the thing I am almost afraid of!" said Sir Edward, smiling. "Uncles and grandmamas are only too kind, and my small family will be quite spoiled with indulgence."

"Not if you leave that old vixen, Mrs. Crabtree, as governor of the nursery," answered Major Graham, laughing. "She ought to have been the drummer of a regiment, she is so fond of beating! I believe there never was such a tyrant since the time when nursery-maids were invented. Poor Harry would pass his life in a dark closet, like Baron Trenck, if Mrs. Crabtree had her own way!"

"She means it all well. I am certain that Mrs. Crabtree is devotedly fond of my children, and would go through fire and water to serve them; but she is a little severe perhaps. Her idea is, that if you never forgive a first fault, you will never hear of a second, which is probably true enough. At all events, her harshness will be the best remedy for your extreme indulgence; therefore let me beg that you and my mother will seldom interfere with her 'method,' especially in respect to Harry and Laura. As for Frank, if all boys were like him, we might make a bonfire of birch rods and canes. He is too old for nursery discipline now, and must be flogged at school, if deserving of it at all, till he goes to sea next year with my friend Gordon, who has promised to rate him as a volunteer of the first class, on board the Thunderbolt."

In spite of Mrs. Crabtree's admirable "system" with children, Harry and Laura became from this time two of the most heedless, frolicsome beings in the world, and had to be whipped almost every morning; for in those days it had not been discovered that whipping is all a mistake, and that children can be made good without it; though some old-fashioned people still say—and such too who take the God of truth for their guide—the old plan succeeded best, and that those who "spare the rod will spoil the child." When Lady Harriet and Major Graham spoke kindly to Harry and Laura about anything wrong that had been done, they both felt more sad and sorry than after the severest punishments of Mrs. Crabtree, who frequently observed that, "if those children were shut up in a dark room alone, with nothing to do, they would still find some way of being mischievous, and of deserving to be punished."

"Harry!" said Major Graham one day, "you remind me of a monkey which belonged to the colonel of our regiment. He was famous for contriving to play all sorts of pranks when no one supposed them to be possible; and I recollect once having a valuable French clock, which the malicious creature seemed particularly determined to break. Many a time I caught him in the fact, and saved my beautiful clock; but one day being suddenly summoned out of the room, I hastily fastened his chain to a table, so that he could not possibly, even at the full extent of his paw, so much as touch the glass case. I observed him impatiently watching my departure, and felt a misgiving that he expected to get the better of me; so after shutting the door, I took a peep through the key-hole; and what do you think Jack had done, Harry? for, next to Mr. Monkey himself, you are certainly the cleverest contriver of mischief I know."

"What did he do?" asked Harry, eagerly; "did he throw a stone at the clock?"

"No! but his leg was several inches longer than his arm, so having turned his tail towards his object, he stretched out his hind paw, and before I could rush back, my splendid alabaster clock had been upset and broken to shivers."

Laura soon became quite as mischievous as Harry, which is very surprising, as she was a whole year older, and had been twice as often scolded by Mrs. Crabtree. Neither of these children intended any harm, for they were only heedless, lively romps, who would not for twenty worlds have told a lie, or done a shabby thing, or taken what did not belong to them. They were not greedy either, and would not on any account have resembled Peter Grey, who was at the same school with Frank, and who spent all his own pocket-money, and borrowed a great deal of other people's, to squander at the pastry-cook's, saying he wished it were possible to eat three dinners, and two breakfasts, and five suppers every day.

Harry was not a cruel boy either; he never lashed his pony, beat his dog, pinched his sister, or killed any butterflies, though he often chased them for fun, and one day he even defended a wasp, at the risk of being stung, when Mrs. Crabtree intended to kill it.

"Nasty, useless vermin!" said she, angrily, "what business have they in the world!

coming into other people's houses with nothing to do! They sting and torment everybody! Bees are very different, for they make honey."

"And wasps make jelly!" said Harry, resolutely, while he opened the window, and shook the happy wasp out of his pocket-handkerchief.

Mrs. Crabtree allowed no pet of any description in her territories, and ordered the children to be happy without any such nonsense. When Laura's canary-bird escaped one unlucky day out of its cage, Mrs. Crabtree was strongly suspected by Major Graham of having secretly opened the door, as she had long declared war upon bulfinches, white mice, parrots, kittens, dogs, bantams, and gold fish; observing that animals only made a noise and soiled the house, therefore every beast should remain in its own home—"birds in the air, fish in the sea, and beasts in the desert." She seemed always watching, in hopes Harry and Laura might do something that they ought to be punished for: and Mrs. Crabtree certainly had more ears than other people, or slept with one eye open, as, whatever might be done, night or day, she overheard the lowest whisper of mischief, and appeared able to see what was going on in the dark.

When Harry was a very little boy, he sometimes put himself in the corner, after doing anything wrong, apparently quite sensible that he deserved to be punished; and once, after being terribly scolded by Mrs. Crabtree, he drew in his stool beside her chair with a funny, penitent face, twirling his thumbs over and over each other, and saying, "Now, Mrs. Crabtree! look what a good boy I am going to be!"

"You a good boy!" replied she, contemptuously: "No! no! the world will be turned into a cream-cheese first!"

Lady Harriet gave Harry and Laura a closet of their own, in which she allowed them to keep their toys; and nobody could help laughing to see that amidst the whole collection, there was seldom one unbroken. Frank wrote out a list once of what he found in this crowded little store-room, and amused himself often with reading it ever afterwards. There were three dolls without faces, a horse with no legs, a drum with a hole in the top, a cart without wheels, a churn with no bottom, a kite without a tail, a skipping-rope with no handles, and a cup and ball that had lost the string. Lady Harriet called this closet the hospital for decayed toys, and she often employed herself as their doctor, mending legs and arms for soldiers, horses, and dolls, though her skill seldom suc-ceeded long, because play-things must have been made of cast-iron to last a week with Harry. One cold winter morning, when Laura entered the nursery, she found a large fire blazing, and all her wax dolls sitting in a row staring at the flames. Harry intended no mischief on this occasion, but great was his vexation when Laura burst into tears, and showed him that their faces were running in a hot stream down upon their beautiful silk frocks, which were completely ruined, and not a doll had its nose remaining. Another time, Harry pricked a hole in his own beautiful large gas ball, wishing to see how the gas could possibly escape, after which, in a moment, it shrivelled up into a useless empty bladder; and when his kite was flying up to the clouds, Harry often wished that he could be tied to the tail himself, so as to fly also through the air like a bird, and see everything.

Mrs. Crabtree always wore a prodigious bunch of jingling keys in her pocket, that rung whenever she moved, as if she carried a dinner-bell in her pocket, and Frank said it was like a rattlesnake giving warning of her approach, which was of great use, as everybody had time to put on a look of good behaviour before she arrived. Even Betty, the under nursery-maid, felt in terror of Mrs. Crabtree's entrance, and was obliged to work harder than any six house-maids united. Frank told her one day that he thought brooms might soon be invented, which would go by steam and brush carpets of themselves, but, in the meantime, not a grain of dust could lurk in any corner of the nursery without being dislodged. Betty would have required ten hands and twenty pair of feet to do all the work that was expected; but the grate looked like jet, the windows would not have soiled a cambric handkerchief, and the carpet was switched with so many tea-leaves, that Frank thought Mrs. Crabtree often took several additional cups of tea in order to leave a plentiful supply of leaves for sweeping the floor next morning.

If Laura and Harry left any breakfast, Mrs. Crabtree kept it carefully till dinner time, when they were obliged to finish the whole before tasting meat; and if they refused it at dinner, the remains were kept for supper. Mrs. Crabtree always informed them that she did it "for their good," though Harry never could see any good that it did to either of them; and when she mentioned how many poor children would be glad to eat what they despised, he often wished the hungry beggars had some of his own hot dinner, which he would gladly have spared to them; for Harry was really so generous, that he would have lived upon air if he might be of use to anybody. Time passed on, and Lady Harriet engaged a master for some hours a-day to teach the children lessons, while even Mrs. Crabtree found no other fault to Harry and Laura, except that in respect to good behaviour their memories were like a sieve, which let out everything they were desired to keep in mind. They seemed always to hope, somehow or other, when Mrs. Crabtree once turned her back, she would never show her face again so their promises of better conduct were all "wind without rain," very loud and plenty of them, but no good effect to be seen afterwards.

Among her many other torments, Mrs. Crabtree rolled up Laura's hair every night on all sides of her head, in large stiff curl-papers, till they were as round and hard as walnuts, after which she tied on a nightcap as tightly as possible above all, saying this would curl the hair still better. Laura could not lay any part of her head on the pillow without suffering so much pain that, night after night, she sat up in bed, after Mrs. Crabtree had bustled out of the room, and quietly took the cruel papers out, though she was punished so severely for doing so, that she obeyed orders at last, and lay wide awake half the night with torture; and it was but small comfort to Laura afterwards, that Lady Harriet's visiters frequently admired the forest of long glossy ringlets that adorned her head, and complimented Mrs. Crabtree on the trouble it must cost her to keep that charming hair in order. Often did Laura wish that it were ornamenting any wig-block rather than her own head; and one day Lady Harriet laughed heartily, when some strangers admired her little granddaughter's ringlets, and Laura asked, very anxiously, if they would like to cut off a few of the longest, and keep them for her sake.

"Your hair does curl like a cork-screw," said Frank, laughing. "If I want to draw a cork out of a beer bottle any day, I shall borrow one of those ringlets, Laura!"

"You may laugh, Frank; for it is fun to you and death to me," answered poor Laura, gravely shaking her curls at him. "I wish we were all bald, like Uncle David! During the night I cannot lie still on account of those tiresome curls; and all day I dare not stir for fear of spoiling them—so they are never out of my head."

"Nor off your head! How pleasant it must be to have Mrs. Crabtree combing and scolding, and scolding and combing, for hours every day! Poor Laura! we must get

Dr. Bell to say that they shall be taken off on pain of death, and then, perhaps, grandmama would order some Irish reapers to cut them down with a sickle."

"Frank! what a lucky boy you are to be at school, and not in the nursery! I wish next year would come immediately, for then I shall have a governess, after which good bye to Mrs. Crabtree, and the wearisome curl papers."

"I don't like school!" said Harry. "It is perfect nonsense to plague me with lessons now. All big people can read and write, so, of course I shall be able to do like others. There is no hurry about it!"

Never was there a more amiable, pious, excellent boy than Frank, who read his Bible so attentively, and said his prayers so regularly every morning and evening, that he soon learned both to know his duty and to do it. Though he laughed heartily at the scrapes which Harry and Laura so constantly fell into, he often also helped them out of their difficulties; being very different from most elderly boys, who find an odd kind of pleasure in teasing younger children—pulling their hair—pinching their arms—twitching away their dinners—and twenty more plans for tormenting, which Frank never attempted to enjoy, but he often gave Harry and Laura a great deal of kind, sober, good advice, which they listened to very attentively while they were in any new distress, but generally forgot again as soon as their spirits rose. Frank came home only upon Saturdays and Sundays, because he attended during most of the week at Mr. Lexicon's academy, where he gradually became so clever that the masters all praised his extraordinary attention, and covered him with medals, while Major Graham often filled his pockets with a reward of money, after which he ran towards the nearest shop to spend his little fortune in buying a present for somebody. Frank scarcely ever wanted anything for himself, but he always wished to contrive some kind generous plan for other people; and Major Graham used to say, "if that boy had only sixpence in the world, he would lay it all out on penny tarts to distribute among half-a-dozen of his friends." He even saved his pocket-money once, during three whole months, to purchase a gown for Mrs. Crabtree, who looked almost good-humoured during the space of five minutes, when Frank presented it to her, saying, in his joyous merry voice, "Mrs. Crabtree! I wish you health to wear it, strength to tear it, and money to buy another!"

Certainly there never was such a gown before! It had been chosen by Frank and Harry together, who thought nothing could be more perfect. The colour was so bright an apple-green, that it would have put anybody's teeth on edge to look at it, and the whole was dotted over with large round spots of every colour, as if a box of wafers had been showered upon the surface. Laura wished Mrs. Crabtree might receive a present every day, as it put her in such good-humour, and nearly three weeks passed without a single scold being heard in the nursery; so Frank observed that he thought Mrs. Crabtree would soon be quite out of practice.

"Laura!" said Major Graham, looking very sly one morning, "have you heard all the new rules that Mrs. Crabtree has made?"

"No!" replied she in great alarm; "what are they?"

"In the first place, you are positively not to tear and destroy above three frocks a-day; secondly, you and Harry must never get into a passion, unless you are angry; thirdly, when either of you take medicine, you are not to make wry faces, except when the taste is bad; fourthly, you must never speak ill of Mrs. Crabtree herself till she is out of the room; fifthly, you are not to jump out of the windows, as long as you can get out at the door"——

"Yes!" interrupted Laura laughing, "and sixthly, when Uncle David is joking, we are not to be frightened by any thing he says!"

"Seventhly, when next you spill grandmama's bottle of ink, Harry must drink up every drop."

"Very well! he may swallow a sheet of blotting-paper afterwards, to put away the taste."

"I wish everybody who writes a book, was obliged to swallow it," said Harry. "It is such a waste of time reading, when we might be amusing ourselves. Frank sat mooning over a book for two hours yesterday when we wanted him to play. I am sure some day his head will burst with knowledge."

"That can never happen to you, Master Harry," answered Major Graham; "you have a head, and so has a pin, but there is not much furniture in either of them."

THE GRAND FEAST

She gave them some tea without any bread,
She whipped them all soundly and sent them to-bed.
NURSERY RHYMES

LADY HARRIET GRAHAM was an extremely thin, delicate old lady, with a very pale face, and a sweet gentle voice, which the children delighted to hear, for it always spoke kindly to them, and sounded like music after the loud, rough tones of Mrs. Crabtree. She wore her own gray hair, which had become almost as white as the widow's cap which covered her head. The rest of her dress was generally black velvet, and she usually sat in a comfortable arm-chair by the fireside, watching her grandchildren at play, with a large work-bag by her side, and a prodigious Bible open on the table before her. Lady Harriet often said that it made her young again to see the joyous gambols of Harry and Laura; and when unable any longer to bear their noise, she sometimes kept them quiet by telling them the most delightful stories about what had happened to herself when she was young.

Once upon a time, however, Lady Harriet suddenly became so very ill, that Dr. Bell said she must spend a few days in the country, for change of air; and, accordingly, she determined on passing a quiet week at Holiday House, with her relations, Lord and Lady Rockville. Meanwhile, Harry and Laura were to be left under the sole care of Mrs. Crabtree; so it might have been expected that they would both feel more frightened for her, now that she was reigning monarch of the house, than ever. Harry would obey those he loved, if they only held up a little finger; but all the terrors of Mrs. Crabtree, and her cat-o'-nine-tails, were generally forgotten soon after she left the room; therefore he thought little at first about the many threats she held out, if he behaved ill; but he listened most seriously when his dear sick grandmama told him, in a faint weak voice, on the day of her departure from home, how very well he ought to behave in her absence, as no one remained but the maids to keep him in order—and that she hoped Mrs. Crabtree would write her a letter full of good news about his excellent conduct.

Harry felt as if he would gladly sit still without stirring, till his grandmama came back, if that could only please her; and there never was any one more determined to be a good boy than he, at the moment when Lady Harriet's carriage came round to the door. Laura, Frank, and Harry, helped to carry all the pillows, boxes, books, and baskets, which were necessary for the journey, of which there seemed to be about fifty; then they arranged the cushions as comfortably as possible, and watched very sorrowfully when their grandmama, after kindly embracing them both, was carefully supported by Major Graham and her own maid Harrison, into the chariot. Uncle David gave each of the children a pretty picture-book before taking leave, and said, as he was stepping into the carriage, "Now, children! I have only one piece of serious, important advice to give you all, so attend to me!—never crack nuts with your teeth."

When the carriage had driven off, Mrs. Crabtree became so busy scolding Betty, and storming at Jack the foot-boy, for not cleaning her shoes well enough, that she left Harry and Laura standing in the passage, not knowing exactly what they ought to do first; and Frank, seeing them looking rather melancholy and bewildered at the loss of their grandmama, stopped a moment as he passed on the way to school, and said, in a very kind, affectionate voice,

"Now, Harry and Laura, listen both of you!—here is a grand opportunity to show everybody that we can be trusted to ourselves, without getting into any scrapes; so that if grandmama is ever ill again, and obliged to go away, she need not feel so sad and anxious as she did to-day. I mean to become nine times more attentive to my lessons than usual this morning, to show how trustworthy we are; and if you are wise, pray march straight up to the nursery yourselves. I have arranged a gown and cap of Mrs. Crabtree's on the large arm-chair, to look as like herself as possible, that you may be reminded how soon she will come back; and you must not behave like the mice when the cat is out. Good bye! Say the alphabet backwards, and count your fingers for half-an-hour; but when Mrs. Crabtree appears again, pray do not jump out of the window for joy."

Harry and Laura were proceeding directly towards the nursery, as Frank had recommended, when unluckily they observed, in passing the drawing-room door, that it was wide open; so Harry peeped in, and they began idly wandering round the tables and cabinets. Not ten minutes elapsed before they both commenced racing about as if they were mad, perfectly screaming with joy, and laughing so loudly at their own funny tricks, that an old gentleman who lived next door very nearly sent in a message to ask what the joke was.

Presently Harry and Laura ran up and down stairs till the housemaid was quite fatigued with running after them. They jumped upon the fine damask sofas in the drawing-room, stirred the fire till it was in a blaze, and rushed out on the balcony, upsetting one or two geraniums and a myrtle. They spilt Lady Harriet's perfumes over their handkerchiefs—they looked into all the beautiful books of pictures—they tumbled many of the pretty Dresden china figures on the floor—they wound up the little French clock till it was broken—they made the musical work-box play its tunes, and set the Chinese mandarins a-nodding till they very nearly nodded their heads off. In short, so much mischief has seldom been done in so short a time; till at last Harry, perfectly worn out with laughing and running, threw himself into a large arm-chair, and Laura, with her ringlets tumbling in frightful confusion over her face, and the beads of her coral necklace rolling on the floor, tossed herself into a sofa beside him.

"Oh! What fun!" cried Harry, in an ecstacy of delight. "I wish Frank had been here, and crowds of little boys and girls, to play with us all day! It would be a good joke, Laura, to write and ask all our little cousins and companions to drink tea here to-morrow evening! Their mamas could never guess we had not leave from grandmama to invite everybody; so I daresay we might gather quite a large party! oh! how enchanting!"

Laura laughed heartily when she heard this proposal of Harry's; and, without hesitating a moment about it, she joyously placed herself before Lady Harriet's writing-table, and scribbled a multitude of little notes, in large text, to more than twenty young friends, all of whom had at other times been asked by Lady Harriet to spend the evening with her.

Laura felt very much puzzled to know what was usually said in a card of invitation; but, after many consultations, she and Harry thought at last that it was very nicely expressed, for they wrote these words upon a large sheet of paper to each of their friends:—

"Master Harry Graham and Miss Laura wish you to have the honour of drinking tea with us to-morrow, at six o'clock.

(Signed)   "HARRY AND LAURA."

Laura afterwards singed a hole in her muslin frock, while lighting one of the Vesta matches to seal these numerous notes; and Harry dropped some burning sealing-wax on his hand, in the hurry of assisting her; but he thought that little accident no matter, and ran away to see if the cards could be sent off immediately.

Now, there lived in the house a very old footman, called Andrew, who remembered Harry and Laura since they were quite little babies; and he often looked exceedingly sad and sorry when they suffered punishment from Mrs. Crabtree. He was ready to do anything in the world when it pleased the children, and would have carried a message to the moon, if they had only shown him the way. Many odd jobs and private messages he had already been employed in by Harry, who now called Andrew up stairs, entreating him to carry out all those absurd notes as fast as possible, and to deliver them immediately, as they were of the greatest consequence. Upon hearing this, old Andrew lost not a moment, but threw on his hat, and instantly started off, looking like the two-penny postman, he carried such a prodigious parcel of invitations; while Harry and Laura stood at the drawing-room window, almost screaming with joy when they saw him set out, and when they observed that, to oblige them, he actually ran along the street at a sort of trot, which was as fast as he could possibly go. Presently, however, he certainly did stop for a single minute, and Laura saw that it was in order to take a peep into one of the notes, that he might ascertain what they were all about; but as he never carried any letters without doing so, she thought that quite natural, and was only very glad when he had finished, and rapidly pursued his way again.

Next morning, Mrs. Crabtree and Betty became very much surprised to observe what a number of smart livery servants knocked at the street door, and gave in cards; but their astonishment became still greater, when old Andrew brought up a whole parcel of them to Harry and Laura, who immediately broke the seals, and read the contents in a corner together.

"What are you about there, Master Graham?" cried Mrs. Crabtree, angrily. "How dare anybody venture to touch your grandmama's letters?"

"They are not for grandmama!—they are all for us! every one of them!" answered Harry, dancing about the room with joy, and waving the notes over his head. "Look at this direction! For Master and Miss Graham! Put on your spectacles, and read it yourself, Mrs. Crabtree! What delightful fun! the house will be as full as an egg?"

Mrs. Crabtree seemed completely puzzled what to think of all this, and looked so much as if she did not know exactly what to be angry at, and so ready to be in a passion if possible, that Harry burst out a-laughing, while he said, "Only think, Mrs. Crabtree! here is everybody coming to tea with us!—all my cousins, besides Peter Gray, Robert Stewart, Charles Forrester, Adelaide Cunningham, Diana Wentworth, John Fordyce, Edmund Ashford, Frank Abercromby, Ned Russell, and Tom——"

"The boy is distracted!" exclaimed Betty, staring with astonishment. "What does all this mean, Master Harry?"

"And who gave you leave to invite company into your grandmama's house?" cried Mrs. Crabtree, snatching up all the notes, and angrily thrusting them into the fire. "I never heard of such doings in all my life before, Master Harry! but as sure as eggs is eggs, you shall repent of this; for not one morsel of cake or anything else shall you have to give any of the party; no! not so much as a crust of bread, or a thimbleful of tea!"

Harry and Laura had never thought of such a catastrophe as this before; they always saw a great table covered with everything that could be named for tea, whenever their little friends came to visit them; and whether it rose out of the floor, or was brought by Aladdin's lamp, they never considered it possible that the table would not be provided as usual on such occasions; so this terrible speech of Mrs. Crabtree's frightened them out of their wits. What was to be done! They both knew by experience that she always did whatever she threatened, or something a greal deal worse, so they began by bursting into tears, and begging Mrs. Crabtree for this once to excuse them, and to give some cakes and tea to their little visiters; but they might as well have spoken to one of the Chinese mandarins, for she only shook her head with a positive look, declaring over and over again that nothing should appear upon the table except what was always brought up for their own supper—two biscuits and two cups of milk.

"Therefore, say no more about it!" added she, sternly, "I am your best friend, Master Harry, trying to teach you and Miss Laura your duty; so save your breath to cool your porridge."

Poor Harry and Laura looked perfectly ill with fright and vexation when they thought of what was to happen next, while Mrs. Crabtree sat down to her knitting, grumbling to herself, and dropping her stitches every minute with rage and irritation. Old Andrew felt exceedingly sorry after he heard what distress and difficulty Harry was in; and when the hour for the party approached, he very good-naturedly spread out a large table in the dining room, where he put down as many cups, saucers, plates, and spoons as Laura chose to direct; but in spite of all his trouble, though it looked very grand, there was nothing whatever to eat or drink except the two dry biscuits, and the two miserable cups of milk, which seemed to become smaller every time that Harry looked at them.

Presently the clock struck six, and Harry listened to the hour very much as a prisoner would do in the condemned cell in Newgate, feeling that the dreaded time was at last arrived. Soon afterwards, several handsome carriages drove up to the door, filled with little Masters and Misses, who hurried joyfully into the house, talking and laughing all the way up stairs, while poor Harry and Laura almost wished the floor would open and swallow them up; so they shrunk into a distant corner of the room, quite ashamed to show their faces.

The young ladies were all dressed in their best frocks, with pink sashes, and pink shoes; while the little boys appeared in their holiday clothes, with their hair newly brushed, and their faces washed. The whole party had dined at two o'clock, so they were as hungry as hawks, looking eagerly round, whenever they entered, to see what was on the tea table, and evidently surprised that nothing had yet been put down. Laura and Harry soon afterwards heard their visiters whispering to each other about Norwich buns, rice cakes, sponge biscuits, and maccaroons; while Peter Grey was loud in praise of a party at George Lorraine's the night before, where an immense plum cake had been sugared over like a snow storm, and covered with crowds of beautiful amusing mottoes; not to mention a quantity of noisy crackers, that exploded like pistols, besides which, a glass of hot jelly had been handed to each little guest before he was sent home.

Every time the door opened, all eyes were anxiously turned round, expecting a grand feast to be brought in; but quite the contrary—it was only Andrew showing up more hungry visiters; while Harry felt so unspeakably wretched, that, if some kind fairy could only have turned him into a Norwich bun at the moment, he would gladly have consented to be cut in pieces, that his ravenous guests might be satisfied.

Charles Forrester was a particularly good-natured boy, so Harry at last took courage and beckoned him into a remote corner of the room, where he confessed, in whispers, the real state of affairs about tea, and how sadly distressed he and Laura felt, because they had nothing whatever to give among so many visiters, seeing that Mrs. Crabtree kept her determination of affording them no provisions.

"What is to be done?" said Charles, very anxiously, as he felt extremely sorry for his little friends. "If mama had been at home, she would gladly have sent whatever you liked for tea; but, unluckily, she is dining out! I saw a loaf of bread lying on a table at home this evening, which she would make you quite welcome to! Shall I run home, as fast as possible, to fetch it? That would, at any rate, be better than nothing!"

Poor Charles Forrester was very lame; therefore, while he talked of running, he could hardly walk; but Lady Forrester's house stood so near, that he soon reached home, when, snatching up the loaf, he hurried back towards the street with his prize, quite delighted to see how large and substantial it looked. Scarcely had he reached tbe door, however, before the housekeeper ran hastily out, saying,

"Stop, Master Charles! stop! sure you are not running away with the loaf for my tea;—and the parrot must have her supper, too. What do you want with that there bread?"

"Never mind, Mrs. Comfit!" answered Charles, hastening on faster than ever, while he grasped the precious loaf more firmly in his hand, and limped along at a prodigious rate: "Polly is getting too fat; so she will be the better of fasting for one day."

Mrs. Comfit, being enormously fat herself, became very angry at this remark,—so she seemed quite desperate to recover the loaf, and hurried forward to overtake Charles;

but the old housekeeper was so heavy and breathless, while the young gentleman was so lame, that it seemed an even chance which won the race. Harry stood at his own door, impatiently hoping to receive the prize, and eagerly stretched out his arms to encourage his friend, while it was impossible to say which of the runners might arrive first. Harry had sometimes heard of a race between two old women tied up in sacks, and he thought they could scarcely move with more difficulty; but at the very moment when Charles had reached the door, he stumbled over a stone, and fell on the ground. Mrs. Comfit then instantly rushed up, and seizing the loaf she carried it off in triumph, leaving the two little friends ready to cry with vexation, and quite at a loss what plan to attempt next.

Meantime, a sad riot had arisen in the dining-room; where the boys called loudly for their tea, and the young ladies drew their chairs all around the table, to wait till it was ready. Still nothing appeared; so everybody wondered more and more how long they were to wait for all the nice cakes and sweetmeats which must, of course, be coming; for the longer they were delayed, the more was expected.

The last at a feast, and the first at a fray, was generally Peter Grey, who now lost patience, and seized one of the two biscuits, which he was in the middle of greedily devouring, when Laura returned with Harry to the dining-room, and observed what he had done.

"Peter Grey!" said she, holding up her head, and trying to look very dignified, "you are an exceedingly naughty boy, to help yourself! As a punishment for being so rude, you shall have nothing more to eat all this evening."

"If I do not help myself, nobody else seems likely to give me any supper! I appear to be the only person who is to taste anything to-night," answered Peter, laughing, while the impudent boy took a cup of milk, and drank it off, saying, "Here's to your very good health, Miss Laura, and an excellent appetite to everybody!"

Upon hearing this absurd speech, all the other boys began laughing, and made signs, as if they were eating their fingers off with hunger. Then Peter called Lady Harriet's house "Famine Castle," and pretended he would swallow the knives, like an Indian juggler.

"We must learn to live upon air, and here are some spoons to eat it with," said John Fordyce. "Harry, shall I help you to a mouthful of moon-shine?"

"Peter! would you like a roasted fly?" asked Frank Abercromby, catching one on the window. "I dare say it is excellent for hungry people,—or a slice of buttered wall?"

"Or a stewed spider?" asked Peter. "Shall we all be cannibals, and eat one another?"

"What is the use of all those forks, when there is nothing to stick upon them?" asked George Maxwell, throwing them about on the floor. "No buns!—no fruit!—no cakes!—no nothing!"

"What are we to do with those tea-cups, when there is no tea?" cried Frank Abercromby, pulling the table-cloth till the whole affair fell prostrate on the floor. After this, these riotous boys tossed the plates in the air, and caught them,—becoming, at last, so outrageous, that poor old Andrew called them a "meal mob!" Never was there so much broken china seen in a dining-room before! It all lay scattered on the floor, in countless fragments, looking as if there had been a bull in a china shop, when suddenly Mrs. Crabtree herself opened the door and walked in, with an aspect of rage enough to petrify a milestone. Now, old Andrew had long been trying all in his power to render the boys quiet and contented. He had made them a speech—he had chased the ringleaders all round the room—and he had thrown his stick at Peter, who seemed the most riotous—but all in vain; they became worse and worse, laughing into fits, and calling Andrew "the police officer and the bailiff." It was a very different story, however, when Mrs. Crabtree appeared, so flaming with fury she might have blown up a powder-mill.

Nobody could help being afraid of her. Even Peter himself stood stock still, and seemed withering away to nothing, when she looked at him; and when she began to scold in her most furious manner, not a boy ventured to look off the ground. A large pair of tawse then became visible in her hand, so very heart sunk with fright, and the riotous visiters began to get behind each other, and to huddle out of sight as much as possible, whispering, and pushing, and fighting, in a desperate scuffle to escape.

"What is all this!" cried she, at the full pitch of her voice; "has bedlam broke loose! who smashed these cups? I'll break his head for him, let me tell you that! Master Peter! you should be hissed out of the world for your misconduct; but I shall certainly whip you round the room like a whipping-top."

At this moment Peter observed that the dining-room window, which was only about six feet from the ground, had been left wide open; so instantly seizing the opportunity, he threw himself out with a single bound, and ran laughing away. All the other boys immediately followed his example, and disappeared by the same road; after which Mrs. Crabtree leaned far out of the window, and scolded loudly, as long as they remained in sight, till her face became red, and her voice perfectly hoarse.

Meantime, the little misses sat soberly down before the empty table, and talked in whispers to each other, waiting till their maids came to take them home, after which they all hurried away as fast as possible, hardly waiting to say "good-bye," and intending to ask for some supper at home.

During that night, long after Harry and Laura had been scolded, whipped, and put to bed, they were each heard in different rooms, sobbing and crying, as if their very hearts would break, while Mrs. Crabtree grumbled and scolded to herself, saying she must do her duty, and make them good children, though she were to flay them alive first.

When Lady Harriet returned home, some days afterwards, she heard an account of Harry and Laura's misconduct from Mrs. Crabtree; and the whole story was such a terrible case against them, that their poor grandmama became perfectly astonished and shocked, while even Uncle David was preparing to be very angry; but before the culprits appeared, Frank most kindly stepped forward and begged that they might be pardoned for this once, adding all in his power to excuse Harry and Laura, by describing how very penitent they had become, and how very severely they had already been punished.

Frank then mentioned all that Harry had told him about the starving party, which he related with so much humour and drollery, that Lady Harriet could not help laughing; so then he saw that a victory had been gained, and ran to the nursery for the two little prisoners.

Uncle David shook his walking-stick at them, and made a terrible face when they entered; but Harry jumped upon his knee with joy at seeing him again, while Laura forgot all her distress, and rushed up to Lady Harriet, who folded her in her arms, and kissed her most affectionately.

Not a word was said that day about the tea-party; but next morning Major Graham asked Harry, very gravely, "if he had read in the newspaper the melancholy accounts about several of his little companions, who were ill and confined to bed from having eat too much at a certain tea-party on Saturday last. Poor Peter Grey has been given over; and Charles Forrester, it is feared, may not be able to eat another loaf of bread for a fortnight!"

"Oh! Uncle David! it makes me ill whenever I think of that party!" said Harry, colouring perfectly scarlet; "that was the most miserable evening of my life!"

"I must say it was not quite fair in Mrs. Crabtree to starve all the strange little boys and girls who came as visiters to my house, without knowing who had invited them," observed Lady Harriet. "Probably those unlucky children will never forget, as long as they live, that scanty supper in our dining-room."

And it turned out exactly as Lady Harriet had predicted; for though they were all asked to tea, in proper form, the very next Saturday, when Major Graham showered torrents of sugar-plums on the table, while the children scrambled to pick them up, and the sideboard almost broke down afterwards under the weight of buns, cakes, cheese-cakes, biscuits, fruit, and preserves, which were heaped upon each other—yet, for years afterwards, Peter Grey, whenever he ate a particularly enormous dinner, always observed, that he must make up for having once been starved at Harry Graham's; and whenever any one of those little boys or girls again happened to meet Harry or Laura, they were sure to laugh and say, "When are you going to give us another

GRAND FEAST?"

THE TERRIBLE FIRE

Fire rages with fury wherever it comes,
If only one spark should be dropped;
Whole houses, or cities, sometimes it consumes,
Where its violence cannot be stopped.

ONE NIGHT, about eight o'clock, Harry and Laura were playing in the nursery, building houses with bricks, and trying who could raise the highest tower without letting it fall, when suddenly they were startled to hear every bell in the house ringing violently, while the servants seemed running up and down stairs, as if they were distracted.

"What can be the matter!"cried Laura, turning round and listening, while Harry quietly took this opportunity to shake the walls of her castle till it fell.

"The very house is coming down about your ears Laura!" said Harry, enjoying his little bit of mischief. "I should like to be Andrew, now, for five minutes, that I might answer those fifty bells, and see what has happened. Uncle David must be wanting coals, candles, tea, toast, and soda-water, all at once! What a bustle everybody is in! There! the bells are ringing again, worse than ever! Something wonderful is going on! what can it be!"

Presently Betty ran breathlessly into the room, saying that Mrs. Crabtree ought to come down stairs immediately, as Lady Harriet had been suddenly taken very ill, and, till the Doctor arrived, nobody knew what to do, so she must give her advice and assistance.

Harry and Laura felt excessively shocked to hear this alarming news, and listened with grave attention, while Mrs. Crabtree told them how amazingly well they ought to behave in her absence, when they were trusted alone in the nursery, with nobody to keep them in order, or to see what they were doing, especially now, as their grandmama had been taken ill, and would require to be kept quiet.

Harry sat in his chair, and might have been painted as the very picture of a good boy during nearly twenty minutes after Mrs. Crabtree departed; and Laura placed herself opposite to him, trying to follow so excellent an example, while they scarcely spoke above a whisper, wondering what could be the matter with their grandmama, and wishing for once, to see Mrs. Crabtree again, that they might hear how she was. Any one who had observed Harry and Laura at that time, would have wondered to see two such quiet, excellent, respectable children, and wished that all little boys and girls were made upon the same pattern; but presently they began to think that probably Lady Harriet was not so very ill, as no more bells had rung during several minutes, and Harry ventured to look about for some better amusement than sitting still.

At this moment Laura unluckily perceived, on the table near where they sat, a pair of Mrs. Crabtree's best scissors, which she had been positively forbid to touch. The long troublesome ringlets were as usual hanging over her eyes in a most teasing manner; so she thought what a good opportunity this might be to shorten them a very little, not above an inch or two; and, without considering a moment longer, she slipped upon tiptoe, with a frightened look, round the table, and picked up the scissors in her hand,—then hastening towards a looking-glass, she began snipping off the ends of her hair. Laura was much diverted to see it showering down upon the floor; so she cut and cut on, while the curls fell thicker and faster, till at last the whole floor was covered with them, and scarcely a hair left upon her head. Harry went into fits of laughing when he perceived what a ridiculous figure Laura had made of herself; and he turned her round and round to see the havoc she had made, saying,

"You should give all this hair to Mr. Mills, the upholsterer, to stuff grandmama's arm-chair with! At any rate, Laura, if Mrs. Crabtree is ever so angry, she can hardly pull you by the hair of the head again! What a sound sleep you will have to-night, with no hard curl-papers to torment you!"

Harry had been told, five hundred times, never to touch the candles, and threatened with twenty different punishments if he ever ventured to do so; but now he amused himself with trying to snuff one, till he snuffed it out. Then he lighted it again, and tried the experiment once more; but again the teasing candle went out, as if on purpose to plague him; so he felt quite provoked. Having lighted it once more, Harry prepared to carry the candlestick with him towards the inner nursery,—though afraid to make the smallest noise, in case it might be taken from him. Before he had gone five steps, down dropped the extinguisher,—then followed the snuffers, with a great crash; but Laura seemed too busy cropping her ringlets, to notice what was going on. All the way along upon the floor, Harry let fall a perfect shower of hot wax, which spotted the nursery carpet from the table where he had found the candle, into the next room,—where he disappeared, and shut the door, that no one might interfere with what he liked to do.

After he had been absent some time, the door was hastily opened again, and Laura felt surprised to see Harry come back, with his face as red as a stick of sealing-wax, and his large eyes staring wider than they had ever stared before, with a look of rueful consternation.

"What is the matter?" exclaimed Laura, in a terrified voice. "Has anything dreadful happened? Why do you look so frightened and so surprised?"

"Oh dear! oh dear! what shall I do?" cried Harry, who seemed scarcely to know how he spoke, or where he was. "I don't know what to do, Laura!"

"What can be the matter? do tell me at once Harry," said Laura, shaking with apprehension. "Speak as fast as you can!"

"Will you not tell Mrs. Crabtree, nor grandmama, nor anybody else?" cried Harry, bursting into tears. "I am so very, very sorry, and so frightened! Laura! do you know, I took a candle into the next room, merely to play with it."

"Well! go on, Harry! go on! what did you do with the candle?"

"I only put it on the bed for a single minute, to see how the flame would look there,—well! do you know it blazed away famously, and then all the bed clothes began burning too! Oh! there is such a terrible fire in the next room! you never saw anything like it! what shall we do? If old Andrew were to come up, do you think he could put it out? I have shut the door that Mrs. Crabtree may not see the flames. Be sure, Laura, to tell nobody but Andrew."

Laura became terrified at the way she saw poor Harry in, but when she opened the door to find out the real state of affairs, oh! what a dreadful sight was there! all the beds were on fire, while bright red flames were blazing up to the roof of the room, with a fierce roaring noise, which it was perfectly frightful to hear. She screamed aloud with terror at this alarming scene, while Harry did all he could to quiet her, and even put his hand over her mouth, that her cries might not be heard. Laura now struggled to get loose, and called louder and louder, till at last every maid in the house came racing up stairs, three steps at a time, to know what was the matter. Immediately upon seeing the flames, they all began screaming too in such a loud discordant way, that it sounded as if a whole flight of crows had come into the passages. Never was there such an uproar heard in the house before, for the walls echoed with a general cry of "Fire! fire! fire!"

Up flew Mrs. Crabtree towards the nursery like a sky-rocket, scolding furiously, talking louder than all the others put together, and asking who had set the house on fire, while Harry and Laura scarcely knew whether to be most frightened for the raging flames or the raging Mrs. Crabtree; but, in the mean time, they both shrunk into the smallest possible size, and hid themselves behind a door.

During all this confusion, old Andrew luckily remembered, that in the morning there had been a great washing in the laundry, where large tubs full of water were standing, so he called to the few maids who had any of their senses remaining, desiring them to assist in carrying up some buckets, that they might be emptied on the burning beds, to extinguish the flames if possible. Everybody was now in a hurry, and all elbowing each other out of the way, while it was most extraordinary to see how old Andrew exerted himself, as if he had been a fireman all his life, while Mrs. Marmalade, the fat cook, who could hardly carry herself up stairs in general, actively assisted to bring up the great heavy tubs, and to pour them out like a cascade upon the burning curtains, till the nursery-floor looked like a duck pond.

Meantime Harry and Laura added to the confusion as much as they could, and were busier than anybody, stealing down the back-stairs whenever Mrs. Crabtree was not in sight, and filling their little jugs with water, which they brought up, as fast as possible, and dashed upon the flames, till at last, it is to be feared, they began to feel quite amused with the bustle, and to be almost sorry when the conflagration diminished. At one time, Laura very nearly set her frock on fire, as she ventured too near, but Harry pulled her back, and then courageously advanced to discharge a shower from his own little jug, remaining stationary to watch the effect, till his face was almost scorched.

At last the fire became less and less, till it went totally out, but not before the nursery furniture had been reduced to perfect ruins, besides which, Betty had her arm sadly burned in the confusion. Mrs. Marmalade's cap was completely destroyed, and Mrs. Crabtree's best gown had so large a hole burned in the skirt, that she never could wear it again.

After all was quiet, and the fire completely extinguished, Major Graham took Laura down stairs to Lady Harriet's dressing-room, that she might tell the whole particulars of how this alarming accident happened in the nursery, for nobody could guess what had caused so sudden and dreadful a fire, which seemed to have been as unexpected as a flash of lightning.

Lady Harriet had felt so terrified by the noise and confusion, that she was out of bed, sitting up in an arm-chair, supported by pillows, when Laura entered,—at the sight of whom, with her well-cropped head, she uttered an exclamation of perfect amazement.

"Why! who on earth is that? Laura! my dear child! what has become of all your hair? Were your curls burned off in the fire, or did the fright make you grow bald? What is the meaning of all this?"

Laura turned perfectly crimson with shame and distress, for she now felt convinced of her own great misconduct about the scissors and curls; but she had been taught on all occasions to speak the truth, and would rather have died than told a lie, or even allowed any person to believe what was not true; therefore she answered, in a low, frightened voice, while the tears came into her eyes, "My hair has not been burned off, grandmama! but—but—"

"Well, child! speak out!" said Lady Harriet, impatiently. "Did some hairdresser come to the house and rob you?"

"Or are you like the ladies of Carthage, who gave their long hair for bows and arrows?" asked Major Graham. "I never saw such a little fright in my life as you look now; but tell us all about it!"

"I have been quite as naughty as Harry!" answered Laura, bursting into tears, and sobbing with grief; "I was cutting off my hair with Mrs. Crabtree's scissors, all the time that he was setting the nursery on fire!"

"Did any mortal ever hear of two such little torments!" exclaimed Major Graham, hardly able to help laughing. "I wonder if anybody else in the world has such mischievous children!"

"It is certainly very strange, that you and Harry never can contrive to be three hours out of a scrape!" said Lady Harriet, gravely; "now Frank, on the contrary, never forgets what I bid him do. You might suppose he carried Mrs. Crabtree in his pocket, to remind him constantly of his duty; but there are not two such boys in the world as Frank!"

"No," added Major Graham; "Harry set the house on fire, and Frank will set the Thames on fire!"

When Laura saw Uncle David put on one of his funny looks, while he spoke in this way to Lady Harriet, she almost forgot her former fright, and became surprised to observe her grandmama busily preparing what she called a coach-wheel, which had been often given as a treat to Harry and herself when they were particularly good. This delightful wheel was manufactured by taking a whole round slice of the loaf, in the centre of which was placed a large teaspoonful of jelly,—after which long spokes of marmalade, jam, and honey, were made to diverge most tastefully in every direction towards the crust, and Laura watched the progress of this business with great interest and anxiety, wondering if it could be hoped that her grandmama really meant to forgive all her misconduct during the day.

"That coach-wheel is, of course, meant for me!" said Major Graham, pretending to be very hungry, and looking slyly at Laura. "It cannot possibly be intended for our little hair-dresser here!"

"Yes, it is!" answered Lady Harriet, smiling. "I have some thoughts of excusing Laura this time, because she always tells me the truth, without attempting to conceal any foolish thing she does. It will be very long before she has any hair to cut off again, so I hope she may be older and wiser by that time, especially considering that every looking-glass she sees for six months will make her feel ashamed of herself. She certainly deserves some reward for having prevented the house to-night from being burned to the ground."

"I am glad you think so, because here is a shilling that has been burning in my pocket for the last few minutes, as I wished to bestow it on Laura for having saved all our lives; and if she had behaved still better, I might perhaps have given her a gold watch!"

Laura was busily employed in eating her coach-wheel, and trying to fancy what the gold watch would have looked like which she might probably have got from Uncle David, when suddenly the door burst open, and Mrs. Crabtree hurried into the room, with a look of surprise and alarm, her face as red as a poppy, and her eyes fixed on the hole in her best gown, while she spoke so loud and angrily, that Laura almost trembled.

"If you please, my lady! where can Master Harry be? I cannot find him in any corner! we have been searching all over the house, up stairs and down stairs, in vain. Not a garret or a closet but has been ransacked, and nobody can guess what has become of him!"

"Did you look up the chimney, Mrs. Crabtree?" asked Major Graham, laughing to see how excited she looked.

" 'Deed, sir, it is no joke!" answered Mrs. Crabtree, sulkily; "I am almost afraid Master Harry has been burned in the fire! The last time Betty saw him, he was throwing a jug of water into the flames, and no one has ever seen or heard of him since! There is a great many ashes and cinders lying about the room, and—"

"Do you think, in sober seriousness, Mrs. Crabtree, that Harry would melt away like a wax doll, without asking anybody to extinguish him?" said Major Graham, smiling. "No! no! little boys are not quite so easily disposed of. I shall find Harry in less than five minutes, if he is above ground."

But Uncle David was quite mistaken in expecting to discover Harry so easily, for he searched and searched in vain. He looked into every possible or impossible place—the library, the kitchen, the garrets, the laundry, the drawing-room, all without success,—he peeped under the tables, behind the curtains, over the beds, beneath the pillows, and into Mrs. Crabtree's bonnet-box—he even opened the tea-chest, and looked out at the window, in case Harry had tumbled over, but nowhere could he be found.

"Not a mouse is stirring!" exclaimed Major Graham, beginning now to look exceedingly grave and anxious. "This is very strange! the house-door is locked; therefore, unless Harry made his escape through the keyhole, he must be here! It is most unaccountable what the little pickle can have done with himself!"

When Major Graham chose to exert his voice, it was as loud as a trumpet, and could be heard half a mile off; so he now called out like thunder, from the top of the stairs to the bottom, saying, "Hollo, Harry, hollo! come here, my boy! Nobody shall hurt you! Harry! where are you?"

Uncle David waited to listen, but all was still—no answer could be heard, and there was not a sound in the house, except poor Laura at the bottom of the stairs, sobbing with grief and terror about Harry having been lost, and Mrs. Crabtree grumbling angrily to herself, on account of the large hole in her best gown.

By this time Lady Harriet nearly fainted with fatigue, for she was so very old, and had been ill all day; so she grew worse and worse, till everybody said she must go to bed, and try if it would be possible to fall asleep, assuring her that Harry must soon be found, as nothing particular could have happened to him, or some person would have seen it.

"Indeed, my lady, Master Harry is just like a bad shilling, that is sure to come back," said Mrs. Crabtree, helping her to undress, while she continued to talk the whole time about the fire, showing her own unfortunate gown, describing the trouble she had taken to save the house from being burned, and always ending every sentence with a wish that she could lay hands on Harry, to punish him as he deserved.

"The truth is, I just spoil and indulge the children too much, my lady!" added Mrs. Crabtree, in a self-satisfied tone of voice. "I really blame myself often for being over-easy and kind."

"You have nothing to accuse yourself of in that respect," answered Lady Harriet, unable to help smiling.

"Your ladyship is very good to say so. Major Graham is so fond of our young people, that it is lucky they have some one to keep them in order. I shall make a duty, my lady, of being more strict than ever. Master Harry must be made an example of this time!" added Mrs. Crabtree, angrily glancing at the hole in her gown. "I shall teach him to remember this day the longest hour he has to live!"

"Harry will not forget it any how," answered Lady Harriet languidly. "Perhaps, Mrs. Crabtree, we might as well not be severe with the poor boy on this occasion. As the old proverb says, 'there is no use in pouring water on a drowned mouse.' Harry has got a sad fright for his pains, and at all events you must find him first, before he can be punished. Where can the poor child be hid?"

"I would give sixpence to find out that, my lady!" answered Mrs. Crabtree, helping Lady Harriet into bed, after which she closed the shutters, put out the candles, and left the room, angrily muttering, "Master Harry cares no more for me than the poker cares for the tongs, but I shall teach him another story soon."

Lady Harriet now feebly closed her eyes, being quite exhausted, and was beginning to feel the pleasant confused sensation that people have before going to sleep, when some noise made her suddenly start quite awake. She sat up in bed to listen, but could not be sure whether it had been a great noise at a distance, or a little noise in the room; so after waiting two or three minutes, she sunk back upon the pillows, and tried to forget it. Again, however, she distinctly heard something rustling in the bed curtains, and opened her eyes to see what could be the matter, but all was dark. Something seemed to be breathing very near her, however, and the curtains shook worse than before, till Lady Harriet became really alarmed.

"It must surely be a cat in the room!" thought she, hastily pulling the bell-rope, till it nearly came down. "That tiresome little animal will make such a noise, I shall not be able to sleep all night!"

The next minute Lady Harriet was startled to hear a loud sob close beside her; and when everybody rushed up stairs to ask what was the matter, they brought candles to search the room, and there was Harry! He lay doubled up in a corner, and crying as if his heart would break, yet still endeavouring not to be seen; for Harry always thought it a terrible disgrace to cry, and would have concealed himself anywhere, rather than be observed weeping. Laura burst into tears also, when she saw what red eyes and pale cheeks Harry had; but Mrs. Crabtree lost no time in pulling him out of his place, being quite impatient to begin her scold, and to produce her tawse, though she received a sad disappointment on this occasion, as Uncle David unexpectedly interfered to get him off.

"Come now! Mrs. Crabtree," said he good-naturedly; "put up the tawse for this time; you are rather too fond of the leather. Harry seems really sorry and frightened, so we must be merciful. The cataract of tears he is shedding now, would have extinguished the fire if it had come in time! Harry is like a culprit with the rope about his neck; but he shall not be executed. Let me be judge and jury in this case; and my sentence is a very dreadful one. Harry must sleep all to-night in the burned nursery, having no other covering than the burned blankets, with large holes in them, that he may never forget

The Terrible Fire!"

THE PRODIGIOUS CAKE

Yet theirs the joy
That lifts their steps, that sparkles in their eyes;
That talks or laughs, or runs, or shouts, or plays,
And speaks in all their looks, and all their ways.
CRABBE

Next day after the fire, Laura could think of nothing but what she was to do with the shilling that Uncle David had given her; and a thousand plans came into her head, while many wants entered her thoughts, which never occurred before; so that if twenty shillings had been in her hand instead of one, they would all have gone twenty different ways.

Lady Harriet advised that it should be laid by till Laura had fully considered what she would like best; reminding her very truly, that money is lame in coming but flies in going away. "Many people can get a shilling, Laura," said her grandmama; "but the difficulty is to keep it; for you know the old proverb tells that 'a fool and his money are soon parted.'"

"Yes, miss! so give it to me, and I shall take care of your shilling!" added Mrs. Crabtree, holding out her hand to Laura, who felt that if her money once disappeared into that capacious pocket, she would never see it again. "Children have no use for money! that shilling will only burn a hole in your purse, till it is spent on some foolish thing or other. You will be losing your thimble soon, or mislaying your gloves; for all these things seem to fly in every direction, as if they got legs and wings as soon as they belong to you; so then that shilling may replace what is lost."

Mrs. Crabtree looked as if she would eat it up; but Laura grasped her treasure still tighter in her hand, exclaiming,

"No! no! this is mine! Uncle David never thought of my shilling being taken care of! He meant me to do whatever I liked with it! Uncle David says he cannot endure saving children, and that he wishes all money were turned into slates, when little girls keep it longer than a week."

"I like that!" said Harry, eagerly; "it is so pleasant to spend money, when the shopkeeper bows to me over the counter so politely, and asks what I please to want."

"Older people than you like spending money, Master Harry, and spend whether they have it or no; but the greatest pleasure is to keep it. For instance, Miss Laura, whatever she sees worth a shilling in any shop, might be hers if she pleases; so then it is quite as good as her own. We shall look in at the bazaar every morning, to fix upon something that she would like to have, and then consider of it for two or three days."

Laura thought this plan so very unsatisfactory that she lost no time in getting her shilling changed into two sixpences, one of which she immediately presented to Harry, —who positively refused for a long time to accept of it, insisting that Laura should rather buy some pretty plaything for herself; but she answered that it was much pleasanter to divide her fortune with Harry, than to be selfish, and spend it all alone. "I am sure, Harry," added she, "if this money had been yours, you would have said the same thing, and given the half of what you got to me; so, now, let us say no more about that, but tell me what would be the best use to make of my sixpence?"

"You might buy that fine red morocco purse we saw in the shop window yesterday," observed Harry, looking very serious and anxious, on being consulted. "Do you remember how much we both wished to have it!"

"But what is the use of a purse, with no money to keep in it?" answered Laura, looking earnestly at Harry for more advice. "Think again of something else."

"Would you like a new doll?"

"Yes; but I have nothing to dress her with!"

"Suppose you buy that pretty geranium in a red flower-pot at the gardener's!"

"If it would only live for a week, I might be tempted to try; but flowers will always die with me. They seem to wither when I so much as look at them. Do you remember that pretty fuchsia, that I almost drowned the first day grandmama gave it me? and we forgot for a week afterwards to water it at all. I am not a good flower-doctor."

"Then buy a gold watch, at once," said Harry, laughing; "or a fine pony, with a saddle, to ride on."

"Now, Harry, pray be quite in earnest. You know I might as well attempt to buy the moon as a gold watch; so think of something else."

"It is very difficult to make a good use of money," said Harry, pretending to look exceedingly wise. "Do you know, Laura, I once found out that you could have twelve of those large ship-biscuits we saw at the baker's shop, for sixpence. Only think! you could feed the whole town, and make a present to everybody in the house besides! I dare say Mrs. Crabtree might like one with her tea. All the maids would think them a treat. You could present one to Frank, another to old Andrew, and there would still be some left for those poor children at the cottage."

"Oh! that is the very thing!" cried Laura, running out of the room to send Andrew off with a basket, and looking as happy as possible. Not long afterwards, Frank, who had returned from school, was standing at the nursery window, when he suddenly called out, in a voice of surprise and amusement.

"Come here, Harry! look at old Andrew! he is carrying something tied up in a towel, as large as his own head! what can it be!"

"That is all for me! these are my biscuits!" said Laura, running off to receive the parcel; and though she heard Frank laughing, while Harry told all about them, she did not care, but brought her whole collection triumphantly into the nursery.

"Oh, fancy! how perfect!" cried Harry, opening the bundle; "this is very good fun!"

"Here are provisions for a siege!" added Frank. "You have at least got enough for your money, Laura!"

"Take one yourself, Frank!" said she, reaching him the largest; and then, with the rest all tied in her apron, Laura proceeded up and down stairs, making presents to every person she met, till her whole store was finished; and she felt quite satisfied and happy, because everybody seemed pleased, and returned many thanks, except Mrs. Crabtree, who said she had no teeth to eat such hard things, which were only fit for sailors going to America or the West Indies.

"You should have bought me a pound of sugar, Miss Laura, and that might have been a present worth giving."

"You are too sweet already, Mrs. Crabtree!" said Frank, laughing. "I shall send you a sugarcane from the West Indies, to beat Harry and Laura with, and a whole barrel of sugar for yourself, from my own estate."

"None of your nonsense, Master Frank! Get out of the nursery this moment! You with an estate, indeed! You will not have a place to put your foot upon soon, except the topmast in a man-of-war, where all the bad boys in a ship are sent."

"Perhaps, as you are not to be the captain, I may escape, and be dining with the officers, sometimes! I mean to send you home a fine new India shawl, Mrs. Crabtree, the very moment I arrive at Madras, and some china teacups from Canton."

"Fiddlesticks and nonsense!" said Mrs. Crabtree, who sometimes enjoyed a little jesting with Frank. "Keep all them rattletraps till you are a rich nabob, and come home to look for Mrs. Frank,—a fine wife she will be! Ladies that get fortunes from India are covered all over with gold chains, and gold muslins, and scarlet shawls. She will eat nothing but curry and rice, and never put her foot to the ground, except to step into her carriage."

"I hope you are not a gipsy, to tell fortunes!" cried Harry, laughing. "Frank would die rather than take such a wife."

"Or, at least, I would rather have a tooth drawn than do it," added Frank, smiling. "Perhaps I may prefer to marry one of those old wives on the chimney-tops; but it is too serious to say I would rather die, because nobody knows how awful it is to die, till the appointed day comes."

"Very true and proper, Master Frank," replied Mrs. Crabtree; "you speak like a printed book sometimes, and you deserve a good wife."

"Then I shall return home some day with chests of gold, and let you choose one for me, as quiet and good-natured as yourself, Mrs. Crabtree," said Frank, taking up his books and hastening off to school, running all the way, as he was rather late, and Mr. Lexicon, the master, had promised a grand prize for the boy who came most punctually to his lessons, which everybody declared that Frank was sure to gain, as he had never once been absent at the right moment.

Major Graham often tried to tease Frank, by calling him "the Professor,"—asking him questions which it was impossible to answer, and then pretending to be quite shocked at his ignorance; but no one ever saw the young scholar put out of temper by those tricks and trials, for he always laughed more heartily than any one else at the joke.

"Now show me, Frank," said Uncle David, one morning, "how do you advance three steps backwards?"

"That is quite impossible, unless you turn me into a crab."

"Tell me, then, which is the principal town in Caffraria?"

"Is there any town there? I do not recollect it."

"Then so much the worse!—how are you ever to get through life without knowing the chief town in Caffraria! I am quite ashamed of your ignorance. Now, let us try a little arithmetic! Open the door of your understanding and tell me, when wheat is six shillings a bushel, what is the price of a penny loaf. Take your slate and calculate that."

"Yes, Uncle David, if you will find out, when gooseberries are two shillings a pint, what is the price of a three-penny tart. You remind me of my old nursery song—

> 'The man in the wilderness asked me,
> How many strawberries grew in the sea;
> I answered him, as I thought it good,
> As many red herrings as grew in the wood.' "

Some days after Laura had distributed the biscuits, she became very sorry for having squandered her shilling, without attending to Lady Harriet's good advice, about keeping it carefully in her pocket for at least a week, to see what would happen. A very pleasant way of using money now fell in her way, but she had been a foolish spendthrift, so her pockets were empty when she most wished them to be full. Harry came that morning after breakfast into the nursery, looking in a great bustle, and whispering to Laura, "What a pity your sixpence is gone! but as Mrs. Crabtree says, 'we cannot both eat our cake and have it!' "

"No!" answered Laura, as seriously as if she had never thought of this before; "but why do you so particularly wish my money back to-day?"

"Because such a very nice, funny thing is to be done this morning. You and I are asked to join the party, but I am afraid we cannot afford it! All our little cousins and companions intend going with Mr. Harwood, the tutor, at twelve o'clock, to climb up to the very top of Arthur's Seat, where they are to dine and have a dance. There will be about twenty boys and girls of the party, but everybody is to carry a basket filled with provisions for dinner, either cakes, or fruit or biscuits, which are to be eat on the great rock at the top of the hill. Now grandmama says we ought to have had money enough to supply what is necessary, and then we might have gone, but no one can be admitted who has not at least sixpence to buy something."

"Oh! how provoking!" said Laura, sadly. "I wonder when we shall learn always to follow grandmama's advice, for that is sure to turn out best in the end. I never take my own way without being sorry for it afterwards, so I deserve now to be disappointed and remain at home; but, Harry, your sixpence is still safe, so pray join this delightful party, and tell me all about it afterwards."

"If it could take us both, I should be very happy, but I will not go without you, Laura, after you were so good to me, and gave me this as a present. No, no! I only wish we could do like the poor madman grandmama mentioned, who planted sixpences in the ground that they might grow into shillings."

"Pray! what are you two looking so solemn about?" asked Frank, hurrying into the room, at that moment, on his way to school. "Are you talking of some mischief that has been done already, or only about some mischief you are intending to do soon?"

"Neither the one nor the other," answered Laura. "But, oh! Frank, I am sure you will be sorry for us when we tell you of our sad disappointment."

She then related the whole story of the party to Arthur's Seat, mentioning that Mr. Harwood had kindly offered to take charge of Harry and herself, but as her little fortune had been so foolishly squandered, she could not go, and Harry said it would be impossible to enjoy the fun without her, though Lady Harriet had given them both leave to be of the party.

All the time that Laura spoke, Frank stood with his hands in his pockets, where he seemed evidently searching for something, and when the whole history was told, he said to Harry, "Let me see this poor little sixpence of yours! I am a very clever conjuror, and could perhaps turn it into a shilling!"

"Nonsense, Frank!" said Laura, laughing; "you might as well turn Harry into Uncle David!"

"Well! we shall see!" answered Frank, taking up the sixpence. "I have put the money into this box!—rattle it well!—once! twice! thrice!—there, peep in!—now it is a shilling! I told you so!"

Frank ran joyously out of the room, being much amused with the joke, for he had put one of his own shillings into the box for Harry and Laura, who were excessively surprised at first, and felt really ashamed to take this very kind present from Frank, when he so seldom had money of his own; but they knew how generous he was, for he often repeated that excellent maxim, "It is more blessed to give than to receive."

After a few minutes, they remembered that nothing could prevent them now from going with Mr. Harwood to Arthur's Seat, which put Laura into such a state of ecstasy, that she danced round the room for joy, while Harry jumped upon the tables and chairs, tumbled head over heels, and called Betty to come immediately, that they might get ready.

When Mrs. Crabtree heard such an uproar, she hastened also into the room, asking what had happened to cause this riot, and she became very angry indeed, to hear that Harry and Laura had both got leave to join in this grand expedition.

"You will be spoiling all your clothes, and getting yourselves into a heat! I wonder her ladyship allows this! How much better you would be taking a quiet walk with me in the gardens! I shall really speak to Lady Harriet about it! The air must be very cold on the top of them great mountains! I am sure you will both have colds for a month after this Tom-foolery."

"Oh no, Mrs. Crabtree! I promise not to catch cold!" cried Harry, eagerly; "and, besides, you can scarcely prevent our going now, for grandmama has set out on her long airing in the carriage, so there is nobody for you to ask about keeping us at home, except Uncle David."

Mrs. Crabtree knew from experience, that Major Graham was a hopeless case, as he always took part with the children, and liked nothing so much for old and young as "a ploy;" so she grumbled on to herself, while her eyes looked as sharp as a pair of scissors with rage. "You will come back, turned into scare crows, with all your nice clean clothes in tatters," said she, angrily; "but if there is so much as a speck upon this best new jacket and trousers, I shall know the reason why."

"What a comfort it would be, if there were no such things in the world as 'new clothes,' for I am always so much happier in the old ones," said Harry. "People at the shops should sell clothes that will never either dirty or tear."

"You ought to be dressed in fur, like Robinson Crusoe, or sent out naked, like the little savages," said Mrs. Crabtree; "or painted black and blue, like them wild old Britons that lived here long ago!"

"I am black and blue sometimes without being painted," said Harry, escaping to the door. "Good bye, Mrs. Crabtree! I hope you will not die of weariness without us! On our return we shall tell you all our delightful adventures."

About half an hour afterwards, Harry and Laura were seen hurrying out of Mrs. Weddel's pastry-shop, bearing little covered baskets in their hands, but nobody could guess what was in them. They whispered and laughed together with merry faces, looking the very pictures of happiness, and running along as fast as they could to join the noisy party of their cousins and companions, almost fearing that Mr. Harwood might have set off without them. Frank often called him "Mr. Punctuality," as he was so very particular about his scholars being in good time on all occasions; and certainly Mr. Harwood carried his watch more in his hand than in his pocket, being in the habit of constantly looking to see that nobody arrived too late. Mail-coaches or steamboats could hardly keep the time better, when an hour had once been named; and the last words that Harry heard, when he was invited, were, "Remember! sharp twelve."

The great clock of St. Andrew's Church was busy striking that hour, and every little clock in the town was saying the same thing, when Mr. Harwood himself, with his watch in his hand, opened the door, and walked out, followed by a dozen of merry-faced boys and girls, all speaking at once, and vociferating louder than the clocks, as if they thought everybody had grown deaf.

"I shall reach the top of Arthur's Seat first," said Peter Grey. "All follow me, for I know the shortest way. It is only a hop, step, and a jump!"

"Rather a long step!" cried Robert Fordyce. "But I could lead you a much better way, though I shall show it to nobody but myself."

"We must certainly drink water at St. Anthony's Well," observed Laura; "because whatever any one wishes for when he tastes it, is sure to happen immediately."

"Then I shall wish that some person may give me a new doll," said Mary Forrester. "My old one is only fit for being lady's maid to a fine new doll."

"I am in ninety-nine minds what to wish for," exclaimed Harry; "we must take care not to be like the foolish old woman in the fairy tale, who got only a yard of black pudding."

"I shall ask for a piebald pony, with a whip, a saddle, and a bridle!" cried Peter Grey; "and for a week's holidays—and a new watch—and a spade—and a box of French plums—and to be first at the top of Arthur's Seat—and—and—"

"Stop, Peter!—stop! you can only have one wish at St. Anthony's Well," interrupted Mr. Harwood. "If you ask more, you lose all."

"That is very hard, for I want everything," replied Peter. "What are you wishing for, sir?"

"What shall I ask for?" said Mr. Harwood, reflecting to himself. "I have not a want in the world!"

"O yes, sir! you must wish for something!" cried the whole party, eagerly. "Do invent something to ask, Mr. Harwood!"

"Then I wish you may all behave well till we reach the top of Arthur's Seat, and all come safely down again."

"You may be sure of that already!" said Peter, laughing. "I set such a very good example to all my companions, that they never behave ill when I am present,—no! not even by accident! When Dr. Algebra examined our class to-day, he asked Mr. Lexicon, 'What has become of the best boy in your school this morning?' and the answer was, 'Of course you mean Peter Grey! he is gone to the top of Arthur's Seat with that excellent man, Mr. Harwood.' "

"Indeed!—and pray, Master Peter, what bird whispered this story into your ear, seeing it has all happened since we left home!—but people who are praised by nobody else, often take to praising themselves!"

"Who knows better!—and here is Harry Graham the very ditto of myself,—so steady he might be fit to drill a whole regiment. We shall lead the party quite safely up the hill, and down again, without any ladders."

"And without wings," added Harry, laughing; "but what are we to draw water out of the well with?—here are neither buckets, nor tumblers, nor glasses!"

"I could lend you my thimble!" said Laura, searching her pocket. "That will hold enough of water for one wish, and every person may have the loan of it in turn."

"This is the very first time your thimble has been of use to anybody!" said Harry, slyly; "but I dare say it is not worn into holes with too much sewing, therefore it will make a famous little magical cup for St. Anthony's Well. You know the fairies who dance here by moonlight, lay their table-cloth upon a mushroom, and sit round it, to be merry, but I never heard what they use for a drinking cup."

Harry now proceeded briskly along to the well, singing as he went, a song which had been taught him by Uncle David, beginning,

> I wish I were a brewer's horse,
> Five quarters of a year,
> I'd place my head where was my tail,
> And drink up all the beer.

Before long the whole party seated themselves in a circle on the grass round St. Anthony's Well, while any stranger who chanced to pass might have supposed from the noise and merriment, that the saint had filled his well with champagne and punch for the occasion, as everybody seemed perfectly tipsy with happiness. Mr. Harwood laughed prodigiously at some of the jokes, and made a few of his own, which were none of the best, though they caused the most laughter, for the boys thought it very surprising that so grave and great a man should make a joke at all.

When Mary Forrester drank her thimbleful of water, and wished for a new doll, Peter and Harry privately cut out a face upon a red-cheeked apple, making the eyes, nose, and mouth; after which they hastily dressed it up in pocket handkerchiefs, and gave her this present from the fairies,—which looked so very like what she had asked for, that the laugh which followed was loud and long. Afterwards Peter swallowed his draught, calling loudly for a piebald pony,—when Harry, in his white trousers and dark jacket, went upon all-fours, and let Peter mount on his back. It was very difficult, however, to get Peter off again; for he enjoyed the fun excessively, and stuck to his seat like Sinbad's old man of the sea, till at last Harry rolled on his back, tumbling Peter head over heels into St. Anthony's Well,—upon seeing which, Mr. Harwood rose, saying he had certainly lost his own wish, as they had behaved ill, and met with an accident already. Harry laughingly proposed that Peter should be carefully hung upon a tree to dry, till they all came down again; but the mischievous boy ran off so fast, he was almost out of sight in a moment, saying, "Now for the top of Arthur's Seat, and I shall grow dry with the fatigue of climbing."

The boys and girls immediately scattered themselves all over the hill, getting on the best way they could, and trying who could scramble up the fastest; but the grass was quite short, and as slippery as ice, therefore it became every moment more difficult to stand, and still more difficult to climb. The whole party began sliding, whether they liked it or not, and staggered, and tried to grasp the turf, but there was nothing to hold,—while occasionally a shower of stones and gravel came down from Peter, who pretended they fell by accident.

"Oh, Harry!" cried Laura, panting for breath, while she looked both frightened and fatigued. "If this were not a party of pleasure, I think we are sometimes quite as happy in our own gardens! People must be very miserable at home, before they come here to be amused! I wish we were cats, or goats, or anything that can stand upon a hill without feeling giddy."

"I think this is very good fun!" answered Harry, gasping, and trying not to tumble for for the twentieth time; "you would like, perhaps, to be back in the nursery with Mrs. Crabtree."

"No! no! I am not quite so bad as that! But Harry! do you ever really expect to reach the top? for I never shall; so I mean to sit down quietly here and wait till you all return."

"I have a better plan than that, Laura! you shall sit upon the highest point of Arthur's Seat as well as anybody, before either of us is an hour older! Let me go first, because I get on famously; and you must never look behind, but keep tight hold of my jacket, so then every step I advance will pull you up also."

Laura was delighted with this plan, which succeeded perfectly well; but they ascended rather slowly, as it was exceedingly fatiguing to Harry, who looked quite happy all the time to be of use,—for he always felt glad when he could do anything for anybody, more particularly for either Laura or Frank. Now, the whole party was at last safely assembled on the very highest point of Arthur's Seat; so the boys threw their caps up in the air, and gave three tremendous cheers, which frightened the very crows over their heads, and sent a flock of sheep scampering down the mountain side. After that, they planted Mr. Harwood's walking-stick in the ground, for a staff, while Harry tore off the blue silk handkerchief which Mrs. Crabtree had tied about his neck, and without caring whether he caught cold or not, he fastened it on the pole for a flag, being quite delighted to see how it waved in the wind most triumphantly, looking very like what sailors put up when they take possession of a desert island.

"Now, for business!" said Mr. Harwood, sitting down on the rock, and uncovering a prodigious cake, nearly as large as a cheese, which he had taken the trouble to carry, with great difficulty, up the hill. "I suppose nobody is hungry after our long walk! Let us see what all the baskets contain!"

Not a moment was lost in seating themselves on the grass, while the stores were displayed, amidst shouts of laughter and applause, which generally followed whatever came forth. Sandwiches, or, as Peter Grey called them, "savages," gingerbread, cakes, and fruit, all appeared in turn. Robert Fordyce brought a dozen of hard-boiled eggs, all dyed different colours,—blue, green, pink, and yellow, but not one was white. Edmund Ashford produced a collection of very sour-looking apples, and Charles Forrester showed a number of little gooseberry tarts; but when it became time for Peter's basket to be opened, it contained nothing except a knife and a fork, to cut up whatever his companions would give him!

"Peter! Peter! you shabby fellow!" said Charles Forrester, reaching him one of his tarts; "you should be put in the tread-mill as a sturdy beggar!"

"Or thrown down from the top of this precipice," added Harry, giving him a cake. "I wonder you can look any of us in the face, Peter!"

"I have heard," said Mr. Harwood, "that a stone is shown in Ireland, called 'the stone of Blarney,' and whoever kisses it, is never afterwards ashamed of anything he does. Our friend Peter has probably passed that way lately."

"At any rate, I am not likely to be starved to death amongst you all!" answered the impudent boy, demolishing everything he could get; and it is believed that Peter ate, on this memorable occasion, three times more than any other person, as each of the party offered him something, and he never was heard to say "No!"

"I could swallow Arthur's Seat if it were turned into a plum-pudding," said he, pocketing buns, apples, eggs, walnuts, biscuits, and almonds, till his coat stuck out all round like a balloon. "Has any one anything more to spare?"

"Did you ever hear," said Mr. Harwood, "that a pigeon eats its own weight of food every day? Now, I am sure, you and I know one boy in the world, Peter, who could do as much."

"What is to be done with that prodigious cake you carried up here, Mr. Harwood?" answered Peter, casting a devouring eye upon it; "the crust seems as hard as a rhinoceros' skin, but I dare say it is very good. One could not be sure, however, without tasting it! I hope you are not going to take the trouble of carrying that heavy load back again?"

"How very polite you are become all on a sudden, Peter!" said Laura, laughing. "I should be very sorry to attempt carrying that cake to the bottom of the hill, for we would both roll down the shortest way together."

"I am not over-anxious to try it either," observed Charles Forrester, shaking his head. "Even Peter though his mouth is constantly ajar, would find that cake rather heavy to carry either as an inside or an outside passenger."

"I can scarcely lift it at all!" continued Laura, when Mr. Harwood had again tied it up in the towel, "what can be done?"

"Here is the very best plan!" cried Harry, suddenly seizing the prodigious cake; and before anybody could hinder him, he gave it a tremendous push off the steepest part of Arthur's Seat, so that it rolled down like a wheel, over stones and precipices, jumping and hopping along with wonderful rapidity, amidst the cheers and laughter of all the children, till at last it reached the bottom of the hill, when a general clapping of hands ensued.

"Now for a race!" cried Harry, becoming more and more eager. "The first boy or girl who reaches that cake shall have it all to himself!"

Mr. Harwood tried with all his might to stop the commotion, and called out that they must go quietly down the bank, for Harry had no right to give away the cake, or to make them break their legs and arms with racing down such a hill. But he might as well have spoken to the east wind, and asked it not to blow. The whole party dispersed like a hive of bees that has been upset; and in a moment they were in full career after the cake.

Some of the boys tried to roll down, hoping to get on more quickly. Others endeavoured to slide; and several attempted to run; but they all fell—and many of them might have been tumblers at Sadler's Wells, they tumbled over and over so cleverly. Peter Grey's hat was blown away, but he did not stop to catch it. Charlie Hume lost his shoe. Robert Fordyce sprained his ankle, and every one of the girls tore her frock. It was a frightful scene; such devastation of bonnets and jackets as had never been known before; while Mr. Harwood looked like the general of a defeated army, calling till he became hoarse, and running till he was out of breath, vainly trying thus to stop the confusion, and to bring the stragglers back in better order.

Meantime, Harry and Peter were far before the rest, though Edmund Ashford was following hard after them in desperate haste, as if he still hoped to over-take their steps. Suddenly, however, a loud cry of distress was heard overhead; and when Harry looked up, he saw so very alarming a sight, that he could scarcely believe his eyes, and almost screamed out himself with the fright it gave him, while he seemed to forget in a moment, the race, Peter Grey, and the prodigious cake.

Laura had been very anxious not to trouble Harry with taking care of her in coming down the bank again, for she saw that during all this fun about the cake, he perfectly forgot that she was not accustomed every day to such a scramble on the hills, and would have required some help. After looking down on every side of the descent, and thinking that each appeared steeper than another, while they all made her equally giddy, Laura determined to venture on a part of the hill which seemed rather less precipitous than the rest; but it completely cheated her, being the most difficult and dangerous part of Arthur's Seat. The slope became steeper and steeper at every step; but Laura always tried to hope her path might grow better, till at last she reached a place where it was impossible to stop herself. Down she went! down! down! whether she would or not, screaming and sliding on a long slippery bank, till she reached the very edge of a dangerous precipice, which appeared higher than the side of a room. Laura then grappled hold of some stones and grass, calling loudly for help, while scarcely able to keep from falling into the deep ravine, which would probably have killed her. Her screams were echoed all over the hill, when Harry, seeing her frightful situation, clambered up the bank faster than any lamplighter, and immediately flew to Laura's assistance, who was now really hanging over the chasm, quite unable to help herself. At last he reached the place where poor Laura lay, and seized hold of her by the frock; but for some time it seemed an equal chance whether she dragged him into the hole, or he pulled her away from it. Luckily, however, by a great effort, Harry succeeded in delivering Laura, whom he placed upon a secure situation, and then, having waited patiently till she recovered from the fright, he led her carefully and kindly down to the bottom of Arthur's Seat.

Now, all the boys had already got there, and a violent dispute was going on about which of them reached the cake. Peter Grey had pushed down Edmund Ashford, who caught hold of Robert Fordyce, and they all three rolled to the bottom together, so that nobody could tell which had won the race; while Mr. Harwood laboured in vain to convince them that the cake belonged neither to the one nor the other, being his own property.

They all laughed at Harry for being distanced, and arriving last; while Mr. Harwood watched him coming down, and was pleased to observe how carefully he attended to Laura, though still being annoyed at the riot and confusion which Harry had occasioned, he determined to appear exceedingly angry, and put on a very terrible voice, saying,

"Hollo! young gentleman! what shall I do to you for beginning this uproar? As the old proverb says, 'one fool makes many.' How dare you roll my fine cake down the hill in this way, and send everybody rolling after it? Look me in the face and say you are ashamed of yourself!"

Harry looked at Mr. Harwood—and Mr. Harwood looked at Harry. They both tried to seem very grave and serious, but somehow Harry's eyes glittered very brightly, and two little dimples might be seen in his cheeks. Mr. Harwood had his eyebrows gathered into a terrible frown, but still his eyes were likewise sparkling, and his mouth seemed to be pursed up in a most comical manner. After staring at each other for several minutes, both Mr. Harwood and Harry burst into a prodigious fit of laughing, and nobody could tell which began first or laughed longest.

"Master Graham! you must send a new frock to every little girl of the party, and a suit of clothes to each of the boys, for having caused theirs to be all destroyed. I really meant to punish you severely for beginning such a riot, but something has made me change my mind. In almost every moment of our lives, we either act amiably or unamiably, and I observed you treat Miss Laura so kindly and properly all this morning, that I shall say not another word about

THE PRODIGIOUS CAKE."

THE LAST CLEAN FROCK

"For," said she, in spite of what grandmama taught her,
"I'm really remarkably fond of the water."

She splashed, and she dashed, and she turned herself round,
And heartily wished herself safe on the ground.

ONCE UPON A TIME Harry and Laura had got into so many scrapes, that there seemed really no end to their misconduct. They generally forgot to learn any lessons—often tore their books—drew pictures on their slates, instead of calculating sums—and made the pages of their copy-books into boats; besides which, Mrs. Crabtree caught them one day, when a party of officers dined at Lady Harriet's, with two of the captains' sword-belts buckled round their waists, and cocked hats upon their heads, while they beat the crown of a gentleman's hat with a walking-stick to sound like a drum.

Still it seemed impossible to make Uncle David feel sufficiently angry with them, though Mrs. Crabtree did all she could to put him in a passion, by telling the very worst; but he made fifty excuses a minute, as if he had been the naughty person himself, instead of Harry or Laura, and above all he said that they both seemed so exceedingly penitent when he explained their delinquencies, and they were both so ready to tell upon themselves, and to take all the blame of whatever mischief might be done, that he was determined to shut his eyes and say nothing, unless they did something purposely wrong.

One night, when Mrs. Crabtree had gone out, Major Graham felt quite surprised on his return home from a late dinner party, to find Laura and Harry still out of bed. They were sitting in his library when he entered, both looking so tired and miserable that he could not imagine what had happened; but Harry lost no time in confessing that he and Laura feared that they had done some dreadful mischief, so they could not sleep without asking pardon, and mentioning whose fault it was, that the maids might not be unjustly blamed.

"Well, you little imps of mischief! what have I to scold you for now?" asked Uncle David, not looking particularly angry. "Is it something that I shall be obliged to take the trouble of punishing you for? We ought to live in the Highlands, where there are whole forests of birch ready for use! Why are your ears like a bell-rope, Harry? because they seem made to be pulled. Now, go on with your story. What is the matter?"

"We were playing about the room, Uncle David, and Laura lost her ball, so she crept under that big table which has only one large leg. There is a brass button below, so we were trying if it would come off when all on a sudden, the table fell quite to one side as you see it now, tumbling down those prodigious books and tin boxes on the floor! I cannot think how this fine new table could be so easily broken; but whenever we even look at anything it seems to break!"

"Yes, Harry! you remind me of Meddlesome Matty in the nursery rhymes,

"Sometimes she'd lift the teapot lid
To peep at what was in it,
Or tilt the kettle, if you did

But turn your back a minute.
In vain you told her not to touch,
Her trick of meddling grew so much."

You have scarcely left my poor table a leg to stand upon. How am I ever to get it mended?"

"Perhaps the carpenter could do it to-morrow!"

"Or, perhaps Uncle David could do it this moment," said Major Graham, raising the fallen side with a sudden jerk,—when Harry and Laura heard a click under the table, like the locking of a door, after which the whole affair was rectified.

"Did I ever—!" exclaimed Harry, staring with astonishment; "so we have suffered all our fright for nothing, and the table was not really broken! I shall always run to you, Uncle David, when we are in a scrape, for you are sure to get us off."

"Do not reckon too certainly on that, Master Harry; it is easier to get into one than to get out of it, any day; but I am not so seriously angry at the sort of scrapes Laura and you get into, because you would not willingly and deliberately do wrong. If any children commit a mean action, or get into a passion, or quarrel with each other, or omit saying their prayers and reading their Bibles, or tell a lie, or take what does not belong to them, then it might be seen how extremely angry I could be; but while you continue merely thoughtless and forgetful, I mean to have patience a little longer before turning into a cross old uncle with a pair of tawse."

Harry sprung upon Uncle David's knee, quite delighted to hear him speak so very kindly; and Laura was soon installed in her usual place there also, listening to all that was said, and laughing at his jokes.

"As Mrs. Crabtree says," continued Major Graham, " 'we cannot put an old head on young shoulders;' and it would certainly look very odd if you could."

So Uncle David took out his pencil, and drew a funny picture of a cross old wrinkled face upon young shoulders like Laura's; and after they had all laughed at it together for about five minutes, he sent the children both to bed, quite merry and cheerful.

A long time elapsed afterwards without anything going wrong; and it was quite pleasant to see such learning of lessons, such attention to rules, and such obedience to Mrs. Crabtree, as went on in the nursery during several weeks. At last, one day, when Lady Harriet and Major Graham were preparing to set off on a journey, and to pay a short visit at Holiday House, Laura and Harry observed a great deal of whispering and talking in a corner of the room; but they could not exactly discover what it was all about, till Major Graham said, very earnestly, "I think we might surely take Laura with us."

"Yes," answered Lady Harriet, "both the children have been invited, and are behaving wonderfully well of late; but Lord Rockville has such a dislike to noise, that I dare not venture to take more than one at a time. Poor Laura has a very severe cough, so she may be recovered by change of air. As for Harry, he is quite well, and therefore he can stay at home."

Now, Harry thought it very hard that he was to be left at home, merely because he felt quite well; so he immediately wished to be very ill indeed, that he might have some chance of going to Holiday House; but then he did not exactly know how to set about it. At all events, Harry determined to catch a cold like Laura's without delay. He would not, for the whole world, have pretended to suffer from a cough if he really had none, because Uncle David had often explained that making any one believe an untruth was the same as telling a lie; but he thought that there might be no harm in really getting such a terrible cold, that nothing could possibly cure it except change of air, and a trip to Holiday House with Laura. Accordingly, Harry tried to remember everything that Mrs. Crabtree had forbid him to do "for fear of catching cold." He sprinkled water over his shirt collar in the morning before dressing, that it might be damp; he ran violently up and down stairs to put himself in a heat, after which he sat between the open window and door till he felt perfectly chilled; and when going to bed at night, he washed his hair in cold water without drying it. Still, all was in vain! Harry had formerly caught cold a hundred times when he did not want one; but now, such a thing was not to be had for love or money. Nothing seemed to give him the very slightest attempt at a cough; and when the day at last arrived for Lady Harriet to begin her journey, Harry still felt himself most provokingly well. Not so much as a finger ached; his cheeks were as blooming as roses, his voice as clear as a bell,—and when Uncle David accidentally said to him in the morning, "How do you do?" Harry was obliged, very much against his will, to answer, "Quite well, I thank you!"

In the mean time, Laura would have felt too happy if Harry could only have gone with her; and even as it was, being impatient for the happy day to arrive, she hurried to bed an hour earlier than usual the night before, to make the time of setting out appear nearer; and she could scarcely sleep or eat for thinking of Holiday House, and planning all that was to be done there.

"It is pleasant to see so joyous a face," said Major Graham. "I almost envy you, Laura, for being so happy."

"Oh! I quite envy myself! but I shall write a long letter every day to poor Harry, telling him all the news, and all my adventures."

"Nonsense! Miss Laura! wait till you come home," said Mrs. Crabtree. "Who do you think is going to pay postage for so many foolish letters?"

"I shall!" answered Harry. "I have got sixpence, and two pence, and a halfpenny, so I shall buy every one of Laura's letters from the postman, and write her an answer immediately afterwards. She will like to hear, Mrs. Crabtree, how very kind you are going to be, when I am left by myself here. Perhaps you will play at ninepins with me, and Laura can lend you her skipping rope."

"You might as well offer Uncle David a hobby-horse," said Frank laughing, and throwing his satchel over his shoulders. "No, Harry! you shall belong to me now. Grandmama says you may go every day to my play ground, where all the school-boys assemble, and you can have plenty of fun till Laura comes back. We shall jump over the moon, every morning, for joy."

Harry brightened up amazingly, thinking he had never heard of such good news before, as it was a grand piece of promotion to play with real big school-boys; so he became quite reconciled to Laura's going away for a short time without him; and when the hour came for taking leave, instead of tears being shed on either side, it would have been difficult to say, as they kissed each other and said a joyous good bye, which face looked the most delighted.

All Laura's clothes had been packed the night before, in a large chaise seat, which was now put into the carriage along with herself, and everything seemed ready for departure, when Lady Harriet's maid was suddenly taken so very ill, as to be quite unfit for

travelling; therefore she was left behind, and a doctor sent for to attend her; while Lady Harriet said she would trust to the maids at Holiday House, for waiting upon herself and Laura.

It is seldom that so happy a face is seen in this world, as Laura wore during the whole journey. It perfectly sparkled and glittered with delight, while she was so constantly on a broad grin laughing, that Major Graham said he feared her mouth would grow an inch wider on the occasion.

"You will tire of sitting so long idle! It is a pity we did not think of bringing a few lesson-books in the carriage to amuse you, Laura," said the Major, slyly. "A piece of needle-work might have beguiled the way. I once knew an industrious lady who made a ball dress for herself in the carriage during a journey."

"How very stupid of her to miss seeing all the pretty trees, and cottages, and farm-houses! I do like to watch the little curly-headed, dirty children, playing on the road, with brown faces, and hair bleached white in the sun; and the women hanging out their clothes on the hedges to dry; and the blacksmith shoeing horses, and the ducks swimming in the gutters, and the pigs thrusting their noses out of the sty, and the old women knitting stockings, and the workmen sitting on a wall to eat their dinners! It looks all so pretty, and so pleasant!"

"What a picture of rural felicity! You ought to be a poet or a painter, Laura!"

"But I believe poets always call this a miserable world; and I think it the happiest place I have ever been in, Uncle David! Such fun during the holidays! I should go wild altogether, if Mrs. Crabtree were not rather cross sometimes."

"Or very cross always," thought Major Graham. "But here we are, Laura, near our journey's end. Allow me to introduce you to Holiday House! Why, you are staring at it like a dog looking at a piece of cold beef! My dear girl, if you open your eyes so wide, you will never be able to shut them again."

Holiday House was not one of those prodigious places, too grand to be pleasant, with the garden a mile off in one direction, and the farm a mile off in another, and the drawing-room a mile off from the dining-room; but it was a very cheerful modern mansion, with rooms large enough to hold as many people as any one could desire to see at once, all very comfortably furnished. A lively, dashing river, streamed past the windows; a small park, sprinkled with sheep, and shaded by fine trees, surrounded the house; and beyond were beautiful gardens filled with a superabundance of the gayest and sweetest common flowers. Roses, carnations, wallflowers, holly-hocks, dahlias, lilies and violets, were assembled there in such crowds, that Laura might have plucked nosegays all day, without making any visible difference; and she was also made free of the gooseberry bushes and cherry trees, with leave to gather, if she pleased, more than she could eat.

Every morning, Laura entered the breakfast room with cheeks like the roses she carried, bringing little bouquets for all the ladies, which she had started out of bed early, in order to gather; and her great delight was to see them worn and admired all the forenoon, while she was complimented on the taste with which they had been selected and arranged. She filled every ornamental jar, basin, and teacup in the drawing-room, with groups of roses, and would have been the terror of any gardener but the one at Holiday House, who liked to see his flowers so much admired, and was not keeping up any for a horticultural show.

Laura's chief delight, however, was in the dairy, which seemed the most beautiful thing she had ever beheld,—being built of rough transparent spar, which looked exactly like crystal, and reminded her of the ice palace built by the Empress of Russia. The windows were of painted glass; the walls and shelves were of Dutch tiles, and in the centre rose a beautiful jet d'eau of clear bright water.

Laura thought it looked like something built for the fairies; but within she saw a most substantial room, the floor and tables in which were so completely covered with cheeses, that they looked like some old Mosaic pavement. Here the good-natured dairy-maid showed Laura how to make cheese, and afterwards manufactured a very small one, about the size of a soup-plate, entirely for the young lady herself, which she promised to take home after her visit was over; and a little churn was also filled full of cream, which Laura one morning churned into butter, and breakfasted upon, after having first practised printing it into a variety of shapes. It was altered about twenty times from a swan into a cow, and from a cow into a rose, and from a rose back to a swan again, before she could be persuaded to leave off her amusement.

Laura continued to become more and more delighted with Holiday House; and she one day skipped about Lady Harriet's room, saying, "Oh! I am too happy! I scarcely know what to do with so much happiness. How delightful it would be to stay here all my life, and never to go to bed, nor say any more lessons, as long as I live!"

"What a useless, stupid girl you would soon become," observed Lady Harriet. "Do you think, Laura, that lessons were invented for no other purpose but to torment little children?"

"No, grandmama; not exactly! They are of use also to keep us quiet."

"Come here, little madam, and listen to me. I shall soon be very old, Laura, and not able to read my Bible, even with spectacles; for, as the Scriptures told us, in that affecting description of old age which I read to you yesterday, 'the keepers of the house shall tremble, and the grinders cease because they are few, and those that look out of the windows be darkened;' what then do you think I can do? because the Bible now is my best comfort, which I shall need more and more every day, to tell me all about the eternal world where I am going, and to show me the way."

"Grandmama! you promised long ago to let me attend on you when you grow old and blind! I shall be very careful, and very—very—very kind. I almost wish you were old and blind now, to let you feel how much I love you, and how anxious I am to be as good to you as you have always been to me. We shall read the Bible together every morning, and as often afterwards as you please."

"Thank you, my dear child! but you must take the trouble of learning to read well, or we shall be sadly puzzled with the difficult words. A friend of mine once had nobody that could read to her when she was ill, but the maid, who bargained that she might leave out every word above two syllables long, because they were too hard for her; and you could hardly help laughing at the nonsense it sometimes made; but I hope you will manage better."

"O, certainly, grandmama! I can spell chrononhotonthologos, and all the other five-cornered words in my 'Reading Made Easy,' already."

"Besides that, my dear Laura! unless you learn to look over my bills, I may be sadly cheated by servants and shopkeepers. You must positively study to find out how many cherries make five."

"Ah! grandmama! nobody knows better than I do, that two and two make four. I shall soon be quite able to keep your accounts."

"Very well! but you have not yet heard half the trouble I mean to give you. I am remarkably fond of music, and shall probably at last be obliged to hire every old fiddler as he passes in the street, by giving him sixpence, in order to enjoy some of my favourite tunes."

"No, grandmama! you shall hear them all from me. I can play Malbrook, and Auld Robin Gray, already; and Frank says if I practise two hours every day for ten years, I shall become a very tolerable player, fit for you and Uncle David to hear, without being disagreeable."

"Then that will be more than seven thousand hours of musical lessons which you have yet to endure, Laura! There are many more things of still greater importance to learn also, if you wish to be any better than a musical snuff-box. For instance, when visiters come to see me, they are often from France or Italy; but perhaps you will not mind sitting in the room as if you were deaf and dumb, gazing at those foreigners, while they gaze at you, without understanding a syllable they say, and causing them to feel strange and uncomfortable as long as they remain in the house."

"No! I would not for the world seem so unkind and uncivil. Pray, let me learn plenty of languages."

"Very well! but if you study no geography, what ridiculous blunders you will be falling into! asking the Italians about their native town Madrid, and the Americans if they were born at Petersburg. You will be fancying that travellers go by steamboats to Moscow, and travel in a day from Paris, through Stockholm to Naples. How ashamed I should be of such mistakes!"

"So should I, grandmama, still more than you; for it would be quite a disgrace."

"Do you remember, Laura, your Uncle David laughing, when he last went to live at Leamington, about poor Mrs. Marmalade coming up stairs to say she did not wish to be troublesome, but she would feel greatly obliged if he would call at Portsmouth occasionally to see her son Thomas. And when Captain Armylist's regiment was ordered last winter to the village of Bathgate near this, he told me they were to march in the course of that morning all the way to Bagdad."

"Yes, grandmama! and Mrs. Crabtree said some weeks ago, that if her brother went to Van Dieman's Land, she thought he would of course, in passing, take a look of Jerusalem; and Frank was amused lately to hear Peter Grey maintain, that Gulliver was as great a man as Columbus, because he discovered Lilliput!"

"Quite like him! for I heard Peter ask one day lately, what side Bonaparte was on at the battle of Leipsic? We must include a little history, I think, Laura, in our list of studies, or you will fancy that Lord Nelson fought at the battle of Blenheim, and that Henry VIII. cut off Queen Mary's head."

"Not quite so bad as that, grandmama! I seem to have known all about Lord Nelson and Queen Mary, ever since I was a baby in long frocks! You have shown me, however, that it would be very foolish not to feel anxious for lessons, especially when they are to make me a fit companion for you at last."

"Yes, Laura! and not only for me, but for many whose conversation will entertain and improve you more than any books. The most delightful accomplishment that a young person can cultivate, is that of conversing agreeably; and it is less attended to in education than any other. You cannot take a harp or piano about with you, but our minds and tongues are always portable and accompany us wherever we go. If you wish to be loved by others, and to do good to your associates, as well as to entertain them, take every opportunity of conversing with those who are either amiable or agreeable; not only attending to their opinions, but also endeavouring to gain the habit of expressing your own thoughts with ease and fluency; and then rest assured, that if the gift of conversation be rightly exercised, it is the most desirable of all, as no teaching can have greater influence in leading people to think and act aright, than the incidental remarks of an enlightened Christian, freely and unaffectedly talking to his intimate friends."

"Well, grandmama! the moral of all this is, that I shall become busier than anybody ever was before, when we get home; but in the meantime, I may take a good dose of idleness now at Holiday House, to prepare me for settling to very hard labour afterwards," said Laura, hastily tying on her bonnet. "I wonder if I shall ever be as merry and happy again!"

Most unfortunately all the time of Laura's visit at Holiday House, she had been, as usual, extremely heedless, in taking no care whatever of her clothes! consequently her blue merino frock had been cruelly torn; her green silk dress became frightfully soiled; four white frocks were utterly ruined; her Swiss muslin seemed a perfect object, and her pink gingham was both torn and discoloured. Regularly every evening Lady Harriet told her to take better care, or she would be a bankrupt in frocks altogether; but whatever her grandmama said on that subject, the moment she was out of sight, it went out of mind, till another dress had shared the same deplorable fate.

At last, one morning, as soon as Laura got up, Lady Harriet gravely led her towards a large table on which all the ill-used frocks had been laid out in a row; and a most dismal sight they were! Such a collection of stains and fractures was probably never seen before. A beggar would scarcely have thanked her for her blue merino; and the green silk frock looked like the tattered cover of a worn-out umbrella.

"Laura," said Lady Harriet, "in Switzerland a lady's wardrobe descends to many generations; but nobody will envy your successor. One might fancy that a wild beast had torn you to pieces every day! I wonder what an old clothesman would give for your whole baggage! It is only fit for being used as rags in a paper manufactory!"

Poor Laura's face became perfectly pink when she saw the destruction that a very short time had occasioned; and she looked from one tattered garment to another, in melancholy silence, thinking how lately they had all been fresh and beautiful; but now not a vestige of their former splendour remained. At last her grandmama broke the awful silence, by saying,

"My dear girl! I have warned you very often lately, that we are not at home, where your frocks could be washed and mended as soon as they were spoiled; but without considering this, you have every day destroyed several; so now the maid finds, on examining your drawers, that there is only one clean frock remaining!"

Laura looked gravely at the last clean frock, and wondered much what her grandmama would say next.

"I do not wish to make a prisoner of you at home during this very fine weather, yet in five minutes after leaving the house, you will, of course, become unfit to be seen; which I should very much regret, as a number of fine people are coming to dinner, whom you would like to see. The great General Courteney, and all his aide-de-camps, intend to be here on their way from a review, besides many officers and ladies who know your papa very well, and wish to see my little granddaughter; but I would not on any account allow you to appear before them, looking like a perfect tatterdemalion, as you too often do. They would suppose you had been drawn backwards through a hedge! Now my plan is, that you shall wear this old pink gingham for romping all morning in the garden, and dress in your last clean frock for dinner; but remember to keep out of sight till then. Remain within the garden walls, as none of the company will be walking there, but be sure to avoid the terrace and shrubberies till you are made tidy, for I shall be both angry and mortified if your papa's friends see you for the first time looking like rag-fair."

Laura promised to remember her grandmama's injunctions, and to remain invisible all the day; so off she set to the garden, singing and skipping with joy, as she ran towards her pleasant hiding-place, planning twenty ways in which the day might be delightfully spent alone. Before long she had strung a long necklace of daisies—she had put many bright leaves in a book to dry—she had made a large ball of cowslips to toss in the air—she had watered the hyacinths with a watering-pot, till they were nearly washed away—she had plucked more roses than could possibly be carried, and eat as many gooseberries and cherries as it was convenient to swallow,—but still there were several hours remaining to be enjoyed, and nothing very particular that Laura could think of to do.

Meanwhile, the miserable pink frock was torn worse than ever, and seemed to be made of nothing but holes, for every gooseberry bush in the garden had got a share of it. Laura wished pink gingham frocks had never been invented, and wondered why nothing stronger could be made. Having become perfectly tired of the garden, she now wished herself anywhere else in the world, and thought she was no better off, confined in this way within four walls, than a canary bird in a cage.

"I should like so much to go if it were only for five minutes, on the terrace!" said she to herself. "How much pleasanter is it than this! Grandmama did not care where I went, provided nobody saw me! I may at least take a peep to see if any one is there!"

Laura now cautiously opened the garden door, and put her head out, intending only to look for a moment, but the moment grew longer and longer, till it stretched into ten minutes.

"What crowds of fine people are walking about on the terrace!" thought she. "It looks as gay as a fair! Who can that officer be in a red coat, and cocked hat with white feathers? Probably General Courteney paying attention to Lady Rockville. There is a lady in a blue cloak and blue flowers! how very pretty! Everybody is so exceedingly smart! and I see some little boys too! Grandmama never told me any children were coming! I wonder how old they are, and if they will play with me in the evening! It would be very amusing to venture a little nearer, and get a better glimpse of them all?"

If Laura's wishes pointed one way and her duty pointed the other, it was a very sad thing how often she forgot to pause and consider which she ought to follow; and on this occasion, as usual, she took the naughty side of the question, and prepared to indulge her curiosity, though very anxious that nothing might happen to displease her grandmama. She observed at some distance on the terrace, a remarkably thick holly-bush, near which the great procession of company would probably pass before long, therefore, hoping nobody could possibly see her there, she stole hastily out of the garden and concealed herself behind it; but when children do wrong, in hopes of not being found out, they generally find themselves mistaken, as Laura soon discovered to her cost. It is very lucky, however, for the culprits, when they are detected, that they may learn never to behave foolishly again, because the greatest misfortune that can happen to any child is, not to be found out and punished when he does wrong.

A few minutes after Laura had taken her station behind the holly-bush, crowds of ladies and officers came strolling along, so very near her hiding-place, that she saw them all distinctly, and felt excessively amused and delighted at first, to be perched like a bird in a tree watching this grand party, while nobody saw her, nor guessed she was there. Presently, however, Laura became sadly frightened when an officer in a scarlet coat happened to look towards the holly-bush, and exclaimed, with some surprise,

"There is surely something very odd about that plant! I see large pink spots between the leaves!"

"Oh no, Captain Digby, you are quite mistaken," answered one of the ladies, dressed in a bright yellow bonnet and green pelisse. "I see nothing particular there. Only a common ugly bush of holly. I wonder you ever thought of noticing it!"

"But, Miss Perceval! there certainly is something very curious behind! I would bet five to one there is!" replied Captain Digby, stepping up close to the holly bush, and peeping over: "What have we here? a ragged little girl, I do believe! in a pink frock!"

Poor Laura was now in a terrible scrape! she started up immediately to run away.

Probably she never ran so fast in her life before, but Captain Digby was a person who enjoyed a joke, so he called out,

"Tally-ho! a race for a thousand pounds!"

Off set the Captain, and away flew Laura. At any other time she would have thought it capital fun, but now she was frightened out of her wits, and tore away at the very top of her speed. The whole party of ladies and gentlemen stood laughing, and applauding, to see how fast they both cleared the ground, while Laura, seeing the garden gate still wide open, hoped she might be able to dart in, and close it; but alas! when she arrived within four steps of the threshold, feeling almost certain of escape, Captain Digby seized hold of her pink frock behind. It instantly began tearing, so she had great hopes of leaving the piece in his hand and getting off; but he was too clever for that, as he grasped hold of her long sash, which was floating far out behind, and led Laura a prisoner before the whole company.

When Lady Harriet discovered that this was really Laura advancing, her head hanging down, her hair streaming about her ears, and her face like a full moon, she could scarcely credit her own eyes, and held her hands up with astonishment, while Uncle David shrugged his shoulders, till they almost met over his head, but not a word was said on either side until they got home, when Lady Harriet at last broke the awful silence by saying,

"My dear girl! you must, of course, be severely punished for this act of disobedience; and is it not so much on account of feeling angry at your misconduct that I mean to correct you, but because I love you, and wish to make you behave better in future. Parents are appointed by God to govern their children as he governs us, not carelessly indulging their faults, but wisely correcting them; for we are told that our Great Father in heaven chastens those whom he loves, and only afflicts us for great and wise purposes. I have suffered many sorrows in the world, but they always made me better in the end, and whatever discipline you meet with from me, or from that Great Being who loves you still more than I do, let it teach you to consider your ways, to repent of your wilfulness, and to pray that you may be enabled to act more properly in future."

"Yes, grandmama," replied Laura, with tears in her eyes, "I am quite willing to be punished, for it was very wrong indeed to make you so vexed and ashamed, by disobeying your orders."

"Then here is a long task which you must study before dinner, as a penalty for trespassing bounds. It is a beautiful poem on the death of Sir John Moore, which every school-girl can repeat; but being rather long, you will scarcely have time to learn it perfectly before coming down to dessert; therefore, that you may be quite ready, I shall ring now for Lady Rockville's maid, and have you washed and dressed immediately. Remember this is your last clean frock, and be sure not to spoil it."

When Laura chose to pay attention, she could learn her lessons wonderfully fast, and her eyes seemed nailed to the book for some time after Lady Harriet went away, till at last she could repeat the whole poem perfectly well. It was neither "slowly nor sadly" that Laura "laid down" her book, after practising it all, in a sort of jig time, till she could rattle over the poem like a rail-road, and she walked to the window, still murmuring the verses to herself with prodigious glee, and giving little thought to their melancholy subject.

A variety of plans suggested themselves to her mind for amusing herself within doors, as she had been forbidden to venture out, and she lost no time in executing them. First, she tried on all her grandmama's caps at a looking-glass, none of which were improved by being crushed and tumbled in such a way. Then she quarrelled with Lady Rockville's beautiful cockatoo, till it bit her finger violently, and after that she teased the old cat till it scratched her; but all these diversions were not sufficiently entertaining, so Laura began to grow rather tired, till at last she went to gaze out at the portico of Holiday House, being perfectly determined, on no account whatever, to go one single step further.

Here Laura saw many things which entertained her extremely, for she had scarcely ever seen more of the country than was to be enjoyed with Mrs. Crabtree in Charlotte Square. The punctual crows were all returning home at their usual hour for the evening, and looked like a black shower over her head, while hundreds of them seemed trying to make a concert at once; the robins hopped close to her feet, evidently accustomed to be fed; a tame pheasant, as fat as a London alderman, came up the steps to keep her company; and the peacock spreading his tail and strutting about, looked the very picture of silly pride and vanity.

Laura admired and enjoyed all this extremely, and crumbled down nearly a loaf of bread, which she scattered on the ground, in order to be popular among her visiters, who took all they could get from her, and quarrelled among themselves about it, very much as boys and girls would perhaps have done in the same circumstances.

It happened at this moment that a large flock of geese crossed the park, on their way towards the river, stalking along in a slow, majestic manner, with their heads high in the air. Laura observed them at a distance, and thought they were the prettiest creatures in the world, with their pure white feathers and yellow stockings, so she wondered what kind of birds these were, having never seen a goose before, except when roasted for dinner, though indeed she was a sad goose herself, as will very soon be told.

"How I should like to examine those large white beautiful birds, a little nearer," thought Laura to herself. "I wonder if they could swim or fly!—oh! how perfect they would look, floating like water-lilies on the river, and then I might take a bit of bread to throw in, and they would all rush after it!"

Laura, as usual, did not wait to reflect what her grandmama might be likely to think! indeed it is to be feared Laura forgot at the moment that she had a grandmama at all, for her mind was never large enough to hold more than one thing at a time, and now it was entirely filled with the flock of geese. She instantly set off in pursuit of them, and began chasing the whole party across the park, making all sorts of dreadful noises, in hopes they might fly; but, on the contrary, they held up their heads, as if she had been a dancing master, and marched slowly on, cackling loudly to each other, and evidently getting extremely angry.

Laura was now quite close to her new acquaintances, and even threw a pebble to hurry them forward, when suddenly an old gander stopped and turned round in a terrible rage. The whole flock of geese then did the same, after which they flew towards Laura, with their bills wide open, hissing furiously, and stretching out their long necks in an angry, menacing way, as if they wished to tear her in pieces.

Poor Laura became frightened out of any wits she ever had, and ran off, with all the geese after her! Anybody must have laughed into fits could they have heard what a triumphant cackle the geese set up, and had they seen how fast she flew away. If Laura had borrowed a pair of wings from her pursuers, she could scarcely have got more quickly on.

In the hurry of escaping, she always looked back to see if the enemy followed, and scarcely observed which way she ran herself, till suddenly her foot stumbled upon a large stone, and she fell headlong into the river! Oh, what a scream Laura gave! it terrified even the old gander himself, and sent the whole flock of geese marching off, nearly as fast as they had come; but Laura's cries also reached, at a great distance, the ears of somebody who she would have been very sorry to think had heard them.

Lady Harriet and all her friends at Holiday House were taking a delightful walk under some fine old fir trees, on the banks of the river, admiring the beautiful scenery, while Miss Perceval was admiring nothing but her own fine pocket handkerchief, which had cost ten guineas, being worked with her name, trimmed with lace, and perfumed with eau de Cologne; and Captain Digby was admiring his own scarlet uniform reflected in the bright clear water, and varying his employment occasionally by throwing pebbles into the stream, to see how far they would go. Suddenly, however, he stopped, with a look of surprise and alarm, saying, "What noise can that be?—a loud scream in the water!"

"Oh dear, no! it was only one of those horrid peacocks," answered Miss Perceval, waving her fine pocket handkerchief. "They are the most disagreeable, noisy creatures in the world! If mama ever keeps one, I shall get him a singing master, or put a muzzle on his mouth!"

"But surely there is something splashing in the river at a great distance. Do you see that?—what can that be?"

"Nothing at all, depend upon it! I could bet the value of my pocket handkerchief, ten guineas, that it is nothing. Officers who live constantly in the barracks are so unaccustomed to the country, that they seem to expect something wonderful shall happen every minute! That is probably a salmon or a minnow."

"I am determined, however, to see. If you are quite sure this is a salmon, will you promise to eat for your dinner whatever we find, provided I can catch it?"

"Certainly! unless you catch a whale! Oh! I have dropped my pocket handkerchief! —pray pick it up!"

Captain Digby did so; but without waiting to examine the pattern, he instantly ran forward, and to his own very great astonishment, saw Laura up to her knees in the river, trying to scramble out, while her face was white with terror, and her limbs trembled with cold, like a poodle dog newly washed.

"Why, here you are again!—the very same little girl that I caught in the morning," cried he, laughing heartily, while he carefully pulled Laura towards the bank, though, by doing so, he splashed his beautiful uniform most distressingly. "We have had a complete game at bo-peep to-day, my friend! but here comes a lady who has promised to eat you up, therefore I shall have no more trouble."

Laura would have consented to be eaten up with pleasure, rather than encounter Lady Harriet's eye, who really did not recognise her for the first minute, as no one can suppose what a figure she appeared. The last clean frock had been covered entirely over with mud—her hair was dripping with water—and her new yellow sash might be any colour in the world. Laura felt so completely ashamed, she could not look up from the ground, and so sorry, she could not speak, while hot tears mingled themselves with the cold water which trickled down her face.

"What is the matter! Who is this!" cried Lady Harriet, hurrying up to the place where they stood. "Laura!! impossible!!!"

"Let me put on a pair of spectacles, for I cannot believe my eyes without them!" said Major Graham. "Ah! sure enough it is Laura, and such a looking Laura as I never saw before. You must have had a nice cold bath!"

"I have heard," continued Lady Harriet, "that naughty people are often ducked in the water as a punishment, and in that respect I am sure Laura deserves what she has got, and a great deal more."

"She reminds me," observed Captain Digby, "of the Chinese bird which has no legs, so it constantly flies about from place to place, never a moment at rest."

"Follow me, Laura," said Lady Harriet, "that I may hear whether you have anything to say for yourself on this occasion. It is scarcely possible that there can be any excuse, but nobody should be condemned unheard."

When Laura had been put into dry clothes, she told her whole history, and entreated Lady Harriet to hear how very perfectly she had first learned her task before venturing to stir out of the room; upon which her grandmama consented, and amidst tears and sobs, the monody of Sir John Moore was repeated without a single mistake. Lady Rockville then came in, to entreat that, as this was the last day of the visit to Holiday House, Laura might be forgiven and permitted to appear at dessert, as all the company were anxious to see her, and particularly Captain Digby, who regretted that he had been the means at first of getting her into a scrape.

"Indeed, my dear Lady Rockville! I might perhaps have agreed to your wishes," answered Lady Harriet, "particularly as Laura seems sincerely sorry, and did not premeditate her disobedience; but she actually has not a tolerable frock to appear in now!"

"I must lend her one of my velvet dresses to destroy next," said Lady Rockville, smiling.

"Uncle David's Mackintosh cloak would be the fittest thing for her to wear," replied Lady Harriet, rising to leave the room. "Laura, you must learn a double task now. Here it is; and at Lady Rockville's request I excuse you this once; though I am sorry that for very sufficient reasons we cannot see you at dessert, which otherwise I should have been most happy to do."

Laura sat down and cried during a quarter of an hour after Lady Harriet had gone to dinner. She felt very sorry for having behaved ill, and sorry to have vexed her good grandmama; and sorry not to see all the fine party at dessert; and sorry to think that next day she must leave Holiday House; and sorry, last of all, to consider what Mrs. Crabtree would say when all her ruined frocks were brought home. In short, poor Laura felt perfectly overwhelmed with the greatness and variety of her griefs, and scarcely believed that any one in the world was ever more miserable than herself.

Her eyes were fixed on her task, while her thoughts were wandering fifty miles away from it, when a housemaid, who had frequently attended upon Laura during her visit, accidentally entered the room, and seemed much surprised, as well as concerned, to find the young lady in such a way, for her sobbing could be heard in the next room. It was quite a relief to see any one; so Laura told over again all the sad adventures of the day, without attempting to conceal how naughty she had been; and most attentively was her narrative listened to, till the very end.

"You see, miss," observed Nelly, "when people doesn't behave well, they must expect to be punished."

"So they should," sobbed Laura; "and I dare say it will make me better! I would not pass such a miserable day as this again, for the world; but I deserve to be more punished than I am."

"That's right, miss!" replied Nelly, pleased to see the good effect of her admonitions. "Punishment is as sure to do us good when we are naughty, as physic when we are ill. But now you'll go down to dessert, and forget it all."

"No! grandmama would have allowed me, and Lady Rockville and everybody was so very kind about inviting me down; but my last clean frock is quite unfit to be seen, so I have none to put on. Oh, dear! what a thousand million of pities!"

"Is that all, miss! Then dry your eyes, and I can wash the frock in ten minutes. Give it to me, and learn your lesson, so as to be ready when I come back."

Laura sprang off her seat with joy at this proposal, and ran—or rather flew—to fetch her miserable object of a frock, which Nelly crumpled under her arm, and walked away with, in such haste that she was evidently determined to return very soon; while Laura took her good advice, and sat down to learn her task, though she could hardly look at the book during two minutes at a time—she watched so impatiently for her benefactress from the laundry.

At length the door flew open, and in walked Nelly, whose face looked as red and hot as a beef-steak; but in her hand she carried a basket, on which was laid out, in great state, the very cleanest frock that ever was seen! It perfectly smelled of soap and water, starch and hot irons, and seemed still almost smoking from the laundry; while Laura looked at it with such delight and admiration, it might have been supposed she had never seen a clean frock before.

When Lady Harriet was sitting after dinner that day, sipping her wine, and thinking about nothing very particular, she became surprised to feel somebody gently twitching her sleeve to attract notice. Turning instantly round to ascertain what was the matter, and who it could be, what was her astonishment to see Laura at her elbow, looking rather shy and frightened.

"How did you get here, child!" exclaimed Lady Harriet, in accents of amazement, though almost laughing. "Am I never to see the last of you to-day! Where did you get that frock! It must have dropped from the clouds! Or did some good fairy give you a new one?"

"That good fairy was Nelly the housemaid," whispered Laura. "She first tossed my frock into a washing-tub; and then at the great kitchen fire she toasted it, and —— ——"

"—— And buttered it, I hope," added Major Graham. "Come here, Laura! I can read what is written in your grandmama's face at this moment: and it says, 'you are a tiresome little puss, that nobody can keep in any order except Uncle David;' therefore sit down beside him, and eat as many almonds and raisins as he bids you."

"You are a nice funny Uncle David!" whispered Laura, crushing her way in between his chair and Miss Perceval's; "nobody will need a tongue now, if you can read so exactly what we are all thinking."

"But here is Miss Perceval, still more wonderful for she knows by the bumps on your head, all that is contained inside. Let me see if I could do so! There is a large bump of reading, and a small one of writing and arithmetic. Here is a terrible organ of breaking dolls and destroying frocks. There is a very small bump of liking Uncle David, and a prodigious one of liking almonds and raisins!"

"No! you are quite mistaken! It is the largest bump for loving Uncle David, and the small one for everything else," interrupted Laura, eagerly. "I shall draw a map of my head some day, to show you how it is all divided."

"And leave no room for anything naughty or foolish! Your head should be swept out, and put in order every morning, that not a single cobweb may remain in your brains. What busy brains they must be for the next ten years! But in the mean time let us hope that you will never again be reduced to your

LAST CLEAN FROCK."

THE LONG LADDER

There was a young pickle, and what do you think!
He lived upon nothing but victuals and drink;
Victuals and drink were the chief of his diet,
And yet this young pickle could never be quiet.

ONE FINE SULTRY DAY in the month of August, Harry and Laura stood at the breakfast-room window, wondering to see the large broken white clouds, looking like curds and whey, while the sun was in such a blaze of heat, that everything seemed almost red hot. The street door had become blistered by the sunbeams. Jowler, the dog, lay basking on the pavement; the green blinds were closed at every opposite house; the few gentlemen who ventured out, were fanning themselves with their pocket handkerchiefs; the ladies were strolling lazily along, under the umbrageous shade of their green parasols; and the poor people who were accustomed in winter to sell matches for lighting a fire, now carried about gaudy paper hangings for the empty grates. Lady Harriet found the butter so melted at breakfast, that she could scarcely lift it on her knife! and Uncle David complained that the sight of hot smoking tea put him in a fever, and said he wished it could be iced.

"I wonder how iced porridge would taste!" said Harry. "I put mine at the open window to cool, but that made it seem hotter. We were talking of the gentleman you mentioned yesterday, who toasted his muffins at a volcano; and certainly yours might almost be done at the drawing-room window this morning."

"Wait till you arrive at the countries I have visited, where, as somebody remarked, the very salamanders die of heat. At Agra, which is the hottest part of India, we could scarcely write a letter, because the ink dries in the pen before you can get it to the paper. I was obliged, when our regiment was there, to lie down in the middle of the day, during several hours, actually gasping for breath; and to make up for that, we all rose at midnight. An officer of ours, who lived long in India, got up always at three in the morning, after we returned home, and walked about the streets of Portsmouth, wondering what had become of everybody."

"I shall try not to grumble about the weather any more," said Laura. "We seem no worse off than other people.

"Or rather we are a great deal better off. At Bermuda, where my regiment stopped on its way to America, the inhabitants are so tormented with high winds, that they build 'hurricane houses'—low, flat rooms, where the families must retire when a storm comes on, as trees, houses, people, and cattle, are all whirled about with such violence, that not a life is safe on the island while it lasts."

"That reminds me," said Lady Harriet, "of a droll mistake made yesterday by the African camel, when he landed at Leith. His keepers were leading him along the high road, to be made a show of in Edinburgh, at a time when the wind was particularly high; and the poor animal, encountering such clouds of dust, thought this must be a simoom of the desert, and threw himself flat down, burying his nose in the ground, according to custom on those occasions. It was with great difficulty that he could at last be induced to face the danger and proceed."

"Quite a compliment to our dust," observed Laura. "But really in such a hot day, the kangaroos and tigers might feel perfectly at home here. Oh! how I should like to visit the Zoological Gardens in London!"

"Then suppose we set off immediately!" said Major Graham, pretending to rise from his chair. "Your grandmama's donkey-carriage holds two."

"Ah! but you could carry the donkey-carriage more easily than it could carry you."

"Shall I try? Well, if we go, who is to pay the turnpikes? for I remember the time, not a hundred years ago, when Harry and you both thought that paying the gates was the only expense of travelling. You asked me then how poor grandmama could afford so many shillings and sixpences."

"We know all about everything now, though," said Harry, nodding in a very sagacious manner. "I can tell exactly how much time it takes going by the public coach to London, and it sleeps only one night on the road."

"Sleeps!" cried Uncle David. "What! it puts on a night-cap, and goes to bed?"

"Yes! and it dines and breakfasts too, Mr. Uncle David, for I heard Mrs. Crabtree say so."

"Never name anybody, unless you wish to see her immediately," said Major Graham, hearing a well known tap at the door. "As sure as you mention an absent person, if he is supposed to be fifty miles off at the time, it is rather odd, but he instantly appears."

"Then there is somebody that I shall speak about very often."

"Who can this Mr. Somebody be?" asked Uncle David, smiling. "A foolish person that spoils you both, I dare say, and gives you large slices of bread and jelly like this. Hold them carefully. Now, good-bye, and joy be with you."

But it was with rather rueful faces that Harry and Laura left the room, wishing they might have remained another hour to talk nonsense with Uncle David, and dreading to think what new scrapes and difficulties they would get into in the nursery, which always seemed to them a place of torture and imprisonment.

Major Graham used to say that Mrs. Crabtree should always have a thermometer in her own room when she dressed, to tell her whether the weather was hot or cold, for she seemed to feel no difference, and scarcely ever made any change in her own attire, wearing always the same pink gown and scarlet shawl, which made her look like a large red flower-pot, while she was no more annoyed with the heat than a flower-pot would have been. On this oppressive morning she took as much pains in suffocating Harry with a silk handkerchief round his neck, as if it had been Christmas, and though Laura begged hard for leave to go without one of her half-a-dozen wrappings, she might as well have asked permission to go without her head, as Mrs. Crabtree seemed perfectly deaf upon the subject.

"This day is so very cold, and so very shivering," said Harry, slyly, "that I suppose you will make Laura wear at least fifty shawls."

"Not above twenty," answered Mrs. Crabtree, dryly. "Give me no more of your nonsense, Master Harry! This is no business of yours. I was in the world long before you were born, and must know best; so hold your tongue. None but fools and beggars need ever be cold."

At last Mrs. Crabtree had heaped as many clothes upon her two little victims as she was pleased to think necessary; so she sallied forth with them, followed by Betty, and proceeded towards the country, taking the sunny side of the road, and raising clouds of dust at every step, till Harry and Laura felt as if they had been made of wax, and were melting away.

"Mrs. Crabtree," said Harry, "did you hear Uncle David's funny story yesterday? One hot morning a gentleman was watching an ant's nest, when he observed that every little insect, as it came out, plucked a small leaf, to hold over its head as a parasol. I wish we could find leaves large enough for us."

"You must go to the Botanical Gardens, where one leaf of a palm-tree was shown to grandmama, which measured fourteen feet long," observed Laura. "How horrid these very warm countries must be, when the heat is all the year like this!"

"You may well say that," answered Mrs. Crabtree. "I would not go to them East Indies—no! not if I were Governess-General—to be running away with a tiger at your back, and sleeping with real live serpents twisted round the bed-post, and scorpions under your pillow. Catch me there! I'm often quite sorry for Master Frank, to think that his ship is maybe going that way! I'm told the very rats have such a smell in that outlandish place, that if they touch the outside of a bottle with their tails, it tastes of musk ever after; and when people are sitting comfortably down, expecting to enjoy their dinner, a swarm of great ants will come, and fall an inch thick, on all the side-dishes. I've no desire whatever to see foreign parts!"

"But I wish to see every country in the universe," said Harry; "and I hope there will be a railroad all round the world before I am grown up. Only think, Mrs. Crabtree, what fun lion-hunting must be, and catching dolphins, and riding on elephants."

The pedestrians had now arrived at the pretty village of Corstorphine, when they were unexpectedly met by Peter Grey, who joined them without waiting to ask leave. Here the hills are so beautifully wooded, and the villas so charming, that Harry, Peter, and Laura stopped a moment, to consider what house they would like best to live in. Near one side of the road stood a large cart of hay, on the top of which were several men, forking it in at the window of a high loft, which could only be entered by a long ladder that leaned against the wall. It was a busy joyous scene, and soon attracted the children's whole attention, who were transfixed with delight, seeing how rapidly the people ran up and down, with their pitchforks in their hands, and tilted the hay from the cart into the loft, while they had many jokes and much laughter among themselves. At last their whole business was finished, and the workmen drove away for another supply, to the neighbouring fields, where they had been raking and tossing it all morning, as merry as crickets.

"What happy people!" exclaimed Harry, looking wistfully after the party, and wishing he might have scrambled into the cart beside them. "I would be a haymaker for nothing, if anybody would employ me; would not you, Peter?"

"It is very strange," said Master Grey, "why little ladies and gentlemen seem always obliged to endure a perfectly useless walk every day, as you and Laura are doing now. You never saw animals set out to take a stroll for the good of their healths! How odd it would be to see a couple of dogs set off for a country walk!"

"Miss Laura!" said Mrs. Crabtree, "Master Harry may rest here for a minute or two with Master Peter, and let them count their fingers, while you come with Betty and me to visit a sick old aunt of mine who lives round the corner; but be sure, boys, you do not presume to wander about, or I shall punish you most severely. We are coming back in two minutes."

Mrs. Crabtree had scarcely disappeared into a small shabby-looking cottage, before Peter turned eagerly to Harry, with a face of great joy and importance, exclaiming, "Only see how very lucky this is! The haymakers have left their long ladder standing on purpose for us! The window of that loft is wide open, and I must climb up immediately to peep in, because never, in all my life, did I see the inside of a hay-loft before!"

"Nor I," added Harry. "Uncle David says, that all round the floor there are deep holes, called mangers, down which food is thrown for the horses, so that they can thrust their heads in to take a bite, whenever they choose."

"How I should hate to have my dinner hung up always before my nose in that way! Suppose the kitchen were placed above your nursery, and that Mrs. Marmalade showered down tarts and puddings, which were to remain there till you eat them, you would hate the sight of such things at last. But now, Harry, for the hay-loft."

Peter scrambled so rapidly up the ladder that he soon reached the top, and instantly vanished in at the window, calling eagerly for Harry to follow. "You never saw such a nice, clean, funny place as this, in all your life!—make haste!—come faster!—never mind crushing your hat or tearing your jacket,—I'll put it all to rights. Ah! there! —that's the thing!—walk up, gentlemen! walk up!—the grand show!—sixpence each, and children half price!"

All this time, Harry was slowly, and with great difficulty, picking his steps up the ladder, but a most troublesome business it was! First, his foot became entangled in a rope,—then his hat got squeezed so out of shape, it looked perfectly tipsy,—next, one of his shoes nearly came off,—and afterwards he dropped his gloves; but at last he stumbled up in safety, and stood beside Peter in the loft, both laughing with delight at their own enterprise.

The quantity of hay piled up on all sides, astonished them greatly, while the nice wide floor between seemed larger than any drawing-room, and was certainly made on purpose for a romp. Harry rolled up a large ball of hay to throw at Peter, while he, in return, aimed at him, so they ran after each other, round and round the loft, raising such a riot, that "the very rafters dirled."

The hay now flew about in clouds, while they jumped over it, or crept under it, throwing handfuls about in every direction, and observing that this was the best play-room they had ever been in.

"How lucky that we came here!" cried Peter. "I should like to stay an hour at least!"

"Oh! two hours,—or three,—or all day," added Harry. "But what shall we do about Mrs. Crabtree? She has not gone to settle for life with that old sick aunt, so I am afraid we must be really hurrying back, in case she may find out our expedition, and that, you know, Peter, would be dreadful!"

"Only fancy, Harry, if she sees you and me clinging to the ladder, about half way down! what a way she would be in!"

"We had better make haste," said Harry, looking around. "What would grandmama say!—I wish we had never come up!"

At this moment Harry was still more brought to his senses, by hearing Mrs. Crabtree's voice exclaiming in loud angry accents, "Where in all the world can those troublesome boys be gone! I must tether them to a tree the next time they are left together! Why, sure! they would not venture up that long ladder into the hay-loft! If they have they had better never come down again, for I shall show who is master here."

"Peter Grey would run up a ladder to the stars, if he could find one," replied Betty. "Here are Master Harry's gloves lying at the bottom of it. They can be gone nowhere else, for I have searched every other place. We must send the town-crier with his bell after them, if they are not found up there!"

Mrs. Crabtree now seemed fearfully angry, while Laura began to tremble with fright for Harry, who was listening overhead; and did not know very well what to do, but foolishly thought it best to put off the evil hour of being punished as long as possible; so he and Peter silently crept in below a great quantity of hay, and hid themselves so cunningly, that even a thief-catcher could scarcely have discovered their den. In this dark corner, Harry had time to reflect and to feel more and more alarmed and sorry for his misconduct; so he said, in a very distressed voice, "Oh Peter! what a pity it is ever to be naughty, for we are always found out, and are always so much happier when we are good!"

"I wonder how Mrs. Crabtree will get up the long ladder!" whispered Peter, laughing. "I would give my little finger, and one of my ears, to see her and Betty scrambling along!"

Harry had to pinch Peter's arm almost black and blue before he would be quiet; and by the time he stopped talking, Mrs. Crabtree and Betty were both standing in the hay-loft, exceedingly out of breath with climbing so unusually high, while Mrs. Crabtree very nearly fell, having stumbled over a step at the entrance.

"Why, sure! there's nobody here!" exclaimed she, in a disappointed tone. "And what a disorderly place this is. I thought a hay-loft was always kept in such nice order, with the floor all swept; but here is a fine mess! Those two great lumps of hay in the corner look as if they were meant for people to sleep upon!"

Harry gave himself up for lost when Mrs. Crabtree noticed the place where he and Peter had buried themselves alive; but to his great relief, no suspicion seemed to have been excited, and neither of the two searchers was anxious to venture beyond the door, after having so nearly tripped upon the threshold.

"They must have been stolen by a gipsy, or perhaps fallen into a well," said Betty, who rather liked the bustle of an accident. "I always thought Master Peter would break his neck, or something of that kind. Poor thing! how distressed his papa will be!"

"Hold your tongue," interrupted Mrs. Crabtree, angrily. "I wish people would either speak sense, or not speak at all. Did you hear a noise among the hay?"

"Rats, I dare say; or, perhaps a dog," answered Betty, turning hastily round and hurrying down the ladder faster than she had come up. "I certainly thought something moved in yon far corner."

"Where can that little shrimp of a boy be hid?" added Mrs. Crabtree, following. "He must have obedience knocked like a nail into his head, with a few good severe blows. I shall beat him to powder when once we catch him."

"You may depend upon it," persisted Betty, "that some gipsy has got the boys for the sake of their clothes. It will be a great pity; because Master Harry had on his best blue jacket and trousers."

No sooner was the loft cleared of these unwelcome visiters, than Harry and Peter began to recover from their panic, and jumped out of the hay, shaking themselves free from it, and skipping about in greater glee than ever.

While they played about as they had done before, and tumbled as if they had been tumblers at Ducrow's, poor Harry got into such spirits, that he completely forgot about the deep holes called mangers, for containing the horses' food, till all at once, when Peter was running after him, he fell, with a loud crash, headlong into one of them. Oh, what a scream he gave!—it echoed through the stable, terrifying a whole team of horses that were feeding there, more particularly Snowball, into whose manger he had fallen. The horse gave a tremendous start when Harry plunged down close to his nose, and not being able to run away, he put back his ears, opened his mouth, and kicked and struggled in the most frightful manner; while Harry, who could not make his escape any more than the horse, shouted louder and louder for help.

Peter did all he could to assist Harry in this extraordinary predicament; but finding it impossible to be of any use, he forgot their terror of Mrs. Crabtree in his fears about Harry, and rushed to the window, calling back their two pursuers, who were walking away at a great distance. He screamed and hallooed, and waved his handkerchief without ceasing, till at last Mrs. Crabtree heard him, and turned round; but never was anybody more astonished than she on seeing him there; so she scolded, stormed, and raged, back to the very foot of the ladder.

"Now, you are the besiegers, and I am the garrison!" cried Peter, when he saw Mrs. Crabtree panting and toiling in her ascent. "We must make a treaty of peace together, for I could tumble you over in a minute, by merely pushing this end a very little more to one side!"

"Do not touch it, Master Peter!" cried Mrs. Crabtree, almost afraid he was in earnest. "There is a good boy,—be quiet!"

"A good boy!" whispered Peter to himself. "What a fright Mrs. Crabtree must be in, before she said that!"

The next moment Mrs. Crabtree snatched Harry out of the manger, and shook him with rage. She then scolded and beat him, till he was perfectly stupified with fright and misery; after which the whole party proceeded towards home, while Harry stumbled along the road, and hung down his head, wishing, fifty times over, that he and Peter Grey had never gone up

"THE LONG LADDER."

THE MAD BULL

There's something in a noble boy,
A brave, free-hearted, careless one;
With his uncheck'd unbidden joy,
His dread of books, and love of fun;
And in his clear and ready smile,
Unshaded by a thought of guile
And unrepress'd by sadness,—
Which brings me to my childhood back,
As if I trod its very track,
And felt its very gladness.
WILLIS

O<small>NE EVENING</small> when Harry and Laura came down to dessert, they were surprised to observe the two little plates usually intended for them, turned upside down, while Uncle David pretended not to notice anything, though he stole a glance to see what would happen next. On lifting up these mysterious plates, what did they see lying underneath, but two letters with large red seals, one directed to "Master Harry Graham," and the other to "Miss Laura Graham."

"A letter for me!!" cried Harry, in a tone of delightful astonishment, while he tore open the seal, and his hand shook with impatience, so that he could hardly unfold the paper. "What can it be about! I like getting a letter very much! Is it from papa? Did the postman bring it?"

"Yes, he did," said Uncle David; "and he left a message that you must pay a hundred pounds for it to-morrow."

"Very likely indeed," said Laura; "you should pay that for telling me such a fine story but my letter is worth more than a hundred pounds, for it is inviting me to spend another delightful week at Holiday House."

"I am asked too! and not Mrs. Crabtree!" cried Harry, looking at his letter, and almost screaming out for joy, whilst he skipped about the room, rubbing his hands together, and ended by twirling Laura round and round, till they both fell prostrate on the floor.

"If that be meant as a specimen of how you intend to behave at Holiday House, we had better send your apology at once," observed Lady Harriet, smiling. "Lord Rockville is very particular about never hearing any noise, and the slamming of a door, or even the creaking of a pair of unruly shoes would put him distracted."

"Yes," added Uncle David, "Holiday House is as quiet as Harry's drum with a hole in it. If a pin drops in any part of the mansion, Lord Rockville becomes annoyed, and the very wasps scarcely dare to buzz at his window so loud as at any other person's. You will feel quite fish-out-of-water-ish, trying to be quiet and hum-drum for a whole week, so let me advise you not to go."

"The meaning of advice always is something that one would rather wish not to do," observed Laura, gravely. "I never in my life was advised to enjoy anything pleasant! Taking physic—or learning lessons—or staying at home, are very often advised, but never playing, or having a holiday, or amusing ourselves!"

"You know, Laura, that Harry's little Shetland pony, Tom Thumb, in my field, is of no use at present, but kicks, and capers, and runs about all day! yet presently he will be led out fastened to a rope, and made to trot round and round in a circle, day after day, till he has no longer a will of his own,—that is education. Afterwards he shall have a bridle put in his mouth, which some little girls would be much the better of also, when he shall be carefully guided ever afterwards in the best ways; and you likewise will go much more steadily for all the reining-in and whipping you have got from Mrs. Crabtree and me, which may, perhaps, make you keep in the road of duty more easily hereafter."

"Uncle David!" said Harry, laughing, "we have read in the Arabian Nights, about people being turned into animals, but I never thought you would turn Laura into a horse! What shall we do with my little Shetland pony if I go away next week?"

"I have thought of a capital plan for making Tom Thumb useful during the whole winter! Your grandmama wants a watch-dog in the country, so we shall build him a kennel—put a chain round his neck, and get some one to teach him to bark."

"Uncle David should be Professor of Nonsense at the University," said Lady Harriet, smiling. "But my dear children, if you are allowed to pay this visit to Holiday House, I hope you will endeavour to behave creditably!"

"Yes," added Major Graham, "I understand that Lord Rockville wished to have some particularly quiet children there, for a short time, so he fixed upon Harry and Laura! Poor, mistaken Lord Rockville! But my good friends, try not to break all his china ornaments the first day—spare a few jars and teacups—leave a pane or two of glass in the windows, and throw none of your marbles at the mirrors."

"I remember hearing," said Lady Harriet, "that when Miss Pelham was married last year, her old aunt, Mrs. Bouverie, sent for her and said, that as she could not afford to give baubles or trinkets, she would give her a valuable piece of advice; and what do you think it was, Laura?"

"I have no idea; do tell me."

"Then I shall bestow it on you, as the old lady did on her niece—'Be careful of china, paper, and string, for they are all very transitory possessions in this world!' "

"Very true, and most judicious," observed Major Graham, laughing. "I certainly know several persons who must have served an apprenticeship under that good lady; many gentlemen, who despatch all their epistles from the club, because there the paper costs them nothing; and a number of ladies, who, for the same good reason, never write letters till they are visiting in a country house."

Having received so many warnings and injunctions about behaving well, Harry and Laura became so quiet during the first few days at Holiday House, that they were like shadows flitting through the rooms, going almost on tiptoe, scarcely speaking above a whisper, and observing that valuable rule for children, to let themselves be seen but not heard. Lord Rockville was quite charmed with such extreme good conduct, for they were both in especial awe of him, and thought it a great condescension if he even looked at them, he was so tall, so grand, and so grave, wearing a large powdered wig and silver spectacles, which gave him a particularly venerable appearance, though Harry was one day very nearly getting into disgrace upon that subject. His lordship had a habit of always carrying two pairs of spectacles in his pocket, and often, after thrusting one pair high upon his forehead, he forgot where they were, and put others on his nose, which had such a droll appearance, that the first time Harry saw it, he felt quite taken by surprise, and burst into a fit of laughter, upon which Lord Rockville gave him such a comical look of surprise and perplexity, that Harry's fit of laughing got worse and worse. The more people know they are wrong, and try to stop, the more convulsive it becomes, and the more difficult to look grave again; so at last, after repeated efforts to appear serious and composed, Harry started up, and in his hurry to escape, very nearly slammed the door behind him, which would have given the last finish to his offences.

Both the little visiters found Lady Rockville so extremely indulgent and kind, that she seemed like another grandmama, therefore they gradually ventured to talk some of their own nonsense before her, and even to try some of their old ways, and frolicsome tricks, which she seldom found any fault with, except when Harry one day eloped with Lord Rockville's favourite walking-stick, to be used as a fishing-rod among the minnows, with a long thread at the end for a line, and a crooked pin to represent the hook; while, on the same day, Laura privately mounted the ass that gave Lord Rockville ass's milk, and rode it all round the park, while he sat at home expecting his usual refreshing tumbler. Still they both passed muster for being very tolerable children, and his Lordship was heard once to say, in a voice of great approbation, that Master and Miss Graham were so punctual at dinner, and so perfectly quiet, he really often forgot they were in the house. Indeed, Harry's complaisance on the day after he had laughed so injudiciously about the spectacles, was quite unheard of, as he felt anxious to make up for his misconduct; and when Lord Rockville asked if he would like a fire in the play-room, as the evening was chilly, he answered very politely, "Thank you, my Lord! We are ready to think it hot or cold just as you please!"

All this was too good to last! One morning when Harry and Laura looked out of the window, it was a most deplorably wet day. The whole sky looked like a large gray cotton umbrella, and the clouds were so low that Harry thought he could almost have touched them. In short, as Lord Rockville remarked, "it rained cats and dogs," so his Lordship knitted his brows, and thrust his hands into his waistcoat pockets, walking up and down the room in a perfect fume of vexation, for he was so accustomed to be obeyed, that it seemed rather a hardship when even the weather contradicted his wishes. To complete his vexation, as "single misfortunes never come alone," his valet, when carelessly drying the Morning Post at a large kitchen fire, had set it in flames, so that all the wonderful news it contained was reduced to ashes, therefore Lord Rockville might well have given notice, that, for this day at least, he had a right to be in extremely bad humour.

Lady Rockville privately recommended Harry and Laura to sit quietly down and play at cat's cradle, which accordingly they did, and when that became no longer endurable, some dominos were produced. Thus the morning wore tediously away till about two o'clock, when suddenly the rain stopped, the sun burst forth with prodigious splendour, every leaf in the park glittered, as if it had been sprinkled with diamonds, and a hundred birds seemed singing a chorus of joy, while bees and butterflies fluttered at the windows and flew away rejoicing.

Harry was the first to observe this delightful change, and with an exclamation of delight, he sprung from his seat, pulled Laura from hers, upset the domino-table, and rushed out of the room, slamming the door with a report like twenty cannons. Away they both flew to the forest, Laura swinging her bonnet in her hand, and Harry tossing his cap in the air, while Lord Rockville watched them angrily from the drawing-room window, saying in a tone of extreme displeasure, "That boy has a voice that might do for the town crier! He laughs so loud it is enough to crack every glass in the room! I wish he were condemned to pass a week in those American prisons where no one is allowed to speak. In short, he would be better anywhere than here; for I might as well live with a hammer and tongs, as with the two children together. They are more restless than the quicksilver figures from China, and I wish they were as quiet; but my only comfort is, that at any rate they come home punctually to dinner at five. Nothing is so intolerable as people dropping in too late and disordering the table."

Meantime, the woods at Holiday House rung with sounds of mirth and gaiety, while Harry scrambled up the trees like a squirrel, and swung upon the branches, gathering walnuts and crab-apples for Laura, after which they both cut their names upon the bark of Lord Rockville's favourite beech, so that every person who passed that way must observe the large, distinct letters. They were laughing and chatting over this exploit, both talking at once, as noisy and happy as possible, and expecting nothing particular to happen, when, all on a sudden, Laura turned pale, and grasped hold of Harry's arm, saying, in a low, frightened voice,

"Hush, Harry!—hush!—I hear a very strange noise. It sounds like some wild beast! What can that be?"

Harry listened as if he had ten pair of ears, and nearly cracked his eye-balls staring round him, to see what could be the matter. A curious deep growling sound might be heard at some distance, while there was the noise of something trampling heavily on the ground, and of branches breaking off the trees, as if some large creature were forcing his way through. Harry and Laura now stood like a couple of little statues, not daring to breathe, they felt so terrified! The noise grew louder and louder, while it gradually became nearer and nearer, till at length a large black bull burst into view, with his tail standing high in the air, while he tore up the ground with his horns, bellowing as loudly as he could roar, and galloping straight towards the place where they stood.

Laura's knees tottered under her, and she instantly dropped on the ground with terror, feeling as if she would die the next minute of fright, while, as for attempting to escape, it never entered her head to think that possible. Harry felt quite differently, for he was a bold boy, not easily scared out of his senses, and instantly saw that something must be done or they would both be lost. Many selfish people would have run away alone, without caring for the safety of any one but themselves, which was not at all the case with Harry, who thought first of his poor frightened companion. "Hollo, Laura! are you hiding in a cart rut?" he exclaimed, pulling her hastily off the ground. "The bull will soon find you here! Come! come! as fast as possible! we must have a race for it yet! That terrible beast can scarcely make his way through the branches, they grow so closely! Perhaps we may get on as fast as he!"

All this time, Harry was dragging Laura along, and running himself into the thickest part of the plantation; but it was very difficult to make any progress, as she had become quite faint and bewildered with fright.

"Oh, Harry!" cried she, trembling all over, "you must get on alone! I am so weak with terror, it is impossible to run a step further."

"Do not waste your breath with talking," answered Harry, still pushing on at full speed. "How can you suppose I would be so shabby as to make my escape without you! No! no! we must either both be caught or both get off!"

Laura felt so grateful to Harry when he said this, that she seemed for a moment almost to forget the bull, which was still coming furiously on behind, while she now

made a desperate exertion to run faster than she had been able to do before, clearing the ground almost as rapidly as Harry could have done, though he still held her firmly by the hand, to encourage her.

The trampling noise continued, the breaking of branches, and the frightful bellowing of this dreadful animal, when at last Harry caught sight of a wooden paling, which he silently pointed out to Laura, being quite unable now to speak. Having rushed forward to it, with almost frantic haste, Harry threw himself over the top, after which he helped Laura to squeeze herself underneath, when they proceeded rather more leisurely onwards.

"That fence will puzzle Mr. Bull," said Harry triumphantly, yet gasping for breath. "We can push through places where his great hoof could scarcely be thrust! I saw him coming along, with his heels high in the air, and his head down, like an enormous wheel-barrow."

Scarcely had Harry spoken, before the infuriated animal advanced at full gallop towards the fence, and after running along the side a little way, he suddenly tore up the paling with his horns, as if it had been made of paper, and rushed forward more rapidly than ever.

Harry now began to fear that indeed all was over, for his strength had become nearly exhausted, when, to his great joy, he espied a large rough stone wall, not very far off, which was as welcome a sight as land to a shipwrecked sailor.

"Run for your life, Laura!" he cried, pointing it out, to encourage her. "There is safety if we reach it."

On they both flew faster than the wind, and Harry having scrambled up the wall, like a grasshopper, pulled Laura up beside him, and there they both stood at last, encamped quite beyond the reach of danger, though the enemy arrived a few minutes afterwards, pawing the air, and foaming and bellowing with disappointment.

"Laura!" said Harry, after she had a little recovered from her fright, and was walking slowly homewards, while she cast an alarmed glance frequently behind, thinking she still heard the bull in pursuit, "you see, as Uncle David says, whatever danger people are in, it is foolish to be quite in despair, but we should rather think what is best to do, and do it directly."

"Yes, Harry! and I shall never forget that you would not forsake me, but risked your own life, like a brave brother, in my defence. I should like to do as much for you another time!"

"Thank you, Laura, as much as if you had, but I hope we shall never be in such a scrape again! If Frank were here, he would put us both in mind to thank a merciful God for taking so much care of us and bringing us safely home!"

"Yes, Harry! It is perhaps a good thing being in danger sometimes, to remind us that we cannot be safe or happy an hour without God's care, so in our prayers to-night we must remember what has happened, and return thanks very particularly."

It was long past five before Harry and Laura reached Holiday House, where Lord Rockville met them at the drawing-room door, looking taller, and grander, and graver than ever, while Lady Rockville rose from her sofa, and came up to them, saying, in a tone of gentle reproach,

"My dear children! you ought to return home before the dinner hour, and not keep his Lordship waiting!"

The very idea of Lord Rockville waiting dinner was too dreadful ever to have entered their heads till this minute; but Harry and Laura immediately explained how exceedingly sorry they were for what had occurred; and to show that it was their misfortune rather than their fault, they told the whole frightful story of the mad bull, to which Lady Rockville listened, as if her very wig were standing upon end, to hear of such doings. She even turned up her eyes with astonishment to think of what a wonderful escape they had made; but his Lordship frowned through his spectacles, and leaned his chin upon his stick, looking, as Harry thought, very like a bear upon a pole.

"Pshaw! nonsense!" exclaimed Lord Rockville, impatiently. "The bull would have done you no harm. He is a most respectable, quiet, well-disposed animal, and brought an excellent character from his last place. I never heard a complaint of him before!"

"It is curious," observed Laura, "that all bulls are reckoned perfectly peaceable and tame, till they have tossed two or three people, and killed them!"

"I thought," added Lord Rockville, looking very grand and contemptuous, "that Harry was grown more a man than to be so easily put to flight. When a bull, another time, threatens to toss you, my boy, seize hold of his tail—or toss him!—or, in short, do anything rather than run away the first time an animal looks at you. This is a mere cock-and-a-bull story, to excuse your keeping me waiting almost a quarter of an hour for dinner!—you should be made a guard of a mail coach for a month, to teach you punctuality, Master Graham."

Lord Rockville gravely looked at his watch, while Harry luckily considered how often his grandmama had recommended him to make no answer when he was scolded; so he nearly bit off the tip of his tongue to keep it quiet, while he could not but wish, in his own mind, that my Lord himself had seen how very fierce the bull looked.

Laura felt more vexed on Harry's account than her own, and the dinner went on as uncomfortably as possible; for even if a French cook has dressed it, if ill-humour be the sauce, any dish becomes unpalatable. Nothing was to be seen reflected on the surface of many fine silver covers, but very cross or very melancholy faces; while Lady Rockville tried to make her own countenance look both cheerful and good-natured. She told Harry and Laura, to divert them, that old Mrs. Bouverie had once been pursued by a furious milch cow along a lane, flanked on both sides by such very high walls that escape seemed impossible; so the good lady, who was fat and breathless, became so desperate, that without a hope of getting off, she seized the enraged animal by the horns, and screamed in its face, till the cow herself became frightened. The creature stared, stepping backwards and backwards, with increasing alarm, till at last, to the old lady's great relief and surprise, she fairly turned tail and ran off.

In the evening, Lord Rockville not having yet recovered his equanimity, went out, rather in bad humour, to take his usual walk before supper. Without once remembering about Harry and the bull, he strolled a great way into the woods, marking several trees to be cut down, and admiring a fine forest which he planted himself long ago, but without particularly considering which way he turned. It was beginning, at last, to grow very dark and gloomy, so Lord Rockville had some thoughts of returning home, when he became suddenly startled by hearing a loud roar not far off, and a moment afterwards the furious bull dashed out of a neighbouring thicket, raging and foaming, and tearing the ground with his horns, exactly as Harry had described in the morning, while poor Lord Rockville, who seldom moved faster than a very dignified walk, instantly quickened his pace, in an opposite direction, striding away faster and faster, till at last,—it must be confessed,—his Lordship ended by running!!!

In spite of all Lord Rockville's exertions, the bull continued rapidly to gain upon him, for his Lordship, being rather corpulent and easily fatigued, stopped every now and then to gasp for breath; till at last, feeling it impossible to get on faster, though the stables were now within sight, he seized the branch of a large oak tree, which swept nearly to the ground, and contrived with great difficulty to scramble out of reach. The enraged bull gazed up into the tree and bellowed with fury, when he saw Lord Rockville so judiciously perched overhead, and he remained for half-an-hour watching to see if his Lordship would venture down again. At last the tormenting animal began leisurely eating grass under the tree, but gradually he moved away, turning his back, while he fed, till Lord Rockville vainly deluded himself with the hope of stealing off unobserved. Being somewhat rested and refreshed, while the enemy was looking in another direction, he descended cautiously as if he had been going to tread upon needles and pins; but, unaccustomed to such movements, he jumped so heavily upon the ground, that the bull, hearing a noise, turned round, and set up a loud furious roar, when he saw his intended victim again within reach.

Now the race began once more with redoubled agility! The odds seemed greatly in favour of the bull, and Lord Rockville thought he already felt the animal's horns in his side, when a groom, who saw the party approaching, instantly seized a pitchfork, and flew to the rescue of his master. Lord Rockville never stopped his career till he reached the stable, and ran up into a loft, from the window of which he gave the alarm and called for more assistance, when several ploughmen and stableboys assembled, who drove the animal with great difficulty into a stall, where he continued so ungovernable, that iron chains were put round his neck, and some days afterwards, seeing no one could manage him, Lord Rockville ordered the bull to be shot, and his carcass turned into beef for the poor of the parish, who all, consequently, rejoiced at his demise; though the meat turned out so tough, that it required their best teeth to eat it with.

Meantime, on that memorable evening of so many adventures, Harry, Laura, and Lady Rockville, wondered often what had become of his Lordship, and, at last, when supper appeared at the usual hour, his absence became still more unaccountable!

"What can be the matter?" exclaimed Lady Rockville anxiously. "This is very odd! His Lordship is as punctual as the postman in general! especially for supper; and here is Lord Rockville's favourite dish of sago and wine, which will become uneatably cold in ten minutes, if he does not return home to enjoy it!"

Scarcely had she finished speaking, when the door opened and Lord Rockville walked majestically into the room. There was something so different from usual in his manner and appearance, however, that Harry and Laura exchanged looks of astonishment; his neck-cloth was loose—his face excessively red—and his hand shook, while he breathed so hard, that he might have been heard at the porter's lodge. Lady Rockville gazed with amazement at all she saw, and then asked what he chose for supper; but when Lord Rockville tried to speak, the words died on his lips, so he could only point in silence to the sago and wine.

"What in all the world has happened to you this evening, my Lord?" exclaimed Lady Rockville, unable to restrain her curiosity a moment longer. "I never saw you in such a way before! Your eyes are perfectly bloodshot—your dress strangely disordered—and you seem so hot and so fatigued! Tell me!—what is the matter?"

"Nothing!" answered Lord Rockville, drawing himself up, while he tried to look grander and graver than ever, though his Lordship could not help panting for breath—putting his hands to his sides—and wiping his forehead with his pocket-handkerchief in an agony of fatigue. Harry observed all this for some time, as eagerly and intently as a cat watches a bird on a tree. He saw that something extraordinary had occurred, and he began to have hopes that it really was the very thing he wished; because, seeing Lord Rockville now perfectly safe, he would not have grudged him a pretty considerable fright from his friend the bull. At last, unable any longer to control his impatience, Harry started off his chair, gazing so earnestly at Lord Rockville, that his eyes almost sprung out of their sockets, while he rubbed his hands with ecstasy, saying,

"I guess you've seen the bull! Oh! I am sure you did! Pray tell us if you have! Did he run after you,—and did you run away?"

Lord Rockville tried more than he had ever done in his life to look grave, but it would not do. Gradually his face relaxed into a smile, till at last he burst into loud peals of laughter, joined most heartily by Harry, Laura, and Lady Rockville. Nobody recovered any gravity during the rest of that evening, for whenever they tried to think or talk quietly about anything else, Harry and Laura were sure to burst forth again upon the subject, and even after being safely stowed in their beds for the night, they both laughed themselves to sleep at the idea of Lord Rockville himself having been obliged, after all, to run away from that "most respectable, quiet, well-disposed animal,

THE MAD BULL."

THE BROKEN KEY

First he moved his right leg,
Then he moved his left leg,
Then he said, "I pardon beg,"
And sat upon his seat.

"O<small>H! UNCLE DAVID! UNCLE DAVID!</small>" cried Laura, when they arrived from Holiday House, "I would jump out of the carriage window with joy to see you again; only the persons passing in the street might be surprised!"

"Not at all! They are quite accustomed to see people jumping out of the windows with joy, whenever I appear."

"We have so much to tell you," exclaimed Harry and Laura, each seizing hold of a hand, "we hardly know where to begin!"

"Ladies and gentlemen, if you both talk at once, I must get a new pair of ears! So you have not been particularly miserable at Holiday House?"

"No, no, Uncle David; we did not think there had been so much happiness in the world," answered Laura, eagerly. "The last two days we could do nothing but play, and laugh, and——"

"And grow fat! Why, you both look so well fed, you are just fit for killing! I shall be obliged to shut you up two or three days, without anything to eat, as is done to pet lap dogs when they are getting corpulent and gouty."

"Then we shall be like bears living on our paws," replied Harry, "and Uncle David, I would rather do that, than be a glutton like Peter Grey. He went to a cheap shop lately, where old cheese-cakes were sold at half price, and greedily devoured nearly a dozen, thinking that the dead flies scattered on the top were currants, till Frank showed him his mistake!"

"Frank should have let him eat in peace. There is no accounting for tastes. I once knew a lady who liked to swallow spiders. She used to crack and eat them with the greatest delight, whenever she could catch one."

"Oh, what a horrid woman! That is even worse than grandmama's story about Dr. Manvers having dined on a dish of mice, fried in crumbs of bread!"

"You know the old proverb, Harry, 'one man's meat is another man's poison.' The Persians are disgusted at our eating lobsters; and the Hindoos think us scarcely fit to exist, because we live on beef; while we are equally amazed at the Chinese for devouring dog pies, and bird's-nest soup. You turn up your nose at the French for liking frogs; and they think us ten times worse with our singed sheep's head, oat cakes, and haggis."

"That reminds me," said Lady Harriet, "that when Charles X. lived in what he called the 'dear Canongate,' his majesty was heard to say, that he tried every sort of Scotch goose, 'the solan goose, the wild goose, and the tame goose, but the best goose of all, was the hag-goose.' "

"Very polite, indeed, to adopt our national taste so completely," observed Uncle David, smiling. "When my regiment was quartered in Spain, an officer of ours, a great epicure, and not quite so complaisant, used to say that the country was scarcely fit to live in, because there it is customary to dress almost every dish with sugar. At last, one day in a rage, he ordered eggs to be brought up in their shells for dinner, saying, 'that is the only thing the cook cannot possibly spoil.' We played him a trick, however, which was very like what you would have done, Harry, on a similar occasion. I secretly put pounded sugar into the salt-cellar, and when he tasted his first mouthful, you should have seen the look of fury with which he sprung off his seat, exclaiming, 'The barbarians eat sugar even with their eggs!' "

"That would be the country for me to travel in!" said Harry. "I could live in a barrel of sugar; and my little pony, Tom Thumb, would be happy to accompany me there, as he likes anything sweet."

"All animals are of the same opinion. I remember the famous rider Ducrow, telling a brother-officer of mine, that the way in which he gains so much influence over his horses, is merely by bribing them with sugar. They may be managed in that way like children, and are quite aware, if it be taken from them as a punishment for being restive."

"Oh! those beautiful horses at Ducrow's! How often I think of them since we were there!" exclaimed Harry. "They are quite like fairies, with fine arched necks, and long tails!"

"I never heard before of a fairy with a long tail, Master Harry; but perhaps in the course of your travels you may have seen such a thing."

"How I should like to ride upon Tom Thumb, in Ducrow's way, with my toe on the saddle!"

"Fine doings, indeed!" exclaimed Mrs. Crabtree, who had entered the room at this moment. "Have you forgotten already, Master Harry, how many of the nursery plates you broke one day I was out, in trying to copy that there foolish Indian juggler, who tossed his plates in the air, and twirled them on his thumb! There must be no more such nonsense; for if once your neck is broke by a fall off Tom Thumb, no doctor that I know of can mend it again. Remember what a terrible tumble you had off Jessy last year!"

"You are always speaking about that little overturn Mrs. Crabtree; and it was not worth recollecting above a week! Did you never see a man thrown off his horse before?"

"A man and horse indeed!" said Uncle David, laughing when he looked at Harry. "You and your charger were hardly large enough then for a toy-shop; and you must grow a little more, Captain Gulliver, before you will be fit for a dragoon regiment."

Harry and Laura stayed very quietly at home for several weeks after their return from Holiday House, attending so busily to lessons, that Uncle David said he felt much afraid they were going to be a pair of little wonders who would die of too much learning.

"You will be taken ill of the multiplication table some day, and confined to bed with a violent fit of geography! Pray take care of yourselves, and do not devour above three books at once," said Major Graham one day, entering the room with a note in his hand. "Here is an invitation that I suppose you are both too busy to accept, so perhaps I might as well send an apology; eh, Harry!"

Down dropped the lesson-books upon the floor, and up sprung Harry in an ecstasy of delight. "An invitation! Oh! I like an invitation so very much! Pray tell us all about it!"

"Perhaps it is an invitation to spend a month with Dr. Lexicon. What would you say to that! They breakfast upon Latin grammars at school, and have a dish of real French verbs, smothered in onions, for dinner every day."

"But in downright earnest, Uncle David! where are we going?"

"Must I tell you? Well! that good-natured old lady, Mrs. Darwin, intends taking a large party of children next week, in her own carriage, to pass ten days at Ivy Lodge, a charming country house about twenty miles off, where you are all to enjoy perfect happiness. I wish I could be ground down into a little boy myself, for the occasion! Poor good woman! what a life she will lead! There is only one little drawback to your delight, that I am almost afraid to announce."

"What is that, Uncle David?" asked Harry, looking as if nothing in nature could ever make him grave again. "Are we to bite off our own noses before we return?"

"Not exactly; but somebody is to be of the party who will do it for you. Mrs. Darwin has heard that there are certain children who become occasionally rather unmanageable! I cannot think who they can be, for it is certainly nobody we ever saw; so she has requested that Mrs. Crabtree will follow in the mail-coach."

Harry and Laura looked as if a glass of cold water had been thrown in their faces, after this was mentioned; but they soon forgot every little vexation, in a burst of joy, when, some days afterwards, Mrs. Darwin stopped at the door to pick them up, in the most curious-looking carriage they had ever seen. It was a very large open car, as round as a bird's nest, and so perfectly crowded with children, that nobody could have supposed any room left even for a doll; but Mrs. Darwin said that whatever number of people came in, there was always accommodation for one more; and this really proved to be the case, for Harry and Laura soon elbowed their way into seats, and set off, waving their handkerchiefs to Major Graham, who had helped to pack them in, and who now stood smiling at the door.

As this very large vehicle was drawn by only one horse, it proceeded very slowly; but Mrs. Darwin amused the children with several very diverting stories, and gave them a grand luncheon in the carriage; after which, they threw what was left, wrapped up in an old newspaper, to some people breaking stones on the road, feeling quite delighted to see the surprise and joy of the poor labourers when they opened the parcel. In short, everybody became sorry when this diverting journey was finished, and they drove up, at last, to the gate of a tall old house, that looked as if it had been built in the year one. The walls were very thick, and quite mouldy with age. Indeed, the only wonder was, that Ivy Lodge had still a roof upon its head, for everything about it looked so tottering and decayed. The very servants were all old; and a white-headed butler opened the door, who looked as frail and gloomy as the house; but before long, the old walls of Ivy Lodge rung and echoed again with sounds of mirth and joy. It seemed to have been built on purpose for hide-and-seek; there were rooms with invisible doors, and closets cut in the walls, and great old chests where people might have been buried alive for a year, without being found out. The gardens, too, were perfectly enchanting. Such arbours to take strawberries and cream in! and such summer houses where they drank tea out of doors every evening! Here they saw a prodigious eagle fastened to the ground by a chain, and looking the most dull, melancholy creature in the world; while Harry wished the poor bird might be liberated, and thought how delightful it would be to stand by and see him soaring away to his native skies.

"Yes! with a large slice of raw meat in his beak!" said Peter Grey, who was always thinking of eating. "I dare say he lives much better here, than he would do killing his own mutton up in the clouds there, or taking his chance of a dead horse on the sea-shore occasionally,"

Harry and Peter were particularly amused with Mrs. Darwin's curious collection of pets. There were black swans with red bills swimming gracefully in a pond close to the window, and ready to rush forward on the shortest notice for a morsel of bread. The lop-eared rabbits also surprised them, with their ears hanging down to the ground, and they were interested to see a pair of carrier-pigeons which could carry letters as well as the postman. Mrs. Darwin showed them tumbler-pigeons too, that performed a summer-set in the air when they flew, and horsemen and dragoon-pigeons, trumpeters and pouters, till Peter Grey at last begged to see the pigeons that made the pigeon-pies, and the cow that gave the butter-milk; he was likewise very anxious for leave to bring his fishing-rod into the drawing-room to try whether he could catch one of the beautiful gold-fish that swam about in a large glass globe, saying he thought it might perhaps be very good to eat at breakfast. Mrs. Darwin had a pet lamb that she was exceedingly proud of, because it followed her everywhere, and Harry, who was very fond of the little creature, said he wished some plan could be invented to hinder its ever growing into a great fat vulgar sheep; and he thought the white mice were old animals that had grown gray with years.

There were donkeys for the children to ride upon, and Mrs. Darwin had a boat that held the whole party, to sail in, round the pond, and she hung up a swing that seemed to fly about as high as the house, which they swung upon, after which they were allowed to shake the fruit-trees, and to eat whatever came down about their ears; so it very often rained apples and pears in the gardens at Ivy Lodge, for Peter seemed never to tire of that joke; indeed the apple-trees had a sad life of it as long as he remained.

Peter told Mrs. Darwin that he had "a patent appetite," which was always ready on every occasion; but the good lady became so fond of stuffing the children at all hours, that even he felt a little puzzled sometimes how to dispose of all she heaped upon his plate, while both Harry and Laura, who were far from greedy, became perfectly wearied of hearing the gong. The whole party assembled at eight every morning, to partake of porridge and butter-milk, after which, at ten, they breakfasted with Mrs. Darwin on tea, muffins, and sweetmeats. They then drove in the round open car, to bathe in the sea, on their return from which, luncheon was always ready, and after concluding that, they might pass the interval till dinner among the fruit-trees. They never could eat enough to please Mrs. Darwin at dinner; tea followed, on a most substantial plan; their supper consisted of poached eggs, and the maid was desired to put a biscuit under every visiter's pillow, in case the young people should be hungry in the night, for Mrs. Darwin said she had been starved at school herself when she was a little girl, and wished nobody ever to suffer, as she had done, from hunger.

The good lady was so anxious for everything to be exactly as the children liked it, that sometimes Laura felt quite at a loss what to say or do. One day having cracked her egg-shell at breakfast, Mrs. Darwin peeped anxiously over her shoulder, saying,

"I hope, my dear, your egg is all right?"

"Most excellent, indeed."

"Is it quite fresh?"

"Perfectly; I dare say it was laid only a minute before it was boiled."

"I have seen the eggs much larger than that!"

"Yes; but then I believe they are rather coarse,—at least we think so, when Mrs. Crabtree gives us a turkey egg at dinner."

"If you prefer them small, perhaps you would like a guinea-fowl's egg?"

"Thank you! but this one is just as I like them."

"It looks rather overdone. If you think so, we could get another in a minute."

"No; they are better well boiled!"

"Then probably it is not enough done. Some people like them quite hard, and I could easily pop it into the slop-basin for another minute."

"I am really obliged to you, but it could not be improved."

"Do you not take any more salt with your egg?"

"No, I thank you."

"A few more grains would improve it."

"If you say so, I dare say they will."

"Ah! now I am afraid you have put in too much! pray do get another."

This long-continued attack upon her egg was too much for Laura's gravity, who appeared for some minutes to have a violent fit of coughing, and ended in a burst of laughter; after which she hastily finished all that remained of it, and thus the discussion closed.

In the midst of all their happiness, while the children thought that every succeeding day had no fault but being too short, and Harry even planned with Peter to stop the clock altogether, and see whether time itself would not stand still, nobody ever thought for a moment of anything but joy; and yet a very sad and sudden distress awaited Mrs. Darwin. One fore-noon she received a letter that seemed very hastily and awkwardly folded,—the seal was all to one side, and surrounded with stray drops of red wax,—the direction seemed sadly blotted, and at the top was written in large letters, the words, "To be delivered immediately."

When Mrs. Darwin hurriedly tore open this very strange-looking letter, she found that it came from her own housekeeper in town, to announce the dreadful event that her sister, Lady Barnet, had been that day seized with an apoplectic fit, and was thought to be at the point of death; therefore it was hoped that Mrs. Darwin would not lose an hour in returning to town, that she might be present on the melancholy occasion. The shock of hearing this news was so very great, that poor Mrs. Darwin could not speak about it; but after trying to compose herself for a few minutes, she went into the play-room, and told the children that, for reasons she could not explain, they must get ready to return home in an hour, when the car would be at the door for their journey.

Nothing could exceed their surprise on hearing Mrs. Darwin make so unexpected a proposal. At first Peter Grey thought she was speaking in jest, and said he would prefer if she ordered out a balloon to travel in this morning; but when it appeared that Mrs. Darwin was really in earnest about their pleasant visit being over so soon, Harry's face grew perfectly red with passion, while he said in a loud, angry voice,

"Grandmama allowed me to stay here till Friday!—and I was invited to stay,—and I will not go anywhere else!"

"Oh, fie, Master Harry!" said Mrs. Crabtree, "do not talk so! You ought to know better. I shall soon teach you, however, to do as you are bid!"

Saying these words, she stretched out her hand to seize violent hold of him; but Harry dipped down and escaped. Quickly opening the door, he ran, half in joke and half in earnest, at full speed up two pair of stairs, followed closely by Mrs. Crabtree, who was now in a terrible rage, especially when she saw what a piece of fun Harry thought this fatiguing race. A door happened to be standing wide open on the second landing place, which, having been observed by Harry, he darted in, and slammed it in Mrs. Crabtree's face, locking and double locking it, to secure his own safety, after which he sat down in the empty apartment to enjoy his victory in peace. When people once begin to grow self-willed and rebellious, it is impossible to guess where it will all end! Harry might have been easily led to do right at first, if any one had reasoned with him and spoken kindly, but now he really was in a sort of don't-care-a-button humour, and scarcely minded what he did next.

As long as Mrs. Crabtree continued to scold and rave behind the door, Harry grew harder and harder; but at length the good old lady, Mrs. Darwin herself, arrived up stairs, and represented how ungrateful he was, not doing all in his power to please her, when she had taken so much pains to make him happy. This brought the little rebel round in a moment, as he became quite sensible of his own misconduct, and resolved immediately to submit. Accordingly, Harry tried to open the door, but, what is very easily done cannot sometimes be undone, which turned out the case on this occasion, as, with all his exertions, the key would not turn in the lock! Harry tried it first one way, then another. He twisted with his whole strength, till his face became perfectly scarlet with the effort, but in vain! At last he put the poker through the handle of the key, thinking this a very clever plan, and quite sure to succeed; but after a desperate struggle, the unfortunate key broke in two, so then nobody could possibly open the door!

After this provoking accident happened, Harry felt what a very bad boy he had been, so he burst into tears, and called through the key-hole to beg Mrs. Darwin's pardon, while Mrs. Crabtree scolded him through the key-hole in return, till Harry shrunk away as if a cannonading had begun at his ear.

Meantime, Mrs. Darwin hurried off, racking her brains to think what had best be done to deliver the prisoner, since no time could be lost, or she might perhaps not get to town at all that night, and the car was expected every minute, to come round for the travellers. The gardener said he thought it might be possible to find a few ladders, which, being tied one above another, would perhaps reach as high as the window, where Harry had now appeared, and by which he could easily scramble down; so the servants made haste to fetch all they could find, and to borrow all they could see, till a great many were collected. These they joined together very strongly with ropes, but when it was at last reared against the wall, to the great disappointment of Mrs. Darwin, the ladder appeared a yard and a half too short!

What was to be done?

The obliging gardener mounted to the very top of his ladder, and Harry leaned so far over the window, he seemed in danger of falling out, but still they did not reach one another, so not a single person could guess what plan would be tried next. At length Harry called out very loudly to the gardener,

"Hollo! Mr. King of Spades! if I were to let myself drop very gently down from the window, could you catch me in your arms?"

"Master Harry! Master Harry! if you dare!" cried Mrs. Crabtree, shaking her fist at him. "You'll be broken in pieces like a teapot, you'll be made as flat as a pancake! Stay where you are! Do ye hear!"

But Harry seemed suddenly grown deaf, and was now more than half out—fixing his fingers very firmly on the ledge of the window, and slowly dropping his legs downwards.

"Oh, Harry! you will be killed!" screamed Laura. "Stop! stop! Harry, are you mad! can nobody stop him?"

But nobody could stop him, for, being so high above everybody's head, Harry had it all his own way, and was now hanging altogether out of the window, but he stopped a single minute, and called out, "Do not be frightened, Laura! I have behaved very ill, and deserve the worst that can happen. If I do break my head, it will save Mrs. Crabtree the trouble of breaking it for me, after I come down."

The gardener now balanced himself steadily on the upper step of the ladder, and spread his arms out, while Harry slowly let himself drop. Laura tried to look on without screaming out, as that might have startled him, but the scene became too frightful, so she closed her eyes, put her hands over her face, and turned away, while her heart beat so violently, that it might almost have been heard. Even Mrs. Crabtree clasped her hands in an agony of alarm, while Mrs. Darwin put up her pocket-handkerchief, and could not look on another moment. An awful pause took place, during which a feather falling on the ground would have startled them, when suddenly a loud shout from Peter Grey and the other children, which was gaily echoed from the top of the ladder, made Laura venture to look up, and there was Harry safe in the gardener's arms, who soon helped him down to the ground, where he immediately asked pardon of everybody for the fright he had given them.

There was no time for more than half a scold from Mrs. Crabtree, as Mrs. Darwin's car had been waiting some time; so Harry said she might be owing him the rest, on some future occasion.

"Yes! and a hundred lashes besides!" added Peter Grey, laughing. "Pray touch him up well, Mrs. Crabtree, when you are about it. There is no law against cruelty to boys!"

This put Mrs. Crabtree into such a rage, that she followed Peter with a perfect hail-storm of angry words, till at last, for a joke, he put up Mrs. Darwin's umbrella to screen himself, and immediately afterwards the car drove slowly off.

When Uncle David heard all the adventures at Ivy Lodge, he listened most attentively to "the confessions of Master Harry Graham," and shook his head in a most serious manner after they were concluded, saying, "I have always thought that boys are like cats, with nine lives at least! You should be hung up in a basket, Harry, as they do with unruly boys in the South Sea Islands, where such young gentlemen as you are left dangling in the air for days together without a possibility of escape!"

"I would not care for that compared with being teased and worried by Mrs. Crabtree. I really wish, Uncle David, that Dr. Bell would order me never to be scolded any more! It is very bad for me! I generally feel an odd sort of over-all-ish-ness as soon as she begins; and I am getting too big now for anything but a birch-rod like Frank. How pleasant it is to be a grown-up man, Uncle David, as you are, sitting all day at the club with your hat on your head, and nothing to do but look out of the window. That is what I call happiness!"

"But once upon a time, Harry," said Lady Harriet, "when I stopped in the carriage for your Uncle David at the club, he was in the middle of such a yawn at the window, that he very nearly dislocated his jaw! It was quite alarming to see him, and he told me in a great secret, that the longest and most tiresome hours of his life are, when he has nothing particular to do."

"Now, at this moment, I have nothing particular to do," said Major Graham, "therefore I shall tell you a wonderful story, children, about liking to be idle or busy, and you must find out the moral for yourselves."

"A story! a story!" cried Harry and Laura, in an ecstasy of delight; and as they each had a knee of Uncle David's which belonged to themselves, they scrambled into their places, exclaiming, "Now let it be all about very bad boys, and giants, and fairies!"

UNCLE DAVID'S NONSENSICAL STORY ABOUT GIANTS AND FAIRIES

"Pie-crust, and pastry-crust, that was the wall;
The windows were made of black puddings and white,
And slated with pancakes—you ne'er saw the like!"

IN THE DAYS OF YORE, children were not all such clever, good, sensible people as they are now! Lessons were then considered rather a plague—sugar plums were still in demand—holidays continued yet in fashion—and toys were not then made to teach mathematics, nor story-books to give instruction in chemistry and navigation. These were very strange times, and there existed at that period, a very idle, greedy, naughty boy, such as we never hear of in the present day. His papa and mama were—no matter who,—and he lived—no matter where. His name was Master No-book, and he seemed to think his eyes were made for nothing but to stare out of the windows, and his mouth for no other purpose but to eat. This young gentleman hated lessons like mustard, both of which brought tears into his eyes, and during school hours he sat gazing at his books, pretending to be busy, while his mind wandered away to wish impatiently for dinner, and to consider where he could get the nicest pies, pastry, ices, and jellies, while he smacked his lips at the very thoughts of them. I think he must have been first cousin to Peter Grey, but that is not perfectly certain.

Whenever Master No-book spoke, it was always to ask for something; and you might continually hear him say, in a whining tone of voice, "Papa, may I take this piece of cake? Aunt Sarah, will you give me an apple? Mama, do send me the whole of that plum-pudding!" Indeed, very frequently, when he did not get permission to gormandize, this naughty glutton helped himself without leave. Even his dreams were like his waking hours, for he had often a horrible nightmare about lessons, thinking he was smothered with Greek Lexicons, or pelted out of the school with a shower of English Grammars, while one night he fancied himself sitting down to devour an enormous plum-cake, and all on a sudden it became transformed into a Latin Dictionary!

One afternoon Master No-book having played truant all day from school, was lolling on his mama's best sofa in the drawing-room, with his leather boots tucked up on the satin cushions, and nothing to do but to suck a few oranges, and nothing to think of but how much sugar to put upon them, when suddenly an event took place which filled him with astonishment.

A sound of soft music stole into the room, becoming louder and louder the longer he listened, till at length, in a few moments afterwards, a large hole burst open in the wall of his room, and there stepped into his presence two magnificent fairies, just arrived from their castles in the air, to pay him a visit. They had travelled all the way on purpose to have some conversation with Master No-book, and immediately introduced themselves in a very ceremonious manner.

The fairy Do-nothing was gorgeously dressed with a wreath of flaming gas round her head, a robe of gold tissue, a necklace of rubies, and a bouquet in her hand of glittering diamonds. Her cheeks were rouged to the very eyes,—her teeth were set in gold, and her hair was of a most brilliant purple; in short, so fine and fashionable-looking a fairy never was seen in a drawing-room before.

The fairy Teach-all, who followed next, was simply dressed in white muslin, with bunches of natural flowers in her light brown hair, and she carried in her hand a few neat small books, which Master No-book looked at with a shudder of aversion.

The two fairies now informed him, that they very often invited large parties of children to spend some time at their palaces, but as they lived in quite an opposite direction, it was necessary for their young guests to choose which it would be best to visit first; therefore now they had come to inquire of Master No-book, whom he thought it would be most agreeable to accompany on the present occasion.

"In my house," said the fairy Teach-all, speaking with a very sweet smile, and a soft, pleasing voice, "you shall be taught to find pleasure in every sort of exertion, for I delight in activity and diligence. My young friends rise at seven every morning, and amuse themselves with working in a beautiful garden of flowers,—rearing whatever fruit they wish to eat,—visiting among the poor,—associating pleasantly together,—studying the arts and sciences,—and learning to know the world in which they live, and to fulfil the purposes for which they have been brought into it. In short, all our amusements tend to some useful object, either for our own improvement or the good of others, and you will grow wiser, better, and happier every day you remain in the palace of Knowledge."

"But in Castle Needless, where I live," interrupted the fairy Do-nothing, rudely pushing her companion aside, with an angry contemptuous look, "we never think of exerting ourselves for anything. You may put your head in your pocket, and your hands in your sides as long as you choose to stay. No one is ever even asked a question, that he may be spared the trouble of answering. We lead the most fashionable life imaginable, for nobody speaks to anybody! Each of my visiters is quite an exclusive, and sits with his back to as many of the company as possible, in the most comfortable arm-chair that can be contrived. There, if you are only so good as to take the trouble of wishing for anything, it is yours, without even turning an eye round to look where it comes from. Dresses are provided of the most magnificent kind, which go on themselves, without your having the smallest annoyance with either buttons or strings,—games which you can play without an effort of thought,—and dishes dressed by a French cook, smoking hot under your nose, from morning till night,—while any rain we have, is either made of cherry brandy, lemonade, or lavender water, and in winter it generally snows iced-punch for an hour during the forenoon."

Nobody need be told which fairy Master No-book preferred; and quite charmed at his own good fortune in receiving so agreeable an invitation, he eagerly gave his hand to the splendid new acquaintance who promised him so much pleasure and ease, and gladly proceeded in a carriage lined with velvet, stuffed with downy pillows, and drawn by milk-white swans, to that magnificent residence Castle Needless, which was lighted by a thousand windows during the day, and by a million of lamps every night.

Thus Master No-book enjoyed a constant holiday and a constant feast, while a beautiful lady covered with jewels was ready to tell him stories from morning till night, and servants waited to pick up his playthings if they fell, or to draw out his purse or his pocket-handkerchief when he wished to use them.

Here Master No-book lay dozing for hours and days on rich embroidered cushions, never stirring from his place, but admiring the view of trees covered with the richest burnt almonds, grottoes of sugar-candy, a jet d'eau of champagne, a wide sea which tasted of sugar instead of salt, and a bright clear pond, filled with gold-fish, that let themselves be caught whenever he pleased. Nothing could be more complete, and yet, very strange to say, Master No-book did not seem particularly happy! This appears exceedingly unreasonable, when so much trouble was taken to please him, but the truth is, that every day he became more fretful and peevish. No sweetmeats were worth the trouble of eating, nothing was pleasant to play at, and in the end he wished it were possible to sleep all day, as well as all night.

Not a hundred miles from the fairy Do-nothing's palace, there lived a most cruel monster, called the giant Snap-'em-up, who looked, when he stood up, like the tall steeple of a great church, raising his head so high that he could peep over the loftiest mountains, and was obliged to climb up a ladder to comb his own hair.

Every morning regularly this prodigiously great giant walked round the world before breakfast, for an appetite; after which he made tea in a large lake, used the sea as a slop-basin, and boiled his kettle on Mount Vesuvius. He lived in great style, and his dinners were most magnificent, consisting very often of an elephant roasted whole, ostrich patties, a tiger smothered in onions, stewed lions, and whale soup; but for a side dish, his greatest favourite consisted of little boys, as fat as possible, fried in crumbs of bread, with plenty of pepper and salt.

No children were so well fed or in such good condition for eating as those in the fairy Do-nothing's garden, who was a very particular friend of the giant Snap-'em-up's, and who sometimes laughingly said she would give him a license, and call her own garden his "preserve," because she allowed him to help himself, whenever he pleased, to as many of her visiters as he chose, without taking the trouble even to count them; and in return for such extreme civility, the giant very frequently invited her to dinner.

Snap-'em-up's favourite sport was, to see how many brace of little boys he could bag in a morning; so, in passing along the streets, he peeped into all the drawing-rooms, without having occasion to get upon tip-toe, and picked up every young gentleman who was idly looking out of the windows, and even a few occasionally who were playing truant from school; but busy children seemed always somehow quite out of his reach.

One day, when Master No-book felt even more lazy, more idle, and more miserable than ever, he lay beside a perfect mountain of toys and cakes, wondering what to wish for next, and hating the very sight of everything and everybody. At last he gave so loud a yawn of weariness and disgust, that his jaw very nearly fell out of joint, and then he sighed so deeply, that the giant Snap-'em-up heard the sound as he passed along the road after breakfast, and instantly stepped into the garden, with his glass at his eye, to see what was the matter. Immediately on observing a large, fat, overgrown boy, as round as a dumpling, lying on a bed of roses, he gave a cry of delight, followed by a gigantic peal of laughter, which was heard three miles off, and picking up Master No-book between his finger and his thumb, with a pinch that very nearly broke his ribs, he carried him rapidly towards his own castle, while the fairy Do-nothing laughingly shook her head as he passed, saying, "That little man does me great credit!—he has only been fed for a week, and is as fat already as a prize ox! What a dainty morsel he will be! When do you dine to-day, in case I should have time to look in upon you?"

On reaching home, the giant immediately hung up Master No-book by the hair of his head, on a prodigious hook in the larder, having first taken some large lumps of nasty suet, forcing them down his throat to make him become still fatter, and then stirring the fire, that he might be almost melted with heat, to make his liver grow larger. On a shelf quite near, Master No-book perceived the dead bodies of six other boys, whom he remembered to have seen fattening in the fairy Do-nothing's garden, while he recollected how some of them had rejoiced at the thoughts of leading a long, useless, idle life, with no one to please but themselves.

The enormous cook now seized hold of Master No-book, brandishing her knife, with an aspect of horrible determination, intending to kill him, while he took the trouble of screaming and kicking in the most desperate manner, when the giant turned gravely round and said, that as pigs were considered a much greater dainty when whipped to death than killed in any other way, he meant to see whether children might not be improved by it also; therefore she might leave that great hog of a boy till he had time to try the experiment, especially as his own appetite would be improved by the exercise. This was a dreadful prospect for the unhappy prisoner; but meantime it prolonged his life a few hours, as he was immediately hung up again in the larder, and left to himself. There, in torture of mind and body,—like a fish upon a hook, the wretched boy began at last to reflect seriously upon his former ways, and to consider what a happy home he might have had, if he could only have been satisfied with business and pleasure succeeding each other, like day and night, while lessons might have come in, as a pleasant sauce to his play-hours, and his play-hours as a sauce to his lessons.

In the midst of many reflections, which were all very sensible, though rather too late, Master No-book's attention became attracted by the sound of many voices laughing, talking, and singing, which caused him to turn his eyes in a new direction, when, for the first time, he observed that the fairy Teach-all's garden lay upon a beautiful sloping bank not far off. There a crowd of merry, noisy, rosy-cheeked boys, were busily employed, and seemed happier than the day was long; while poor Master No-book watched them during his own miserable hours, envying the enjoyment with which they raked the flower borders, gathered the fruit, carried baskets of vegetables to the poor, worked with carpenter's tools, drew pictures, shot with bows and arrows, played at cricket, and then sat in the sunny arbours learning their tasks, or talking agreeably together, till at length, a dinner bell having been rung, the whole party sat merrily down with hearty appetites, and cheerful good humour, to an entertainment of plain roast meat and pudding, where the fairy Teach-all presided herself, and helped her guests moderately, to as much as was good for each.

Large tears rolled down the cheeks of Master No-book while watching this scene; and remembering that if he had known what was best for him, he might have been as happy as the happiest of these excellent boys, instead of suffering ennui and weariness, as he had done at the fairy Do-nothing's, ending in a miserable death; but his attention was soon after most alarmingly roused by hearing the giant Snap-'em-up again in conversation with his cook; who said, that if he wished for a good large dish of scolloped children at dinner, it would be necessary to catch a few more, as those he had already provided would scarcely be a mouthful.

As the giant kept very fashionable hours, and always waited dinner for himself till nine o'clock, there was still plenty of time; so, with a loud grumble about the trouble, he seized a large basket in his hand, and set off at a rapid pace towards the fairy Teach-all's garden. It was very seldom that Snap-'em-up ventured to think of foraging in this direction, as he never once succeeded in carrying off a single captive from the enclosure, it was so well fortified and so bravely defended; but on this occasion, being desperately hungry, he felt as bold as a lion and walked, with out stretched hands, straight towards the fairy Teach-all's dinner table, taking such prodigious strides, that he seemed almost as if he would trample on himself.

A cry of consternation arose the instant this tremendous giant appeared; and as usual on such occasions, when he had made the same attempt before, a dreadful battle took place. Fifty active little boys bravely flew upon the enemy, armed with their dinner knives, and looked like a nest of hornets, stinging him in every direction, till he roared with pain, and would have run away, but the fairy Teach-all, seeing his intention, rushed forward with the carving-knife, and brandishing it high over her head, she most courageously stabbed him to the heart!

If a great mountain had fallen to the earth, it would have seemed like nothing in comparison of the giant Snap-'em-up, who crushed two or three houses to powder beneath him, and upset several fine monuments that were to have made people remembered for ever; but all this would have seemed scarcely worth mentioning, had it not been for a still greater event which occurred on the occasion, no less than the death of the fairy Do-nothing, who had been indolently looking on at this great battle, without taking the trouble to interfere, or even to care who was victorious; but being also lazy about running away, when the giant fell, his sword came with so violent a stroke on her head, that she instantly expired.

Thus, luckily for the whole world, the fairy Teach-all got possession of immense property, which she proceeded without delay to make the best use of in her power.

In the first place, however, she lost no time in liberating Master No-book from his hook in the larder, and gave him a lecture on activity, moderation, and good conduct, which he never afterwards forgot; and it was astonishing to see the change that took place immediately in his whole thoughts and actions. From this very hour, Master No-book became the most diligent, active, happy boy in the fairy Teach-all's garden; and on returning home a month afterwards, he astonished all the masters at school by his extraordinary reformation. The most difficult lessons were a pleasure to him,—he scarcely ever stirred without a book in his hand,—never lay on a sofa again,—would scarcely even sit on a chair with a back to it, but preferred a three-legged stool,

—detested holidays,—never thought any exertion a trouble,—preferred climbing over the top of a hill to creeping round the bottom,—always ate the plainest food in very small quantities,—joined a Temperance Society!—and never tasted a morsel till he had worked very hard and got an appetite.

Not long after this, an old uncle, who had formerly been ashamed of Master No-book's indolence and gluttony, became so pleased at the wonderful change, that, on his death, he left him a magnificent estate, desiring that he should take his name; therefore, instead of being any longer one of the No-book family, he is now called Sir Timothy Bluestocking,—a pattern to the whole country round, for the good he does to every one, and especially for his extraordinary activity, appearing as if he could do twenty things at once. Though generally very good-natured and agreeable, Sir Timothy is occasionally observed in a violent passion, laying about him with his walking-stick in the most terrific manner, and beating little boys within an inch of their lives; but on inquiry, it invariably appears that he has found them out to be lazy, idle, or greedy, for all the industrious boys in the parish are sent to get employment from him, while he assures them that they are far happier breaking stones on the road, than if they were sitting idly in a drawing-room with nothing to do. Sir Timothy cares very little for poetry in general; but the following are his favourite verses, which he has placed over the chimney-piece at a school that he built for the poor, and every scholar is obliged, the very day he begins his education, to learn them:

Some people complain they have nothing to do,
And time passes slowly away;
They saunter about with no object in view,
And long for the end of the day.

In vain are the trifles and toys they desire,
For nothing they truly enjoy;
Of trifles, and toys, and amusements they tire,
For want of some useful employ.

Although for transgression the ground was accursed,
Yet gratefully man must allow,
'T was really a blessing which doom'd him at first,
To live by the sweat of his brow.

"Thank you a hundred times over, Uncle David!" said Harry, when the story was finished. "I shall take care not to be found hanging any day, on a hook in the larder! Certainly, Frank, you must have spent a month with the good fairy; and I hope she will some day invite me to be made a scholar of too, for Laura and I still belong to the No-book family."

"It is very important, Harry, to choose the best course from the beginning," observed Lady Harriet. "Good or bad habits grow stronger and stronger every minute, as if an additional string were tied on daily, to keep us in the road where we walked the day before; so those who mistake the path of duty at first, find hourly increasing difficulty in turning round."

"But, grandmama!" said Frank, "you have put up some finger-posts to direct us right; and whenever I see 'no passage this way,' we shall all wheel about directly."

"As Mrs. Crabtree has not tapped at the door yet, I shall describe the progress of a wise and a foolish man, to see which Harry and you would prefer copying," replied Lady Harriet, smiling. "The fool begins, when he is young, with hating lessons, lying long in bed, and spending all his money on trash. Any books he will consent to read, are never about what is true or important; but he wastes all his time and thoughts on silly stories that never could have happened. Thus he neglects to learn what was done and thought by all the great and good men who really lived in former times, while even his Bible, if he has one, grows dusty on the shelf. After so bad a beginning, he grows up with no useful or interesting knowledge; therefore his whole talk is to describe his own horses, his own dogs, his own guns, and his own exploits; boasting of what a high wall his horse can leap over, the number of little birds he can shoot in a day, and how many bottles of wine he can swallow without tumbling under the table. Thus, 'glorying in his shame,' he thinks himself a most wonderful person, not knowing that men are born to do much better things than merely to find selfish pleasure and amusement for themselves. Presently he grows old, gouty, and infirm—no longer able to do such prodigious achievements; therefore now his great delight is, to sit with his feet upon the fender, at a club all day, telling what a famous rider, shooter, and drinker, he was long ago; but nobody cares to hear such old stories; therefore he is called a 'proser,' and every person avoids him. It is no wonder a man talks about himself, if he has never read or thought about any one else. But at length his precious time has all been wasted, and his last hour comes, during which he can have nothing to look back upon but a life of folly and guilt. He sees no one around who loves him, or will weep over his grave; and when he looks forward, it is towards an eternal world, which he has never prepared to enter, and of which he knows nothing."

"What a terrible picture, grandmama!" said Frank, rather gravely. "I hope there are not many people like that, or it would be very sad to meet with them. Now pray let us have a pleasanter description of the sort of persons you would like Harry and me to become."

"The first foundation of all is, as you already know, Frank, to pray that you may be put in the right course and kept in it, for of ourselves we are so sinful and weak that we can do no good thing. Then feeling a full trust in the Divine assistance, you must begin and end every day with studying your Bible, not merely reading it, but carefully endeavouring to understand and obey what it contains. Our leisure should be bestowed on reading of wiser and better people than ourselves, which will keep us humble while it instructs our understandings, and thus we shall be fitted to associate with persons whose society is even better than books. Christians who are enlightened and sanctified in the knowledge of all good things, will show us an example of carefully using our time, which is the most valuable of all earthly possessions. If we waste our money we may perhaps get more—if we lose our health it may be restored—but time squandered on folly, must hereafter be answered for, and can never be regained. Whatever be your station in life, waste none of your thoughts upon fancying how much better you might have acted in some other person's place, but see what duties belong to that station in which you live, and do what that requires with activity and diligence. When we are called to give an account of our stewardship, let us not have to confess at the last that we wasted our one talent, because we wished to have been trusted with ten; but let us prepare to render up what was given to us, with joy and thankfulness, perfectly satisfied that the best place in life, is where God appoints, and where He will guide us to a safe and peaceful end."

"Yes," added Major Graham. "We have two eyes in our minds as well as in our bodies. With one of these we see all that is good or agreeable in our lot—with the other we see all that is unpleasant or disappointing; and you may generally choose which eye to keep open. Some of my friends always peevishly look at the troubles and vexations they endure; but they might turn them into good, by considering that every circumstance is sent from the same hand, with the same merciful purpose—to make us better now and happier hereafter."

"Well, my dear children," said Lady Harriet, "it is time now for retiring to Bedfordshire; so, good-night."

"If you please, grandmama, not yet!" asked Harry, anxiously. "Give us five minutes longer!"

"And then in the morning you will want to remain five minutes more in bed. That is the way people learn to keep such dreadfully late hours at last, Harry! I knew one very rich old gentleman formerly, who always wished to sit up a little later every night, and to get up a little later in the morning, till at length he ended by hiring a set of servants to rise at nine in the evening, as he did himself, and to remain in bed all day."

"People should regulate their sleep very conscientiously," added Major Graham, "so as to waste as little time as possible; and our good king George III. set us the example, for he remarked that six hours in the night were quite enough for a man, seven hours for a woman, and eight for a fool. Or perhaps, Harry, you might like to live by Sir William Jones's rule:

'Six hours to read, to soothing slumber seven,
Ten to the world allot—and all to Heaven.' "

THE ILLUMINATION

A neighbour's house he's slyly pass,
And throw a stone to break the glass.

ONE FINE MORNING, Peter Grey persuaded a party of his companions to spend all the money that they had on cakes and sugar-plums, and to make a splendid entertainment under the trees in Charlotte Square, where they were to sit like a horde of gipsies, and amuse themselves with telling fortunes to each other. Harry and Laura had no one with them but Betty, who gladly joined a group of nursery-maids at a distance, leaving them to their own devices; upon which they rushed up to Peter and offered their assistance, subscribing all their pocket money, and begging him to set forth and obtain provisions for them as well as for himself. Neither Harry nor Laura cared for eating the trash that was collected on this occasion, and would have been quite as well pleased to distribute it among their companions; but they both enjoyed extremely the bustle of arranging this elegant dejeuné, or "*disjune*," as Peter called it. Harry gathered leaves off the trees to represent plates, on each of which Peter arranged some of the fruit or sweetmeats he had purchased, while they placed benches together as a table, and borrowed Laura's white India shawl for a table cloth.

"It looks like that grand public dinner we saw at the Assembly Rooms one day!" exclaimed Harry, in an ecstasy of admiration. "We must have speeches and toasts, like real gentlemen and officers. Peter! if you will make a fine oration, full of compliments to me, I shall say something wonderful about you, and then Laura must beat upon the table with a stick, to show that she agrees to all that we observe in praise of each other."

"Or suppose we all take the names of some great personages," added Peter; "I shall be the Duke of Wellington, and Laura, you must be Joseph Hume, and Harry, you are Sir Robert Peel, that we may seem as different as possible; but here comes the usher of the black rod to disperse us all! Mrs. Crabtree hurrying into the square, her very gown flaming with rage! what can be the matter? she must have smelled the sugar-plums a mile off! One comfort is, if Harry and Laura are taken away, we shall have the fewer people to divide these cakes among—and I could devour every one of them for my own share."

Before Peter finished speaking, Mrs. Crabtree had come close up to the table, and without waiting to utter a word, or even to scold, she twitched up Laura's shawl in her hand, and thus scattered the whole feast in every direction on the ground, after which she trampled the sugar-plums and cakes into the earth, saying,

"I knew how it would be, as soon as I saw whose company you were in, Master Harry! Peter Grey is the father of mischief! he ought to be put into the monkey's cage at the *Geo*logical gardens! I would not be your maid, Master Grey, for a hundred a-year."

"You would need to buy a thrashing machine immediately," said Peter, laughing; "what a fine time I should have of it! you would scarcely allow me, I suppose, to blow my porridge! How long would it take you, Mrs. Crabtree, to make quite a perfectly good boy of me? Perhaps a month, do you think? or, to make me as good as Frank, it might possibly require six weeks."

"Six weeks!" answered Mrs. Crabtree; "six years, or sixty would be too short. You are no more like Master Frank than a shilling is to a guinea, or a wax light is to a dip. If the news were told that you had been a good boy for a single day, the very *statutes* in the streets would come running along to see the wonder. No, no! I have seen many surprising things in my day; but them great pyramuses in Egypt will turn upside down before you turn like Master Frank."

Some days after this adventure of Harry and Laura's, there arrived newspapers from London containing accounts of a great battle which had been fought abroad. On that occasion the British troops of course performed prodigies of valour, and completely conquered the enemy, in consequence of which it was ordered by government that, in every town, and every village, and every house throughout the whole kingdom, there should be a grand illumination.

Neither Harry nor Laura had ever heard of such a thing as an illumination before, and they were full of curiosity to know what it was like; but their very faces became lighted up with joy, when Major Graham described that they would see crowds of candles flaming in every window, tar-barrels blazing on every hill, flambeaux glaring at the doors, and transparencies, fireworks, and coloured lamps shining in all the streets.

"How delightful! and walking out in the dark to see it," cried Harry, "that will be best of all! oh! and a whole holiday! I hardly know whether I am in my right wits, or my wrong wits, for joy! I wish we gained a victory every day!"

"What a warrior you would be, Harry! Caesar was nothing to you," said Frank. "We might be satisfied with one good battle in a year, considering how many are killed and wounded."

"Yes, but I hope all the wounded soldiers will recover."

"Or get pensions," added Uncle David. "It is a grand sight, Frank, to see a whole nation rejoicing at once! In general, when you walk out and meet fifty persons in the street, they are all thinking of fifty different things, and each intent on some business of his own, but on this occasion all are of one mind and one heart."

Frank and Harry were allowed to nail a dozen little candlesticks upon each window in the house, which delighted them exceedingly; and then, before every pane of glass, they placed a tall candle, impatiently longing for the time when these were to be illuminated. Laura was allowed to carry a match, and assist in lighting them, but in the excess of her joy she very nearly made a bonfire of herself, as her frock took fire, and would soon have been in a blaze, if Frank had not hastily seized a large rug and rolled it round her.

In every house within sight, servants and children were to be seen hurrying about with burning matches, while hundreds of lights blazed up in a moment, looking as if all the houses in town had taken fire.

"Such a waste of candles!" said Mrs. Crabtree, angrily; "can't people be happy in the dark?"

"No, Mrs. Crabtree," answered Frank, laughing. "They cannot be happy in the dark! People's spirits are always in exact proportion to the number of lights. If you ever feel dull with one candle, light another; and if that does not do, try a third, or a fourth, till you feel merry and cheerful. We must not let you be candle-snuffer to-night, or you will be putting them all out. You would snuff out the sun itself, to save a shilling."

"The windows might perhaps be broken," added Laura; "for whatever pane of glass does not exhibit a candle, is to have a stone sent through it. Harry says the mob are all glaziers, who break them on purpose to mend the damage next day, which they will be paid handsomely for doing."

There were many happy, joyous faces, to be seen that evening in the streets, admiring the splendid illumination; but the merriest party of all was composed of Frank, Harry, and Laura, under the command of Uncle David, who had lately suffered from a severe fit of the gout; but it seemed to have left him this night, in honour of the great victory, when he appeared quite as much a boy as either of his two companions. For many hours they walked about in the streets, gazing up at the glittering windows, some of which looked as if a constellation of stars had come down for a night to adorn them; and others were filled with the most beautiful pictures of Britannia carrying the world on her shoulders; or Mars showering down wreaths of laurel on the Duke of Wellington, while victory was sitting at his feet, and fame blowing a trumpet at his ear. Harry thought these paintings finer than any he had ever seen before, and stood for some moments entranced with admiration, on beholding a representation in red, blue, yellow, and black, of Europe, Asia, Africa, and America, all doing homage to St. George mounted on a dragon, which breathed out fire and smoke like a steamboat. Nothing, however, occasioned the party such a burst of delightful surprise, as when they first beheld the line of blazing windows more than a mile long, from the bottom of the Canongate to the highest pinnacle of the Castle, where they seemed almost to meet the stars shining above, in their perpetual glory. "You see," remarked Major Graham, when he pointed them out to his young companions, "there is a fit emblem of the difference between earth and heaven. These lights are nearer and brighter to us at present, but when they have blazed and glittered for one little hour, they come to an end; while those above, which we see so dimly now, will continue to shine for ages and generations hereafter, till time itself is no more."

Occasionally, during their progress, Harry felt very indignant to observe a few houses perfectly dark; and whether the family were sick, or out of town, or whatever the reason might be, he scarcely became sorry when a frequent crash might be heard, as the mob, determined to have their own way this night, aimed showers of stones at the offending windows, till the very frames seemed in danger of being broken. At last Uncle David led his joyous little party into Castle Street, in which not a light was to be seen, and every blind seemed carefully closed. A crowd had assembled, with an evident intention to attack these melancholy houses, when Major Graham suddenly caught hold of Harry's arm, on observing that he had privately picked up a large stone, which he was in the very act of throwing with his whole force at one of the defenceless windows. And now the whole party stood stock-still, while Uncle David said in a very angry and serious voice,

"Harry! you heedless, mischievous boy! will you never learn to consider a moment before you do what is wrong? I am exceedingly displeased with you for this! What business is it of yours whether that house be lighted up or not?"

"But, Uncle David! surely it is very wrong not to obey the government, and to be happy like everybody else! Besides, you see the mob will break those windows at any rate, so it is no matter if I help them."

"Then, for the same reason, if they were setting the house on fire, I suppose you would assist the conflagration, Harry. Your excuse is a bad one; when you hear what I have to say about this house, let it be a lesson for the rest of your life, never to judge hastily, nor to act rashly. The officer to whom it belonged, has been killed in the great battle abroad; and while we are rejoicing in the victory that his bravery helped to gain, his widow and children are weeping within those walls, for the husband and father who lies buried on a foreign shore. Think what a contrast these shouts of joy must be to their grief."

"Oh, Uncle David! how sorry I am!" said Harry. "I deserve to go home this moment, and not to see a candle again for a week. It was very wrong of me, indeed. I shall walk all the way home with my eyes shut, if you will only excuse me."

"No, no, Harry! that is not necessary! If the eyes of your mind are open, to see that you have acted amiss, then try to behave better in future. When people are happy themselves, they are too apt to forget that others may be in distress, and often feel quite surprised and provoked at those who appear melancholy; but our turn must come like theirs. Life is made up of sunshine and shadow, both of which are sent for our good, and neither of them last, in this world, for ever; but we should borrow part of our joys, and part of our sorrows, from sympathy with all those we see or know, which will moderate the excess of whatever is our portion in life."

At this moment the mob, which had been gradually increasing, gave a tremendous shout, and were on the point of throwing a torrent of stones at the dark, mournful house, which had made so narrow an escape from Harry's vengeance, when Major Graham, forgetting his gout, hastily sprung upon a lamp-post, and calling for attention, he made a speech to the crowd, telling of the brave Captain D——, who had died for his country, covered with wounds, and that his mourning family was assembled in that house. Instantly the mob became as silent and motionless as if they had themselves been turned into stones; after which, they gradually stole away, with downcast eyes and mournful countenances; while it is believed that some riotous people, who had been loudest and fiercest at first, afterwards stood at the top of the little street like sentinels for more than an hour, to warn every one who passed that he should go silently along, in respect for the memory of a brave and good officer. Not another shout was heard in the neighbourhood that night; and many a merry laugh was suddenly checked, from reverence for the memory of the dead, and the sorrow of the living; while some spectators remarked, with a sigh of melancholy reflection, that men must ever join trembling with their mirth, because even in the midst of life they are in death.

"If we feel so much sorrow for this one officer and his family, it shows," said Frank, "what a dreadful thing war is, which costs the lives of thousands and tens of thousands, in every campaign, by sickness and fatigue, and the other sources of misery that accompany every army."

"Yes, Frank! and yet there has scarcely been a year on earth, while the world has existed, without fighting in some country or another; for, since the time when Cain killed Abel, men have been continually destroying each other. Animals only fight in temporary irritation when they are hungry, but pride, ambition, and folly of every kind have caused men to hate and massacre each other. Even religion itself has caused the fiercest and most bloody conflicts, though, if that were only understood and obeyed as it ought to be, the great truths of Scripture would produce peace on earth, and good-will among all the children of men."

The whole party had been standing for some minutes opposite to the Post-Office, which looked like a rainbow of coloured lamps, and Harry was beginning, for the twentieth time, to try if he could count how many there were, when Major Graham felt something twitching hold of his coat pocket behind, and on wheeling suddenly round, he perceived a little boy, not much older than Harry, darting rapidly off in another direction, carrying his own purse and pocket-handkerchief in his hand. Being still rather lame, and unable to move very fast, Major Graham could only vociferate at the very top of his voice, "Stop thief! stop thief!" but not a constable appeared in sight, so the case seemed desperate, and the money lost for ever, when Frank observed also what had occurred, and being of an active spirit, he flew after the young thief, followed closely by Harry. An eager race ensued, up one street, and down another, with marvellous rapidity, while Frank was so evidently gaining ground, that the thief at last became terrified, and threw away the purse, hoping thus to end the chase; but neither of his pursuers paused a moment to pick it up, they were so intent upon capturing the little culprit himself. At length Frank sprung forward and caught him by the collar, when a fierce conflict ensued, during which the young thief was so ingenious, that he nearly slipped his arms out of his coat, and would have made his escape, leaving a tattered garment in their hands, if Harry had not observed this trick, and held him by the hair, which, as it was not a wig, he could not so easily throw off.

At this moment a large, coarse, ruffianly-looking man hurried up to the party, evidently intending to rescue the little pickpocket from their custody; so Frank called loudly for help, while several police officers who had been sent by Major Graham, came racing along the street, springing their rattles, and vociferating "Stop thief!"

Now, the boy struggled more violently than ever to disentangle himself, but Frank and Harry grasped hold of their prisoner, as if they had been a couple of Bow Street officers, till at length the tall fierce man thought it time to be off, though not before he had given Harry a blow on the face, that caused him to reel back and fall prostrate on the pavement.

"There's a brave little gentleman!" said one of the constables, helping him up, while another secured the thief. "You ought to be knighted for fighting so well! This boy you have taken is a sad fellow! He broke his poor mother's heart a year since by his wicked ways, and I have long wished to catch him. A few weeks on the treadmill now, may save him from the gallows in future."

"He seems well practised in his business," observed Major Graham. "I almost deserved, however, to lose my pocket-book for bringing it out in a night of so much crowding and confusion. Some lucky person will be all the richer, though I fear it is totally lost to me."

"But here is your pocket-handkerchief, Uncle David, if you mean to shed any tears for your misfortune," whispered Laura; "how very lucky that you felt it going!"

"Yes! and very surprising too, for the trick was so cleverly executed! That little rascal might steal the teeth out of one's head without being noticed! When I was in India the thieves there were so expert that they really could draw the sheets from under a person sleeping in bed, without disturbing his slumbers."

"With me, any person could do that, because I sleep so very soundly," observed Frank. "You might beat a military drum at my ear, as they do in the boys' sleeping rooms at Sandhurst, and it would not have the smallest effect. I scarcely think that even a gong would do!"

"How very different from me," replied Laura. "Last night I was awakened by the scratching of a mouse nibbling in the wainscot, and soon after it ran across my face."

"Then pray sleep to-night with your mouth open, and a piece of toasted cheese in it, to catch the mouse," said Major Graham. "That is the best trap I know!"

"Uncle David," asked Frank, as they proceeded along the street, "if there is any hope of that wicked boy being reformed, will you try to have him taught better? Being so very young, he must have learned from older people to steal!"

"Certainly he must! It is melancholy to know how carefully mere children are trained to commit the very worst crimes, and how little the mind of any young boy can be a match for the cunning of old, experienced villains like those who lead him astray. When once a child falls into the snare of such practised offenders, escape becomes as impossible as that of a bird from a lime twig."

"So I believe," replied Frank. "Grandmama told me that the very youngest children of poor people, when first sent to school in London, are often way-laid by those old women who sell apples in the street, and who pretend to be so good-natured that they make them presents of fruit. Of course they are very acceptable, but after some time, those wicked wretches propose that the child in return should bring them a book, or anything he can pick up at home, which shall be paid for in apples and pears. Few little boys have sufficient firmness not to comply, whether they like it or not, and after that the case is almost hopeless, because whenever the poor victim hesitates to steal more, those cruel women threaten to inform the parents of his misconduct, which terrifies the boy into doing anything rather than be found out."

"Oh, how dreadful!" exclaimed Laura. "It all begins so smoothly! No poor little boy could suspect any danger, and then he becomes a hardened thief at once!"

"Grandmama says, too, that pickpockets in London used to have the stuffed figure of a man hung from the roof of their rooms, and covered all over with bells, for the boys to practise upon, and no one was allowed to attempt stealing on the streets, till he could pick the pocket of this dangling effigy, without ringing one of the many bells with which it was ornamented."

"I think," said Harry, "when the young thieves saw that figure hanging in the air, it might have reminded them how soon they would share the same fate. Even crows take warning when they see a brother crow hanging dead in a field."

"It is a curious thing of crows, Harry, that they certainly punish thieves among themselves," observed Major Graham. "In a large rookery, some outcasts are frequently to be observed living apart from the rest, and not allowed to associate with their more respectable brethren. I remember hearing formerly, that in the great rookery at Ashgrove, when all the other birds were absent, one solitary crow was observed to linger behind, stealing materials for his nest from those around; but next morning a prodigious uproar was heard among the trees,—the cawing became so vociferous, that evidently several great orators were agitating the crowd, till suddenly the enraged crows flew in a body upon the nest of their dishonest associate and tore it in pieces."

"Bravo!" cried Frank. "I do like to hear about all the odd ways of birds and animals! Grandmama mentioned lately, that, if you catch a crow, and fasten him down with his back to the ground, he makes such an outcry, that all his black brothers come wheeling about the place, till one of them at last alights to help him. Immediately the treacherous prisoner grapples hold of his obliging friend, and never afterwards lets him escape; so, by fastening down one after another, we might entrap the whole rookery."

"I shall try it some day!" exclaimed Harry, eagerly. "What fun to hear them all croaking and cawing!"

"We shall be croaking ourselves soon with colds, if we do not hurry home," added Uncle David. "There is not a thimbleful of light remaining, and your grandmama will be impatient to hear all the news. This has really been a most adventurous night, and I am sure none of us will soon forget it."

When the whole party entered the drawing-room, in a blaze of spirits, all speaking at once, to tell Lady Harriet what had occurred, Mrs. Crabtree, who was waiting to take a couple of little prisoners off to bed, suddenly gave an exclamation of astonishment and dismay as she looked at Harry, who now, for the first time since the robber knocked him down, approached the light, when he did, to be sure, appear a most terrible spectacle! His jacket was bespattered with mud, his shirt frill torn and bloody, one eye almost swollen out of his head, and the side of his face quite black and blue.

"What mischief have you been in now, Master Harry?" cried Mrs. Crabtree, angrily; "you will not leave a whole bone in your body, nor a whole shirt in your drawer!"

"These are honourable scars, Mrs. Crabtree," interrupted Major Graham. "Harry has been fighting my battles, and gained a great victory! we must illuminate the nursery!"

Uncle David then told the whole story, with many droll remarks about his purse having been stolen, and said that, as Harry never complained of being hurt, he never supposed that anything of the kind could have occurred; but he felt very much pleased to observe how well a certain young gentleman was able to bear pain, as boys must expect hard blows in the world, when they had to fight their way through life, therefore it was well for them to give as few as they could, and to bear with fortitude what fell to their own share. Uncle David slyly added, that perhaps Harry put up with these things all the better for having so much practice in the nursery.

Mrs. Crabtree seemed rather proud of Harry's manly spirit, and treated him with a little more respect than usual, saying, she would fetch him some hot water to foment his face, if he would go straight up stairs with Laura. Now it very seldom happened, that Harry went straight anywhere, for he generally swung down the bannisters again, or took a leap over anything he saw on the way, or got on some of the tables and jumped off, but this night he had resolutely intended marching steadily to bed, and advanced a considerable way, when a loud shout in the street attracted his attention. Harry stopped, and it was repeated again, so seizing Laura by the hand, they flew eagerly into Lady Harriet's dressing-room, and throwing open a window, they picked up a couple of cloaks that were lying on a chair, and both stepped out on a balcony to find out what was going on; and in case any one should see them in this unusual place, Harry quietly shut down the window, intending to remain only one single minute. Minutes run very fast away when people are amused, and nothing could be more diverting than the sight they now beheld, for at this moment a grand crash exploded of squibs and rockets from the Castle-hill, which looked so beautiful in the dark, that it seemed impossible to think of anything else. Some flew high in the air, and then burst into the appearance of twenty fiery serpents falling from the sky, others assumed a variety of colours, and dropped like flying meteors, looking as if the stars were all learning to dance, while many rushed into the air and disappeared, leaving not a trace behind. Harry and Laura stood perfectly entranced with admiration and delight, till the fireworks neither burst, cracked, nor exploded any more.

A ballad-singer next attracted their notice, singing the tune of "Meet me by moonlight," and afterwards Laura showed Harry the constellation of Orion mentioned in the Bible, which, besides the Great Bear, was the only one she had the slightest acquaintance with. Neither of them had ever observed the Northern Lights so brilliant before, and now they felt almost alarmed to see them shooting like lances across the sky, and glittering with many bright colours, like a rainbow, while Laura remembered her grandmama mentioning some days ago, that the poor natives of Greenland believe these are the spirits of their fathers going forth to battle.

Meantime, Lady Harriet called Frank, as usual, to his evening prayers and reading in her dressing-room, where it was well known that they were on no account to be disturbed. After having read a chapter, and talked very seriously about all it was intended to teach, they had begun to discuss the prospect of Frank going abroad very soon to become a midshipman, and he was wondering much where his first great shipwreck would take place, and telling Lady Harriet about the loss of the Cabalvala, where the crew lived for eight days on a barren rock, with nothing to eat but a cask of raspberry jam, which accidentally floated within their reach. Before Frank had finished his story, however, he suddenly paused, and sprung upon his feet with an exclamation of astonishment, while Lady Harriet, looking hastily round in the same direction, became terrified to observe a couple of faces looking in at the window. It was so dark, she could not see what they were like, but a moment afterwards, the sash began slowly and heavily opening, after which two figures leaped into the room, while Frank flew to ring a peal at the bell, and Lady Harriet sunk into her own arm-chair, covering her face with her hands, and nearly fainting with fright.

"Never mind, grandmama! do not be afraid! it is only us!" cried Harry; "surely you know me!"

"You!!!" exclaimed Lady Harriet, looking up with amazement. "Harry and Laura!! impossible! how in all the world did you get here! I thought you were both in bed half an hour ago! Tiresome boy! you will be the death of me some time or other! I wonder when you will ever pass a day without deserving the bastinado!"

"Do you not remember the good day last month, grandmama, when I had a severe toothache, and sat all morning beside the fire? Nobody found fault with me then, and I got safe to bed, without a single 'Oh fie!' from noon till night."

"Wonderful, indeed! what a pity I ever allowed that tooth to be drawn; but you behaved very bravely on the occasion of its being extracted. Now take yourselves off! I feel perfectly certain you will tell Mrs. Crabtree the exact truth about where you have been, and if she punishes you, remember that it is no more than you deserve. People who behave ill are their own punishers, and should be glad that some one will kindly take the trouble to teach them better."

THE POOR BOY

Not all the fine things that fine people possess
Should teach them the poor to despise;
For 'tis in good manners, and not in good dress,
That the truest gentility lies.

THE FOLLOWING SATURDAY MORNING, Frank, Harry, and Laura, were assembled before Lady Harriet's breakfast hour, talking over all their adventures on the night of the illumination; and many a merry laugh was heard while Uncle David cracked his jokes and told his stories, for he seemed as full of fun and spirits as the youngest boy in a play-ground.

"Well, old fellow!" said he, lifting up Harry, and suddenly seating him on the high marble chimney-piece. "That is the situation where the poor little dwarf, Baron Borowloski, was always put by his tall wife, when she wished to keep him out of mischief, and I wonder Mrs. Crabtree never thought of the same plan for you."

"Luckily there is no fire, or Harry would soon be roasted for the Giant Snap-'em-up's dinner," said Frank, laughing; "he looks up there like a Chinese mandarin. Shake your head, Harry, and you will do quite as well!"

"Uncle David!" cried Harry, eagerly, "pray let me see you stand for one moment as you do at the club on a cold day, with your feet upon the rug, your back to the fire, and your coat-tails under your arms! Pray do, for one minute!"

Uncle David did as he was asked, evidently expecting the result, which took place, for Harry sprung upon his back with the agility of a monkey, and they went round and round the room at full gallop, during the next five minutes, while Lady Harriet said she never saw two such noisy people, but it was quite the fashion now, since the King of France carried his grandchildren in the same way, every morning, a picture of which had lately been shown to her.

"Then I hope his majesty gets as good an appetite with his romp as I have done," replied Major Graham, sitting down. "None of your tea and toast for me! that is only fit for ladies. Frank, reach me these beef-steaks, and a cup of chocolate."

Harry and Laura now planted themselves at the window, gazing at crowds of people who passed, while, by way of a joke, they guessed what everybody had come out for, and who they all were.

"There is a fat cook with a basket under her arm, going to market," said Harry. "Did you ever observe when Mrs. Marmalade comes home, she says to grandmama, 'I have desired a leg of mutton to come here, my lady! and I told a goose to be over also,' as if the leg of mutton and the goose walked here arm-in-arm of themselves."

"Look at those children going to see the wild beasts," added Laura, "and this little girl is on her way to buy a new frock. I am sure she needs one! That old man is hurrying along because he is too late for the mail-coach; and this lady with a gown like a yellow daffodil, is going to take root in the Botanical Gardens!"

"Uncle David, there is the very poorest boy I ever saw!" cried Harry, turning eagerly round; "he has been standing in the cold here, for ten minutes, looking the picture of misery! he wears no hat, and has pulled his long hair to make a bow about twenty times. Do come and look at him! he is very pale, and his clothes seem to have been made before he began to grow, for they are so much too small, and he is making us many signs to open the window. May I do it?"

"No! no! I never give to chance beggars of that kind, especially young able-bodied fellows like that, because there are so many needy deserving people whom I visit, who worked as long as they could, and whom I know to be sober and honest. Most of the money we scatter to street beggars goes straight to the gin-shop, and even the very youngest children will buy or steal, to get the means of becoming intoxicated. Only last week, Harry, the landlord of an ale-house at Portobello was seen at the head of a long table, surrounded with ragged beggar boys about twelve or fourteen years of age, who were all perfectly drunk, and probably your friend might be of the party."

"Oh no! Uncle David! this boy seems quite sober and exceedingly clean, though he is so very poor!" replied Laura. "His black trowsers are patched and repatched, his jacket has faded into fifty colours, and his shoes are mended in every direction, but still he looks almost respectable. His face is so thin you might use it for a hatchet; I wish you would take one little peep, for he seems so anxious to speak to us."

"I dare say that! we all know what the youngster has to tell! Probably a wife and six small children at home, or, if you like it better, he will be a ship-wrecked sailor at your service. I know the whole affair already; but if you have sixpence to spare, Laura, come with me after breakfast, and we shall bestow it on poor blind Mrs. Wilkie, who has been bed-ridden for the last ten years; or old paralytic Jemmy Dixon the porter, who worked as long as he was able. If you had twenty more sixpences, I could tell you of twenty more people who deserve them as much."

"Very true," added Lady Harriet. "Street beggars, who are young and able to work, like that boy, it is cruelty to encourage. Parents bring up their children in profligate idleness, hoping to gain more money by lying and cheating than by honest industry and they too often succeed, especially when the wicked mothers also starve and disfigure these poor creatures to excite more compassion. We must relieve real distress, Harry, and search for it, as we would for hidden treasures, because thus we show our love to God and man; but a large purse with easy strings will do more harm than good."

"Do you remember, Frank, how long I suspected that old John Davidson was imposing upon me?" said Major Graham. "He told such a dismal story always, that I never liked to refuse him some assistance; but yesterday, when he was here, the thought struck me by chance to say, 'What a fine supper you had last night, John!' You should have seen the start he gave, and his look of consternation, when he answered, 'Eh, sir! how did ye hear of that? We got the turkey very cheap, and none of us took more than two glasses of toddy.' "

"That boy is pointing to his pockets, and making more signs for us to open the window!" exclaimed Laura. "What can it all mean! he seems so very anxious!"

Major Graham threw down his knife and fork—rose hastily from breakfast—and flung open the window, calling out in rather a loud, angry voice "What do you want, you idle fellow? It is a perfect shame to see you standing there all morning! Surely you don't mean to say that an active youngster like you would disgrace yourself by begging?"

"No, sir! I want nothing!" answered the boy respectfully, but colouring to the deepest scarlet. "I never asked for money in my life, and I never will."

"That's right, my good boy!" answered the Major, instantly changing his tone. "What brings you here, then?"

"Please, sir, your servants shut the door in my face, and everybody is so hasty like, that I don't know what to do. I can't be listened to for a minute, though I have got something very particular to say, that some one would be glad to hear."

Major Graham now looked exceedingly vexed with himself, for having spoken so roughly to the poor boy, who had a thoughtful, mild, but careworn countenance, which was extremely interesting, while his manner seemed better than his dress.

Frank was despatched as a most willing messenger, to bring the young stranger up stairs, while Uncle David told Harry that he would take this as a lesson to himself ever afterwards, not to judge hastily from appearances, because it was impossible for any one to guess what might be in the mind of another; and he began to hope this boy, who was so civil and well-spoken, might yet turn out to be a proper, 'ndustrious little fellow.

"Well, my lad! Is there anything I can do for you?" asked Major Graham, when Frank led him kindly into the room. "What is your name?"

"Evan Mackay, at your service. Please, sir, did you lose a pocket-book, last Thursday, with your name on the back, and nine gold sovereigns inside?"

"Yes! that I did, to my cost! Have you heard anything of it?"

The boy silently drew a parcel from his pocket, and without looking up or speaking, he modestly placed it on the table, then colouring very deeply, he turned away, and hurried towards the door. In another minute he would have been off, but Frank sprung forward and took hold of his arm, saying, in the kindest possible manner, "Stop, Evan! Stop a moment! That parcel seems to contain all my uncle's money. Where did you get it? Who sent it here?"

"I brought it, sir! The direction is on the pocket-book, so there could be no mistake."

"Did you find it yourself, then?"

"Yes! it was lying in the street that night when I ran for a doctor to see my mother, who is dying. She told me now to come back directly, sir, so I must be going."

"But let us give you something for being so honest," said Frank. "You are a fine fellow, and you deserve to be well rewarded."

"I only did my duty, sir. Mother always says we should do right for conscience' sake, and not for a reward."

"Yes! but you are justly entitled to this," said Major Graham, taking a sovereign out of the purse. "I shall do more for you yet, but in the mean time here is what you have honestly earned to-day."

"If I thought so, sir,"——said the poor boy, looking wistfully at the glittering coin. "If I was quite sure there could be no harm——, but I must speak first to mother about it, sir! She has seen better days once, and she is sadly afraid of my ever taking charity. Mother mends my clothes, and teaches me herself, and works very hard in other ways, but she is quite bed-ridden, and we have scarcely anything but the trifle I make by working in the fields. It is very difficult to get a job at all sometimes, and if you could put me in the way of earning that money, sir, it would make mother very happy. She is a little particular, and would not taste a morsel that I could get by asking for it."

"That is being very proud!" said Harry.

"No, sir! it is not from pride," replied Evan; "but mother says a merciful God has provided for her many years, and she will not begin to distrust Him now. Her hands are always busy, and her heart is always cheerful. She rears many little plants by her bedside, which we sell, and she teaches a neighbour's children, besides sewing for any one who will employ her; for mother's maxim always was, that there can be no such thing as an idle Christian."

"Very true!" said Lady Harriet. "Even the apostles were mending their nets and labouring hard, whenever they were not teaching. Either the body or the mind should always be active."

"If you saw mother, that is exactly her way, for she does not eat the bread of idleness. Were a stranger to offer us a blanket or a dinner in charity, she would rather go without any than take it. A very kind lady brought her a gown one day, but mother would only have it if she were allowed to knit as many stockings as would pay for the stuff. I dare not take a penny more for my work than is due, for she says, if once I begin receiving alms, I might get accustomed to it."

"That is the good old Scotch feeling of former days," observed Major Graham. "It was sometimes carried too far then, but there is not enough of it now. Your mother should have lived fifty years ago."

"You may say so indeed, sir. We never had a drop of broth from the soup-kitchen all winter, and many a day we shivered without a fire, though the society offered her sixpence a week for coals; but she says 'the given morsel is soon done;' and now, many of our neighbours who wasted what they got, feel worse off than we, who are accustomed to suffer want, and to live upon our honest labour. Long ago, if mother went out to tea with any of our neighbours, she always took her own tea along with us."

"But this is being prouder than anybody else," observed Frank, smiling. "If my grandmama goes out to a tea-party, she allows her friends to provide the fare."

"Very likely, sir! but that is different when people can give as good as they get. Last week a kind neighbour sent us some nice loaf bread, but mother made me take it back, with her best thanks, and she preferred her own oat cake. She is more ready to give than to take, sir, and divides her last bannock, sometimes, with anybody who is worse off than ourselves."

"Poor fellow!" said Frank compassionately; "how much you must often have suffered!"

"Suffered!" said the boy, with sudden emotion. "Yes! I have suffered! It matters nothing to be clothed in rags,—to be cold and hungry now! There are worse trials than that! My father died last year, crushed to death in a moment by his own cart-wheels,—my brothers and sisters have all gone to the grave, scarcely able to afford the medicines that might have cured them,—and I am left alone with my poor dying mother. It is a comfort that life does not last very long, and we may trust all to God while it lasts."

"Could you take us to see Mrs. Mackay?" said Major Graham, kindly. "Laura, get your bonnet."

"Oh sir! that young lady could not stay half a minute in the place where my mother lives now. It is not a pretty cottage such as we read of in tracts, but a dark, cold room, up a high stair, in the narrowest lane you ever saw, with nothing to sit on but an old chest."

"Never mind that, Evan," replied Major Graham. "You and your mother have a spirit of honour and honesty that might shame many who are lying on sofas of silk and damask. I respect her, and shall assist you if it be possible. Show us the way."

Many dirty closes and narrow alleys were threaded by the whole party, before they reached a dark ruinous staircase, where Evan paused and looked round, to see whether Major Graham still approached. He then slowly mounted one flight of ancient, crumbling steps after another, lighted by patched and broken windows, till at last they arrived at a narrow wooden flight, perfectly dark. After groping to the summit, they perceived a time-worn door, the latch of which was lifted by Evan, who stole noiselessly into the room, followed by Uncle David, and the wondering children.

There, a large cold room nearly empty, but exceedingly clean, presented itself to their notice. In one corner stood a massive old chest of carved oak, surrounded with a perfect glow of geraniums and myrtles in full blossom; beside which were arranged a large antique Bible, a jug of cold water, and a pile of coarsely-knitted worsted stockings. Beyond these, on a bed of clean straw, lay a tall, emaciated old woman, apparently in the last stage of life, with a face haggard by suffering; and yet her thin, withered hands, were busily occupied with needle work, while in low, faltering tones, she chanted these words,

"When from the dust of death I rise,
To claim my mansion in the skies,
This, this shall be my only plea,
Jesus hath lived and died for me."

"Mother!" said Evan, wishing to arouse her attention. "Look, mother!"

"Good day, Mrs. Mackay," added Major Graham, in a voice of great consideration, while she languidly turned her head towards the door. "I have come to thank you for restoring my purse this morning."

"You are kindly welcome, sir! What else could we do!" replied she, in a feeble tremulous voice. "The money was yours, and the sooner it went out of our hands the better."

"It was perfectly safe while it stayed there," added Major Graham, not affecting to speak in a homely accent, nor putting on any airs of condescension at all, but sitting down on the old chest as if he had never sat on anything but a chest in his life before, and looking at the clean bare floor with as much respect as if it had been a Turkey carpet. "Your little boy's pocket seems to be as safe as the Bank of Scotland."

"That is very true, sir! My boy is honest; and it is well to keep a good conscience, as that is all he has in this world to live for. Many have a heavy conscience to carry with a heavy purse; but these he need not envy. If we are poor in this world, we are rich in faith; and I trust the money was not even a temptation to Evan, because he has learned from the best of all teachers, that it would 'profit him nothing to gain the whole world, and lose his own soul.' "

"True, Mrs. Mackay! most true! We have come here this morning to request that you and he will do me the favour to accept of a small recompense."

"We are already rewarded, sir! This has been an opportunity of testifying to our own hearts that we desire to do right in the eye of God. At the same time, it was Providence who kindly directed my son's steps to the place where that money was lying; and if anything seems justly due to poor Evan, let him have it. My wants are few, and must soon be ended. But, oh! when I look at that boy, and think of the long years he may be struggling with poverty and temptation, my heart melts within me, and my whole spirit is broken. Faith itself seems to fail, and I could be a beggar for him now! It is not money I would ask sir, because that might soon be spent; but get him some honest employment, and I will thank you on my very knees."

Evan seemed startled at the sudden energy of his mother's manner, and tears sprung into his eyes while she spoke with a degree of agitation so different from what he had ever heard before; but he struggled to conceal his feelings, and she continued with increasing emotion,

"Bodily suffering, and many a year of care and sorrow, are fast closing their work on me. The moments are passing away like a weaver's shuttle; and if I had less anxiety about Evan, how blessed a prospect it would appear; but that is the bitterness of death to me now. My poor, poor boy! I would rather he was in the way of earning his livelihood, than that he got a hundred a year. Tell me, sir!—and oh! consider you are speaking to a dying creature—can you possibly give him any creditable employment, where he might gain a crust of bread, and be independent!"

"I honour your very proper feeling on the subject, Mrs. Mackay, and shall help Evan to the best of my ability," replied Major Graham, in a tone of seriousness and sincerity. "To judge of these fine geraniums, he must be fond of cultivating plants; and we want an under gardener in the country; therefore he shall have that situation without loss of time."

"Oh, mother! mother! speak no more of dying! You will surely get better now!" said Evan, looking up, while his thin pale face assumed a momentary glow of pleasure. "Try now to get better! I never could work as well, if you were not waiting to see me come home! We shall be so happy now!"

"Yes! I am happy!" said Mrs. Mackay, solemnly looking towards heaven, with an expression that could not be mistaken. "The last cord is cut that bound me to earth! May you, sir, find hereafter the blessings that are promised to those who visit the fatherless and widows in their affliction."

THE YOUNG MIDSHIPMAN

When hands are link'd that dread to part,
And heart is met by throbbing heart;
Ah! bitter, bitter is the smart
Of them that bid farewell.
HEBER

NEXT MONDAY MORNING, at an early hour, Frank had again found his way with great difficulty to the house of Widow Mackay, where he spent all his pocket-money on two fine scarlet geraniums. If they had been nettles or cabbages, he would have felt the same pleasure in buying them; and his eyes sparkled with animation when he entered Uncle David's room, carrying them in his hand, and saying, "I was so glad to have some money! I could spare it quite well. There is no greater pleasure in being rich than to help such people as Evan Mackay and his poor sick mother!"

"Yes, Frank, I often wonder that any enjoyment of wealth can be considered equal to the exercise of kind feelings, for surely the most delightful sensation in this world is, to deserve and receive the grateful affection of those around us," replied Major Graham. "What a wretched being Robinson Crusoe was on the desert island alone, though he found chests of gold! and yet many people are as unblest in the midst of society, who selfishly hoard fortunes for themselves, unmindful of the many around who ought to be gratefully receiving their daily benefits."

"I was laughing to read lately of the West India slaves, who collected money all their lives in an old stocking," said Frank, "and who watched with delight as it filled from year to year; but the bank is only a great stocking, where misers in this country lay up treasures for themselves which they are never to enjoy, though too often they lay up no treasures for themselves in a better world."

"I frequently think, Frank, if all men were as liberal, kind, and forbearing to each other as the Holy Scriptures enjoin, and if we lived as soberly, temperately, and godly

together, what a paradise this world would become; for many of our worst sufferings are brought on by our own folly, or the unkindness of others. And certainly, if we wish to fancy the wretchedness of hell itself, it would only be necessary to imagine what the earth would become if all fear of God and man were removed, and every person lived as his own angry, selfish passions would dictate. Great are the blessings we owe to Christianity, for making the world even what it is now, and yet greater would those blessings be, if we obeyed it better."

"That is exactly what grandmama says, and that we must obey the Gospel from love and gratitude to God, rather than from fear of punishment or hope of reward, which is precisely what we saw in poor Widow Mackay and Evan, who seemed scarcely to expect a recompense for behaving so honestly."

"That was the more remarkable in them, as few Christians now are above receiving a public recompense for doing their duty to God. Men of the world have long rewarded each other with public dinners and pieces of plate, to express their utmost praise and admiration, but of late I never open a newspaper without reading accounts of one clergyman or another, who has been 'honoured with a public breakfast!' when he is presented by an admiring circle with 'a gold watch and appendages!' or a Bible with a complimentary inscription, or a gown, or a pair of bands, worked by the ladies of his congregation! and all this, for labouring among his own people, in his own sphere of duty! What would Archbishop Leighton and the old divines have said to any one who attempted to rouse their vanity in this way, with the praise of men!"

"What you say reminds me, Uncle David," said Frank, "that we have been asked to present our Universal-Knowledge-Master, with a silver snuff-box, as a testimonial from the scholars in my class, because he is going soon to Van Dieman's Land, therefore, I hope you will give me half-a-crown to subscribe, or I shall be quite in disgrace with him."

"Not one shilling shall you receive from me, my good friend, for any such purpose! A snuff-box, indeed! your master ought to show his scholars an example of using none! a filthy waste of health, money, and time. Such testimonials should only be given, as Archbishop Magee says, to persons who have got into some scrape, which makes their respectability doubtful. If my grocer is ever presented with a pair of silver tongs, I shall think he has been accused of adulterating the sugar, and give over employing him directly."

"Laura," said Frank, "you will be having a silver thimble voted to you for hemming six pocket-handkerchiefs in six years."

"I know one clergyman, Dr. Seton, who conscientiously refused a piece of plate, which was about to be presented in this way," continued Major Graham; "he accidentally heard that such a subscription was begun among the rich members of his congregation, and instantly stopped it, saying, 'Let your testimonial consist in a regular attendance at church, and let my sole reward be enjoyed hereafter, when you appear as my crown of joy and rejoicing in the presence of our Lord Jesus Christ at his coming.'"

Sir Edward Graham's particular friend, Captain Gordon, at last wrote to say, that the Thunderbolt, 74, having been put in commission for three years, was about to sail for the African station, therefore he wished Frank to join without delay; and as a further mark of his regard, he promised that he would endeavour to keep his young protegé employed until he had served out his time, because a midshipman once paid off, was like a stranded whale, not very easily set afloat again.

Lady Harriet sighed when she read the letter, and looked paler all that day, but she knew that it was right and necessary for Frank to go, therefore she said nothing to distress him on the occasion, only in her prayers and explanations of the Bible that evening, there was a deeper tone of feeling than ever, and a cast of melancholy, which had rarely been the case before, while she spoke much of that meeting in a better world, which is the surest hope and consolation of those Christians who separate on earth, and who know not what a day, and still less what many years, may bring forth.

Major Graham tried to put a cheerful face on the matter also, though he evidently felt very sorry indeed about parting with Frank, and took him out a long walk to discuss his future prospects, saying, "Now you are an officer and a gentleman, entitled therefore to be treated with new respect and attention by all your brother-officers, naval or military, in his Majesty's service."

Frank himself, being a boy of great spirit and enterprise, felt glad that the time had really come for his being afloat, and examining all the world over with his own eyes; but he said that his heart seemed as if it had been put in a swing, it fell so low when he thought of leaving his dear happy home, and then it rose again higher than ever at the very idea of being launched on the wide ocean, and going to the countries he had so often read of, where battles had been fought and victories won.

"Frank!" said Peter Grey, who was going to join the Thunderbolt, in about a fortnight afterwards, "you have no idea how beautiful I looked in uniform to-day! I tried mine on, and felt so impatient to use my dirk, I could have eat my dinner with it, instead of employing a common knife."

"You never forget to be hungry, Peter," said Frank, laughing. "But now you are like the old Lord Buchan, who used to say he could cook his porridge in his helmet, and stir it with his broad-sword."

"I hope," said Major Graham, "you both intend to become very distinguished officers, and to leave a name at which the world grows pale."

"Certainly," answered Peter. "All the old heroes we read of shall be mere nobodies compared to me! I mean to lose a leg or an arm in every battle,"——

"Till nothing is left of you but your shirt-collar and shoe-strings," interrupted Frank, laughing.

"No! no! What remains of me at last shall die a Peer of the realm," continued Peter. "We must climb to the top of the tree, Frank! What title do you think I should take?"

"Lord Cockpit would suit you best for some time, Peter! It will not be so easy a business to rise as you think. Every one can run a race, but very few can win," observed Major Graham. "The rarest thing on earth is to succeed in being both conspicuous and respectable. Any dunce may easily be either the one or the other, but the chief puzzle with most men is, how to be both. In your profession there are great opportunities, but at the same time let me warn you, that the sea is not a bed of roses."

"No, Uncle David! but I hope it will become a field of laurels to us," replied Frank, laughing. "Now tell me in real earnest who you think was the greatest of our naval heroes till now, when Peter is to cut them all out."

"He must wait a few years. It is a long ladder to run up before reaching the top. In France, the king's sons are all born Field Marshals, but nobody in this country is born an Admiral. The great Lord Duncan served during half a century before gaining his most important victory, but previous to that, he paved the way to success, not by mere animal courage alone, but by being so truly good and religious a man, that his extraordinary firmness and benevolence of character gained the confidence of all those who served with him, and therefore half his success in battle was owing to his admirable conduct during peace."

"So I have heard!" replied Frank; "and when there was mutiny in every other ship, the Admiral's own crew remained faithful to him. How much better it is to obeyed from respect and attachment than from fear, which is a mean feeling that I hope neither to feel myself, nor to excite in others. I wish to be like Nelson, who asked, 'What is fear? I never saw it.' "

"Yes, Frank! Nelson was said to be 'brave as a lion, and gentle as a lamb.' Certainly both he and Lord Duncan were pre-eminently great; but neither Lord Duncan nor any other enlightened Christian would have said what Lord Nelson did, with his latest breath—'I have not been a great sinner!' No mortal could lift up his eyes at the day of judgment, and repeat those words again; for every man that breathes the breath of life is a great sinner. We are living in God's own world without remembering him continually; and amidst thousands of blessings we disobey him. The chief purpose for which men are created, is to glorify God, and to prepare for entering his presence in a better world; but instead of doing so, we live as if there were no other object to live for, than our own pleasures and amusements on earth. How then can we be otherwise than great sinners? I hope, Frank, that you will endeavour to be, like Lord Duncan, not merely a good officer, but also a good Christian; for, besides fighting the battles of your country, you must gain a great victory over yourself, as all men must either conquer their own evil dispositions, or perish for ever."

Lady Harriet was particularly earnest in entreating Frank to write frequently home, observing, that she considered it a religious duty in all children to show their parents this attention, as the Bible says, that "a wise son maketh a glad father," and that "the father of the righteous shall greatly rejoice;" but on the contrary, too many young persons leave their parents to mourn in suspense and anxiety as to the health and happiness of those whom they love more than they can ever love any one else.

"Tell us of everything that interests you, and even all about the spouting whales, flying fish, and dying dolphins, which you will of course see," said Laura. "Be sure to write us also, how many albatrosses you shoot, and whether you are duly introduced to Neptune at the Cape."

"Yes, Laura! But Bishop Heber's Journal, or any other book describing a voyage to the Cape, mentions exactly the same thing. It will quite bring me home again when I speak to you all on paper; and I shall be able to fancy what everybody will say when my letter is read. Mrs. Darwin sent for me this morning on particular business; and it was to say that she wished me, in all the strange countries where the Thunderbolt touched, to employ my spare moments in catching butterflies, that as many as possible might be added to her museum."

"Capital! How like Mrs. Darwin!" exclaimed Major Graham, laughing. "You will of course be running all over Africa, hat in hand, pursuing painted butterflies, till you get a *coup de soleil*, like my friend Watson, who was killed by one. Poor fellow! I was with him then, and it was a frightful scene. He wheeled round several times in a sort of convulsion, till he dropped down dead in my arms."

"I shall gild the legs and bills of some ducks before leaving home, and send them to her as a present from Sierra Leone," said Peter. "The wings might be dyed scarlet, which would look quite foreign; and if an elephant falls in my way, it shall be stuffed and forwarded by express."

"Uncle David! Do you remember what fun we had, when you sent Mrs. Darwin that stuffed bear in a present! I was desired to announce that a foreigner of distinction had arrived to stay at her house. What a bustle she was in on hearing that he brought letters of introduction from you, and intended to remain some time. Then we told her that he could not speak a word of English, and brought 'a Pole' with him; besides which he had once been a great dancer. Oh! how amusing it was, when she at last ventured into the passage to be introduced, and saw her fine stuffed bear."

"Whatever people collect," said Peter, "every good-natured person assists. I mean to begin a collection of crooked sixpences immediately; therefore, pray never spend another, but give me as many as you can spare; and the more crooked the better."

"Sing a song of sixpence!" said Frank, laughing. "Laura should begin to collect diamonds for a necklace, and perhaps it might be all ready before she comes out. I shall return home on purpose to see you then, Laura."

"Pray do, Master Frank," said Mrs. Crabtree, with more than usual kindness; "we shall have great rejoicings on the occasion of seeing you back—an ox roasted alive, as they do in England, and all that sort of Tom-fooleries. I'll dance a jig then myself for joy!—you certainly are a wonderful good boy, considering that I had not the managing of you."

Frank's departure was delayed till after the examination of his school, because Mr. Lexicon had requested that, being the best scholar there, he might remain to receive a whole library of prize-books and a whole pocketful of medals; for, as Peter remarked, "Frank Graham deserved any reward, because he learned his lessons so perfectly, that he could not say them wrong even if he wished!"

Harry and Laura were allowed to attend on the great occasion, that they might witness Frank's success; and never, certainly, had they seen anything so grand in their lives before! A hundred and forty boys, all dressed in white trousers and yellow gloves, were seated in rows, opposite to six grave learned-looking gentlemen, in wigs and spectacles, who seemed as if they would condemn all the scholars to death!

The colour mounted into Harry's cheeks with delight, and the tears rushed into his eyes, when he saw Frank, whose face was radiant with good humour and happiness, take his place as head boy in the school. All his companions had crowded round Frank as he entered, knowing that this was his last appearance in the class; while he spoke a merry or a kind word to each, leaning on the shoulder of one, and grasping the hand of another with cordial kindness, for he liked everybody, and everybody liked him. No one envied Frank being dux, because they knew how hard he worked for that place, and how anxious he had been to help every other boy in learning as cleverly as himself; for all the boobies would have become duxes if Frank could have assisted them to rise, while many an idler had been made busy by his attention and advice. No boy ever received, in one day, more presents than Frank did on this occasion from his young friends, who spent all their pocket-money in pen-knives and pencil-cases, which were to be kept by Frank, in remembrance of them, as long as he lived; and some of his companions had a tear in their eye on bidding him farewell, which pleased him more than all their gifts.

Major Graham took his place, with more gravity than usual, among the judges appointed to distribute the prizes; and now, during more than two hours, the most puzzling questions that could be invented were put to every scholar in succession, while Frank seemed always ready with an answer, and not only spoke for himself, but often good-naturedly prompted his neighbours, in so low a tone that no one else heard him. His eyes brightened, and his face grew red with anxiety, while even his voice shook at first; but before long Frank collected all his wits about him, and could construe Latin or repeat Greek with perfect ease, till at length the whole examination was concluded, and the great Dr. Clifford, who had lately come all the way from Oxford, was requested to present the prizes. Upon this he rose majestically from his arm-chair, and made a long speech, filled as full as it could hold of Latin and Greek. He praised Homer and Horace for nearly twenty minutes, and brought in several lines from Virgil, after which he turned to Frank, saying, in a tone of great kindness and condescension, though at the same time exceedingly pompous,

"It seems almost a pity that this young gentleman—already so very accomplished a scholar—who is, I may say, a perfect *multum in parvo*, should prematurely pause in his classical career to enter the navy; but in every situation of life his extraordinary activity of mind, good temper, courage, and ability, must render him an honour to his country and his profession."

Dr. Clifford now glanced over the list of prizes, and read aloud—"First prize for Greek—Master Graham!"

Frank walked gracefully forward, coloured, and bowed, while a few words of approbation were said to him, and a splendidly-bound copy of Euripides was put into his hands by Dr. Clifford, who then hastily read over the catalogue of prizes to himself, in an audible voice, and in a tone of great surprise.

"First prize for Latin!—Master Graham! First for algebra,—first for geography,—first for mathematics,—all Master Graham!!!—and last, not least, a medal for general good conduct, which the boys are allowed to bestow upon the scholar they think most deserving—and here stands the name of Master Graham again!!"

Dr. Clifford paused, while the boys all stood up for a moment and clapped their hands with enthusiasm, as a token of rejoicing at the destination of their own medal.

For the first time Frank was now completely overcome,—he coloured more deeply than before, and looked gratefully round, first at his companions, then at his master, and last at Major Graham, who had a tear standing in his eye when he smiled upon Frank, and held out his hand.

Frank's lip quivered for a moment, as if he would burst into tears, but with a strong effort he recovered himself, and affectionately grasping his uncle's hand, hastily resumed his place on the bench, to remain there while his companions received the smaller prizes awarded to them.

Meantime Harry had been watching Frank with a feeling of joy and pride, such as he never experienced before, and could scarcely refrain from saying to every person near him, "That is my brother!" He looked at Frank long and earnestly, wishing to be like him, and resolving to follow his good example at school. He gazed again and again, with new feelings of pleasure and admiration, till gradually his thoughts became melancholy, while remembering how soon they must be separated; and suddenly the terrible idea darted into his mind, "Perhaps we never may meet again!" Harry tried not to think of this; he turned his thoughts to other subjects; he forced himself to look at anything that was going on, but still these words returned with mournful apprehension to his heart, "Perhaps we never may meet again!"

Frank's first action, after the examination had been concluded, was hastily to gather up all his books, and bring a sight of them to Harry and Laura; but what was his astonishment when, instead of looking at the prizes, Harry suddenly threw his arms round his neck and burst into tears!

"My dear, dear boy! what has happened!" exclaimed Frank, affectionately embracing him, and looking much surprised. "Tell me, dear Harry, has anything distressed you?"

"I don't know very well, Frank! but you are going away,—and—and—I wish I had been a better boy! I would do anything you bid me now!—but I shall never be so happy again—no! never, without you."

"But, dear Harry! you will have Laura and grandmama, and Uncle David, all left, and I am coming back some day! Oh! what a happy meeting we shall have then!" said Frank, while the tears stood in his eyes; and drawing Harry's arm within his own, they walked slowly away together.

"I am very—very anxious for you and Laura to be happy," continued Frank, in the kindest manner; "but, dear Harry, will you not take more care to do as you are bid, and not always to prefer doing what you like! Mrs. Crabtree would not be half so terrible if you did not provoke her by some new tricks every day. I almost like her myself; for as the old proverb says, 'her bark is worse than her bite;' and she often reminds me of that funny old fable, where the mice were more afraid of the loud, fierce-looking cock, than of the sleek, smooth-looking cat, for there are people carrying gentler tongues yet quite as difficult to deal with. At the same time, seeing how uncomfortable you and Laura both feel with Mrs. Crabtree, I have written a letter to papa, asking as my last and only request on leaving home, that he will make a change of ministry, and he is always so very kind, that I feel sure he will grant it."

"How good of you, Frank!" said Harry. "I am sure it is our own faults very often when we are in disgrace, for we are seldom punished till we deserve it; but I am so sorry you are going away, that I can think of nothing else."

"So am I, very sorry indeed; but my best comfort, when far from home, would be, to think that you and Laura are happy, which will be the case when you become more watchful to please grandmama."

"That is very true, Frank! and I would rather offend twenty Mrs. Crabtrees than one grandmama; but perhaps Uncle David may send me to school now, when I shall try to be like you, sitting at the top of the class, and getting prizes for good behaviour."

"Well, Harry! my pleasantest days at school have been those when I was busiest, and you will find the same thing. How delightful it was, going over and over my tasks till they were quite perfect, and then rushing out to the play-ground, where my mind got a rest, while my body was active; you know it is seldom that both mind and body work at once, and the best way of resting the one is to make the other labour. That is probably the reason, Harry, why games are never half so pleasant as after hard study."

"Perhaps," replied Harry, doubtfully; "but I always hate anything that I am obliged to do."

"Then never be a sailor, as I shall be obliged to do fifty things a day that I would rather not; for instance, to get up in the middle of the night, when very likely dreaming about being at home again; but as grandmama says, it is pleasant to have some duties, for life would not get well on without them."

"Yes—perhaps—I don't know!—we could find plenty to do ourselves, without any-body telling us. I should like to-morrow, to watch the boys playing at cricket, and to see the races, and the Diorama, and in the evening to shoot our bows and arrows."

"My good sir! what the better would you, or anybody else, be of such a life as that! Not a thing in this world is made to be useless, Harry; the very weeds that grow in the ground are for some serviceable purpose, and you would not wish to be the only creature on earth living entirely for yourself. It would be better if neither of us had ever been born, than that the time and opportunities which God gives us for improving ourselves and doing good to others, should all be wasted. Let me hope, Harry, when I am away that you will often consider how dull grandmama may then feel, and how happy you might make her by being very attentive and obedient."

"Yes, Frank! but I could never fill your place!—that is quite impossible! Nobody can do that!"

"Try!—only try, Harry! Grandmama is very easily pleased when people do their best. She would not have felt so well satisfied with me, if that had not been the case."

"Frank!" said Harry, sorrowfully, "I feel as if ten brothers were going away instead of one, for you are so good to me! I shall be sure to mention you in my prayers, because that is all I can do for you now."

"Not all, Harry! though that is a great deal; you must write to me often, and tell me what makes you happy or unhappy, for I shall be more interested than ever, now that we are separated. Tell me everything about my schoolfellows, too, and about Laura. There is no corner of the wide world where I shall not think of you both every day, and feel anxious about the very least thing that concerns you."

"My dear boys!" said Major Graham, who had joined them some moments before, "it is fortunate that you have both lived always in the same home, for that will make you love each other affectionately, as long as you live. In England, children of one family are all scattered to different schools, without any person seeming to care whether they are attached or not, therefore their earliest and warmest friendships are formed with strangers of the same age, whom they perhaps never see again, after leaving school. In that case, brothers have no happy days of childhood to talk over in future life, as you both have,—no little scrapes to remember, that they got into together,—no pleasures enjoyed at the same moment to smile at the recollection of, and no friction of their tempers in youth, such as makes everything go on smoothly between brothers when they grow older; therefore, when at last grown up and thrown together, they scarcely feel more mutual friendship and intimacy than any other gentlemen testify towards each other."

"I dare say that is very true," said Frank. "Tom Brownlow tells me when his three brothers come home from Eton, Harrow, and Durham, they quarrel so excessively, that sometimes no two of them are on speaking terms."

"Not at all improbable," observed Major Graham. "In everything we see how much better God's arrangements are than our own. Families were intended to be like a little world in themselves—old people to govern the young ones—young people to make their elders cheerful—grown-up brothers and sisters to show their juniors a good example—and children to be playthings and companions to their seniors, but that is all at an end in the present system."

"Old Andrew says that large families 'squander' themselves all over the earth now," said Frank, laughing.

"Yes! very young children are thrust into preparatory schools—older boys go to distant academies—youths to College—and young men are shipped off abroad, while who among them all can say his heart is in his own home? Parents, in the mean time, finding no occupation or amusement in educating their children, begin writing books, perhaps theories of education, or novels; and try to fill up the rest of their useless hours with plays, operas, concerts, balls, or clubs. If people could only know what is the best happiness of this life, it certainly depends on being loved by those we belong to; for nothing can be called peace on earth, which does not consist in family affection, built on a strong foundation of religion and morality."

Sir Edward Graham felt very proud of Frank, as all gentlemen are of their eldest sons, and wrote a most affectionate letter on the occasion of his going to sea, promising to meet him at Portsmouth, and lamenting that he still felt so ill and melancholy he could not return home, but meant to try whether the baths in Germany would do him any good. In this letter was enclosed what he called "Frank's first prize-money," the largest sum the young midshipman had ever seen in his life, and before it had been a day in his possession, more than the half was spent on presents to his friends. Not a single person seemed to be forgotten except himself; for Frank was so completely unselfish, that Peter Gray once laughingly said, "Frank scarcely remembers there is such a person as himself in the world, therefore it is astonishing how he contrives to exist at all."

"If that be his worst fault, you show him a very opposite example, Peter," said Major Graham, smiling; "Number One is a great favourite with you."

"Frank is also very obliging!" added Lady Harriet; "he would do anything for anybody."

"Ah, poor fellow! he can't help that," said Peter, in a tone of pity. "Some people are born with that sort of desperate activity—flying to assist every one—running up stairs for whatever is wanted—searching for whatever is lost—and picking up whatever has been dropped. I have seen several others like Frank, who were troubled with that sort of turn. He is indulging his own inclination in flying about everywhere for everybody, as much as I do in sitting still!—it is all nature!—you know tastes differ, for some people like apples and some like onions."

Frank had a black shade of himself, drawn in uniform and put into a gilt frame, all for one shilling, which he presented to his grandmama, who looked sadly at the likeness when he came smiling into her dressing-room, and calling Harry to assist in knocking a nail into the wall, that it might be hung above the chimney-piece. "I need nothing to remind me of you, dear Frank," observed Lady Harriet, "and this is a sad exchange, the shadow for the substance." Frank gave a handsome new red morocco spectacle-case to Uncle David, and asked leave to carry away the old one with him as a remembrance. He bought gowns for all the maids, and books for all the men-servants. He presented Mrs. Crabtree with an elegant set of teacups and saucers, promising to send her a box of tea the first time he went to China; and for Laura and Harry he produced a magnificent magic lantern, representing all the stars and planets, which cost him several guineas. It was exhibited the evening before Frank went away, and caused great entertainment to a large party of his companions, who assembled at tea to take leave of him, on which occasion Peter Grey made a funny speech, proposing Frank's health in a bumper of bohea, when the whole party became very merry, and did not disperse till ten.

Major Graham intended accompanying Frank to Portsmouth, and they were to set off by the mail next evening. That day was a sad one to Harry and Laura, who were allowed a whole holiday; but not a sound of merriment was heard in the house, except when Frank tried to make them cheerful, by planning what was to be done after he came back, or when Major Graham invented droll stories about the adventures Frank would probably meet with at sea. Even Mrs. Crabtree looked more grave and cross than usual; and she brought Frank a present of a needle-case made with her own hands, and filled with thread of every kind, saying, that she heard all "midshipmites" learned to mend their things, and keep them decent, which was an excellent custom, and ought to be encouraged; but she hoped he would remember, that "a stitch in time saves nine."

Lady Harriet stayed most of the time in her dressing-room, and tried to conceal the traces of many tears when she did appear; but it was only too evident how sadly her time had been passed alone.

"Grandmama!" said Frank, taking her hand affectionately, and trying to look cheerful; "we shall meet again; perhaps very soon!"

Lady Harriet silently laid her hand upon the Bible, to show that there she found the certain assurance of another meeting in a better world; but she looked at Frank with melancholy affection, and added, very solemnly and emphatically,

> "There is no union here of hearts,
> That finds not here an end.' "

"But, grandmama! You are not so very old!" exclaimed Laura, earnestly. "Lord Rockville was born ten years sooner, and besides, young people sometimes die before older people."

"Yes, Laura! young people may die, but old people must. It is not possible that this feeble aged frame of mine can long remain in the visible world. 'The eye of him that hath seen me shall see me no more.' I have many more friends under the earth now, than on it. The streets of this city would be crowded, if all those I once knew and still remember, could be revived; but my own turn is fast coming, like theirs, and Frank knows, as all of you do, where it is my hope and prayer that we may certainly meet again."

"Grandmama!" said Frank, in a low and broken voice, "it wants but an hour to the time of my departure; I should like much if the servants were to come up for family prayers, and if Uncle David would read us the 14th chapter of St. John."

Lady Harriet rung the bell, and before long the whole household had assembled, as not one would have been absent on the night of Master's Frank's departure from home, which all were deeply grieved at, and even Mrs. Crabtree dashed a tear from her cheek as she entered the room.

Frank sat with his hand in Lady Harriet's, while Major Graham read the beautiful and comforting chapter which had been selected, and when the whole family kneeled in solemn prayer together, many a deep sob, which could not be conquered, was heard from Frank himself. All being over, he approached the servants, and silently shook hands with each, but could not attempt to speak; after which Lady Harriet led him to her dressing-room, where they remained some time, till, the carriage having arrived, Frank hastened into the drawing-room, clasped Harry and Laura in his arms, and having, in a voice choked with grief, bid them both a long farewell, he hurried out of their presence.

When the door closed, something seemed to fall heavily on the ground, but this scarcely attracted any one's attention, till Major Graham followed Frank, and was shocked to find him lying on the staircase perfectly insensible. Instead of calling for assistance, however, Uncle David carefully lifted Frank in his own arms, and carried him to the carriage, where, after a few moments, the fresh air and the rapid motion revived his recollection, and he burst into tears.

"Poor grandmama! and Harry and Laura!" cried he, weeping convulsively. "Oh! when shall I see them all again!"

"My dear boy!" said Major Graham, trying to be cheerful; "do you think nobody ever left home before? One would suppose you never expected to come back! Three years seem an age when we look forward, but are nothing after they have fled. The longer we live, the shorter every year appears, and it will seem only the day after to-morrow when you are rushing into the house again, and all of us standing at the door to welcome you back. Think what a joyous moment that will be! There is a wide and wonderful world for you to see first, and then a happy home afterwards to revisit."

"Yes, dear, good, kind Uncle David! no one ever had a happier home; and till the east comes to the west, I shall never cease to think of it with gratitude to you and grandmama. We shall surely all meet again. I must live upon that prospect. Hope is the jewel that remains wherever we go, and the hope to which grandmama has directed me, is truly compared to a rainbow, which not only brightens the earth, but stretches to heaven."

THE AMUSING DRIVE

I would not enter on my list of friends
(Though graced with polish'd manners and fine sense,
Yet wanting sensibility) the man
Who needlessly sets foot upon a worm.
COWPER

LADY HARRIET was confined to bed for several days after Frank's departure from home, and during all that week Harry and Laura felt so melancholy, that even Mrs. Crabtree became sorry for them, saying, it was quite distressing to see how quiet and good they had become, for Master Harry was as mild as milk now, and she almost wished he would be at some of his old tricks again.

On the following Monday a message arrived from Lady Rockville, to say that she was going a long drive in her phaeton, to visit some boys at Musselburgh school, and would be happy to take Harry and Laura of the party, if their grandmama had no objection. None being made by anybody, they flew up stairs to get ready, while Harry did not take above three steps at a time, and Laura, when she followed, felt quite astonished to find Mrs. Crabtree looking almost as pleased herself, and saying she hoped the expedition would do them both good.

Before five minutes had elapsed, Harry was mounted on the dickey, where Lady Rockville desired him to sit, instead of the footman, who was now dismissed, as room could not be made for them both; so after that Harry touched his hat, whenever any of the party spoke to him, as if he had really been the servant.

Laura, meanwhile, was placed between Lady Rockville and Miss Perceval, where she could hardly keep quiet a minute for joy, though afraid to turn her head or to stir her little finger, in case of being thought troublesome.

"I am told that the races take place at Musselburgh to-day," said Lady Rockville. "It is a cruel amusement, derived from the sufferings of noble animals; they have as good a right to be happy in the world as ourselves, Laura; but we shall pass that way, so Harry and you will probably see the crowds of carriages."

"Oh, how enchanting! I never saw a race-course in my life!" cried Laura, springing off her seat with delight. "Harry! Harry! we are going to the races!"

"Hurra!" exclaimed Harry, clapping his hands, "what a delightful surprise! Oh! I am so dreadfully happy!"

"After all, my dear Lady Rockville," said Miss Perceval, yawning, "what have horses got legs for, except to run!"

"Yes, but not at such a pace! It always shocked me—formerly at Doncaster, where the jockeys were sometimes paid L.1000 for winning—to see how the poor animals were lashed and spurred along the course, foaming with fatigue, and gasping till they nearly expired. Horses, poor creatures, from the hour of their birth till their death have a sad time of it!"

"Grandmama once read me a beautiful description of a wild horse in his natural state of liberty," said Laura. "Among the South American forests he was seen carrying his head erect, with sparkling eyes, flowing mane, and splendid tail, trotting about among the noble trees, or cropping the grass at his feet, looking quite princely, and doing precisely what he pleased."

"Then look at the contrast," said Lady Rockville, pointing to a long row of cart-horses with galled sides, shrivelled skins, broken knees, and emaciated bodies, which were all dragging their weary load along. "Animals are all meant for the use of man, but not to be abused, like these poor creatures."

"As for racing," said Miss Perceval, "a thoroughbred horse enters into the spirit of it quite as much as his rider. Did you never hear of Quin's celebrated steed, which became so eager to win, that when his antagonist passed he seized him violently by the leg, and both jockeys had to dismount that the furious animal might be torn away. The famous horse Forrester, too, caught hold of his opponent by the jaw, and could scarcely be disengaged."

"Think of all the cruel training these poor creatures went through before they came to that," added Lady Rockville; "of the way in which horses are beaten, spurred, and severly cut with the whip; then, after their strength fails, like the well known 'high-mettled racer,' the poor animal is probably sold at last to perpetual hard labour and ill-usage."

"Uncle David showed me yesterday," said Laura, "that horrid picture which you have probably seen, by Cruikshanks, of the Knacker's Yards in London, where old horses are sent to end their miserable days, after it is impossible to torture them any longer into working. Oh! it was dreadful! and yet grandmama said the whole sketch had been taken from life."

"I know that," answered Lady Rockville. "In these places the wretched animals are literally put to death by starvation, and may be seen gnawing each other's manes in the last agonies of hunger."

"My dear Lady Rockville," exclaimed Miss Perceval, affectedly, "how can you talk of such unpleasant things!—there is an act of Parliament against cruelty to animals, so of course no such thing exists now. Many gentlemen are vastly kind to old horses, turning them out to grass for years, that they may enjoy a life of elegant leisure and rural retirement, to which, no doubt, some are well entitled; for instance, the famous horse Eclipse, which gained his owner L.25,000! I wish he had been mine!"

"But think how many are ruined when one is enriched, and indeed both are ruined in morals and good feeling; therefore I am glad that our sex have never taken to the turf. It is bad enough, my dear Miss Perceval, to see that they have taken to the moors; for were I to say all I think of those amazons who lately killed their six brace of grouse on the 12th of August, they would probably challenge me to single combat. Lord Rockville says, 'What with gentlemen doing worsted work, and ladies shouldering double-barrelled guns, he scarcely thinks this can be the same world that he was born in long ago.' "

The carriage at this moment began to proceed along the road with such extraordinary rapidity, that there seemed no danger of their following in the dust of any other equipage, and Miss Perceval became exceedingly alarmed, especially when Lady Rockville mentioned that this was one of the first times she had been driven by her new coachman, who seemed so very unsteady on his seat, she had felt apprehensive, for some time, that he might be drunk.

"A tipsy coachman! Dear Lady Rockville, do let me out! We shall certainly be killed in this crowd of carriages! I can walk home! Pray stop him, Miss Laura! I came to look on at a race, but not to run one myself! This fast driving is like a railroad, only not quite so straight! I do verily believe we are run off with! Stop, coachman!—stop!"

In spite of all Miss Perceval's exclamations and vociferations, the carriage flew on with frightful rapidity, though it reeled from side to side of the road, as if it had become intoxicated like the driver himself, who lashed his horses and galloped along, within an inch of hedges and ditches all the way, till at last, having reached the race-course, he pulled up so suddenly and violently, that the horses nearly fell back on their haunches, while he swore at them in the most furious and shocking manner.

Lady Rockville now stood up, and spoke to the coachman very severely on his misconduct, in first driving her so dangerously fast, and then being disrespectful enough to use profane language in her presence, adding, that if he did not conduct himself more properly, she must complain to Lord Rockville, as soon as the carriage returned home. Upon hearing this, the man looked exceedingly sulky, and muttered angrily to himself in a tipsy voice, till at last he suddenly threw away the reins, and, rising from the box, he began to scramble his way down, nearly falling to the ground in his haste, and saying, "If your ladyship is not pleased with my driving, you may drive yourself!"

After this the intoxicated man staggered towards a drinking-booth not far off, and disappeared, leaving Miss Perceval perfectly planet-struck with astonishment, and actually dumb during several minutes with wonder at all she heard and saw. There sat Harry, alone on the dickey, behind two spirited blood-horses, foaming at the mouth with the speed at which they had come, and ready to start off again at the slightest hint, while noises on every side were heard enough to frighten a pair of hobby-horses. Piemen ringing their bells—blind fiddlers playing out of tune—boys calling lists of the horses—drums beating at the starting post—ballad-singers squalling at the full pitch of their voices—horses galloping—grooms quarrelling—dogs barking—and children crying.

In the midst of all this uproar, Harry unexpectedly observed Captain Digby on horseback not far off. Without losing a moment, he stood up, waving his handkerchief, and calling to beg he would come to the carriage immediately, as they were in want of assistance; and Lady Rockville told, as soon as he arrived, though hardly able to help laughing while she explained it, the extraordinary predicament they had been placed in. Captain Digby, upon hearing the story, looked ready to go off like a squib with rage at the offending coachman, and instantly seizing the driving-whip, he desired his servant to hold the horses' heads, while he proceeded towards the drinking-booth, flourishing the long lash in his hand as he went in a most ominous manner. Several minutes elapsed, during which Harry overheard a prodigious outcry in the tent, and then the drunken coachman was seen reeling away along the road, while Captain Digby, still brandishing the whip, returned, and mounting the dickey himself, he gathered up the reins, and insisted on driving Lady Rockville's phaeton for her. Before long it was ranged close beside a chariot so full of ladies it seemed ready to burst, when Harry was amused to perceive that Peter Grey and another boy, who were seated on the rumble behind, had spread a table-cloth on the roof of the carriage, using it for a dining-table, while they all seemed determined to astonish their appetites by the quantity of oysters and sandwiches they ate, and by drinking at the same time large tumblers of porter. Lady Rockville wished she could have the loan of Harry and Laura's spirits for an hour or two, when she saw how perfectly bewildered with delight they were on beholding the thousands of eager persons assembled on the race-ground,—jockeys riding about in liveries as gay as tulips—officers in scarlet uniform—red flags fluttering in the breeze—caravans exhibiting pictures of the wildest-looking beasts in the world—bands of music—recruiting parties—fire-eaters, who dined on red-hot pokers—portraits representing pigs fatter than the fattest in the world—giants a head and three pair of shoulders taller than any one else, and little dwarfs, scarcely visible with the naked eye—all of which were shown to children for half-price!

Lady Rockville very good-naturedly gave Harry half-a-crown, promising that, before leaving the race-ground, he should either buy some oranges to lay the dust in his throat, after so long a drive, or visit as many shows as he pleased for his half-crown; and they were anxiously discussing what five sights would be best worth sixpence each, when the loud hurra was heard, the drums beat, and five horses started off for the first heat. Harry stood up in an ecstasy of delight, and spoke loudly in admiration of a jockey on a gray horse, with a pink jacket, who took the lead, and seemed perfectly to fly, as if he need never touch the ground; but Harry exclaimed angrily against the next rider, in a yellow dress and green cap, who pulled back his own bay horse, as if he really wished to lose. To Laura's astonishment, however, Captain Digby preferred him, and Miss Perceval declared in favour of a light blue jacket, and chestnut horse. Harry now thought everybody stupid not to agree with him, and called out in the height of his eagerness, "I would bet this half-crown upon the pink jacket!"

"Done!" cried Peter, laughing. "The yellow dress and green cap for my money!"

"Then I shall soon have five shillings!" exclaimed Harry in great glee; but scarcely had he spoken, before a loud murmuring sound arose among the surrounding crowd, upon hearing which he looked anxiously about, and was astonished to see the green cap and yellow dress already at the winning post, while his own favorite gray horse cantered slowly along, far behind all the others, carrying the jockey with the pink jacket, who hung his head, and was bent nearly double with shame and fatigue.

Peter Grey gave a loud laugh of triumph when he glanced at Harry's disappointed angry countenance, and held out his hand for the half-crown, saying, "Pay your debt of honour, Master Harry! It is rather fortunate I won, seeing that not one sixpence had I to pay you with! not a penny to jingle on a mill-stone. You had more money than wit, and I had more wit than money, so we are well met. Did you not see that the gray horse has fallen lame? Good-bye, youngster! I shall tell all the giants and wild beasts to expect you another day!"

"Harry!" said Lady Rockville, looking gravely at his enraged countenance, "it is a foolish fish that is caught with every bait! I am quite relieved that you lost that money. This is an early lesson against gambling, and no one can ever be rich or happy who becomes fond of it. We were wrong to bring you here at all; and I now see you could easily be led into that dreadful vice, which has caused misery and ruin to thousands of young men. If you had possessed an estate, it would have been thrown away quite as foolishly as the poor half-crown, making you perhaps miserable afterwards for life."

"I thought myself quite sure to win!" exclaimed Harry, still looking with angry astonishment after Peter, who was making odd grimaces, and holding up the half-crown in the most teazing manner. "I would rather have thrown my money into the sea than given it to Peter."

"Think, too, how many pleasanter and better ways there are, in which you might have spent it!" added Lady Rockville. "Look at that poor blind man whom you could have relieved, or consider what a nice present you should have given to Laura! But there seem to be no more brains in your head, Harry, than in her thimble!"

"Peter is quite a little black-leg already," observed Miss Perceval. "I never saw such a boy! So fond of attracting notice, that he would put on a cap and bells if that would make him stared at. Last Saturday he undertook for a bet, to make a ceremonious bow to every lamp-post along Prince's Street, and I wish you could have seen the wondering crowd that gradually collected as he went along, performing his task with the most perfect composure and impudence."

"For cool assurance, I hope there are not many boys equal to him," said Lady Rockville. "He scattered out of the window lately, several red-hot halfpence among some beggars, and I am told they perfectly stuck to the poor creatures' fingers when trying to pick them up; and he was sent a message, on his pony, one very cold day lately, to Lady De Vere's, who offered when he was taking leave, to cut him one of her finest camellias, to which he replied, 'I would much rather you offered me a hot potatoe!' "

"Peter feels no sympathy in your disappointment, Harry," added Miss Perceval; "but we might as well expect wool on a dog, as friendship from a gambler, who would ruin his own father, and always laughs at those who lose."

"Go and cut your wisdom teeth, Harry!" said Captain Digby, smiling. "Any one must have been born blind not to observe that the gray horse was falling behind; but you have bought half-a-crown's worth of wisdom by experience, and I hope it will last for life. Never venture to bet even that your own head is on your shoulders, or it may turn out a mistake."

"Harry is now the monkey that has seen the world and I think it will be a whole year of Saturdays before he ever commits such a blunder again," continued Lady Rockville. "We must for this once, not complain of what has occurred to Lady Harriet, because she would be exceedingly displeased, but certainly you are a most ingenious little gentleman for getting into scrapes!"

Harry told upon himself, however, on his return home, because he had always been accustomed to do so, knowing Major Graham and his grandmama never were very angry at any fault that was confessed and repented of, therefore he went straight up stairs and related his whole history to Uncle David, who gave him a very serious exhortation against the foolish and sinful vice of gambling. To keep him in mind of his silly adventure that day, Harry was also desired, during the whole evening, to wear his coat turned inside out, a very frequent punishment administered by Major Graham for small offences, and which was generally felt to be a terrible disgrace.

THE UNEXPECTED EVENT

His shout may ring upon the hill,
His voice be echo'd in the hall,
His merry laugh like music trill,
I scarcely notice such things now.
WILL

Some weeks after Frank had left home, while Lady Harriet and Major Graham were absent at Holiday House, Harry and Laura felt surprised to observe, that Mrs. Crabtree suddenly became very grave and silent,—her voice seemed to have lost half its loudness, —her countenance looked rather pale,—and they both escaped being scolded on several occasions, when Harry himself could not but think he deserved it. Once or twice he ventured to do things that at other times he dared not have attempted, "merely as an experiment," he said, "like that man in the menagerie, who put his head into the lion's mouth, without feeling quite sure whether it would be bit off the next moment or not;" but though Mrs. Crabtree evidently saw all that passed, she turned away with a look of sadness, and said not a word.

What could be the matter? Harry almost wished she would fly into a good passion and scold him, it became so extraordinary and unnatural to see Mrs. Crabtree sitting all day in a corner of the room, sewing in silence, and scarcely looking up from her work; but still the wonder grew, for she seemed to become worse and worse every day. Harry dressed up the cat in an old cap and frock of Laura's,—he terrified old Jowler by putting him into the shower bath,—and let off a few crackers at the nursery window, —but it seemed as if he might have fired a cannon without being scolded by Mrs. Crabtree, who merely turned her head round for a minute, and then silently resumed her work. Laura even fancied that Mrs. Crabtree was once in tears, but that seemed quite impossible, so she thought no more about it, till one morning, when they had begun to despair of ever hearing more about the business, and were whispering together in a corner of the room, observing that she looked duller than ever, they were surprised to hear Mrs. Crabtree calling them both to come near her. She looked very pale, and was beginning to say something, when her voice suddenly became so husky and indistinct, that she seemed unable to proceed; therefore, motioning with her hand for them to go away, she began sewing very rapidly, as she had done before, breaking her threads and pricking her fingers at every stitch, while they became sure she was sobbing and crying.

Laura and Harry silently looked at each other with some apprehension, and the nursery now became so perfectly still, that a feather falling on the ground would have been heard. This had continued for some time, when at last Laura upon tiptoe stole quietly up to where Mrs. Crabtree was sitting, and said to her, in a very kind and anxious voice, "I am afraid you are not well, Mrs. Crabtree! Grandmama will send for a doctor when she comes home. Shall I ask her?"

"You are very kind, Miss Laura!—never mind me! Your grandmama knows what is the matter. It will be all one a hundred years hence," answered Mrs. Crabtree, in a low husky voice. "This is a thing you will be very glad to hear!—you must prepare to be told some good news!" added she, forcing a laugh, but such a laugh as Harry and Laura never heard before, for it sounded so much more like sorrow than joy. They waited in great suspense to hear what would follow, but Mrs. Crabtree, after struggling to speak again with composure, suddenly started off her seat, and hurried rapidly out of the room. She appeared no more in the nursery that day, but next morning when they were at breakfast, she entered the room with her face very much covered up in her bonnet, and evidently tried to speak in her usual loud bustling voice, though somehow it still sounded perfectly different from common. "Well, children! Lady Harriet was so kind as to promise that my secret should be kept till I pleased, and that no one should mention it to you but myself.—I am going away!"

"You!" exclaimed Harry, looking earnestly in Mrs. Crabtree's face. "Are you going away?"

"Yes, Master Harry,—I leave this house to-day! Now don't pretend to look sorry! I know you are not! I can't bear children to tell stories. Who would ever be sorry for a cross old woman like me?"

"But perhaps I am sorry! Are you in real earnest going away?" asked Harry again with renewed astonishment. "Oh no! It is only a joke!"

"Do I look as if this were a joke?" asked Mrs. Crabtree, turning round her face, which was bathed with tears. "No no! I am come to bid you both a long farewell! A fine mess you will get into now! All your things going to rack and ruin, with nobody fit to look after them!"

"But, Mrs. Crabtree! we do not like you to go away," said Laura, kindly. "Why are you leaving us all on a sudden? it is very odd! I never was so surprised in my life!"

"Your papa's orders are come. He wrote me a line some weeks ago, to say that I have been too severe. Perhaps that is all true. I meant it well, and we are poor creatures who can only act for the best. However, it can't be helped now! There's no use lamenting over spilt cream. You'll be the better behaved afterwards. If ever you think of me again, children, let it be as kindly as possible. Many and many a time shall I remember you both. I never cared for any young people but yourselves, and I shall never take charge of any others. Master Frank was the best boy in the world, and you would both have been as good under my care,—but it is no matter now!"

"But it does matter a very great deal," cried Harry eagerly. "You must stay here, Mrs. Crabtree, as long as you live, and a great deal longer! I shall write a letter to papa all about it. We were very troublesome, and it was our own faults if we were punished. Never mind, Mrs. Crabtree, but take off your bonnet and sit down! I am going to do some dreadful mischief to-night, so you will be wanted to keep me in order."

Mrs. Crabtree laid her hand upon Harry's head in silence, and there was something so solemn and serious in her manner, that he saw it would be needless to remonstrate any more. She then held out her hand to Laura, endeavouring to smile as she did so, but it was a vain attempt, for her lip quivered, and she turned away, saying, "Who would believe I should make such a fool of myself! Farewell to you both! and let nobody speak ill of me after I am gone, if you can help it!"

Without looking round, Mrs. Crabtree hurried out of the nursery and closed the door, leaving Harry and Laura perfectly bewildered with astonishment at this sudden event, which seemed more like a dream than a reality. They both felt exceedingly melancholy, hardly able to believe that she had ever formerly been at all cross, while they stood at the window with tears in their eyes, watching the departure of her well-known blue chest, on a wheel-barrow, and taking a last look of her red gown and scarlet shawl as she hastily followed it.

For several weeks to come, whenever the door opened, Harry and Laura almost expected her to enter, but month after month elapsed, and Mrs. Crabtree appeared no more, till one day, at their earnest entreaty, Lady Harriet took them a drive of some miles into the country, to see the neat little lodging by the sea-side where she lived, and maintained herself by sewing, and by going out occasionally as a sick-nurse. A more delightful surprise certainly never could have been given than when Harry and Laura tapped at the cottage door, which was opened by Mrs. Crabtree herself, who started back with an exclamation of joyful amazement, and looked as if she could scarcely believe her eyes on beholding them, while they laughed at the joke till tears were running down their cheeks. "Is Mrs. Crabtree at home!" said Harry, trying to look very grave.

"Grandmama says we may stay here for an hour while she drives along the shore," added Laura, stepping into the house with a very merry face. "And how do you do, Mrs. Crabtree?"

"Very well, Miss Laura, and very happy to see you. What a tall girl you are become! and Master Harry, too! looking quite over his own shoulders!"

After sitting some time, Mrs. Crabtree insisted on their having some dinner in her cottage; so making Harry and Laura sit down on each side of a large blazing fire, she cooked some most delicious pancakes for them in rapid succession, as fast as they could eat, tossing them high in the air first, and then rolling up each as it was fried, with a large spoonful of jam in the centre, till Harry and Laura at last said, that unless Mrs. Crabtree supplied fresh appetites, she need make no more pancakes, for they thought even Peter Grey himself could scarcely have finished all she provided.

Harry had now been several months constantly attending school, where he became a great favourite among the boys, and a great torment to the masters, while for his own part, he liked it twenty times better than he expected, because the lessons were tolerably easy to a clever boy, as he really was, and the games at cricket and foot-ball in the play-ground put him perfectly wild with joy. Every boy at school seemed to be his particular friend, and many called him "the holiday maker," because if ever a holiday was wished for, Harry always became leader in the scheme. The last morning of Peter Grey's appearing at school, he got the name of "the copper captain," because Mr. Lexicon having fined him half-a-crown, for not knowing one of his lessons, he brought the whole sum in half-pence, carrying them in his hat and gravely counting them all out, with such a pains-taking, good-boy look, that any one, to see him, would have supposed he was quite penitent and sorry for his misconduct, but no sooner had he finished the task and ranged all the half-pence neatly in rows along Mr. Lexicon's desk, than he was desired in a voice of thunder, to leave the room instantly, and never to return, which accordingly he never did, having started next day on the top of the coach for Portsmouth; and the last peep Harry got of him, he was buying a perfect mountain of gingerbread out of an old man's basket to eat by the way.

Meantime Laura had lessons from a regular day-governess, who came every morning at seven, and never disappeared till four in the afternoon, so, as Mrs. Crabtree remarked, "the puir thing was perfectly deaved wi' edication," but she made such rapid progress that Uncle David said it would be difficult to decide whether she was growing fastest in body or in mind. Laura seemed born to be under the tuition of none but ill-tempered people, and Madame Pirouette appeared in a constant state of irritability. During the music-lessons she sat close to the piano, with a pair of sharp-pointed scissors in her hand, and whenever Laura played a wrong note, she stuck their points into the offending finger, saying sometimes, in an angry foreign accent, "Put your toe upon 'dis note! I tell you put your toe upon 'dis note!"

"My finger, I suppose you mean?" asked Laura, trying not to laugh.

"Ah! fingare and toe! dat is all one! Speak not a word! take hold of your tongue."

"Laura!" said Major Graham, one day, "I would as soon hear a gong sounding in my ear for half an hour, as most of the fine pieces you perform now. Taste and expression are quite out of date, but the chief object of ambition is, to seem as if you had four hands instead of two, from the torrent of notes produced at once. If ever you wish to please my old-fashioned ears, give me melody,—something that touches the heart and dwells in the memory,—then years afterwards, when we hear it again, the language seems familiar to our feelings, and we listen with deep delight to sounds recalling a thousand recollections of former days, which are brought back by music (real music) with distinctness and interest which nothing else can equal."

During more than two years, while Harry and Laura were rapidly advancing in education, they received many interesting letters from Frank, expressing the most affectionate anxiety to hear of their being well and happy, while his paper was filled with amusing accounts of the various wonderful countries he visited; and at the bottom of the paper, he always very kindly remembered to send them an order on his banker, as he called Uncle David, drawn up in proper form, saying, "Please to pay Master Harry and Miss Laura Graham the sum of five shillings on my account. Francis Arthur Graham."

In Frank's gay, merry epistles, he kept all his little annoyances or vexations to himself, and invariably took up the pen with such a desire to send cheerfulness into his own beloved home, that his letters might have been written with a sunbeam, they were so full of warmth and vivacity. It seemed always a fair wind to Frank, for he looked upon the best side of everything, and never teased his absent friends with complaints of distresses they could not remedy, except when he frequently mentioned his sorrow at being separated from them, adding, that he often wished it were possible to meet them during one day in every year, to tell all his thoughts, and to hear theirs in return, for sometimes now, during the night watches, when all other resources failed, he entertained himself by imagining the circle of home all gathered around him, and by inventing what each individual would say upon any subjects he liked, while all his adventures acquired a double interest, from considering that the recital would one day amuse his dear friends when their happy meeting at last took place. Frank was not so over-anxious about his own comfort, as to feel very much irritated and discomposed at any privations that fell in his way, and once sitting up in the middle of a dark night, with the rain pouring in torrents, and the wind blowing a perfect hurricane, he drew his watch-coat round him, saying good-humouredly to his grumbling companions, "This is by no means so bad! and whatever change takes place now, will probably be for the better. Sunshine is as sure to come as Christmas, if you only wait for it, and in the mean time we are all more comfortably off than St. Patrick, when he had to swim across a stormy sea, with his head under his arm."

Frank often amused his messmates with stories which he had heard from Uncle David, and soon became the greatest favourite imaginable with them all, while he frequently endeavoured to lead their minds to the same sure foundation of happiness which he always found the best security of his own. He had long been taught to know that a vessel might as well be steered without rudder or compass, as any individual be brought into a haven of peace, unless directed by the Holy Scriptures; and his delight was frequently to study such passages as these: "When thou passest through the waters, I will be with thee; and through the rivers, they shall not overflow thee; when thou walkest through the fire thou shalt not be burned; neither shall the flame kindle upon thee. For I am the Lord thy God, the Holy One of Israel thy Saviour."

AN UNEXPECTED VOYAGE

Full little knowest thou, that hast not tried,
How strange it is in "steamboat" long to bide,—
To fret thy soul with crosses and with cares,
To eat thy heart through comfortless despairs,
To speed to-day—to be put back to-morrow—
To feed on hope—to pine with fear and sorrow.
                    SPENSER

As HARRY AND LAURA grew older, they were gradually treated like friends and companions by Lady Harriet and Major Graham, who improved their minds by frequent interesting conversations, in which knowledge and principle were insensibly instilled into their minds, not by formal instruction, but merely by mentioning facts, or expressing opinions and sentiments such as naturally arose out of the subjects under discussion, and accustoming the young people themselves to feel certain that their own remarks and thoughts were to be heard with the same interest as those of any other person. No surprise was expressed, if they appeared more acute or more amusing than might have been expected,—no angry contempt betrayed itself if they spoke foolishly, unless it were something positively wrong; and thus Major Graham and Lady Harriet succeeded in making that very difficult transition from treating children as toys, to becoming their confidential friends, and most trusted, as well as most respected and beloved associates.

Frank had been upwards of five years cruising on various stations abroad, and many officers who had seen him, gave such agreeable reports to Major Graham of his admirable conduct on several occasions, and of his having turned out so extremely handsome and pleasing, that Lady Harriet often wished, with tears in her eyes, it were possible she might live to see him once again, though her own daily increasing infirmities rendered that hope every hour more improbable. She was told that he spoke of her frequently, and said once when he met an aged person at the Cape, "I would give all I possess on earth, and ten times more, if I had it, to see my dear grandmother as well, and to meet her once more." This deeply affected Lady Harriet, who was speaking one day with unusual earnestness of the comfort it gave, whatever might be the will of Providence in respect to herself, that Frank seemed so happy, and liked his profession so well, when the door flew open, and Andrew hastened into the room, his old face perfectly wrinkled with delight, while he displayed a letter in his hand, saying in a tone of breathless agitation as he delivered it to Major Graham, "The post-mark is Portsmouth, sir!"

Lady Harriet nearly rose from her seat with an exclamation of joy, but unable for the exertion, she sunk back, covering her face with her hands, and listened in speechless suspense to hear whether Frank had indeed returned. Harry and Laura eagerly looked over Major Graham's shoulder, and Andrew lingered anxiously at the door, till this welcome letter was hurriedly torn open and read. The direction was certainly Frank's writing, though it seemed very different from usual, but the contents filled Major Graham with a degree of consternation and alarm, which he vainly endeavoured to conceal, for it informed him that, during a desperate engagement with some slave-ships off the coast of Africa, Frank had been most severely wounded, from which he scarcely recovered before a violent attack of fever reduced him so extremely, that the doctors declared his only chance of restoration was to be invalided home immediately; "therefore," added he, "you must all unite a prayer for my recovery with a thanksgiving for my return, and I can scarcely regret an illness that restores me to home. My heart is already with you all, but my frail, shattered body must rest some days in London, as the voyage from Sierra Leone has been extremely fatiguing and tedious."

Lady Harriet made not a single remark when this letter was closed, but tears coursed each other rapidly down her aged cheeks, while she slowly removed her hands from her face, and gazed at Major Graham, who seated himself by her side, in evident agitation, and calling back Andrew when he was leaving the room, he said in accents of unusual emotion, "Desire John to inquire immediately whether any steamboat sails for London to-day."

"You are right!" said Lady Harriet, feebly. "Oh! that I could accompany you! But bring him to me if possible. I dare not hope to go. Surely we shall meet at last. Now indeed I feel my own weakness when I cannot fly to see him. But he will be quite able for the journey. Frank had an excellent constitution,—he—he was—"

Lady Harriet's voice failed, and she burst into a convulsive agony of tears.

A few hours, and Uncle David had embarked for London, where, after a short passage, he arrived at his usual lodgings in St. James' Place; but some days elapsed, during which he laboured in vain to discover the smallest trace of Frank, who had omitted, in his hurried letter from Portsmouth, to mention where he intended living in town. One evening, fatigued with his long and unavailing search, Major Graham sat down, at the British Coffee-house, to take some refreshment before resuming his inquiries, and was afterwards about to leave the room, when he observed a very tall interesting young man, exceedingly emaciated, who strolled languidly into the room, with so feeble a step, that he seemed scarcely able to support himself. The stranger took off his hat, sunk into a seat, and passed his fingers through the dark masses of curls that hung over his pale white forehead, his large eyes closed heavily with fatigue, his cheek assumed a hectic glow, and his head sunk upon his hand. In a low subdued voice he gave some directions to the waiter, and Major Graham, after gazing for a moment with melancholy interest at this apparently consumptive youth, was about to depart, when a turn of the young man's countenance caused him to start; he looked again more earnestly—every fibre of his frame seemed suddenly to thrill with apprehension, and at last, in a voice of doubt and astonishment, he exclaimed, "Frank!"

The stranger sprung from his seat, gazed eagerly round the room, rushed into the arms of Major Graham, and fainted.

Long and anxiously did Uncle David watch for the restoration of Frank, while every means were used to revive him, and when at length he did regain his consciousness, no time was lost in conveying him to St. James' Place, where, after being confined to bed and attended by Sir Astley Cooper and Sir Henry Halford during four days, they united in recommending that he should be carried some miles out of town, to the neighbourhood of Hammersmith, for change of air, till the effect of medicine and diet could be fully tried. Frank earnestly entreated that he might be taken immediately to his own home, but this the doctors pronounced quite impossible, privately hinting to Major Graham that it seemed very doubtful indeed whether he could ever be moved there at all, or whether he might survive above a few months.

"Home is anywhere that my own family live with me," said Frank in a tone of resignation, when he heard a journey to Scotland pronounced impossible. "It is not where I am, but who I see, that signifies; and this meeting with you, Uncle David, did me more good than an ocean of physic. Oh! if I could only converse with grandmama for half-an-hour, and speak to dear Harry and Laura, it would be too much happiness. I want to see how much they are both grown, and to hear their merry laugh again. —Perhaps I never may! But if I get worse, they must come here. I have many, many things to say! Why should they not set off now?—immediately! If I recover, we might be such a happy party to Scotland again. For grandmama, I know it is impossible; but will you write and ask her about Harry and Laura? The sooner the better, Uncle David, because I often think it probable——"

Frank coloured and hesitated; he looked earnestly at his uncle for some moments, who saw what was meant, and then added,

"There is one person more, far distant, and little thinking of what is to come, who must be told. You have always been a father to me, Uncle David, but he also would wish to be here now. Little as we have been together, I know how much he loves me."

Frank's request became no sooner known than it was complied with by Lady Harriet, who thought it better not to distress Harry and Laura, by mentioning the full extent of his danger, but merely said, that he felt impatient for the meeting, and that they might prepare on the following day, to embark under charge of old Andrew and her own maid Harrison, for a voyage to London, where she hoped they would find the dear invalid already better. Laura was astonished at the agitation with which she spoke, and felt bewildered and amazed by this sudden announcement. She and Harry once or twice in their lives caught cold, and spent a day in bed, confined to a diet of gruel and syrup, which always proved an infallible remedy for the very worst attacks, and they had frequently witnessed the severe sufferings of their grandmama, from which, however, she always recovered, and which seemed to them the natural effects of her extreme old age; but to imagine the possibility of Frank's life being in actual danger, never crossed their thoughts for an instant, and, therefore, it was with a feeling of unutterable joy that they stood on the deck of the Royal Pandemonium, knowing that they were now actually going to meet Frank.

Nothing could be a greater novelty to both the young travellers than the scene by which they were now surrounded; trumpets were sounding—bells ringing—sailors, passengers, carriages, dogs, and baggage all hurrying on board pell-mell, while a jet of steam came bellowing forth from the waste pipe, as if it were struggling to get rid of the huge column of black smoke vomited forth by the chimney. Below stairs they were still more astonished to find a large cabin, covered with gilding, red damask, and mirrors, where crowds of strange-looking people, more than half sick, and very cross, were scolding and bustling about, bawling for their carpet-bags, and trying to be of as much consequence as possible, while they ate and drank trash, to keep off sea-sickness, that might have made any one sick on shore—sipping brandy and water, or eating pepper-mint drops, according as the case required. Among those in the ladies' cabin, Laura and Harry were amused to discover Miss Perceval, who had hastened into bed already, in case of being ill, and was talking unceasingly to any one who would listen, besides ordering and scolding a poor sick maid, scarcely able to stand. Her head was enveloped in a most singular night-cap, ornamented with old ribbons and artificial flowers—she wore a bright yellow shawl, and had taken into the berth beside her a little Blenheim spaniel—a parrot—and a cage of canary birds, the noisy inhabitants of which sung at the full pitch of their voices till the very latest hour of the night, being kept awake by the lamp which swung from side to side, while nothing could be compared to their volubility except the perpetual clamour occasioned by Miss Perceval herself.

"I declare these little narrow beds are no better than coffins! I never saw such places! and the smell is like singed blankets and cabbages boiled in melted oil! It is enough to make anybody ill! Mary! go and fetch me a cup of tea; and, do you hear! tell those people on deck not to make such a noise—it gives me a headache! Be sure you say that I shall complain to the captain. Reach me some bread and milk for the parrot,—fetch my smelling-bottle,—go to the saloon for that book I was reading,—and search again for the pocket-handkerchief I mislaid. It cost ten guineas, and must be found. I hope no one has stolen it! Now do make haste with the tea! What are you dawdling there for? If you do not stop that noise on deck, Mary, I shall be exceedingly displeased! Some of those horrid people in the steerage were smoking too, but tell the captain that if I come up he must forbid them. It is a trick to make us all sick and save provisions. I observed a gun-case in the saloon too, which is a most dangerous thing, for guns always go off when you least expect. If any one fires, I shall fall into hysterics. I shall, indeed! What a creaking noise the vessel makes! I hope there is no danger of its splitting! We ought not to go on sailing after dusk. The captain must positively cast anchor during the night, that we may have no more of this noise or motion, but sleep in peace and quietness till morning."

Soon after the Royal Pandemonium had set sail, or rather set fire, the wind freshened, and the pitching of the vessel became so rough, that Harry and Laura, with great difficulty, staggered to seats on the deck, leaving both Lady Harriet's servants so very sick below, that instead of being able to attend on them, they gave nine times the trouble that any other passenger did on board, and were not visible again during the whole voyage. The two young travellers now sat down together, and watched, with great curiosity, several groups of strangers on deck; ladies, half sick, trying to entertain gentlemen in seal-skin travelling caps and pale cadaverous countenances, smoking cigars; others opening baskets of provisions, and eating with good seafaring appetite; while one party had a carriage on the deck so filled with luxuries of every kind, that there seemed no end to the multitude of Perigord pies, German sausages, cold fowls, pastry, and fruit that were produced during the evening. The owners had a table spread on the deck, and ate voraciously, before a circle of hungry spectators, which had such an appearance of selfishness and gluttony, that both his young friends thought immediately of Peter Grey.

As evening closed in, Harry and Laura began to feel very desolate, thus for the first time in their lives alone, while the wide waste of waters around made the scene yet more forlorn. They had enjoyed unmingled delight in talking over and over about their happy meeting with Frank, and planned a hundred times how joyfully they would rush into the house, and with what pleasure they would relate all that happened to themselves, after hearing from his own mouth the extraordinary adventures which his letters had described. Laura produced from her reticule several of the last she had received, and laughed again over the funny jokes and stories they contained, inventing many new questions to ask him on the subject, and fancying she already heard his voice, and saw his bright and joyous countenance. But now the night had grown so dark and chilly, that both Harry and Laura felt themselves gradually becoming cold, melancholy, and dejected. They made an effort to walk arm-in-arm up and down the deck, in imitation of the few other passengers who had been able to remain out of bed, and they tried still to talk cheerfully, but in spite of every effort, their thoughts became mournful. After clinging together for some time, and staggering up and down, without feeling in spirits to speak, they were still shiveringly cold, yet unwilling to separate for the night, when Harry suddenly stood still, grasping Laura's arm with a look of startled astonishment, which caused her hastily to glance round in the direction where he was eagerly gazing, yet nothing became visible but the dim outline of a woman's figure, rolled up in several enormous shawls, and with her bonnet slouched far over her face.

"I am certain it was her!" whispered Harry, in a tone of breathless amazement; "almost certain!"

"Who?" asked Laura, eagerly.

Without answering, Harry sprung forward, and seized the unknown person by the arm, who instantly looked round.——It was Mrs. Crabtree!

"I am sorry you observed me, Master Harry! I did not intend to trouble you and Miss Laura during the voyage," said she, turning her face slowly towards him, when, to his surprise, he saw that the traces of tears were on her cheek, and her manner appeared so subdued, and altogether so different from former times, that Laura could yet scarcely credit her senses. "I shall not be at all in your way, children, but I—— ——I must see Master Frank again. He was always too good for this world, and he'll not be here long—Andrew told me all about it, and I could not stay behind. I wish we were all as well prepared, and then the sooner we die the better."

Harry and Laura listened in speechless consternation to these words. The very idea of losing Frank had never before crossed their imaginations for a moment, and they could have wished to believe that what Mrs. Crabtree said was like the ravings of delirium, yet an irresistible feeling of awe and alarm rushed into their minds.

"Miss Laura! if you want help in undressing, call to me at any time. I was sure that doited body Harrison would be of no service. She never was fit to take care of herself, and far less of such as you. It put me wild to think of your coming all this way with nobody fit to look after you, and then the distress that must follow."

"But surely, Mrs. Crabtree, you do not think Frank so very ill?" asked Laura, making an effort to recover her voice, and speaking in a tone of deep anxiety. "He had recovered from the fever, but is only rather too weak for travelling."

"Well, Miss Laura, grief always comes too soon, and I would have held my tongue had I thought you did not know the worst already. If I might order as in former days, it would be to send you both down directly, out of this heavy fog and cold wind."

"But you may order us, Mrs. Crabtree," said Harry, taking her kindly by the hand; "we are very glad to see you again! and I shall do whatever you bid me! So you came all this way on purpose for us! How very kind!"

"Master Harry, I would go round the wide world to serve any of you! who else have I to care for! But it was chiefly to see Master Frank. Let us hope the best, and pray to be prepared for any event that may come. All things are ordained for good, and we can only make the best of what happens. The world must go round,—it must go round, and we can't prevent it."

Harry and Laura hung their heads in dismay, for there was something agitated and solemn in Mrs. Crabtree's manner, which astonished and shocked them, so they hurried silently to bed; and Laura's pillow was drenched with tears of anxiety and distress that night, though gradually, as she thought of Frank's bright colour and sparkling eyes, his joyous spirits and unbroken health, it seemed impossible that all were so soon to fade away, that the wind should have already passed over them, and they were gone, till by degrees her mind became more calm; her hopes grew into certainties; she told herself twenty times over, that Mrs. Crabtree must be entirely mistaken, and at last sunk into a restless agitated slumber.

Next day the sun shone, the sky was clear, and everything appeared so full of life and joy, that Harry and Laura would have fancied the whole scene with Mrs. Crabtree a distressing dream, had they not been awakened to recollection before six in the morning, by the sound of her voice, angrily rebuking Miss Perceval and other ladies, who with too good reason were grumbling at the hardship of sleeping, or rather vainly attempting to sleep, in such narrow uncomfortable dogholes. Laura heard Mrs. Crabtree conclude an eloquent oration on the subject of contentment, by saying, "Indeed, ladies! many a brave man, and noblemen's sons too, have laid their heads on the green grass, fighting for you, so we should put up with a hard bed patiently for one night."

Miss Perceval turned angrily away, and summoned her maid to receive a multitude of new directions. "Mary, tell the Captain that when I looked out last, there was scarcely any smoke coming out of the funnel, so I am sure he is saving fuel, and not keeping good enough fires to carry us on! I never knew such shabbiness! Tell the engineer, that I insist on his throwing on more coals immediately. Bring me some hot water, as fast as possible. These towels are so coarse, I cannot, on any account, use them. After being accustomed to such pocket-handkerchiefs as mine, at ten guineas each, one does become particular. Can you not find a larger basin? This looks like a soup-plate, and it seems impossible here to get enough of hot water to wash comfortably."

"She should be put into the boiler of the steamboat," muttered Mrs. Crabtree. "I wish them animal-magnifying doctors would put the young lady to sleep till we arrive in London."

"Now!" continued Miss Perceval, "get me another cup of tea. The last was too sweet, the one before not strong enough, and the first half cold, but this is worse than any. Do remember to mention, that yesterday night the steward sent up a tin tea-pot, a thing I cannot possibly suffer again. We must have the urn too, instead of that black tea-kettle; and desire him to prepare some butter-toast—I am not hungry, so three rounds will be enough. Let me have some green tea this time; and see that the cream is better than last night, when I am certain it was thickened with chalk or snails. The jelly, too, was execrable, for it tasted like sticking-plaster—I shall starve if better can't be had; and the table-cloth looked like a pair of old sheets. Tell the steward all this, and say he must get my breakfast ready on deck in half an hour; but meantime I shall sit here with a book while you brush my hair."

The sick persecuted maid seemed anxious to do all she was bid; so after delivering as many of the messages as possible, she tried to stand up and do Miss Perceval's hair, but the motion of the vessel had greatly increased, and she turned as pale as death, apparently on the point of sinking to the ground, when Laura, now quite dressed, quietly slipped the brush out of her hand, and carefully brushed Miss Perceval's thin locks, while poor Mary silently dropped upon a seat, being perfectly faint with sickness.

Miss Perceval read on, without observing the change of abigails, till Harry, who had watched this whole scene from the cabin-door, made a hissing noise, such as grooms do when they curry-comb a horse, which caused the young lady to look hastily round, when great was Miss Perceval's astonishment to discover her new abigail, with a very pains-taking look, brushing her hair, while poor Mary lay more dead than alive on the benches. "Well! I declare! was there ever anything so odd!" she exclaimed in a voice of amazement. "How very strange! What can be the matter with Mary! There is no end to the plague of servants!"

"Or rather to the plague of mistresses!" thought Laura, while she glanced from Miss Perceval's round, red, bustling face, to the poor suffering maid, who became worse and worse during the day, for there came on what sailors call "a capful of wind," which gradually rose to a "stiff breeze," or what the passengers considered a hurricane; and, towards night, it attained the dignity of a real undeniable "storm." A scene of indescribable tumult then ensued. The captain attempted to make his voice heard above the roaring tempest, using a torrent of unintelligible nautical phrases, and an incessant volley of very intelligible oaths. The sailors flew about, and every plank in the vessel seemed creaking and straining, but high above all, the shrill tones of Miss Perceval were audibly heard exclaiming,

"Are there enough of 'hands' on board? Is there any danger? Are you sure the boiler will not burst? I wish steamboats had never been invented! People are sure to be blown up to the clouds, or sunk to the bottom of the ocean, or scalded to death, like so many lobsters. I cannot stand this any longer! Stop the ship, and set me on shore instantly!"

Laura clung closer to Harry, and felt that they were like two mere pigmies, amid the wide waste of waters, rolling and tossing around them, while his spirits, on the contrary, rose to the highest pitch of excitement with all he heard and saw, till at length, wishing to enjoy more of the "fun," he determined to venture above board. By the time Harry's nose was on a level with the deck, he gazed around, and saw that not a person appeared visible except two sailors, both lashed to the helm, while all was silent now, except the deafening noise made by the wild waves, and the stormy blast, which seemed as if it would blow his teeth down his throat. Harry thought the two men looked no larger than mice in such a scene, and stood, clinging to the bannisters, perfectly entranced with astonishment and admiration at the novelty of all he saw, and thinking how often Frank must have been in such scenes, when suddenly a wave washed quite over the deck, and he felt his arm grasped by Mrs. Crabtree, who desired him to come down immediately, in a tone of authority which he did not even yet feel bold enough to disobey; therefore, slowly and reluctantly he descended to the cabin, where the only living thing that seemed well enough to move, was Miss Perceval's tongue.

"Steward!" she cried, in sharp angry accents, "Steward! here is water pouring down the sky-lights like a shower bath! Look at my band-box swimming on the floor! Mary! tiresome creature! don't you see that! My best bonnet will be destroyed! Send the captain here! He must positively stop that noise on deck; it is quite intolerable! My head aches, as if it would burst like the boiler of a steamboat! Stupid man! Can't he put into some port, or cast anchor? How can he keep us all uncomfortable in this way! Mary! Mary! I say! are you deaf? Steward! send one of the sailors here to take care of this dog! I declare poor Frisk is going to be sick! Mary! Mary! This is insufferable! I wish the captain would come and help me to scold my maid! I shall certainly give you warning, Mary."

This awful threat had but little effect on one who thought herself on the brink of being buried beneath the waves, besides being too sick to care whether she died the next minute or not; and even Miss Perceval's voice became drowned at last in the tremendous storm which raged throughout the night, during which the captain rather increased Laura's panic, if that were possible, by considerately putting his head into the cabin now and then to say, "Don't be afraid, ladies! There is no danger!"

"But I must come up and see what you are about, Captain!" exclaimed Miss Perceval.

"You had better be still, ma'am," replied Mrs. Crabtree. "It is as well to be drowned in bed as on deck."

Nothing gives a more fearful idea of the helplessness of man, and the wrath of God, than a tempestuous sea during the gloom of midnight; and every mind on board became awed into silence and solemnity during this war of elements, till at length, towards morning, while the hurricane seemed yet raging with undiminished fury, Laura suddenly gave an exclamation of rapture, on hearing a sailor at the helm begin to sing Tom Bowling. "Now I feel sure the danger is over," said she, "otherwise that man could not have the heart to sing! If I live a century, I shall always like a sailor's song for the future."

It is seldom that any person's thankfulness after danger bears a fair proportion to the fear they felt while it lasted; but Harry and Laura had been taught to remember where their gratitude was due, and felt it the more deeply next day, when they entered the Yarmouth Roads, and were shown the masts of several vessels, appearing partly above the water, which had on various occasions been lost in that wilderness of shoals, where so many melancholy catastrophes have occurred.

After sailing up the Thames, and duly staring at Greenwich Hospital, the hulks, and the Tower of London, they landed at last; and having offered Mrs. Crabtree a place in the hackney coach, they hurried impatiently into it, eager for the happy moment of meeting with Frank. Harry, in his ardour, thought that no carriage had ever driven so slowly before. He wished there had been a railroad through the town; and far from wasting a thought upon the novelties of Holborn or Piccadilly, he and Laura gained no idea of the metropolis, more distinct than that of the Irishman who complained he could not see London for the quantity of houses. One only idea filled their hearts, and brightened their countenances, while they looked at each other with a smile of delight, saying, "Now at last, we are going to see Frank!"

THE ARRIVAL

What is life?——a varied tale,
Deeply moving, quickly told.
WILLIS

"OH! WHAT A lovely cottage!" exclaimed Laura, in an ecstasy of joy, when they stopped before a beautiful house, with large airy windows down to the ground; walls that seemed one brilliant mass of roses; rich flowery meadows in front, and a bright smooth lawn behind stretching down to the broad bosom of the Thames, which reflected on its glassy surface innumerable boats, filled with gay groups of merry people.

"That is such a place as I have often dreamed of, but never saw before! It seems made for perfect happiness!"

"Yes, how delightful to live here with Frank and Uncle David!" added Harry. "We shall be sailing on the water all day!"

The cottage gate was now opened, and Major Graham himself appeared under the porch; but instead of hurrying forward, as he always formerly did, to welcome them after the very shortest separation, he stood gravely and silently at the door, without so much as raising his eyes from the ground; and the paleness of his countenance filled both Harry and Laura with astonishment. They flew to meet him, making an exclamation of joy; but after embracing them affectionately, he did not utter a word, and led the way with hurried and agitated steps into a sitting-room.

"Where is Frank?" exclaimed Harry, looking eagerly round. "Why is he not here? Call him down! Tell him we are come!"

A long pause ensued; and Laura trembled when she looked at her uncle, who was some moments before he could speak, and sat down taking each of them by the hand, with such a look of sorrow and commiseration, that they were filled with alarm.

"My dear Harry and Laura!" said he solemnly, "you have never known grief till now; but if you love me, listen with composure. I have sad news to tell, yet it is of the very greatest consequence that you should bear up with fortitude. Frank is extremely ill; and the joy he felt about your coming, has agitated him so much, that he is worse than you can possibly conceive. It probably depends upon your conduct now, whether he survives this night or not. Frank knows you are here; he is impatient for you to embrace him; he becomes more and more agitated every moment the meeting is delayed; yet if you give way to childish grief, or even to childish joy, upon seeing him again, the doctors think it may cause his immediate death. You might hear his breathing in any part of this house. He is in the lowest extreme of weakness! It will be a dreadful scene for you both. Tell me, Harry and Laura, can you trust yourselves? Can you, for Frank's own sake, enter his room this moment as quietly as if you had seen him yesterday, and speak to him with composure?"

Laura felt, on hearing these words, as if the very earth had opened under her feet,—a choking sensation arose in her throat,—her colour fled,—her limbs shook,—her whole countenance became convulsed with anguish,—but making a resolute effort, she looked anxiously at Harry, and then said, in a low, almost inaudible voice,

"Uncle David! we are able,—God will strengthen us. I dare not think a moment. The sooner it is done the better. Let us go now."

Major Graham slowly led the way without speaking, till he reached the bed-room door, where he paused for a moment, while Harry and Laura listened to the gasping sound of Frank struggling for breath.

"Remember you will scarcely know him," whispered he, looking doubtfully at Laura's pallid countenance; "but a single expression of emotion may be fatal. Show your love for Frank now, my dear children. Spare him all agitation,—forget your own feelings for his sake."

When Harry and Laura entered the room, Frank buried his face in his hands, and leaned them on the table, saying, in convulsive accents, "Go away, Laura!—oh go away just now! I cannot bear it yet!—leave me!—leave me!"

If Laura had been turned into marble at the moment, she could not have seemed more perfectly calm, for her mind was wound up to an almost supernatural effort, and advancing to the place where he sat, without attempting to speak, she took Frank by the hand—Harry did the same; and not a sound was heard for some moments, but the convulsive struggles of Frank himself, while he gasped for breath, and vainly tried to speak, till at length he raised his head and fixed his eyes on Laura. Then, for the first time, was she struck with the dreadful conviction, that this meeting was but a prelude to their immediate and final separation. The pale ashy cheek, the hollow eye, the sharp and altered features, all told a tale of anguish such as she had never before conceived, and a cold tremor passed through her frame, as she stood amazed and bewildered with grief, while the past, the present, and the future seemed all one mighty heap of agony. Still she gazed steadily on Frank, and said nothing, conscious that the smallest indulgence of emotion would bring forth a torrent which nothing could control, and determined, unless her heart ceased to beat, that he should see nothing to increase his agitation.

At length, in a low, faint, broken voice, Frank was able to speak, and looking with affectionate sympathy at Laura, he said, "Do not think, dear sister, that I always suffer as you see me now. This joy has been too much for me. I shall soon feel easier."

Major Graham observed a livid paleness come over Laura's countenance, when she attempted to answer and seeing it was impossible to sustain the trial a moment longer, he made a pretext to hurry her away. Harry instantly followed, and rushing into a vacant room, he threw himself down in an agony of grief, and wept convulsively, till the very bed shook beneath him. Hours passed on, and Major Graham left them to exhaust their grief in weeping together, but every moment seemed only to increase their agitation, as the conviction became more fearfully certain, that Frank was indeed lost to them for ever. This then was the meeting they had so often and so joyously anticipated! Laura sunk upon her knees beside Harry, and prayers were mingled with their tears, while they asked for consolation, and tried to feel resigned. "Alas!" thought she solemnly, "how truly did grandmama say, 'If the sorrows of this world are called 'light afflictions,' what must be those from which Christ died to save us!' It is merciful that we are not forbid to weep, for, oh! who ever lost such a brother?—the kindest—the best of brothers!—dear, dear Frank!—can nothing be done! Uncle David," added Laura, clinging to Major Graham, when he entered the room, "oh! say something to us about Frank getting better,—do you think he will? May we have a hope?—one single hope to live upon, that Frank may possibly be spared;—do not turn away—do not look so very sad—think how young Frank is,—and the doctors are so skilful—and—and—oh, Uncle David! he is dying! I see it! I must believe it!" continued she, wringing her hands with grief. "You cannot give us one word of hope, though the whole world would be nothing without him."

"My dear,—my very dear Laura! remember that consoling text in holy Scripture, 'Be still, and know that I am God;'—we have no idea what He can do in saving us from sorrow, or in comforting us when it comes, therefore let us seek peace from Him, and believe that all shall indeed be ordered well, even though our own hearts were to be broken with affliction. Frank has seen old Nurse Crabtree, and is now in a refreshing sleep, therefore I wish you to take the opportunity of sitting in his room, and accustoming yourselves, if possible, to the sight of his altered appearance. He is sometimes very cheerful, and always patient, therefore we must keep up our own spirits and try to assist him in bearing his sufferings, rather than increase them by showing what we feel ourselves. I was pleased with you both this morning—that meeting was no common effort, and now we must show our submission to the Divine will, difficult as that may be, by a deep heartfelt resignation to whatever He ordains."

Harry and Laura still felt stupified with grief, but they mechanically followed Major Graham into Frank's room, and sat down in a distant corner behind his chair, observing with awe and astonishment his pallid countenance, his emaciated hands, and his drooping figure, while scarcely yet able to believe that this was indeed their own beloved Frank. After they had remained immoveably still for some time, though shedding many bitter tears, as they gazed on the wreck of one so very dear, he suddenly started awake, and glanced anxiously round the room, then with a look of deep disappointment, he said to Uncle David in low, feeble accents,

"It was only a dream! I have often dreamed the same thing, when far away at sea—that would have been too much happiness! I fancied Harry and Laura were here!"

"It was no dream, dear Frank! we are here," said Laura, trying to speak in a quiet, subdued voice.

"My dear sister! then all is well; but pray sit always where I can see you. After wishing so long for our meeting, it appears nearly impossible that we are together at last."

Frank became exhausted with speaking so much, but pointed to a seat near himself, where Harry and Laura sat down, after which he gazed at them long and earnestly, with a look of affectionate pleasure, while his smile, which had lost all its former cheerfulness, was now full of tenderness and sensibility. At length his countenance gradually changed, while large tears gathered in his eyes, and coursed each other silently down his cheeks. Thoughts of the deepest sadness seemed passing through his mind during some moments, but checking the heavy sigh that rose in his breast, he riveted his hands together, and looked towards heaven with an expression of placid submission, saying these words in a scarcely audible tone though evidently addressed to those around,

"Weeping endureth for a night, but joy cometh in the morning." "We know that if our earthly house of this tabernacle be dissolved, we have a building of God, an house not made with hands, eternal in the heavens." "Weep ye not for the dead, neither bemoan him; *but* weep sore for him that goeth away: for he shall return no more, nor see his native country."*

These words fell upon the ear of Harry and Laura like a knell of death, for they now saw that Frank himself believed he was dying, and it appeared as if their last spark of hope expired when they heard this terrible dispensation announced from his own lips. He seemed anxious now that they should understand his full meaning, and receive all the consolation which his mind could afford, for he closed his eyes, and added in solemn accents,

"I must have died at some time, and why not now? If I leave friends who are very dear on earth, I go to my chief best friend in heaven. The whole peace and comfort of my mind rest on thinking of our Saviour's merits. Let us all be ready to say, 'the will of the Lord be done.' Think often, Harry and Laura, of those words we so frequently repeated to grandmama formerly:

> 'Take comfort, Christians, when your friends
>   In Jesus fall asleep;
> Their better being never ends,
>   Why then dejected weep?
> Why inconsolable as those
>   To whom no hope is given?
> Death is the messenger of peace,
>   And calls 'my' soul to Heaven.' "

Frank's voice failed, his head fell back upon the pillows, and he remained for a length of time, with his eyes closed in solemn meditation and prayer, while Laura and Harry, unable so much as to look at each other, leaned upon the table, and wept in silence.

Laura felt as if she had grown old in a moment,—as if life could give no more joy—and as if she herself stood already on the verge of the grave. It appeared like a dream that she had ever been happy, and a dreadful reality to which she was now awakened. "Behold, God taketh away! who can hinder him? who will say unto him, What doest thou?" "Cease ye from man, whose breath is in his nostrils." These were texts which forced themselves on her mind, with mournful emphasis, while she felt how helpless is earthly affection when the dispensations of God are upon us. All her love for Frank could not avert the stroke of death,—all his attachment to her must now be buried in the grave,—and the very tenderness they felt for each other, only embittered the sorrow of this dreadful moment.

From that day, Harry and Laura, according to the advice of Uncle David, testified their affection for Frank, not by tears and useless lamentations, though these were not always to be controlled in private, but by the incessant, devoted attention with which

---

*Jeremiah xxii. 10.

they watched his looks, anticipated his wishes, and thought every exertion a pleasure which could in the slightest degree contribute to his comfort. Frank, on his part, spared their feelings, by often concealing what he suffered, and by speaking of his own death, as if it had been a journey on which he must prepare with readiness to enter, reminding them, that never to die, was never to be happy, as all they saw him endure from sickness, became nothing to what he endured from struggling against sin and temptation, which were, the great evils of existence,—and that from all these he would be for ever freed by death. "Those who are prepared for the change," added he solemnly, "can neither live too long, nor die too soon; for when God gives us his blessing, He then sends heaven, as it were, into the soul before the soul ascends to heaven; and I trust to being gifted with faith and submission for all that may be ordained during my few remaining hours upon earth."

Yet, with every desire to feel resigned, Frank himself was sometimes surprised out of his usual fortitude, especially when thinking that he must never more hope to see Lady Harriet, towards whom he cast many a longing and affecting thought, saying once, with deep emotion, "If I could only see grandmama again I should feel quite well!" One evening, as he sat near an open window, gazing on the rich tints of twilight, and breathing with more than usual ease, a wandering musician paused with her guitar, and sung several airs with great pathos and expression. At length she played the tune of "Home! sweet home," to which Frank listened for some moments with intense agitation, till, clasping his hands and bursting into tears, he exclaimed, in accents of powerful emotion,

"Home! That happy home! Oh! never—never more,—*my* home is in the grave."

Laura wept convulsively while he added in broken accents, "I shall still be remembered——still lamented——you must not love me too well, Laura,—not as I love you, or your sorrow would be too great; but long hence, when Harry and you are happy together, surrounded with friends, think sometimes of one who must for ever be absent,—who loved you better than them all,—whose last prayer will be for you both. Oh! who can tell what my feelings are! I can do nothing now but cause distress and anguish to those who love me best!"

"Frank, I would not exchange your affection for the wealth of worlds. As long as I live, it will be my greatest earthly happiness to have had such a brother, and if we are to suffer a sorrow that I cannot name and dare not think of, you are teaching me how to bear it, and leaving us the only comfort we can have in knowing that you are happy."

"Many plans and many hopes I had for the future, Laura," added Frank; "but there is no future to me now in this world. Perhaps I may escape a multitude of sorrows, but how gladly would I have shared all yours, and insured my best happiness, by uniting with Harry and you in living to God. If you both learn more by my death than by my life, then, indeed, I do rejoice. With respect to myself it matters but little a few years or hours sooner, for I may say, in the words of Job, 'though He slay me, yet will I trust in him.' "

Frank's sufferings increased every day, and became so very great at last, that the doctor proposed giving him strong doses of laudanum, to bring on a stupor and allay the pain; but when this was mentioned to him he said, "I know it is my duty to take whatever you prescribe, and I certainly shall, but if we can do without opiates, let me entreat you to refrain from them. Often formerly at sea I used to think it very sad how few of those I attended in sickness, were allowed by the physician to die in possession of their senses, on account of being made to take laudanum, which gave them false spirits and temporary ease. Let me retain my faculties as long as they are mercifully granted to me. I can bear pain,—at least, God grant me strength to do so,—but I cannot willingly enter the presence of my Creator in a state little short of intoxication."

Many days of agony followed this resolution on the part of Frank, but though the medicine, which would have brought some hours of oblivion, lay within reach, he persevered in wishing to preserve his consciousness, whatever suffering it might cost; and though now and then a prayer for bodily relief was wrung from him in his acute agony, the most frequent and fervent supplications that he uttered night and day were, in an accent of intense emotion, "God have mercy upon my soul."

Harry and Laura were surprised to find the fields and walks near London so very rural and beautiful as they appeared at Hammersmith, and to meet with much more simplicity and kindness among the common people than they had anticipated. The poorer neighbours, who became aware of their affliction, testified a degree of sympathy which frequently astonished them, and was often afterwards remembered with pleasure, one instance of which seemed peculiarly touching to Laura. Frank always suffered most acutely during the night, and seldom closed his eyes in sleep till morning, therefore she invariably remained with him, to beguile those weary hours, while any remonstrance on his part against so fatiguing a duty became a mere waste of words, as she only grew sadder and paler, saying, there would be time enough to take care of herself, when she could no longer be of use to him. The earliest thing that gave any relief to Frank's cough every day, generally was, a tumbler of milk warm from the cow, which had been ordered for him, and was brought almost as soon as the dawn of light. Once, when Frank had been unusually ill, and sighed in restless agony till morning, Laura watched impatiently for day, and when the milkman was seen at six o'clock, slowly trudging through the fields, and advancing leisurely towards the house, Laura hurried eagerly down to meet him, exclaiming in accents of joy, while she held out the tumbler, "Oh, I am so glad you are come at last!"

"At last, miss!! I am as early as usual!" replied he gruffly. "It's not many poor folks that gets up so soon to their work, and if you had to labour as hard as me all day, you would maybe think the morning came too soon."

"I am seldom in my bed all night," answered Laura, sadly. "My poor sick brother cannot rest till this milk is brought, and I wait with him, hour after hour till daylight, wearying for you to come."

The old dairyman looked with sorrowful surprise at Laura, while she, thinking no more of what had passed, hurried away; but next morning, when sitting up with Frank, she became surprised to observe the milkman a whole hour earlier than usual, plodding along towards his cattle at a peculiarly rapid pace. He stayed not more than five minutes, only milking one cow, though all the others gathered round him, and as soon as he had filled his little pail, he came straight towards Major Graham's cottage and knocked at the door. Laura instantly ran down to thank him with her whole heart for his kind attention, after which, as long as Frank continued ill, the old dairyman rose long before his usual time, to bring this welcome refreshment.

Frank desired Laura to beg that he would not take so much trouble, or else to insist on his accepting some remuneration, but the old man would neither discontinue the custom, nor receive any recompense.

"Let me see this kind good dairyman, to thank him myself," said Frank, one night, when he felt rather easier; and next morning, Laura invited poor Teddy Collins to walk up stairs, who looked exceedingly astonished, though very much pleased at the proposal, saying, "Maybe, ma'am, the poor young gentleman would not like to see a stranger like me!"

"No one is a stranger who feels for him as you have done," replied Laura, leading the way, and Frank's countenance lighted up with a smile of pleasure when they entered his room. He held out his thin emaciated hand to Teddy, who looked earnestly and sorrowfully in his face as he grasped hold of it, saying, "You look very poorly, sir! I'm afraid indeed you are sadly ill."

"That I am! as ill as any one can be on this side of eternity! My tale is told, my days are numbered; but I would not go out of this world without saying how grateful we both feel for your attention. As a cup of cold water given in Christian kindness shall hereafter be rewarded, I trust also that your attention to me may not be forgotten."

"You are heartily welcome, sir! It is a great honour for a poor old man like me to oblige anybody. I shall not long be able for work now, seeing that I am upwards of threescore and ten, and my days are already full of labour and sorrow."

"To both of us, then, the night is far spent, and the day is at hand," replied Frank—"How strange it seems, that, old as you are, I am still older; my feeble frame will be sooner worn out, and my body laid at rest in the grave! Let me hope that you have already applied your heart to wisdom, for every child of earth must sooner or later, find how short is everything but eternity. While I appear before you here as a spectacle of mortality, think how soon and how certainly you must follow. May you then find, as I do, that even in the last extreme of sickness and sorrow, there is comfort in looking forward to such blessings as 'eye hath not seen, nor ear heard.' Farewell, my kind friend! In this world we shall meet no more, but there is another and a better."

The old man, apparently unwilling to withdraw, paused for some moments after Frank had ceased to speak. He muttered a few inaudible words in reply, and then slowly and sorrowfully left the room, while Frank's head sunk languidly on the pillows, and Laura retired to her room, where, as usual, she wept herself to sleep.

When Harry and Laura first arrived at Hammersmith, Frank felt anxious that they should walk out every day for the benefit of their health; but finding that each made frequent excuses for remaining constantly with him at home, he invented a plan which induced them to take exercise regularly.

Being early in June, strawberries were yet so exceedingly rare, that they could scarcely be had for any money; but the doctor had allowed his patient to eat fruit. Frank asked his two young attendants to wander about in quest of gardens where a few strawberries could be got, and to bring him some. Accordingly, they set out one morning; and after a long, unsuccessful search, at last observed a small green-house near the road, with one little basket in the window, scarcely larger than a thimble, containing two or three delicious King's seedlings, perfectly ripe. These were to be sold for five shillings; but hardly waiting to ascertain the price, Laura seized this welcome prize with delight, and paid for it on the spot. Every morning afterwards, her regular walk was to hasten with Harry towards this pretty little shop, where they talked to the gardener about poor

Frank being so very ill, and told him that this fine fruit was wanted for their sick brother at home.

One day the invalid seemed so much worse than usual, that neither Harry nor Laura could bear to leave him a moment; so they requested Mrs. Crabtree to fetch the strawberries, which she readily agreed to do; but on drawing out her purse in the shop, and saying that she came to buy that little basket of fruit at the window, what was her astonishment when the gardener looked civil and sorry, answering that he would not sell those strawberries if she offered him a guinea apiece.

"No!" exclaimed Mrs. Crabtree, getting into a rage; "then what do you put them up at the window for? There is no use pretending to keep a shop, if you will not sell what is in it! Give me these strawberries this minute, and here's your five shillings!"

"It is quite impossible," replied the gardener, holding back the basket. "You see, ma'am, every day last week, a little master and miss came to this here shop, buying my strawberries for a young gentleman who is very ill; and they look both so sweet and so mournful like, that I would not disappoint them for all the world. They seem later to-day than usual, and are, maybe, not coming at all; but if I lose my day's profits, it can't be helped. They shall not walk here for nothing if they please to come!"

When Mrs. Crabtree explained that she belonged to the same family as Harry and Laura, the gardener looked hard at her to see if she were attempting to deceive him; but feeling convinced that she spoke the truth, he begged her to carry off the basket to his young friends, positively refusing to take the price.

THE LAST BIRTH-DAY

Mere human power shall fast decay,
And youthful vigour cease;
But they who wait upon the Lord
In strength shall still increase.

FRANK FELT no unnatural apathy or indifference about dying, for he looked upon it with awe though not with fear; nor did he express any rapturous excitement on the solemn occasion, knowing that death is an appointed penalty for transgression, which, though deprived of its sharpest sting by the triumphs of the cross, yet awfully testifies to all succeeding generations, that each living man has individually merited the utmost wrath of God, and that the last moment on earth, of even the most devoted Christian, must be darkened by the gloom of our original sin and natural corruption. Yet, "as in Adam all die, so in Christ are all made alive;" and amidst the throng of consolatory and affecting meditations that crowded into his mind on the great subject of our salvation, he kept a little book in which were carefully recorded such texts and reflections as he considered likely to strengthen his own faith, and to comfort those he left behind—saying one day to Major Graham,

"Tell grandmama, that though my days have been few upon the earth, they were happy! When you think of me, Uncle David, after my sufferings are over, it may well be a pleasing remembrance, that you were always the best, the kindest of friends. Oh! how kind!—but I must not—cannot speak of that——. This is my birth-day! my last birth-day! Many a joyous one we kept together, but those merry days are over, and these sadder ones too shall cease; yet the time is fast approaching, so welcome to us both,

'When death-divided friends at last
Shall meet to part no more.' "

In the evening, Major Graham observed that Frank made Mrs. Crabtree bring everything belonging to him, and lay it on the table, when he employed himself busily in tying up a number of little parcels, remarking, with a languid smile,

"My possessions are not valuable, but these are for some old friends and messmates, who will be pleased to receive a trifling memorial of one who loved them. Send my dirk to Peter Grey, who is much reformed now. Here are all the letters any of you ever sent me; how very often they have been read! but now, even that intercourse must end; keep them, for they were the dearest treasures I possessed. At Madras, formerly, I remember hearing of a nabob who was bringing his whole fortune home in a chest of gold, but the ropes for hoisting his treasure on board were so insufficient, that the whole gave way, and it fell into the ocean, never to be recovered. That seemed a very sudden termination of his hopes and plans, but scarcely more unexpected than my own. 'We are a wind that passeth away and cometh not again.' Many restless nights are ordained for me now, probably, that I may find no resource but prayer and meditation. Others can afford time to slumber, but I so soon shall sleep the sleep of death, that it becomes a blessing to have such hours of solitary thought, for preparing my heart, and establishing my faith, during this moment of need."

"Yes, Frank, but your prayers are not solitary, for ours are joined to yours," added Laura. "I read in an old author lately, that Christian friends in this world might be compared to travellers going along the same road in separate carriages—sometimes they are together—often they are apart—sometimes they can exchange assistance, as we do now—and often they jostle against each other, till at last, having reached the journey's end, they are removed out of these earthly vehicles into a better state, where they shall look back upon former circumstances, and know even as they are known."

Laura was often astonished to observe the change which had taken place in her own character and feelings, within the very short period of their distress. Her extreme terror of a thunder-storm formerly had occasioned many a jest to her brothers, when Harry used, ocasionally, to roll heavy weights in the room above her own, to imitate the loudest peals, while Frank sometimes endeavoured to argue her out of that excessive apprehension with which she listened to the most distant surmise of a storm. Now, however, at Hammersmith, long after midnight, the moon, on one occasion, became completely obscured by dense heavy clouds, and the air felt so oppressively hot, that Frank, who seemed unusually breathless, drew closer to the window. Laura supported his head, and was deeply occupied in talking to him, when suddenly a broad flash of lightning glared into the room, followed by a crash of thunder that seemed to crack the very heavens. Again, and again, the lightning gleamed in her face with such vividness, that Laura fancied she could distinguish the heat of it, and yet she stirred not, nor did a single exclamation, as in former days, arise on her lips.

"Pray shut the window, Laura," said Frank, languidly, raising his eyes; "and be so kind as to close the shutters!"

"Why, Frank?—you never used to be alarmed by thunder!"

"No! nor am I now, dear Laura. What danger need a dying person fear? Some few hours sooner or later would be of little consequence—

> Come he slow, or come he fast,
> It is but death that comes at last.

Yet, Laura, do you think I have forgotten old times! Oh! no!—not while I live. You attend to my feelings, and surely it is my duty to remember yours."

"Never mind me, Frank!" whispered Laura. "I have got over all that folly. When real fears and sorrows come, we care no more about those that were imaginary."

"True, my dear sister; and there is no courage or fortitude like that derived from faith in a superintending providence. Though all creation reel, we may sleep in peace, for to Christians, 'danger is safe, and tumult calm.' "

When Frank grew worse, he became often delirious. Yet as in health he had been habitually cheerful, his mind generally wandered to agreeable subjects. He fancied himself walking on the bright meadows, and picking flowers by the river side,—meeting Lady Harriet, and even speaking to his father, as if Sir Edward had been present; while Harry and Laura listened, weeping and trembling to behold the wreck of such a mind and heart as his. One evening, he seemed unusually well, and requested that his armchair might be wheeled to the open window, where he gazed with delight at the hills and meadows,—the clouds and glittering water,—the cattle standing in the stream,—the boats reflected on its surface,—and the roses fluttering at every casement.

"Those joyous little birds!—their song makes me cheerful," said he, in a tone of placid enjoyment. "I have been in countries where the birds never sing, and the leaves never fade; but they excited no sympathy or interest. Here we have notes of gladness both in sunshine and storm, teaching us a lesson of grateful contentment,—while those drooping roses preach a sermon to me, for as easily might they recover freshness and bloom as myself. We shall both lie low before long in the dust, yet a spring shall come hereafter to revive even the 'ashes of the urn.' Then, Uncle David, we meet again,—not as now, amidst sorrow and suffering, with death and separation before us, but blessed by the consciousness that our sins are forgiven,—our trials all ended,—and that our afflictions, which were but for a moment, have worked out for us a far more exceeding, even an eternal weight of glory."

Some hours afterwards, the doctor entered. After receiving a cordial welcome from Frank, and feeling his pulse, he instantly examined his arms and neck, which were covered entirely over with small red spots, upon observing which the friendly physician suddenly changed countenance, and stole an alarmed glance at Major Graham.

"I feel easier and better to-day, doctor, than at any time since my illness," said Frank, looking earnestly in his face. "Do you think this eruption will do me good? Life has much that would be dear to me, while I have friends like these to live for. Can it be possible that I may yet recover?"

The doctor turned away, unable to reply, while Frank intensely watched his countenance, and then gazed at the pale agitated face of Major Graham. Gradually the hope which had brightened in his cheek began to fade,—the lustre of his eye became dim,—his countenance settled into an expression of mournful resignation,—and covering his face with his hands, he said, in a voice of deep emotion,

"I see how it is!—God's will be done!"

The silence of death succeeded, while Frank laid his head on the pillow and closed his eyes. A few natural tears coursed each other slowly down his cheek; but at length, an hour or two afterwards, being completely exhausted, he fell into a gentle sleep, from which the doctor considered it very doubtful if he would ever awaken, as the red spots indicated mortification, which must inevitably terminate his life before next day.

Laura retired to the window, making a strenuous effort to restrain her feelings, that she might be enabled to witness the last awful scene; and fervently did she pray for such strength to sustain it with fortitude, as might still render her of some use to her dying brother. Her pale countenance might almost have been mistaken for that of a corpse, but for the expression of living agony in her eye; and she was sunk in deep, solemn thought, when her attention became suddenly roused by observing a chariot and four drive furiously up to the gate, while the horses were foaming and panting as they stopped. A tall gentleman, of exceedingly striking appearance, sprung hurriedly out, walked rapidly towards the cottage door, and in another minute entered Frank's room, with the animated look of one who expected to be gladly welcomed, and to occasion an agreeable surprise.

Harry and Laura shrunk close to their uncle, when the stranger, now in evident agitation, gazed round the room with an air of painful astonishment, till Major Graham looked round, and instantly started up with an exclamation of amazement, "Edward! is it possible! This is indeed a consolation! You are still in time!"

"In time!!" exclaimed Sir Edward, grasping his brother's hand with vehement agitation. "Do you mean to say Frank is yet in danger?"

Major Graham mournfully shook his head, and undrawing the bed-curtains, he silently pointed to the sleeping countenance of Frank, which was as still as death, and already overspread by a ghastly paleness. Sir Edward then sunk into a chair, and clenched his hands over his forehead with a look of unspeakable anguish, saying, in an under tone, "Worn out, as I am, in mind and body, I needed not this to destroy me! Say at once, brother, is there any hope?"

"None, my dear Edward! None! Even now he is insensible, and I fear with little prospect of ever becoming conscious again."

At this moment, Frank opened his eyes, which were dim and glassy, while it became evident that he had relapsed into a state of temporary delirium.

"Get more candles! how very dark it is!" he said. "Who are all those people? Send away everybody but grandmama! I must speak to her alone. Never tell papa of all this, it would only distress him—say nothing about me. Why do Harry and Laura never come? They have been absent more than a week! Who took away Uncle David too?"

Laura listened for some time in an agony of grief, till, at last, unable any longer to restrain her feelings, she clasped Frank in her arms, and burst into tears, exclaiming in accents of piercing distress, "Oh Frank! Frank! have you forgotten poor Laura?"

"Not till I am dead!" whispered he, while a momentary gleam of recollection lighted up his face.

"Not even then! Laura! we meet again."

Sir Edward now wished to speak, but Frank had relapsed into a state of feeble unconsciousness, from which nothing could arouse him; once or twice he repeated the name of Laura in a low melancholy voice, till it became totally inaudible—his breath became shorter—his lips became livid—his whole frame seemed convulsed—and some hours afterwards, all that was mortal of Frank Graham ceased to exist. About four in the morning his body was at rest, and his spirit returned to God who gave it.

The candles had burned low in their sockets, and still the mourners remained, unwilling to move from the awful scene of their bereavement. Mrs. Crabtree at length, who laid out the body herself, extinguished the lights, and flung open the window curtains. Then suddenly a bright blaze of sunshine streamed into the room, and rested on the cold pale face of the dead. To the stunned and bewildered senses of Harry and Laura, the brilliant dawn of morning seemed like a mockery of their distress. Many persons were already passing by—the busy stir of life had begun, and a boy strolling along the road whistled his merry tune as he went gaily on.

"We are indeed mere atoms in the world!" thought Laura, bitterly, while these sights and sounds fell heavily on her heart. "If Harry and I had been dead also, the sun would have shone as brightly, the birds sung as joyfully, and those people been all as gay and happy as ever! Nobody is thinking of Frank—nobody knows our misery—the world is going on as if nothing had happened, and we are breaking our hearts with grief!"

Laura's agony became calm as she gazed on the peaceful and almost happy expression of those beautiful features, which had now lost all appearance of suffering. The eyes from which nothing but kindness and love had beamed upon her, were now closed for ever; the lips which had spoken only words of generous affection and pious hope, were silent; and the heart which had beat with every warm and brotherly feeling, was for the first time insensible to her sorrows; yet Laura did not give way to the strong excess of her grief, for it sunk upon her spirit with a leaden weight of anguish, which tears and lamentations could not express, and could not even relieve. She rose, and kissed, for the last time, that beloved countenance which she was never to look upon again till they met in heaven, and stole away to the silence and solitude of her own room, where she tried in vain to collect her thoughts. All seemed a dreary blank. She did not sigh—she could not weep; but she sat in dark and vacant abstraction, with one only consciousness filling her mind—the bitter remembrance that Frank was dead—that she could be of no further use to him—that she could have no future intercourse with him—that even in her prayers she could no longer have the comfort of naming him; and when at last she turned to his own Bible which he had given her, to seek for consolation, her eyes refused their office, and the pages became blistered with tears.

After Frank's funeral, Sir Edward became too ill to leave his bed; and Major Graham remained with him in constant conversation; while Harry and Laura did everything to testify their affection, and to fill the place now so sadly vacant.

On the following Sunday, several of the congregation at Hammersmith observed two young strangers in the rector's pew, dressed in the deepest mourning, with pale and downcast countenances, who glided early into church, and sat immoveably still, side by side, while Mr. Palmer gave out for his text the affecting and appropriate words which Frank himself had often repeated during his last illness, "In an hour that ye think not, the Son of man cometh."

Not a tear was shed by either Harry or Laura,—their grief was too great for utterance; yet they listened with breathless interest to the sermon, intended not only to console them, but also to instruct other young persons from the afflicting event of Frank's death.

Mr. Palmer took this opportunity to describe all the amiable dispositions of youth, and to show how much of what is pleasing may appear before religion has yet taken entire possession of the mind; but he painted in glowing colours the beautiful consistency and harmony of character which must ensue after that happy change, when the Holy Spirit renews the heart, and influences the life. It almost seemed to Harry and Laura as if Frank were visibly before their eyes, when Mr. Palmer spoke in eloquent terms of that humility which no praise could diminish,—that benevolence which attended to the feelings, as well as the wants of others,—that affection which was ever ready to make any sacrifice for those he loved,—that docility which obeyed the call of duty on every occasion,—that meekness in the midst of provocation which could not be irritated,—that gentle firmness in maintaining the truths of the gospel, which no opposition could intimidate,—that cheerful submission to suffering which saw a hand of mercy in the darkest hour,—and that faith which was ever "forgetting those things which are behind, and reaching forth unto those things which are before, pressing toward the mark for the prize of the high calling of God in Christ Jesus."

It seemed as if years had passed over the heads of Harry and Laura during the short period of their absence from home—that home where Frank had so anxiously desired to go! All was changed within and around them,—sorrow had filled their hearts, and no longer merry, thoughtless young creatures, believing the world one scene of frolicsome enjoyment and careless ease; they had now witnessed its realities,—they had felt its trials,—they had experienced the importance of religion,—they had learned the frailty of all earthly joy,—and they had received, amidst tears and sorrow, the last injunction of a dying brother, to "call upon the Lord while He is near, and to seek Him while He may yet be found."

"Uncle David," said Laura one day, several months after their return home, "Mrs. Crabtree first endeavoured to lead us aright by severity,—you and grandmama then tried what kindness would do, but nothing was effectual till now, when God Himself has laid His hand upon us. Oh! what a heavy stroke was necessary to bring me to my right mind, but now, while we weep many bitter tears, Harry and I often pray together that good may come out of evil, and that we who mourn so deeply, may find our best, our only comfort from above."

> Unthinking, idle, wild and young,
> I laugh'd, and talk'd, and danced, and sung;
> And proud of health, and frolic vain,
> Dream'd not of sorrow, care, or pain,
> Concluding in those hours of glee
> That all the world was made for me.
> But when the days of trial came,
> When sorrow shook this trembling frame,
> When folly's gay pursuits were o'er,
> And I could dance or sing no more;
> It then occurr'd how sad 'twould be
> Were this world only made for me.
>
> PRINCESS AMELIA

The Fairy Bower,
or
The History of a Month
A Tale

By HARRIET MOZLEY

Harriet Mozley (1803–1851) was the eldest daughter of the Newman family, born two years after her celebrated brother, John Henry Newman, to whom she was warmly attached throughout their childhood and youth. Her husband, Thomas Mozley, like Newman, was a fellow of Oriel College, Oxford, the center after 1833 of the Oxford Movement, sometimes called "Tractarian" after the series of *Tracts for the Times* written by its leaders. The *Tracts* sought to propagate among the public the belief that the Church of England was the true Catholic Church, in direct succession to that founded by the Apostles of Christ. They combatted the influence of the state in the affairs of the church and opposed the growth of "Protestant" or "Evangelical" or "Latitudinarian" tendencies. In 1841, after *Tract 90*, in which Newman asserted the compatibility with Roman Catholic theology of the Thirty-nine Articles of Faith of the Church of England, the Tractarians, who had aroused intense public controversy, were forbidden to publish further. After an anguished additional four years of soul-searching, Newman became a Catholic in 1845 and embarked upon four and a half decades of activity as a Catholic writer and apologist.

After John Henry Newman's conversion to Catholicism, his beloved sister Harriet Mozley never spoke to him again, a blow he keenly felt. Two years before she lost her brother to the Church of Rome, she had almost lost her husband, Tom, a man of far less intellect and stability than Newman. In 1843 he was temporarily so attracted by some friendly Catholic priests he had met that he threatened to go over to their faith. Tom Mozley did, however, remain in the Church of England; but it may have been in part because of the struggle Harriet had undergone with him that she so desperately resented her brother's apostasy.

Her remarkable story for children, *The Fairy Bower*, and its sequel, *The Lost Brooch*, both appeared in 1841, the very year of *Tract 90*, before either her husband or her brother had made an overt move toward Rome. So in these two books Harriet Mozley did not focus her attention upon the Catholics, whose threat to her own peace of mind did not yet so vitally concern her, but upon the Evangelical or "Low Church" tendencies against whose prevalence within the Church of England the Oxford Movement was striving.

While it may seem ponderous to introduce a story for children with so dense a summary of family history and of contemporary religious strife, it is truly impossible to understand and enjoy *The Fairy Bower* without appreciating its author's place in the contemporary intellectual world and recognizing the overpowering importance of religious questions in her life. With much justice, Charlotte Yonge remarked about *The Fairy Bower*, "Only a Newman could have written it."

The Fairy Bower is the story of a lie—the lie that Harry and Laura Graham of *Holiday House* would never have told, despite their naughtiness—the sin that (together with theft) seemed so heinous to the Victorians. The lie is told by a girl of about twelve, Mary Anne Duff, who allows herself to be given credit for an idea that originated with Grace Leslie, age ten, the heroine of the book: the idea of decorating a room for a Twelfth-Night party with garlands of artificial flowers and many lights, to serve as a "fairy bower" for a pet parrot. When the decorations prove a sensational success, the grown-ups crown Mary Anne queen of the evening. Grace, unwilling to expose Mary Anne's deception, says nothing, much to the guilty child's surprise and relief. Mary Anne's cousin, Emily Ward, eventually must reveal the truth—if she did not, she too would be telling a lie—and the record is set straight. But during the long period in which the mystery is being cleared up, Grace suffers because her own veracity is under a cloud. All the personages—adults and children alike—discuss the question of the fairy bower as if there were no other possible subject of conversation.

Like Catherine Sinclair with *Holiday House*, Harriet Mozley set *The Fairy Bower* in pre-Victorian times. (Grace's mother remarks, "Now we look upon the Prince Regent almost as King; but *I* cannot feel it the same. . . .") So George III is still alive, and one must date the action in the Regency Decade, 1820–1830.* As the wife of a Tractarian in 1841, at a moment when their party was under fire as too sympathetic to Rome, Harriet Mozley could more easily carry out her intention of satirizing the Evangelicals if she fixed the date of her story well before the controversies of the thirties and forties had begun.

The leading characters of *The Fairy Bower* are children—the five Duffs: Campbell (thirteen), Mary Anne (twelve), Constance and Fanny (twins, about ten), and Charlotte (younger); the three eldest Wards, cousins of the Duffs: George (thirteen), Emily (twelve), and Ellen (somewhat younger); and an additional Ward cousin, on the other side of the family, Isabella (about fourteen), daughter of a recently created peer, Lord Musgrove. In the course of the short novel, each of these many children emerges as a character in his own right: Campbell serious and stable, Mary Anne easily swayed and not very intelligent, with a "bad spirit and a wrong temper," Constance intensely religious and arrogantly self-confident, Fanny romantically foolish, sentimental, and self-dramatizing, Charlotte already showing signs of steadiness and maturity; George Ward good-natured and witty, Emily kind and impulsive, Ellen grave and reflective, Cousin Isabella affected and pretentious, so given to exaggeration that she often is on the verge of lying without realizing it. Nor does Harriet Mozley merely describe these qualities; she shows us each child talking and acting in character.

Grace Leslie, the heroine, is preternaturally good by any standard: regular and devoted in her habits of study, deeply fond of her widowed mother—whom she tries to protect against the world—already pondering in bed her own "past and present being; the existence and character of God, the true meaning of . . . Eternity," and the difficulty of reconciling the concept of an all-loving, all-powerful God with the idea of eternal punishment. Thus philosophical at the age of ten, Grace is also well-read enough to respond in kind when publicly addressed in extempore verse by her erudite godfather: twice she aptly caps his verses calling her a grace and a muse. But, reassuringly, she cannot do it every time. Kind, considerate, naturally pious, determined to search her soul before acting and to do what is right, Grace only just avoids priggishness. She is credible only in her setting: a world where other children show "a deep sense of religion at four," or are so steeped in "sensibility" (which Harriet Mozley deplores) that they weep at captive butterflies and screech helplessly when their mothers are unwell; by contrast, Grace, with proper presence of mind, goes quietly upstairs and fetches the necessary medicine.

---

*Yet Grace's father was killed four years before the story opens, early in the Nepalese War, which began in 1814; so this would date *The Fairy Bower* in 1818. The discrepancy is Harriet Mozley's and cannot be reconciled. In any case, she clearly intended to date her story at least twenty years earlier than the time of its publication.

Part of the secret of Grace's virtue is that Mrs. Leslie has never studied education. In *The Fairy Bower*, those who have studied it, and applied what they have learned, are hopeless failures. The Duff children are brought up by an Evangelical governess, Miss Newmarsh, who will allow her charges no dancing or dice or cards (she is deeply distressed when they see a conjurer doing card tricks), and who is so strict a Sabbatarian that she follows the Sabbath customs of the Jews, as some Low Church Anglicans did, and will never perform any activity after seven o'clock on Saturday evening. For entertainment her pupils have Bible riddles: "they 'cap' in the Bible, and make crambo verses out of it, and play at forfeits with texts." Miss Newmarsh never punishes her charges for their faults, but rewards them instead with additional privileges. She endorses the system at a boys' boarding-school where the boys are prevented from talking to one another by the constant vigilance of the masters and are kept under a surveillance so rigid that they never fight or cheat. A Tory High Anglican assures Miss Newmarsh that boys so treated will "burst with pent up folly and evil," and will be "fit for the gallows."

Indeed, Miss Newmarsh's principles bear ill fruit. Her pupil, Mary Anne Duff, is the liar whose pious education cannot prevent her from committing the crime of laying claim to Grace's idea. Yet for punishment Miss Newmarsh decrees that for three months Mary Anne "is to be down stairs every morning a quarter of an hour later than her sisters," and "to sit up the same space later," so that she may have leisure to reflect upon her sin. Into the mouth of Mary Anne, Harriet Mozley puts an Evangelical denunciation of country clergymen, the backbone of her own Tractarian party:

> "I know in the country [says Mary Anne] all clergymen are old and dull . . . and all the people who live there call them your reverence, and bow before them almost as the Catholics do before *their priests*, and the squire of the village pays them the same respect . . . so that every body thinks all they do and say quite right, and nobody dare speak of them as we do of our preachers. . . . country parsons are old-fashioned ignoramuses; they sit with the squire drinking wine after dinner, or play at back-gammon night after night. . . ."

Mary Anne's father, Mr. Duff, a successful businessman, lives with his family at "Winterton," which is surely Clapham, the London suburb where the leading Evangelical families lived; so in fact Mary Anne can know nothing about the countryside and its clergy. By satirizing the stubborn conviction of the Evangelicals that there had been no change in the rural church since the eighteenth century, Harriet Mozley by indirection was condemning their views.

Mary Anne's sister Fanny, by contrast, embarks upon an exaggeratedly sentimental friendship with Isabella Ward. The girls plan to run off together and seek solitude, declaring that they love each other as lovers do. When the gushing Fanny rhapsodizes about nuns, "most unfortunate and interesting creatures," wretchedly wandering about all night in long black garments with streaming white veils, Ellen Ward warns Fanny that the nuns would cut off her hair, bury her, and keep her forever behind iron bars. Grace adds that if Fanny then tried to talk to her parents alone, the nuns would wall her up in the cellar and leave her to starve. So through Grace, Harriet Mozley gave new currency among children to ancient popular superstitions about the wicked Roman Catholics. Of Miss Newmarsh's pupils, Constance Duff is the most aggressively pious. In her diary she writes edifying comments on the unhappy "fall" of her sister Mary Anne, never reproaching her except (!) to compare her to Peter denying the Lord.

So Evangelical education is detestable. But Harriet Mozley gets in a dig at fashionable girls' schools also. Isabella Ward, the peer's daughter, is at a school so exclusive that, she declares, she knows only three of the eight girls there. Each girl has her own study and music room; each master sends in his calling card, and the girl receives him for a lesson only if the state of her social engagements permits. This proves to be one of Isabella's exaggerations, but it is obvious that Harriet Mozley had no use for such establishments either. Nor does tutoring boys at home produce good results: we meet a deplorable youth in *The Fairy Bower* who has been hopelessly spoiled by this system. Boys should be sent to Public School. Campbell Duff will be saved from Miss Newmarsh by Eton, and so spared the disastrous bringing-up that has been so bad for his sisters. For girls, a systematic study of French and music at home, preferably under the direction of a tenderhearted but demanding mother like Mrs. Leslie, is the answer. Grace, though far poorer than the Duffs, is far more happily started in life. At the house of the rich, pious Duffs, the children at a dinner party get drunk and break the dishes; even Harry and Laura Graham in *Holiday House* smashed crockery only in an excess of high spirits. With all their Evangelical piety the Duffs are great snobs, welcoming the absurd (and possibly dangerous) friendship between their daughter Fanny and Isabella Ward only because Isabella's father is Lord Musgrove.

In 1869 and again in 1899, Charlotte Yonge wrote warmly of *The Fairy Bower*, remembering how its appearance had coincided with the height of the Tractarian movement, welcoming its "peculiar suggestiveness of portraiture" and the way in which the children's conversations were made realistic and central to the tale. But the Tractarian Miss Yonge indirectly criticized Harriet Mozley for not coming out more directly in behalf of Tractarian principles and for contenting herself with anti-Evangelical satire. Miss Yonge was disappointed that, having broached the problem of the proper education for children, Harriet Mozley had not provided more definite answers; and she felt that the questions of conscience raised by the book were on the whole too subtle for young readers. Almost a century later, in 1965, Margaret Kennedy rightly criticized the clumsiness of Harriet Mozley's narrative style, and her inability to control her satirical weapons. But, while recognizing its faults, both Charlotte Yonge and Margaret Kennedy, like other discerning readers, praised the book for its authenticity and its conviction. At its best, *The Fairy Bower* is comparable to the best work of Charlotte Yonge herself, and at times its wittiest conversations provide echoes of Jane Austen.

In the same year *The Fairy Bower* appeared, 1841, Harriet Mozley followed with *The Lost Brooch*, which reintroduces the same characters more than six years later. Grace Leslie, now sixteen, is spending a month at the seaside with the Duffs and the Wards. Twice as long as *The Fairy Bower*, the narrative of the sequel is far less tightly woven: the lost brooch of the title is not even mentioned until the story is far advanced, and does not become the center of attention until well along in Volume 2. It is a coral brooch, the only piece of jewelry still possessed by the deeply pious Constance Duff, earlier Miss Newmarsh's favorite pupil, now at sixteen portrayed as a full-fledged religious fanatic.

"Almost in a state of monomania," as Harriet Mozley herself puts it, Constance insists on blaming the theft of the brooch upon an innocent servant girl named Jessie Baines, whom she wishes to become the first inmate of a new women's penitentiary that she plans to found. Constance does not perceive her own cruelty as she hounds her victim, trying to prevail upon Jessie's new employer to discharge her, and threatening her with the police. Grace Leslie intervenes to thwart the plan, with the help of Charlotte Duff, who emerges as a strong character, and of Campbell, so broadened by Eton and Oxford that he sees the wickedness of Constance's behavior. Emily and George Ward obtain evidence that the brooch is still in Constance's own work box, where they cause her dramatically to rediscover it: Jessie has been innocent all along, and the whole sorry episode has been Constance's fault.

But Constance shows no remorse. As George Ward summarizes her view,

> "if a person was unspiritual, it did not matter whether he were a murderer or a thief, or simply unspiritual, for . . . all were in the same condition; and . . . if *she* [Constance] thought, much more pronounced, a person unspiritual, he or she *was* unspiritual; and that further she did pronounce Jessie Baines unspiritual; therefore Jessie was so; and it was impossible for her to injure Jessie by any thing of any kind she could say against her; therefore she had not injured the said Jessie, and she did not think better or worse of her than she did before. Q.E.D."

Indeed, Constance persecutes Jessie in part because Jessie refuses to attend a religious meeting of Dissenters to which Constance invites her. A devout member of the Church of England, Jessie wants nothing to do with Dissenters. But Constance, like many Evangelicals, finds more spiritual affinity with Dissenters than with her fellow Anglicans. Constance now prefers the Quakers to any other sect.

So *The Lost Brooch* pursues Harriet Mozley's feud with the Evangelicals. Her husband, Tom, wrote that it was the greatest "shew-up" (i.e., exposure) of Evangelical foibles ever attempted. This unremitting satire, all directed against the same target, makes the book far duller than its predecessor. Although Constance has developed into the girl she had promised to become half a dozen years earlier, and the boys too have grown up, Grace, at sixteen, is still only the embodiment of the virtues she had displayed at ten. The natural and entertaining conversations of *The Fairy Bower* here grow tedious. Certain that everything they do is aimed at someone else's good, the Duffs have allowed a rich worldly woman more or less to adopt Fanny and are quite able to overlook the fact that Fanny will inherit her money. And Fanny embarks upon a sentimental attachment to an unsuitable young man, as silly as her childhood passion for Isabella. The Low Church Duffs, though far richer than the High Church Wards, somehow give away only a fifth as much to charity, and then always to favorite Evangelical causes—"Bible, Tract, Missionary, Jews' Societies"—while the Wards give to their parish and neighborhood good causes in the proper way.

At times, *The Lost Brooch* is intensely theological. Constance argues for the favorite Evangelical tenets of justification by faith and imputed righteousness: "My sins are washed away by His blood, and my heart renewed by His spirit; I renounce my own righteousness, and His righteousness is imputed to me." Faith in Christ brings regeneration, and only the "inner witness" can assure a belief that in fact he does believe. Constance's High Church cousin, Ellen Ward, argues (as Harriet Mozley would have argued) that by attending Dissenters' meetings Constance is disobeying the authority of the Church of England and fostering division within it; and Constance's own brother, Campbell, says to her, "If you profess to be of the church, you must submit to her teaching." To be a consistent Christian, these young Tractarians argue, one must be a consistent churchman; but Constance retorts that they are "dwelling forever" on the Church, while she speaks "only of those who love the Lord Jesus." Constance's arrogation to herself of the right to pronounce on spirituality or its lack, on innocence or guilt, has led her to think of herself as infallible. Yet she makes a thoroughly dishonest proposal to raise money to pay the debts of a young spendthrift and professed convert by advertising in a religious magazine to obtain cash contributions for his personal benefit.

All this was the stuff of daily controversy and polemic among intellectual Victorians; it was the stuff of novels for adults, where it is often made to come alive for modern readers. But it is not the stuff of children's literature. So *The Lost Brooch* here deserves no more than this brief note, designed to relieve the curiosity of those readers of *The Fairy Bower* who may wish to know how its personages turned out when they had grown into young people in their teens.

The text of The Fairy Bower *is reprinted from an American edition (New York and Philadelphia: D. Appleton and Company, 1847) based on the third English edition.*

ADVERTISEMENT

IT IS HOPED that the following Tale may be looked upon as an attempt rather to represent characters as they really are, than to exhibit moral portraitures for unreserved imitation or avoidance.

In this respect it may perhaps differ from most publications of the same class, and though it may not possess their poetical beauty, it may perhaps have the advantage over them, that it introduces young persons to those scenes and situations of life, which are their actual sphere and trial.

Should this story meet with encouragement, a further history of the youthful actors may perhaps appear, presenting them in a more confirmed and developed stage of character.

CHAPTER I

. . . little body with a mighty heart.
SHAKSPEARE

"MY DEAR!" said Mr. Ward, putting in just his head at the breakfast-room door, prepared as he was for his cold winter's drive to London,—"my dear! you may as well write that note to Mrs. Leslie, to-day."

"To-day, George," exclaimed his lady, "why it is only the 29th, and the children's party is not till the 6th!"

"But now all the cousins are coming on New Year's day," answered Mr. Ward, "you may as well give Grace the opportunity of joining them, and getting a little acquainted with the rest before Ellen comes; you know Grace is younger than them all, and a quiet timid little girl seemingly."

"Certainly," returned Mrs. Ward, "it is rather formidable for her, coming among so many strangers, poor child! and such high-spirited creatures as George and Emily!"

"Then you'll write, my dear?" continued the gentleman; "and then, will you to-morrow, when you get Mrs. Leslie's answer, send out the dinner invitations, for the 8th; it is very short notice, but as it is, I doubt if we catch the Freemantles in London—Good by to ye, my dear!"

"I say!" added Mr. Ward, re-opening the door, "you understand! I sleep in Grosvenor Square to-night!—but I shall dine at home to-morrow, and perhaps drive Everard down," and he finally left the room.

"Mr. Everard will be a willing guest of ours now," thought Mrs. Ward, as she prepared to write her note to Mrs. Leslie, "he is little Grace's godfather."

Mr. Ward was in business in London, but he resided entirely in its neighbourhood, and usually went up every morning and returned to dinner. He was a brother of Lord

Musgrove, who had been lately raised to the Peerage. Mr. and Mrs. Ward had a family of several children; they were hospitable people, and their house was constantly full of company. Mrs. Ward was always much engaged with visitors either at home or abroad, and sometimes she had bad health, so that neither herself nor their papa saw a great deal of the children. George was the eldest living; he was at this time about thirteen, and was at home for his holidays. Emily, the next, was about a year his junior; she also went to school. Ellen, the third, was at her grandmamma's, where she was almost domesticated. There were besides some little ones under the age of eight, who need not be more particularly mentioned. These young people had a large family of cousins of the name of Duff, with whom they were very intimate; Mrs. Duff was Mrs. Ward's sister. The two eldest of these, Mary Anne and Campbell, were now spending a weak or two with their young friends at Fulham; and Mrs. Ward was writing to ask Mrs. Leslie, an old friend of Mr. Ward's, and her little daughter Grace, to join the party.

Mrs. Leslie had been left a young widow, with this one little girl; she had never mixed much in the world since the death of her husband. Major Leslie was a rising young officer, who fell very honourably in leading on a forlorn hope, in one of the first engagements in the dreadful Nepaul war. His early and unexpected death left his widow but moderately provided for, and this, together with the grief his loss had occasioned, had made her live in much retirement. She would willingly have continued to do so, but she had often thought her little Grace was injured by being so much secluded; she therefore, without hesitation, accepted Mrs. Ward's invitation, though she was aware it would be the means of leading herself again into society.

We will now take a view of Mrs. Leslie's drawing-room, just after she has written her answer to Mrs. Ward's invitation. Grace had been amusing herself with reading, while her mamma was engaged with her note. As Mrs. Leslie folded it up, she called upon Grace to bring her the taper. Grace was so intent on her book that she was not roused, till again her mamma called, "Grace, my dear, did you not hear me?"

"Oh, yes, dear mamma,—the taper!" cried the little girl, running for it. "I beg your pardon, the words did not reach me; really this story of Mrs. Leicester's is so very interesting; I think it is the prettiest of all—it is almost as good as being with the party themselves!"

"Well, my dear child," answered Mrs. Leslie, "if you think it good to be among such a party, you will be pleased with what I have to tell you. This note is to accept an invitation for you."

"For *me*, mamma!" exclaimed the little girl, her eyes glistening, and the bright colour rushing into her cheeks, "you know I never had an invitation in my life!"

"Perhaps you never had what you call a regular invitation in your life, but you have paid visits, you know."

Grace looked puzzled, and after a moment's thought, said, "Oh, mamma, you mean at aunt Williams's. Yes, I have often been there, but then *they are only my cousins*, and my aunt just says, 'Will you come to-morrow or next day?' that is not like a real invitation."

"It is true, my love," said her mamma, "this is a more *formal* invitation than any you have hitherto received; yet I remember one you had more *particular* in some respects than this, because that was to *yourself* alone, without me."

"Oh, mamma," said Grace, colouring, and looking down with an uneasy movement, "I know when you mean; it was Mrs. Marsden's; that was a year ago last Michaelmas. What a little girl I was then—only eight years old. I wonder I was not afraid to go among strangers, and such clever little girls as the Miss Marsdens are; you know that beautiful ottoman they worked in tapestry, and Ellen Marsden's drawings, and their governess, Miss Cook, who was so clever, and spoke I don't know how many languages! I wished very much to see Miss Cook, I had then never seen a governess."

"Why, Grace," said her mother, rather surprised at her mode of noticing an event that had passed away in half an hour's conversation, and had never again been alluded to, "you speak as if you had really gone there."

"Oh, I know I did not go," replied Grace, "I never saw the little Marsdens, or Miss Cook, and only Mrs. Marsden that once, you know, when she called to ask me. She was to come some day the next week; did not she say so, mamma," added Grace, timidly, "and to take me home, and I was to have stayed several days?"

"Something of the kind was talked of, my dear," answered Mrs. Leslie, "but Mrs. Marsden wished to have taken you back with her that very day, only your dear aunt, you remember, was with us just before her marriage, and I did not like you to go from home till she left."

"I did not wish to go away while aunt was here that last time, but I did wish, though, mamma, *very much indeed*, to go to Richmond, and I listened every day all the next week to every carriage that drove past," replied Grace, rather ashamed of herself. She then added, "Do you think, mamma, she forgot it? Was it a *promise*, mamma?" then after a pause, in which Mrs. Leslie felt perplexed to answer, and also surprised at what seemed a new mood in her child, Grace rejoined, "but people never forget *promises*, do they, mamma?"

"I should be very sorry indeed," said Mrs. Leslie, gravely, "that my little girl should ever forget a promise; as to Mrs. Marsden, you must not think about it; mistakes are often made by word of mouth, and either we did not understand one another, or something occurred to prevent Mrs. Marsden from coming, which was a satisfactory reason to herself."

"Well but, mamma, I *will* ask one thing," said Grace, with an air of resolution, the colour mounting to her very forehead; then hesitating, she was silent.

Mrs. Leslie, thinking she had best perhaps not be made to put her thought into words, only added seriously, "Always remember, Grace, grown people have a right to judge for themselves." After a slight pause, Mrs. Leslie rejoined, "Now, Grace, my dear, ring the bell for this note to go to the post; you seem to have forgotten all about the invitation."

"Oh, no! I have not, mamma; but when is it? I know *you* are going too, by what you said just now."

"Yes, I am; and we are to stay a fortnight; it is at Mr. Ward's, at Fulham; you have seen Mr. and Mrs. Ward, Grace: the little Wards have two of their cousins—the Duffs—staying with them, and there may be some other young people, so you will be a large party."

"When are we to go, mamma?"

"I have appointed Thursday, which you know is New Year's Day; so you will begin the year with quite a new scene. But now, my dear child," said Mrs. Leslie, "go and finish your favourite story; I am going to be busy. You must not let this pleasure in store unsettle you, Grace, we must go on to-morrow as usual."

Away ran Grace to her book, and finished her story with composure and interest; we do not say that there was not a consciousness of something exciting in her mind, and that when at leisure it turned to the new prospect before her with curiosity and high expectation. But the steady uninterrupted routine of daily lessons, which her mamma pursued with her, had already accustomed her mind to do with ease, what many older cannot do with difficulty;—to concentrate her small powers upon the subject she had in hand, and not to be diverted from her task by outward objects. Mrs. Leslie had not studied the subject of education, like some mothers, and did not feel capable of forming any original plans. She only had a strong idea of the value of regular daily lessons; she had no plans about it; she did not talk about it; but she practised it. *Nothing*, we may say, interfered with the morning business. A mother differently circumstanced, could not herself have undertaken the office of instructress, with such unrelenting regularity. But Mrs. Leslie had only to do with her own circumstances, and was not of a disposition to interfere with the plans or opinions of any one else.

Since Grace speaks very little for herself, and has no young companions, like the rest of our party, to draw her out, it may be necessary occasionally to give her thoughts. During the active portions of the day, she had not much time for speculation and wonderment; at least in her little life, unvaried by events, or much society, to call out her thoughts, she had not occasion as yet, to pause, and become bewildered with the multitude of thoughts within her. But there were two especial seasons when she gave full range to her reflections; the one we may call for speculations *retro*spective; the other for speculations *pro*spective. She was accustomed to go to bed early, and she soon slept—the light, but not the sound, sleep of childhood; she invariably woke early, and in the summer part of the year especially, used to lie for hours before she was allowed to rise, watching the dawning day, or the full burst of sunshine about the room, or pursuing the path of the clouds across the sky: with such thoughts and reveries on her past and present being; the existence and character of God; the true meaning of that, to her, most awful word—Eternity; the fearful sense of the doctrine of eternal punishment; the difficulty of reconciling it with the love of the Almighty Creator of the world; and numberless topics of the same nature, as, with her respective comments and imaginings, would prove that there is the germ of philosophic yearning, and heretical wanderings in the mind, as soon as it is capable of embracing a thought, or receiving any revealed doctrine. After a time, these speculations gave way in a great measure, on a somewhat maturer understanding of the Great Truths, which are calculated to subdue them. The other season, in which she indulged less abstract fancies, was after the age of six, when she began music. Her hour of practice was also an hour of eager wonderment and anticipation; over all the words she heard that seemed to introduce her to the world without; over all the little incidents of the day, and the pleasures either of occupation or amusement that were in store for her. But her dearest and fondest theme was the love of her mother—on this she could dwell under every sort of form. It entered into all her wild religious and metaphysical speculations, from her earliest years. She would think, "What a small creature I am! but what great things I can think, and nobody knows my thoughts! Yes, I suppose God knows them. I am sure He does, though I cannot think how; and besides, I think mamma knows them; I think all mothers must have the power of knowing their children's thoughts. She does not say so, but I think mamma knows all mine." Then she would get bewildered in the mazes of metaphysics. At the time of her father's death she felt more perplexity than sorrow. She had never known him, nor had she been led to expect his return, or to dwell upon the thought of seeing him some day. "What is the difference to me?" she would think; "Why is papa dead? Why is he more dead to me to-day than last week or last month? Besides he has been dead now five months, though we have but just heard of it. He was quite dead to me before. What is the difference to him, I wonder?" Then she would go on till the tears fell fast, thinking of her mamma's dear face of sorrow, and the sigh that haunted her beyond all the rest. "There must be some difference," she thought, "because mamma thinks so."

It may be necessary to state a few facts, to account for the different nature of Grace's feeling towards her parents. Captain Leslie embarked for India when his little girl was two years old, and it is not to be expected she could have a personal remembrance of him. Her mother parted with him, under a melancholy foreboding that she should never see him again; and the more her own thoughts were absorbed by his memory, the less she could bring herself to cherish it in the mind of her child, by any cheerful mention of his name. Indeed, it is very doubtful if she ever recalled him as one likely to be seen again, so that her allusions to him, before and after his death, were of the same character, and were always tinctured with the solemnity, which is apt to accompany the mention of a lost parent, to a child. The death of Major Leslie made no difference in their mode of living. They continued in the same place and the same house. The only outward signs Grace perceived, was the garb of mourning themselves and their household were made to assume. It was hardly clear to those about her, if she associated her mother's more serious face and the frequent sigh, which never failed to catch her ear, as she amused herself about the room, with the event that clothed them in black.

CHAPTER II

Alas! what kind of grief should thy years know?
BEAUMONT AND FLETCHER

IF IT WILL NOT detain the kind reader too long from our young friends at Fulham, we would in this place transcribe a conversation that passed between Grace's aunt, Mrs. Leslie's sister, and another lady, which may serve to throw a light on the child's feelings and character.

Miss Winton was of a more lively, energetic nature than her sister, and her spirit had not been in the same way oppressed by early anxieties of her own, and subdued by solitude. It seemed as if she penetrated and understood the character of her little niece better than her own mother. But it not infrequently happens with children, as with their seniors, that traits of character, and qualities for good and evil, discover themselves often to a stranger or a visitor, when they remain for years hidden to the eyes of relatives, who are in daily and hourly intercourse;—so it might be in this instance. Be that as it may, Miss Winton had a stronger and more decided view of Grace's heart and mind than her sister, though she was not in the habit of disclosing her opinion. Mrs. Bell was a lady in the neighbourhood; she had several children, but only one girl, about the age of Grace, and she was often in the habit of comparing them.

The following conversation between these two ladies, took place a few months after the death of Major Leslie. After some preliminary discourse, Mrs. Bell asked, "if little Grace had latterly shown more feeling on her papa's death?"

"She is a reserved child at all times," answered Miss Winton, "but I really hardly know what are her feelings on the subject, or whether she at all comprehends the loss she has had."

"But, my dear Miss Winton," said Mrs. Bell, "why do you not question her? You might bring out her feelings, and that would be such a great thing for her, poor child."

"As far as I can judge," returned Miss Winton, "I should say her affection at present is almost entirely exercised on her mamma."

"Affection for her mamma! my dear Miss Winton, how can you say so? I never in my life saw a little creature so perfectly insensible to her mamma's feelings. Why, the other day, when I was calling there, I had an instance. I had been some time talking to Mrs. Leslie, and telling her the high compliment his brother officers paid to the Major's honourable conduct in India, and how he was loved and respected by all who came near him; poor Mrs. Leslie's eyes filled with tears, and at last she gave a deep sigh. Grace, who was close by with my little girl, suddenly looked up, and I am sure she saw her mamma was in distress, yet, would you believe it? the little insensible thing, immediately began talking as fast as she could, even going on to laugh quite loud, tossing her doll about,—(which, by the bye, she is such an odd child she never plays with,—it was only brought down to show my Anna) and talking to it in a strange wild way; I assure you I felt so shocked I did not know what I was saying, and I got up and left as soon as I could. Well, and further to show you this was no accident, but a real want of heart, I can tell you another anecdote; once before, when I was calling, poor Mrs. Wilson came in—you know it was just after her husband had had that disappointment about a place in the Treasury, which would quite have set them up again; Mrs. Wilson, poor thing, was quite overpowered, and at last burst into tears. Grace observed it, I saw she did; immediately she ran, or rather skipped all across the room to me—and you know she is such an unaccountable child, she never speaks to one of herself;—well, she ran to me with her book in her hand, to show me a picture, and ask if Anna had it, 'it was such a pretty book,' and a great deal more, chattering away in a way that would have been quite pleasant at any other time, while she stood in the rudest manner—quite unnecessary, with her back to Mrs. Wilson, as if she was determined to show what a little hard heart she had got. I never could bear that child; I am sure it would break my heart if my dear Anna showed so little sensibility. Why she cries at the least appearance of distress; do you know, one day she came in sobbing as if her little heart would break, because she was afraid she had hurt a 'poor, poor butterfly,' she had been in vain trying to catch; and if she thinks me unhappy, or even displeased, I am sometimes afraid she will go into fits. But then she has a very tender heart, and such wonderfully refined feelings for a child of her age."

"I do not know much of your little girl," said Miss Winton, "but you must let me say one word for our poor Grace, which may perhaps convince you she is not quite so devoid of feeling as you imagine, and that she *has* affection of some sort for her mamma. In the first place, at the time the news of her papa's death reached us, *I* observed that Grace was unusually serious for some days. One may say, you know, she had *never* seen him, so one could not expect the sorrow that even at such early years, a child is capable of feeling; but from that time she has been alive in an extraordinary degree, to any show of sadness in her mamma; I have seen her watch her face, when she seemed all the time intent on her book or her work; and when she thought nobody perceived it, she would creep round and stand by her, and begin to read or talk, or do any thing that she saw did not annoy her. But it is her mamma's sigh that seems most to attract her; my sister has often said to me, that both before and after her husband's death, little Grace's soft low whisper of 'don't sigh, mamma,' has done more to fortify her and recall her to herself, than any human help she ever received."

"Well," said Mrs. Bell, "that is rather different from my notion of her, but I have heard others think as I do; and one lady told me she thought Grace was quite as incapable of religious feeling as she was of human."

"You must look with some indulgence, my dear madam, on a child of her tender years, and. . . ."

"She is *six* years old," interrupted Mrs. Bell, "and *my* little Anna showed a deep sense of religion at four;—the lady I spoke of said she should be miserable if her children could not talk with some readiness of their spiritual state, and religious frames, at six or seven. Why you know little Miss Barker wrote, or rather talked, for she could not write, a whole book full of such things before she was five years old; and I have heard very sensible people say, not quite of Dr. Barker's way of thinking, that the language and sentiments were really surprising;—but she was a little saint, and a prodigy besides, certainly—no wonder she did not live. Now I don't expect Grace, or even Anna, to do any thing of that kind, but I think at six years old a child ought to have some feeling about religion."

"Well, I should be sorry that you should think our dear Grace a little heathen, and so I will tell you an anecdote that I never mentioned to any creature, not even to her own mother," replied Miss Winton; "I was staying with my poor sister when the news of her husband's death arrived, and we had two or three friends passing the afternoon with us. My dear sister read a letter that was brought her, and put it aside; she joined a word or two in the conversation, I thought with an altered tone, and that she looked pale: presently she rose, as to leave the room; before she reached the door the effort was too great, and she fell down in a swoon; in a moment she had quite fainted away. Of course we were in great confusion, and presently all the servants came in; nobody thought of little Grace, who was present. After other remedies failed, I ran up stairs for the hartshorn. The medicine chest was in my sister's dressing-room, which was also then Grace's room. I burst in, and there I found little Grace by her bed-side, upon her knees, with her face buried in her hands; she was sobbing, and so intent, that I don't think she heard me. I found no hartshorn in the chest, and I ran down asking where it was. One of the servants persisted it was there; another said she saw Miss Grace standing about with a bottle when her mistress first fainted, and on looking we found it close by. She had, it seems, run up immediately her mamma fell, I suppose having remembered hartshorn was proper in fainting; but finding us all engaged with other remedies, she had left it, and silently retired. I can never think otherwise than with great hope of a child whose affectionate feeling first prompted her with presence of mind to active measures, and which afterwards, when she found herself of no use, sent her on her knees alone to her chamber. I think, my dear madam, you would have been satisfied with such a trait in your Anna."

"Oh, *my* dear child is such a peculiar disposition, she would never do a thing of that kind," said the other lady, "poor dear love! once when I was on the point of fainting, she clung about me and screamed so frightfully that every body was obliged to leave me and see to her, in another room. I came to myself all alone, and had nearly fainted again when I found the state she was in; she was in strong hysterics; we were quite alarmed for her; we sent for Mr. Coleman, and she was in bed for a week. Her feelings are too much for her, poor little thing! and ever since that I have been very careful to keep her out of the way of all excitement. But to return to your little niece: I am glad to hear any thing that shows something like feeling; but what was the reason of her distress?"

"Indeed, I can only guess: she had heard of her father's death, for one of the servants had told her that it was the cause of her mamma's fainting. Myself I feel sure her distress arose simply from the situation she saw her mother in."

"But, my dear Miss Winton, do you really mean to say you never questioned her?"

"No, I did not."

"Is it possible that you could let pass such an opportunity of cherishing a feeling that appeared once, and was then past for ever?"

"I do not mean to say I did right," said Miss Winton; "I know many would have done differently; but I could not bring myself to break in upon the sacredness of the sorrow of that sweet child, whom I saw on her knees. Mine was an accidental intrusion; I have never mentioned it or noticed it, and I fear I shall regret having done so now."

"Indeed, my dear Miss Winton, I feel all amazement; you talk as if your niece were more than a grown person, instead of a weak child committed to your hands for instruction and guidance."

"In my youth," answered Miss Winton, "I was a much harder and more obstinate little thing than ever poor Grace has been, and if I did not respect the sanctuary of a child's heart, I should find a warning in the memory of my irritated and wounded feelings when I thought any body had intruded upon them in an unauthorized manner."

"Unauthorized! you amaze me! you are her aunt!"

"Well, my dear madam, I do not say I was right; I don't know if I should have done otherwise if it had come into my head, and I am not at all clear that it did. I never wished to recall that painful scene to my dear sister's memory, so I have never mentioned the circumstance even to her."

"Well, I repeat," said Mrs. Bell, "I am better satisfied with Grace, and I will, if I can, forget her cold manner."

"Oh, Mrs. Bell!" exclaimed Miss Winton, and she was going to assure her poor Grace's manner was not cold to those who knew her; but she had a notion that there was a mutual estrangement between the parties, and she could not be surprised, for Mrs. Bell exercised a surveillance over Grace, which a child like her would feel, though not understand; and the misconceptions that ensued were easily accounted for.

CHAPTER III

Gay hope is theirs, by Fancy led. . . .
Wild wit! Invention ever new.
GRAY

I<small>T IS HIGH TIME</small> to take a peep at our young party at Fulham, and we find them assembled together in the library, which room was appropriated to their use.

"There is two o'clock striking," cried George; "they were to be here between two and three; but I wish there were more coming than this Grace; and besides she is such a little girl!"

"Yes," said his cousin Mary Anne Duff, "younger than any of us; she is only ten years old."

"But," said Emily, "papa, who knows most about her, says she is a very nice child, and old of her age, and that she is like what her aunt was when she was young, and we all have heard what a clever woman Mrs. Stanley is."

"Yes, and good-natured too," cried Campbell, in his honest hearty tone. "I don't care for your clever people, and clever women particularly, I think them all very great bores."

"Oh, oh!" exclaimed the whole party, and George especially; "oh, oh! let the honourable gentleman be called to order!—explain! explain!"

"Well, I will explain," said Campbell, "I do think your clever men and women, with their politics, and arts and sciences, and rates and taxes" . . . Here they all burst out laughing, and cried, "What do you mean, Campbell?"

"Well, I mean rents and tithes," blundered on Campbell, "and all their jargon of high pressure, and low pressure, which I'm sure some of them don't understand themselves, very tiresome, and I think there's a great deal of humbug in it, and I'm glad when they're gone; and I like a good-natured pleasant lady like Mrs. Stanley, who smiles and nods, and does not look a bit clever, ten times as well, and all I can say is, that if Grace is like her aunt, I shall like her very much and she shall be my wife."

"Ha, ha, capital! well done, Campbell!" shouted George.

"But, Campbell," said Emily, "you don't know what you're talking about. Have you never heard that Mrs. Stanley is a very clever woman indeed? I believe she understands Latin, but I *know* she knows," counting on her fingers, "French, Italian, Spanish, German—oh, I know there are some more—six languages there should be, and then she understands several things I don't know the names of. . . ."

"Lots of 'ologies,' I dare say, like Miss Newmarsh," interposed George.

"No, not *ologies*, harder names than those," continued Emily, "and you know how well she sings and draws; besides she has written a book, a real book, which has been printed and sold."

"Well, master Campbell, what have you to say to all this?" asked George.

"Why I say that I never heard a word of all this cleverness, and I need not believe it except I choose, and that if it is true I don't care, and shall like her just as well. I don't mind people being clever, if nobody knows any thing about it, and they have not got that nasty clever face and way with them."

"Oh, Campbell, how strange you are!" said his sister Mary Anne, "and how oddly you express yourself! Now there's Mrs. Lenham. . . ."

"Oh, no! no!" interrupted Campbell, "I won't talk of your Mrs. This and Mrs. That; I know what I mean; I like some people, and I don't like others, and I know the reason I *like* people; it is because they are good-natured, and if they are good-natured, I don't care whether they're clever or not; and as to some cleverness, why its all botheration and humbug!"

"Campbell, really you are so queer there's no talking with you," again said Mary Anne; "and Campbell you're a funny fellow," said his cousin Emily, when the door opened, and brought a summons to the young party to assemble in the drawing-room, in order to receive their expected companion.

"What a bore to go into the drawing-room, and play the *good!*" said George, making his queer face, and drawing a deep sigh; "but there's one good thing, there'll be plenty of company to quiz! perhaps Mrs. Musprat will be there, and her bonnet—that will be rich!"

"Oh, George," said Mary Anne, "how naughty you are! how often have I told you you ought to quiz nobody!"

"Yes, I know you have, my pretty cousin," said he, "come along!" and drawing her arm within his, he led the way, marching her along in an absurd manner, chanting,

> "O, this pace,
> Is all for this Grace!
> And this chase
> For her grace,
> For in very short space
> This famous Grace
> Is a coming to this place!"

The young people were so convulsed with laughter at this witticism, that they were obliged to stop in the passage and recover themselves, before they proceeded to the drawing-room.

"Oh, George, you'll kill me!" screamed Mary Anne, throwing herself against the wall.

> "That would be base!"

returned George in his chant.

"George!" gasped his sister, panting for breath, "we really shall behave so bad in the drawing-room!"

> "What a disgrace!"

still chanted George.

"Do please let us recover!" added she.

> "Then your nerves you must brace!"

continued the inexorable George, bringing his chant to a close.

Here Campbell, who had been laughing as heartily as any of them, interfered. By degrees the party composed themselves, and they entered the drawing-room with tolerable sobriety.

CHAPTER IV

Confused and quick my introduction passed.
CRABBE.

THERE WAS A ROOM full of company; several visitors were making morning calls, and some staying in the house. The children were all noticed and spoken to. "Oh, you have got your cousins with you!" said one lady to Emily; "how d'ye do, my dear? I hope your papa and mamma are well! Upon my word, Miss Mary Anne is growing a fine young lady!" added she, turning to Mrs. Ward. "Master Campbell, come and shake hands, you have not spoken to me! how do you go on at school? have you got another prize this half year? and how is your friend, that pleasant boy, young Freeman? have you had another battle with him? or can you go on liking him now without? What strange boys those are, Mrs. Ward! do you know. . . ."

By this time Campbell had escaped rather unceremoniously into the back ground, —the door opened, and Mrs. Leslie was announced. For some time there was the confusion of greeting and introduction; and Grace, the expected of the children, was quite lost in the crowd. At length every body was seated again, and the elder ladies and gentlemen began talking. Grace stood by her mamma's side. The group of children had withdrawn themselves into one of the windows.

"How small she is!" said Mary Anne. "But how very pretty!" Emily. "She looks very shy, I'm afraid she's stupid," George. At this moment Grace raised her eyes and looked steadily across the room at their party, and Campbell completed the remarks by, "I don't know *that*."

Mrs. Ward here called to the young folks, who came forward. She mentioned to Grace each of their names and their relationship, adding, "but I dare say you will soon find each other out in the other room." She then went on talking to her elder guests. The children all stared at each other, and had not a word to say before "company," till George very politely placed a chair for Grace and requested her to sit down. He then began: "Miss Leslie, don't you think that's a very pretty bonnet?" pointing out a lady on the other side of the room.

Grace looked at him, and he repeated his question, with a queer wink at the bonnet. She then answered readily, "No, not very pretty, but very warm and comfortable this cold weather."

"So's a chimney-pot, but one would not go about in it!"

"But a chimney-pot's *red*," said Grace.

"No, a chimney-pot's black."

"It's black and smoky *inside*."

"And it's black and rusty outside, and so's that bonnet, *Q. E. D.*" said George. "Miss Leslie shall have all she likes *here*; so Emily," added he, in a whisper, "please send for the bricklayer directly, and let him bring down one of the chimney-pots, Miss Leslie wants it for a Sunday bonnet."

This set all the young people giggling, and Grace, who had not been too amazed for amusement, now laughed audibly. Mrs. Ward turned to them, and said good-naturedly,

"Do, young folks, run away to your room; it's a shame to keep you here smothering your laugh; run away and enjoy yourselves!" and away they went.

"Miss Leslie," said George, when they had reached the library, "pray how d'ye mean to trim your new bonnet?"

"With French ribbon, *vapeur couleur* and *flamme de ponche*, I suppose," returned Grace, rather ashamed of her wit.

"Oh, none of your French;" cried George, "construe! construe!"

"Fashionable French ribbons," cried Emily, "smoke and flame coloured; you know they are all the rage in Paris just now."

"Very good indeed, very suitable!" cried George, "with a couple of pokers for feathers, and a sheet of lead for a veil! What a swell Miss Leslie will be! and what an improving on this dull thing!" pointing to her simple bonnet.

"By the bye, talking of bonnets," said Emily, "Miss Leslie, will you not take off yours for the present? we need not go up stairs yet;" and she assisted Grace in removing her out-door apparel, while the latter said, "Please don't call me Miss Leslie; call me by my name."

"What! *Grace?*" said George, with a certain look that reminded the rest of his late poetic effusion. She assented. They then requested her to do the same by them, and so this this matter was satisfactorily settled. George however went on, "Well, *Grace*, you are not like Isabella Ward; do you know, though she's our cousin, she doesn't like us to call her 'Isabella,' but wants us to say Miss Ward."

"What stuff it is!" cried Campbell.

"Why," added his sister, "you must remember her papa is a Lord, and she is the *Honorable* Miss Ward, and that makes a difference."

"A difference! why should it make a difference?" asked Emily; "her papa is Lord Musgrove, it is true, but he has not been raised to the peerage above two years, and then she was plain Belle to us always."

"Yes, and broad Belle, and bold Belle, and bouncing Belle, and every thing but bonny Belle," cried George.

"But," persisted Mary Anne, "now she's an 'honorable' it would not do to call her any of those names, or Bella, or even Isabella, I think."

"Nonsense!" exclaimed her brother, "why you know it's all the same thing, especially when people are cousins."

"Besides," pursued George, "it's all a chance; *we* might just as well have been '*Honorable*' as Isabella and James and the rest of them. If my uncle had only been papa's father instead of his brother, *he* would have been '*Honorable*,' and that's very near *us*. How well it would have sounded, 'The Honorable Mr. George Ward!'"

"The Honorable *Mr.* Ward, or the Honorable George Ward," interposed Mary Anne, in a tone of correction.

"Well, the Honorable Mr. Ward, let it be," cried George, and in a moment he was out of the room, flung open the door, announced in a thundering voice, "The Honorable Mr. Ward," disappeared and entered again, bowing and shrugging, going up to Grace, and mincing in an affected manner, "My dear Madam, I hope I have the felicity of seeing you quite well. The governor and my mother, Lord and Lady Musgrove, regret they cannot have the honour of waiting upon you, but Lord Musgrove is laid up with a slight pain in the little finger, and Lady Musgrove's favourite lap-dog is under Dr.

Sickamore's care—I fear dangerously indisposed; her Ladyship felt quite unfit to encounter a party under such peculiar and distressing circumstances!"

This sally was received, as may be imagined, with peals of laughter, which continued
for some time. Grace had scarcely recovered herself, when George asked her, in his
natural tone, if he should not make a capital "Honorable."

"Why," answered Grace, laughing, "I never saw any noble-man or honorable-man in a
room, but if they are all like *that*, they are more amusing than any people I have yet met
any where."

George bowed very low indeed, and looked really pleased. Emily exclaimed, "There,
George! what a compliment! Did you ever receive such a one before?"

Poor Grace felt inexpressibly confused; she saw she had said something she did not
intend, but could not recall the sense of her words; so at once she asked, "What have I
said?"

"Oh, don't be frightened," answered Emily, "only something exceedingly kind and
pretty; you paid George a very fine compliment indeed."

"I am sure I am very sorry," said Grace, with great *naïveté*, "but really I did not mean
it."

This occasioned another laugh; Emily exclaimed, "So much the better," and Campbell,
"that's a kiss on one cheek and a blow on the other, George!" whilst George, in a
theatrical manner, entreated the gracious Grace not to repent of her graciousness. "By
the bye," added he, "we had a choriambic to celebrate your arrival just before you came,
and as I had the honour of its composition, I hope I may consider this graceful
graciousness of the gracious Grace, as an especial reward for my choriambic!"

"*What* do you call it?" asked Mary Anne.

"A choriambic, my learned cousin, from two Greek words, which I dare say I need
not explain to Miss Leslie—I beg your pardon—to Grace, I mean—no doubt you
understand Greek?"

Grace laughed at the idea, but did not think it worth while to deny, till he repeated his
question.

"No? indeed!" said he, "I thought all young ladies educated at home were classical
scholars now-a-days. Here is this cousin of mine has begun *Latin*, at any rate: come,
Mary Anne, hic, hæc, hoc, hujus—come?" giving her a jog, "what comes next?"

"Oh, George, how tiresome you are!" said Mary Anne, "I wish you'd *not*."

"Ah, you don't know!" cried George, "that comes of the *no-flogging* system: when
young ladies meddle with boys' learning, they ought not to object to boys' punishments:
no Latin was ever learned without being well *beat* in, and either you have been beat or
you don't know!"

"But I do, though," replied Mary Anne, rather provoked.

"If you knew, you'd say," retorted George; "come, hic, hæc, hoc, hujus. . . ."

"Huic, hunc, hanc, hoc," continued Mary Anne.

"Well! there's a good girl, she shan't be flogged! Do you know, Grace," continued he,
"their governess does not approve of punishments; she says that she teaches 'all by love;'
so when they're naughty and won't say their 'as in presenti,' or their French verbs, or
any of their 'ologies,' instead of the old-fashioned corner, or a fool's cap, or bed, which
naughty good girls used to have once upon a time, what do you think she does?"

"Really, I cannot guess," replied Grace, finding he waited for an answer, and not at all able to find out if he was in jest or earnest.

"No! nor any one else, I'll answer for it!" said George. "Why, she has three modes of punishment: if they are simply naughty, or obstinate, she helps them at dinner to all the titbits, and gives them more sweets and cake than all the rest put together. I believe she keeps a box called the 'naughty box,' full of barley-sugar and lollypops, for the bad children. If they are *very* naughty, she makes them a present of very pretty picture-books, with gilt edges; and if they are very naughty indeed, and deserve a rare flogging, she goes to Mrs. Sell's and chooses the prettiest toy in the whole shop, and gives it to this naughty girl or boy, with a smile and a kiss."

"Oh, George!" cried Mary Anne, "how can you be so ridiculous!"

"I don't say it is not ridiculous," said George, "but I do say it is true—now is it not? Is not Fanny the worst among you, and has she not a library full of these little books? and is not Charlotte the best among you, and has she not—not got one?"

"Charlotte has got none, but I do not know that she is the best among us, only you always choose to say so," replied his cousin.

"Well," said George, "I'll tell you what we'll do; we'll have a trial about it when we are all together to-night."

"I'll tell you what," said Campbell, "I think you are all very unfair about Miss Newmarsh; I'm sure if you would only do as she bids you, you'd be all very good girls."

"Yes, that's all true enough, I dare say," said George, "but you see they *won't;* and then they get rewarded for being disobedient. We must have the trial; that's poz! and then we can decide once for all. Reginald Freemantle shall be judge, and the rest jury; and I'll be the barrister, and examine my witnesses. You'll see it will be capital fun!"

Here the dressing-bell rang, and broke up the conference.

CHAPTER V

Il est vrai qu'elle est plus formée qu'on ne l'est ordinairement à son age.... Par exemple,
sa facilité à contrefaire tout le monde, est une chose que je n'ai vue qu'à elle.
MADAME DE GENLIS

THE YOUNG PEOPLE dispersed, in order to be ready for dinner. Emily conducted Grace up stairs; she showed her the room meant for her, and after a little talk, took her to her mamma's room where she left her. In a few minutes, Mrs. Leslie came in.

"Oh, mamma, I am so glad you have come!" cried Grace, "I thought I should hardly have time to speak to you; but first, Emily says, if you approve it, she and I are to have the same room;—have you any objection?"

"No, my dear; you are old enough, Grace, to act for yourself, and I can trust you not to lie awake, talking *too* long," said her mamma, smiling, "and not to gossip."

"Thank you, dear mamma," answered Grace. Mrs. Leslie then inquired how she had got on with her new friends. "Oh, I have been thinking it all over before you came in," said Grace, "you can't think, mamma, how clever and amusing they are! it is just like reading a story to sit by and listen—and George, he is the drollest boy I ever saw! I have been laughing loud by myself, thinking of his odd faces and ways; and Emily, too, I see can be very amusing; but George is quite the head when they are all together."

"Well, and the cousins?" asked her mamma.

"Oh, I should think they are very clever too, but quite in a different way: do you know, mamma, Mary Anne Duff learns Latin! But George told such odd stories, I hardly know whether to believe them or not."

"Well, and how did you get on with them?" asked Mrs. Leslie, "did you talk at all?"

"Oh, no, not at all!" answered the little girl; "I could not talk as they do; it is just like a book, and when I did speak, I made such blunders that they were all quite amused; I said just the wrong thing, and then made bad worse,—I was so glad, mamma, that you were not by."

"Why, my dear?" asked Mrs. Leslie.

"Why, mamma, I should never mind *telling* you of my mistakes," said Grace, rather abashed, "but I could not bear you to see them, I should feel so much more ashamed of them."

Here the maid answered the bell, and after a few necessary arrangements, Grace followed her and her wardrobe, and proceeded to take possession of her new apartment. We trust the good reader will allow us to take a peep at the young ladies at their toilet, as their conversation will spare us some tedious narrative, and serve to introduce the expected party. After some little talk, on the house and such topics, Emily turned to Grace, who was making an orderly arrangement of her little wardrobe, and warned her not to put on her 'best frock,' as this was not their grandest party.

"We are to have *our* grand party on Twelfth Day," said she.

"And who is coming to-day," asked Grace; "what sort of party is it—big or little?"

"Oh," replied Emily, "it's big and little, large and small; it's nothing and every thing. It's neither all big people for papa and mamma, nor all little people for us; but it's a little of both: mamma said it was an accident, and could not be helped, and that two parties had got into one day. So we are all to dine down stairs with company; we have never done such a thing before. I don't like it much,—particularly *to-day*, for there's a gentleman, a very clever man indeed, to be there;—by the bye he knows your mamma very well, and papa says he wanted to marry her once. He wears spectacles, and has such a voice when he chooses; we are all so frightened at him;—sometimes he takes no notice of us, and at other times he will turn suddenly upon one of us—generally me, because I am the eldest, and ask some puzzling question, or say something in a terrible voice; his words are not so cross,—indeed Mary Anne says, he pays very great compliments; but I am always too frightened to hear what he says. Do you know, he is the only person in the world I am afraid of; I can take off every body else, but not him. Now," continued she, "I'll show you another of the company," and she jumped up, put on a face, bowed as though accosting somebody, repeating the words, "Very well? very well? Mrs. Ward? the children? quite well? that's well, that's well;" she then planted herself before the fire, and contrived with the help of her dressing-gown, to look more like a rather large gentleman, than any one could well imagine who has not seen a little girl possessed of this power. Then resuming her own manner, she said, "Now you will see that gentleman to-night,—I won't tell you his name,—and then you'll be sure I could take off Mr. Everard as well; but I could not for the world, I am so afraid of him."

"Mr. Everard!" said Grace, "Mr. Everard is my god-papa, I wonder if it is the same."

"Oh, I have no doubt it is," replied Emily, "and I am so glad, because now he will take notice of you, and not of us."

After a time, the conversation on the evening was continued, and Grace asked if there were to be any young people. "Oh, yes, several," said Emily, "there are all the Duffs; oh, by the bye, their governess, Miss Newmarsh, is to come with them; you know George told you of her just now; I would show you her in a minute, only I'm afraid we shall be late," and as she spoke, she drew her face for one moment into a new expression, in a manner that seemed quite magical to Grace. "Well," continued she, "there are the Duffs—you must learn them—Constantia, Fanny, Charlotte, and the little ones, who don't signify; Constance and Fanny are twins; well, then there's Newton Gray, his mamma comes with him; he is older than any of us, above fourteen; but I won't tell you about him, for I should like to see what you think of him;—is it not odd, his name is Newton Newton Gray?—besides these, there are the Wards, Isabella and James Ward, our cousins."

"What a number there seems!" said Grace.

"Oh, I have forgotten one," continued Emily, "Reginald Freemantle; he is a sort of betweenity, for he is seventeen or eighteen, but he always comes to *us;* he is a very nice fellow indeed; so witty and clever; he and George together sometimes make us die with laughing. But I was going to count them—not the little ones—only ourselves; three Duffs, two Wards, Newton Gray, Reginald Freemantle, and our five selves: yes, twelve," concluded she, assenting to Grace's reckoning, "not so many you see."

"Yes, but then there's all the company besides," said Grace.

"Oh, never mind them, it is *our* party properly, and mamma said we should have the back drawing-room all to ourselves." Grace inquired if these Wards were those of whom they were talking down stairs; "Oh, yes, the same; *the Honorable Miss Ward,*" replied Emily, in a comic tone, which set Grace laughing, "or bouncing B, as George sometimes will call her."

"And what is she like, really?" asked Grace.

"Oh, she's very good-natured, and cannot ever be really angry, though she tries: she's silly sometimes, and very affected, and then we laugh her into good humour again. But do you know, though she's hardly older than I, she's quite a little woman, and often gets treated as if she was *out;* but then she dresses just like a woman, and gives herself such airs that the people don't know she's not one. But you won't see her in her glory now, because, you know, we cannot wear coloured dresses: she has been quite angry with the mourning, and says she will dress this holidays like us '*children,*'—in white, with black ribands. I dare say she will have white crape on to-night."

"Is she clever?" asked Grace.

"No—yes—a little," said Emily. "Oh! I'll tell you what she does very well, she plays beautifully, and that makes her seem old; for she sits down and plays waltzes and quadrilles without end—all without book; but then, you know, she goes to such a grand school: her papa pays three or four hundred pounds a-year for her. Oh, I could tell you such a good story!" continued she, presently, "but really we shall be late;" and she went on to plait her hair very fast. Then, after a minute, she cried, "Grace, look here!"

Grace turned, and started with surprise; she could not for some seconds be sure it was Emily. She had stuck up her hair, and tucked up her gown behind, and looked regularly French. She then walked a few steps, with her toes outward, and said with a true French air, "Mais, fi donc, Mademoiselle!—There!" continued she, pulling down her hair again, "that is Isabella's French teacher; I wish you could see her."

"Oh!" cried Grace, "please don't make me laugh so, I shall never be dressed!"

"Why, you *are* dressed," answered Emily, "I have been wondering at you all the time; I never saw any thing like you; some of our girls are very quick, but not like you! I cannot think how you can tie your own frock and sash in that way: I wish I could; how did you learn it?"

"By getting up early, you know, I'm obliged," replied Grace.

"Obliged! how?"

"Why, when I get up before the servants and mamma, there's nobody to help me, and I must dress myself."

"But why are you obliged to get up?"

"I am not *obliged*," answered Grace, "but when I have got any thing to do, I *must*, you know."

"Why, my dear Grace, what do you mean?" said Emily, laughing; "you are obliged, and you *must*, and you are not obliged, at the same time; does your mamma order you in this way?"

"I am not obliged to get up early," said Grace, seeing the puzzle, "but I *am* obliged to fasten my frock myself if I do."

"But do you mean to say you get up before you are made?" asked Emily.

"To be sure I do," answered Grace, "particularly in summer. When I was a very little girl mamma did not wish it; but when I began music, she said I was old enough to do as I pleased in that respect."

"But what can you do?—all alone, too!"

"Oh, I never can get through half I have to do, and am so sorry when the clock strikes seven, and I must go and practise."

"What! are you up before seven? why it is worse than being at school; we only get up at seven."

"But do you not practise before breakfast, at home?" asked Grace.

"Oh, I never do lessons at home," said Emily; "and at school we have to scramble through our tasks before breakfast. I'm never very long at that: some of the girls learn their lessons in bed, and some get up when they are called; but I open my books when I am plaiting my hair, and gabble them over a little; that does well enough for me."

"But," said Grace, "you cannot know them well in that way."

"I say them better than half the girls," replied Emily, "and am oftener than any, even than Selina Carey, at the top of the classes, and last year I got the prize for being at the top."

Grace said nothing, but stood at her dressing-table, musing over Emily's cleverness, which altogether seemed to her more amazing than any thing she ever heard of. Emily roused her by calling out, "Oh, Grace, dear! please come and fasten my frock; it's a great deal past the half hour, but the second bell never rings when there's company; and people will not be here yet. But I'am rather in a fuss, for I have got to find my gloves, and tie my sandals, and one, I know, is off."

"Let me sew on your sandal," said Grace, at her little box in a moment; "see, how fortunate! here's black silk ready threaded; you look for your gloves, and I will sew your sandal in a minute."

But Emily had found her gloves and tied her sandal before Grace had completed her task; and hearing several steps on the stairs, Emily caught the shoe from her, broke off the thread, put in a pin, and said, "La! it doesn't signify; there now I'm ready." Then, springing up and running for her handkerchief, she added,

> " 'A pin in need
> Is a friend indeed,'

as we often say at school."

Grace followed her in silence: she thought of the old adage, "A stitch in time saves nine:" but she did not feel inclined to say it.

CHAPTER VI

Vociferated logic kills me quite,
A noisy man is always in the right.
COWPER

THE PARTY EXPECTED in the evening, was, as Emily had explained, of a heterogeneous character. Mrs. Ward had failed in finding the Freemantles able to meet Mrs. Leslie on the 8th. This family had formerly been neighbours of Mrs. Leslie, and knew her before her marriage. Sir Richard Freemantle was in a well known banking house in the city, but he had a family seat in the country, where he usually resided: they had all come up to London for a month before Christmas-day, and intended to have returned to Lacklands several days before Mrs. Ward's proposed dinner party. Lady Freemantle had therefore requested Mrs. Ward to allow them to see Mrs. Leslie the very first day of her arrival, and they settled to put off their journey till the day after. This caused a great change in Mrs. Ward's arrangements; she was obliged to get together a few dinner guests in haste; she also asked a few elder young people for the evening. There was the children's New Year's day party previously arranged, to be added to this. The young people also always dined with their parents on that day, and were promised not to be disappointed. There are only three other dinner guests necessary to be noticed: the Mr. Everard, of whom Emily spoke with so much alarm, was one. He was something of a "terrible Turk" to children, but if we may be allowed the expression, "his bark was worse than his bite." He had always a sly liking for little folks, especially if he saw any thing either good or clever in them; but he could be severe on those who did not please him. Mr. and Mrs. Russell completed the dinner guests. Mr. Russell was a man well known in the literary and political world: he had till latterly been for many years the editor of a Whig periodical: he was a very pleasant man, and an acceptable guest at most tables.

Having introduced the reader so far to his new acquaintance, we must proceed to give a slight sketch of the plan of the house, which may serve to facilitate the understanding, both of this complicated party and of future scenes. Mr. Ward's house, or rather cottage, for it was built on that model, was large and very commodious. It had been in the possession of several occupants before Mr. Ward; each of whom had added to it; and, except lofty rooms, it had all the advantages of size, without the appearance of it. All the sitting-rooms were on the ground-floor; the entrance was behind, which led into a square saloon, usually called the hall; in this were five doors, which led respectively to the stair-case on the right hand, the dining-room on the left, the two drawing-rooms opposite, and one communicating with a passage which led to the library and one or two small rooms. The windows of the drawing-rooms opened into the garden, and looked down upon a sloping lawn, which reached to the borders of the river Thames. These two rooms also had folding doors between them, and though they were both on a line, the smaller one had got distinguished by the children by the name of the "back drawing-room," on account of their having been accustomed to this term in the house where they formerly resided in London. There was also a small ante-room connected with the last by an arch which led to a long conservatory.

Having despatched these necessary, though tedious details, we will proceed to the front drawing-rooms, where we find the ladies of the house already seated. They were soon joined by Mr. Ward, who had driven Mr. Everard from London. The children were talking and laughing in the back drawing-room, and though seen, and occasionally heard, through the doors, which were open, they were far enough removed to feel quite at their ease. Emily, however, was anxious that Grace should see the entrance of the gentleman she had taken off, and had therefore moved her to the most conspicuous place, so as to command a full view of the front drawing-room. Here they sat and chatted in a low voice, and we shall take no notice of them for the present, only feeling sure that Grace was watching for the terrific Mr. Everard, and often looking at the door. Before long it opened, and Mr. Everard made his appearance; he walked up to Mrs. Ward, bowed and greeted her, and said in a sonorous tone, "Madam, your servant and your slave;" he then turned to Mrs. Leslie, bowed lower, waved his hand, placed it on his heart, and said, "Fair lady of our reverence, we greet you well." Mrs. Ward then addressed him, and feared they had had a very cold drive from London; to which Mr. Everard replied, "Cold was the drive, but warm the welcome awaiting us," and he hummed in an indifferent manner the first lines of a ballad then fashionable, expressive of a similar sentiment. He then began fingering the ornaments on the mantel-piece, holding them very close to his eyes, and presently admired a beautiful bouquet of flowers, asking leave, "like Beauty's beast to steal a rose;" he then repeated the hackneyed lines of Romeo's, of "a rose by any other name," in such a manner as to make them sound new to every body; such is the charm of a voice. This was his usual style of conversation, if such it could be called; a sort of soliloquy, addressed to any thing, or any body at hand; he seldom joined in a general conversation, but would argue with one person sometimes with great force, or he would put in a pithy remark, either of assent or dissent, on subjects that were being discussed, sometimes with great point or wit. His present audible musings however were disturbed by the entrance of Sir Richard, Lady, and Miss Freemantle, and though Grace had quite forgotten Emily's representation, and was absorbed by Mr. Everard's voice, she in a moment recognized this gentleman as its original. Mr. and Mrs. Russell followed soon after, and Mr. Ward rang the bell for dinner. Immediately these last entered, Mr. Everard turned to Mrs. Leslie, and asked after her "little maiden," his god-daughter, remarking he had seen her but once. Hearing she was with the rest of the children, in the next room, he would not allow Mrs. Leslie to stir, but said he would go and make acquaintance with her himself, adding, "the maiden's name is Grace, I know." The children felt considerable alarm at his approach, not unlike that of a flock of sheep at the casual appearance of a strange dog amongst them, only our little party felt the more certain assurance that their enemy was advancing for their actual annoyance, and there was no means of escape in their power. Emily's late feeling of triumph, at reading in Grace's face the acknowledgement of her successful power of mimicry, sunk before the dreaded presence of her foe. But to her great relief, he approached Grace, whom she had seated in the most conspicuous place, as we have before explained. He placed himself before her, and addressed her with suitable action as follows:—

> "Fair Grace! the sweetest Grace of earthly sphere,
> If of our earth thou art—I prithee tell,
> Child of great Jove, which of the sisters three
> May claim the honour of a name from thee?
> Thalia, 'Glaia, or Euphrosyne?"

Poor Grace was much more alarmed than became her godlike extraction; luckily, however, it did not appear, and more luckily, there came a line to her assistance, which she simply rehearsed, and was never more relieved than when she had got to the end of it; she replied:—

> "Thalia I! a grace and muse at once."

"Then," returned her tormentor,

> "Then graceful Grace and Muse—scarcely of *Comedy*,
> Thalia! take this rose,—thy humble votary's gift,"

and he presented the rose. Poor Grace had no friendly line rise to her lips this time; she saw too that the "company" in the other room were silently looking in at the scene, and feeling very foolish and very awkward, she merely took the rose, and placed it in her sash. Poor Grace! her annoyance was not at an end.

> "Better than words, thy deeds, intent
> On kindly thoughts, sweet Grace, in silence eloquent,"

continued her tormentor. How glad was Grace when the door opened and dinner was announced! but what was her dismay when, regardless of Mrs. Ward's summons to him, Mr. Everard declared himself, "Thalia's votary," and insisted on "attending her winged steps." He took her hand, and Grace was compelled to be conducted in form to dinner by this formidable gentleman; and before she had well recovered, she found herself seated between him and Miss Freemantle. George was disappointed, for he thought he should sit next her, and wanted to make her laugh at some of the company, especially Sir Richard Freemantle. But "grown people" themselves are constrained frequently to submit to equally bitter disappointments of the same sort, and with a better grace than

George, who certainly looked rather black on the occasion. He, however, sat next to his cousin Mary Anne; this, which would have quite satisfied him, had not the novelty of a new acquaintance interfered, he considered better than being placed between two seniors. The children of course did not enjoy the party as if there had been no strangers, but it was a great novelty to them. George was ready to amuse himself with the peculiarities of any or all of the company. Emily congratulated herself that she was not in Grace's situation, at whom she now and then tried to get a peep, to see how she got on; Campbell made himself contented and satisfied, as he usually did, wherever he went; while Grace by degrees forgot her embarrassment, since her terrible neighbour did not continue to address her in his heroic strain, only now and then in a few words of the same character, he offered to supply her wants from the dishes before them; however there was a great deal of talking going on, and nobody was looking at or thinking of her, so she did not care. But, alas! she was not destined to escape so easily. During a remove, and in the midst of a dead pause in the conversation, Mr. Everard turned upon her, and in a hollow sepulchral voice, that made many start, he let drop slowly from his lips, the words:—

> "Wilt thou the gay Thalia's part forget,
> And pledge with me a cup like dire Melpomene?"

Fortune once more favoured Grace, for a slight movement among the servants, created a diversion in her favour, and something like a line seemed to spring up within her. In a tone, rather in contrast to that of her persecutor, she made answer:—

> "I am no Janus, double-faced."

> "Then, wittiest Grace of Graces, pledge with me
> A simple cup of love and amity,"

returned Mr. Everard, pouring out some wine. Now poor Grace had never taken a glass of wine with any body in her life, and at any other time it would have been formidable to her; but now it seemed quite a deliverance, and she did not care for all Mr. Everard's gesticulations, so long as he did not address her. But soon after she was relieved from his notice, at the expense of the rest of the party; nobody knew how the dispute began, but suddenly Mr. Everard answered Mr. Russell, who sat opposite to him, in his most sonorous tone, "Sir, I say he is a blot on the escutcheon of his country, a reproach to the face of his King, a dishonour to himself, and a pest to society."

There was a pause for a short space, when Mr. Russell replied with much temper and ease, "If so, sir, I am sure you are very right in not becoming a Whig."

"Sir," almost vociferated Mr. Everard, "a Whig does not know himself, he wears a mask, though not Thalia's," added he, in a changed tone, turning to his small neighbour, then, in his startling voice, again he went on:—"I say, sir, he is bringing ruin and destruction on his country, and pulling down the gigantic fabrics, raised by the *wisdom of our forefathers*, about our ears;" then muttering between his teeth, but quite distinct enough to be heard all over the room, he repeated the line:—

> "Come woe, destruction, ruin, loss, decay!"

when he made a pause, which no one seemed disposed to break, and he completed the couplet thus;—

> "The cat will mew; the dog will have his day."

His tone was quite altered, but no one could tell whether he was in jest or earnest, and an uncomfortable silence ensued till this singular man turned to his little companion, and gave a sudden sharp bark, so like that of a dog that the whole company were startled. The children, however, most quickly recovered, and with George at their head, they received the sally, which seemed especially directed to them, with acclamations of merriment. A great relief it was to the whole party, for no one knew what to expect next. This took place after dinner, and Mr. Everard ceased to torment Grace by long speeches, only occasionally with devoted actions he offered "his Lady Grace" fruits and cakes of all sorts, which at first she was afraid to decline. But she had now a new series of persecutions to endure. Miss Freemantle, who had been till the late outbreak incessantly chatting with her other neighbour, now began to take notice of Grace, and "her admirer," as she called Mr. Everard; she kept whispering to her continually. "There! Grace, don't you see he wants you to thank him for the rose? Now thank him, there's a good girl; it is very unkind to receive his gifts so coldly;—I dare say he wants a kiss," whispered she very low. "Don't you know he is your *admirer*? he wants you to be his wife; you must marry him now, you know, that you have accepted his rose, that was a trial; and then just now he said 'love' to you, and you did not say 'no,' so you must have him now."

Grace looked dreadfully frightened, though she did not believe a word; and this teazing young lady went on to say, "Oh, you cannot draw back now, you have promised, Grace."

"Oh, no! I have not promised indeed," cried Grace, in her momentary alarm hurried out of all considerations; then she thought how foolish she had been, for she knew quite well this young lady was only in jest. Poor little girl! she thought she had never been so glad as when dinner was announced; but now she heard with ten-fold pleasure, Mrs. Ward propose moving into the drawing-room, which she did rather early, on account of the young people who would shortly arrive. The seniors and juniors took respective possession of the two rooms, and soon were in full conversation.

CHAPTER VII

"He will remove most certainly from evil," said the Prince, "who shall devote himself to that solitude which you have recommended by your example."
RASSELAS

"WHAT A STRANGE MAN that Mr. Everard is!" exclaimed Mrs. Ward, as she stirred the fire, while the other ladies stood before it; "he certainly does imitate Dr. Johnson, as people say, but I think I never saw him so rude before."

"It is a great pity, indeed," said Mrs. Leslie, "that he allows himself in such eccentricities; he would not deliberately be rude, I am sure."

This was said on Mrs. Russell's account. Mrs. Ward smiled: she might have rallied Mrs. Leslie on her defence, but she was always a little afraid of that lady, though she was not likely to think so; she therefore said nothing.

"Oh, he is an odious man!" cried Miss Freemantle; "I declare I was frightened out of my wits; I am sure, Mrs. Leslie, your little girl must have wonderful nerves to stand his attacks as she did. He was teasing her all dinner time."

"Most children I know would have cried," remarked one lady, who sat opposite at dinner.

"But not Grace a bit," returned the young lady. "I sat near her, and heard all, which no one else could. I can assure you she answered very well indeed, in a way that a grown-up girl would not be ashamed of. And really," she added, laughing, "she seems quite at home among all the gods and goddesses; I had to brush up my old lessons to keep pace at all with her."

Mrs. Leslie smiled, and replied she was glad her little girl remembered her *Catechism* of Mythology, when it was required.

"I can assure you," replied Miss Freemantle, "she has it all at her fingers' ends. It was the same before dinner: I sat near the door and heard all that passed. I am sure that horrid man and his tremendous voice was enough to frighten away all her senses; but she looked as quiet as possible, and acknowledged her relationship to the Graces and Muses, as if she had been born and bred among them. For my part, I don't know a Grace from a Muse, nor remember their hard, long names, though I learned it all at school; but then I hated it with all my heart."

"I am rather surprised," answered Mrs. Leslie, "at what you tell me of Grace, for she had a great dislike to her Mythology lesson at first, and never seems to take to it as she does to some others."

"It surprises me, Mrs. Leslie," said Mrs. Ward, "how you can undertake that child all by yourself. Certainly," she added, "if you had assistance it would not be much better: a home education must be a nuisance any way; there is no end to the troubles with the children; we tried it once, but Mr. Ward did not like it, and it did not answer at all. Emily is so high-spirited, school is the only place for her; and the rest were so young. So when we found Ellen was so constantly with her grandmamma, and when we left London, we gave up the home plan, and mean to send all to school as soon as they are old enough. I found it an amazing relief: with my health, it really was too much for me, and I was in a constant fever. My sister, Mrs. Duff, however, thinks very differently; she would not let a girl of hers go to school for the world: but, you know, she's very peculiar in her notions of education, and has got a governess who carries out her plans to her heart's content, I should think." "Do you know," continued she, "I'm almost surprised they let the children come at all to see their cousins. At one time I really thought we must give it up, but we have compounded now, and it is settled that the little Duffs *may* come to us, provided I do not allow them to dance, or to play at cards, or to have dice."

"Why, how can you amuse children night after night," asked Miss Freemantle, "without such helps? Poor little things! I quite pity them."

"Oh!" said Mrs. Ward, laughing, "you need not do *that*; George and Emily, you know, are very clever and amusing, and can keep them in a roar from morning to night. I have given them the library, for they used to disturb the whole house when they were in any of these rooms; and then, you know, they *may* play at *some* games, and have forfeits and amusements of that kind."

"But I thought Miss Newmarsh did not quite approve of games of any sort?" said one of the ladies.

"Why, no, she does not, but my sister has rather too much sense to consent to *that*. Miss Newmarsh has tried very hard to confine the exercise of the girls to their 'Calisthenic movements,' and their amusements to the 'Bible riddles,' 'New Testament puzzles,' and other entertainments of the same sort."

"What are these riddles and puzzles?" said Lady Freemantle; "I never heard of them."

"Why, they are all manner of riddles and cross-readings, and curious questions in the Bible. I have never seen them, but I hear the children talk of them sometimes: George laughs at them, and Emily can hardly help it; but Ellen one day nearly cried, when they were explaining them to her: then they 'cap' in the Bible, and make crambo verses out of it, and play at forfeits with texts: it's a very good thing in one respect, for those children know the Bible nearly by heart; yet I don't know if it does them any good after all."

Here they were disturbed by the arrival of guests, till the whole party had assembled. Of course the seniors and juniors allotted themselves into the two rooms respectively. There were, however, two dubious cases: the first was Reginald Freemantle; but he very soon settled the matter by joining the young people. The other was a more delicate case—"Miss Ward." She did not choose to do more than ask "where the *children* were," look in, and nod good-naturedly; but finding nothing but dull conversation going on for some time among the elder people, she longed to adjourn to the young party; and this she effected with a good grace on the entrance of Mr. Everard, who seldom waited for the rest of the gentlemen. The moment he appeared, she protested she could not "stay in the same place with that unaccountable being," and withdrew into the next room. Here we will leave her for the present, and take up the conversation in the drawing-room, where Mr. Everard found it on his entrance. Mrs. Leslie was saying, "It is at any rate only an experiment as yet; we cannot fairly pronounce a judgment either way."

Mr. Everard asked, "What, fair lady, may this experiment be on which you speak with your wonted wisdom and caution?"

Mrs. Leslie explained, that in a boys' school at Halston a new plan had just been adopted, principally affecting the play hours. "But," added she, "I have only just heard of it, and cannot well explain it: this lady, who understands all about it, can do justice to it better than I."

Mr. Everard very politely applied to Miss Newmarsh for explanation.

"The plan is very simple," said that lady, "and easily explained. Dr. Barker has had great experience of boys, and he found they got a great deal more harm by themselves in play hours than at any other time. He heard of a plan, and was immediately resolved to engraft the principle into his system, and being a man of great grasp of mind, he has effected his purpose in a very able manner. His object was to prevent two boys from speaking together without the presence of a master. As he had above a hundred boys, this seemed almost impossible; but by adding some new ushers to his establishment, and himself and his eldest son, who is in the school, taking their part in the watchings, they have attained their end. He has by this means ten or twelve masters in the house."

"That must be a very expensive plan," interrupted a gentleman standing by; "I wonder how it can answer his purpose, with a hundred boys."

"His terms are high," returned Miss Newmarsh, "and his extra masters, such as French, music, and drawing, having been first-rate, were very expensive. He now has engaged *accomplished* men, but not *professors*. These reside in the house, and with the assistance of himself, his son, and all the masters, they do very well."

"But what are these watchings?" asked some one.

"Why he divides the school into decades," answered Miss Newmarsh; "to every decade there is a Decadian, which is one of the masters, whose business it is *to be sure* that those ten boys never speak together out of his hearing, and are never left together for one moment. Besides this, they are never allowed to speak any thing but Latin. He hopes to effect modern languages in time. He tried French at first, but found it did not do; only a boy here and there knew any thing of French, and many of the masters themselves did not speak it."

"But," said the same objector, "some of the masters of drawing, music, &c. cannot speak Latin, I suppose."

"He endeavours to obtain such as do, and wishes them to learn if they do not; but for the present he puts such over the little classes who cannot yet speak Latin. Besides his object is to discourage talking *entirely* among the boys, and to make them feel instead a confidence and love towards their teachers, who are constantly with them, and as ready to sympathize in all their little pleasures, as they are to lead them to profitable discourse, when they are inclined for it; and at such times the Decadian has the power of dispensing with Latin; indeed that is his prerogative. Dr. Barker is exceedingly strong, on giving to his masters most full discretionary powers; without which nothing can be done in education."

"Well, but at night they may chatter away, and make up for the day's constraint."

"Oh, my dear sir," replied Miss Newmarsh, smiling, "Dr. Barker understands young people too well, not to be aware of the dangers that may arise on that point; and he has made provision to meet them, supposing such an emergency should occur. The beds are already placed in decades; five on each side, and a Decadian's bed could be inserted at the feet of the two ranges of beds; at right angles, between each row; besides, the heads of the boys' beds are set alternately head and feet against the wall;—do you understand?"

"Oh, perfectly," replied the gentleman, "like so many pairs of soles."

"By this means," continued Miss Newmarsh, "the boys could not speak to each other in a whisper or low voice, and the Decadian would have as full command over them by night as by day."

"But," persisted her invincible objector, "suppose the poor Decadian, wearied by his hard day's labour, at any time should sleep so soundly, and snore so roundly, that the one should wake the boys and the other give them the liberty of talking?"

"Dr. Barker has made provision for that too," answered Miss Newmarsh. "In each dormitory are four decades, and when the nocturnal watchings are put in practice, to each of these dormitories four Decadians would be attached. His rule then would be, that if one Decadian snored, another should rise and wake him, and see what was going on in that part of the gallery."

"But how could they tell a Decadian's snore from a boy's snore?" asked the gentleman.

"Oh," replied Miss Newmarsh, "they could easily distinguish a boy's snore from a man's snore."

"I am not so sure of that," said the gentleman; "besides, every body does not snore, and suppose a Decadian sleeps soundly without."

"Dr. Barker justly observes," replied the lady, "that when a man's heart is in his business or profession, there is no fear of his failing in his duty. The soldier wakes at the first sound of the drum; the peasant is at his work before the dawn, without any summons at all, then why should not his masters be in the same way alive to the claims of duty? he studies besides, even now, to assist them in the habit of light sleeping, by diligently attending to the subject of dieting, in which he greatly excels. However, Dr. Barker does not anticipate difficulties in this part of his arrangements, and he says if they arise (he spares no expense), he would hire three watchmen for the three dormitories."

"Three watchmen?" exclaimed the gentleman, in a tone of doubt.

"Not real *Watchmen*," answered Miss Newmarsh, "that would only be their title; they must of course be trustworthy and superior people, whose business it would be to give an alarm at a snore among the Decadians, or any talking among the boys."

"Then the poor Decadians would not be released?"

"Oh, by no means," returned Miss Newmarsh, "*I* consider the nocturnal watchings the most important point in the system, and long for their adoption: you think it hard upon the Decadians, I suppose? but Dr. Barker has thought of *that*, and has arranged so that each of the Decadians would have one night out of seven to himself; he calls this night their 'Sabbakin,' and the room that he is building for their use the 'Sabbatarium;' and rather than that they should any of them lose their Sabbakin, he himself would take share in the nocturnal watchings."

"I am very troublesome," said the gentleman, "but may I ask why Dr. Barker does not call his masters *Deans* rather than *Decadians*?"

"I am quite aware," replied Miss Newmarsh, "that *Dean* is the proper title, but he had that office already in his establishment, and he could not re-appropriate it."

"I see that Dr. Barker is armed at all points," remarked the gentleman, "pray how long has he tried his plan?"

"Three-quarters of a year; he began last Easter," replied Miss Newmarsh, "and it has answered beyond our most sanguine hopes, for before he came the school had got into a dreadful state of insubordination among the individuals; in less than a month the reformation was most signal, and now the boys are in the quietest state possible, and many of them in a very interesting frame of mind."

"But what do the boys say to it?" asked the same gentleman; "how they must hate it!"

"Indeed, my dear Sir," replied Miss Newmarsh, "you are very much mistaken; the boys like it better than their masters even."

"Why they are obliged to say so, of course, or they'd be flogged!" said the gentleman.

"Flogged!" repeated Miss Newmarsh, "Dr. Barker *never* flogs! But you're mistaken again; I know that many of the boys have said the same at home, and have remarked that *now* they never cheat, nor quarrel, nor fight, nor get into any troubles or punishments, and that they are quite happy, and don't want the old system back again. I know one sweet little fellow said to his mamma, 'Dear mamma, I'm so happy and good now at school; and I always do right—there's no harm in my saying I always do right, because, you know, I could not do wrong if I wished it ever so much.' Another clever fellow remarked, it was exactly like walking in a narrow path with a high wall on each side."

"*Well, then,* all I can say is, that boys must be different now from what they were in my day," said the gentleman, as though giving up the question.

"Oh, no, not different, dear Sir, only they have been led to better ways by kindness and reasonable treatment, and not frightened and beaten into deceit and disobedience." She then appealed to Mr. Everard, and asked what was his opinion.

"Madam," said he, in his decided tone, "when your boys come out of your school they'll be fit for the gallows!"

Miss Newmarsh, nothing daunted, asked, "Why?"

To this he replied, "What happens to a kettle when you stop up its apertures?"

"It bursts," answered Miss Newmarsh.

"So will these boys, madam," said he, "they will burst with pent up folly and evil; and it will not be Dr. Barker's fault, I say, if they are not fit for the gallows."

"Well, I suppose they will not all be hung!" remarked the same gentleman that had before spoken.

"I did not say they would all *come* to the gallows," said Mr. Everard, "I said they would be fit for the gallows."

"Well," returned the other, "you know Hamlet says, 'Use every man after his desert, and who shall 'scape whipping?' "

"Whipping's not hanging," replied Mr. Everard, "I said nothing against whipping."

"But do you not think, Sir," pursued Miss Newmarsh, "human nature is so prone to evil that if we can keep the seeds of evil from springing up we are doing great things?"

"How do weeds grow in a garden?"

"They come up."

"Of themselves?"

"Yes."

"How do you get rid of them?"

"By pulling them up."

"If you shut up earth in a box, will weeds spring up?"

"I suppose not."

"And *I* suppose not, madam, but open that box to the air, and weeds *will* spring up, as readily as—aye, perhaps more readily, than in the open field; so with the hearts of these young people: bring them in contact with the world and the world's temptations, evils will spring up, and they will have less root in themselves, than many, who, on *the old system,* have been tried in their own little world, and have, weed by weed, plucked out each as it appeared."

"But how few have done that!" remarked Miss Newmarsh.

"*None* ever can on your system, madam, because you will not give them the opportunity."

"But do you not think, Sir," continued Miss Newmarsh, "if we can keep boys from the evil example of others, we are bound to do so?"

"Madam," cried Mr. Everard, in rather an elevated tone, "you talk like a foolish mother."

"Which I am *not,*" said the lady.

"Madam," continued Mr. Everard, "I did not say that you *were* a foolish mother, I said you talked like one." He then took a seat next Mrs. Leslie, and hoped the fair Grace was not to be brought up under any *new* systems; adding, he need scarcely ask, since she had not a foolish mother to fight against common sense and the established maxims of wisdom. Mrs. Leslie laughed, and said her little girl was indebted to having a mother not clever enough to devise or follow any new or original plans. The conversation now became less general.

CHAPTER VIII

Within her gilded cage,
I saw a dazzling Belle,
A parrot of that famous kind
Whose name was Nonpareil.
WORDSWORTH

W E MUST NOW take a view of what has been going on in the other room since dinner-time. The young people had scarcely discussed the scenes that passed at dinner, before their expected guests began to arrive. The Duffs were first. Grace thought the twins so alike, and so like Mary Anne, that she should never know any of them apart; they all had very dark smooth hair, which was braided close to the face, and though all so young, their hair behind was tied up. Still they looked like children; they had good complexions, with a rather high colour, and were every where called "very fine young ladies." The twins were much slighter than Mary Anne, and in this respect they became less alike every day. When they came to be known, Fanny was certainly the prettiest and most delicate of the three. Mary Anne, if she had not been under control, with, on her own part, a great fear of displeasing, would have been thought rather bold. Charlotte looked more than only one year younger than her two sisters. There was a family likeness, but her effect was very different; her hair was two shades lighter, and from an invincible propensity to curl, the attempt of dressing it like the others was at length given up, very much against Miss Newmarsh's wishes. It always looked so rough and untidy next theirs, that her mamma said she could bear it no longer. It was, therefore, cut short again, and allowed to take its own course. James Edward, as he was always called, because his papa's name was James, was quite young, and he took his place among the small ones, who had bricks and other amusements in one corner of the room. The conversation continued in the same strain, as soon as the new guests had got settled.

"Oh," cried George to his cousins, "how I wish you had dined with us—we had such fun!" and he began to take off several of the company—their bows, their ways, their tone of voice; especially Mrs. Russell, who, he said, could not say "bo to a goose." He called her a "poor body," and some other names. Grace felt more and more uncomfortable as he went on, particularly when he took off her courtesy. She found she could not laugh, though it was all very like, and she had always laughed before; she felt very uneasy. George then began upon Sir Richard Freemantle, whom he called "the Alderman," though he was not one; he seized his sister's fan, and a paper-cutter on the inkstand, drew a china card-basket before him, and showed how Sir Richard ate and drank. Grace still could not join in the laugh. Emily remarked it this time, and said that Mr. Everard had frightened Grace out of her wits, and she did not wonder at it.

"Oh, no!" said Grace, "I had quite forgotten Mr. Everard."

"Then what's the matter?"

Grace was silent, felt very awkward, and stared in Emily's face. "Now, what's the matter?" repeated George, "what makes you look so? you *shall* tell, for you look almost as stupid as Constance," said he, looking towards his cousin, who was still arranging the little ones in the corner of the room. "What were you thinking of? we *will* know!"

Grace replied, with a feeling that her thought might be very silly, "I was thinking perhaps Sir Richard Freemantle might be very kind."

"Very kind!" cried George, "well I dare say he is, but what then?"

"I thought perhaps as kind as Mrs. Russell," said Grace.

"What do you know of Mrs. Russell?" asked Emily.

"I never saw her before," replied Grace, "but going down stairs I trod on her dress, and she turned to me and smiled, and spoke so kindly, and I thought she looked for a moment like my aunt Stanley."

"Well, but what has all this to do with Sir Richard Freemantle and his dinner?" said George, "you disturbed him—he had not half finished." He attempted to go on, but the young party had received a damp, and only a faint laugh ensued. George threw up his knife and fork, and said, very much provoked, "What flats you all are! and as for you, Grace, you have become almost as sanctimonious as Constance; I think the sight of her has bewitched you," added he, as Constance drew near.

"How you have been laughing!" cried she, "I can't think, George, how you always can go on so."

"Why we meet to laugh, don't we?" asked he.

"No," said she, disdainfully.

"Well, what do we meet for, then? you won't let us dance, or play at cards, and now you won't let us laugh!"

"Oh, no," said she, "I wouldn't prevent your laughing, but we don't *meet* to laugh."

"Well, what *do* we meet for, my sage cousin?"

"Why,—every body knows that," replied she, hesitating a little.

"No, *I* don't," said George.

"Oh, George," cried several, "I'm sure you do."

"I know what *I* think we meet for," said George, "but not what *she* thinks; but I must examine;" then assuming a grave look, and pretending to settle his spectacles, he asked, "my sapient young lady, do we meet for business?"

"No."

"Do we meet for pleasure?"

"No;—yes *you* do, I suppose."

"Well, but *yourself?*" persisted George.

"Oh, *I* don't care about it."

"Well, then," said George, "to come to the point at once, what do *you* think we ought to meet for?"

"Why for edification," replied Constance, gravely.

"Wheugh," cried George, with a whistle, "there!" motioning to Grace and Constance, "you *two* may go together, you will suit very well, I fancy—*we* meet for pleasure, you *sanctimonious* young ladies, for *'edification,'* " and he drew his face down to a prodigious length, and made all laugh but Constance, who remained quite silent and still. George was satisfied, having raised a laugh again.

"Here comes Reginald Freemantle," cried Emily; "I am so glad you have come to us, I have been watching you some time."

"Well, youngsters," said he, shaking hands and greeting them all, while the small ones left their corner, "what can I do for you?"

"Oh, any thing *you* like will do—any thing you like," cried several voices, while George took him aside, and proposed a trial on Miss Newmarsh's reward system.

"No! no!" said Reginald, good-naturedly, I'll have nothing to do with *that.*"

"But why not?" asked George, "it will be such fun! why not?"

"Because I don't choose, my good fellow," said Reginald. He then mixed with the rest, and all were soon deeply engaged settling the preliminaries of a new amusement he was teaching them. It was a French game, called "Mufti." Reginald was to be Mufti, and when he said, *"Mufti fait comme ci,"* all the rest were to do as he did. When he said *"Mufti fait comme ça,"* they were to do nothing, and stand still. Those who failed were put aside, and he called them "dead men." Just as they were practising, Isabella Ward entered their room, and walked slowly towards the merry group. "Here's bouncing B.," cried George, "she shall play! Come, Belle, here's a famous new game, come, you must play."

"George, you're very rude; I shall *not.*"

"Oh, it's the best fun in the world; if *he* says 'Mufti fait commi ci,' and hops, we must all hop; and if he hops all round the room, we *must* all follow; and if he wags his fingers or head, we must do the same; it's the best fun in the world, we've been trying it."

"Well, I'll look at you, children, but I shall not play," answered his cousin.

Here Reginald came forward and explained the game. He said that *he* was Mufti, and that he was used to the office, and had had the honour of leading many young ladies; that he would promise her he would not make her jump over the moon, or do any impossibilities. But Miss Ward was not persuaded by the persuasive Reginald's handsome face; she wished it all the time, and if the folding doors had been shut, perhaps it would have been different;—so much does dignity cost.

"Well," said George, maliciously, "certainly your satins, and pearls, and flummery, don't look very fit for a game of romps."

"Oh," said one of the Duffs, "that is a reproach for our dress."

"You all do very well, and are fit either for a game of romps or a dance," replied George.

They then began, and a laughable game it was to look at. Reginald made a capital 'mufti,' and very wisely managed his resources; he kept it easy for some time for the little ones, or any unapt, and then got harder and more complicated. Fanny Duff was out first of all, then some of the little ones, then Mary Anne, then Newton Grey, then Emily, from laughing and fatigue, and the rest one by one; the two last that remained were Constance and Grace; and for some time it seemed as if neither would miss; but at last Grace did, and Constance, as Reginald said, proved herself worthy her name; not that Grace had not done the same. The young people sat down to rest themselves, and by degrees recovered their breath and comparative gravity. But there was plenty of talking; George was teasing Belle, and saying she looked yellow from jealousy, and that her white satin set off her complexion, and that she would have given her ears, not to speak of her fine pearl ear-rings, to have been in the game; and that if she had, she would have been the very first out; because first, she was bouncing B., and second, clumsy Cousin.

"George, you're very rude indeed; I wonder you're not ashamed of yourself," said Miss Ward, and she turned away, and walked in a grand manner towards a sofa, where were Emily, Grace, and two or three more. Grace was rested by this time, but had lost the animated colour she had just now in the game, and from the fatigue looked rather paler than usual; she *did*, however, always look very different at rest, and in talking or exercise, and Miss Ward did not know her as the little girl she had just now wondered at.

"And who's this little dear?" asked she of Emily, in a patronizing tone;—Emily told her.—"What a darling! oh, you must let me take you in my lap," said she, raising her and kissing her, "what a love! who curls these pretty curls, my dear child? and what a lovely chain, and a miniature, I protest," said she, drawing a locket from poor Grace's band, which had lain quite unperceived; "an officer! what a handsome man! oh, you sly. . . . . ."

"Please don't take it;—please don't talk of it," cried Grace, in a tone so earnest and distrest, that even Isabella was checked, and silenced in her intended raillery; she let Grace take the picture, and replaced it as before. Both were silent, and the Honourable Miss Ward never found herself in a more awkward situation in her life. There was something in Grace's tone and manner, so out of keeping with the style in which she had been addressing her, and with the situation she had made her assume, that even Isabella, who was not very quick in such matters, felt she had made a false step; but the question was, how to get her off her lap. The *little* girl seemed to grow heavier every moment, and older too, and she wondered how she had ever dreamed of placing her there; this put a happy thought into the young lady's head; "how old is she?" asked she of Emily; for she felt some repugnance in addressing Grace herself.

"Between ten and eleven, I believe," said Emily, who all along had marvelled at her cousin's want of tact.

"Is it possible?" cried Isabella, "I should have taken her for five or six. How young she looks of her age!" and Grace very willingly slid off her lap, both being mutually pleased to part. There was now a group of the elder girls on the sofa, who began talking together. Emily asked Isabella, if she went back to the school after the holidays.

"Yes; I think I shall go for one more term," replied her cousin.

"Ah! it's always one more and one more," remarked Emily; "I thought you'd go back."

"Why, I thought I had better give one more term to my music and dancing; else, I had made up my mind to leave."

"But do you settle it all for yourself?" asked Constance.

"Lady Musgrove ostensibly decides it, but she always applies to me for my opinion, and does as I wish," replied Isabella, carelessly.

"Don't believe her!" said Emily, "she's a better girl than *that*, she does as her papa and mamma *wish*."

"Emily, you are very . . . ," Isabella began, but finding herself in a scrape, and knowing she was not at all a match for Emily, she made a dead stop. Emily continued, "people don't know themselves, and I can tell you she has always been a good child: comes when she's called; does as she's bid; and shuts the door after her."

"Emily," said her cousin, "I am surprised how you can be so vulgar; you are always repeating proverbs, and those vulgar sayings. Mrs. Jenkinson would not take a young lady who would bring such ways into her house."

"Well," returned her cousin, "I really don't want to come."

"I can't believe *that*, when you know in what different style *we* have things from your *school*," said Isabella, disdainfully. "It is almost the same as being at home."

"I can never think school the same as home," answered Emily.

"But Mrs. Jenkinson's is *not* a school," said Isabella.

"What is it then? an Establishment?" asked Constance.

"No, she does not like *that*," replied Isabella.

"She calls it nothing; she says it is her *house*."

"I am sure you must be often put to for a name," said Emily.

"There again! my dear Emily!" exclaimed Isabella, " 'put to'—what a vulgar expression! Now I am only doing what Mrs. Jenkinson does with us; it was quite *ennuyant* at first; she is so very particular."

"Yes, I know," replied Emily, "she made you speak all your 'a's' in the way you do now, and gave you that languishing drawl. You know how George used to quiz you at first."

"*Quiz!* again, my dear child," said Isabella, "it would be daggers to me, if you talked in that way in our coterie."

"Is that your new name for your schoolfellows?" asked Emily, "by the bye, have you any new girls?"

"Schoolfellows! girls!" cried her cousin, as much shocked as Emily could wish; "it is no use teaching you better ways! Emily, you would exasperate Mrs. Jenkinson to the verge of madness!"

"Well," replied Emily, in precisely her cousin's tone, drawl, and manner, "since, my dear Isabella, it affects your nerves so distressingly, I will imitate your better way, to the best of my capacity. I cannot then fail of giving you satisfaction. I protest," cried she, changing her tone to Isabella's lively air, "you have got on your new set of pearls, and I have not noticed them! how *etourdie!* how *barbare* you must think me! what loves! what dainty loves! Excuse my raptures, but they are positively *bijoux* of darlings!"

Awe kept the Duff part of the audience from laughter; politeness, Grace; and of course, anger, Isabella; yet she dared not show it, because she felt she had brought this upon herself, and she dreaded Emily's powers. So she forced a sort of laugh, and turned upon Fanny, who was the nearest to her. "How beautifully you all dress your hair!" she cried; "I have been admiring it this hour past, but I think yours is the smoothest," stroking it with her hand. "My maid cannot dress mine after that mode; she has spent hours and hours trying."

"Do you waste hours so unworthily?" asked Constance; "but, perhaps," she added, "you are not particular, for just now you said, 'this hour past,' when we have not been sitting together one quarter of that space."

Mary Anne seemed uneasy, and fidgeted; Fanny touched her sister, and whispered in a shocked tone, "Oh, Constance," and Isabella answered:—

"I see you are what Mrs. Jenkinson calls, 'a matter of fact' young lady; she says such are not fit for the world, and is always labouring to teach them better ways, and she invariably effects her purpose; she says she likes to give an enthusiastic spirit, where Nature has denied it."

Mary Anne, fearing this would lead to a regular dispute between her sister and Isabella, and seeing Emily had disappeared, now ventured on her first speech, and inquired, carefully wording her sentence, "How many young ladies there were at Mrs. Jenkinson's."

"Our society consists of eight," replied Isabella.

"It must be quite a family party," remarked the other, "have you any friends among them?"

"Oh," replied Isabella, carelessly, "I am only acquainted with three. I do just know the others by sight; but mere bowing acquaintances."

"What *can* you mean?" asked Constance; and the young lady explained as follows:—

"Mrs. Jenkinson does not approve of a numerous society; she therefore divides her establishment; different suites of rooms are appropriated to each society, and we never see each other; the other night, at a party at Lord Polestone's, I was introduced to a young lady, who I found had been three years at Mrs. Jenkinson's; and last summer, I discovered that Lady Emily Fainton, a very particular friend of mine, had been there a long time, and we had never known it, although Lord and Lady Musgrove are most intimate friends of the Faintons: it was *'penible'* to the last degree! Indeed there are many things I do not approve of in Mrs. Jenkinson's arrangement; but when one is under a lady's roof, one cannot be so rude as to interfere with her domestic appointments."

"But," inquired Grace, who had been intently listening, "do you really never see your friend, Lady Emily, at all?"

"Occasionally, I send her in an invitation; but it interferes so much with my plans, that I cannot indulge myself much in the pleasure of her society. It is so different from being in the same coterie."

"Certainly," observed Grace, thoughtfully, "Mrs. Jenkinson is very right in not calling it a school, for it is quite different from any I ever heard of;—how do you learn? have you masters?"

"Our studies are regulated by our own convenience and inclination; we each have our library and piano in our study, and masters attend every day; my maid brings me in their cards, and if I am inclined to see any of them, I admit them; if my engagements have been such as not to allow of my preparing for them, I do not. But to speak candidly, my genius has so decidedly declared itself for music and dancing, that I think it hardly fair to tax the patience of any professors, but of those accomplishments."

"Do you take your lessons in private?" asked Mary Anne.

"*Most certainly.*"

"But your dancing lessons?" said Grace, "surely you do not each dance alone."

What Isabella's answer would have been, cannot be determined, since the conversation received a turn. Fanny had taken a seat on a low stool by her side, immediately after the patronizing stroke of the hand, and by degrees, had become more and more bold—receiving many gracious notices of encouragement; after a long examination of the hand, adorned with rings, which hung down carelessly, she at length ventured to touch it, and gently say, "How beautiful!" this apostrophe coinciding with Grace's

question, and being perhaps pleasanter as well as easier to answer, obtained the favoura-
ble notice of Miss Ward.

"Which?" said she, smiling graciously, "the rings or the hand?"

"Both," replied Fanny, gently.

"That, I suppose," said Isabella, "is a return for my compliment on the lovely hair;
and in this strain the conversation went on;—Fanny, in short space, lovingly reclining
against Isabella's soft satin, and Isabella's beautiful hand and rings, pressed against her
new friend's lovely hair. So, we must leave them. But it may be proper to say a few
words as to Miss Ward's personal appearance, else it is difficult, as Emily observed, to
believe she is not a woman. The fact was, she looked more so among grown persons,
than among those of her own age. Her manners were more than *womanly;* and so
anxious was she for her dignity, that with children, they appeared little less than a piece
of acting. The presence of Emily or George alone subdued her a little on such occasions.
Well bred people readily accord the deference that is claimed of them, and the Honourable Miss Ward was not backward or sparing in her demands. She generally obtained
the observation she desired, when alone among strangers, but not at her aunt Ward's,
who resolutely persisted in classing her with *the children,* and whose treatment in this
respect she avoided, at the risk of encountering instead, her cousins' raillery. She was
not particularly tall of her age, but of a plump round figure, and if a stranger were told,
at a little distance, she was not *near* twenty *years* of age, he might be at a loss whether to
class her with matrons or children. It was therefore her manners, her dress, and her
music—not to speak of the distinction attached to her name, which Mary Anne so fully
appreciated, to which she was indebted for the success she occasionally met with. At
school (she must pardon us), however, it was very different. We will just add, she
promised to be a fine showy girl, fair and bright, but not very delicate-looking, or
lady-like; and that she had really a pretty white hand, which some day would be too
plump for the rings which so ornamentally graced it.

CHAPTER IX

Who shall decide when Doctors disagree?
POPE

W E WILL NOW pass to the other room and take a view of what is passing there. The
younger part of the company had gathered round the piano, where music and talk went
on pretty nearly incessantly; else, certainly the folding doors would have been closed
during the performance of Mufti. The graver part of the company sat about the fire
where we left them.—Lady Freemantle enjoying the vicinity of her formerly "young
friend" Mrs. Leslie, whom she much esteemed, and Mr. Everard still in the seat he took
after the argument with Miss Newmarsh. But it seemed as though some malicious fate
were ever at hand to bring these two opposite spirits into collision. Several times had

they clashed, and though Miss Newmarsh only seemed to give her opponent a new opportunity of emitting, as it were, sparks of fire, and extinguishing by his more effective style of argument her less dazzling blaze, she still continued to dare the contact; Lady Freemantle was telling Mrs. Leslie of the pleasant society they continued to have about them at Lacklands, how glad her old friends would be to see her again, and new comers to make her acquaintance. Mrs. Leslie remarked it was no new habit of Lady Freemantle's to find pleasant neighbours wherever she went.

"Well, I do think we are uncommonly fortunate," answered that lady; "I hear complaints in other neighbourhoods of want of pleasant society, but we have never found it."

"You must indeed be fortunate," remarked Miss Newmarsh, "I am sure my experience has been far otherwise, and Mrs. Duff makes the same complaint every day. But she is very particular; especially now her children are getting of an age to be considered."

"I am sure she is very right to be particular," returned Lady Freemantle, "and in or near London, one can in a measure choose one's society, but in the country one must take what comes; and if one's neighbours are respectable, must be content with whatever we can get beside."

"People affix such different meanings to the word '*respectable*,'" remarked Miss Newmarsh.

"I mean, I suppose," replied Lady Freemantle, "such as are correct in their religious and social duties."

"That would not satisfy me," said Miss Newmarsh, "I could never enter into society of a worldly character or of an unprofitable nature."

"I wish we had Mrs. Ward here," said Lady Freemantle, "she would be able to argue the matter with you at length, which I will not pretend to do." Seeing Miss Newmarsh looked perplexed towards their hostess, she added, "Mrs. General Ward of Langham, I mean."

"You do not approve then of mixing in society?" asked Mr. Everard.

"Not indiscriminately," said Miss Newmarsh.

"I suppose not," returned the gentleman; "you would not, for instance, visit an unbeliever."

"Except to do him good," said Miss Newmarsh.

"Madam, you ought not to visit him to do him good," said Mr. Everard.

"Surely, sir, you cannot be in earnest," remarked the lady.

"Evil communications, madam, corrupt good manners," returned Mr. Everard, "he might do you harm, but you would never do him good."

Miss Newmarsh, who took this rather personally, asked if Mr. Everard thought there was not any use in discussions with such persons.

"No, madam, not in the way of visiting; a guest is not only on a par with, but beneath his host. A christian should never voluntarily place himself either on a par with, or beneath an unbeliever."

"But, my dear sir, the christian slaves formerly."

"They did not place *themselves*, madam, but that is not to the purpose, those are matters of necessity and duty, *we* talk of choice and pleasure."

"Excuse me," returned Miss Newmarsh, "*I* talk of duty."

"Then, madam, you hold it a matter of duty to exchange hospitalities with an infidel or a reprobate, but to refuse the same towards those of more religious and orderly habits; I am happy, madam, to hear you complain of the want of society you have felt in all the neighbourhoods you are acquainted with."

Miss Newmarsh had allowed herself to be pushed farther than she meant, or was perhaps aware of, and explained her meaning to be, "that society should be conducted on the basis of mutual edification, or profit to one party or other."

"Very true," said Mr. Everard, "I grant you, madam; and these ends are attained by cultivating kindly feelings among neighbours—you know I have made my exclusions."

"But my exclusions are greater than yours," said the lady; "I exclude the world."

"Remember, madam, yourself is one of the world."

"I may be *in* the world, but not *of* the world," replied Miss Newmarsh.

"There, madam, you have me!" cried Mr. Everard, apparently rather pleased than otherwise, "but the truth of the matter is, our terms are undefined. Combatants of all sorts should measure their weapons before they come into the field."

Miss Newmarsh expressed her willingness to recommence on any terms he chose to propose.

"No, madam," said he, "I consider it *unprofitable* according to your rule; *I shall do you no good.*"

"But, sir," replied the lady, "you should *try.*"

"Well, madam, to please you I will try," said Mr. Everard, courteously, "and I will do, what in some cases I fancy you would approve—I will give you a sermon, instead of an argument. Madam, I honour your conscientiousness, but you aim more at doing good, than doing right; I respect, madam, your zeal, but you have done with your practice what papists and heretics have with their doctrines; you have allowed one side of your duties to grow out. Let us be content, madam, with doing our duty *in* our station, rather than seeking for ways of doing it *out* of it."

Surprising as it may seem, Mr. Everard could throw so much politeness into his manner, that unlike the dinner scene, not only were the audience at ease and unannoyed, but Miss Newmarsh herself felt no uneasiness, and seemed to take the piece of advice as rather a compliment than otherwise: any further discussion, however, was put aside by a sudden disturbance in the next room, which had been particularly quiet for some time. First, voices were raised as in anger, and presently a scuffle; it increased so much that some of the gentlemen went in to ascertain the cause. One soon returned to quiet the alarm of one or two ladies, especially Mrs. Newton Grey, who anxiously inquired what was the matter.

"Only two of the young fellows sparring in play," said he, "nothing of consequence."

Presently the disturbance was stilled, and the other gentlemen one by one returned.

"Do not be alarmed," said one, seeing Mrs. Newton Grey's anxiety, "no harm! only a little sparring between your boy and young Duff."

"Upon my word," said another, "he's a fine fellow! how he laid into him! and not half his size!"

"What was it about? who struck the first blow?" asked Mrs. Newton Grey, "that Campbell Duff is such a rude fellow! those public schools are the ruin of boys."

One of the gentlemen had stepped in to satisfy her, and returned, saying, young Duff had struck the first blow.

"Ah," said the lady, "I was certain of it! I was sure my dear boy would never do such a thing!" and here the affair ended. There were a good many young people present, and before this interruption, some one had proposed getting up a quadrille. The room required some arranging for this purpose, since no dance had been previously designed. After some delay all were in their places. The sight, however, made a greater sensation in Miss Newmarsh's mind, than the late misdemeanour of Campbell, for she did not feel responsible for him as for her own pupils. She walked rapidly across the room to Mrs. Ward, and expostulated with her for breaking thus the conditions of the treaty. Mrs. Ward replied that the dancing was among the grown young people and in another room—the children would have nothing to do with it. After a good deal of talk on the subject, Miss Newmarsh walked into the other room, sat down, took a book from the table, and began reading. But finding the music and dancing distract her, she rose, and with some difficulty closed the folding doors. The young people had all been thickly congregated together at one corner of the room, apparently intently absorbed in something that was going on. After a time, Miss Newmarsh's anxiety was excited, and she called and beckoned to Constance, who was outermost, and inquired what it was.

"A conjurer," said Constance.

"A conjurer!" repeated Miss Newmarsh, rising and going towards the scene, "you do not mean so!"

"It is, indeed," exclaimed she, turning away, "and I do declare, a pack of cards! my dear child come here with me!" and she carried her pupil into the small ante-room. "I really do wonder," continued she, when they were seated, "that your mamma allows you to go to these parties! but, indeed, it is not her fault; for the conditions are broken! dancing in one room, and cards in another!"

"They are not *playing*," said Constance, "and they have only a few cards."

"But, my dear child, conjurers are very wrong, and nobody should encourage such people; what has he been doing!"

"Some curious tricks with the cards, and other things."

"Well, it is very wrong; you know how unhappy I always am to think that any of you have only seen a card."

Constance, who thought she should discover how the tricks were done, and was rather disappointed at being carried away, took the conjurer's part rather more than she might have done under any other circumstances, and said, "it was all in jest, and that some of them said it was Reginald Freemantle, since he and Emily had disappeared for some time, only he was so well dressed up nobody could be sure."

At this moment, Emily, who had eyes for every thing, and had seen and understood all Miss Newmarsh's movements, ran in and whispered a few words in that lady's ear; they did not seem satisfactory, for she merely shook her head and remained unmoved. Emily hastened back again to her young friends. The conjurer had done several curious, and sometimes astonishing tricks;—cards, shillings, and handkerchiefs, seemed to be endued with life and invisibility, and many a young spectator was startled and provoked at being discovered to be the repository of the missing article. One after another persisted, he or she would not become a victim, but the more positive they were, the more certain seemed their fate. Miss Ward was among the most vehement of the protesters, and indeed it did seem as though she would escape, for time after time passed and she continued unmarked; at last the conjurer declared a handkerchief that had disappeared would be found in some white satin reticule; no one else had such a thing, and as hers hung upon her arm, she triumphantly opened it, and to her utter amazement, drew out the handkerchief; the next was a shilling, and that was found in the same young lady's band; the next was a precious ancient small coin, belonging to one of the young guests; it had suddenly disappeared, so the ear told, out of a long-necked china vessel; the question was, "where is it?" The conjurer confessed himself ashamed to trouble the same young lady, but as the coin was very precious, he must announce where it was to be found. Isabella was quite sure it had not been transported to her this time; the conjurer persisted, and said that it was within the left satin slipper. Most certainly there she found it, and very indignant she was. She considered the whole affair as a great liberty, and with offended step she walked away from the party, to the other end of the room. She found the folding doors closed, and heard music and dancing. She would have been glad to enter, but did not choose to run the risk of standing a mere spectator, and she knew her aunt would not promote her interest in the way of a partner. She therefore turned away and felt lonely. Presently she caught sight of Miss Newmarsh and Constance in the ante-room. At any other time she would have disdained both or either; Constance had offended her, and Miss Newmarsh was not a person of fashion. But her present feeling of desertion prompted her to seek protection, and her love of patronage and desire of esteem of some kind or other, enabled her to enter the ante-room and accost them with a graciousness that ensured her welcome. Fanny, who had been watching the steps of her patronizing friend, immediately followed her, and presently took her seat by her side.

CHAPTER X

> . . . Strong affection
> Contends with all things and overcometh all things.
> Will I not live with thee? will I not cheer thee?
> Wouldst thou be lonely then? wouldst thou be sad?
> JOANNA BAILLIE

"OH!" CRIED ISABELLA as she entered, "how happy and delightful you look in your lovely retirement! I hope I may come and partake your peaceful retreat," and she threw herself at length on a settee.

"It is indeed a sweet little room," answered Miss Newmarsh, "here we may sit, withdrawn from worldly scenes:

'The world forgetting, by the world forgot.' "

"What a charming line!" cried Isabella, "what a delicious sentiment, and how sweetly repeated; I never heard it before, but I shall never forget it—'The world forgetting—by the world forgot:' I shall adopt it for my motto. How pleasant it is to sit here! how wise you two have been! I wish I had known of your retreat earlier; did you come away on purpose?"

"Yes," replied Miss Newmarsh, "while there was dancing in one room, and folly in another, Constance and myself thought we were better employed here—engaged in a little quiet discourse."

"Oh, how true that is," said Isabella, "how much better than all the nonsense we have been engaged in! How I should like a sweet little cottage on the top of one of the mountains in Wales, and there live as you say;—

'The world forgetting, by the world forgot;'

Should not you, dear?" she asked of Fanny, who was again reclining upon her.

"Not quite at the top of the mountain," replied her new friend, gently, "but nicely sheltered from the winds, and surrounded by trees, full of birds singing all day, and owls hooting all night; and a stream with a waterfall on one side, and nothing to be seen but cows and sheep all about, and one old woman in a red cloak, picking up sticks."

"Oh, how exactly our tastes agree!" cried the young lady with enthusiasm, "*you* shall choose our cottage and the spot, and we will go and live together; will you come?"

"Oh, yes," answered Fanny, "I will go and live and die there!"

"Not die quite yet," interposed Constance.

"No, but some day," said Fanny, softly.

"Well, how can we find a cottage?"

"Oh," answered Fanny, "there are plenty every where in the country—very small and rather old; very low roof and ceilings, all thatch and moss-grown, and the rain sometimes coming in."

"Oh, no," objected Miss Ward, "not the rain coming in; I should not like that, I think."

"Well, then, we can have that mended," replied her friend, "but it must *look* very old, and be covered with roses and jessamine; and there shall be flowers of all sorts in the garden; but they must all be scented."

"Except lilies," said Isabella, "lilies and roses you know always go together—we must have lilies."

"Well, we'll have lilies, and they *do* smell a little too," returned Fanny.

"But do you two mean to live together?" asked Constance; "you are so young, and what will you do for servants?"

"Oh, we can get the old woman in the red cloak to do all we want," said Fanny, "you know we shall never want any dinner or things of that sort."

"But we can't do without dinner," said Isabella, "we must eat, you know."

"Yes, we must eat, I know," replied her friend, who seemed to have bestowed some thought upon the subject, "we must eat, but not dinner; I mean no meat, or any thing that requires cooking; there are no butchers or people of that kind," added she, with a look of disgust, "in places of that kind! you know Edwin says,

'No flocks that range the mountains free
To slaughter I condemn.'

We shall eat nothing but roots and fruits, and drink nothing but milk, though, you know *Edwin* says again,

> 'A scrip with herbs and roots supplied,
>   And *water* from the spring.'

But I think I should like *milk,* because then we must have a cow."

"Well, I was going to ask you where you would get your milk," said her sister; "but who would take care of your cow?"

"Oh, Constance!" said Fanny, "what a silly question! a cow lives in a field, and does not want any body to take care of her. Cows go grazing about, you know, and give no trouble to any body."

"Well, but your cow must be milked!"

"Yes, to be sure," said Fanny, "that's the best part; I don't care for the milk, only the milking. I would have such a nice little stool, and such a pretty pair of milk-pails with a yoke; and then I would make the butter with a churn,—not one of the churns people use now, but one of those nice high churns, such as you see in old-fashioned picture books, like Jemima Placid's. And then, you know, we should have poor people, who have lost their way, cold and hungry, come for food and lodging. Edwin says,

> 'Here to the houseless child of want
>   My door is open still;
> And though my portion is but scant,
>   I give it with good will!'

And again in the Traveller,

> 'And haply too some pilgrim thither led,
>   With many a tale repays the nightly bed.'

And you know the country parson, which is just the same as we should be:

> '*His* house was known to all the vagrant train.'

And,

> 'The long remembered beggar was his guest,
>   Whose beard descending swept his aged breast.'

And 'the ruined spendthrift' and 'the broken soldier' the same. You know they all

> 'Sat by his fire and talked the night away.'

So it would not be dull, we should have plenty of amusement."

"Well, all that is very well in poetry and long ago," said Constance, "but it would not do now to have beggars and people of that sort, who may be thieves and robbers, come and sit with one and sleep in the house."

"Oh," said Isabella, who before Constance spoke was inclined to take her view of the matter, "you know beggars in the country are very different from our beggars in London."

"To be sure," said Fanny; "the men are all good old people with long white beards, and the women have clean plaitings to their caps, with aprons white as the driven snow, and their cloaks, though tattered, are quite bright and red. You know they have all been unfortunate, and chased out of their cottages by

> 'Men of wealth and pride,'

like those

> 'Poor exiles! every pleasure past,'

from sweet Auburn. Or else they are brave old soldiers on their way to their children, covered with wounds and scars, with broken arms and legs, and crutches.—It says, you know,

> 'Shouldered his *crutch* and showed how fields were won!' "

"Fanny, you are very inconsiderate," said Constance, "you never could go on living in that way.—I am sure," she added, addressing Isabella, "*you* would want your carriage, and your maid, and your satins, and all the things you have been used to."

"Oh, you do not know me!" cried Isabella, piqued; "it's all very well when these things come, but I can do just the same without them. Now, I will give you a proof!" added she, rising; and going to a mirror, she took off all her ornaments one by one,—earrings, necklace, aigrette, and even rings. "There, now!" said she, triumphantly, "I shall not put on one of them again the rest of the evening!"

Miss Newmarsh praised her resolution, and said it was a good beginning towards indifference on such matters. The conversation now took a more serious turn, and Miss Newmarsh bore the principal share in it. It was broken up by supper being announced, and all the party assembled in the supper room. We shall here leave our young friends, having no doubt, that as nothing has reached us to the contrary, the rest of the evening went off undisturbed, though with less to relate than the hours that preceded it.

CHAPTER XI

Who comprehends his trust; and to the same
Keeps faithful with a singleness of aim.
WORDSWORTH

GRACE ACCOMPANIED her mamma to her room that night, and as soon as they had reached it, Mrs. Leslie said, "Well, Grace, I am sure this has been a new day for you."

"Indeed, mamma," said the little girl, almost sighing with its weight, "it has been a wonderful day."

"But I hope you have enjoyed it, my dear child."

"Oh yes, mamma, very much indeed; every thing has been so new and so pleasant—every thing," she added, "but one or two things."

"By the bye," asked her mamma, "what was that sad disturbance after tea? I am afraid Campbell Duff is a strange quarrelsome fellow."

"Oh, mamma," said Grace, warmly, "it was not Campbell's fault, I admire his conduct very much!"

"Then he did *not* strike the first blow? they told me he did," said Mrs. Leslie.

"Yes, mamma, he did,—he *did* strike the first blow; I forgot that," said Grace, sorrowfully.

"I am surprised then at you admiring his conduct, Grace; how is that?"

"He was *very much* provoked *indeed*," said Grace, with emphasis.

"But, my dear, he should be able to control his temper better than that—with the help of his sisters and all you young ladies standing round—in the drawing-room too!"

"Oh, mamma, *that* made it worse, I think! *better* I mean for poor Campbell; *better* that he should have struck the first blow!"

"Well, my dear, I am a little surprised that *you,* who do not like even to read of battles and violence, should admire any thing of this kind. Can you tell me how it all happened?"

"Oh, mamma," said Grace, alarmed, "I don't think I can!"

"Well, my dear, you shall not, if you do not wish," replied Mrs. Leslie; "and I am sure it is too late to talk over these things to-night: I am afraid you will be quite knocked up to-morrow with these late hours.—Good night, my dear. I would advise you, Grace, not to sit up long talking to-night, but to get to bed and to sleep in good time. Good night, my dear girl," she repeated, stooping and kissing her child, "God bless you!"

Grace walked to her new room with a very thoughtful step. She had a great deal to think of, but Campbell's affair now quite put aside every thing else. "How sorry I should be if he was wrong!" thought she; "oh, I hope he was not wrong!" She found Emily waiting very impatiently for her to come and take possession of the day nursery, which was next her room, and where a fire had been kept up for them by Mrs. Ward's desire. Grace found this was a treat to Emily as well as herself. She learned several little pieces of domestic news, interesting to her. Ellen was to come home on Saturday. Emily said *she* did not care for her sister's being so much at her grandmamma's, because she herself was at school, and this was the first time Ellen had not been with them the whole of the holidays. Hanson, her nurse, had not been well, and could not come up with her before. Hanson was a nurse who had formerly lived with them, but when they left London she followed Ellen, and went to Mrs. Ward, at Langham. Grace asked Emily if Ellen was like *her.*

"Oh, not in the least," said Emily, "neither in face nor any thing else. Ellen is quite fair and has light hair, and she is as quiet and slow as I am the contrary: yet she is very odd sometimes, and so droll; but one cannot at all tell if she means to be so or not. Mamma says she does not, but I am sure she does sometimes."

Grace found that Mary Anne and Campbell were only to stay a week longer; they were to leave on the night of the grand party. At a convenient pause, Grace rose and said now she must go.

"Go! where?" cried Emily.

"To bed and to sleep," said Grace; "why, how late it is!"

"But we have only just come," said Emily; "and look at the fire! brighter than ever, and I have a hundred things to say!"

"So have I," said Grace, "but mamma wishes me not to sit up."

"Not generally; but to-night," returned Emily, "she did not desire you to go away so soon, did she?"

"Not exactly, but she advised me to get to bed in good time," answered Grace.

"But will she be angry with you if you sit up a little?"

"Oh, no," said Grace, "not angry, mamma is never angry with me."

"Well, then, there can be no harm," replied Emily; "I would not ask you if your mamma would be angry."

"But indeed," said Grace, "I had rather do as mamma advises me."

"But I have so many things to say," returned Emily, "and this is the best time; I wanted to talk a great deal about the party, and that disagreeable boy Newton Grey, and Campbell. Oh, Grace, you must do me a favour, and stay a little longer!"

Poor Grace, what could she do? It seemed unkind to refuse, when she knew her mamma did not care for five or ten minutes; but she also knew if once they began talking again there would be no opportunity of making off, and all this would come over again. "Oh," thought she, "if there was but a watch in the room!" and she immediately hit upon a substitute. "Well, I will stay a little longer," said she; "I will stay till that coal falls down upon the hearth."

Emily was amused and quite satisfied at the contract, for the coal looked pretty secure for the present, and she thanked Grace, saying she was afraid she was going to be as obstinate as Constance. "You know," she proceeded, "if Constance once says a thing, if it is ever so absurd, she will do it,and it is quite impossible to laugh her out of any thing."

"I think that quite right," answered Grace, "do not you? and what I have seen of Constance I admire so very much!"

There was a pause. "And do you like Isabella?" said Emily.

"Oh, she is so very different, I cannot think of them together," said Grace.

"Well, do you like Miss Newmarsh?"

Grace looked surprised, and said, "Why she is grown up!"

"Well, what then?" said Emily, laughing, "you may like her, I suppose."

"Yes, but quite differently, you know, from ourselves;—and besides, she is so clever!"

"But still you may like her, may you not?"

"Yes, of course, I do like her, and should like her," replied Grace, "but you know I have nothing to do with her, she is not my governess."

"No, nor mine, thank goodness," said Emily.

Presently Emily introduced the subject of the fight, and they were beginning upon it, Grace eagerly desirous of hearing an opinion that might clear Campbell from all blame, when—down came the signal coal. Again Emily entreated with the same arguments; but Grace said, "You promised, you know, to let me go," and rose and retired to her room. Emily was soon tired of being alone, and presently followed her.

CHAPTER XII

Make not too rash a trial of him,
He's gentle and not fearful.
SHAKESPEARE

Would you your son should be a sot, or dunce, . . .
Train him in public, with a mob of boys, . . .
Thou wouldst not, deaf to nature's tenderest plea,
Turn him adrift upon a rolling sea,
Nor say—Go thither—conscious that there lay
A brood of asps, or quicksands in the way.
Then governed only by the self-same rule
Of natural pity—send him not to school.
COWPER

OUR LITTLE FRIEND Grace had never been in a situation where her usual morning lessons were systematically omitted; and before leaving home she had many doubts about it, as it seemed to her a thing impossible. At last she ventured to ask her mamma, and was told there would be so much to do and to see, that it should be quite a holiday to her, as it was to the rest, except—supposing it could be managed without disturbing any arrangement in the family—her hour's practice. "And of course, Grace," her mamma added, "you and I shall read the psalms and lessons together as usual."

When they parted at night Mrs. Leslie had told her little girl to come to her room about ten o'clock for this purpose; and at that hour, which was not long after breakfast, Grace's gentle tap was heard at the door.

"Well, Grace," said her mamma, "I am really glad of this opportunity of a little quiet for you; for many days together like yesterday would quite unsettle you."

"Oh, I hope not, mamma," said Grace, quite alarmed, "I would not get unsettled for all the world!"

"Well, I hope not too," said her mamma, "and I think coming to me every morning and having a little quiet, besides our reading, will be a means of keeping you steady, though our usual habits are broken into. I think, however, Grace, we must give up the hour's practice, because I do not see how you can manage it, and it may make you seem *particular* to your young friends—you know I never wish that."

"But, mamma, if you have no objection, I think I can manage it," said Grace.

"I have no objection, my dear, but as I shall have you every morning a little, perhaps your young friends may think you absent from them too long."

Grace answered, that she could practise before breakfast as she did at home; that she had seen the night before a piano in the day nursery which was seldom used; that Emily had assured her she would disturb nobody; therefore she *had* practised her hour that morning before Emily was up; that she got to bed and to sleep soon, and that breakfast was so late here that she could always do so. "And then, mamma," she added, "it will all be over before any body is up, and I shall have the whole day to myself afterwards."

Her mamma consented to this plan, but told her she might do as she pleased any morning. She then inquired if she had made acquaintance with any of the young visitors the night before.

"Not much acquaintance, mamma, but I know one from the other; and though

Constance and Fanny are so much alike, I knew them apart before the end of the evening."

"And who do you think you shall like best?"

"Why I can't tell yet," said Grace, "but," she added, almost reverentially, "I do admire Constance so very much—she is so very good, mamma."

"How have you found it out so soon, my dear, and what do you admire her so particularly for?"

"Because, mamma, she is so very bold."

"Bold! my dear Grace, what has come to you?" said her mamma, almost alarmed, "last night you admired a young gentleman because he was violent and rude, and to-day a young lady because she is bold!"

"I am glad," said Grace, "I can defend Constance better than I did poor Campbell; I don't mean *bold*—forward—but she's not afraid to speak, and says exactly what she thinks to every body."

"I think that seems much the same thing," returned her mamma, "but you had better give me an instance, if you can remember one."

Grace remembered several, but none pleasant to repeat, because she must have seemed to find fault with some others; and except in Newton's case, of which it gave her a thrill of horror to think, she was not sure it was right to do so. She therefore said, "Why, mamma, if she saw me do any thing wrong she would tell me of it directly, and so seriously that I must mind her."

Mrs. Leslie here spoke of Mr. Everard, laughed about his compliments! and asked Grace how she liked them.

"Compliments! mamma," repeated Grace, "were they compliments? they did not sound to me like compliments, and that is what Emily said, I remember."

"Why you know, my dear, it was a *compliment* to compare you to Graces and Muses and such fine people," said Mrs. Leslie, smiling, "and then his talking so much to a little girl like you, and handing you down stairs, was a favour."

"To be sure, mamma, I did not think of that; but then, you know, it was not a very pleasant favour to me, because it made every body look at me, and it only came from my name happening to be 'Grace.' "

"Very true," replied Mrs. Leslie, "I was glad, however, that you found something to answer him, and were not quite silent and awkward."

"Did you see me or hear me, mamma?" asked Grace, alarmed.

"I saw you a little, and I heard that you showed you understood Mr. Everard, and that you were not too frightened to bring your mythology to your assistance."

"If you had been near, though, mamma, you would have seen how frightened and awkward I was—it was all chance what I said."

"Well, what *did* you say?"

"Why, Mr. Everard asked me what Grace I was; so I said Thalia. I have always wished to be Thalia, you know, because that is the name of a Grace and a Muse, and it is a prettier name and easier to say than the others: then he talked of a mask and two faces; so that put me in mind of Janus, who was 'double-faced,' as my Catechism says;—it was very lucky he just asked me the only two questions I could answer."

"Well," said her mamma, "I am glad you had presence of mind enough to find the answers in time: it is so much better to answer a little properly on such occasions, than to laugh like some little girls, or cry like others."

"Well, mamma," said Grace, "do you know, I really think I might have cried, if you had not told me long ago to get rid of what you called that foolish propensity."

"Did Mr. Everard distress you so very much, my poor child?" said Mrs. Leslie, half compassionately, half laughing.

"Oh, not Mr. Everard, mamma," said Grace, "though I was very much afraid any one should look at me,—but Miss Freemantle,—she teazed me a great deal more, and I was so glad when dinner was over."

Mrs. Leslie told her little girl she must not mind such things too much; and after a little more talk, she proposed reading, and Grace immediately brought the books. As Grace is in the habit of giving accounts of passing events to her mamma, and seems to continue to be pretty honest towards herself, and not unkind towards others, it may not be out of place here to introduce, by way of contrast, Newton Grey's behaviour and conversation with his mother on the late unfortunate occasion; and in order to do so, it will be necessary to relate the affair of the evening before with Campbell Duff, which Grace was so unwilling to mention or allude to. It was as follows. The young party had been talking and amusing themselves in groups, till by degrees they were attracted to be mere listeners of Campbell and Newton, who had got into a conversation, the tone of which seemed rather doubtful. Campbell went to a public school, and Newton had been asking him about many of his school-fellows, who were friends of his. Several were in Campbell's form. To all the inquiries an answer to the same effect followed: "I don't know him much, he's no friend of mine."

"Why you seem to know nobody," said Newton.

"No wonder," replied Campbell, "when you ask me after the worst fellows in the school!"

"Worst! what do you mean?" returned the other, "these are all *good boys*, or have plenty of money!"

"But that does not make them my friends," said Campbell.

"Well! who are your friends? I don't believe you have any! The fact is," continued he, in a provoking tone, "the grapes are sour! these 'bad boys' don't like *you!* if you *have* any friends, who are they?"

"I have some," said Campbell, coolly.

"I don't believe it," answered Newton, contemptuously, "tell me *one!*"

"Spencer Freeman," replied Campbell.

"Oh! Spencer Freeman," cried Newton, laughing rudely, "I see your set! *I've* heard of him—he's a flat! besides, who is he? the son of a poor country parson!"

Thus the dispute went on. At last Newton, in an insulting manner, called Campbell and his friends "flats and saints."

Constance here spoke, to the surprise of some of the young ladies, and asked Newton what was the meaning of those words.

Newton laughed most provokingly, and said, "Flats were not sharps, and saints were fellows who were bullies and cowards, and dared not fight, and had no spirit for any thing."

In this reply he made use of some expressions too bad to be written down. Many of the by-standers were very much shocked, and there was a pause. Constance broke it by rebuking Newton for the impropriety of his language. He very angrily turned upon her and said something worse; adding, that girls could say any thing, because they knew nobody would fight them. He then repeated his offence, and turning to Campbell, he called him the same as a girl, and a saint, adding much more which we shall omit. Campbell had had for some time the greatest difficulty in restraining his spirit; his indignation seemed at its height at the insult offered to his sister, and he could bear no more. He now cried, "Is that like a girl?" and gave him a blow so unexpected and violent that the recipient well nigh reeled underneath it, though nearly twice his size.

Newton had not the slightest expectation of such an attack; he really believed what he said; that is, he believed that for some reason or other "flats and saints" would never fight, much less strike the first blow, and Campbell's coolness continued to assure him. He could scarcely recover the balance of body or mind. He essayed two or three blows, which fell rather awkwardly and inefficiently, and no one was more satisfied than Newton when the gentlemen interfered and parted the combatants.

Mrs. Newton Grey was a very kind and a very anxious mother. She had been left a widow early with only this one boy, and she was in all respects his sole guardian. He was some day to have a comfortable, but not a large fortune. She had decided to educate him for the law, both for the purpose of giving him a profession, and also in the hope that he would thereby increase his worldly means. She had most anxiously debated within herself whether or not to send him to a public school, or to a school at all. Some of her friends urged school strongly, but they were not of such strict religious principles as herself, and she did not think herself justified to take their advice on so important a subject. She therefore, by letter, consulted a clergyman, whom she greatly respected, who had himself been at a public school, and had also taken pupils, many of them from schools of different sorts. He sent her his own opinion, and that of several of his friends. Only one was in favour of a public education. This gentleman had several sons, and had sent them all to Eton. One had just passed through his career at College, and had not only distinguished himself, (which Mrs. Newton Grey did not care for comparatively,) but had escaped—even blame,—and had gained the good opinion both of his tutors and companions. Another seemed following his brother's steps, and was intended for the Church. But this instance Mrs. Newton Grey did not think a fair one, since, she said, these youths came of a family who were almost without exception steady, and did not seem to possess the lively disposition of most boys. She therefore decided on a strictly private education, and immediately set about inquiring after a tutor to reside in the house. After much trouble she met with one exactly suited to her purpose—a very grave and very kind man—not young. He had not, however, been used to so young a boy. Newton was at this time six, and in his turn was not used to be managed by a gentleman. It did not answer, and after a year Mrs. Newton Grey was glad that Mr. Finch decided to quit. After this she got a younger man, accustomed to the Pestalozzi system, and they went on very comfortably; but after a time Newton became so unmanageable and impertinent, that nothing could be done with him, and his mamma, after expostulating in vain with her refractory boy, thought it advisable to part with the tutor, since she saw it was impossible any good could be done. Newton made a joke of all his lessons; made puns upon them, instead of saying them; made rhymes of every thing, and even went on to take the same liberties with his tutor's name, to his face. His mother saw his sense of the absurd was too great for the Pestalozzi plans; so gave up that and got another tutor, who was most highly recommended in all respects. But this gentle-man was too resolved on his own plans, and the trio were mutually satisfied to part. The next she got answered better than all; but she was told he was a very poor scholar, and indeed by what she saw, Newton made as little progress under him in his classical as in other studies. So Mrs. Newton Grey, quite tired with changes, gave up this plan, and removed into a new neighbourhood, in order to be near a clergyman she knew and respected, who would see Newton every day, and entirely superintend his education, but not reside in the house. This plan had been going on steadily the last three years, and she considered her boy in every respect improving. Her ideas of *private education* had never interfered with his mixing with other children, or—now with youths. She did not dread their contact in their home circles; it was only the mixed multitude at schools which excited her fears. Newton had therefore many friends of his own age, whom he constantly saw both at home and abroad. Mrs. Newton Grey hitherto had liked herself to accompany him on his visits, not to be a spy upon him, but merely for the satisfaction of being near at hand. But she did not make a point of this. She was aware of the objections to private education for boys, and was anxious to avoid its errors. She especially wished him not to become what is vulgarly called a "milksop," or a "mamma's darling," and was always on the watch to instill manly habits. His dress accordingly was always on the advance of his companions, and also from his very early years, she had unwillingly, though resolutely, given up his calling her *mamma*.

Having thus given an account of the position of the mother and son with respect to each other, we will relate the conversation which took place between them after they got home on the night of the fracas between Newton and Campbell. She began to question him upon it, according to her custom on such occasions. "My dear Newton," said she, "what was your dispute about with Campbell Duff?"

"Oh, mother," replied he, "we had some words about some of his schoolfellows, —Lord Henry, James Jenkins, and the rest of them."

"Well, but why should you fight about them?"

"*I* did not fight, mother."

"Well, what did he fight for? I am afraid you provoked him in some way, my dear boy: now tell me, Newton, exactly," she added, seriously.

"Well, mother, I will," replied he, frankly, "I *did* provoke him, certainly, because I laughed in return at his friend Spencer Freeman, that *poor* fellow, you know, Lord Henry and young Forbes told us all about! Campbell was very angry, and told me my friends were the worst fellows in the school; this made *me* angry, and I defended them, and then I called his set 'flats,' or something of the kind, I can't remember all my words, for Campbell flew upon me and gave me a blow that nearly stunned me, I feel it now."

"Did you return it?" asked his mother.

"Yes, I defended myself, and would have put into him well, only he is such a small fellow, I did not like, and there was not much time, for the gentlemen came and parted us."

"Now, Newton, you are sure you have told me all that passed?" inquired his mother.

"Oh, no, dear mother, not all the *words*, but this is the principal part—one of his sisters interfered—she had no business—she asked me what a flat was."

"And what did you answer?"

"Oh, I believe I laughed and said a flat was not a sharp."

"Well, and what then?"

"Why I think it was just about then that Campbell gave me the blow."

"Newton," said his mother, "I fear you must have been very provoking in your manner, or Campbell would never have behaved so ill."

"I dare say I was, mother," said Newton, "one cannot judge of one's own manner, but I am sure Campbell was provoking enough to *me,* and I could not help his striking me."

"Well, my dear boy," answered his mother, "you must take particular care in future not to vex or provoke your companions. Remember you must bear and forbear."

After a pause she added, "And now, my dear boy, you must think it all over to-night before you go to bed, be sorry for what you have done wrong, and avoid it in future. Also you must not bear malice against Campbell Duff; remember he has a right to his feelings about his friends, as well as you." She then wished him good night, and inquired into the bruises he had received.

We will just beg our young readers to compare Newton's account of this affair with what actually happened. It will be found correctly true, to the letter—and even more. But there are omissions which entirely alter the character of the actions of all parties. Again, Grace constantly makes omissions in her relations of things to her mamma. Grace's omissions are from tenderness to others, Newton's from tenderness to himself.

CHAPTER XIII

Let other Bards of Angels sing,
Bright Suns without a spot;
But thou art no such fearful thing,
Rejoice that thou art not!
WORDSWORTH

WE MUST NOW return to our young friends at Fulham, and will enter the library with Grace after she had left her mamma's room. "Oh, Grace," cried Emily, "I thought you would never come! what a time you have been! Do you do lessons with your mamma now?"

Grace said, "No, but her mamma wanted her," and asked what they were going to do.

She was told the boys were tired of waiting for her, and had gone out for a little skating, and that if she liked it, they were to go and look on.

This was agreed to, and the three young ladies were soon ready and at the spot. George skated well, and Campbell very fairly: they cut some very pretty figures together, while the young ladies looked on. Grace hardly observed it was cold, till Emily cried out, "La! how cold it is! I can't bear this!" and she ran and began jumping backwards and forwards over a low gate, that led from the garden to the small piece of water, by the side of which they stood.

Grace looked at her instead of the skaters, and was admiring the ease with which she did it. Emily then called to Mary Anne and Grace to come and do the same. "How foolish you are!" said she, "I am warm already! are you not cold?"

Poor Grace was very cold: she knew she could very well leap a gate like that, for she had often done greater feats at home and with her cousins. She would have liked to do it,—she wished to do it; but she felt rather strange here, and she was not sure it was quite *the thing*. While she was thinking about it and wondering what Mary Anne would do, George took off his skates, and joined them. He began asking Mary Anne to leap and join his sister—said she would do it so well, and that they would look like two beautiful greyhounds. To all of which Mary Anne answered, "Nonsense, George, I wish you would not tease so."

Again and again George tried with the same success, and Grace thought, "How lucky it was *I* did not go; if Mary Anne does not like it, how much worse it would be in me—a stranger."

Now George altered his tone, and said he knew very well her reasons, that she *could* not—and no wonder—she was twice as heavy as Emily; he'd take any bet that she could not do it.

"Oh, George," said Mary Anne, "it is not right to bet, you should not say so."

"Ah," said he, "all that's very fine, but you are afraid of losing your money, because you know you could not leap that gate."

Mary Anne said she could, but she did not choose.

"What nonsense!" cried George, "what reason can you have, except that," added he, laughing provokingly and drolly, "except that you can't?"

Again Mary Anne said she could, she had often leapt higher.

"Then why not now? I *say*," cried George, emphatically, "Mary Anne could not jump that gate three times, or if she could she'd do it."

Mary Anne immediately ran and leapt it pretty well the three times, though not so lightly as Emily. Grace was utterly amazed. This was the second time Mary Anne had been teased into doing a thing. She could not understand why she was first unwilling, and then consented because George dared her. While she was pondering over it, George's compliments to his cousin on her feat were ended; and he turned to Grace and wished her to do the same. "Then," said he, "we'll all leap, and it will be capital fun, like the men over the horses at Astley's."

Grace was still wondering whether it was over particular of her to refuse,—Emily and Mary Anne had both consented. "But then," thought she, "they are sisters and cousins, and they all know each other very well." Again, she remembered her mamma always said she did not wish her to seem "particular," and this might be an instance; then she remembered how she disliked what she called rude or forward little girls, whenever she had seen them, and that she had rather be any thing than that. She felt very confused and uncomfortable.—Poor Grace; what will she do in the end?

George meanwhile had not hurried her. He waited patiently while he thought she was debating; he did not laugh and tease her aloud, as he had his cousin; he spoke only to *her*. At length he said he had only asked Mary Anne for the sake of persuading *her*, because he knew she was as light as a bird, and could fly if she pleased. Now George was a young gentleman who, like many much older than himself, believed he was clever enough to persuade *any* body to do any thing he chose, especially any young lady; and he often boasted if he could not gain his end by one means he could by another. He thought now he had tried one mode long enough with Grace, and gave it up;—the fact was, his last speech had a little checked Grace in her wish of pleasing him—she did not like it, though she hardly knew why. He misunderstood Grace's character. He changed his tone, and though not so boisterous as he was to his cousin, he treated her in the same way; he *dared* her to it. And now Grace felt her task quite easy. To George's surprise she exclaimed, "Oh, no, now you have dared me to it! I can't!"

"Can't!" cried he, "why not?" To which she only answered, she never could. He tried all the means in his power, but quite in vain. He persisted she could not. He called her sulky, which made her laugh; and he almost laughed too at his charge, so animated and good humoured was she looking all the time. She then ran to her two friends, and proposed a good fast walk to get warm; but George still persecuted her, and she was obliged to say more gravely, "You know I have *said* I can't."

"You mean *won't*," said George, very much displeased, and turning away to leave them, added, "she's as obstinate as a mule."

Poor Grace did not quite like this, and felt all the time as if she had been doing wrong. Campbell ran for a new dog they had, and was very anxious that Grace should lead him by his chain. She was glad to do so, and more glad of a little run round the garden. The four young people and the dog Pincher had a pleasant race, and this somewhat restored the spirits of the party, especially of Grace and Emily, who was fond of her brother, and sorry he should be vexed. Grace however still felt as the offender, and rather dreaded seeing George. After some time it was proposed to go in-doors again, and for that purpose they walked towards the house more slowly. Emily suddenly asked Campbell how he was after his blows last night, and if he felt them. Campbell scarcely answered, but released Grace from the care of Pincher, and ran away to chain him up again. The three girls entered the house, and retired to the library. "How strange it is of Campbell," said Emily, "he can't bear to have last night's business alluded to."

Grace thought it not at all strange, but said nothing. Mary Anne said that if Campbell was ashamed, Newton Grey should be more so.

"Oh," said Emily, "we all know what Newton is; he is a shocking fellow, and so mean, we all hate him, and I was so glad that he got two or three good blows from Campbell; I am sure they must have hurt him."

"Now, Emily," said Mary Anne, "you have said a great many wrong things. You know we should not hate any body, nor be glad when they are hurt, and we cannot say it was right of Campbell to fight."

"Do you mean to say," asked Emily, quickly, "that I am not to hate a boy that used such language as Newton, and insulted Constance as he did? and am I not to be glad when he gets well beaten for it? I am sure if no one else had done it, I should like to have given him a cuff myself!" cried Emily, with action suited to the words, that almost made Grace smile in spite of her serious feelings at the beginning of Emily's speech.

"Oh, Emily, for shame!" said her cousin, "how you talk!"

"Well, now, Grace," said Emily, "you shall be judge; what did you think about it?"

"Oh, please don't ask me," cried poor Grace, quite frightened, "I really don't know what is right."

"Nonsense!" said Emily, "you can tell quite well enough. Now don't you think Newton deserved a good pummelling?"

"I think he deserved a very severe punishment," replied Grace, in a low serious tone.

"Punishment! yes!" returned Emily, "but how was he to get it there? do you mean he should be flogged? you know he is educated at home, and there's no one there to flog him, and I believe his mamma never has him flogged; besides none of us would go tell!"

"How glad I am," thought Grace to herself, "that I did not tell mamma; I did not think it would be telling tales."

"Well, Grace," continued Emily, after waiting, "what do you think? do you agree with Mary Anne that it is wrong to be glad when bad people are punished?"

"Oh, no," cried Grace, quickly, "at least, I don't know if I am right, but I am sure I am very glad sometimes; you know how glad one is in stories and history, when very wicked people indeed and tyrants are punished or dethroned, and it must be the same sort of thing, I suppose."

"To be sure," said Emily; "why it's the beauty of fairy tales and all those stories; I could sometimes clap my hands for joy when I come to those wicked enchanters being destroyed, and all the beautiful princesses they have shut up being released; and then, you know, how one admires the knight who has done it all alone by his bravery and courage!"

"Yes," said Mary Anne, "but all that is a story, and it is not Christian."

"Ah!" said Emily, "now we've got to the 'no-punishment system' again, and we want George here to set things right. Now, Grace," continued she, "do you think it right that naughty boys and girls should never be punished?"

"Oh, no, of course," replied Grace, "who thinks so?"

"Why," answered Emily, "did you not hear yesterday that Miss Newmarsh never punishes the Duffs?"

Grace said she thought it all in jest.

Emily assured her it was quite true, and Mary Anne did not contradict it.

"I suppose they are all very good, and do not deserve being punished," said Grace, "you know they cannot do very wrong at home."

"Indeed you are mistaken, they are not so good," returned Emily, "and what do you mean by 'can't do very wrong at home?' you know children can be naughty any where."

"No, not at home, I think," said Grace, "one can't help being good—I mean—not being very bad at home."

"Why, then, are you never naughty? or does your mamma never punish you?"

"Mamma never punishes me," said Grace, rather ashamed of never being punished.

"There!" cried Mary Anne, triumphantly, "you see your mamma does just the same as Miss Newmarsh!"

"Then I can understand it very well," said Grace.

"But do you really mean to say, Grace," said Emily, "*upon your word*, that your mamma never punished you in her life?"

Grace looked very serious, and after some time said, "I can only remember once."

"And when was that?"

"One day," said Grace, colouring very much, "that she would not let me go with her to see my cousins."

"And what had you done?"

"I had not attended to my music."

"Was that all?"

"I had been careless the day before, and mamma said if I did not do better the next day, she would leave me behind."

"And you were really left behind?"

Grace assented.

"And were you not very angry?"

"No, not angry," said Grace, "I could not be angry, because I knew I deserved it."

"Then you were sorry, I suppose."

"Yes," replied Grace, hesitating, "but. . . ."

"But what?"

"But not so sorry as I might have been."

"Now do go on, Grace, please, without so much 'pumping,' " said Emily, "because why?"

"Because," said Grace, "mamma was so very kind as to *promise* me she would not tell my aunt."

"But then," said Emily, "after all it was not much of a punishment—only just for once not seeing your cousins."

"Oh, yes," said Grace, "but it was; for they were all going to the Tower to see the wild beasts, and the King's crown, and every thing else, and I have never been there yet."

"But why did you not say that that was the punishment at first?" asked Mary Anne, surprised.

"I did not remember it," said Grace, "till Emily reminded me: at the time I thought of nothing but my aunt hearing of it."

The tears had been in poor Grace's eyes almost ever since she spoke of her mamma's kindness; and now that her young friends ceased to question her, she drew a long breath, and seemed quite relieved to be allowed to be silent. Soon after, the boys came in, for it was near dinner time. George was in very good humour, and Grace had answered him several times, and laughed at his droll ways, before she remembered she had been dreading to see him again. His kindness made her a great deal more sorry for what she had done, and she resolved to please him whenever she could, to make up for her offence. The rest of the day went on in the same way—no company—and the young people went into the dining-room and drawing-room; also they enjoyed the time they had together in the library, and Grace found no drawbacks. She and Emily had a pleasant talk together at night; the fire was kept up for them, and Grace was not in such a hurry as the night before. They talked of Ellen, who was coming the next day; and Emily gave some amusing accounts of her schoolfellows. Grace also discovered that Emily went to school at Richmond, and that she knew the Miss Marsdens,—that they came every week to dance; and according to Emily's report they were the most disagreeable girls in the world; that they spoke to *her*, because, "you know," said she, "my uncle is Lord Musgrove; but they turn their backs on some of the girls, and are so rude, you don't know! but then their papa and mamma are just the same; and since they had that large fortune left them, they have cut all their old friends. How I do hate such stuff!"

Grace was pondering over the new and wonderful things that she heard every minute, and Emily asked what she was thinking of.

"I was only wondering at all you have been telling me," said Grace, "but I want to ask you what you meant just now by saying that Selina Carey was a favourite at school, *though* she is so good: I should have thought you meant *because* instead of *though*."

"Oh, you know," replied Emily, "some good girls are so tiresome and fidgety, they won't let one do or say any thing, and are always telling tales."

After a pause, Emily introduced quite another subject, and in due time the little friends again sought their room. Grace did not get to sleep so soon this night; she thought a good deal about Campbell's affair, and their talk about it; also the garden scene and Emily's words just now made her quite uneasy. "I wonder," thought she, "if I should be one of those disagreeable girls that every body dislikes if I was at school." Then she thought, how glad she was not to be at school and disliked by all the girls; then again, that it was all the same thing if she was that sort of character, and here became lost, as usual, in the depth of metaphysics. At length she considered it was foolish to spend her thoughts and make herself uneasy about what she *might* be under any other circumstances, but resolved to try and do as well as she could under those in which she was placed; and thus she came home, as it were, to her dear mamma, and thought over the pieces of advice she gave her, in such a kind and useful way. "Now," thought she, "if mamma every day were to tell me the same good things one after another, all at once, I never should remember half, and should be quite confused; but she says *now and then* a very few easy words, as things occur, and that shows me exactly what she means, and I can keep it in my head for another time when the same sort of thing happens, just as that day a long time ago, when Anna and Edward Bell were so tiresome and changeable in choosing their orange, mamma said to me afterwards, 'Grace, always have a choice, even in small matters;' that gave me a rule for a long time, and helped me to say *Thalia* the other day to Mr. Everard. How right and safe mamma always is!" and she fell asleep thinking over many such little anecdotes of her dear mamma's wisdom.

CHAPTER XIV

George was a boy with a spirit strong and high,
With handsome face, and penetrating eye.
CRABBE

Next morning at ten, Grace went to her mamma's room, but found her not yet there. After about a quarter of an hour, Mrs. Leslie came in. "Oh, my dear Grace," said she, "I knew you would be here, and I was sorry to keep you, but Mrs. Ward was talking to me on particular business, and I could not leave her; I am glad, however, you have not been waiting doing nothing;"—for Grace's little fingers were fast at work at a chain she was making.

"Oh, mamma," said she, "it has not seemed long, and I want you, please, to do me a favour."

In answer to her mamma's inquiries, Grace explained that she wished to finish this chain, and that she should like to bring it and work at it a little for a day or two after they had read together, for that she wished to finish it for George, and not to let it be seen till done.

"For George!" said her mamma; "why, yesterday Campbell seemed your favourite!"

Grace was puzzled for the moment at this view of the case; she certainly had seen much more to like, according to her understanding of the word, in Campbell than George, but she soon remembered how it came to pass. "Why, mamma," said she, "I have twice vexed George, and I was afraid he would think me very ill-natured."

"I am sorry," said her mamma, "that you should vex any of your companions; how did that happen?"

Grace had not at all expected this question, and hardly knew how to answer it. She said, however, that she did not mean to vex him, but it was an accident.

"Well, my dear Grace," said her mamma, "if you think it right and fair to tell me, I should like to know how it was you vexed George *one* of the times you allude to—would it be unfair?"

Poor Grace was quite perplexed. "Really, mamma, I don't know, I wish you could tell me," said she: then she thought perhaps her mamma would think it was something much worse than it was; so after a little thought, she chose her first offence, and answered, "Why, mamma, you know George is very clever and can take off any body, and after the dinner party he took off some of the company; I did not like it just after we had seen them and been dining with them, and I could not laugh as I had done before. George observed it, and seemed very much vexed."

"And I suppose," said her mamma, "the other time was the same sort of thing—I don't wish to hear it."

"Yes, something of the same sort, I think," answered Grace.

"Well, my dear Grace," said her mamma, "you are old enough to know how to behave; never let high spirits make you forget yourself."

"Mamma," said the little girl, timidly, "would you be so very kind as to tell me if you think I did right?"

"My dear child," answered Mrs. Leslie, "I cannot quite tell without having been present; young people together are apt to become rude or forget themselves, and if one can put a little check upon the rest without being tiresome, it is very right and proper."

"Ah, mamma," said Grace, despondingly, "there is the difficulty—'without being tiresome!' "

"It is a difficulty, my dear girl," said her mamma, "and you must not be discouraged when I say you must be *tiresome* sometimes, especially at first; but in the *long run*, Grace, they will understand you, because I think my little girl would always have a good and a kind reason for what she does."

Mrs. Leslie here proposed reading, and Grace remarked it was the third day of the month. "How is it you know the day of the month so much better than the day of the week, my dear?" asked Mrs. Leslie, alluding to something that passed at breakfast.

"Because," said Grace, rather more slowly, "it begins with my favourite psalm, and I have been thinking of it all the time we were talking."

Mrs. Leslie found that this psalm had become her favourite from one verse it contained, and Grace placed her finger on the fifth as that verse. She said she had observed it ever since they began reading the psalms together, and that she always was glad when she awoke on the morning of the third day of the month, because of that verse.

Mrs. Leslie said she wondered Grace had never happened to mention it, and Grace told her mamma she very nearly had done so, when they were talking the other day about people keeping promises.

Mrs. Leslie then said, "There is one more remark I will make before we begin, and that is, Grace, that people who admire this psalm should be very particular in observing the verse before your favourite one—of course you know the meaning of 'setteth not by himself?' "

"I used to be so puzzled, mamma, about that verse," said Grace; "I used to think it ought to be *sitteth,* and that it meant *sitting* alone in the same way that the Pharisee *stood* alone and looked down on the Publican; but I suppose it means the same sort of thing—not setting himself up above others. Is that right?"

"Yes, my dear, quite right, I believe; and now let us read."

Mrs. Leslie felt rather surprised at her little girl's silent observation, but made no further remark. After they had read, Grace found she had not explained her wish about the chain fully to her mamma, and accordingly did so. She said that George yesterday brought his chain to his sister, and asked her to make him a new one, for that his was quite worn out. Emily said she would at school, but that she had no time in the holidays. George was very droll indeed about her having no time in the holidays, and Grace remembered this chain of hers already begun, which her mamma had advised her to bring, in case she wanted a little idle work of that kind. She had worked half an hour at it, besides her practice, that morning, and if she might secure an hour or so besides for the two remaining days, she thought she could get it finished by Tuesday, the day of the party, for George had been pretending to cry because his chain was so shabby for "company." Mrs. Leslie made no objection to Grace's wish, and all was settled to her satisfaction. She had a nice long talk with her mamma, and while this is going on, it may be as well to relate part of the conversation which passed in the library among the cousins meanwhile. George had gone out, and said he should return about the time "the face of a Grace" made its appearance. In about an hour he came in, and a great racket he made at not finding her yet down stairs. Emily remarked that not one of them yet had·given any opinion about Grace, and asked what they thought of her. Mary Anne answered, that for her part she saw nothing at all in her, and thought her like any other little girl.

"Well, I can't say *that,*" said Emily; "I know a great many little girls, both at school and at home, and I have been thinking that there is not one I can compare her to;" and Emily spoke in favour of her: she told them of her getting up in the morning and practising, all in the cold and dark almost.

"Well," said Mary Anne, "that's only what we do at home; we do not practise, but we are always at our lessons, or something of that sort."

"But then why are you not so here?" asked George.

"Oh, because I have no lessons, and am not obliged."

"Well, and Grace is not obliged," said Emily, "and yet she does it."

"But I suppose her mamma tells her," said Mary Anne.

"She need not practise unless she likes," said Emily.

"That's a good one!" cried George; "you may depend upon it, her mamma would flog her if she did not!"

"It's no such thing, George," said Emily, quickly; "besides, if she chose not to practise, how would her mamma or any body else know?"

"Why, of course," said George, "her mamma asks her every morning—'Grace, have you practised an hour?' and if she said, '*No,*' she would punish her."

"She might practise a little, and make that do, if she chose to do so," said Emily.

"Oh, no," returned her brother, "Grace is a good girl, and would not tell a fib; she is a regular prude, in every thing, you may be sure."

Emily defended her against the charge of prudery.

George persisted, "But I say she is a prude, and she shows it every minute."

"Ah," said Emily, "that is all because you could not make her do as you pleased yesterday in the garden."

George rather warmly replied, that he could easily have made her, but the fact was, she could not leap, so it was no use trying; that in other things he had seen she was a prude; at dinner, the first day, he sat opposite her and tried all he could to make her laugh at the company, but she would not. At first he thought she was stupid, then that she was shy, but that since he saw she was neither of these, so he was quite sure she was a prude.

Emily laughed at her brother for his inconsistency in being in such a fidget for Grace to come all the morning, and at the same time disliking her so much.

"Well," said George, "that's the very reason; I mean to have some fun with her, and I'm determined to cure her of her prudish ways."

Emily again laughed at him; said he was very inconsistent—that just now he had confessed he could not make Grace do as he pleased, and that now he seemed to think he could have it all his own way.

"And so I can," said George, "do you think I can't make any girl do as I please? and especially such a little girl as Grace? Why, here's Mary Anne, who is so religious, and much older than Grace, yet she always does just as I choose."

Mary Anne burst out into a defence of her independence, and reminded him of her constant habit of correcting him and telling him when he was doing wrong.

"Ha! ha! my pretty cousin," cried George, "you tell me when I'm wrong! I know you do—make signs at me! frown! shake your head when I'm quizzing!—why all that makes me do it more, because I know it pleases you."

"For shame, George," cried Mary Anne, "you know it makes me very angry."

"Then why do you laugh and look at me?"

"I can't help laughing sometimes, you are so ridiculous," said Mary Anne; "mamma says that is the most remarkable point about me—my sense of the ridiculous is so very strong!"

"Then you should not look at me," said George, "if you don't like it and can't help laughing."

"I look at you," returned his cousin, "to stop you and correct you, for it is very wrong to be laughing at people's oddities; we ought to pity them and. . . ."

"Ha, ha!" cried George, "to stop me!—why I tell you it makes me worse: if you want to stop me, you should do as Grace does, for she does not let me catch her eye. I know she has seen me twenty times, and I have made all the faces I could."

"Well, and does she keep her countenance at your odd faces?" asked Mary Anne.

"No, she sometimes quite laughs at them, but I want to make her laugh at the company, and I'm determined I will—she's only shy at first: you were very 'prettily behaved' at first, Mary Anne, but are no prude now, certainly."

Mary Anne was displeased at this, and almost pleaded guilty of prudery.

"No, no, my pretty cousin," cried George, looking very good-natured, and giving her an encouraging tap under the chin, "I know you better and I like *you* better than your words: believe me, you were never made for a prude, and as to Grace she's a regular little old maid."

Campbell here interfered and objected to George's expression. George laughed, and said, "Well, Campbell, you know you need not be offended, for Grace will never be really an old maid, because we all know she is to be your wife."

This raised a good laugh, and quite silenced poor Campbell. George, elated with his victory, repeated in a louder and more decided tone, "I say she's a little old maid, and a tiresome squeamish prude."

While he said this, the door opened, and Grace entered. She came in with almost a laugh on her face, saying, "How you have been laughing as I came along the passage!"

There was a little pause; but Emily, who had a safe conscience, had readiness enough to reply, "Yes, we were laughing at Campbell."

Grace turned to Campbell, who certainly looked rather foolish. She had observed they were apt to laugh at him, generally on account of his bluntness and honesty, and she had no doubt it was so in this instance; so she said, very good-naturedly, "Well, Campbell, we shall find some opportunity to laugh at them some day."

There was another little pause, rather awkward; for George was more stunned by Grace's sudden appearance and unsuspicious manner, than he could have believed beforehand. In the meanwhile the words Grace had *heard* but not observed on her entrance, came to her ear; and she too felt uncomfortable, hardly knowing why. However, she was the first to speak, and she asked what they were going to do.

"Why," said Emily, "you must ask George; he has been pining after you ever so long, and I suppose had something in his head."

George felt a little angry and awkward, and began a reply, not however with his usual readiness. Just then small and quick steps were heard in the passage, the door opened, and in came the three little Duffs.

CHAPTER XV

... Not only ... "See how these Christians love one another," but the still nobler com-
mendation, "See how these Christians love all the world."
REV. J. W. CUNNINGHAM

THE PLEASURE of this visit was unexpected, and at this moment the cousins were received with a double welcome; the spirit of the party was restored, and talking recommenced with animation. Mrs. Duff was coming to see her sister, and had put the little girls into the carriage. Fanny said Miss Newmarsh did not like giving them a holiday, since they were having so many just now; but they had left her on their way at her friend Dr. Barker's, and were to call for her on their return; "which you know," she added, "always pacifies her."

Constance rebuked her sister for her mode of speaking of Miss Newmarsh, and Fanny said if she was as great a favourite as Constance, perhaps she would speak differently.

"Well, Fanny," said George, "I am sure you've no right to complain; you've got a good library of books and all manner of pretty toys from Miss Newmarsh."

"Yes," said Fanny, "but that's not like being the favourite; there's Constance always closeted up with Miss Newmarsh, and I do believe she tells her all her secrets—I don't like it at all—it is not fair to have Constance always against us."

"Does Constance tell?" asked George.

"What is there to tell?" said Mary Anne, "I am sure I don't know."

"Nothing particular to *tell*," answered Fanny, "only you know we sometimes speak of Miss Newmarsh as I did just now, and if she knew it she would be very cross."

"Well, but," said George, "she would not punish you, would she?"

"Yes, sometimes she gives us verses to learn."

"Oh, then, she does punish after all!"

"Only for impertinence," said Constance, "and nobody gets impositions but Fanny."

"And does Fanny go on getting more rewards than any of you for being naughty?" asked George.

Fanny said she had not had any thing lately.

George said he was glad to hear it, and hoped she'd grow a better girl; and then, to Grace's great satisfaction, he continued, "Well, now you're all together, will you tell the history of the books and the skipping-rope?—but first, Mary Anne, putting yourself out of the question, who's the best among you?"

She answered, "Charlotte."

"And putting yourself out of the question, who's the worst among you?"

She answered, "Fanny."

He then asked Constance the same questions, and got the same answers. Then he continued to Mary Anne, "Who has the most pretty books with gilt edges?"

She answered, "Fanny."

"And who the fewest?"

"Charlotte."

He then asked Fanny what sort of books, and got her to say they were pretty story books, full of amusing tales,—some were graver, but she never read them—they were given her after she had been naughty—she once had a story called "Temper" given her after she had been cross to Charlotte, and another time "Industry ahd Idleness," when she had been lying on the lawn under a tree, instead of preparing her realization lesson—that the skipping-rope was some time ago, soon after Miss Newmarsh came. Constance took up the story here, and said it ought to be explained, on Miss Newmarsh's account—that Fanny had been very naughty, and that Miss Newmarsh said, on the old system she would have been flogged, so she gave her a *cord*, such as people used to flog themselves with, and she thought Fanny could never use her skipping-rope without remembering how naughty she had been and avoiding her fault in future.

George then asked if Charlotte had any thing at all.

They said, "Yes, a few little books given her by her mamma."

"Ah," said George, "she's always the best of you, and she gets neither praise nor blame."

After this they talked of the party the other night, and of Newton Grey. Campbell was fidgety here. The rest agreed to dislike him. Even Constance, who was always ready to take the unpopular side, spoke unfavourably of him. George remarked that Grace was the only one silent, and said he really believed Grace liked Newton Grey.

"I!" exclaimed Grace, "what can make you think so?"

"Because, perhaps, you think it is wrong to find fault with any body;—but don't you like him?"

Grace coloured, as she said deliberately, "I can't bear him, and if he was in the room, I don't think I could speak to him."

George looked surprised, and all seemed a little struck. Constance broke the pause by saying, "Well, I don't think that is christian; it is not right to be as unforgiving as that."

Grace looked very serious, and Constance continued, "Now he has offended *me* more than any of you, but I would not only speak to him, but do any thing kind for him."

After a little thought, Grace said, "Yes, but you know he has not offended me!"

"Well done!" cried George, "capital!" thinking it a repartee on Grace's part, for which she did not mean it. It however made a turn in the conversation, and presently they got upon "Miss Ward." Fanny admired her—thought her such a delightful creature—had thought of nothing else ever since; and Constance praised her, though not so warmly, yet highly. Emily opened her eyes with surprise; "Why, Constance!" said she, "do you really like Isabella? I thought you would hate her!"

"Hate!" exclaimed Constance, shocked, "I never hate any body! much less your cousin, who seems to have so much that is promising about her!"

"What *do* you mean?" asked Emily, "her dress, for instance! how hard you always are on the Newtons and many others for their dress, and they are not half so smart! and how often you have laughed at little girls wearing rings and ornaments!"

"Oh, Emily," said Constance, "you are unreasonable! you don't consider!—your cousin is not a little girl, and her rank gives her a right to dress differently from other people; besides, she sits quite loose to all these things—you can't think," said she, smiling at the scene, "how sweetly she got up and took off all her ornaments!"

"Well," said Emily, "I wondered what that whim was for! I saw she had got them off at supper, but could not get at her to ask why."

"It was to prove to me," said Constance, "that she did not care about such things, and when I came with her for her ornaments before she left, she took my hand, and in the sweetest manner asked me if I was satisfied."

"Ho, ho!" exclaimed George, "I thought you were going to say, asked you to accept of them!"

"Oh, George," said Emily, "you could never expect Belle would do such a thing!"

"Why, I was surprised, but after all that passed, I really expected it."

"What a foolish thought!" said Constance, "I should never be so ridiculous as to wear such things."

"The grapes are sour, as Newton said," cried George, "you must wait till you have them, before you despise them; you'd be as fine as Belle if you could!"

Emily rebuked her brother, and said, that certainly Constance was not fond of dress, and that she never spent any of her money in ornaments of any kind.

"Well, better that she should," answered the unreasonable George, "Why does she not do like others?"

"How unfair you are," said Grace, "nothing seems to please you!"

He then turned upon Grace, and asked how she spent her money.

She really could not tell; and the more she tried to think, the less she could remember. Constance asked gravely, "Don't you spend your money on principle?"

George suggested that Grace perhaps had none to spend, while Emily said she was sure *she* could not answer the same question if asked.

"Well," continued George, "Belle could, well enough, for, though her papa and mamma are always giving her real jewels, and things of that sort, she spends all she can get in gimcracks besides."

"I should think," remarked Constance, "that school she goes to is a bad thing for her, and I dare say the young ladies there dress very much."

"Oh, no such thing!" said Emily, "though she's the youngest there, she dresses more than any of them. Mrs. Jenkinson does not like the young ladies to dress, and will not let Belle wear any of her fine things there,—but Belle will put them on whenever she can. Mrs. Jenkinson is a very elegant woman, and very sensible, I have heard mamma say so often; and besides, she is in some things very much of Miss Newmarsh's way of thinking. She used to go to Congreve chapel, but when Mr. Temple went away and Mr. Allan came, she left, and now she always goes to Park Street chapel, to hear Mr. De Lisle, though it is so far from her house; and there is a clergyman comes once a fortnight to read and......oh! what do you call it, Constance? you know Mr. Bishop is always doing it."

"Do you mean *expound*?" said Constance, doubtingly.

"Yes, to read and expound to the girls."

"Indeed!" cried Constance, "Miss Ward's account seemed quite different."

"Oh!" said Emily, "you must not mind what she says!"

"Do you mean to say," said Constance, remembering her first impression of Isabella, "that she does not speak the truth?"

"Not exactly that," returned Emily, "but she rhodomontades at a famous rate, and thinks it all very fine; but what stuff has she been telling you?"

"Oh, she gave a very grand account of Mrs. Jenkinson's school and house and servants."

"Well," said Emily, "it is rather grand for a school, but tell me all she said."

"Why," said Constance, "she said there were eight young ladies, and that Mrs. Jenkinson kept two regular sets of rooms and servants for them; she had two carriages, two pair of horses, two coachmen, several footmen in livery, and eight lady's maids for the young ladies; that there were also sixteen rooms, besides the four dining and drawing rooms; for that each young lady had a bed-room and study, with a piano in it, and that they took their lessons all separate."

Mary Anne interrupted her sister several times in this relation; first, at the two carriages and several footmen, saying she did not hear Miss Ward say so. Constance proved it from her saying they got into the *wrong carriage:* the same with the eight lady's maids, (to which Mary Anne also objected;) because Isabella said, "*My* maid."

Emily waited till the end of this account, and then said, "And really Belle told you all this stuff! that was because I was away; she'd no more dare to say such things before George or me, than she'd give you her fine pearls. Now, I'll just tell you how it is: Mrs. Jenkinson has a large house, and she keeps a footman; she also has a carriage, and she takes the young ladies to dance at D'Egvilles, and also to the church I just now spoke of; the girls are all together, just like any other school, but they have drawing and practising rooms, which put the eight studies into her head."

"But," said Constance, "how could she say they lived separate by four and four?"

"Because they have two tables at tea and breakfast, where they sit four and four, and I have often heard mamma laugh about it: she says Mrs. Jenkinson always manages that the girls of the highest rank should sit together; and they are in all ways more favoured. Some half years she classes them according to age, and others to merit, but generally speaking it is so contrived. Now it happens that Isabella is the youngest of the whole set, and so excessively idle and stupid, except in music, that if Mrs. Jenkinson wished it ever so much, she could not displace Miss Corrie, who is three years older than Isabella, and very clever. Miss Corrie is the daughter of a baronet, and the only one at the highest table beneath Belle in rank. All at Belle's table are only the daughters of gentlemen; two are sisters, and very nice girls; the other thinks of nothing but her studies, and despises Belle for her indolence. Belle is always longing to be at the high table, and what she meant by never seeing or knowing them, was that they scarcely ever spoke to her, and she had very little to do with them."

"So it was a sort of a fable!" exclaimed Fanny, in admiration, "what imagination she must have! I shall like her better than ever!"

"Oh, how can you say that!" said Grace, "you know if she did so in every thing, one could not tell whether to believe her or not!"

Constance remarked, that Grace was offended with Miss Ward because she took her for such a little girl, and so of course would not like her. This silenced Grace, whilst Emily reminded Constance *she* did not like Isabella at first.

Constance allowed this, but said she had since seen so much that was interesting in Miss Ward, that she saw good reason for changing her opinion, and especially since now she found Mrs. Jenkinson was such a religious woman.

The young people had more talk on Ellen's expected arrival, which seemed to rejoice Charlotte the most. They also discussed the party for the next Tuesday, and after all dining together, Mrs. Duff was ready to go, and the three little sisters departed.

In the evening Ellen arrived, escorted by Hanson, who had formerly been nurse at the Wards. Grace had always heard her spoken of with great affection by the children, as old nurse Hanson, or old nurse; she had fancied she must be like Jemima Placid's old nurse, and was therefore surprised at finding her not at all an old woman, and very quiet and respectful in her manners, though she seemed very glad to see every one of them again. Ellen was certainly very different from her sister. She had great simplicity of character, and yet, when she chose it, a drollery and quaintness in its way quite as amusing as her brother's or sister's. She was always a singular child, and very few persons understood her—so much so, that most thought her, "a very odd child;" many had "no patience with her;" and some even hinted that "she was wanting." Her mamma was inclined to the two first opinions, and always wondered, though she was pleased, at Mrs. General Ward's preference for Ellen. She was her godmamma as well as her grandmamma, and had very early taken a fancy to the little girl. When the Wards moved from London, and Emily went to school, this lady made a more formal matter of Ellen's constant visits to Langham, and it was generally understood that she would become an adopted child. Mrs. Ward was General Ward's second wife, and now a widow; she was therefore no relation whatever of any of the family.

Having now introduced the reader to a new acquaintance, we shall leave the meeting between the parties to be imagined—how pleased all were—how all laughed and talked at once—how surprised every body was at Ellen's growth, and how in turn she was surprised at the same in her brothers and sisters—how Grace stood in the back ground and was interested in the scene, and how, after a time she was remembered and brought forward; and then the little check the appearance of a stranger gave for a short time to Ellen's ease and freedom, and her recovery of the same. Then came tea, all together, and Ellen fell into her more usual way. She asked some questions that made them all laugh, and George began to make fun of her. Her mamma cried, "Oh, Ellen, always the same! when will that child cease to be a baby!" while Emily exclaimed, "What an odd girl you are, Ellen!" However they all seemed very happy together, and Grace had quite a new sort of evening, almost pleasanter than what had gone before. But at last the evening came to an end, and nurse Hanson insisted on Miss Ellen not sitting up that night with Miss Emily, since she had had a long day's fatigue, and to-morrow was Sunday, and she must not get knocked up and tired; so she waited while Ellen wished Emily and Grace good night and said a few words, and then took her off to her room.

"How tiresome old nurse always is!" said Emily, "she will have her own way, and I know it's no use speaking to her."

Grace agreed it was disappointing, but reminded Emily that Ellen was going to stay a long time. "It is not as if we had only one day—then it would be tiresome indeed."

"Oh, Grace," cried Emily, "you are always full of reasons for every thing being right; and really," she added, "if I were much with you I think I should grow quite a good girl."

CHAPTER XVI

On Sunday Heaven's Gate stands ope,
Blessings are plentiful and rife,
More plentiful than Hope.
GEORGE HERBERT

T HE NEXT MORNING was Sunday, and a very fine day. After breakfast the young party retired as usual to the library, and it was proposed to go out in the garden. Grace, however, found it was half-past nine, and said she could not accompany them, since she must go to her mamma.

"Why, to-day's Sunday!" said George, "what *can* your mamma want you for? you don't do lessons on Sunday, do you?"

"No," said Grace, "not lessons, but mamma told me to come at half-past nine, and it is just that time now."

George teazed to know what for; and added, "It is very wrong, you know, to do any thing on Sunday, and if you do, Grace, Mary Anne will not speak to you."

Mary Anne corrected him here, and said, "she wished George would take care to say what was true, for she should do no such thing."

"Well, then," said George, "you would not cut her, but you would say behind her back that she was a *very wicked little girl,* and Constance would tell her so to her face."

A few more sentences were exchanged between the young people on this subject; meanwhile Grace had slipped out of the room; Ellen found she was gone, and overtook her in the hall—"Grace, Grace," she called softly, "will you please to tell me, if you've no objection, what you are going to do with your mamma?" Seeing Grace hesitate, she added, in her slow mysterious tone, "Do tell me, for I have a very particular *reason* for wanting to know!"

Grace told her she was going to say the Catechism, and then went up stairs to her mamma's room.

Ellen ran back to the dining-room door. Here she found her mamma with Mrs. Leslie. She jumped on a stool, and whispered something in her mamma's ear. Mrs. Ward answered her aloud, "Yes, my dear, if Mrs. Leslie has no objection."

It was then explained to that lady that Ellen wished to say her Catechism with Grace. The request was granted, and Ellen was desired to go up to Grace.

"What a strange child that is!" said Mrs. Ward, as the little girl closed the door; "do you know, she takes as much delight in reading and saying the Catechism, and things of that sort, as if it was all her own choice. She is quite different from the rest of my children—then she's not of their lively turn."

"I suppose she has been used to such things at her grandmamma's," remarked Mrs. Leslie.

"Yes, but before that she used always to be teazing me to hear them the Catechism on Sundays, as her aunt Duff was accustomed to do. Only think," added Mrs. Ward, laughing, "the idea of my hearing George and the rest of them the Catechism! and reading the Bible with them!"

Mrs. Leslie remarked that it was the custom in many families.

"I do not mean that it should not be done," said Mrs. Ward, "their governess, of course, used to attend to those things, and now I send them to school—only *I* could not do it. It is all very well, if people are as religious as my sister, Mrs. Duff—and their children are not so lively as mine; but you know George would almost make me laugh; and besides, how could I, with my quick temper, hear and teach them their duty to their neighbour, and all the rest? oh, no! I'm not so bad as that; I know my own faults too well, and could never set myself up as a pattern to my children, as some mothers I know do—no better than myself after all!"

"Indeed," said Mrs. Leslie, rather perplexed for an answer, "indeed I think you mistake the thing altogether—I have never looked upon it in that light."

"Oh," said Mrs. Ward, "*you* cannot judge in this case; you have one quiet little girl, who gives you no trouble at all, and you have a placid temper by nature; just think of the difference—here was I with two wild boys, when poor Edward was alive at the head of the rest, and Emily nearly as bad; how could I, with my health, too, call them all together, and hear them the Catechism, and make them read the Bible?—why, you know, I know no more of it than they do; I am no divine, and I was not brought up under the religious system of the present day: besides, I was never made for a teacher—I have not the patience—it would drive me wild; and then, what an example for the children!"

"But have you an objection to Ellen reading with Grace to-day?"

"Oh, none in the world; I should not *choose* such ways for her, but her grandmamma likes them, and will be delighted to hear that she keeps them up. Mrs. General Ward entirely undertakes Ellen, and has every right to prescribe her education; I should be sorry that Emily should take such a turn, but as for Ellen, some day she will be able to afford to do as she pleases, so it does not matter. But now you must be going to your little pupils."

Mrs. Leslie here rose and proceeded to her room, where she found the two little girls, who seemed to have been in very earnest conversation. They read with her till church time. The children dined between services. After dinner George went to Campbell in the garden, and proposed a good long walk. Campbell remarked, it was just church time.

"Why," said George, "we *have* been to church to-day."

His cousin reminded him of afternoon service.

"Oh," said George, "we never go to that; nobody ever goes to afternoon service!"

"How can you tell that," said Campbell, "if you are never there?"

"Because every body says so; why, what's the use of going twice, it's all the same thing over again?"

"It is not all the same thing over again," said Campbell; "it is much shorter, and there are prayers instead of the litany, and the lessons and psalms are quite different—only a small part is the same: besides, the sermon is never the same."

"Well," said George, "what good does the sermon and all the rest do you? can you attend to all the prayers and understand the sermon?"

"No, not to all," replied his cousin.

"Then what's the use of it all?" said George, "you'll be just as good if you come and walk with me and enjoy this beautiful day out of doors, as if you go and shut yourself up in a church with nobody but servants and shop-keepers."

"No," said Campbell, "I must go to church."

"Why," cried George, "you *are* a complete *saint,* as Newton said, and as bad as Constance; I thought that now you had been at Eton so long, you'd be cured of those home, girl's ways."

"Whatever ways they are," said Campbell, "they are right ways, and I don't want to be cured of them."

"Well," replied his cousin, "I know you are so obstinate, that when once you've got a thing into your head there's no beating it out, so good-bye, I must go by myself;" and he walked out of the garden. He thought perhaps Campbell would follow him, but was mistaken. The rest went to church with Mrs. Leslie. Emily was not accustomed to do so, but could do as she pleased in such matters; so she went with them. After they returned, Grace and Ellen continued together some time up stairs, having got into some talk that interested them both. The rest came down stairs, and George soon returned from his walk. He boasted of the pleasant time he had had. He had been on the road seeing all the coaches and carriages pass to and from London, and afterwards had been looking at people from London skating—such fun, he said, so many tumbles, such roars of laughter, and a famous crowd and bustle.

Mary Anne said that George was very wrong to go, and they were very wicked people.

"Ah," cried George, "I said you would call Grace a wicked little girl behind her back, as you do these people; and I suppose you call me wicked for not going to church twice. Now, Mary Anne," continued he, "tell me if I am wicked for not going twice, what am I for not going at all?"

"Why, it's just the same," said Mary Anne.

"No, no," said Campbell, "it's much worse not to go at all."

"Why so?" asked George, "and why do you go at all?"

"Because," said Campbell, "all good people do; and the prayer-book has two services, one for morning and the other for evening."

"If you went by the prayer-book," said George, "you'd go *twice every day.*"

"What nonsense you talk!" cried Mary Anne, "I never heard of such a thing! At some churches there is morning service on Wednesdays and Fridays—I believe there is at our old church—I know there is in Lent, because we always go to the lecture, but I never heard of church every day."

"Well, there ought to be, if you go by the prayer-book," persisted George.

"What do you mean, George?" said Emily.

George took up a prayer-book from the table, pointed to one of the rubrics, and desired them to read it.

"*That* is not in my prayer-book," said Mary Anne; and she began looking.

"It's in every prayer-book, I can tell you," said George, "and there are also lessons and psalms for every day in the year; I know it all well enough; so you see, Mary Anne, with all your religion, I know more about the prayer-book than you do."

"I never observed it before," said Emily, "how came you to know it, George?"

"Oh," said George, "I know all about those things in the prayer-book: I have read those pieces of small print through and through, out of a very large prayer-book in our pew at school; while Mr. Markwell goes on preaching his one sermon Sunday after Sunday."

Mary Anne rebuked her cousin for this, and he replied, that he had profited more by his way, than she had by all the sermons she had listened to, since he had been able to teach her something.

Mary Anne persisted he ought to listen to the sermon; and he in turn asked what was the use, when he could not understand a word, and there was nothing in it.

There seemed likely to be no end to the argument—but Grace and Ellen came in, and George appealed to the former to settle it, explaining the matter, and concluding, "Now is it not better to attend to what you *can* understand, than try to make out a sermon you can't, or stare about and think of every thing around you?"

"Well, George," said Emily, "I don't know what you do at school, but I am sure you do that at home."

"That has nothing to do with it, I am asking Grace a question—now, Grace!"

"Well," answered Grace, "I have been thinking about it. Mr. Fuller, our clergyman, preaches such very easy sermons that I cannot well judge—for there is no reason to attend to any thing else."

"Well then," said Ellen, "suppose the sermon was in Latin, what would you do?"

"No, that is not fair," said Grace, "you ought to say, suppose it were some parts in Latin and some in English;—Why, then, I think," continued she, "I should watch for the English pieces, and try to understand them."

"Well, George," cried Emily, "there is an answer for you, you should watch for the easy parts, and profit by them."

"But suppose there are no easy, or rather no useful parts?"

"Oh, George," said Ellen, "all sermons are good!"

"How can you say so?" said Mary Anne, "why there's Dr. Gosset in our parish church, who every body says is a mere stick!"

"Well then," said Ellen, very gravely, "it is just what he ought to be, and I should like to see him rise up and beat you, for talking in that way of your clergyman."

No one could smile, for Ellen spoke seriously.

"Ah," said Mary Anne, "that's the way *you* talk, who live in the country, and have only a church to go to!"

"What do you mean?" asked Ellen.

"Why you know we have an old church, and a new church, and two chapels, all close by; so we can choose, and one likes one preacher, and one another, but there's only one good for any thing, Mr. Taylor, and we go to him."

"Mary Anne," returned Ellen, "I am quite ashamed of you; I never heard any one talk in such a way."

"No," said Mary Anne, "I dare say not; I know in the country all clergymen are old and dull, like the Vicar of Wakefield, or Dr. Syntax, and all the people who live there call them your reverence, and bow before them almost as the Catholics do before *their priests*, and the squire of the village pays them the same respect, just like Sir Roger de Coverly, so that every body thinks all they do and say quite right, and nobody dare speak of them as we do of our preachers."

"Mary Anne," said Ellen, "you really know nothing about it, you know you have never been in the country."

"But I have read, and heard people talk who have been there, and I know all about it just as well," returned her cousin; "I know that country parsons are old-fashioned ignoramuses; they sit with the squire drinking wine after dinner, or play at backgammon night after night, and their wives are fat and vulgar, and their daughters do all the work of the house, and try to look smart."

"Mary Anne," cried Campbell, "what stuff you are talking! why, don't you know that Spencer Freeman is the son of a country clergyman? and what can be more different from his father, mother, and sisters, than what you have been saying?"

"Yes," said Ellen, "and all round about us at Langham; it makes me laugh to think of Mr. Bradshaw being old and ignorant, or Mrs. Palmer being fat and vulgar."

"Well, Mary Anne," said George, "what have you to say to this?"

"Why, that Mr. Freeman is quite an exception; he was not born and brought up in the country like other country clergymen, and I dare say those that Ellen mentions are the same."

"But what do you mean," said Ellen, "by being born and brought up in the country? don't you know that all clergymen must go to college; and if they choose they can get very clever and learned there?"

"Yes, but then the clever ones become good preachers, and come in or near London, and the dull stupid ones go into the country; I *know* it is so, for I have often heard people say, that except a very few clergymen, like Mr. Taylor, of Appletree—that every body knows—and a few more of the same kind, there is not a sermon fit to be heard preached in any parish church in the country, all through England."

"Really, Mary Anne," said Ellen, "you talk very great nonsense; I know grandmamma thinks many of the clergymen about us very good preachers, and there are two not far from us she often asks to lend her their sermons."

"Yes," said Mary Anne, "but then, is your grandmamma religious?"

"Religious!" cried Ellen, looking much amazed, "why to be sure she is!"

"But just now," replied her cousin, "you said all sermons were good, and perhaps you think in the same way all grandmammas are religious."

"I know *my* grandmamma is religious," said Ellen, "and very particular too—a great deal more particular in some things with me than your governess is with you."

"Well, what does she do?" asked Mary Anne, "beat you when you are naughty, as I know they do at all charity schools in the country."

"Well," said George, "and a good thing too. I should like to have you beat for laughing at grandmamma; I know she's very kind to all of us, and never comes here without giving me half a guinea, and she sends me cake and fruit and good things twice a year to school, and that is being quite religious enough for me. Your Miss Newmarsh would never do such a thing—except," added he, correcting himself, "I had been very naughty."

"Now, George," said Ellen, "you have been wrong in turn, you have no business to speak in that way of Miss Newmarsh, when you were correcting Mary Anne for the very same thing."

"Well," said George, "when Miss Newmarsh gives me half a guinea and sends me good things to school, I will speak well of her, and not allow any body else to find fault with her."

This sort of conversation went on some time. At last Mary Anne called it unprofitable, and proposed some of her Bible questions, &c. George said they would be good fun. Ellen objected strongly, and Emily said she would not play if George was in the room, for he always made her laugh. Mary Anne objected to Emily's word *"play,"* and Emily asked what else to call it.

We shall leave the young people to settle the matter at their leisure, and to conclude their evening, having given the above as a specimen of their Sunday's conversation.

CHAPTER XVII

Order is Heaven's first law! . . .
POPE

THE NEXT DAY was much given up to preparations for the grand twelfth-night party. Emily had the characters to cut and fold up, and a great many little affairs of that sort to arrange: besides, she had a plan in her head for the evening, about which she sought George early after breakfast to propose it. It was to make a list of suitable games for the evening, and arrange their entertainments so that there should be no confusion. She applied to George for his assistance and memory. George laughed at her plan, called it nonsense, and a great bore to think of things beforehand, and asked why now more than ever before, when they had always done very well.

"Why, George," said his sister, "you don't consider, we are to have no dancing and cards to-night, and we must amuse them all with games of different sorts, and this is a very large party for that. Besides, the Harrises, and Thompsons, and that Newton, are always ready for mischief, and if they begin as they do at other houses, what shall we do?"

"Well, trust to me," said George, "I could keep them amused for more than one night—trust to me!"

"I will trust to you afterwards," replied his sister, "only help me to make out this list; you cannot keep fifty or sixty amused all night, but if we make a plan, and divide them into rooms, we can do it very well among us. See, I have got pen and ink all ready, and it won't take you a quarter of an hour. I talked it all over with Grace on Saturday night, and she advised me to set about it the first thing this morning."

"Well," said George, "I wondered where you got such a tiresome notion from—it's just like Grace and her prudish ways."

"Nonsense, George," said his sister, "it's a very good way, and you'll be glad of it when the time comes."

George objected that any plan made beforehand would spoil the spirit of the evening, and Emily said Grace had answered that objection by saying they need not keep exactly to the list, but it would be a guide for them, and would help her to provide every thing necessary, and the same in the forefeits. "For you know," added she, "if Reginald Freemantle is here he thinks of such queer forfeits, and then we should have every thing at hand."

"Well, then," said George, "if it must be, why do you come to *me?* why does not Grace come to help you? it's all her plan."

"It's her idea, but my plan," said Emily, "and she will help me all she can afterwards; but she's now with her mamma, and I want *you* to help me with the list, and then *we* will arrange every thing afterwards. Now, George, there's a dear boy! tell me, what shall I write down first?"

"Well," replied her brother, "oranges and lemons."

"No, no," said Emily, "that will not do; it will make the boys so rude, we shan't know what to do with them the rest of the evening."

"Now, you see," replied George, "you ask me, and then object to what I propose."

Emily explained to her brother that their party would be too large for such a game, and it would end just as one she reminded him of at a neighbour's last Christmas. —"And you did not forget that for a week," said she.

After this George gave the plan a little thought, and soon entered into it very cleverly and good-naturedly. He made several alterations and suggestions, and then advised Emily to write it out afresh in proper order, and that he should like a copy of it, for he confessed he should be sorry that their party got into such confusion as the Thompsons or the Duffs; and he reminded Emily of their large party last year, the only one they had had without dancing, which was all confusion and dispute as to what they should do and what should come next.

Emily said it was talking over that party which made Grace propose this plan to her.

"Well," said George, "I think it was a clever thought for such a little girl, but after all it's a regular prudish idea, as I said at first: I am sure you would never have thought of such a thing."

"I don't think I should," said Emily, "but I can do it when it is put in my head, and I shall remember it for another time."

Grace meanwhile was up stairs with her mamma, and after their reading she set hard to work at her chain. "I do hope, mamma," said she, "to get it finished by breakfast time to-morrow, but I must work very hard, and Emily wants me as soon as I can come; she has a great many proposals to make for to-morrow."

Grace was rather in trouble about her chain; she wanted a clasp fastened on, which she had by her, and she had heard of a man in the place who could do such a thing, but she had no time to go, even if her mamma would be so kind as to go with her. She had, however, a great many plans, which she proposed. Mrs. Leslie advised her to have no clasp, but to sew up her chain and put a ring and slide. Grace knew how to make a slide, and her mamma said she would let her have her steel ring from her chain, and Grace should some day repay it with another. Also she gave her leave to sit up with her that night and finish her chain, and the slide could be done to-morrow morning, before breakfast. Grace was delighted at these arrangements, wondered she had forgotten her favourite slide, and exclaimed, "What good thoughts you always have for every thing, mamma! it is always the best way to consult you, though I sometimes like to surprise you, too! but I do not quite like to take your handsome cut ring—suppose I cannot get one like it?"

Mrs. Leslie assured Grace that she could, and told her the price, which Grace was quite satisfied with.

Soon after this she joined her young friends in the library, and was very busy helping Emily and Ellen. George talked and amused them. Mary Anne did not do much, but every now and then had scruples on the unprofitableness of their occupations.

"What stuff!" said Emily; "why, you know, if you ask people, you must find something to amuse them. Now I should like to know how you would like to come to a party and find nothing to eat, for instance?"

"Oh, I should not care at all," said Mary Anne.

Here George gave a great whistle, and said Mary Anne liked plum-cake as well as any one, and eat quite as much; he would back her against all her sisters.

Mary Anne said she took it when it came; it would be rude to refuse when such things were provided, and indeed she thought it was very unkind not to take them.

"Yes, to be sure," said George, "you ought to stuff as hard as ever you can, and as fast as you can, and never say 'thank you,' for it's all for kindness! I know who taught you that—it is just one of Miss . . ."

"Now, George, hold your tongue," said Emily, interrupting him, "you see you prevent Mary Anne from helping us, for she cannot talk and work as we can—just look at Grace! she folded all that heap just now while she was talking to you and laughing."

Mary Anne said she could if she chose, but that she was not quite sure it was a profitable employment, so she did not like to do it.

"I declare, Mary Anne," cried Emily, "you are enough to try the patience of Job! you have no objection to join in all our games and be amused, but you will give every body else the trouble of preparing for them. Constance is better than you, though it's more disagreeable; she will not help at the time, and pretends not to enjoy afterwards."

"Well," said Mary Anne, "it is all very unprofitable, and I think all these parties are very wrong; you know we have quite given them up. Mamma said she would never have another after ours last Christmas."

"And I don't wonder at it," said Emily, "I never saw such a scene! and perhaps it would have been prevented if you had prepared amusements, as we are doing now."

"I never saw such a bear-garden in my life!" said George.

"I am sure," said Ellen, "I sat down and cried; I could not help it; the little Davises and many others were as if they were mad!"

"Well, they were tipsy," said George.

"Yes, but that was after supper," said Mary Anne.

"Ah, but they were pretty fresh before," returned George.

"What do you mean?" asked Grace, exceedingly amazed, "do you mean they were really tipsy?"

"To be sure I do," said George, "why you know it's only following up Mary Anne's plan of eating and drinking as much as one can—it was only '*kindness*' to the Duffs, and the Davises are very religious children indeed, so of course they were the kindest, that is, they got the tipsiest."

"I am ashamed of you, George," said his cousin.

"Well, now, I ask you all," said George, "were not the little Davises the tipsiest of the party?"

"Oh, nobody else was tipsy, George," said Emily.

"Well, and are not their papa and mamma very religious people?—they never go to parties themselves."

"Well, and no wonder," said Ellen, "if all parties were like that one; I am sure if they knew of their children's behaviour it would be enough to break their hearts."

"Mrs. Davis did know it," said Mary Anne, "for Miss Newmarsh thought it quite right to inform her."

"And what did she say?" asked Grace, anxiously.

"She said one could not expect children to be as grave as judges, and that we could not put old heads on young shoulders."

"But Emily—Ellen—not George—for he only laughs," said Grace, "do you mean they were *really* tipsy?"

"Yes, *really*," said Emily, "there were three boys, and they got at a bottle of wine on a side table, and emptied it in no time: then their sister behaved ill too, and they stamped, and kicked, and thumped the table for cake and sweets; and the boys fell to snatching at every thing, and made some of the rest as bad as themselves, till the dishes were quite emptied, and almost all the glasses and plates broken to pieces; and such a noise! no wonder poor Ellen sat and cried, for it frightened all of us nearly out of our wits."

"And did their mamma know all this?" asked Grace.

"Yes," said Mary Anne, "and a great deal more, for when Miss Newmarsh found she did not care, she told her every thing; and the beginning of the evening the Davises objected to every thing we proposed, and emptied the trays of negus and cake before the servants could get into the room: they upset a tray, and broke a great many of mamma's best tea service."

"But did she know they were really tipsy?" persisted Grace.

"Yes, yes, yes!" replied George, "why you know it's very easy to get tipsy at a party; you could get tipsy to-morrow evening if you please!"

Grace hardly knew whether to laugh or be shocked at the idea, and George continued, "Why, Grace, I thought you expected some of us to get tipsy to-morrow."

"I!" exclaimed Grace, "why?"

"Why!" said George, "because you burned the tipsy man just now in the characters, and would not let us fold him up with the others."

"But how did that show I expected you to be tipsy?" asked Grace.

"Why, I supposed you thought the sight of a tipsy man, hopping about as he was, with a red nose and a pot in his hand, would hurt our feelings if we were any of us tipsy."

Grace laughed.

"Well, then, what was the reason? you seemed quite serious about it, and burned the poor man with a great deal of pleasure."

"Yes," said Grace, "because I was much obliged to you all for letting me do so."

"Then why did you burn him?" asked George.

"Because," answered Grace, "I did not like to make a joke of what is so very wrong."

"Ah, you've no sense of the ridiculous," said Mary Anne, decidedly.

This sort of conversation went on with a good deal of amusement between whiles all the day, and the young ladies were all busily employed helping Emily one way or other. In the evening they were all for a time with the elder part of the family in the drawing-room. Grace and Mary Anne, who seldom had been alone together, were on a sofa. Mary Anne was talking of their home doings, and describing her sisters, and what they did. Grace was amazed at their cleverness, especially Constance, who seemed quite a prodigy. She also was astonished to hear that Fanny wrote verses—such beautiful verses, Mary Anne said, that a gentleman they knew, wanted to have them printed.

"How very clever she must be!" exclaimed Grace, "can you remember any of her verses?"

"Yes," said Mary Anne, "I know one poem."

"Oh, do say it, please!" cried Grace.

Mary Anne said it was to a Bird, and repeated the following lines:—

> Dear little Bird, I love you so,
>   I'd rather be with thee,
> And to the farthest corners go
>   Of utmost Araby.
>
> I'd rather go away with you
>   And travel like a dove,
> And live with nought but sky in view,
>   On solitude and love.
>
> Yes, I would leave my halls of state,
>   And live in bowers with thee,
> And link with thee my desolate fate,
>   In far-off Araby.

"How very pretty!" exclaimed Grace, "how very clever Fanny must be! is it all her own?"

"Yes, all," replied Mary Anne.

"It sounds very pretty!" again said Grace.

"Yes," returned the other, "but the sentiment too is very sweet!"

Grace said she should like to hear it again, and Mary Anne again repeated it. Grace again admired it, but remarked on the word "desolate," and asked why Fanny used it.

"Oh, you know all poets are gloomy and desolate," said Mary Anne, "you could not be a poet without—it is not true, you know."

"But I suppose Fanny meant really that she liked a free happy life," said Grace, "and that a bird's life must be a very pleasant one,—and so it must: you know how swift they fly and how joyfully they sing. I often watch them and listen to them, and I always think they seem to have more real happiness than any other creatures in the world. I always fancy they could fly away from any trouble, and that they never can have much— singing all day long as they do; they seem like the Angels of Animals."

"Yes, that is just what Fanny meant," said Mary Anne.

"Then she did mean it for herself?" asked Grace.

"Yes, to be sure."

"Then how could she be desolate with all of you, and her papa and mamma and brothers? is she unhappy?"

"Oh, no," replied Mary Anne, "why will you think so?"

"Because she says '*desolate*,'" returned Grace.

"You cannot understand any thing about poetry if you talk in that way," said Mary Anne, decidedly; "you seem to think it is all true; you know you must pretend to be wretched and miserable, or else you can never be a poet."

Here was a pause, which Grace broke, by saying, "Do you know, it was very curious, but before you repeated those lines and we talked of birds, I was thinking what a pretty sort of cage the ante-room could be made. If I was Emily I would fit it up for to-morrow, and bring in her beautiful paroquet, and I would call it, 'the Fairy Bower.' "

"How would you do it?" asked Mary Anne.

"I would bring in, if I might, a good many of the plants from the conservatory," answered Grace, "and get evergreens from the garden, to hide the walls. Then I would get as many real flowers as I could to mix with them, and make flowers from paper to help them out. . . ."

"Flowers from paper!" interrupted Mary Anne, "what are those?"

"Have you never seen them?" said Grace, "they are cut out of coloured papers and tied up with wire, and they look very well indeed at a little distance, and by candelight. Well, I would make festoons of roses all across the arch to confine Madge in her cage, and prevent any body from teazing her, and the arch would look very pretty indeed with drooping flowers all round it." And she rose to explain her idea more fully; "that is not all," continued she, "I would put lights behind in different parts, which would complete it. And Madge on her pole would look so well, she is so pleased with light, and likes to be looked at; then, I say, I would call it 'the Fairy Bower.' "

"And then," said Mary Anne, "if they got tired of her they could easily put her away into the conservatory, and the room would be a pretty one for ourselves."

Grace remarked, they could not do that, because the door would be covered with branches and flowers, and they must not injure the plants. Presently they spoke of something else.

CHAPTER XVIII

When thou dost purpose aught within thy power
Be sure to do it, though it is but small.
GEORGE HERBERT

AFTER A TIME, Emily joined them and proposed some amusement, as usual, in the Library. Mrs. Leslie called to Grace as she was leaving the room, and advised her privately to go up stairs and finish her chain, as it was getting late and she did not wish her to sit up long. Grace therefore excused herself from accompanying her young friends, and went up to her mamma's room. Her chain was completed when her mamma came up, and according to her advice, she went immediately to her own room. She found Emily in bed and asleep; she woke up for a moment, and complained of Grace being so long, and told her she had something to talk to her about, but now she could not, she was so sleepy. Grace was sorry to have disappointed her friend, but hoped it would do to-morrow morning; and though she had a great many things she wished to lie awake thinking of, she tried to get to sleep as quickly as she could, that she might be up as soon as daylight, and finish the slide on which she had set her heart, so as not to take her away from her young friends, who might want her to assist them. Poor Grace! she got up before the sun rose, and was dressed, but still it was so dark she was obliged to practise, for there was not light enough for any thing else: however, at the first gleam of day she sat down to her task, and to her joy got it finished just at breakfast time.

"Why, Grace," said Mrs. Ward, as she entered, "you are late to-day, I suppose you have been resting for to-night; Emily has been up and at work this hour past."

"Ah," said Emily, "I am up early for a wonder to-day, but Grace is early every morning."

"Well," said her mamma, "it's a pity Grace did not know you were busy, for she would have been up this morning to help you."

Poor Grace felt very uncomfortable; she felt what she called her childish propensity coming on, and thought she should have cried; first, at what she felt was Emily's kindness, and second, at Mrs. Ward's manner, which was more severe than her words; however she managed to keep down her tears, and only looked very much ashamed; she could not have spoken if she had wished it ever so much, and her heart beat very fast, but she knew nobody could see these things, and before long they went off. Still, however, she felt very uncomfortable; Grace had too keen a sense of injustice, and without constant watchfulness and self-control, it would become her snare and her torment as she came into the world, and grew to be a woman. This was almost the first trial of the kind she had experienced. Instead of the pleasure she had anticipated, she carried her chain to her mamma with a very heavy heart. Mrs. Leslie did not perceive Grace's dullness; she had observed what passed at breakfast, but did not take it seriously: many mammas would have been vexed, and would have comforted their little girl, and told her not to mind being misunderstood if she did right, but Mrs. Leslie was of a different character, and considering Grace's disposition, this was happy for her.

"Well, Grace," said her mamma, cheerfully, "so you've really finished your chain. I give you joy.—By the bye," added she, "I suppose you were hard at work at it instead of helping Emily this morning. I wondered why you did not give up your practice."

"I did not know Emily was up," said Grace, rather downcast.

"Well," said her mamma, smiling, "you see you got a little *hit*. We must pay for our pleasures, Grace," she added, rather more gravely, "we seldom have a pleasure without pain of some kind."

Mrs. Leslie now gave Grace the ring, and the chain looked very nice and complete. "Now, my dear child," said she, "this is your pleasure at present, so you must enjoy it, and I hope George deserves it, for it is a pretty present, and has cost a good deal of kind labour."

Grace's desire for tears was now quite dispelled by her mamma's manner; first, by her smiling at what Grace thought Mrs. Ward's unkindness; second, by her telling her that pleasure was seldom without pain, and she would have been quite ashamed that her mamma should have thought she had nearly been so silly; she now, therefore, could receive her mamma's kind kiss with a stout and happy heart.

"Now," thought she, "if mamma had kissed me, and spoken of *that* at breakfast, when I first came into the room, I could not have helped bursting out crying, and I dare say I should have gone on till now."

Grace only staid to-day for their reading, since Mrs. Leslie said her young companions might want her. Grace kept her chain very snug, and ran down to the Library. As she reached the passage she remembered she had to present it, and she did not know *how;*

however she found the library door open and nobody there. Mrs. Ward was alone in the dining-room; poor Grace felt a little uncomfortable at speaking to her. To-day was not the first time Mrs. Ward had spoken what Grace thought "unkindly;" one day when Grace was laughing and playing with the rest, Mrs. Ward came in, and after looking at them, she turned to leave, and said to a lady with her, of Grace, "It's quite a treat to see that child laugh, or look like other children;" this and some other things, made Grace believe that Mrs. Ward disliked her, and she fancied now she spoke angry to her, when she told her that Emily and the rest were in the drawing-room. When Grace entered, what was her surprise! she found the four cousins in the ante-room, which was being prepared just as she had suggested the evening before! Grace stood quite still, and they all laughed.

"Ah," said Emily, "I thought you'd be surprised; I was so angry with you for not coming last night till I was asleep, and then I thought I would do it and surprise you; but you are earlier than usual, and we thought it would be finished before you came down. Is it not pretty? It is all Mary Anne's thought; we are to have my paroquet here, and lights behind; was it not a good thought of Mary Anne's?"

There was a little pause, and Mary Anne said,

"You know I told you that Grace and I talked it over together."

Emily told Grace that directly Mary Anne suggested it, she asked her mamma, and got leave to remove certain plants and flowers into the ante-room, and that Thomas had been helping them, but that there was a great deal to be done yet, and they had a great many difficulties.

"Well now, Mary Anne," cried George, "for your lights, how are they to be placed?"

Mary Anne suggested a plan, which George called very awkward, and Ellen reminded her they must not put in any nails. Mary Anne said it could not be done without nails—it was impossible.

"Oh," said Emily, "how soon you give up things; there are a hundred ways besides nails;—you might tie the lights behind the branches of the trees, or—or . . ."

"Or festoon them with strings from the rods and the bellwires," said Grace, while Emily was hesitating.

Emily said that was the best possible plan, and produced a fine ball of string she had sent for the first thing in the morning. But presently they were stopped for lights, —should they be lamps or candles? where could they get them? Grace asked if they had sockets, or what is called save-alls, in the house. George remembered there were once many such used in London at an illumination, and made interest with nurse Hanson, who in a short time let him have several, which were joyfully received by the young company; they also coaxed her to tell Thomas to bring up the steps, and herself to come and put candles into the sockets. There was some difference of opinion among the young people as to the mode of lighting up. Grace had suggested a mode of concentrating the light from the sides of the entrance door of the ante-room. Mary Anne's notion was to disperse the light about behind the branches and flowers. It probably arose from her having misunderstood the application of Grace's word, "behind," the evening before. Mary Anne's plan was the most popular, but Grace succeeded so far as to be allowed also to place as many sockets as she pleased in her favourite spot, opposite the conservatory door. After this they appealed to Mary Anne for her festoons of flowers, and how to make them of paper. She had no more resources than on the lights. Emily began cutting from coloured paper, leaves like a rose, and tied them up with cotton; it looked something like, but made them all laugh.

"Is this what you mean?" said she, showing it to Mary Anne.

"Oh, I never made one," said Mary Anne, "but they look more like real than that."

Emily said, "Oh, they must be real artificial flowers, which nobody can make; have you ever seen them, Grace?"

Grace said she had helped her cousins to make a great many, and they looked very well by candlelight.

Emily now appealed to Grace for instruction, and found it required many little things;—different paper from the common sort, wire, gum, green cotton, &c. Grace said the paper was called flower paper, and made on purpose. Ellen gave news of a great deal of that thin coloured paper in a certain portfolio; she used to hear it called *flower* paper, and she always thought it was *flour* paper, like rice paper. They got permission to use this; the other materials were got together, and all the young ladies set to work, while Campbell and George were changing and arranging the ante-room, and making improvements according to their fancy. Grace was called in to consult on some point, and presently she found a good opportunity of giving George the chain. In a rather hurried, and certainly not very graceful manner, she pushed it towards him, and said, "George, there's a chain for you."

George looked exceedingly surprised, and poor Grace thought he did not like it.

"Do you mean this for me?" said he, "have you really bought this for me?"

"No," said Grace, "I did not buy it, I made it."

"And did you make it for me?"

"Most of it," said Grace, "but it was begun before I came here; you said you wanted a new one for to-day, so I finished it."

"Well, really," said George, "I am very much obliged to you; how well you have done it, it is just like a bought one." Then recovering his usual air, he came forward and said, "I'll tell you what, Grace is the best girl I ever knew."

"What's the matter, now?" said Emily, while Mary Anne coloured like scarlet. Grace saw it, and fancied she knew the reason. George hid his hands behind him, and asked them to guess what he had there. Grace wished to relieve Mary Anne's embarrassment, so she said, "Oh, it's only something I have been making George," and George produced the chain with a great air.

"Did you really make this?" said Emily, "it's a great deal better done, and much prettier than any that the girls do at school; it looks like a bought one; how did you make the slide?"

"Oh, she must have bought the slide," said Mary Anne, quite forgetting her late panic, and obligation to Grace, "you might as well ask if she made the ring?"

"Yes, what a handsome ring!" said Emily, while all were examining it, "but did you buy the slide?"

"No, I made the slide; it is not at all hard to do it like that," said Grace, "I could teach you in a minute, as mamma taught me; you see it is not well done when you look close to it, but I was rather in a hurry this morning."

"Well, then," said Emily, "I suppose that is the reason you have not practised these two mornings. You see, Mary Anne," added she, turning to her cousin, "you were *not* right about Grace this time."

Campbell meanwhile examined it very carefully, and as he put it aside, said mournfully, "I have no watch."

"Well, Campbell," said Grace, "I promise you that when you have a watch, I will, if I can, make you a chain for it."

"Thank you, Grace," said Campbell, as if he had actually got it, "for I know you will not forget it."

"You know, I say *if I can*," said Grace.

"Well," said George, "it is mine, give it to me; I am very proud of it;" and he fastened his watch to it, making Grace a very low bow; he then tossed his old chain to his sister, saying, "there, Emily, take your nasty old thing."

"Oh," said Grace, "it was not always nasty and old; and I dare say, you were as pleased with it at first as you are with mine now, and some day you will toss mine away in the same way."

"No, no!" said George, "that I never shall; why you know it's a great honour for *you* to make it for me; because you are not my sister, or even my cousin; I should not care half so much for one that Mary Anne made me, because she's my cousin; but there's no fear of that; for she's not clever enough to make such a thing as yours, and she's too fond of her money."

Mary Anne, whose conscience was in an irritated state, and whose temper therefore had been disturbed several times, replied sharply to this affront. George laughed, called her his "pretty cousin in a pet," and gave her his usual tap under the chin. Seeing she was still offended, he called to Campbell to take their walk, and left the room.

"How disagreeable George is, I'm sure I wish he'd not!" said Mary Anne, "he's always teazing every body."

"No, not every body," said Emily, "only you."

"Well, then, I wish he'd not," repeated Mary Anne.

"If you don't like it," said Grace, "why do you let him?"

"Let him!" said Mary Anne, "how can I help it—he will—though I'm always telling him I can't bear it."

"Oh," said Grace, "I'm sure you could prevent him if you chose."

"Why, how can I help it?"

"Oh, I don't know how exactly," said Grace, "but you can *show* you don't like it, and no boys are rude then."

"But George is not rude," said Mary Anne.

"Why, Mary Anne, how you change," said Ellen, "just now you complained of him."

"Yes, but not because he was rude—he is so tiresome, I don't like it."

"Well," pursued Ellen, "and Grace was saying you could prevent it if you wished, and so you can."

"I cannot," said Mary Anne, "it's all very well for Grace to talk; she thinks because he don't teaze her so, that I could prevent it, but she don't remember that I'm his cousin, and he is not so fond of her as he is of me."

"Then," persisted Ellen, "you think people are disagreeble and tiresome when they are fond of you."

"Oh, nonsense," cried Emily, "how can you go on, Ellen, don't you know that Mary

Anne likes George to teaze her in that way, and would be very much vexed if he was to leave off—I think you're all stupid. Now, Mary Anne, don't say another word, for it's all stuff and nonsense, and we had better talk of something else."

She then began consulting with Grace about the first wreath of flowers and evergreens, which was completed, and they retired into the ante-room, to hang it up and admire it.

CHAPTER XIX

A sweet behaviour and a solid mind.
DRYDEN

W E MUST NOW pass to the dining-room, where the two mammas were seated at work. Emily had just run in to ask leave about the flower paper and other things; when she left, Mrs. Ward said, "I'm sure I would not have to do all that Emily has for something! she has fifty children to amuse to-night, and without dancing and cards, I quite dread it, for they get so unruly sometimes; but George and Emily have such spirit, they seem able to do any thing. Is your little girl clever at such times, Mrs. Leslie?"

"Yes, pretty well," said Mrs. Leslie, "she's very handy, and exceedingly thoughtful beforehand; but you know she has not had the practice of your children; only now and then a party at her cousins'. They always beg and pray for her to come and help them, so I suppose she assists."

"She seems so very quiet that I cannot fancy her being very fond of such things," remarked Mrs. Ward.

"She's not quite so quiet as she looks *here*," said Mrs. Leslie, smiling, "you know you always see her before company."

"Well, I was surprised to see her one day in the Library," said Mrs. Ward; "but she is too grave for a child, though Emily tells me she is fond of fun and very clever; and Emily, though such a girl, is a good judge generally." This conversation was disturbed by the door opening, and Mrs. Newton Grey being announced, much to the surprise of Mrs. Ward, for it was early, and she expected her and her boy in the evening. Mrs. Newton Grey looked agitated and wearied, as if she had passed a sleepless night, which was very true. Mrs. Ward felt alarmed, and exclaimed, "What's the matter?—I hope nothing is the matter—is Newton with you?—has he gone to the children?"

By this time Mrs. Newton Grey had recovered herself, and she said, smiling faintly, "Oh, nothing particular is the matter; but I think we are not coming to-night, so I thought I would call and explain." "But," she said, "I think the best way would be, for you to read this letter I had yesterday from Miss Newmarsh"—"a very kind and candid letter, indeed," added Mrs. Newton Grey, "and Mrs. Leslie, I shall ask you to be so kind as to read it too, as I am about to ask your assistance in a rather painful business." Mrs. Ward took the letter and began to read. It was as follows:—

MY DEAR MADAM,

Though I have not the pleasure of much personal acquaintance with you, yet, from the character you bear, and from the free interchange of sentiment I enjoyed with you last week, I venture to address you, assured that the subject I have to bring before you, however painful, will be received as it is offered—in a Christian spirit.—Believe me, my dear Madam, my present task is to me no pleasant one. A mother's feelings demand the highest respect and tenderness, and nothing but a deep sense of duty and Christian faithfulness could prompt me to such a line of action. I will make no farther apology, but proceed to the subject of my letter. I must still, however, trespass on your patience, as a little previous explanation is necessary. It is always my custom to require my pupils every night before going to bed, to write an account of the events, or rather the feelings, of the day; with a view of leading them to amend what has been contrary to the life of a Christian. This diary is shown to me and to their mamma every Saturday, and furnishes a subject for improvement for the Sunday following. By this means I have become acquainted with some part of the behaviour of your son, on that unfortunate night of the party at Fulham, and I feel bound to acquaint you with it. If you are already aware of it, I shall have discharged my conscience without inflicting a new wound upon you; if not, I am sure you will agree that it is a mistake of kind but misguided friends to keep you in ignorance of such a circumstance. Constance, who has the most sensitive conscience of all my dear pupils, thus alludes to the incident in her diary:—"After I left the party I could think of nothing but Newton Grey's sin. I sat up long, and prayed that he might be brought to a sense of it. I felt thankful that I was not afraid to rebuke him before so many.—I hope I was not proud of it. I believe I should not have done so for his bad language alone; but I felt strengthened when he scoffed at religion, and called us and others 'saints,' &c." Fanny does not notice the incident, and Charlotte seems to feel nothing but distress at "dear C.'s fight with N. G." and says "the disturbance quite spoilt the pleasure of the evening." Mary Anne is still at Fulham. Now, my dear Madam, I am sure you will acquiesce in the propriety of noticing any thing so deserving of rebuke as this in the conduct of your son. That he should have acquired habits of bad language is sufficiently to be lamented, but it can indeed be nothing but the evil of an unrenewed nature that can lead him to scoff at the Saviour, as reflected in the persons of the little ones of his flock.

As I believe you agree pretty much with me on the subject of punishment, I feel the less scruple in speaking openly, since I subject your poor boy to no pain, and do not run the risk of his being ruined and hardened by severe treatment. But I am confident, dear Madam, that you will consider the trait of character thus brought to light worthy of your most serious attention and anxious watchfulness. With my most sincere prayers for your comfort in the future well-doing of your dear boy, allow me to subscribe myself,

Dear Madam,

Yours respectfully and faithfully,

M. A. NEWMARSH.

Jan. 5, Winterton.

While Mrs. Ward read this letter, the other two ladies carried on a discourse some-what apart. Mrs. Newton Grey shortly explained the charge against Newton: she said at the first moment she was very miserable, and was about to speak to him directly, but on consideration she thought she would come first to Fulham, and ascertain the *truth* of the story; for her boy was of a very lively disposition, and the little Duffs did not at all understand such ways. Then, as to Constance, she did not think she knew what bad language was; that she was so particular in every thing, and that if Newton called any body "a double X flat," or "a rapscallion of a donkey," or any other of his queer expressions, she would think it the same as the worst language. She said she was most distressed about Newton allowing himself to speak slightingly of religious people, and was shocked to think of his using the word "saint" as a term of reproach. At the same time, she said she should like to ascertain the circumstances of his doing so;—"and now, my dear Mrs. Leslie," she added, "it is here I wish to ask your assistance. Before I speak to Newton, I wish to be *sure* of all that passed, and I thought perhaps your little girl might have told you all about it."

Mrs. Leslie assured her that Grace had scarcely alluded to the circumstances she had just mentioned, and had not given her the least idea of what took place.

"And do you not think," said Mrs. Newton Grey, "that is a sure proof that nothing so bad went on: a nice well-behaved little girl like yours, never away from you, would, of course, be sure to mention such a thing to you, do you not think so?"

"Not *sure*, I think," answered Mrs. Leslie, remembering Grace's disgust.

"Well, but I do wish you would be so kind," said Mrs. Newton Grey, "as to question your little girl about it, for I could trust to *her,* but I could not trust to the other children: the Duffs are brought up *very* strictly, and cannot understand Newton's high spirits; and then, poor dear boy! he was so unfortunate once as to offend the Wards, and they have never forgotten it; so, you see, I can look to no one but your little girl for a correct report."

By this time Mrs. Ward had finished the letter, and handed it to Mrs. Leslie.

"What do you think of it?" asked Mrs. Newton Grey.

"Why, you know," answered Mrs. Ward, "some parents would think nothing at all of it, but, though I am not so particular as others, I do not like my boys to use bad language; it is a disgraceful, shocking habit, and if he was my boy, I would have him corrected, flogged—I suppose they always flog boys, don't they, when they do wrong?"

"Oh," said poor Mrs. Newton Grey, dreadfully shocked, "Newton has never been flogged—that would never do—I never thought of such a thing for a moment; and besides, I think the bad language may be quite exaggerated. Newton has no habit of that sort—it is the other charge that I think most of."

"What is that?" asked Mrs. Ward.

"Why, laughing at the Duffs, and calling them 'saints.' "

"Do you really mean so?" said Mrs. Ward; "I scarcely observed it. Why, you know, all boys at school, and grown people too, do that; and as for Constance, she's such a provoking little puss, that I don't wonder at a boy being irritated by her tiresome ways. I often wonder George puts up with her, but he is so good-humoured, he laughs it off."

"Well, *I* thought Constance very likely might have teazed poor Newton; he's of an open, frank disposition, and cannot control himself always as he ought," replied Mrs. Newton Grey, "and though I mean to talk very seriously to him, I do confess I think

Miss Newmarsh rather hard upon him; she does not say a word about the furious attack of Campbell upon him. I can assure you I was quite alarmed at the blow: there was a place as large as the palm of my hand, and frightfully black. You know, poor fellow, he is all alone, and has no brothers and sisters, like the rest, to stand by him."

"I am sure I have always wondered you did not send him to school," said Mrs. Ward.

"Oh, I have such a horror of schools, I could not have answered it to myself," replied Mrs. Newton Grey.

"Well, I could not have undertaken such a charge at home," remarked Mrs. Ward, "with no gentlemen, too, to superintend."

"I have seen so much of schools, I know what they are too well," said Mrs. Newton Grey: "two brothers of my husband's and one of my own, and some cousins of mine, were all ruined by being sent to public schools, and I saw such specimens of school-boys in my childish days, that when I grew up I resolved no boy of mine should ever be thrown into such a world of wickedness."—Seeing that Mrs. Leslie had finished the letter, Mrs. Newton Grey went on to ask her what she would have done if Grace had been a boy; "so careful as you are, you would never have sent a boy to school, would you?"

"Indeed," replied Mrs. Leslie, "it is a serious charge, and I have often felt thankful my little Grace was a girl; it is a great trial and a risk, but I think I should have sent a boy to school."

"Do you really think so?" said the other lady.

"I have not the mind or the energy of many mothers," returned Mrs. Leslie, "and I never could have undertaken the responsibility of a boy's education at home, I think."

"But, you know, I never pretend to interfere," said Mrs. Newton Grey, "and I do not, like you, consider school a *risk*, but *certain* ruin."

"I cannot quite feel that," said Mrs. Leslie; "I had four brothers all at school, and they all turned out well; and as a girl, I used to see a good deal of their companions, and cannot find the faults you do."

"Well," said Mrs. Newton Grey, "I wish I had your experience. But," added she, reverting to her first subject, "what do you say to Miss Newmarsh's letter? what would you advise me to do, Mrs. Leslie? what would *you* do? now, will you be so good as to put yourself in my place and tell me?—remember, Newton is not a *schoolboy*."

"Indeed," said Mrs. Leslie, "it is so impossible to judge for another person, and really I do not understand boys."

"Oh, but you could try to think," said Mrs. Newton Grey, beseechingly, "for I really am quite at a loss."

"You have a tutor for your boy, have you not?" asked Mrs. Leslie.

"Yes, certainly—not in the house—Mr. Taylor, the clergyman of our chapel," replied Mrs. Newton Grey.

"Well, I think I should talk to Newton myself first, and see what sort of a frame he was in, and then hand him over to his tutor, begging him to judge, and inflict as severe a punishment as he thought necessary: it should not be passed over and forgotten in a moment, especially if Newton has got into such a shocking habit."

"Then you would believe it all at once, and make no inquiries?" asked Mrs. Newton Grey.

"I think I *should*, but I say I should question Newton; of course you can trust to him, even against himself."

"Oh, most entirely," said the other lady; "he has the simplest, frankest heart in the world; he told me he was wrong in the matter, and very provoking the other day, quite of his own accord."

"But did he tell you of his bad language?" asked Mrs. Ward.

"No, he did not; but you know a boy in a passion does not know what he says; and if he *did* remember it, I could not expect he would tell me without being questioned. —Well, Mrs. Leslie, I will abide by your advice, and I am greatly obliged to you: I should not have done exactly so myself, but I am quite satisfied; I will talk to Newton, and according to what passes, I will refer him over to his tutor, though hitherto Mr. Taylor has had nothing to do with any thing that passes out of lecture time."

Mrs. Leslie entreated Mrs. Newton Grey not to follow her counsel—it was quite forced from her.

The other lady said she saw her unwillingness to bring her little girl forward in the matter, and she had no other means of judging.

Mrs. Leslie did not offer to sacrifice her little Grace, and so it ended. Mrs. Newton Grey took her leave; after which Mrs. Ward exclaimed with some impatience of her mismanagement of her son, "Why is *he* more precious than other boys, and why not send him to school? he is the plague and the pest of every body! my children will shout for joy when they hear he is not coming to-night."

"He is a nice looking boy, and not at all shy or spoiled seemingly," remarked Mrs. Leslie.

"Oh! do you think so? I can't bear the boy," said the other lady; "he has fine dark eyes, and a bright complexion, and handsome black hair, certainly," continued she, "but then you don't know him as I do; he's the meanest wretch in the whole world, and thinks nothing at all of a lie; I was quite angry with myself afterwards for taking his part against even that disagreeable little puss Constance. And really," added she, very much provoked, "I could hardly contain myself when you and she were comparing notes about your brothers—her brothers and yours! it is really too absurd. Her brothers and her husband's were the veriest raffs in the schools they went to; and as to one of the cousins she alluded to, he went to the same school as your brothers. I dare say they would scarcely speak to such a fellow, though they would know his name well enough; do you ever remember hearing them mention the name of Walter Johnson?"

"Walter Johnson—to be sure," said Mrs. Leslie, "I know the name better than my own; poor boy! he used to be my model for every thing shocking and wicked; I have often wondered if it was mere school-boy talk, though my brothers never gossipped much, and I was their eldest sister, and they could trust to me."

"He was a shocking fellow, and turned out worse.— Well, this cousin and her brother used to bring home from different schools a set just like themselves; and then she judges all schools and all school-boys by these disgraceful fellows, that no decent boy would associate with; you know, I'm not over particular; I don't want George to be too precise, he'll never get on in the world if he is, but it's quite as bad to be intimate with the very bad set, as the very strict ones (the 'saints,' as they call them.) I have no patience with people judging of schools in this way, while all the time their own boys, just like Newton, are worse than the worst set in a school; and do you know, this Newton picks up the worst boys he falls in with every where, and they visit him, and he them. He is a clever fellow, and keeps on decent terms before his mamma; and, as you say, his manner can look very well. She has had such a fear of his being a milksop, that she let him go out into all companies very early, and she has taken him to watering places, and encouraged him to make all the connexions he can, in order to make him manly. But I have always observed he chooses the worst companions he can get hold of; indeed no respectable boy will remain long his friend."

Just at this point Miss Newmarsh entered. The young folks had joined their cousins. She said she met Mrs. Newton Grey in the hall, and they had had a talk about Newton's sad affair. "I have been doing all I could to persuade dear Mrs. Newton Grey to send her boy to Dr. Barker," added Miss Newmarsh, "it would be the making of him, and the only thing to be done."

"Poor Mrs. Newton Grey," said Mrs. Ward, laughing, "every body is advising her! and I am sure I would beg her by no means to send him *there*, for flogging is the only thing for that boy, you may depend upon it, and he ought to be flogged every day within an inch of his life!"

"Oh, Mrs. Ward," cried Miss Newmarsh, quite shocked, "who could suppose you were a mother!"

"Perhaps," said Mrs. Ward, "if you had been a mother, and plagued as I have been by unruly boys, you would think with less horror of flogging. If boys are good without, I don't want them flogged; but every body knows what a good-for-nothing fellow that Newton is. Now, there's Reginald Freemantle, I don't believe he was ever flogged once the whole time he was at school. You know he has always been a regularly good boy, though lively, and is a pride and an honour to his family and masters."

Miss Newmarsh sighed, and said, "Flogging will not change the heart."

"But, you know, the old proverb says, 'Spare the rod and spoil the child,' and the Bible says something of the same kind, somewhere," answered Mrs. Ward quickly.

"You mean, 'a rod for a fool's back,' I suppose," said Miss Newmarsh, "but I consider that figurative, and it is under the old dispensation.—'Train up a child in the way he should go' is more agreeable to the spirit of the Gospel."

"Oh, I can't fight you with texts," said Mrs. Ward, "I know you are a walking Concordance."—And here the conversation turned upon other matters.

CHAPTER XX

Words followed words, from question answer flowed,
And talk of various kind deceived the road.
PARNELL

W E WILL NOW visit our young friends in the back drawing-room, towards the afternoon. The Duffs, and Isabella and James Ward, had arrived according to the previous arrangement. The boys were gone out skating, and the young ladies were all more or less busy in completing the decoration of the ante-room, which began to look so pretty as to interest them exceedingly. The Wards arrived first, and were surprised and charmed. Isabella said it was very like a boudoir at Lord Polstone's, at a party one night when she was there.

Emily said she was glad she liked it, and told her it was Mary Anne's idea.

"Well, Miss Duff," said Isabella, "I give you infinite credit. It is really designed with surprising taste," added the young lady, receding, and taking up her glass; "the effect is most pleasing, but I suppose you have a Chinese lamp for the centre."

The rest of the plan was explained to her, and she expostulated with Mary Anne on the Chinese lamp. Mary Anne entered into the new plan at once; said it was much prettier, and proposed to take down the sockets.

"Oh, pray do," cried Isabella, "and I will send the coachman to Dodd and Robson's for one of their splendid Chinese lamps. There's plenty of time to send to London," added she, looking at her watch.

"It shall not be done," said Emily, decidedly, "George has put up the sockets, and he will be very angry with us if we touch them."

"What do I care for George?" said Mary Anne, "he is not my master."

"No, but he has helped us," returned Emily, "and we must not change the plan without consulting him. And I'll tell you what," continued she, turning to Isabella, "if you interfere with his arrangements, George will find some way of revenging himself this evening."

This representation had the effect of arresting Isabella in her progress towards the bell. "Well," said she, turning, and again taking up her glass, "on a second view, I see it is too small for those lamps. Lady Polstone's boudoir was three or four times as large." She then suggested other improvements, which Emily opposed, and Mary Anne approved of.

"It is very strange, Emily," said Isabella, "that you will not adopt ideas that Miss Duff approves of, when she is the original designer of the whole: she must know best what will do justice to her own idea."

"But this is not her first idea; I have adopted that, and we all liked it, but we don't want coloured lamps and transparencies, it would not do here; and besides, we have no time to get them."

"Oh, I would manage all that," said Isabella, and again she appealed to Mary Anne, and got her approval of the coloured lamps and farther changes. Then she urged Mary Anne's authority; she said her idea was most tasteful, and it ought to be fully carried out.

"We all liked the idea, but I must say Mary Anne has not been so clever in helping in the execution," said Emily; "Grace Leslie has been at the head of all that. Grace has suggested every plan." "I am sure, Mary Anne," added she laughing, "you have been so stupid in this part, and Grace so clever, that I should think the idea was hers rather than yours."

This was neither the first, nor will it be the last time that the old proverb, "there's many a true word spoken in jest," is fulfilled; and it made two individuals very uncomfortable; indeed it is doubtful which felt the most so, the innocent or the guilty. Grace had associated her feelings on the subject all through the morning with the idea of guilt, and her whole thoughts were bent on warding off a discovery of the truth. She almost fancied she had said to Mary Anne, "Don't be afraid, I will take care nobody finds it out," and she watched Mary Anne anxiously, lest she should betray her secret. This threw poor Grace into a most uneasy state of conscience, and we are not sure if an exposure had taken place whether Grace would not have experienced the sensations of shame at a detected fraud. She saw that Mary Anne coloured furiously at Emily's remark, and was rejoiced that a diversion was made by the entrance of the Duffs. They burst in with joyful news—"Do you know," said they, "Newton Grey is not coming to-night!"

"You don't mean so!" said Emily, "how do you know?"

"Why," said Charlotte, "we met Mrs. Newton Grey, and she told us."

"He's afraid of another of Campbell's blows," said Emily, "and I am sure, if so, we are very much obliged to Campbell."

Isabella was here perceived and properly greeted. With Fanny she was especially affectionate, and turned her by the hand she still held, towards the ante-room, claiming her approbation. Fanny was in raptures, and it even met with Constance's approbation; she said it was so simple and lovely.

"Yes," said Fanny, softly, to Isabella, "it is just like the talk we had in that dear room; I wanted something to distinguish it, though I should never forget it without;" and she pressed the pretty be-ringed hand, still held in hers.

"You darling *mignonne!*" whispered her friend.

"I am glad you like our bower, Constance," said Emily, "I was afraid you might not."

"Not!—why?" said Constance.

"Oh, I thought you would think it silly."

"Silly! how little you understand me," returned the other, "silly to make a graceful use of the beauties of nature!"

"Yes, but then, you know, that some of these flowers are paper, not real, and I thought you would call that waste of time and unprofitable."

"I did not know they were not real," said Constance; "certainly it is an unprofitable use of money—why, it must have cost several pounds."

"Several pence," said Emily, "and some hours; we have three or four dozen sheets of paper, and some yards of ribbon-wire."

"Did you make them yourselves?" cried all at once.

"Yes, did you not understand that?" said Emily; "look, here is our table and materials; we have not finished yet, and we want all of you to come and help us."

They said they were willing—only some thought it too hard.

"Oh, no," said Emily, "George, and Campbell, and Mary Anne, have been cutting out for us three, and you can do the same if you like; we shall not make up faster than you cut out, for Grace has to leave off to give patterns of different flowers; she understands it better than Mary Anne, though it's all Mary Anne's plan."

"Mary Anne's plan!" cried the sisters, "did you, Mary Anne, really invent this?"

Mary Anne was not only covered with confusion, but totally at a loss for an answer. What she would have said if Grace had not been present cannot be told—that is, whether she was prepared to assert a downright falsehood; but the more forbearing Grace was, the less she understood her; she could not believe she meant to keep the secret, and she might only be waiting to expose her more fully. Once or twice she thought Grace really forgot that the idea was her own, or that she did not care about it; but now that it got so much admired, she thought Grace would claim it, and perhaps contradict her; she stooped down to hide her face, and picked up her scissors, which she had dropped; she wished it had been a needle, that she could have called the rest to help—to such shifts are the deceitful exposed. But before an answer was absolutely necessary, Grace had relieved her from her embarrassment. Grace felt more uneasy every moment at Mary Anne's falsehood—perhaps the admiration all the strangers had expressed might increase her sense of it. She thought Mary Anne must feel the same, and would be glad of an opportunity of disclaiming the idea. But how could she do so now, publicly? If there was a chance of speaking to her alone, Grace thought something might be done; meanwhile she would shield her as well as she could. At this point she said, "Invent! no, Mary Anne did not invent them; I have often made them, but I did not invent them." Now, thought she, surely Mary Anne will take this opportunity of saying something like the truth.

Poor Grace! she did not calculate on what her quixotic generosity might bring upon her.

"But did Mary Anne plan ornamenting the ante-room in this way?" said Constance.

What could Grace answer? she could not say what was absolutely not true, to serve any one; and to say what was true seemed equally impossible. She stared in Constance's face without saying a word, while she thought for something she dared to say, and the words, "Emily told me so," came to her lips almost mechanically; while Mary Anne forgot her fright and her obligation to Grace, in satisfaction at it having passed off so well.

Constance and the other sisters turned to express surprise and admiration at Mary Anne's great taste, and asked her where she had seen, and learned to make these flowers.

She said she had never made them before, but she had heard of them. Emily here called to them all, and told them that herself and Ellen had placed all their seats and planned their tasks, and they must come and set hard to work. Isabella took the seat nearest the fire, and made a change in the arrangements. Fanny sat next her, and they declared they would only work at the same flower. Emily objected, because Grace must then cut out two patterns of every flower; but Grace said she could easily arrange it, if they would be so kind as to undertake all the roses of different colours.—"You know we can never have too many roses; and I dare say," she added, with a good-natured smile, "you and Fanny had rather weave a wreath of roses together than any thing else."

"Oh, delightful!" exclaimed Fanny, "dear, dear roses! don't you love them?"

Grace actually kept these two at work by her lively skill, in spite of the interruption of their loving ways, and somewhat indolent habits. She began making up moss rosebuds, and as she finished them, placed them in order before the two leaf cutters, so that they really seemed to imagine it was all their own doing; then she got them to have patience, and let her begin upon roses; and at last to help her to wreath them into a festoon with evergreens, and hang them up. They bent over it with delight, and talked of it as the work of their own hands.—The trio were equally satisfied. Meanwhile the following conversation went on, interrupted with occasional breaks of inquiries of the experienced, and calls for assistance at different points of the occupation. Constance was particularly eager in assisting, and insisted in making up the flowers, saying, any body could cut the leaves; and some one of the three were constantly teaching her the secrets of the art. She was not so neat handed as either of Grace's morning pupils, Emily or Ellen, but did pretty well. Emily remarked again, she was glad that Constance took so much to the art—she expected she would refuse to assist, as she always had done before.

"Why," returned her cousin, "you never before had any employment so rational and useful—how little you know of me! I love sweet flowers, and admire even their lovely shadows—these are their shadows!"

"Rational it may be," replied Emily, "but I cannot see how it is *useful* in your sense."

"I do not usually make use of words without meaning," answered Constance—"I mean *useful*. Do you think I am taking such pains to learn, merely for that pretty toy-room, which will fade to-morrow?—No, I hope I have rather more consistency than that!"

"What are you driving at?" asked Emily, coolly.

"Why, I am quite amazed at Mary Anne," answered Constance, "for not mentioning this art before. Mary Anne, how could you forget it for Bodstock last month?"

"I did not know it then," said Mary Anne.

"When did you hear of it?"

"Only since I have been here," said Mary Anne.

"Oh, Mary Anne," cried Ellen, "just look! you have blown away my whole heap of leaves that I had just arranged for my beautiful striped carnations."

"Oh, I beg your pardon," cried Mary Anne, "it was this sheet of paper; let me help you to pick them up, and arrange them again for you."

"Well," said Ellen, "I can't scold you, you are so kind and good-natured."

Perhaps Mary Anne was quite as much obliged to the opportune waft of air, as Ellen was for Mary Anne's good-nature.

"But, Constance," said Emily, "you were going to tell me the great usefulness of this new art."

"Why," said Constance, "I consider it quite a discovery for missionary purposes."

"For missionary purposes!" exclaimed Isabella, "what can you mean?"

"Don't you know the meaning of missionary purposes?" asked Constance, with something of a tone of superiority.

"No, not in the least, I protest," said Isabella; "missionaries, I know, are sent abroad to convert the heathen; I know Mrs. Jenkinson has a box for our forfeits, with blackamoors and texts upon it, but I can't think what artificial flowers can have to do with converting the heathen."

"Is it possible!" exclaimed Constance, "I thought Mrs. Jenkinson was very religious; does she never make you work for missionary purposes?"

"No, never," replied Isabella, "I protest I am quite in the dark."

"In the dark, indeed!" exclaimed Constance, "and cannot you guess?"

"No," replied the young lady,—"except," she added, more doubtingly than in jest, "you send them over roses to crown the new made converts with."

Emily, who had some time been very much tickled at the manner of the parties, now burst into a scarcely restrained laugh, which was less visibly echoed by one or two of the others. Miss Ward had not the tact to join it, and it might have become a serious affair—"How can you be so absurd!" cried Emily, half stifled.

"Who's absurd?" asked Isabella.

"Why, all of you," answered her cousin, still laughing, "you've no idea how absurd you've been the last quarter of an hour."

"I am really quite ashamed of you, Emily," said Constance, who had kept her countenance immovable during the whole scene; "what can you find to laugh at in our discourse?"

"I am not laughing at the missionaries," said Emily,—"I know you think I am—but at your words and faces, and Isabella's idea of crowning them with flowers!—oh, dear!" cried she, stifled with laughter, and holding up a festoon, "just think of sending this wreath all the way to India to put on the head of a poor black!"

"For shame, Emily," cried Constance, with the most unmoved countenance, while all the rest, even Isabella and Fanny, were infected by Emily's hearty merriment.

Presently Emily added, as she recovered, "Well, I'm sure I don't wonder at Isabella, who could ever guess what paper roses had to do with preaching to the heathen?"

She got through this pretty composedly, but was constantly bursting into little repressed laughs as they went on talking.

"Really," said Constance, "I see nothing so ridiculous in sending over presents to the new converts; if you discovered brothers and sisters in a distant land, would you not like to show your affection for them?"

"Yes," replied Emily, "but think of these paper roses! and their black faces!—oh, dear! Constance, how can you be so silly!"

The more Emily laughed the graver Constance became, and she now said with earnestness, "Well, I declare I had rather work for those dear negroes than for all the fine ladies and gentlemen in the land!"

"Oh, yes," cried Fanny, who had followed Isabella's lead, and was now grave, "the dear, dear negroes! do you not love them?"

"Love them!" cried Miss Ward, "what, love their horrid black faces! what do you mean, *mignonne?*"

"I mean," said Fanny, "that I love them so much I should like to go and preach to them; I had rather do that, than even live in our cottage in Wales. Oh, should you not like to go over and convert them all? you know we should only want plenty of Bibles and little tracts, and we should dress quite plain, and only just talk to them, for they are so simple and affectionate, they don't want being preached to like other heathens, but they say, 'Yes, massa,' and believe in a minute. Would you not like to go?"

"You darling, *mignonne,*" cried Isabella, kissing her, "I should like to go any where with you; you are positively a little enthusiast."

"Fanny," said Constance, "you speak like a child; you don't consider the cost of a missionary's life when you talk in that way."

"Besides," said Ellen, "*you* could not convert them; you can't convert the heathen without a clergyman."

"What can you mean?" said Constance, "could not Fanny teach the way of salvation to the perishing heathen just as well as the wisest man?"

"Why, she could help a very little by reading, because they cannot read," said Ellen, "but I mean there must be a clergyman to baptize them and teach them afterwards." After a pause, she continued, "But will you, Constance, please say what you meant just now by 'missionary purposes?' "

"I do not wonder," said Constance, "that *you* should not know, because you are shut up in the country, and that is always a hundred years behind London; but I am surprised that Mrs. Jenkinson should not have introduced to her young ladies an invention which is the honour of the age we live in."

"Well, but what is it?" asked Ellen.

"It is, that ladies, instead of using their accomplishments for purposes of vanity and folly, turn them to account in works of a more lasting description, and send the money to the missionary and Bible societies, and others of the same kind."

"Well, I don't understand you now," said Ellen.

"I'll explain," said Emily; "a party of ladies join together for what they call a 'Fancy Fair;'—they make pin-cushions, housewives, and pretty things of that sort, and sell them for these purposes. Some have a stall always in their drawing-room; whoever calls they make buy something or other, and if they can, make every body promise to work for them too; and you know Constance is delighted with these flowers because it is a new idea for these Fairs."

"Well," said Isabella, "I think it a very good idea; I am sure we ought to do something sometimes for those poor starving negroes."

"I am delighted to hear you say so," cried Constance, "perhaps you will do us the honour of adding to our stores—we are just beginning a drawing-room table."

"I shall be most happy," replied the young lady, "but I am really such a useless creature; I never made a pin-cushion in my life."

"Oh, but a drawing, or any thing, as *yours*, would be most valuable."

"Do dear, sweet *amie*," whispered Fanny, softly, "do use this pretty white hand in our service," and she raised the white hand and kissed it.

"You darling enthusiast," cried Isabella, "I cannot refuse *you*.—Well, I'll tell you what I can do, I will cut out one of those shades of Bonaparte's face."

"Oh, delightful!" cried the Duffs.—"And," said Constance, "I shall not sell it, but I shall keep it hid, and show it *as yours* to every body, at so much per head; it will bring us in a regular income. We have hardly set about asking any body yet, but, Emily, I was thinking these flowers will be of no use to you after to-night, so we may as well have them; you'll take care they're not hurt, please."

Emily said she could not part with them, since her mamma wished for them if they were at all nicely done for a similar occasion.

Constance pressed it, and said she would ask her aunt about it herself, and the three Duffs and Isabella took part against Emily.

Emily said she could ask, but she did not think her mamma would agree;—"particularly," added she, "after mamma has seen the ante-room, for I am sure she'll be very much surprised; it has never been ornamented any thing like so tastefully, and I know she will like to keep them for some of her own parties."

"Well, then," said Constance, rising, "I will go this moment and ask before she has seen it."

"Well, go," said Emily, laughing, "I know the answer you will get."

"I am not often refused," remarked Constance, gravely, "when once I make up my mind to ask a favour."

"Well, go," repeated Emily, "why don't you go?"

"Why, on second thoughts," said she, resuming her seat, "I do not think it would be quite fair before my aunt has seen it; you know she might wish to change her mind."

"What a discovery!" cried Emily, "a happy thought, just in time, was it not, Grace?"

"I was very glad Constance remembered it," replied Grace, "for it did not seem right."

"Then why did you not tell me so?" asked Constance.

"I thought you would not do it," replied Grace.

"And why did you think so?"

"Because," said Grace, hesitating, "because you seem always so . . ."

"Well, so what?" said Constance, coolly.

"So determined to do what is right," said poor Grace, in some confusion, she hardly knew why.

"Grace does not say you always do right, but you are always determined to do right," remarked Emily.

"But," pursued Constance, without noticing her cousin's remark, "why do you think me so very good? you know very little of me."

"I have heard you talk a good deal, you know," replied Grace, afraid every thing she said was wrong.

"You must have a great deal of observation," remarked Constance.

"Why, to be sure she has," cried Emily, "don't you know Grace is cleverer than all of you put together?"

"How do you know that?" said Mary Anne, "nobody is cleverer than Constance."

"I can tell you a person, Mary Anne, that Grace is both cleverer and better than," said Emily, in a tone that alarmed two of the party; then catching Grace's eye, she turned it into a laugh, and exclaimed, "Grace, you are the oddest girl I ever saw in my life."

"What are you talking of, Emily?" said Ellen, "who do you mean?

"Oh, La! never mind," cried Emily, "only Grace is a regular goose!"

"And yet she's cleverer than all of us!" said Constance.

"Well, she's both, and a gaby into the bargain, I have no patience with her!" continued Emily. After which there was a little pause.

"Really, Emily," said Isabella, "I do wish you would cure yourself of those vulgar words and expressions; it is no use talking to you, I have been quite ashamed of you all the morning, and now you have used four all at once."

"Well, what are they?" said her cousin.

"You said, '*Oh, La!*'—'*goose!*'—'*gaby!*'—and '*into the bargain!*' it is really quite shocking."

"Indeed it is, as you justly remark," said Constance; "I have told Emily, I am sure, almost every time I see her, of her breaking the third commandment in the way she constantly does."

"I don't break the third commandment," said Emily, "I only say '*La,*'—that is not breaking the third commandment."

"It is," said Constance, "and I have told you over and over again, but it's no use."

"If it is of no use, why do you go on?" said Emily; "I can't help it, and every body does it."

"No, nobody does it," said Isabella; "Mrs. Jenkinson will not allow any of the young ladies to make use of such an expression; she says it is not at all genteel, and that no well-bred people do so."

"Then why are you always saying, 'good gracious!' and 'my goodness!' " said Emily.

"I do not," replied the other, indignantly, "I may say 'gracious me' sometimes, Mrs. Jenkinson does not object to that, but she says the others are quite vulgar."

"I dare say," cried Emily, "the girls say them all behind her back as much as I do; I don't think we say any thing of the sort before the Miss Carters."

"I hope you don't mean to compare your school to Mrs. Jenkinson's."

"Yes, to be sure I do," said Emily, "all schools may be compared together."

"Well, then," said Isabella, "I will compare yours to a charity school."

"Well, do," returned the other, "and what will you say of them?"

"Why, I'll say," returned the young lady, "that they are just alike, and that you are all an odious vulgar set."

"Very likely," replied Emily, not more provoking than provoked, "but remember you are cousin to one of the set."

The Duffs were ready to exclaim at Emily's rudeness, when the door opened, and the boys came in. This made an interruption, for some of the party had to greet—the two Jameses having stopped by the way and joined the skating party. Then came admiration of the ante-room, and the festoons being pretty nearly completed, the boys assisted to finish the work. Madge was brought in and installed in her place of honour, of which she seemed very proud, marching and sliding up and down her perch, and talking and looking round as if she approved of the labour of her young friends. In about half an hour, just at dusk, it was finished, and all stood round much satisfied. Emily unfolded a cloth she had prepared to conceal their handiwork till the evening, when the candles would be lit and all exhibited to perfection. She then despatched all, to be ready for dinner, as they were to dine all together at five to-day, and herself stayed behind with Hanson to gather together their numerous materials, and clear the room for the evening.

CHAPTER XXI

What matter? if the waymarks sure
On every side are round us set,
Soon overleaped, but not obscure,
'Tis ours to mark them or forget.
The Christian Year

ELLEN TOOK GRACE to her own room, since they had not to dress before dinner. "Only look at my hands," said she, "they are covered with gum, and as black as tinkers', are not yours?"

"Not very bad," said Grace.

"Why, I declare they are as clean as if you had washed them; how did you manage that, Grace?"

Grace said she was used to handle gum, and Ellen would do the same with a little practice.

By this time they had reached Ellen's room, and when they were ready for dinner, Ellen, after a silence, said, in her mysterious tone, "Grace, I want to ask you something."

"Well," said Grace, "what is it?"

"You'll not be angry, will you?"

"No," said Grace.

"Well, it's about what they were talking of just now—the third commandment, you know—do you think it right to use those expressions? I hope you're not angry with me, Grace, dear, but I really want to know what you think."

"Why, I don't know," said Grace, "I never heard any body say."

"Yes, but what do you think? I have never heard you use them, do you ever?"

"No," said Grace, "I do not."

"Then why do you not? have you never heard them?"

"I have often heard them," said Grace, "a great many little girls I have met use them."

"Then why do not you? is it, as Mrs. Jenkinson says, because they are vulgar."

"No, I never thought of that," said Grace, "I did not know they were vulgar."

"Then, why?"

"I always thought it did not seem quite right; I don't know the meaning of some of them, but I was always afraid to use them."

"Well," said Ellen, "that is just what I used to feel; I am so glad!—But I should like to tell you what made me think *seriously* about it first;—I must tell you I was very silly indeed three or four years ago; it was when Emily first went to school, and I was with her for a few days: it was all so new, I liked it very much indeed, and the girls were so kind to me, because, you know, I was not there as a pupil—so they made me their plaything; all they did and said seemed so grand to me—and this is where I was so silly—I wished to do the same; among other things I thought it would be so fine to say, 'Oh, La,' and 'good gracious,' and 'bless me,' as some of them did, at every thing. Emily caught it in a minute, and I tried to do it very often, but some how or other I could not; one day I was running in the garden, and my frock caught in a bush; I cried out, 'Good gracious! Emma, I have torn my frock!' I found it much easier to say than I thought it would be, but I felt so ashamed that I never said it again. In a few days Hanson came for me—you know nurse Hanson—and we three were in the room while my bonnet and handkerchief were being put on. Emily was in a great hurry, and she said, 'La, Ellen, what a time you are.' Hanson said, 'Miss Emily, you should not make use of that expression, you know what it is.' Emily said just the same as she did just now down stairs. I felt so much obliged to Hanson—I did not tell her so, but I have always liked her since; I am sure it prevented me ever again wishing to use any of those words. Are you tired of my talking, Grace?"

"Oh, no," said Grace, "not at all."

"Well, then," added she, "there are two or three other things about it very curious indeed, which I should like to tell you, for I never mentioned them to any body. The next Sunday, the second morning lesson was those words of our Saviour, 'Let your yea be yea,'—you know them, I dare say. I never understood them before, and I thought very much of 'whatsoever is more than these cometh of evil;' do you think it means such expressions as these?"

"I always think *perhaps* it does, and that it is better not to use them."

"Well, I thought so too; but then, Grace, there was another curious coincidence: the next day I went to grandmamma's, where, you know, I live now much more than I do at home, and two or three days after she took me to a neighbour's—I know them now very well; the little girls took me into their school-room, and I took down some of their books: they told me that was their Sunday shelf, and I presently opened a little volume, which was Sermons for Children, twenty-two, I think, by a Lady. There was a sermon on each of the commandments, and I opened at the third: it said just the same as Hanson, and just what I had been thinking of,—I cannot remember the words, for every body was talking to me all the time, and I was in a hurry, but I have never fogotten the sense,—now don't you think these things all coming together were very curious?"

"Yes," said Grace, "but I think they are always happening. Mamma often says things that are of use to me, sometimes the very next minute; I quite expect it, and keep her words in my head."

"I had another thing to say, Grace, but I hope you won't think it very wrong, and that is, that so many people use those words; what do you say to that?"

"Why," said Grace, "you know we cannot help what other people do; we must take care to do right ourselves; don't you think so?"

"Yes, certainly," replied Ellen, in an unsatisfied tone.

"Why, you know, we might become every thing that is bad if we went by that rule," continued Grace, "because there are some very wicked people in the world."

"Yes, but what I mean," said Ellen, "is that I do not like to see people do what I think it wrong to do myself; do you, Grace?"

"No," said Grace, "not all."

"And what do you do? do you tell them?"

"I! oh no," said Grace, "I could not do so for all the world!"

"Well, but I do sometimes," said Ellen, "do you think it is wrong?"

"Oh, not wrong! it can't be wrong; I do wonder at Constance, and admire her every minute; I wish I could do as she does—how very good she is!"

"Yes," said Ellen, "but I can't do as she does at all; it is only some people I can speak to—children, I mean, like myself; and then it's all by chance—you know I could not do it if I thought of it beforehand, I should not be able to open my lips, and should feel quite choked. But, Grace, I want to say one more thing to you, will you let me?"

"Yes, certainly."

"Do you think it right to object to those expressions because they are vulgar?" asked Ellen, "or to use one and not another?"

"You mean what your cousin said of Mrs. Jenkinson," remarked Grace; "I thought perhaps she had not mentioned all her governess said to her."

"Then you did think *that* not a right reason, did you?" asked the determined Ellen.

"I think it cannot be," replied Grace, "because, you know if a thing is wrong, it cannot signify if it is vulgar or not, for it must not be done."

"But then there are some things," said Ellen, "not exactly wrong, that 'vulgar' would do to correct—such as speaking loud or being boisterous, or any thing of that kind, don't you think so?"

"Yes, I suppose so," said Grace, "but you know people might do all such very small things, because they are *right*, if they pleased, either because their mamma told them not, or because they saw they hurt or offended some of their friends."

"I don't think I ever thought of that reason for such little things before," said Ellen, "yet I never like to hear people say, 'Do not do so and so, because it is vulgar,' or 'do so and so, because it is genteel,' do you?"

"Mamma never says so to me," replied Grace, "and I do not think I ever heard it said till to-day. Mamma sometimes says to me such a thing is rude, it might hurt people's feelings—or such a thing was forward, and I understand these words much better than the others,—but I always understand mamma."

Here the bell rang for dinner, and the young friends hastened down.

We ought not perhaps to pass over the drawing-room conversation between the young ladies without a few remarks. It was not like young ladies, and what is far worse, it was not like young Christians. Mary Anne shows constantly a very bad spirit and wrong temper, not to speak at present of her grand piece of falsehood; she does not seem to check the beginnings of evil, but yields to temptation in a moment. Isabella is silly and affected, and what is worse, suffers these follies to lead her into exaggeration and almost downright falsehood; she talks in such a random manner, that when she is wishing to exhibit her own importance, she scarcely knows truth from falsehood; there was a first beginning to all this—alas! why did she allow it? Fanny lets foolish thoughts and feelings take hold of her, so that she is ready to be satisfied with such a one for a friend as Isabella, without waiting to see if she is likely to be worthy of her regard; their friendship has begun in flattery, so it is very likely there is not much sincerity in it; such characters as Fanny's very often end in discontent and suspicion of every body, because they place their affections on unworthy and unstable characters, and will not believe the opinion of persons who have the means of knowing the truth better than themselves. Emily has a great many good qualities, but she has not yet brought them into order; and besides, she has some faults—she is provoking, and she tries her cousin's temper too much—then she confesses she allows herself in a wrong habit, "because she cannot help it." If she cannot correct herself, even outwardly, she is not fit to correct others at present. Ellen felt very sorry after she had made use of an expression she heard from others—she found it easy to do so, but felt ashamed—she left it off, and never did so again; every day proofs occurred of her judgment being right—she joyfully acquiesced in them and kept to her resolution. Emily and Ellen were sisters; they had much the same training; the same circumstances in this instance occurred to both; both witnessed the same scenes for a fortnight; both had the same temptations; both had the same warning from Hanson; both heard the same chapter read on the next Sunday; but both did not make the same use of these kind providences—one resisted the bad habit, the other yielded, and now makes for excuse, "she cannot help it;" alas! why did she ever begin?

CHAPTER XXII

Ce n'est que le premier pas qui conte.
FRENCH PROVERB

MR. EVERARD came down to dinner, but it was quickly despatched, and the young people dispersed to their toilets. Grace had thought before dinner of trying to speak to Mary Anne herself, but it was quite impossible to do so without all being aware of it, since the Duffs dressed together in the same room, and Mary Anne, not having seen her sisters so long, kept particularly close to them. Grace was in her room first, and she was deeply musing on her late conversation with Ellen, when Emily came into their room. The moment she entered she ran up to Grace and seized her by both her hands, saying, "You naughty, deceitful child—Grace, I am quite ashamed of you!"

Grace did not know whether she was in jest or earnest, and looked distressed.

"Why you know you are," continued Emily, "but I know all about it, you can't deceive me!"

"What do you mean?" said Grace.

"Why, you know well enough; what does your conscience tell you?"

"Indeed I don't know," said Grace, whose memory kept running over her late conversation with Ellen.

"Well, I believe you, Grace, though you have been deceiving us all the morning; I really don't know which is worse, Mary Anne or you."

"Oh, Emily!" cried poor Grace, colouring crimson, and covering her face with her disengaged hands.

"Well, I'm glad you are ashamed at last," said Emily.

Emily did not understand Grace's feelings, and was now amazed and concerned to see Grace was in much distress. She believed Emily thought she had been acting very deceitfully, and was afraid it was true, yet she could not say a word of any sort because of betraying Mary Anne; she therefore turned away silently and supported herself by the bed-post. Emily went to her and said, "Oh, Grace, dear Grace, are you really distressed? don't you know I'm only in jest? Grace, do speak to me; why you are trembling so, you can hardly stand;" and she ran for a chair—"What can be the matter, Grace? do answer me; is it what I have said?"

"What did you mean?" said Grace, recovering herself as well as she could, and speaking very calmly, though some little girls, under her feelings, would have burst into a passion of tears, and almost gone into hysterics.

"Why I mean," said Emily, deceived by Grace's self-command, and returning to her usual high spirits, "I mean that I know as well as if I had heard it, that the ante-room was all your idea, and that Mary Anne has stolen the credit of it from you."

"Oh, Emily!" exclaimed Grace again.

"It is no use your pretending it is not so; I found it out of myself; I wondered at Mary Anne's taste, for she has none in the world, but I never doubted the truth till by chance I said that about its being your idea instead of hers; she coloured so much and looked so cold, I could not help remarking it; and some time after, when she upset the flowers, I was sure. Then I tried you both, and it was only your imploring look that prevented my exposing her; I should never have understood your look, you are such a strange girl, only you did just the same by Isabella the other day, in making me promise not to expose her folly and exaggerations."

"I did not know I looked at you," said Grace.

"But you did though, and I could have laughed, only you seemed so uneasy—more uneasy than Mary Anne, I think. But now, Grace," continued she, in a more serious tone, "you *must* confess it is as I say;" and on Grace giving no answer, she added, "You may as well, for if you do not I will tell all the company in the middle of the evening, just as Mary Anne has got all the credit, for I know the ante-room will be greatly admired. Now, was it not your idea?"

"Oh, Emily," cried poor Grace, "you are very cruel!"

"Confess!" said Emily, "who proposed the plan? did she?—only yes or no!"

"No," sighed Grace.

"Did you?—I certainly will tell to-night," added Emily, seeing Grace's hesitation—"yes or no!"

"Yes," said Grace. "Now, Emily," she continued, recovering her spirit, "you have forced it from me unfairly, and you are bound to promise me to say nothing about it one way or other."

"I don't see that at all," said Emily; "do you think I can bear to see that shabby Mary Anne take all the credit?—she shall not."

"Well, then, you will destroy all the pleasure of my evening, and I do not think I shall ever be able to look Mary Anne in the face again."

"Why, Grace, are you crazy?" said Emily, "you speak as if Mary Anne and you had changed places."

"Oh, no!"—think how poor Mary Anne will feel when it has all gone so far; and you know if I had meant to tell, I ought to have done it at first, and not let it go so long; you know Mary Anne never *said* it was her idea, every body would have it so, and I think I was as bad as she, for you know I told very nearly a story about it.—Oh, Emily, do have a little pity upon me! I do not think I can begin dressing till you promise me."

"But," said Emily, "it is worse and worse to go on; you know there is no end to it."

Grace had not thought of this, and she added to herself, "Yes, and Mary Anne is made more and more wrong." "Oh," said she, aloud, "what a shocking thing it is to take the first wrong step!"

"Yes, but now you can prevent Mary Anne from taking a third and fourth."

"I did not mean Mary Anne," said Grace.

"Then, who?"

"Myself," replied Grace.

"You silly girl!" cried Emily, "what nonsense you are talking! why, how could you help it?"

"I don't know," said Grace, despondingly, "but you see I am in such a situation that I cannot do right."

"What a strange girl you are, Grace," said Emily, "and how you seem to puzzle yourself about things; I never heard any body talk so much about right and wrong as you do."

"Do you think I puzzle myself?" asked Grace, with some hope, "do you see what ought to be done?"

"Why," said Emily, "I never think of making such a fuss about such things as you do; you know at school this sort of thing happens constantly."

"And what do you do!" asked Grace.

"Oh, *then* I don't tell, because the girls would hate me and call me tell-tale; but if this happened among ourselves, as now, I should not think about it, but feel that Mary Anne had behaved shabbily, and deserved to be exposed, so I should expose her; besides, you know, she will take all the credit from you."

"But, Emily, only think—just suppose for a moment; suppose you had done something of the same kind—you must fancy so just for a moment; well now, suppose in the middle of a large party I were to expose you just as you wish me to do Mary Anne,—just think how shocking—should you like it?"

"But," said Emily, "I don't think I ever should do such a thing as Mary Anne."

"I did not mean that you would, but you must try to fancy that you had; now, would you not think me very unkind, and a great deal worse, when I had said nothing all the morning, and not even spoken to yourself?"

"Well," said Emily, "I do see now that it would not be quite fair."

"Then you will say nothing?" exclaimed Grace, joyfully.

"No, I will not promise, I will not have her carry away all the credit from you."

"Oh, Emily, I wish you would not talk of credit, it is quite nonsense; you know it was only a thought—quite passed in a moment; if there is any credit for such a small thing it belongs to those who have worked at it afterwards.—I am sure," added she, sorrowfully, "I wish I could give what you call the credit all away to Mary Anne. Oh, how I wish she had thought of it first."

Emily had become almost as perplexed as poor Grace, and a pause ensued—Emily wondering at Grace's strange feelings, yet every moment finding something more reasonable in them than at first she could have thought possible. Grace remained on the chair, leaning her head against the friendly bed-post. Emily was making progress in her dressing. Presently Grace burst out with, "Well, Emily, will you do this? you know you discovered it all quite by yourself, so you have as much right to speak to Mary Anne as you had to me; will you speak to her all alone, before people come, and I dare say she will be as glad as I am to give up what you call the credit; why should we speak of the *idea?* we have all worked at it together, and that is the principal part; do you think there would be any thing wrong in doing so?"

"Oh, certainly not," said Emily, "and it would be very easy if we had begun so, but, you know, all down stairs think it is Mary Anne's, and Constance and Fanny never neglect to puff off their sister, and it will be all over the room in a minute; you know nothing else was talked of all dinner time, and papa is quite anxious to see it."

"Well but, Emily, if Mary Anne chose, you know, she could manage to put off a great deal upon the rest, and by degrees it could come to very nearly the truth indeed; at any rate, you know, it would be a great relief to her to get such a weight off her mind, and what would be better than all, she would not be going farther wrong; will you promise to speak to her?—but alone, Emily, and not in the drawing-room,—up in her room, or some room alone, please, will you?"

"Well, said Emily, "I promise I will *if I can.*"

"Thank you, dear Emily, how good you are!" said Grace, quite relieved; and she got up and walked to the fire, where Emily was standing nearly dressed, for they had one in their room to-day.

"It is not *I* that am good," said Emily, more seriously than she had ever spoken to Grace, "I am sure it's a shame that so silly a girl as Mary Anne should give you so much trouble," and she took Grace's hand and kissed her, almost immediately exclaiming, "Why, Grace, you are as cold as ice, and how you tremble! I never felt any thing like you! what is the matter? you must be very ill."

"Oh, no, not ill," said Grace, now smiling and quite at her ease, "I was very uncomfortable just now, but now I know what to do I shall soon be as usual again."

"But just feel," said Emily, placing her hand on Grace's temples and neck, "it is not trembling now, I see—it is throbbing, all over you—you must be very ill—do let me go and tell your mamma."

"Oh, no, Emily, pray come back—indeed I am not ill; I know very well what it is, I am often the same—indeed mamma can do nothing, and I shall be quite as usual presently."

"Well, but you must have something."

"No, indeed," said Grace, "I know what it is, and I could have cured it before, only we went on talking so long. But I believe," added she presently, "now I must just lie down a little; luckily I have very little dressing, and ten minutes lying down will take this off; it is only a beating of the heart, and I know exactly all about it."

Emily helped her to lie down on her bed, and warmed a shawl and threw over her.

"Oh, thank you," said Grace, "that is better than all the rest."

Grace lay very still for a few minutes, when presently Emily turned round, looking very much alarmed. "Why Grace," said she, going towards her, "is it possible!—is that your heart beating? why I hear it here."

"Yes, it is," said Grace, "but Emily, please don't look so frightened, you will make me laugh, your eyes look quite terrified; I am so used to it, I think nothing about it."

Emily again begged Grace to let her fetch her mamma, and proposed some hartshorn and water—did she never take any thing?

Oh, never she said, only once her mamma gave her sal volatile and water, but she had rather not, and she should be quite well after tea.

Emily said that would be a long time to wait, and then remember most likely coffee was made, and she said she would go down and get Hanson to give her a cup of coffee.

Grace was so fearful of a report being raised that she was not well, and so little used to take any thing, that she opposed it, but Emily ran out of the room, while Grace said, "Please do not say I am ill."

"Oh," thought Grace, when she was left alone, "what a sad thing deception is! I am afraid of saying a word, lest all should be discovered." And then she began to think of Mary Anne's part. "I dare say," thought she, "Mary Anne did not mean to deceive at first, but was led into it by Emily's praise, and so she has gone on, finding it each moment harder and harder; how careful we should be about the beginnings." Then she remembered that she herself had, as it were, helped on the falsehood, and feared she had done almost as wrong as Mary Anne; but she knew there was a difference. "She put me in a difficulty certainly," thought she, "what could I have said when they told me it was Mary Anne's? I could never have said, 'Oh, no, it is mine!' Besides, it never came into my head till now; then every instant it has got worse and worse. But I do hope Emily will speak to Mary Anne, and that things will be better than I expect; mamma said one day we should not 'meet troubles,' and that is the same, I suppose, as those words of our Saviour's, 'Sufficient unto the day is the evil thereof.' "

It may be mentioned here that Grace's surmise as to the mode in which Mary Anne had suffered herself to be tempted, was pretty nearly correct. Mary Anne did not find thoughts come into her head so readily as others, and instead of taking pains to improve in this respect, she gave way to indolence, and so from year to year became worse instead of better. She was often called dull, and stupid, and awkward, because she would exert neither body nor mind; she therefore grew listless in both; yet she wished very much to appear good and clever, and was always trying short cuts to each. She took as much pains sometimes to do this as would have served *really* to improve herself. She would take advantage of her sister's exercises, and avail herself of opportunities which certainly were not quite right. By these and other means she was becoming a weak, useless character, and was ready to give way to almost any temptation that fell in with her peculiar failings. As they were going up to bed on the Monday night, Mary Anne had said to Emily, casually, as they passed through the hall, "What would you say to ornamenting the ante-room with flowers and evergreens for to-morrow, Emily?"

Emily said they sometimes did so, but not in winter, it took so many flowers, and so few were blown.

"But I meant to *make* flowers out of paper, and mix them, and put festoons and lights behind, and then I would bring in your paroquet."

Emily took very much to the idea, if they could make flowers, and Mary Anne made very light of this part. Emily praised Mary Anne's idea much more than she would have done any one's else, because she was surprised at her thinking of such a plan. This emboldened the other, and she talked more freely about it, saying once, rather faintly, that she and Grace had been talking it over. Emily longed for Grace that evening, but she did not come, she took the step we have already related.

CHAPTER XXIII

Hoddy Doddy sat on a wall,
Hoddy Doddy had a great fall,
Not all the King's horses and all the King's men
Could set Hoddy Doddy up again.
ANCIENT RIDDLE

Grace was disturbed in her reflections by a tap at the door; she thought Emily had returned for something, but found it was Hanson. "Miss Emily," cried she, as she entered, looking round, "I thought you answered me."

"It was I," said a soft little voice, proceeding apparently from nowhere.—"Here, Hanson," said Grace, raising herself a little.

"Oh, Miss Leslie! Are you there? Dear! dear!" cried Hanson, "are you ill?"

"Oh, no, Hanson," said Grace, "I am not ill, only I promised to lie here till Emily came back."

"Not ill! my dear young lady," said Hanson, feeling her pulse, and seeing how all her pulses throbbed, "what can be the matter?" and she seemed quite alarmed, examined her as to what she had had for dinner, and wanted to get her some specifics of her own; but Grace told her she would lie still and have a cup of coffee, and Hanson then recommended her to lie quiet as long as she could, and promised to come up in time to dress her, the very last thing. Grace undertook to remain quite still upon the bed till some of them came to her. Hanson asked where Miss Emily was, and found she must just have missed her, as Emily went out to seek her to get dressed, before she got the coffee. The coffee was not quite ready, but Hanson said Grace should have a cup as soon as possible. Grace was then left some time alone, and from the entire rest and cessation from talking, her ailments greatly abated, and by the time Emily returned the palpitation was nearly gone.

"I have been very long," said Emily, "but I had to wait, and George called me in about the lights; we want you sadly, Grace, to advise us, but you cannot come down yet. Now, drink this cup of coffee. Hanson will come and dress you, and then you shall come in and see all is right, before we let papa and mamma and the rest see our *Fairy Bower,* for now I understand the meaning of the title, I do want you so to come."

This revived a little poor Grace's painful remembrances, and she was wondering if Emily had spoken to Mary Anne, when Emily continued, "I said nothing about your being ill, Grace, though Ellen and the rest wondered you could not fasten my frock.—"I don't know how it is, but I cannot help doing as you wish; I never minded any body so much before."

"I am sure you are very kind," said Grace, "and you have made me quite well with that cup of coffee—now kiss me, Emily!—how nice you look! Hanson finished you, I suppose?"

"Yes, she would tie my sash all over again," replied Emily; "by the bye she told me I must look at my hair, for it was not quite right, and no one can do that but myself. Now give me your cup." And Emily went to the glass.

"I never saw any one with hair dressed like yours," said Grace.

"It is foreign," replied Emily, "my aunt brought it from the Continent, and tried to dress Isabella's so, but nobody liked it, and every body likes mine, because mine was always out of curl."

"I am sure it always looks nice now," said Grace, "and is no trouble at all." Presently she added, "Emily, dear, I wish you would move the cup and saucer a little, I am afraid you will whisk them off that stand."

"Yes, I will directly," said Emily, "I must just tie this bow afresh."

Grace watched the cup anxiously, for it was very beautiful china, and looked very jealously at Emily's quick and not very guarded movements. She had placed the cup on a toilette stand. Grace longed to speak again; she would gladly have risen and moved it, but she thought that would be troublesome. Emily however had moved a little, and Grace was more satisfied, when in a moment down came stand and all on the floor, and of course the cup and saucer were broken to pieces.

"Oh, dear," cried poor Emily, "how I wish I had moved it as you told me! but yet I did not whisk it off—I don't know how it was."

"I see," said Grace, "it was your chain round the foot of the stand."

"Yes," said Emily, "I was just putting on my chain, and caught it up in a hurry; but do you know, it is the best china, and it cannot be matched. It was all that tiresome Hannah—Hanson would not have given me the best china.—I know mamma will be so angry about it."

"Well," said Grace, "it is all my fault; you could not help it."

"Why *I* broke it," said Emily.

"Yes, but it would not have been there, except for me," said Grace.

"I cannot replace it, that is the worst! Oh, how I wish I had minded you, Grace!" said Emily.

"I dare say," returned the other, "you were hurrying to mind me, and that was the cause of the accident."

"Yes; but if I had moved it at once," sighed poor Emily, "it would not have been broken."

"Well, it *is* better, certainly, as you say," answered Grace, "to do a thing at once; but it cannot be helped now, and if it teaches us that lesson for our whole lives—I mean, to do a thing at once, it will be a good accident after all; I have learned some things so already."

"Grace, you always make every thing right," said Emily; "I wish I was like you!"

"Oh, pray don't say that!" cried poor Grace, thinking of some of her great defects.

Emily gathered together the unfortunate remains of the beautiful cup, and laid them on the toilette stand; she then prepared to leave the room, and herself told Grace she should try and speak to Mary Anne, before it was quite impossible. She added, "It is a very great bore indeed, and I would do it for nobody but you, Grace."

Her friend thanked her warmly, and once more she was left alone.

After a time Hanson came in, and was very glad to find Grace seeming well again. She had recovered her colour which was a very pretty one, and her eyes looked bright and laughing. Hanson said she thought the cup of coffee had done great things.

"Oh, Hanson," said Grace, "that is the worst part! a great deal worse than my palpitation, for we have broken that beautiful cup and saucer!"

"Dear! dear! I am very sorry, indeed; what a pity!" cried Hanson; "I declare, here it is, all to pieces! How did you do it, Miss Grace?"

But for the morning's experience, Grace might have let it pass as her personal accident, but that had given her a shock, and she said, "I did not do it myself exactly, but it was my fault, it was brought up for me.—I am afraid," added she, "Mrs. Ward will be very much vexed; what do you think I could do, Hanson?—you know best about such things; do you think you could get a cup at all like it for me?"

"Well, I don't know but I might," said Hanson, examining it; "it is Spode's china, I see, and I have a friend in the works—if it is to be had, he could get it for me."

Grace's joy was excessive: she told Hanson that Emily had said it could not be matched.

Hanson said it was very true, but that her friend was good-natured and clever, and had managed to match several breakages for her very well.

This was joyful news to Grace, and made her forget all her other troubles. We have seen Grace was a little afraid of Mrs. Ward, and she really thought every thing was going to be unfortunate for her, for Mrs. Ward might very properly be angry that a little girl like Grace should take the liberty of getting a cup of coffee in the best china. Grace asked when Hanson thought she could know about this cup and saucer, and if she could give a guess as to the price.

Hanson said in a few days,—but she could not tell about the price.

Poor Grace asked if it would be more than two guineas.

Hanson assured her not near so much, and promised she would not forget it.

Grace had never been so regularly *drest* since she was quite a little girl, as now, by Hanson, who was very particular indeed. Though Grace's frock and slip were simple enough, yet she was a long time fastening them and setting the bow of the sash. Grace felt terribly impatient, for she wished to get down stairs; but she considered, it was very good of Hanson to take such pains to make her look proper. She longed to jump away, and say, "Oh, that will do, I can fasten it myself in a minute;" but she repressed her impatience, and thanked Hanson before she left the room.

"What a dear little lamb that is!" thought Hanson, as she folded the broken pieces carefully in a piece of paper; "I was really ashamed I was so long, but this finger of mine makes me very awkward—yet there she stood, as gentle as a dove—not a pull, or a twist, or an impatient word, like some young ladies! Miss Ellen, though she's a darling, would not have been as good as that, and Miss Emily would have been off like a shot long ago—why, I could hardly keep her for a quarter of the time just now!"

CHAPTER XXIV

Nor sullen lip, nor taunting eye,
Deforms the scene when thou art by.
AKENSIDE

GRACE WAS RECALLED to the remembrance of her grand trouble by finding her mamma had left her room. She did not, however, avoid seeing her mamma by going into the back drawing-room: she went straight to the other room, and as she expected, Mrs. Leslie remarked on her not coming to her as usual, and asked why she had been so long.—Mrs. Ward said, "Grace is unfortunate to-day; it is the second time that Emily has been hard at work before her." Grace was rather a favourite of Mr. Ward's, because he fancied her like her mamma and her aunt Stanley; so he said, "Well, I dare say Grace could give a good reason for it—why, look at all these folds," said he, taking hold of Grace's white muslin frock, "this must have taken an age to put on!"

Grace was obliged to both Mr. and Mrs. Ward for speaking, for it spared her accounting to her mamma for her absence; and in a few minutes she was dismissed to her young friends, and charged not to go through the folding doors,—for Mr. Ward said they were going to have a great surprise in this wonderful device of Mary Anne's, and that he was told Mary Anne would be very angry indeed if they caught a glimpse before the proper time. Mrs. Ward began saying she was quite glad to find Mary Anne had some taste, and was appealing to Miss Newmarsh about it as Grace closed the door.

When Grace entered the other room she was herself surprised.—The blaze of light, the bank of evergreens, the brilliant bird raised high on her perch, and especially the festoons of roses, which seemed to confine her in her bower, with the pendant bright flowers, hanging around the arch of the ante-room, together with the group of snowy, thin dresses, had a most striking effect, and Grace forgot all drawbacks in the pleasure of admiration. Grace was warmly greeted on her entrance, and she could hardly satisfy them with her praises.—"You cannot think," said she, "how nice you all looked standing round! the thin white dresses, and your cousin's gray satin, set it off so very well, and the black dresses help too."

"But what do you think of the lights?" said George; "are they right?"

"Yes, pretty well, I think," said Grace; but presently she found it was not quite to her taste, and she proposed to Emily to extinguish all the lights on that side of the room. Emily did it, and a general exclamation of disappointment ensued. Emily said they were trying a new effect; and Constance replied that she ought to consult Mary Anne before they made any changes.

"Mary Anne has not helped a bit in the lighting," said George, "and we have been waiting for Grace's opinion."

Isabella was quite against the "new effect," and Mary Anne very strong the same way. Grace remarked to the first, if she would come to the end of the room she thought she would approve of it, and added, "You know we can light all again directly if you do not like it. You see it is quite a blaze here, and the light falls so well on the dresses." She then went to George and asked him to be so good as to light the lights again for his cousin to see, and begged the rest to come and see the difference.

It was a *fact* that the grand point in the scene, namely, the ante-room, showed far more brilliantly under Grace's "new effect;" and the manner in which Grace had consulted every body's feelings as well as taste, gained the day. Isabella protested it was a great improvement, at this end of the room; the rest followed, and Mary Anne was not disposed to contend the point with such odds against her. It was therefore voted unanimously that the lights should be again extinguished, and a deputation was forthwith formally despatched to acquaint the Grandees that the "Fairy Bower" was ready for public inspection. Meanwhile Grace and Emily were grouping the parts for the first general view. The doors were thrown open, and the surprise and admiration of the seriors, equalled the highest expectation of the juvenile *artistes*. Mr. Ward said he had never seen any thing more elegantly devised at the very best houses. Mrs. Ward said she should not have known her own room. Miss Newmarsh remarked it was a most graceful imitation of the beauties of nature; whilst Mr. Everard asked for the "fair architect," addressed Mary Anne by the title of "Bright Flora," saying that she had "with rosy fingers made their winter spring." All agreed that it was a most happy idea, executed with the greatest taste and promptitude. After a time Mr. Everard observed that Mrs. Leslie had not joined in the praises, and asked her if she did not approve the fairy design.

"It is," said she, "remarkably pretty."

Mr. Everard here rallied her on her cool praise, and she answered, it was really simple surprise, for it was so like in style and execution the little devices of her nephews and nieces, at their cottage at Hampstead, that she was amazed at the coincidence of thought—"but," she added, "Grace must have helped in it, because she is used to make such flowers as those with her cousins, and I recognize a great many little devices as her own."

Mr. Everard was much surprised to hear that the flowers were artificial, much more that they were the work of the young people, and he stepped onwards to examine them. When he came back, Mrs. Leslie hoped the disclosure had not lost the young people his approbation—she knew he was so fond of real flowers.

He assured her not at all, just the contrary; he admired their cleverness and industry greatly.—"Better let your little girl do such things than addle her brain and lose her health, poring all day long over the arts and sciences."—"But," added he, "of one thing I am tolerably sure, from my examination of yon pretty Bower, and that is, that it is all one idea; no one at this time of year, without a real fairy bed of roses, or a fairy purse, or the fancy flowers, would have thought of such a thing; so, my good friend, I would have you keep an eye, and if your fair Grace is the sole proprietor of the patient, she may prove Flora as well as Thalia, and be double-faced in two or three senses, in spite of her disclaiming the attribute, as she did to me the other day. Do not trust to what I say, but do not forget it. *Verbum sapienti.*"

Mr. Everard was a quick discerner; he did not speak from mere guess; something had passed at dinner that struck him, and Mrs. Leslie's surprise and remark had brought it again to his remembrance. Soon after this the young party began to assemble: there was a mixture of elder persons among them—the papas and mammas, or grown-up members of some of the family. Of course the Fairy Bower was the grand object of attraction on the entrance of each party; the young people flocked round to admire it and talk to Madge. Emily found it a wonderful relief to her; for the younger children, who usually were troublesome to amuse while the party were assembling, and often got to romping, were ready to stand and converse with Madge and feed her all night. She, too, was highly pleased, and favoured the company with all her speeches, some of which were highly complimentary: one had been taught her formerly by Hanson,—"You are a pretty little lady;" and some by the boys came in amusingly, though not so amiably. After a time Emily and George began to make their arrangements, as settled beforehand. The *quite* young folks were conducted into the hall, or the saloon, as it was called at parties, when it was usually used for dancing. Clara,—who was the eldest of the younger portion of the Ward family, and a quick child, something like her sister Emily,—had been instructed, and had joyfully undertaken the generalship of this small band; and Hanson and some of the steady servants, had been requested to be at hand, and keep order if necessary. The tea was therefore poured out in this room, and a very merry and orderly little troop filled it. Nothing at all occurred to occasion an uncomfortable remembrance; one game or amusement went on after another, and every body seemed wonderfully disposed to obey. By this arrangement Emily despatched above twenty of her guests, and had only occasionally to look in upon them, in turn with Ellen and Grace, who were appointed to this office. Mary Anne, Emily had relieved from her share, not very unwillingly, since it had been agreed in the morning that she had done her part in designing the Fairy Bower. On the whole every thing went off in the other two rooms most successfully. There were a few difficulties now and then with the formidable Thompsons and Davises, but the absence of Newton Grey was Emily's grand support. She found her task easy when there was no big bold boy to fan every spark into a flame.—Besides, she discovered a mode in which to quiet any rising discontents or tumults. She observed how easily Grace seemed to manage and persuade their own party about the lights, and it struck her she must have a skill that way which herself did not possess; so whenever any unpleasantness seemed ready to arise, she got Grace to come and smooth matters for her. Grace was very successful in her attempts this evening—indeed she generally was, for she set about such things the right way. She always entered into people's feelings very quickly, and was ready to please them and accommodate them as nearly as possible in their own way. She did not do this in a patronizing way, or in a formal way, or in a cunning way, or in a clever way, but in a simple way, thinking very little about it, but trying to satisfy them, and giving up her own preferences, if they were only preferences. Another thing that helped Grace was her appearance, though she was not nearly so handsomely dressed as some of the young ladies: but face and manner has a great deal to do with every body's appearance, though dress has also considerable weight in affairs such as Grace undertook this evening; for instance, if Isabella had set her authority against Grace's, we would not give much, generally speaking, for Grace's chance of success. But fortunately Grace had gained Miss Ward's favour for the moment by consulting her about the lights, and by two or three more acts of essential service she had been able to do her in the course of the evening. Still Grace was no favourite of Miss Ward's, nor likely to become such. Grace's most arduous task was the following,—Emily came to her in much distress, and summoned her to assist in the next room, for a party of boys had assembled together, and declared they would have a good game. They only laughed at her, and if George interfered it would be a regular dispute she was sure; she had left them debating what game it should be, and entreated Grace to go and do as well as she could—she said John Thompson was at the head of all. Grace found a party of young gentlemen gathered round, having cleared a space before them. They were standing in attitudes most suspiciously approaching to a game of leap-frog, but had not yet begun. It happened fortunately that in the beginning of the evening, one of these boys in the press towards the Fairy Bower, had by some means or other pushed against Grace, trodden not very lightly upon her foot, and torn her dress to an extent that looked very alarming. This was not the first accident of the sort he had ever met with, for he was a careless, and therefore a clumsy boy; and it had so happened that each time before he had got very black looks, and some angry words. On this occasion, however, just as he was about to laugh—more from awkwardness and not knowing how to apologize, than from actual ill-nature—Grace turned round, looked very good-natured, and assured him he had not hurt her any thing to speak of. This checked him, but he had not manners enough to say any thing. Presently she spoke to him again, and said she wished he would try and prevent those behind pressing and pushing so violently, for some of the little ones near her were quite frightened. This prevented himself from pushing, and protected Grace in some degree; and also he spoke to others, rather roughly certainly, "*to be quiet*," but they attended to him. Some little time after this he was standing still, and he heard George say to Grace, "Why, what's the matter, Grace? you have been going about limping like a lame duck?"

"Yes," said Grace, laughing, "I know I limp."

"But how did it happen?" said George, "have you been like the cow jumping over the moon? you know you would not jump in the garden the other day!"

"Somebody trod on my foot in the press," said Grace, "but it is nearly well now."

Grace did not know any one overheard this little discourse. On her joining the leap-frog group, she asked what they were going to do. Her manner was such that the answer was given rather in a foolish tone, as if they knew they were about an unsuitable action. She then spoke a little aside to this young Thompson, and so persuasive were her representations, that after about three minutes' conversation, he turned to the rest, and said, "I say, this will be flat work here; we shall break our heads against the chairs and all these gimcracks, and shall set all the girls screaming; come away, there's some fun going on in the other room."

Emily said afterwards to Grace, "You are a wonderful girl, Grace, I watched your face all the time, and you did nothing but laugh and smile, and yet that uncouth boy minded all you said in a moment."

"Why," said Grace, "very luckily he tore my frock in the beginning of the evening, and I know he remembered it by something he said."

"Why, I'm sure," said Emily, "he did not say much."

"No, not much, but it was to the purpose. But we must not stay here, for I promised him, as you gave me leave, the new game of mufti, and George and Reginald Freemantle are already preparing and teaching them in the hall."

This game had been under debate between George and Emily the day before. Emily was against it, because they had it the other evening. George was for it, because so few of the same party were present, and because it was quite a new game; so it was settled that if Reginald Freemantle came they would have mufti, and that it should come just before supper; that the whole party, little and big, should play, and that it should take place in the hall, as being the freest space. A game they had, and a very comic one it was. The elder part of the company were spectators, and seemed as much entertained as the rest. It is a game which in description, and at the onset, seems poor, but in action, and with a judicious mufti, is one of the most amusing of such entertainments. Emily's list was of the greatest use; indeed the idea of the leap-frog crept in, while George and Emily were by an accident absent together, and there was no one to take the lead in a proposition. Every other time they had taken care to be at hand, and had two or three proposals ready, the most popular of which was immediately adopted. We must now relate the most important scene of the evening, though we have been forestalling it by others far less so.

CHAPTER XXV

The trumpets sound; stand close, the Queen is coming!
SHAKESPEARE

THE FAIRY BOWER had abundantly attracted the notice of the elder part of the company. Every body was full of admiration: it was visited and inspected, the flowers examined, and the whole pronounced elegantly devised and executed. A party of the seniors were talking it over in the drawing-room the beginning of the evening, and it was mentioned as entirely the work of the young people—the idea only suggested the night before. It did indeed seem incredible; but a dozen pair of hands, more or less willing, can sometimes effect wonders. Lord and Lady Musgrove were especially pleased, and the latter asked if it was Emily's notion. She was told, No—her cousin Mary Anne Duff's, who was staying in the house.

"Oh," said Lady Musgrove, "I have been looking at the Duffs; they are fine girls, and our Isabella has taken a great fancy to one—is that Mary Anne?"

Miss Newmarsh said she rather thought not; she believed Constance was her favourite.

Lady Musgrove said she should like to speak to them some time in the evening, especially to the young designer.

"Well," said one of the gentlemen, "it really is a most tasteful plan, and I think the fair *artiste* should receive some honour at our hands—what do you say," said he, "to crowning her with her own flowers?"

It was thought a very pretty idea, and some of the party walked into the next room to arrange it. It was near the end of some game, and these gentlemen had a slight conference with Reginald Freemantle. He took to the idea immediately, and undertook the whole management. At a proper moment he stepped forward and made a loud flourish of trumpets, which was an art he excelled in, and having obtained silence, he made a proclamation, demanding in the name of the aristocracy of the other room, that Mary Anne, the fair *artiste* of the Fairy Bower, should be forthwith consigned to his hands; for it was the will and pleasure of the higher powers that more than the praise of words should be awarded to one so accomplished, and that he was the happy herald commissioned to proclaim, that she was to be crowned "Queen of the Fairy Bower," in the sight of the assembled multitude. He then summoned all, high and low, to witness the coronation of the Queen of the Fairy Bower, and ended by again demanding the fair Mary Anne to be brought forward. He then closed with his military flourish. Reginald's proclamation was sufficiently clear, yet no one stirred. Emily, Grace, and George were standing near together, as they were on the point of proposing some new arrangement. "Oh, Emily!" cried Grace, in a low voice, "then you did not speak to Mary Anne!"

"No," said Emily, "she was gone down stairs, and I found them all waiting for me here."

"Well," thought Grace, "then it cannot be helped; we tried to do something—that is a comfort."

Again came a flourish, and the herald called upon Emily, the lady of the revels, and her lady-in-waiting, the fair Grace, forthwith to conduct Mary Anne, the Queen of the Fairy Bower, to his presence.

There was again a pause.—"Oh, Emily," whispered Grace, in great agitation, "what can we do? we must go!"

"Grace," said Emily, decidedly, "*I will not*, whatever are the consequences."

Poor Grace! all fell upon her—what could she do! After waiting due time, the herald repeated his summons. It was really a very solemn scene, and to the three individuals in question must have been, from different causes, a most exciting one. The consequences rushed across Grace's mind; she saw the whole transaction exposed, and Mary Anne publicly degraded, and without another thought she turned to George and asked him to take an answer from them, any thing he chose to say, and to ask permission to depute himself and Campbell to the office proposed for herself and Emily.

George stepped forward, and in due form announced that he had the honour of bearing a message from the ladies Emily and Grace—that they begged to assure the herald it was no disrespect to the higher powers, that they had not immediately hastened to perform their commands; but that their feelings were so excited on the occasion of the unexampled honour, proposed to be conferred on their amiable friend, that they entreated to be allowed to name his unworthy self and his cousin Campbell, as deputies in their place. The herald highly commended the feelings of the young ladies, and assured them they would be equally appreciated by his illustrious employers. Here came another flourish of trumpets, and George withdrew in due form. He sought Campbell, and they conducted Mary Anne between them, across the room, before the herald.—"Fair maiden," said he, "the trumpet of Fame has announced to the puissant powers of the other room, that yon brilliant bower, commonly designated 'The Fairy Bower,' boasts its origin from the elegant stores of your mind, and is the child of your genius; say, fair maiden, does Fame speak truly?"

Mary Anne said nothing; she hung her head and looked what is called foolish, but her manner and appearance was not any thing unusual, and excited no remark among either friends or strangers. Finding he got no answer, the herald continued, "Fair maiden, be assured we all respect your modesty and humility, nor shall they be disturbed by the rudeness of forms and of courts. Your maidenly silence shall be accepted as it is meant, and proclamation shall be issued accordingly." He then in due form announced that the fair Mary Anne, now before them, "is the true and sole architect of the Fairy Bower, and it is the sovereign will and pleasure of the puissant powers of the other room, that she shall forthwith be crowned Queen of the same: I therefore hereby cite the ladies before mentioned, Emily and Grace, and in the name of my illustrious employers command them, to prepare from the fairest of the wreaths of yon bower, a chaplet for the fair brows of the new Queen."—And here came another flourish.

Grace again whispered to Emily, and Emily again refused to assist,—"Oh, Emily!" cried Grace, much distressed, "is it kind to me?"

"I don't know," replied the other, "but don't make me go, I shall throw the chaplet at her head; I cannot go, and so it's no use asking me."

Grace moved mechanically towards the Bower, and asked one of the young gentlemen to cut her down a certain festoon, which was all white roses and buds. She then approached the group at the other end of the room.—"Obedient maiden," said the herald, "in the name of my puissant employers, I greet you! and command you to weave the purest of chaplets, for the fair brows of the Queen of the Fairy Bower."

Poor Grace with rather trembling, but not at all ungraceful hands, began to arrange the wreath she held in a suitable garland for the head, having possessed herself of the knife, which her knight, young Thompson, used in her service. As she began, the following words in a fine sonorous tone, dropped slowly from a voice which every one at once recognized as Mr. Everard's:—

Weave a chaplet, maiden mine,
Fit for Queen of Fairy line,

Soft as dew, and pure as snow,
Let it grace the rightful brow.
Many a crown is fraught with thorns
For the brow that it adorns;
But no thorn, while Grace has power,
E'er shall mar her roseate dower.
What high nature should she be,
Candidate for Queen's degree;
Not a breath of pride or art
In her bosom must find part
Gracious, courteous, gentle, bland,
Beyond all daughters in the land:
Yet her steps attended aye,
By wisdom meek and dignity.
Weave a chaplet, maiden fair,
For a royal Fairy's hair:
Keep the loveliest blossoms, Grace,
Cast away the mean and base!
Let the fairy chaplet be,
Emblem, Grace, befitting thee;
Pure and simple, firmly blent,
Modest, sweet, and elegant!
Fame at best is poor and vain,
Man's decoy and woman's bane.
Fame beside is blind and dull,
Mammon's slave and Error's fool,
Scarcely right and often wrong,
Gives what does not all belong:
Rightful goods she takes away,
Maidens, watch, lest she betray!
The woof is wove, the web is spun,
Herald, see the work is done!

This prompt and apt effusion had a most admirable, and to two of the party, a most startling effect. Grace was so amazed at almost every line, that she did not dare look up. She thought the whole transaction was betrayed to every creature,—how Mr. Everard became acquainted with the history, was however to her a profound mystery. He must have known it some time she felt sure, for so many appropriate lines could never, she thought, have been unpremeditated—what was to come next was now her perplexity. With an outwardly composed demeanour, however, she placed her elegant little garland in the hands of the herald. During the ode, Mary Anne stood where she had been placed, and continued pretty still—only fidgeting now and then with her hands, in a way not quite befitting the candidate for a crown; but this was her usual manner. We have remarked she had not control of either body or mind in any great extent; and indeed, as is usual with those whose thoughts are very much on themselves, she felt most especially awkward when brought into more notice than usual, however much she desired, or as we may unhappily say with truth, *coveted* that sort of distinction. It is the most humble, generally speaking, who are the most self-possessed, and on whom distinction seems to fall naturally without puffing them up. It is doubtful if the unhappy circumstances of Mary Anne's present distinction at all affected her outward manner, or if at this moment they much even affected her mind. She was pleased, and in her sad way satisfied, at being publicly honoured. So blunted were her feelings by self, that she did not even perceive the drift of Mr. Everard's verses, which Grace thought so plain, that no one could mistake. Her mind was confused by vanity and the novelty of her situation; she thought all eyes were upon her, admiring her; and she took Mr. Everard's lines as entirely complimentary to herself; she did not perceive that herself was barely alluded to, and Grace was made much more prominent; nor did she guess, that every eye was fixed on Grace and the chaplet she was dexterously weaving, and that herself was quite secondary in the scene.

Emily was the other individual to whom we alluded, as being amazed at the hints contained in Mr. Everard's effusion. No one else in the room observed them, which is not to be wondered at, as to the uninitiated they contain no more than a moral maxim clothed in poetical language. Many observed he made Grace more the heroine of the scene than Mary Anne: some thought it not fair—others did not wonder. We must however recall the reader to the spectacle, for such it was really becoming.—The herald has the crown in his hand; again he sounds his trumpet, and issues a proclamation for the coronation of the queen of the Fairy Bower; adding, that in the name of his puissant employers, he appointed the fair Grace to the office of placing the crown on the royal head. Grace was bewildered beyond expression at this announcement. She found all was *not* discovered, as at first she supposed; she wished she could hear those verses again, and ended by thinking that she had as Emily said, puzzled herself so that she turned every thing into a meaning of her own. Whatever might be the cause, however, she felt greatly relieved, and proceeded to discharge the office imposed on her without hesitation. Grace had felt no awkwardness in doing any thing that had fallen to her lot. If she had been told beforehand that she would be called on to do such things, she would have felt uncomfortable and anxious—just as she did on a less public occasion in the morning, when she thought of giving George his chain; but her present offices had come upon her naturally and suddenly, and all were things she could easily do. She was bid to do them, and she did them without thinking about it. Before placing the crown, the herald withdrew and cleared a circle before the folding doors; where stood the range of the elders, who had witnessed the whole scene. A cushion was placed, on which the half-created Queen was desired to kneel: she did, upon both knees,—Grace, we think, would have been content with one,—and meanwhile the following coronation chorus fell from the ready lips of the inexhaustible Bard, while Grace had the good sense to wait for the proper moment, according to the verses, for placing the crown on the royal head.

> Gentlest of Graces, and meekest of maids,
> Weaver of garlands whose freshness ne'er fades,
> Thine 'tis to place on the brow of the Queen
> Thine own fairy garland of white and of green.
> Sure if a crown is a hand's worthy prey,

Fitly that hand may bestow it away!
Diamonds are brilliant, gold too is rare,
But crowns of such texture are weighty with care:
Blossoms are lovely, and lighter than gems,
But quickly they wither and fall from their stems.
Grace bears a coronet, wrought by her skill,
Precious as diamonds, lovelier still;
Hers is no crown to embarrass with woe,
Goodness its virtue, kindness its show;
No sad emotion weighs the head down,
Heavy and sleepless, that carries her crown.
Yet—if a bosom is tainted with art,
'Tis not this crown could clear the soiled heart:
No! let us keep the heart safely within,
Then never fear where we end or begin:
All have a friend while their conscience is clear,
Conscience, the monarch of Queen and of Peer.
Gentlest of Graces, and meekest of friends,
Raise now the Crown as the Fairy Queen bends;
Set on her head the pure chaplet of snow,
Let not its honours encumber her brow;
Crowned by a Grace, with leaf and with flower,
Hail her now Queen of the bright Fairy Bower!

It was a very pretty group; the two young gentlemen duly supported the Queen and the attendant, and Grace exactly suited her actions to the words of the ode. It was the same in the former address,—at the line, "Cast away the mean and the base!" she took care to follow the lead, and the action was followed by plaudits, which, after this burst agreeably interrupted the recital at fitting times. At the conclusion of the whole, the herald blew his trumpet, the multitude cheered, and the ladies waved their handkerchiefs. Many voices were loud in Mary Anne's praises. One lady, a Mrs. Mason, the same that had admired her in a morning call one day, exclaimed, "A fine young lady indeed Miss Mary Anne is! and how prettily she did her part! just like a little queen!"

"The Grace would have borne such honours more meekly, if not more worthily," muttered Mr. Everard in reply.

"That little girl is a vast favourite of yours, Mr. Everard," returned this lady, "but surely you must think Miss Mary Anne a much finer girl!"

"Not one of my sort," replied Mr. Everard; "fine and smooth—smooth and false," added he, in an almost inaudible tone, as he walked away.

After the acclamations had somewhat subsided, the herald stepped forward and conducted the young Queen into the presence of the elders, especially introducing her to Lord and Lady Musgrove, and saying her Ladyship had expressed a wish to have an audience of the new Queen.

"Indeed," said Lord Musgrove, "we are highly honoured by her Majesty's condecension, and we hope the Queen of the Fairy Bower will to-night enjoy the honour she has so richly deserved."

A few such sentences passed, which Mary Anne received but awkwardly; not that she need have replied much, but her mode of receiving them was any thing but simple—as Grace's would have been, or clever, as Emily's. However she presently fell more into herself, and as she went on, her *manner* rather improved. The reader must judge for himself as to the more important part. Lady Musgrove admired her taste and her skill displayed in the Fairy Bower very much, and asked her how the idea first came into her head—had she been used to such decorations?

Mary Anne answered only, "No," and looked sheepish, for she had never before been spoken to by a Lord or a Lady, and she thought it a very great honour; and so it was, but not exactly as Mary Anne felt it.

"How did you plan it, my dear?" said Lady Musgrove, "by yourself, or did you talk it over with Emily?"

"Emily and I talked of it afterwards," answered Mary Anne.

"But" pursued Lady Musgrove, "was it quite your own idea, or had you ever seen any thing of the sort before?"

"I had never seen any thing of the sort before," replied Mary Anne, who was beginning to be very much on her guard, or what in her case may be called by the unpleasant word *cunning*.

"Did you," continued her Ladyship, "think of the bower for the bird or the bird for the bower?"

"The bower for the bird," said Mary Anne, obliged to answer, and remembering it rose in that way with Grace.

"Well, that was a very pretty idea," returned Lady Musgrove, "and really has a good deal of genius in it; and did anything put it in your head?"

"I think," said Mary Anne, getting bolder, and thinking now she could afford a little of her fame to her family, "I think it might be some poetry of my sister Fanny's."

"Does your sister write poetry?" asked Lady Musgrove, surprised, "I thought you were the eldest."

"Yes, I am," said Mary Anne, proud to recommend her sister, "Fanny is younger than me."

"Is it Fanny that Isabella has taken a fancy to?"

"Yes," returned Mary Anne, "I believe so."

Miss Newmarsh felt very much disappointed.

"Well, can you repeat your sister's lines, or say what they were about?"

"They were about a bird—wishing to be like a bird."

"But was there any thing about a bower?" asked this inquisitive lady.

"Yes, one line," replied Mary Anne,—

> "And live in bowers with thee."

"Well, it is a very pretty line; and that put it into your head, I suppose?"

"I think so," said Mary Anne, getting quite hardened.

"Then what made you call it a 'fairy bower,' and not a bird's bower?" again asked the lady.

"It was not I invented that name," said Mary Anne, candidly, "it was done by the rest when the room was finished, and the lights were lit. I had nothing to do with the lighting, Emily and George managed all that—Emily is so very clever."

Mary Anne now thought she had established her character for taste and genius, she might try at goodness, and introduce her cousin, as she had her sister.

"Oh, yes," said Lady Musgrove, "I know Emily is very clever, but she would not have planned such a bower as that; I dare say, however, she helped you in the execution."

"Oh, yes," cried Mary Anne, quite in her own manner, "she and all the rest helped in the flowers, and did a great deal more than I did."

"Well," said Lady Musgrove, "you have passed a very good examination, and have shown that you can be good as well as clever.—True genius has no envy. Now, my dear, I will not keep you from your companions; here is Ellen waiting quite impatiently till I have done with you."

Mary Anne did not know Ellen or any of the young people were within hearing, and she started to find she was close at her elbow. She could not be sure she had not said some dangerous things before Ellen. She had rather it should have been Grace than Ellen; for though she could not understand Grace, she felt now sure she did not mean to betray her; and as long as Grace kept it all to herself, she did not care for the rest. What a shocking state of mind she must have been in! But Mary Anne's examinations were not at an end: as Ellen was leading her off, Miss Newmarsh stopped them, and said, "Mary Anne, I am amazed at you for not thinking of these flowers for our Bodstock fair."

"Oh," said Mary Anne, "I did not hear of them till long afterwards."

"Why, when did you hear of them?"

"Since I have been here," replied the young lady.

"And who told you?"

Mary Anne all along had the craft or conscience to avoid Grace's name entirely, and if now she announced it, she knew the whole affair was likely to be discovered. She remembered she had in the morning, before Ellen, said simply she heard of them "since she had been here." She therefore answered warily, that she could not tell who told her.

"Why, that is very strange," said her governess, "you have been here little more than a week, and have been out very little; cannot you remember when it was, or where?"

"It must have been when I first came," said Mary Anne, thinking it best to put off the time before Grace's arrival, as well as Ellen's.

"When you first came!" said Miss Newmarsh, "I wonder you did not mention it to your sisters, when they came to see you; you know we are all very busy now upon the drawing-room table stall, and I charged you to look about for any new ideas. But cannot you at all remember who told you? because it is very important to know from what quarter it comes, that we may not be forestalled."

"It must have been somewhere that I called with Emily," said Mary Anne, alarmed at committing herself to times and places, for she well knew she had only been to two houses before Grace came,—"or it might be," added she, "sombeody calling here."

"Cannot you tell what room it was in, or whether it was a lady or a child that told you, or any thing at all about it?" pursued her governess.

"No, really I cannot," said Mary Anne, "it all passed in a moment."

"Well," said Miss Newmarsh, "it is very unaccountable, Mary Anne, and very unfortunate; but go, my dear child, I am sorry to have kept you, but it is an important subject, and I wish to know whence the idea came."

The two cousins then returned to the back drawing-room, and mingled in the sports.

The Queen was hailed as she joined the young band, and her spirits now rose to an unrestrained height. Every body but Emily and Grace paid her a sort of homage, addressing her by her title, and consulting her with a deference, which, though avowedly mock, was very agreeable to her; and she was the liveliest—perhaps we ought to say the most boisterous—among the throng. Emily, even, wondered at her, though she had seen the same sort of thing at school; but poor Grace was quite aghast; she began to think she was in a dream—she must have made a mistake—that Mary Anne really devised the Fairy Bower—and she ended with believing as a betweenity, that Mary Anne had either persuaded herself that she had, or that she thought so from the very first. This idea restored Grace to herself while it lasted, and accounted for every thing. How else could Mary Anne have gone through all she had that evening? How else stood Mr. Everard's appalling voice, exerted with solemn effect, especially at the word "conscience," and the awful pause he made after those two lines? several times it had thrilled herself to her very heart, and that poor little heart at the same time bled for Mary Anne. "But," thought she, "if Mary Anne believes herself the designer, of course she would not notice these things." Without this persuasion, and the necessity Grace was under of being in constant activity, she would have sat still in a corner, and gazed with surprise all the evening at Mary Anne—full of enjoyment and laughter as she was, her face highly excited with pleasure and notice.

Different amusements filled up the rest of the time, and after the highly popular game of "mufti," the whole party adjourned to the supper room.

CHAPTER XXVI

"We do not always find visible happiness in proportion to visible virtue."
RASSELAS

THE QUEEN was conducted to her seat in due form; there was a flourish of trumpets preceding her, and a procession of her more immediate court. The supper tables were a very pretty sight as the party entered. They were placed in the form of a T, and in the centre, conspicuously raised, stood one of Birch's best twelfth cakes—the kind Christmas present of grandmamma Ward. The supper went off as well as the rest of the evening. Emily thought that Grace happening to sit next John Thompson was a fortunate circumstance; she felt quite sure that Grace kept him in good order; how she managed it she could not imagine, for if Emily ever attempted to interfere with any of his ways, his usual answer was something like, "What's that to you?" "I wish you'd mind your own business!" but we are happy to say, neither such as these nor any other uncomfortable incidents, disturbed the outward serenity of the evening, and every body seemed happy and pleased. The internal disquiets are better known to the reader than to any of the guests, and of this portion of the history we are about to speak.

In the course of the supper, the propriety of drinking the health of the Queen of the

Fairy Bower, was discussed among some of the good-natured gentlemen, and Reginald Freemantle was deputed to manage the affair. He rose and proposed it. The idea was received with great approbation; some of the gentlemen were so kind as to enter into the amusement, for so it must be called, and one by one they rose to second the resolution. Several very ingenious and entertaining speeches were made; the Fairy Bower was dissected and discussed in all its bearings, but all turned into a compliment to the Queen. Several very pretty allusions were made to her crown being formed from her own works. Another said her genius in its loveliness disdained fairy tiaras or costly gems, and took the form most appropriate to its simplicity and modesty. Another again compared her to Flora, and talked of her carpeting the earth with flowers, for wherever she stepped bright flowers sprang up. At length it was observed that Mr. Everard had not spoken, and every one knew that speaking on any subject, was an art he peculiarly excelled in. An intimation of the popular wishes on the subject was therefore given him. He excused himself, saying he had done his part in the pageant, by discharging the office of poet laureate. But the public would not be content, and he was called on by general acclamation. He rose and said he could not refuse such a flattering appeal, but he had thought he had sufficiently trespassed on the patience of the company, by his two coronation odes; and besides, he felt he could not add any thing worthy the notice of such a company, after the able speakers who had preceded him; truly indeed might they have been said to have exhausted the mine. However it must be confessed that to courtiers the praises of majesty, and to poets the praises of beauty and nature were mines *in*exhaustible; and though he neither wished nor dared to account himself on the one hand a courtier, nor on the other a poet, he should be ashamed to be found without loyalty to the line of sovereigns, or without admiration of the forms of beauty. He would therefore with willing lips second the proposition. He would also propose that congratulations should be presented to her youthful Majesty, on her elevation to so high an office; for he confessed he considered the honours she had attained, however merited by genius and taste, a distinction and a dignity which might assist to direct her destinies through life. "I cannot look upon that white coronet of fair flowers," continued the orator, "without myself being reminded of the purity of Truth and the loveliness of Virtue! What is purer than snow? What is lovelier than flowers? Has not this coronet been chosen to grace the brows of the Queen of the Fairy Bower? And has not her present Majesty been selected to her high post of honour by the voice of those who had the right, as well as the will, to distinguish her? Am I then unduly pressing a conclusion when I say, that the bearer of such a crown ought to be mindful in every action of her coming life, to be the representative of the Grace of Truth and the Grace of Virtue? To use the words of a poet, no doubt familiar to her Majesty's ear,—

> 'Princes and Peers may flourish and may fade,
> A breath may make them as a breath hath made.'

"But I would add,

> 'But bright unsullied Truth, our noblest pride,
> When once destroyed can never be supplied.'

"Let us then with dutiful loyalty beg to lay these observations at the feet of youthful Majesty; and the trifling incident of an evening dedicated to lighter amusement, may become to the sovereign of an hour and her juvenile court, a monitor for the employments, whether light or serious, of a coming life."

This address was received with murmurs of approbation. They however quickly subsided on its being perceived, that the orator continued on his legs. He continued, "I have but one word to add, and that is, to propose the health of the person, whether young lady or gentleman, who suggested the title of 'The Fairy Bower;' and I humbly recommend that immediate measures may be taken, to ascertain the individual to whom we are indebted, for such a suitable and elegant designation."

Some one rose to second the motion, but proposed that the Queen's health should be first drunk.

This was accordingly done, with great enthusiasm. The plaudits and cheers continued for a considerable space. It was afterwards signified to Mary Anne, that she must return an address of thanks; but that she might depute a champion to the office. She accordingly chose Reginald Freemantle, who sat next her. After a slight conference with her, he rose. He said he had the honour of being selected by her Majesty, to convey to the company her Majesty's sense of the distinction just received; he felt how unequal he was to the task, and he felt how difficult it was to do justice to the modesty of her Majesty's sentiments, without expressing himself in a manner that might seem unsuitable to her high office. "But rather," continued he, "would I suffer in your estimation, however painful such a result would be to my feelings, than that the humility of her Majesty's sentiments should not meet a just interpreter. I will therefore venture to say in her name, that her sense of the unexampled condescension of the aristocracy, who appointed her to the high office she now bears, and of the gratifying loyalty of her assembled subjects, in the late enthusiastic expression of their sentiments, will not quickly pass away from her remembrance, but will recall this evening to her as one of the most agreeable of her life. She would confess freely that she feels these honours, the mere abundance of your kindness, showered down upon her for a very small service on her part; indeed she would say, as far as any thing she had done to merit them, they were totally undeserved; but at the same time she accepts these your flattering marks of approbation for her poor doings, with the profoundest respect and the deepest gratitude."

He then begged to say he was commissioned by her Majesty to state, that the *name* of the Fairy Bower did *not* originate with herself. In conclusion, he hoped he was not stepping out of his office, if he said, in the name of himself and the young court, that the eloquent and able address of an honourable and learned gentleman who had preceded him, should not pass disregarded. He hoped that none would recall this evening to memory—untainted, as it was, by a single pain—without remembering the lesson then so ably enforced. Crowns, indeed, without Truth and Virtue, are honours undeserved, and crumble to dust; whilst Virtues flourish and abide, and are themselves the brightest coronet, that can sit upon the brow of either Queen or Peasant.

Before Reginald began this speech, he had some talk with Mary Anne. He told her what he should say, and was rather puzzled at a sort of hesitation in her manner when he said he should talk of the honours being "undeserved."

"Why should I say so!" said he, in answer to her,—"why not?—you do not think the Fairy Bower called for all this, I suppose." Mary Anne saw every word she spoke was dangerous, but she felt more anxiety at that part of Reginald's speech than any thing that had happened. One reason was, she attended to what was so nearly connected with herself; whereas she carelessly listened to the rest, only turning every thing she could to her own honour and praise. Reginald also thought she ought to disclaim giving the title of the Fairy Bower; if she did not, it would be supposed she had; and now he asked her if she had named it or not, for she must state the fact publicly through him. Mary Anne was thrown into consternation by this announcement. She could not feel sure she had not committed herself. She knew she had told Lady Musgrove, and that many besides heard, that she had not invented the name. She knew also that Ellen heard; but she could not remember if she had reported her invention to Emily, by that name on the night of Monday. She thought she had *not*, or that if she had, Emily had forgotten it. It was never mentioned by that name the whole morning; they called it simply the ante-room; and the "Fairy Bower" sprung up as quite a new title among a group she joined after the lighting was finally settled. How it began she knew not, and her conscience prevented her then asking a word or making a remark, because she could not be sure whether or not she had made that name an original part of her communication with Emily. The fact was, she could not realize the effect of the lights, so the title had quite gone out of her head, till she heard every body calling it the Fairy Bower, and then she saw the appropriateness of the name, especially after the extinguishing the rival lights. What was she to do when Reginald asked her this simple question?—to hesitate was most dangerous; to say she did not know, or could not remember, fatal; to say "yes," equally fatal, as far as regarded Lady Musgrove and the elders; and to say "no," might be so as regarded all the rest. Besides, Ellen might be able to light the whole train. One device struck her: she said to Reginald, "Why say any thing about it?" He looked rather surprised, and answered, "Why not? it is much more proper that you should notice it; just tell me yes or no." She was obliged to say "No," as that word contained less of certain destruction than the other.—Who can guard all the endless points of falsehood? Till this moment Mary Anne had suffered herself to enjoy the triumphs of her situation unbroken, except with just an uneasy thought or two after the discovery of Ellen at her side. Her present uneasiness may be imagined; but we believe we may safely say her greatest suffering of the evening, did not equal a small part of Grace's. Virtue is not always its own reward, as some pretend. Virtue, or right action and feeling, sometimes endures sufferings of mind, similar to those of actual guilt. Grace had felt this in a degree all day; and now she seemed to partake and deserve those which properly belonged to Mary Anne.

Meanwhile the question was whispered about among the young people, "Who invented the title of the Fairy Bower?"—"Did you?"—"Did you?"—"I thought it was Mary Anne"—Nobody knew. Every body said every body was using it suddenly, just after the lighting, and of course all thought it was Mary Anne's name. One of the gentlemen now made the inquiry, and the result of these whispers was reported—"Nobody knew."

Mary Anne gathered hope. Again and again inquiry was made, and it began to look very mysterious.

Mr. Everard suggested it must have been a real fairy stepped in among the young folks for a few minutes. "Possibly," added he, "the same artifice employed by Oberon. —The likeness of our bower to his must strike every one—and though his fame was great in fairy land, he may well be unknown here—Let us call to mind an account of him and one of his works." Here he repeated the following lines from the Flower and the Leaf:—

"Rich sycamores with eglantine were spread,
A hedge about the sides, a covering over head;
And so the fragrant brier was wove between,
The sycamore and flowers were mixed with green,
That Nature seemed to vary the delight,
And satisfied at once the smell and sight:
The master workman of the bower was known
Thro' fairy-lands and built for Oberon."

"Who knows," continued he, "that if we search for our *incognita* as carefully as the same poet searched his bower for his Nightingale, we may be as successful—he says presently,

'At length I waked, and looking round the bower,
Searched every tree and pryed in every flower,
If any where by chance I might espy
The rural poet of the melody;
For still methought she sung not far away,
At last I found her on a laurel spray,
Close by my side she sat, and fair in sight,
Full in a line against her opposite.' "

Mr. Everard pronounced these lines with great emphasis. Grace felt amazed and miserable, for she sat next, though not close to the reciter, and opposite Mary Anne. Mr. Everard's powers of invention and adaptation seemed to her the most fairy-like events of the evening.

Meanwhile Mary Anne's hopes strengthened; she thought these effusions of Mr. Everard's would make a diversion; but Mr. Everard intended no such thing—and soon revived the inquiry, "who invented the title of the Fairy Bower?" which indeed had still been going on in the quarters most interested. After a considerable time, a murmur of small whispers, carried up something promising from the farthest end of the table, and it was reported that little Clara said she knew "*who.*"

"Is it true," asked one of the gentlemen, in a loud voice, "that the little Clara can clear this mystery?—let her send up word!"

In a short space an answer travelled up again. Clara said "*it was Emily.*"

"Emily!" said her papa, "did you give that name to the Bower?"

"No, papa," said Emily, in a very determined voice, "it was Grace Leslie."

Poor Grace! she felt as if she was shot quite through. She felt a thrill all over her, and though she did not know it, she turned exceedingly pale. "Now," thought she, "all *is* discovered! Oh, Emily!"

"Grace!" said Mr. Ward, gently—he always spoke so to her—"did you devise that pretty name?"

Grace gathered up her breath, and answered in a tone, mournful to those who were near enough to hear her, "I believe I thought of it first."

"Does she say, 'yes?' " said Mr. Ward; and her answer was reported to him, and handed down and all round the table.

"Then it is Grace, after all, who is our Fairy!" said the other gentleman; "that is greater than a Queen." While the young people began whispering, "Was it Grace? was it Grace?—I thought it was Mary Anne, did not you?"

"Why," said Constance, "you make as much fuss as if Grace had invented the *Bower*, instead of only the name; did you not hear that Mary Anne just now told Reginald Freemantle to say she had *not* invented the name?"

"Well," said Ellen, "and were you not surprised?—I am sure I was; I thought the name went with the Bower, and that Mary Anne invented both."

"Well," returned Constance, "you see she did *not*, and she says so; why will you not let Grace have the merit of the name?—not that there's much in it, it is not like the Bower."

The elder part of the company also expressed surprise at the manner in which this little fact had come out. Lady Musgrove and others praised Mary Anne highly. Several of them had heard her disclaim the title of her own accord; and her conduct seemed very "pretty," as the lady observed, with whom Mary Anne was always a favourite, —"Very pretty, indeed," she said, "Miss Mary Anne has a very fine spirit."

"It is more," said Mrs. Ward, in a low tone, "than I would say of Grace Leslie; I do not like that sly way for children, of keeping such things secret—why could she not confess at once?—and why did not every body know it was her name? it is very unnatural for a child to be so close."

"Well, I don't know," said Lady Musgrove, "it was rather modest of her to keep silence, and not to trumpet her own praises."

"And you know," said Mr. Ward, "if you blame her, you must blame Emily; for it seems she knew all the time.—By the bye, I wonder she did not speak at once; Emily is very fond of Grace, I know; and Emily is a warm-hearted girl. I certainly do wonder, my dear," said he to his wife, "that Emily did not speak without so much pumping."

"Oh," said Lady Musgrove, "it is easily accounted for; you could not expect a young girl like Emily, to be able to speak like any of you gentlemen, before a large party like this."

"Very true," replied Mr. Ward, "but Emily has a good spirit of her own, and spoke boldly enough when she did speak."

"But you remember," said Lady Musgrove, "she was afraid to come forward and crown the Queen, and let that little Grace do it all by herself; I am sure I wondered at her more than I did at Emily: it was very formidable."

Such remarks were interrupted by Mr. Everard rising, and proposing the health of Grace Leslie. He gave the reason for so doing, and made a short simple speech. Grace felt very glad it was so soon over. She now was uneasy at feeling the eyes of every body turned upon her; for she really had the feeling of taking something that did not belong to her; and her thoughts altogether began to be so confused, that she hardly knew whether the next step would not be the discovery of the rest of the deception. She could not understand Emily's declaration, or how the name could be separated from the rest of the invention; however she found the company could do so, and she gladly acquiesced. Her health was drunk, and according to the form, she had to return thanks. She deputed George as her champion; that seemed to her the most proper thing, since he was, as it were, her host; and she asked him to say as little as possible—only that she was very much surprised.

George represented he must say, 'pleased and gratified.'

"Well, so I am, I suppose," said Grace, "but I had a great deal rather it should not have been, though you know I think it very kind indeed."

George was a much better hand at a droll speech than a grave one; to make the latter in public would rather have frightened him—the former he could do with ease; and this was a tempting opportunity. He told the company that he rose in obedience to his friend Grace Leslie, who had done him the favour to appoint him her champion. He assured them from herself, she felt deeply the honour she had just received at their hands, or rather at their glasses; but so amazed was she at their unexpected kindness, that she had not time or power to ascertain her own feelings.—She supposed, however, she was both pleased and gratified. He was quite sure the company would understand his fair friend's sentiments, especially when he added, she would have much rather it had never happened; yet at the same time her gratitude was inexpressible, and therefore he would cease attempting to express it, only hoping, in her name, that some day each individual of the company present, might enjoy such honours as were now showered down upon her.

George was a great favourite, and his manner was very amusing; his speech was therefore very favourably received. When he sat down, Grace whispered to him, "Oh, George, how could you do so? I felt so very much ashamed!"

"Well," answered George, "shall I say so? you know I only said just what you told me." Grace could not deny this.

The rest of the supper went off without any thing worth relating. All seemed to enjoy themselves. Mary Anne again recovered her thoughtlessness, now she saw all had passed so safely, and she congratulated herself on her wariness and skill.

CHAPTER XXVII

Ann Boleyn.—I swear again, I would not be a Queen
For all the world.
SHAKESPEARE

ALL SUPPERS must however come to an end, and so at length did this. By degrees the room was thinned. Party after party departed, and the more domestic circle alone remained. This was the three sets of cousins. All the young ladies went up together to put on cloaks and shawls, &c., and as usual at such times, some of the events of the past evening were discussed. Isabella said she was sure Mary Anne had had honours enough, and compliments without end.

"Indeed," said Mary Anne, "it is very disagreeable; I can't bear compliments; I wonder people can like them!"

"Particularly, if they don't deserve them!" observed Emily, as coolly as she could.

Grace looked at her.

"Well, but Mary Anne did deserve all that happened tonight," said Constance.

"You don't mean to say, I suppose," said Ellen, "that every body who has a pretty idea come into her head deserves to be crowned a Queen, though certainly Mary Anne does deserve very great praise for the plan of the Bower. I suppose, Mary Anne, you mean that you feel as Grace did, according to George's droll way of expressing it."

"Yes," said Mary Anne; "but it is so ridiculous to dress you up, and call you a Queen, and be paying such compliments to you: how ridiculous it was of Mr. May to talk of my genius, taste, and modesty! and of Mr. Parry to compare me to Flora! and all the rest who spoke of my fair face and lovely brow!—such stuff, you know; and then Mr. Everard, worse than all, he talked of my beauty and loveliness, and went on more than any body, calling me 'her Majesty!'—it's so very disagreeable, when every body's looking at you, too!"

"Well, Mary Anne," said Emily, restraining her indignation for Grace's sake, "you need not complain of Mr. Everard, for I am sure he did not pay *you* any very great compliments."

"But I am sure he did though!" said Mary Anne; "and you would have thought so, if they had been to you."

"Well," returned her cousin, "I had rather you should have had such than I."

"Ah!" said Mary Anne, "that's nothing but spite, I know well enough; for you have not once treated me like the rest, or called me 'your Majesty,' the whole evening."

"Why, Mary Anne," remarked Ellen, in her dry, quiet way, "you are very unreasonable; first, you blame every body for calling you Queen, and paying you that amusing mock sort of honour, and now you blame Emily for not doing so; now, what do you *really* wish?"

"Oh, I only wish people would not be so ridiculous!" said Mary Anne, feeling she had made herself silly, and hoping to get out of the scrape.

"Yes, but, about *Emily*," persisted Ellen,—"why, then, do you blame Emily?"

"Because," said Mary Anne, "I know she was vexed, and wanted some share in the praise about the Bower; she would not come and help to crown me—I observed it all; and I know Emily has been grudging me my honours all the evening, because she thought more praise should be given to her for her part in the execution. I tried that it should be so, for I told Lady Musgrove that the others had done more than I had; but Lady Musgrove did not think so, for she said Emily could never have thought of any thing as pretty as the Bower—did she not, Ellen?"

"Yes," said Ellen; "but she said she was sure Emily helped you a great deal in the execution—and so she did; and I am sure Emily has been quite the life of every thing to-night,—and Grace too," added she, "only Grace is so quiet, one never observes what she does, only sees the effect. She is just like our river at Langham: it is a beautiful, clear, quiet stream, running silently underneath tall reeds; we can hardly see a glimpse of the water, only where the sun shines upon a few little open spots now and then, but the meadows on each side are beautifully green and bright. This little stream, too, supplies the whole village with water, making no show at all, but springing out between the stones. Now is not that just like Grace?"

Grace had not spirits to answer her kind friend as she might have done another time. The rest of the Duffs and Isabella were not disposed to join in the praise of Grace, for different reasons, and Emily was still burning with indignation at Mary Anne's late consummate impudence and affectation. At last, Charlotte Duff, who never interfered in any thing scarcely, said, "What a pretty idea that is of Ellen's! it would make a subject for Fanny to write verses upon."

"It may be pretty or not," said Ellen, "I do not care for that; but I want you to say it is true of Grace."

"To be sure it is true of Grace!" cried Emily at last, "and the only reason they don't say so is, because it is *too* true."

Charlotte meanwhile had stolen quite close to Grace, and ventured to take her hand.—"Well," thought poor Grace, "I ought to care for nothing, when I have three such dear, kind friends—how can I ever make them understand how much I love them? how much better this honour of Ellen's is, than the honour they paid me down stairs."—Yet she felt ashamed that others heard it, because she knew it was Ellen's and Emily's kind exaggeration, which others would not understand, though it was delightful to herself in proving their affection for her.

Nothing else particular passed, except at the immediate parting, which took place in the dining-room. The reader will remember that Mary Anne's and Campbell's visit to their cousins was at an end, and they were to return home to-night with their brothers and sisters. Glad enough was Mary Anne that it was so: she thought she should escape any unacceptable examination on the Fairy Bower, and it would die away naturally. Had she not been leaving, she might not have been so bold. But just before going, she remembered she must take leave of Grace, and should be expected to kiss her. She could hardly tell why she felt it so entirely impossible to do this; yet to go without would be so very remarkable. The same difficulty had struck Grace, some time before, and she thought she should see by it what Mary Anne really thought. All had taken leave—Mary Anne was in a hurry and confusion—she had lost one of her gloves—every body looked for it—it was found, and she was running after some of her party who had gone,—when Mr. Everard called her back, and reminded her she had not taken leave of the fair Grace, who had so dexterously woven her crown for her.

Mary Anne was forced to check her steps and return. With a hurried movement she approached Grace, took her hand, and quickly kissed her.—"Good bye, Grace," said she.

Grace coloured crimson in a moment—Mary Anne, scarlet; and she ran as fast as she could into the hall, to join her party. Grace felt very uneasy at finding the eyes of Mr. Everard and Mrs. Ward fixed steadily upon her. She knew she looked very remarkable, and was much relieved to withdraw from their gaze as soon as possible. Grace attended her mamma to her room, and Mrs. Leslie began talking to her. Presently she said, to Grace's surprise, "Grace, my dear, I hope you have had a pleasant evening—has any thing happened? you seemed enjoying yourself very much."

"Yes, I did, mamma, very much," answered Grace.

"But then, my dear, why are you so dull now?" asked her mamma.

Poor Grace said she did not know that she was dull.

Her mamma then very kindly asked if she was well.

Grace answered, "Yes, quite well."

Mrs. Leslie then told her she must be quite tired and excited by all her dissipation, and advised her to go to bed, and not to sit up talking at all with Emily, though they must have a great deal to say. "Else, my dear child," added she, "I shall have you quite ill; or perhaps one of those sad palpitations will come on; so good night, my dear little girl," and she gave her a kiss.

Poor Grace! her mamma's words recalled *all* her troubles; how she wished she might tell her all! but that she knew was more impossible than any thing. She knew her mamma never encouraged her to tell any thing unfavourable of her companions, yet she thought she never could feel easy with such a great bar between herself and her mamma. "It is not," thought she, "like George's quizzing people, or any thing else that has ever happened before to me: this is such a *great* thing, and so many other events are tangled together in it—my palpitation and the broken cup; and then Hanson is connected, besides Emily's part; then those strange words of Mr. Everard's, and I cannot think why he would find out the person who invented the name of the Fairy Bower!"

By this time Grace had reached her room, where was Emily. Emily had not begun undressing, but was walking up and down the room. There was a strange contrast between the appearance of the two young friends. Emily was highly excited, and looked quite fresh and ready to begin the evening again. Grace's motives for exertion had ceased; namely, the pleasure of assisting to entertain others, and the desire of not betraying that any thing was wrong by her manner; and now that she was alone with the only person who knew the secret, she no longer struggled against the sad feelings that oppressed her. She looked very worn and sorrowful. "Oh, Grace!" cried Emily, "I have been so impatient for you! who could ever have supposed such things would have happened? I am really nearly wild with anger; and I am angry too with you, for it was all your fault. It was all for your sake I was silent; and up-stairs, too, I was just going to tell all, only you looked at me so imploringly."

"Indeed," said Grace, "I know it is all my fault, and I am very sorry indeed that you are angry with me."

Emily now scolded Grace for her simplicity, and told her there was nobody to blame but "that mean and false Mary Anne." "I had no idea," said she, "Mary Anne was so bad, though I knew she was silly and vain; besides I really did not think she was clever enough for such a deception."

Emily did not remember that much of Mary Anne's cleverness, was owing to her own and Grace's silence. Mary Anne had not been *clever* enough to deceive Emily, who had a great deal of observation; besides, indolent people, who seem to have no wit or cleverness, and are thought very dull, or even stupid, have sometimes cleverness, or cunning, enough to deceive others a great deal wiser, better, and cleverer than themselves. A very little cleverness goes a great way in a fraud, because good sort of people are not suspicious; they think others like themselves, till they find out any person false. And again, this sort of cleverness is soon learned, and is less trouble to acquire than any other. Mary Anne had gained all she had in less than twenty-four hours! but then she had prepared her mind for it *silently* for many years; as we before said, she availed herself of her sisters' talents and labours; she chose to learn duets, that she might play and be praised with less trouble before company; and she had at times done sly things, which nobody knew, to get admired. All these practices, and the habit of mind she had thereby acquired, prepared her for this almost incredible piece of falsehood. Step by step she had led herself into it; and even when in the midst, she felt very little pain of conscience; she felt pain and fear a very few times, but it was *lest all should be discovered*. The sin in the sight of God,—the wrong to her neighbour,—the injury she was doing her own soul, never distressed her; though she was every day hearing all these things, and had been doing so all her life, with her mamma and her governess, Miss Newmarsh. She had been blunting her conscience; even Mr. Everard's words, startling as they might be thought to one under her circumstances, scarcely touched her: she was thinking of herself and her situation. Part of his addresses she did not even hear,—part she did not understand,—other parts she mistook, and turned to compliments to herself, as may be seen by the remarks she made to her young companions afterwards. In what a different state was Grace's conscience! She therefore could not understand any thing at all about Mary Anne; it quite frightened her to allow her mind to dwell upon her conduct or feelings, and she turned away to any other point in the transaction as a relief. If she could not *think* of Mary Anne's conduct, much less could she speak of it; and she could find no reply to Emily's last remark.

Emily went on observing and lamenting Grace's dulness, and saying she was wishing to have a long talk, for she was not tired at all:

Grace said *she* was not tired, but that her mamma desired her to go to bed, because perhaps she would be ill.

Emily remembered how ill poor Grace seemed before the party began, and then wondered how she had gone through every thing as well as she had. Very kindly and properly she gave up her wish for sitting up, and before long the young friends sought their beds.

CHAPTER XXVIII

Oh, that our lives, which flee so fast,
In purity were such,
That not an image of the past,
Should fear that pencil's touch!
WORDSWORTH'S *Memory*

THE DEPARTURE of the two cousins made a change in the proceedings of those left behind. The three girls were much more in the drawing-room, with their two mammas, and George sometimes went out for skating, or amusing himself with some young gentlemen in the neighbourhood. They usually however passed their evenings together in the study. There was another change, namely, that invitations were accepted to some houses for the children. While Mary Anne and Campbell were with them, they could go no where, where there was dancing or cards,—several such parties were now in prospect. This morning Grace was with her mamma about ten o'clock, as usual. Grace had not her own lively, easy manner, but her mamma made no remark, thinking she was tired after yesterday's excitement and fatigue. They read the psalms and lessons, as usual, together. Grace was exceedingly amazed at many passages in both, especially in the psalms; they seemed so applicable to what went on yesterday. Yet she shrank from allowing it, even to herself. The first words that struck her were, "*They imagine deceitful words*, &c." The idea of Mary Anne came painfully into her head as she read that verse, for it came to her turn, and she wished she could get rid of it. But the beginning five verses of the following psalm, were very much more striking to her, and she almost wished they had not come to-day. Also she seemed never before to have noted so particularly the evening psalm, which is a peculiarly beautiful one; the thirty-eighth verse she thought she should now never forget. "But then," thought she, "have I 'kept innocency' in this case?—oh! I am afraid not; though I have tried to take heed unto the thing that is right." One of these lessons was about Abraham not saying Sarah was his wife. She thought this very remarkable to come to-day; it seemed so like what she had done. "Ah!" thought she, "I must not blame Mary Anne, I see, for I have done the same!—no, not *quite* the same, added she, in thought, "I know my fault is not quite the same, but still I am afraid it is very bad." Grace found something more of comfort for herself in the second morning lesson; it was part of the sermon on the mount, and though she knew it very well, (it was a very favourite chapter of hers, and contained the very verse Ellen had spoken of to her the day before,) she now thought those words of our Saviour's more beautiful than ever; and as she read, "Blessed are they that mourn, for they shall be comforted," the tears filled her eyes, so that she was afraid she could not have gone on: but she got over it, and went through above half the chapter, when her mamma stopped her, as she sometimes did, and said she would finish reading, for she saw Grace was tired.

Grace thought she had never before observed so much the meaning of the psalms and lessons which she read. "How good," thought she, "it is of mamma to read these with me every day!—ah, if Mary Anne's mamma did so with her:—especially the psalms, I am sure she could never have done such a thing; the psalms speak so much against deceit and falsehood, and indeed against every thing wrong."

Mrs. Leslie talked to her little girl on the yesterday's proceedings. There was a great deal Grace could talk freely about; but she felt very uncomfortable at the constant watchfulness she was obliged to keep up, lest she should say any thing that should betray Mary Anne. "This cannot be right," thought she.

Once her mamma said, "So I find Fanny Duff writes verses! have you seen any, Grace?"

Grace was almost afraid what her answer might lead to, but she replied she had—they were about a bird.

"Ah," said her mamma, "that is what I heard of; and it was from one line that Mary Anne got her pretty idea of the Bower—do you remember that line, Grace?—

'And live in *bowers* with thee.' "

"Yes, mamma, very well," said Grace—"Ah!" thought she, "*that* line was the beginning of all my troubles; for if I had not heard it perhaps I should never have mentioned my idea of the unfortunate Fairy Bower."

Mrs. Leslie then remarked, "How like Mary Anne's Bower is to the plans of your cousins in Hampstead; but I suppose, Grace, you *did* help a good deal: in the flowers, I know you did, because of that fine long tendril, which you remember every body was so amused about."

This danger had never before struck Grace,—that her mamma would recognize her style of workmanship. She now wondered her mamma did not suspect, since it was well known that the decorations at Hampstead originated with Grace; and ever since she first showed her skill that way, her cousins were very anxious she should come and assist in the preparations. But every thing was at present surprising to Grace: she answered her mamma's question as truly and simply as she could, and some other subject was introduced.

Mrs. Leslie was in some respects like her daughter Grace; or rather, the daughter inherited some of the mother's excellencies: one was a great simplicity of mind, and a heart perfectly unsuspicious,—not that Mrs. Leslie was wanting in sense; she had common sense to a most uncommon degree, but she had not that quality usually called *knowledge of the world,* which quickly discovers evil and low motives in every action. Like the genius of our country's law, she believed every body innocent, till proved guilty; and though often rallied on her simplicity, she never yet had lost it. Many other mammas would have put Mr. Everard's remark, the discovery of the originator of the name of the Fairy Bower, and her own surprise, together, and would have got a notion of the truth. Had such an idea of so young a girl as Mary Anne—so strictly brought up, too—come into her head, she would have almost discarded it again. She did not *forget* Mr. Everard's remark, but as yet it had made no impression.

This week the dinner party took place, which was intended to greet Mrs. Leslie. It was a large party, and several guests joined it in the evening. The children had very little to do with it, but were for some time in the room. Grace was more noticed by old and new friends of her mamma, than she ever had been before. There was a good deal of music, and Mrs. Leslie sang. Grace was delighted at this, for she thought no one but her aunt Stanley, and one celebrated public singer she once heard, sung like her mamma. Grace, though such a child, and a fond daughter, was not quite wrong in her judgment. Mrs. Leslie *was* a very beautiful singer, and the whole room was perfectly charmed. Afterwards she was warmly thanked, and congratulated on not having given up her singing.

Mrs. Leslie said she did not mean to do that, and she had kept it up more than any thing, for the sake of her little girl, who she thought some day would sing.

Some one asked if Grace had begun yet.

"Not regularly," said Mrs. Leslie, "but she likes to sit and hear me, and she shows a taste for it."

A gentleman present shrugged his shoulders, and asked if it was possible that Mrs. Leslie could waste such a voice and such science on a child.

"I do not call it *waste*," replied Mrs. Leslie, smiling, "but then, you know, I am a fond mamma."

The gentleman answered that a hurdy-gurdy, or a ballad singer, would please a child equally; and that it was distressing to think of such powers as hers being so spent.

Mrs. Leslie laughed, and assured him her little girl was a better judge than that, and showed a decided taste for music of all sorts, and especially for singing. "I can assure you," she added, "she knows as well as I do, when I am out of practice; and when it is so, often prepares the piano and opens my books of a morning, as a sort of hint. I dare say she will have observed I have a cold to-night."

"Well," said the gentleman, politely, "she must be a greater critic than any one here, for no one else could have discovered it."

Mrs. Leslie was made to sing more than once again; and in one song, an English ballad, a great favourite of Grace's, the little girl crept round the company, and at last got close to her mamma's side. After it was finished, little Grace whispered, "Mamma, I am afraid you have a cold."

Mrs. Leslie saw the gentleman heard this whisper, and did not wish it to be brought into general talk, so answered, "Yes, my dear, I have a little cold," and began playing an air.

CHAPTER XXIX

Remember when the judgment's weak
The prejudice is strong.
SONG

MEANWHILE A CONVERSATION was going on at a sofa, between Mrs. Ward and Mrs. Mason, the lady who had always spoken in praise of Mary Anne Duff. They began talking of Mrs. Leslie's singing, and Mrs. Ward said she was glad to hear it again, and to find that Mrs. Leslie had lost nothing.—"She really gives up so much to her little girl, that I was quite afraid she would neglect it, though she told me she did not mean to lose her singing, for Grace's sake."

"That child is very little of her age, and not a very fine looking girl," remarked Mrs. Mason.

"Not at all *fine*, I should say delicate," returned Mrs. Ward; "yet she can be animated too, and sometimes her eyes are very expressive when she looks full at you; but I do not admire them in a child, it is too much like a grown person to be pleasant."

"You make me laugh," said the other lady, "to call that little girl like a grown person; I can hardly fancy her ever grown up. Now your Emily, in manner, or Mary Anne Duff, in person, are much more like young women: Mary Anne is a fine promising girl."

"Yes, but her manners are not what I like," said Mrs. Ward, "she is as much deficient in self-possession as Grace is overburdened with it."

"Do you call that little girl womanly and self-possessed?" exclaimed this lady.

"To be sure I do," returned her hostess; "why, only think how she went through that scene of the coronation! a very formidable scene, for a child! with every eye fixed upon her, and Mr. Everard paying her every compliment he could think of. She seemed to mind it no more than if she was alone in the room; while Mary Ann looked so silly and sheepish, I was quite ashamed of her.—You see," said she, laughing, "I am rather unreasonable, but I do believe Emily would just hit the right medium, only she would have been much cleverer—more theatrical than Grace."

"Certainly she did go through all that very well," said Mrs. Mason, "but you would not compare Emily and that little Grace; there must be several years difference between them."

"About two, I think," said Mrs. Ward.

The lady was much surprised, and began to think of Grace with a little more respect. Yet she said she could not admire her as much as Emily or her cousins, the Duffs. —"But," she added, "they are all fine girls, and so very clever."

"Grace is clever, certainly," said Mrs. Ward, "but I don't quite know what to make of her. I think her mamma is deceived in her, though she is so much with her. I think Grace rather a close character, and not quite to be trusted. Her mamma has the most implicit confidence in her: she tells me, and she *believes*, that Grace practises now every morning an hour, before breakfast; but I have my reasons for thinking it is not the case: Mary Anne found out something of the kind by questioning Emily one morning. I did not choose to tell her mamma. Besides, I don't know what *you* thought the other night, but *I* was not at all satisfied with that business about the Fairy Bower; there was something very odd about it, and I cannot help thinking Grace got more credit about it than she deserved; she turned so pale when she said she invented the name, that I could not help noticing it; and when she took leave of Mary Anne that night, the colour rushed into her cheeks, and she looked as guilty as possible, and could not at all bear my eye. Besides, the children were so exceedingly amazed—they were so sure before that it was Mary Anne's own naming. It was *not* hers, because you know she said so before us all in the drawing-room; but I cannot believe it is Grace's, somehow or other, and I am sure there is some mystery about it."

Mrs. Mason agreed that the long silence about it at supper was very strange, and reminded Mrs. Ward of her husband's remark at the time, about Emily's behaviour.

"It was *that* remark," replied Mrs. Ward, "that first put these notions into my head, though I noticed Grace's turning so pale before that. Emily is very fond of her new friend, and if Grace had hinted the name was her own idea, Emily might wish to give her the chance of the distinction. Emily is a generous girl to those she loves."

"Well, really," said Mrs. Mason, "what you say seems very likely; what a shabby little thing she must be! I never liked her looks much, as you might see."

"I do not say it *is* so," answered Mrs. Ward, "but I shall keep a watch. Oh!" added she, "one other incident I forgot: the morning after the party, the three girls were sitting at work with us, and talking over the evening, when Ellen, who you know is as simple as an infant, asked how it was that *Grace* had invented the name of the Fairy Bower; and she reminded Emily of '*what she said*' (I don't know what it was) on the Monday night. Emily was silent, though I saw she tried to answer once or twice. Ellen again pressed the subject, and Emily said, in some confusion, 'Whatever I said then, was a mistake; for Grace *did* invent the name.' Ellen persisted in her inquiries, and said, 'Then I suppose, Grace, you and Mary Anne talked it over together, and you then suggested *that* name for it,—was it so?' Grace answered, 'Something of that kind,' and seemed very much annoyed, especially as I had all the time fixed my eyes upon her. Ellen then remarked, that it was very clever of Grace, for that nobody could have guessed by daylight it would be such an appropriate name; for though it looked very pretty, there was nothing *Fairy* in it, till the lights were lit, and she appealed to me. I could with truth agree; for next morning, when the bird was gone, and all the real flowers dead or withered, and the ends of candle and sockets appearing here and there, with a good deal of grease about it, it did look really deplorable; I could hardly believe it was that elegant little device we had so much admired.—I cannot understand this affair, I say, but I am sure all is not as it should be."

Mrs. Mason agreed in this opinion, and some other subject was started.

CHAPTER XXX

Give unto me made lowly wise,
The spirit of self-sacrifice.
WORDSWORTH

T HE MORNING AFTER the juvenile party, Emily and Grace had a long talk together, on their unfortunate secret. Emily's wish for revealing it was a good deal abated—the *eclat* she had anticipated, and which in the event had so greatly surpassed her anticipation, had passed away; nothing could restore it to Grace; and Mary Anne too was gone,—her exposure must now be private. Yet Emily did wish the truth should be known, though she was not so pressing for it as yesterday. There was another reason that had some weight with her—the broken cup and saucer. Grace had told her, her hopes about Hanson's undertaking. Hanson was going that day to visit among her friends, and had promised to go to John Edwards, the workman at Spode's, the very first thing. She had taken the broken pieces with her, to match. Grace, as well as Emily, had had a private conference with her just before she left. Grace had been some time talking to Emily, to persuade her to let them mention the accident to her mamma. Emily was against this, because she said if Hanson got a new cup, it would be so much better to tell the accident, and give the cup all at once.—"Why should we vex mamma and make her angry with us, when we can do without?" said she; "mamma will not care for it, and will be very much pleased when she sees the cup."

Grace had thought of this too, but it seemed to her more proper to mention the accident. She could not make her friend think so; she therefore tried another way, more like Emily's own arguments, and said, "But suppose Hanson cannot match the china after all; how much worse it will be to have to tell it then than now.—And besides, it may be very long perhaps after I have gone," added she, quite alarmed at the thought.

"Well," said Emily, "you need not look so frightened, suppose it is! you know you would only escape a scolding, and it would all come upon me,—if I am not gone to school first."

Grace next represented, that it might be discovered meanwhile, for the servants must know.

Emily said nobody knew but Hanson, and that she said she had told nobody, and did not mean to do so; that she was gone, and had taken the broken pieces away. She likewise reminded Grace that the mention of this accident, would very likely lead to a discovery of the affair of the Fairy Bower, since Mrs. Leslie would hear of Grace not being well, and would find everything out by her questions. She also remarked that Grace was fond of interfering with other people,—that if she had not, the affair of the Fairy Bower would have come out long ago, through herself; and that now it was the same about the cup. She said it was very unkind of Grace to refuse her request, when she had so faithfully kept *her* secret; that she should also remember that it was much more her business than Grace's, for she had broken the cup; and that the fault was towards her own mamma, not Grace's.

All this was true, and some of it reasonable. Grace felt the last representations as a little rebuke; she was much ashamed of having urged the motives above-mentioned for telling of the accident, since her arguments had not been successful; she therefore said nothing, and acquiesced. She however felt more doubt and pain about it than any thing else she had done. She was herself a little afraid of Mrs. Ward: she would have preferred not telling her, on that account: it would, as Emily said, be *pleasanter* to have a cup to replace the broken one with. Again, she was aware of the danger of a discovery of the whole secret, and she shrank from nothing so much as being the means of this,—from *nothing* so much, except herself telling a falsehood, or doing any thing she knew to be wrong. To do Grace justice, however, in spite of these two motives, she had much rather have told Mrs. Ward; she would gladly have gone that moment and told it herself, if Emily would have let her; and it was this strong wish she felt, that rather satisfied Grace she was not doing quite wrong in consenting to act by her friend's wishes, rather than her own. Emily, too, was afraid of her mamma; and this it was that induced her, as it were, to make a compact with Grace, that the one secret should be set against the other. Emily did not mean any deceit; she thought her meaning and feeling very fair and natural. It was natural, and it *might* be fair, but it was not quite right, if she thought her mamma expected to be told of such accidents; and Grace's judgment concerning it was a much safer one. It is right to be prudent, and to look forward as to the consequences of our actions. Our Lord bids us be "wise as serpents." It is right also *not* to be prudent, and not to look forward to the consequences of our actions. Our Lord also says the children of this world, are in their generation *wiser* than the children of light. He would not have us wise in this sense. God has given us *sense* to discover when we are to do the one or when the other; and he has promised us His Holy Spirit, to enlighten our natural sense, and to enable us to bear consequences, whatever they may be. He also who can still the raging wind and tempest, can, in one moment, turn away from us consequences, however unavoidable and dreadful they may seem to us; so that we need never fear, if we are, as Grace said, "keeping innocency, and taking heed unto the thing that is right." This temper is called forth much more in small trials, such as the one before us, than in great ones; because great actions and trials are usually more public; indeed that makes them called *great*. Just so, large and coarse paintings have much more effect to a greater number of spectators, than small delicate ones. The broad strokes *tell* more, and look much bolder and brighter; they may also have cost much less labour. This actually was the case with Mary Anne and Grace. Mary Anne's conduct and manner, even though not very good, *told* well. Lady Musgrove, Mrs. Mason, and others in the room, praised her very much indeed. She contrived to patch up, as it were, enough goodness for that one public night. But *her* goodness would not stand the test of every day's small trials. The observant reader will have noticed this in her sad envy of Grace—before this grand piece of wickedness,—in her desire of her cousin George's attention, and in very many pieces of folly she allowed herself to indulge in. People who go through daily trials well, will go through great trials well—of that we may be sure. There is an old proverb, "Take care of the pence; the shillings and pounds will take care of themselves." Nothing is more true than this sentiment, as applied to matters of conduct. It certainly would have been safer if Emily had done as her friend wished, and not deferred telling her mamma. Grace perhaps could press it no farther.

CHAPTER XXXI

New scenes arise . . .
THOMPSON

T HIS WEEK was one of the children's parties at a neighbour's house. Grace of course accompanied them, and we had best hear her account of it to her mamma, when she returned. They had had such a very pleasant evening! every thing was right. Mrs. Wallis and her grown-up daughter were so kind and good, and arranged every thing so nicely. They had dancing and cards, and Grace had both danced and played at cards.

Mrs. Leslie asked her little girl if they played for money, and if she had any with her.

"We did not play for money, mamma," said Grace, "Mrs. and Miss Wallis came and arranged it all; and in one game they set up a pretty glass ship for the winner, and a nice little girl, the youngest among us, got it, which pleased them all very much, for she could hardly play at all, and some one or other was obliged to tell her. Then the dancing was quite as pleasant; we had some quadrilles, and then country dances: some were very odd; there was one half a slow tune, and half quick, very funny indeed, and very pretty; but I did not dance in that."

"Who played for you?" asked her mamma.

"Miss Wallis, all the time, but once," answered Grace, "and then she was tired: and mamma, you will be almost frightened to hear what I did, *I* played that one tune for them."

The next week another party of the same kind occurred, and Grace was full of anticipation. It was to be in London, and she was sorry to hear she should see none of those who were at the last party, and very few who were at the Wards. The young people came in from this party full of disgust. The three Wards were very open in expressing it. George said he would not go there again, there was such cheating at cards. Emily said that it was as bad in the dancing, and that she was black and blue with being shoved and pushed about; while Ellen dwelt upon the scenes at supper time.

Mr. Ward remarked upon Grace having said nothing, and asked whether she looked grave because she was shocked at the party, or at his children's accounts of it?

Grace felt confused at being thus publicly called on, and said it was not such a nice party as that at Mrs. Wallis's; she had never been at such a noisy one before.

"And I suppose," said Mr. Ward, "you will be as displeased with it as the others, when you talk it over alone with them."

Grace certainly felt displeased enough, and told her mamma a good deal of what went on; she felt it much easier to do so than if she had known the young people there. Of some she did not even know the names, though the names of the leaders of mischief, at such parties, usually transpire and are bandied about. "Oh, mamma," said Grace, "I have quite changed my mind since the other day; then, I wondered why Mrs. Duff and Miss Newmarsh could object to cards and dancing, and now I quite agree with them; I do not wish ever to see cards or dancing again.—You cannot think how shocking it was! And first I thought it was because they played for money, and then I remembered the other night they played for a ship, and might have been violent and unfair if they had liked. Then I thought the fault in the dancing was because we had only country dances, but we had them too last week."

Mrs. Leslie asked what was so very bad; and Grace said, "It was nothing but a romp at first, and a fight at last: some of the young ladies would be always at the top, and danced up and down in a sad boisterous way; and after a great deal of pushing and shoving, some of the boys got to fighting. Then the cards were as bad; what George said, mamma, was really true; they *did* cheat,—I saw them; but I think it was in fun at first. Then when it was discovered, they began to quarrel and were so violent that *we* got out of the way. I am sure I hope there will be no more parties while I am here."

Mrs. Leslie reminded her little girl, that there were two ways of doing all things that were proper—a right way and a wrong way. "But you know, my dear Grace," added she, "that I am always afraid of too much dissipation for you." She then told her little girl it was time for her to go to bed.

There was one remark of Emily's, in their conversation on the morning after the grand party at home, which had made a great impression on Grace. This was her saying that Grace was fond of interfering with other people's actions. She thought over the whole transaction of the Bower, and she found that was the case; but then, in excuse for herself, she remembered that Emily had not only spoken of it to her, but forced the secret from her. "Ah!" thought she, "if Emily had taken it all upon herself, i should not only *not* have prevented it, but should have been really glad, on *some* accounts;" meaning her present reserve towards her dear mamma. Emily's remark however led her to reflect on several things; and one was the difference betweenwhat should be her *own* part and feelings, and Emily's. She then tried to put herself in Emily's plae, when she first suspected the deceit. She saw in a moment that she should not have been able to rest, till she had made it certain one way or other. What a dreadful injury to Mary Anne, though only in thought. She next saw that the means Emily took to ascertain the fact, were the readiest and most natural in her power. It was much more unpleasant to find out the truth through Mary Anne, even if Emily could get at her alone, than through herself; and looking on it so, Emily's conduct seemed much more fair to her now than it did at the time. She thought how angry she should be if any one took away Emily's *credit* in any thing; and though at the time, and even now, she thought the *credit* nothing worth speaking of, still Emily was right in wishing it to come upon the proper owner. When she thus distinguished her own feelings and line of conduct from Emily's, she saw she might have been very wrong in compelling Emily, as she did, to act according to her own views. "How much *thought*," said she to herself, "it requires to act right! Now several days have passed, and I have only just discovered this! yet I wanted it at a moment's warning. I hope, I am sure, it will be a lesson to me, as mamma always says, and that I shall remember it all the rest of my life, not to interfere with other people's actions. I see now it was right for Emily to wish Mary Anne exposed, and to try and see the matter set right, and it was right of me to wish to shelter Mary Anne."

Grace got a little comfort by this discovery: she thought her small piece of deceit *might* be, perhaps, more than excused,—it might be right. But the comfort she might gain on one sight, she lost, poor little girl, on the other; for there was now a new point doubtful in her conduct,—her having unduly interfered. She was not, however, of that weak cast of heart, which would make herself more guilty than she was; nor did she brood over such things. Hers was a healthy habit of mind, that turned her failings, her pains, and her pleasures even, to some good account, present or future. She therefore rose relieved by these reflections; especially after reading that morning with her mamma;

—for she found a verse in the Psalms, which seemed to show, it might be right at one time to "hold the tongue," and at some other time (or as she interpreted it, some other person would be right) to reprove and set their evil ways before those who had erred.

It was this morning that Mrs. Leslie said to her little girl, that she hoped in all this dissipation, she did not forget her prayers, night and morning.

Grace said she did not, and she added, "I think, mamma, dissipation, as you call it, must make people remember them more than ever."

Mrs. Leslie was rather surprised at her child's remark, for it was not exactly one herself would have made. It had been trouble and trial with her that had led her to think more and more seriously; perhaps had she known all her little daughter's present feelings and experience, she would have found it was not *quite* so different from her own; there *was* pain of some kind in both. Mrs. Leslie said, "I am glad, my dear Grace, that you think so; I asked you because I did not quite know about Emily."

"Oh, mamma," cried Grace, warmly, "I can assure you Emily is much more particular in that respect than I am.—And," she added, in a lower tone, "do you know, she has four lines taken from that verse in the psalms, 'I will lay me down in peace and take my rest; for it is Thou, Lord, only that makest me to dwell in safety.' She says she could not go to sleep she is sure without saying these lines. I wish I could have learnt them, but I did not like to ask her to say them over again."

Mrs. Leslie said she was glad to hear all this of Emily; and added, that Grace had no temptation in that respect.

"No, indeed, mamma, I have not," said Grace, "and I admire Emily so very much about it; you cannot think how right and proper she has always been; I am sure Constance could not have been more so."

"Then, my dear, you still retain your admiration of Constance."

"Yes, indeed, mamma, I do; I think she is quite wonderful, though only a little girl."—Then there came suddenly into Grace's head a thought how shocked Constance would be if she knew of her sister's conduct—if it should ever come out! She paused, and something like a sigh escaped her.

Her mamma asked her what she was thinking of.

She said she was thinking how shocked Constance would be at any body about her doing any thing wrong.

Her mamma said, "That was an odd thought, Grace; for in such a large family the little ones must often be naughty, and Fanny, I hear, is not always very good."

"I meant, mamma," said Grace, "any thing *very* bad."

"My dear child," said Mrs. Leslie, "what could put such an idea into your head? why do you think it likely any of the little Duffs should do any thing *very bad?*"

Poor Grace found how dangerous the most common conversation could become, under any circumstances of mystery. This reflection turned her mind on her own misdoings, and she thought how wrong Constance would think she had been, and that herself would never have got into such a situation. She however answered, "I was only thinking, mamma, if they *did*, how shocked Constance would be."

"Well, my dear," said Mrs. Leslie, half smiling, "I think you have rather odd thoughts just now."

Grace was afraid of saying another word.

CHAPTER XXXII

Little again! nothing but low and little!
SHAKESPEARE

WE HAVE FORESTALLED some of the events of the next week, and must now continue them. Grace accompanied her young friends to another party close by; it was a small and a quiet one,—no cards and no dancing; there were puzzles and quiet games. George found out that Grace could play at chess, and played with her. She was a better player than he expected, and she beat him the two first games: the first he thought accident, but the second he was provoked about, and determined to take more pains. Grace was very anxious about this third game, certainly, for George had been rather provoking and contemptuous. At first he wanted to take off his queen, and then to give her the move. She thought this only good-natured; but after being beaten the first game, he talked of its being "all chance, as if he could not beat any *little* girl!" Grace *was* a little girl, and she did not care for being thought so; but she did not like to be called so by George before strangers. George made such a racket about it, that a good many of the company were attracted, and two or three gentlemen came and looked over. Grace was very glad to beat, but said nothing. One of the gentlemen was very much pleased, and said, "Why don't you crow? why don't you clap your wings, little bird? if I were you I should stand upon the table and crow!"

Grace laughed, but she *was* very much pleased.

George would have another game, and a very tough one it was. Grace lost her queen, and George triumphed in rather an unmanly manner. Soon after, Grace forked George's queen with her knight. It was neatly done, and the gentlemen were delighted. After this the game became tiresome, and some gave over looking on. It was a drawn game. Grace was more than satisfied: she did not expect to win, for she saw George was a better player than she was. The gentlemen however made a good deal of her play. Grace had good sense; she was not persuaded to believe she played a bit better than she thought before. As they put away the men, for they were very handsome, and there was a box for them, Grace said to George, he must beat *her* some other time.

"Ah, you think I can't," said George, "but I can, and you'll see!"

Grace said she did not think so—that she knew he would beat in the end, for he played a better game than she did.

George neither believed her sincerity nor her judgment. He did not think her *good* enough for the one, nor *clever* enough for the other. He did her wrong. Grace saw it, and it made her smile to herself.

This evening also the elders of the family dined out; and Mrs. Leslie told Grace that some old friends of hers wished to see her little girl, and she must take her some day. Grace wondered very much why people should like to see children, and said she was sure they only said so from kindness.—"I am sure, mamma," continued she, "I know some ladies, who had rather I was not in the room to be spoken to, and yet they talk to me, and to you of me."

Mrs. Leslie told her little girl she had better not say things of that kind, nor think them,—but speak when she was spoken to, try never to be in the way, and be obliged to any body who was kind to her.

"But, mamma," said Grace, "I really cannot help liking some people, even if they are grown up, better than others I hope that is not wrong. Now I am sure I should like aunt William and aunt Stanley, if they were not my aunts; and I should like you, if you were not my mamma;" and the tears started into poor Grace's eyes at the supposition.—"And then," continued she, "I am sure there are other people I should not like much if they were my aunts; is this wrong, mamma?"

"It depends on your reasons, my dear child; but you know you have not much now to do with grown people, so you need not think about it."

After a pause of consideration, Grace said, "What a good remark, mamma, that is of yours, for now I think of it, I always can tell my reasons for not liking any body of my own sort of age, but I never can find out exactly why I don't like grown up people. Of course it is as you say, and I need not think about it. Do you think I shall be able to tell why I do not like grown people when I am grown up myself?—can you, mamma?"

"Of course, my dear child, I think I have reason for liking some people better than others, for else, you know, I should never have married your papa?"

This answer was a great comfort to Grace; but it was also a great distress. She thought, "Then of course mamma must have loved papa better than any body else in the whole world; and yet mamma never saw him after I was two years old." She had never before realized her mamma's loss; and she lost herself in thinking how thought-less she must have been till this moment. Seeing so many families, with both parents living, prepared her for these thoughts; besides a little incident which had very much contributed to the first part of her conversation. At the small party she had just been at, was Mrs. Mason, who talked a good deal to Grace. She made her come and sit with her on the sofa, praised her hair and her eyes, and alluded to Mr. Everard's *compliments* to her, as she called them. Grace did not like this, and longed to be rude and run away, but she thought her mamma would not approve of her doing so; she therefore sat still. Mrs. Mason then went on telling her, that she did not wonder at Mr. Everard admiring her so much, for that once he admired her mamma very much, and she should not wonder if he were to be her papa after all.—"Should you like Mr. Everard for a papa, my dear?"

Grace stared at the lady in such a way, that Mrs. Mason felt the meaning of Mrs. Ward's remark, that Grace's eyes were like those of a grown person. At length she said, "Mr. Everard is my godpapa."

"Yes, my dear, I know *that*," said the lady, "but I mean your *papa*—your real papa."

Grace still fixed her eyes in Mrs. Mason's face, and replied with a very proper tone and manner, "What do you mean!—my papa is dead!"

Grace had never before mentioned her papa to any stranger, and she felt as if she had been wrong in doing so now. Mrs. Mason actually was annoyed, and though an unusual circumstance with her, was at a loss for an answer. She however said, "I know it, my dear; but don't you know people can marry again? and if your mamma married Mr. Everard, he would be your papa?"

Grace did not think, this time, whether her mamma would approve it or not, but as soon as she could, she slid off the sofa, and escaped to the other end of the room. —Soon after her games of chess began. Mrs. Mason's remarks had made her very uncomfortable; she had never chanced to have heard such made before. When her mamma alluded to her papa, she felt very much re-assured, and thought it exceedingly singular, since Mrs. Leslie very rarely mentioned him. She did not dislike Mr. Everard, or even feel much afraid of him now. She had seen a good deal of him, and understood him a little, and she saw he was kind to *her*; but when she went to bed, she got an opportunity, when Emily did not see her, of having a long look at her papa's picture, and felt very much satisfied at the conclusion she came to, that it was not in the least like Mr. Everard. Few persons can understand the effect of remarks of this kind upon an observant and sensitive child, in Grace's circumstances; if they did, they would not be so cruel as lightly to inflict such pain. The ignorance a child is conscious of in such matters, adds to the sting, and should be its protection. There is an injustice, too, both to parents and children, as the effect of such communications unadvisedly made, may produce lasting and irremediable evils, and every parent has a right to make such an important communication in the way that seems most suitable to the dispositions of children. But Mrs. Mason was not of a character to take such things into consideration; she was of social disposition, and had very little to do besides finding all the amusement she could among her neighbors.

CHAPTER XXXIII

How partial parents' doting eyes,
No child was e'er so fair and wise.
GAY'S *Fables*

THE NEXT DAY there was another large dinner party at home. The guests were principally neighbours of Mr. and Mrs. Ward, and strangers to Mrs. Leslie. Mr. Everard, however, was there,—also Mrs. Mason. The children appeared, as usual at such times, only in the drawing-room. After the gentlemen came up, there was music. Mr. Everard, who was very fond of music, and understood it thoroughly, was near the piano, as usual; he asked Mrs. Leslie if Grace played well enough to be asked to sit down.

"Indeed she does," said a nice-looking young lady—the Miss Wallis, before mentioned; "Mrs. Leslie, I was quite surprised at your little girl the other evening at our house; the children were dancing, and some one proposed a new dance, with a slow air and a country dance. I really did not wish to undertake it, for I dare not play for dancing without the notes before me. Emily went and brought up your little girl; she said she was not afraid, and I assure you she played for a good half hour without a single mistake, as steady as old Time."

Mrs. Leslie was pleased to hear Grace could do such a thing, as it was quite new to her. She said Grace had mentioned playing one dance for them. She asked what slow air she played, and heard it was "God save the King." Mr. Everard said he had rather hear Grace play that, than any thing; and Mrs. Leslie went herself to speak to Grace, who was just finishing some game. Grace was much more alarmed at the idea, than on the former occasion; because, she said now that it was music,—then it was dancing, and nobody listened. Her mamma reminded her that, since it had been requested, people would be more pleased by her obedience than by her skill, and she need only suppose she was practising. Grace followed her mamma, sat down, and played "God save the King," through, with more touch and force than is commonly met with in a child. Every head was turned to the piano at the first notes of the well-known anthem, and every one was surprised to see there a little girl,—and so small a one. She was made to play it over again. At the end, Mr. Everard praised her very simply, and so as not to annoy Grace at all. He asked her who taught her her chords, for they were particularly correct.

Grace put her fingers on the minor chord in a sort of nervousness, and looked at her mamma, who was good enough to answer for her.—She had heard a gentleman play it in that way once, some time ago, and Grace found the notes out afterwards.

"I suppose you liked those chords and the bass?" asked Mr. Everard.

Grace said, "Yes, much better than the old ones."

Miss Wallis said she had observed the difference immediately, and asked Grace to show her, which she did. Miss Wallis then played it, and Grace had to set her right twice; also she made some remarks on her own mode of bringing in the parts, which showed a good deal of taste and judgment.

"But why," said the young lady, "do you not play those chords every time, and why not the same bass, which has a much richer effect?"

"Because," answered Grace, "there would be too much of it, and because, you know, it comes in so much better the second time."

Miss Wallis said she had an excellent ear, and she wished she had half Grace's taste. Some other persons round the piano also praised her. Mr. Everard said he hoped Grace would not trust to ear, or taste, but practise as her mamma and aunt had done before her,—"Depend upon it," said he, "nothing is like practice for a lady's play."

Grace was allowed to escape to the other end of the room. Some little girls would have been injured by this sort of praise—Grace was not likely to be: she was accustomed to remember advice more than praise; and she often received praise as a piece of politeness to her mamma, which, in fact, the praises of children usually are. Grace, then, carried away Mr. Everard's advice alone. "That is just what mamma often says," thought she; "nothing is to be done without practice." Then one uncomfortable thought passed her mind, of what Mrs. Mason said last night, and mechanically she turned her head where that lady sat. Mrs. Mason's eyes, and those of the lady to whom she was talking, seemed looking at her.

We will take the liberty of hearing what they have been talking about.—"Well, I do declare!" said Mrs. Mason, "Mrs. Leslie is leading her little girl up to the piano; I do wonder at mothers,—they do all think their children such prodigies! and as for that little Grace, I am quite sick of her name; every body is saying something or other of her; one talks of her dancing, another of her chess, another of her manners, and now, I suppose, we shall have her music!"

"*I* can speak of her music," said a lady on the sofa, "for I was quite pleased at her talent, yet perfect simplicity, the other night, at my house."

"Well, you may talk of her simplicity, if you please," returned Mrs. Mason; "but I must say I can see nothing of it; in my opinion, there is a great slyness about that child, and I am not the first to notice it. I assure you, many persons have spoken to me of what took place here the night of their grand juvenile party; and my opinion is, that Mary Anne Duff could tell tales that would make that little Grace blush!"

"It was Mary Anne Duff that devised the Fairy Bower, and was crowned queen, was it not?" asked a third lady, who sat on the sofa.

"Yes," replied Mrs. Mason, "and she deserved it, for a very pretty notion it was. —But," added she, looking significantly, "it is my opinion that *some* that night got more than they deserved."

The lady inquired farther, and Mrs. Mason became more explicit. Mrs. Wallis was shocked at the idea of such falsehood in so nice a looking child as Grace; and Mrs. Mason supported her opinion by declaring many had the same thoughts, and assured Mrs. Wallis she would hear of them before long. She also said she had heard, from very good authority, other stories of Grace's duplicity, and she was sure her mamma was quite deceived in her, adding, mothers always were, affection blinded them to every thing!

Mrs. Wallis said that Mrs. Leslie was not a person of that sort, and she never could believe any child of hers could be guilty of such a mean, base action.

Mrs. Mason replied, that Mrs. Leslie was such a vast favourite every where, that she had no doubt many would think the same; but if people were bold enough to speak their thoughts, it would be found that pretty nearly all the company that night were of her opinion.—"Not Mr. Everard, of course," she added. Then looking at the piano, where the party of whom she was speaking were grouped, she continued her remarks in another direction. She soon, however, returned to Grace, who was then showing Miss Wallis the chords, called her a conceited little thing, and wondered any body could see any thing in her manners; for her part, she thought her the rudest and most disagreeable child in the world; and she gave her version of the conversation between them the evening before.—"I saw she was all alone, with no one to speak to, so I got her by me on the sofa; I did every thing to please her: I chose out the nicest cakes, and praised her, as you know one does children, talked to her ever so long,—when, would you believe it! I turned to take a cup of tea, and this rude little thing had got off the sofa, and was at the other end of the room, when I turned round!"

Mrs. Wallis did not receive all this as Mrs. Mason expected; so she continued in the same strain to the other lady. But we have heard enough to see that Mrs. Mason did not like either Grace or her mamma, and was not very scrupulous in the means she took to make others of her own opinion. No one had spoken first of the supper scene to her but Mrs. Ward; but she had that morning been making calls, and for want of something better, had made it a subject of conversation and mystery. It was a great pity that Mrs. Ward made any remark in the first instance, till she was more certain, especially to any person she could not be sure of. Grace was her guest; and though but a small one, in a measure under her protection. Mrs. Ward did not like Grace, and suffered that feeling to make her forget proprieties she ought to have observed. Good breeding would have taught this, or true Christian feeling,—they are the same thing outwardly, and that is the reason they are sometimes mistaken one for the other. Mrs. Mason's mode of talking is what is generally called *gossip;* perhaps hers might go a little farther, Mrs. Wallis did not gossip, as far as we have seen.

CHAPTER XXXIV

'Tis the sublime of man,
Our noontide majesty, to know ourselves.
COLERIDGE

Fear to stop and shame to fly.
GRAY

T HE NEXT DAY Mrs. Ward and Ellen were going to London; the latter to pay a visit to the dentist, and her mamma to make calls. It was not necessary for Emily to visit Mr. Parkinson, and she disliked his room too much to wish to accompany them. Her mamma was surprised at her readiness to stay at home, for Emily was generally always ready for a day's excursion, or any change. She found it was not mere politeness to Grace,—she said she wished to stay with her, for she liked her.

"My dear Emily," said her mamma, "I do think you are bewitched with that little girl; are you going to become a sentimental young lady?"

"Well, mamma, I cannot help liking Grace," said Emily, "and I shall enjoy a morning with her alone; for it is some time since I have had a talk with her."—(Ellen had joined their evening toilet since Mary Anne left.) "Especially," added she, "now she is going away so soon,—there is scarcely a week left."

After Grace had read this morning, her mamma told her she had a letter to write, and Grace went down to Emily with her work. Emily was pleased, and said they should have a nice comfortable chat together. Grace rather wondered at her feeling; for she was never alone with Emily, without the sense of their secret becoming tenfold more painful to her.

"Why are you so grave, Grace?" said Emily.

"I was thinking of a great many things, Emily," answered Grace, "and one is, that I am glad to be alone with you, for I want very much to thank you for something."

"Thank me!" cried Emily, "what have I done for you?"

"Not *done* any thing exactly; but *said*,—you said something that I shall never forget, and I am very much obliged to you."

"What can you mean?" asked Emily, seeing Grace quite in earnest.

"Why, you told me I interfered, and so I did, and I wish you to be so kind as to say you forgive me."

"Why, Grace, I never shall get to know you! you are certainly the oddest girl I ever knew!" said Emily, "what do you mean?"

"Grace then explained and said she could not help it now, for the time was past, and whatever came of it all, she must bear it, for she knew she had done wrong, and only asked Emily to forgive her. The tears stood in Grace's eyes;—Emily was amazed,—was perplexed, and could say nothing. Grace said, "Then, Emily, you will not say you forgive me?"

"How can I forgive you?" said Emily, "I have nothing to forgive; I hardly remember what I said; I spoke in a great pet, and I ought rather to ask you to forgive me; only I never do such things."

Grace explained what she meant more clearly; and ended with saying, "Now, if I had let you tell all about it, as you wished, you know all that has happened afterwards would never have occurred; so now will you forgive me?—besides you know it is going on now."

Emily said she would do or say any thing to please her, adding, "you are so strange, Grace, like nobody else; you seem to think all the faults of every body about you, belong to you."

Emily said this more seriously than usual, and added, "I am sure I don't know what would become of you, if you went to school."

"Is school so very bad?" asked Grace.

"Very bad! to be sure it is! why, I am almost a good girl there; though some are a good deal better than me too!"

"You? yes, of course," said Grace, rather timidly.

"I, good, Grace? why I am sure you must think me very bad indeed; and lately, that you have seen more of me, I have often wondered you will speak to me—but that is the difference between you and Constance and some other good girls; I don't know what it is exactly though, I don't like them but I know I like you."

Grace's eyes glistened with pleasure at this confession, and she said she was so glad that Emily liked her—she longed to kiss her friend—and some how or other she managed it. Emily was a good deal affected, but she got over it, and said, "Well, now, Grace, that we have got so far, you shall tell me, don't you think me very bad?"

Grace looked exceedingly amazed; she longed to say how good and how clever she thought her; and she remembered the difference she felt between her and her brother George, with some pain, but said nothing.

"Now, Grace," continued Emily, with some vehemence, "I have asked you, and you *shall* tell! Don't you think me very bad?"

"No! to be sure I do not," answered Grace.

"Well, but do you mean to say I have never done or said any thing which you call '*wrong*,' since you have been here?"

Grace began going over the events of the Fairy Bower, which were always ready to start forward with her, and she could remember nothing—she was thinking whether not speaking of the broken cup, was sufficient; but she considered that, now, as much her own doing, as Emily's; when suddenly, she knew not how, Emily's habit of exclamation came to her mind. She coloured very much, and felt confused.

"Well," said Emily, as quietly as she could, "say what it is; I ought to be satisfied, you have been so long finding it out, I thought there would be a hundred things in a moment."

"Oh, Emily!" cried Grace.

"Well," returned the other, "say at once; it is much worse to be kept guessing, as I am."

"Do you really wish it?" asked Grace.

Emily assured her she did.

"But I know," said Grace, "you do not think it wrong, so it is no use my telling you, I have heard you say, you don't think it wrong; I know many people do not."

Emily assured her she really wished to hear, and would not be the least offended. Grace then reminded her of the conversation that they had all together, the morning of the party; when Isabella and Constance both objected to what she said. Emily now remembered and understood; she said, rather satisfied, "Oh, is that all? I thought it was something much worse."

"Ah!" said Grace, rather disappointed, "I said you did not think it wrong." There was a pause, and Grace ventured to add, "How I wish you would!"

"Why do you care about it?" asked Emily.

"Because," replied Grace, I cannot bear people I am with, especially if I like them, to do what I think wrong. I am afraid you will say that is *interfering* again; but I do not think I shall ever be able to help that;" and the glistening tears in her eyes, proved her sincerity.

"But," said Emily, "if you were at school, you would see how impossible it is to avoid it. Every body does it."

"But you know, Emily, even if every body does, *we* must not, if it is a wrong thing; but you think it right."

"Right!" said Emily, "no, I don't say right; neither right nor wrong, because every body does it. Why, Grace, I am sure you do not think of every thing you do; *you*, even, must do a great many little things without thinking whether they are right or wrong."

"Yes, *little* things," said Grace, "and great ones too, I dare say, if I knew them," and she thought of her late mistake; "and I should do a great many more if I were at school, I know; but I do not call this a *little* thing; because I think, you know, it has, *perhaps* to do with one of the Commandments; but I know you do not think so." Grace was surprised that Emily did not assent. The truth was, Emily had too much sense to give the light answer to Grace she had before done; for she knew well enough that it was not a fair one. Having no answer, Grace continued rather timidly, "And I think if we do not quite know whether a thing is right or wrong, it seems so much better not to do it; then afterwards, if we are sure either way, it is so much more comfortable, either to begin doing it, or not to have done it at all: don't you think so, Emily?"

Emily said gravely, she had never thought so much of right and wrong, as Grace. "If I like a thing," continued she, more in her own way, "and it is not very bad, I do it; and if I don't, I don't want to do it;—why you know, I could never get on at school, if I did your way; there would be no end of it; and I must stand debating all day."

Poor Grace was always alarmed at the *terra incognita* of *school*—she pleaded guilty to knowing nothing about it; and was only so glad her mamma did not send her to school. However, she was clear-headed enough to keep to her point, and remarked, that school had nothing to do with what they were talking of. Emily said it *had*, because every body did it there, and it was so catching; and it was impossible to express your feelings without exclamation of some sort or other. Grace agreed to this, and said it was very difficult—she often wanted words for the purpose. "But," continued she, "do you mean that really every girl at your school uses such words?" Grace just then remembered a remark Ellen had made of Selina Carey, and was afraid she too might have forgotten her first thoughts.

"Oh, not quite *all*," said Emily. "I know there are two who never do, because they have been watched and teazed. Elenor Brown sets every body to rights, and one day she took this up, and some of the girls said what I do, that every body did. Elenor said that Selina Carey did not, so we set about watching those two, and I never heard them say any thing of the sort, certainly. The other girls, also, set upon watching all the school, and kept a list, but I did not care about it. Elenor Brown, though, is a very disagreeable girl, really. I am almost sure you would not like her, Grace; though perhaps you might, too. Selina Carey, every body likes; but she is particular in all things, and is no rule, because she is like nobody else."

"But," returned Grace, "if she is very particular and very good, and attentive to her lessons, as you have said before, and every body likes her, I should think she is a very good rule."

"Well, so she would be, for *you*, Grace, she is something like you; I often compare you, and yet you are quite different; I like her—but not as I like you. You know, I could not say all I have been saying to you now, to *her*;—oh, no. If she was forced to object to any thing I did—these words, for instance—she never did, though—I should call her a 'dear particular thing,' give her a kiss, and run away; and when Elenor Brown found fault with me, I said, why we only say 'La;' and we all went on arguing, just to provoke her, as long as we could; but then, I always make myself a great deal worse than I am, to provoke Elenor—it is such fun." Grace looked grave, though Emily's manner was very droll and trying. "Now, Grace," continued Emily, "you want to give me a lecture, and you are as bad as Elenor;—no, not as bad, either,—or as good, I suppose—but now you see, as I told you just now, how bad I am, and it is better you should know it at first; for I am not likely to change, and then you know you can throw me off, and hate me at once—which will be much better; I know you will in the end, for no good girl ever liked me, and you are the only one I ever took a fancy to." There was some passion in Emily's manner as she said this; and she went on with more vehemence, "Now, Grace, say it at once; say you hate me!"

Poor Grace was exceedingly affected; she could only throw her arms round her friend's neck, and say nothing. Emily's tears, too, began to fall fast. At last she said, "You don't mean to say, Grace, that you can like me after all I have told you."

"I do," said Grace, "and I always shall, I am sure,—only, Emily, please do not talk in that way of yourself and of me,—I cannot bear it."

"Well, but you must find out the difference between us, sooner or later," returned Emily, "and I had rather you should know what I am at once."

"But if you think you are wrong, Emily," said Grace, very much puzzled , "why do you not change? you *can*, you know, if you please; do you *really* think yourself wrong?"

"Yes, to be sure I am—I am wrong, and bad, and what you would call wicked."

"Oh, Emily!" cried Grace, very much shocked, "how can you talk so? I have never seen any thing to blame but that one thing."

"Well," replied Emily, "that is partly your own blindness, and partly because I can keep pretty well before you. I always should, I think. Why, you know, I shall not use any of those words before you; at least, I shall try not."

"Oh, dear Emily!" cried Grace, distressed, "that is worse than all!"

"Why?" said the other, "I thought you would like it."

"If it is wrong to be done at all, it is always wrong,—and I think," added Grace, doubtfully, "it is almost worse to do as you say, than to do it *always*. No," continued she, "not *worse*, because it might get you into a habit of leaving it off; but then you know it is of no use to do any thing of that kind only to please any body like me. It is not like your papa or mamma, or any body of that sort."

"But papa and mamma don't tell me," said Emily.

"But suppose the third commandment does?" answered Grace, very seriously; "do think of that, please, Emily; I only ask you to think of it—it may be so, you know!"

Emily said she *could* think of it; but it was no use; if she let off these things she must go on leaving off others, and the girls would all find it out, and she should have no peace; it was much worse to make a turn, than to begin right at first, though that was very disagreeable, and that if she made any turn, it must be when she left school, and could do as she pleased.

Grace had sense enough to know if people wish to correct themselves of any thing, it is best to begin at once, and not defer, and she said so. But Emily persisted that Grace could not judge, as she had never been at school. After a long pause, Grace said, timidly, "But I suppose school is not worse than when we are grown up, and have a great deal to do, and a great many people to see, is it?"

"Yes," replied Emily, "it is; because then, you know, we shall be old, and may do as we please."

"But still, then we may not do wrong," said Grace.

"Oh," said Emily, "right and wrong are quite different to us at school, and to grown up men and women."

Grace still could not think so, but her ignorance of schools and of grown up people made her diffident; and besides, she thought she was quite teazing Emily, and had some time felt uncomfortable. She therefore only said, presently, that she hoped she had not said any thing to vex Emily, who assured her she had not, and reminded her that the conversation was brought on by herself. A few kind words passed between the young friends, and then another subject was started. When the clock struck twelve, Grace said she must go to her mamma, and told Emily she was to ask her if she would like to go out with them, for they were going to walk before the beauty of the day was over. Emily was quite disposed, and went to prepare. Grace found her mamma folding the letter she had been writing, and she bade her light a taper. As Grace waited by her mamma's side, she saw the direction was to Mr. Everard; she was just going to remark on it, with pleasure—for she liked Mr. Everard now, and wished to say so, since at first she had been alarmed at his manner—when Mrs. Mason's words came into her head, and she could not speak. Thus—if there was really any truth in the insinuation—did that lady deprive a mother for ever of the comfort which such a spontaneous testimony from her child would have been to her heart.

When Grace was at leisure, she thought a good deal of her conversation with Emily. "How good she is!" was her first thought, "how little she thinks of herself,—and how well of other people,—how I wish I was like her!" Then she considered with some surprise her way of talking, and going on to do a thing, when she knew it was wrong. If it had not been for the one specimen Grace had actually seen, she would have believed it was a misunderstanding of words, and only that Emily was much more particular than herself,—but this puzzled her a little, and she could not understand it. Then came her unknown world—*school*—and put an end to her speculations. She could only think, as usual, how glad she was that she was not there.

Grace told Ellen, the other day, she never could tell people of their faults. She was mistaken; she had done so before in her way, and had been doing so now, but she did not know it. It came to her hand, to do, and in the same way, no doubt, as she grew older, she would be able to correct others, when proper.

CHAPTER XXXV

Lord! Polly, only think—
Miss has danced with a Lord!
EVELINA—*Letter lv*

T HE YOUNG PEOPLE were to dine with the elder part of the family to-day, since Ellen was to have that pleasure, having spent the day in London; and as the party did not return as soon as Emily expected, she proposed getting dressed ready; for Ellen would have a good deal to say. Just as they were beginning, however, the carriage drove up, and presently Ellen found them out, in their room. She came in with all manner of pretty things in her hands, for they had been to the Bazaar. Emily began helping her to put them down, and was exclaiming, "What have you got—let us see—how very pretty!" when Ellen said, "I have got something to tell you that will surprise you more than all in these papers!"

"What is it?" cried Emily, in a tone of pleased expectation, "I like to be surprised."

"Well, you shall guess," said her sister, "because I am sure you never can!—I must give you one hint, though; you know we have been to Grosvenor Square; now, you shall have three guesses."

"Well, it's about Isabella, I am sure," said Emily; "Isabella is going to leave school, and coming out."

"No!" said Ellen, "but you'll never guess, except I give you one more hint,—it has something to do with the Duffs."

"You don't mean that they are all coming to Isabella's grand party?"

"No! but try once more."

"Well, then, Isabella has given Fanny her beautiful pearl brooch."

"No! but you burn," said Ellen; "really, Emily, you have been very near indeed.—It is, that Fanny is going to stay in Grosvenor Square—not going only to the party, but going to *stay*, you know, more than a whole week!"

"Well! I *am* surprised," said Emily, in a manner very satisfactory to Ellen. "Why, you know, *we* never go and stay there!—Really *going!* do you say? What will they do about the dancing and cards?"

"Oh, I suppose Fanny will not dance or play;—you know she can't; but mamma said that would not signify *there*; because, you know, the Duffs have wished so much to get acquainted with the Wards; and now Isabella has taken such a fancy to Fanny—it's very pleasant. Mamma was more surprised than you, and has talked of nothing else, all the way home. She is very much pleased, and thinks it will be such a nice thing for the Duffs."

"And I was thinking," said Grace, "what a nice thing it would be for Isabella; I mean, if Constance knew her well."

"Oh, the Duffs will be the most pleased of the two," said Emily, "but it is only *Fanny*, you know, not *all* of them."

"Yes, but mamma says the others will come afterwards, and she has always wished so much that they should be acquainted," replied Ellen, "indeed, it seems very odd to me that they should not; you know they are both our cousins, and we know both so very well.

I could hardly believe, till you reminded me, the other night, that Isabella and the Duffs had never met till that week, since they were quite little things; and that my uncle and aunt had never seen them at all."

"Well, but how did it all happen?" asked Emily.—"Isabella, I suppose, persuaded her mamma, as she sometimes can."

"Yes; I will tell you about that presently; but you shall hear first, what my aunt said to mamma. She began talking of our party, and she said she never was at one so nicely managed; she was quite amazed, without dancing or cards, how an evening of children could be so spirited, and yet not boisterous. Then she said a great deal was owing to that elegant Fairy Bower, for it threw a grace and quiet over the scene, which the children felt insensibly—(I tell you her very words.) This led her to talk of Mary Anne Duff, and how clever she was, and she admired all the Duffs; she said they were very superior to what she had expected, for she had never heard they were pretty; and she thought their manners good—especially Fanny's; then she talked of Fanny's writing verses, which Mary Anne told her; I was by then, and heard her."

"Stop!" cried Emily, "I don't understand,—what do you mean by *then?*"

"Why, after the Coronation of the Queen of the Fairy Bower, you know, I went to lead Mary Anne into the back drawing-room, and found my aunt was talking to her; Mary Anne was giving her an account of the idea of the Fairy Bower first coming into her head; and she said it was from some verses of Fanny's, and repeated one line, which you know: my aunt was very much surprised at Fanny's cleverness, and spoke to Isabella about it, that evening. Well! now I come to Isabella's part; she immediately set upon Fanny, about her verses, and said she wished she would write some to *her*. Fanny said she would with all her heart, and that she would do them by the time of her grand party, on the 28th; which, you know, Isabella was always talking of. After some more talk between them, Isabella settled that she would do all she could to persuade her mamma to ask Fanny, to come and stay with her, to write these verses, to be ready for the grand party: my aunt liked Fanny, and at last agreed, and Fanny is to go next Monday."

"And the party is Tuesday week," said Emily. "Well, we shall hear all about it, to-morrow night, as the Duffs. I really quite long for it."

"To-morrow!" cried Ellen, "I thought it was Saturday we were going."

"So it was; but did you not know, the other day, mamma had a note from my aunt Duff, saying that she could not persuade Miss Newmarsh as she thought she could, and so the party must be either to-morrow, or next week; so mamma chose to-morrow."

"But why did Miss Newmarsh object?" asked Ellen.

"Why, you know, it was Saturday, and Miss Newmarsh never does any thing after seven o'clock on Saturday evening, because of Sunday," replied her sister.

"If it was a large party it would be different," said Ellen, "but you know it is only just ourselves, and one neighbour's family, and we should leave quite early.—I am so sorry, because of the little Wallises: but why did mamma say Friday?"

"It is lucky mamma did say Friday, else, you know, Grace might have been gone; for I want Grace to go to the Duffs."

"Grace, gone!" cried Ellen, "what do you mean? I thought Grace was staying at least a week longer; and we hoped she would go with us to Isabella's party; my aunt sent a message to your mamma, Grace, about you and herself too; but she told mamma she did not like to make a formal invitation of it, to Mrs. Leslie, as it was a juvenile party. When does Grace go?"

"Next Tuesday," said Grace, "mamma changed her mind, and settled it rather earlier, this morning."

"Oh, how sorry I am!" cried Ellen; "that is worse than all. I never once thought of your going away, Grace."

"I am very sorry, indeed," said Grace; "I seem to know you all so well, now, I do not like to leave at all;—but mamma says she must go home on Tuesday, and so it cannot be helped. Mamma said, too, that perhaps I should see you again before you go to school, so I have been thinking of that."

"But don't you think your mamma will go, or like you to go, to this party, Grace? because, I remember mamma said that she hoped it would tempt Mrs. Leslie to stay;—for it will be a very grand one; several little lords and ladies, as there always are, you know."

"I don't know, really," said Grace; "mamma generally does as she says at first; and you know, if she has business at home, she *must* go."

"Well, I hope she will not," said Ellen; and here the dinner-bell summoned the young people.

It was, as the conversation between the young folks showed, quite a new thing for the Duffs to make acquaintance with the elder branch of the Ward family. Lady Musgrove had for many years steadily, though not unpolitely, avoided any intercourse, and it was only the sight of the young people, hearing of their talents, and the proof of what she considered an elegant taste in the Fairy Bower, which induced her to listen to Isabella's entreaties. Isabella was resolved on her point, and had various methods for gaining it still in store; but her mamma spared her the use of them by consenting, after a moderate degree of teazing. Lady Musgrove did not ask all the family to the party. She told Isabella to write to Fanny, and say she wrote by her mamma's request, to ask her to come on Monday or Tuesday, and stay a week, but not to mention the party. Isabella accordingly wrote as affectionate a note as her circumscribed task allowed; for her mamma would let nothing be said but what alluded to the invitation. Isabella had great difficulty in writing this note.—It may be thought singular, that so accomplished a young lady should be at a loss in this respect; she could have written an affectionate epistle, and have run on to any length; or she could have copied a formal invitation, from the note tray. But any thing between these, did not come within the range of her powers. The note, at length, ran thus:—

MY OWN BELOVED FANNY,

Mamma desires me to write, and send her compliments to your mamma, and she hopes she will allow you to come to us at the beginning of next week, and stay a week with me, in Grosvenor Square. Papa and mamma both desire their compliments to Mr. and Mrs. Duff. You know how glad I shall be to see you,

My darling mignonne,

Your own ISABELLA

This was shown to Lady Musgrove, who said it would do pretty well; but made Isabella date it very fully, and add her surname to her signature; also, she presided over the direction. Isabella was about to write, simply Miss Fanny Duff, Winterton;—it became eventually,—

> *Miss F. Duff, James Duff, Esq.,*
> *Winterton,*
> *Surrey.*

CHAPTER XXXVI

Defer not the least virtue.
GEORGE HERBERT

THE NEXT MORNING which was Friday, Emily and George went out after breakfast, in order to make a new arrangement, in consequence of Mrs. Leslie's leaving on the following Tuesday. She came for a fortnight, and had stayed nearly three weeks; still every one had hoped she would yet prolong the visit,—both Mrs. Leslie and Grace being acceptable in their respective circles. Mrs. Ward certainly expected that the invitation to Grosvenor Square would be an inducement, and she considered Mrs. Leslie's neglect of it, as another proof of her very unaccountable simplicity. At first, she thought that Mrs. Leslie was offended at receiving no regular invitation, and she explained fully Lady Musgrove's reason; but she found this made no difference in Mrs. Leslie, who, however, was so easy and pleasant about it, that it was impossible to be angry with her, as Mrs. Ward felt inclined to be. When Mrs. Leslie and Grace came down this morning, with their work, they found Ellen alone in the room; and they heard where George and Emily were gone; Mrs. Leslie said to Ellen, it was a very kind of them to take so much trouble for Grace's sake. "I assure you, my dear Ellen," aded she, "Grace and I shall talk a great deal over this visit, so much pleasure will last Grace for a very long time."

Ellen could speak of nothing but her sorrow that the visit was at an end; and they went on, talking on the past and future. Grace was delighted to hear her mamma say, she hoped now they would often meet in holidays.

After some time Mrs. Ward came in; she presently said, "Do you know, the most extraordinary thing has happened, I ever met with. Thomas just now came to me with a very long face, and told me that one of the coffee cups and saucers of the best tea service has disappeared;—nobody in the house knows any thing about it."

"Somebody must have broken it," said Mrs. Leslie.

"But then, you know, the pieces would have been found in one of the rooms, next morning. I know I can trust Thomas, and I think I can, the rest of the servants; and they say, that really and truly they know nothing about it. Thomas says he did not put away any of the best things till yesterday, because we were having parties so often; and yesterday, he first counted them over, and could not make them right; but as he was in a hurry to be ready to go with us to London, he said nothing, hoping to find the missing one, among some other set; but he and all the maids have looked every where.—I saw no cup broken; did you?"

"No," said Mrs. Leslie.

"No," said Ellen.

Poor Grace! we hope the reader feels a little for her.

"You may think it strange," continued Mrs. Ward, "that I should think so much about a cup and saucer; but, besides their being really very handsome, they were the gift of my poor mother, on our marriage; and she took a great deal of pains, indeed, about the pattern and form; besides, several have unfortunately been broken, and mostly coffee cups; so that they become very precious now. I told Thomas when he first came, he might break any thing in the house, rather than that tea service."

"As you cannot find the pieces, I cannot help hoping the cup and saucer may be found whole," said Mrs. Leslie.

"No, indeed, I quite give that up for, I feel pretty sure some one has broken them, and is afraid to tell. I mean to question all the children;—of course I should not care so much if they could be matched; but I have tried different people at Spodes', and they all say it cannot be done."

After this the subject was dropt. Grace felt very miserable, and longed for Emily's return. Other matters were talked of, but Grace thought of but one; and when she heard the hall door open, she went and caught Emily, and made her come at once up stairs, to take off her bonnet. Here she told her what had just happened, and she said, "Now, Emily, do, pray let us—or me—do once right in this unfortunate business;—let me tell I broke the cup."

"But you did *not*," said Emily, (Grace always fancied she actually had,) "it was *I*, you know, and you agreed that it was my business."

Grace remembered her lesson about interfering, and was silenced. "I'll tell you what I'll do," continued Emily, "if mamma asks me, I will tell her at once; but, you know, Hanson is to come to-morrow, and then we shall know about it; and it is a great pity to tell now, when Saturday is so near, and we have been waiting so long."

"May I just say one thing?" asked Grace, fearfully.

Emily gave her leave, and she said, that "the cup was brought up for *me*, and you cannot think how uncomfortable I have been down stairs, all the time your mamma was inquiring about it."

Emily still persisted it was her affair, and repeated, she would tell if questioned; also reminded Grace of the certainty of the whole affair of the Fairy Bower coming out by this disclosure; representing very strongly that her mamma would be much more angry and sorry that the acquaintance between the two families of cousins should be checked, or most likely put an end to, than that the breakage of a cup should be concealed; and she also said it would be more ill-natured than ever, *now* to betray Mary Anne, or to do the least thing that might lead to a discovery. Grace had never thought of all this; she saw now that confessing this small accident would almost certainly lead to a breach for ever between these two families; and she had seen, that Mrs. Ward was very anxious indeed, for some reason or other, that the acquaintance should take place. Her new rule, however, came to her relief, and she resolved *not to interfere;* as, without doubt, in this matter, Emily had the greatest right to direct. She, therefore, only asked Emily what she was to do if Mrs. Ward questioned her, adding, "then, I *will* tell; only you shall say how."

Emily said, "Tell mamma *I* know all about it."

"And then, Emily, about my own mamma; I must tell her if she asks me!"

Emily said she could do as she pleased about that; but hoped Mrs. Leslie would not tell. She also explained that *she* should not care herself that Mary Anne's deceit should all come out, but that her mamma would be very much vexed that any thing should occur just at this moment, and certainly it was not fair that Fanny should suffer for her sister's fault; "However," she added, "it is not at all unlikely, for my uncle is very particular in such things, and my aunt, I know, would be very glad to get rid of Fanny's visit altogether."

After this, Emily endeavoured to console Grace a little, by its not being likely that any thing farther should occur to-day, about the cup, for it was just one o'clock, when they were to dine in the library, and then be off directly for Winterton, and that she had other things to talk of to her mamma—about the little party for Monday, and so on. This was true; and besides Mrs. Ward had a note to write to her sister, for the young people to take; for, from the change of day, the elders were not able to go to Winterton, as before arranged, since they were engaged to dinner at a neighbour's, in Fulham. Mrs. Ward regretted this much, as she wanted to talk over Fanny's projected visit, and other things, with her sister. Mrs. Ward, therefore, wrote her note, instead of coming in to luncheon, as usual, and the children departed without any questions being asked.

CHAPTER XXXVII

Judge before friendship; then confide till death.
YOUNG

GRACE FELT her other trouble coming on as she approached Winterton. It was above an hour's drive, especially now the roads were heavy, and they reached the house rather before five o'clock. Grace quite dreaded seeing Mary Anne; and much more from the feelings she imagined must be hers, than from any thing else. The parting scene had convinced her that Mary Anne was conscious of some delinquency, and now that lasting results seemed likely to be the consequence of her deceit, Grace wondered more and more how she felt, and how she looked. She soon had a view of the latter, at any rate; but, became only more and more perplexed as to the former. Mary Anne greeted Grace among the rest, and all began talking. Fanny was in very high spirits, and her new prospects soon became the topic of conversation.

"I suppose you have heard," said she, "that I am going to stay a week in Grosvenor Square, with your cousin Isabella."

They assented.

"Ah, Fanny is very much pleased," said her mamma; "but she should remember it was all Mary Anne's doing, and it is rather hard on Mary Anne that her generous feeling should not get its reward; but I tell Mary Anne she must not mind, her turn will come some day."

"I am sure," said Constance, "*I* should not think it much of a reward to go to Lord Musgrove's, they are all very worldly people, and mix in very worldly society; besides, I dare say there will be cards and dancing, every night."

"I don't care for the cards or dancing, or any body I shall see, but dear Isabella," said Fanny, "and she will be all the world to me!"

"All the world, Fanny! what a false sentiment and expression!" said her sister.

"Ah! Constance, that is because you love nobody, as I do Isabella, and you do not understand that feeling," returned Fanny. "Isabella and I love each other, just as Edwin and Angelina did; only they were man and woman; and just as Damon and Pythias did, only they were two men. She says to me;

'No, never from this hour to part,
We'll live, and love so true.'

And I say to her,—

'The sigh that rends thy constant heart,
Shall break thy Fanny's too.' "

"How can you be so ridiculous, Fanny?" exclaimed Constance.

"You may call it ridiculous if you please," said Fanny, "but it is quite true, and you would have been very glad to go to Lord Musgrove's, if Isabella had taken the fancy to you, she has to me; you know how much you talked of her and liked her at first, when you and Miss Newmarsh fancied *you* were her favourite. *I* knew how it was, all the time, and could have laughed at you!"

"Fanny, you do not understand me," said Constance, with great command of temper. "I liked Isabella then, because there seemed a great deal promising about her; and I should *then*, and would *now*, do any thing to do her good; but I would not go to such a house as *that*, for mere fancy and pleasure, as you are doing; I hope I am not so inconsistent."

"Well, and why may not *I* do Isabella good?" asked Fanny.

"Nonsense, Fanny," returned her sister, "you know very well, *that* is not your reason for going, and you do not think about it."

"No," said Fanny, "because I love Isabella too much to think of any thing but seeing her: don't you know that the presence of the beloved object is every thing? why! don't you know that people *die* willingly for those they love, as Angelina says when she thought Edwin *had* died for her,—

'And there forlorn, despairing hid,
I'll lay me down and *die*,
'Twas so for me that Edwin did,
And so for him will I.'

You see she is quite ready to die for him, as I am for Isabella."

"How ridiculous you are, Fanny," cried Constance, "talking of dying in that way; why should you die for Isabella's sake? I'm sure she would not die for you. I dare say she cares very little about you."

"But she does, though," said Fanny, "else why has she asked me, for a whole week?

the fact is, you do not understand what true friendship is, and you say, like Edwin, when he was vexed,

> 'And what is friendship but a name?—
> A charm that lulls to sleep,
> A shade that follows wealth or fame,
> But leaves the wretch to weep.' "

"I am sure," replied Constance, "I say no such stuff."

"Fanny just knows Edwin and Angelina," said Mary Anne, "and can quote nothing else."

"Well, no wonder, that is all Miss Newmarsh's fault," replied Fanny. "I should be glad enough to have more poetry like that; but *that*, and Henry and Emma, are the only two pieces, in all our poetry, at all to my taste—yes! and the rest of Goldsmith, and a piece here and there, perhaps, in other books. Miss Newmarsh is so cross, she lets us have no poetry at all."

"No poetry at all! what do you mean?" said Constance, "why, we have all Milton, and four volumes of that sweet Cowper, and all Goldsmith besides, and several collections of the extracts from all our best poets, modern and ancient!"

"Yes, I know that, and I say I like pieces here and there, and some of Cowper; I like that line,—

> 'Oh, for a lodge in some vast wilderness!'

So beautiful it is! that is what Isabella and I are to do—to fly like my bird, far away from all the bustle and evil of the world, and live quite happy, all alone!"

Here George, who had been with Campbell and some other boys, came into the room, and joined the party.

"Live quite happy, all alone, Fanny!" cried he, "*that* I'm sure you would never do! why, you'd have nobody to talk and quote poetry to."

"By *quite alone*, I mean just *one* more," said Fanny.

"That is, by 'one,' you mean 'two;' and by 'two,' you mean 'three,' and so on. But pray who is this '*one more*' to be?—Isabella, or me? oh, not poor me; I see by your look of contempt; oh! oh! dear me! dear me, what shall I do?" continued he, pretending to cry. "Fanny likes Isabella, whom she has seen just twice, better than me, whom she has known all her life! ah! well does her favourite poet say all that about Friendship!" and he rehearsed the stanza Fanny had just before done, but in very different style; repeating the last line, and ending, "ah, to weep! to weep! how true that is! cruel Fanny!"

Of course, this gave a turn to the tone of the conversation; no one could help laughing at George, for he was very droll, and very good-natured; but Fanny was a little provoked.

"Well, *Fanny, dear!*" continued he, "don't be angry, it's I, you know, that should be angry."

"Why should you be angry?" asked Fanny.

"Because," replied George, "I see, as plain as a pikestaff, that you are going to cast me and all of us off, for your *darling Isabella;* and as I don't care for bouncing B one half so much as I care for myself and all the rest of us, of course I am very angry, and think you a very silly girl."

"I am sure, George, you are very rude to speak of your cousin in that way," said Fanny.

"Well, then she has no business to be *my cousin*," replied George, "for you know, Fanny, I am not more polite than necessary to any of my *cousins*."

"Indeed you are not!" cried Fanny, "and I hope before long you will learn better manners!"

"Weugh!" exclaimed George, with a long whistle, "my dear pretty Fanny, I see we must have a little serious talk together." Then assuming a graver air, he asked her whether she thought there were any such people in the world, as those of whom Edwin speaks—

'Who leave the wretch to weep.' "

She said, "Yes, all bad people."

"Well, *Fanny dear*," said he, "take care you don't make another of these *'bad people.'* "

"Do you mean," cried Fanny, indignantly, "that I shall deceive and desert Isabella, and leave her to weep and to die?"

"No, not exactly that," answered George, "but that you will desert all of us, and leave us to die,—you know, you have made me weep already."

"George, what nonsense you talk!" cried Fanny, impatiently.

"Well! and pray *why* have not *we* quite as much right to die, if we please, as Isabella?" said George, "and as to nonsense, I appeal to the company! Now, Grace, you are no relation to any of us, and are, besides, always the fairest judge in the world: have I talked more nonsense than this cousin of mine?"

Grace had now become used to being appealed to by George, and generally found something to say; she was rather afraid now, as she saw to her surprise, that Fanny was really provoked; she answered, "Why there is a great difference between you! one is in jest, and the other in earnest."

"Very good—sapient judge!" cried George; "Fanny is in earnest in her folly; I am in jest in mine."

"Not in her *folly;* in her *sense*," returned Grace, "you may keep your folly to yourself, George."

"Sense! sense! do you use that word in two *senses?*" said George. "A *pun* I do declare! but a very vile one, for nobody but you, would have thought of either sense or meaning, from the lips of my fair cousin there; don't look shocked, Grace!" continued he; "you don't know Fanny yet—she will not be offended; she sets up for being a young lady, with sentiment instead of sense, and poetry instead of meaning."

"Well, and are not sentiment and dear poetry worth all the dull things in the world put together?" exclaimed Fanny.

"There!" cried George, triumphantly, "what more would you have? You see, Grace, Fanny would not let you help her off! so you might have spared your pains."

The young people were here summoned to a very plentiful tea, which broke in upon the conversation. George was too fond of amusement at all times, and not very serious; yet he gave Fanny some hints in this conversation, which might have been of use to her all her life, had she attended to them; but it was rarely that she took in or considered, the advice and opinion of her elders and instructors; much less would she listen to those of her companions, if they were disagreeable to her. Now, especially, she was more elated than she had ever been in her whole life, and George had perceived this.

CHAPTER XXXVIII

Thus conscience does make cowards of us all.
SHAKSPEARE

THERE WERE PUZZLES and riddles for the young people after tea. All the party amused themselves with them; meanwhile, the following conversation took place.

"So, Fanny," said Emily, "I find you and Isabella settled this visit together, the other night."

Fanny said that Isabella proposed it, and talked it over.

"And how was it your mamma and Miss Newmarsh consented?" asked Emily.

"Miss Newmarsh was very much against it," replied Mary Anne; "she said, if it was Constance, she should have been glad, because *she* had principle and firmness, and would do Isabella good, but that Fanny was quite unfit."

"And she said too," added Constance, "that it was a great slight to ask Fanny, and not Mary Anne, who was the beginner of it all, and whose elegant fancy was so conspicuous the other night; by the bye, we have been trying to make those flowers, and we cannot do it at all, the tiresome people send us the wrong paper and wire; and the gum will not hold, and nobody can cut out the leaves properly; we have tried in vain, and now have quite given it up. How did we manage the other day? it seemed as easy as possible."

"Oh, the paper was the right sort, and so was the gum and the wire, and there were so many of us," said Mary Anne, hoping to put off any dangerous remarks.

"And you know Grace helped us," said Ellen, "and cut out all the patterns, and taught us how to make them up; you know she knew more about the flowers, a great deal than you, Mary Anne, though it was all your plan; oh, by the bye, Mary Anne, I wanted to ask you, when I saw you, how it was about the Fairy Bower,—the name I mean."

While Ellen was speaking, Mary Anne was reaching over for the snuffers. It has been before remarked, that she was not handy; and the confusion and alarm into which Ellen's impending question threw her, increased her natural clumsiness. In her hurry and agitation, she upset one of the candles, on the puzzle Ellen was putting together. "Oh, Mary Anne," cried several voices, "see what you have done! how could you be so awkward?"

"Mary Anne always is awkward," said Fanny.

Every body was disturbed; the bell was rung; the damage, that table, puzzle, and candle had sustained, rectified; and Ellen went up stairs with the maid, to do the best she could with her frock and her hands, both of which had severely suffered. As soon as

Mary Anne had seen things pretty straight in the drawing-room, she said she would see after Ellen, and left the room.

"I have no patience with her!" said Emily, in a lowered voice, to Grace, as they walked to a sofa at the other end of the room, "and if it was not for mamma, I would tell all this moment."

Constance and Fanny, finding the party at their end of the table broken up, presently followed them.

"Why, Emily," cried Fanny, whose spirits seemed constantly rising, "I am surprised at you, who always laugh at me! I am sure you are quite as sentimental, with Grace Leslie, as I am with Isabella! how you have been whispering to her!"

"Well, and why not? may not I have a 'darling *mignonne*' as well as Isabella?" cried Emily, taking off that young lady to the life.

"Fanny is so delighted at what she considers her good fortune," remarked Constance, "that she cannot contain herself; you cannot think how ridiculous she has been! she carries the note close to her heart, and is every minute saying something or other to us, to try and provoke us. Poor Mary Anne cannot bear it; for she is very much vexed, certainly, and says it is very hard the reward should all fall upon Fanny, who has done nothing."

"Done nothing! indeed!" cried Fanny.

Her sister, without heeding the interruption, continued, "But *I* don't care the least in the world for it. I would not go to Lord Musgrove's house, if they were all to come here and ask me."

"But you would to do Isabella good, you *said* so," remarked Grace, in an inquiring tone.

"Yes, but that would be done in quite a different way," said Constance. "I would not go for mere pleasure, or to the party which Fanny is always talking about. If I had had more serious talk with Miss Ward, and she had taken a fancy to me, and asked me to come, I might perhaps have gone then."

"Well, and that is just what she has done with me," cried Fanny.

"Nonsense, Fanny!" said her sister, "you know, you talk nothing but ridiculous stuff to *her*, as well as to every body else."

"Well, but just remember, Constance," returned the other, "that you and I, both had what you called a serious talk with Isabella in the ante-room, before it was the Fairy Bower, and that you were very much pleased with her, and Miss Newmarsh too, and if she had liked your seriousness as well as mine, you would be so still."

"I shall always be ready to do her good, I hope," said Constance, with her usual command of temper, "but I do not consider yours the right way. I should just as soon think of going to a regular dance and card party at the house, which nothing would induce me to do."

"Nothing but an invitation, I suppose," said Fanny.

"Fanny, you are very contemptuous, but I forgive you," returned her sister.

"Do you mean to go on in this way, Constance?" said Emily; "I declare if you do, by the time you are grown up, you will be fit for nothing but a monastery, and you must leave the world, and shut yourself up in a convent."

"I hope I shall leave the world," returned her cousin, "but I hope I shall not shut myself up in a convent, and be any thing so shocking as a nun."

"Not be a nun!" cried Fanny, "not be a dear beautiful nun! Oh, I had rather be a nun than any thing else in the whole world!"

"Really, Fanny, I am quite ashamed of you," said her sister. "Do you know what you are saying? don't you know a nun is a Roman Catholic?"

"Oh, but a nun is the most unfortunate and interesting creature in the whole world!" cried Fanny, "and they all look so miserable, and wander about and sing all night, and they wear long black garments, with a streaming white veil, and an immense long string of beads, with a cross at the end of it; and they go about curing all sick people, and binding up their wounds."

"Fanny!" cried Emily, "what a medley you are making! I know what it is all from. *I* told you of a nun in one of Mrs. Ratcliff's novels, and some one else has been talking to you of Madame de Genlis's 'Siege of Rochelle,' I am sure; but all that is not true of nuns!"

"No, to be sure not!" said Ellen, "first they would cut off all your hair, and then bury you, and shut you up in a convent, with bars, and you could never get out again."

"Yes," continued Grace, "and they would never let you see any of your friends, except before the abbess, and several others; they would not even let you speak alone to your papa or mamma, or brothers and sisters, and if you tried to do so, or to get out, they would clap you up in mortar, in a cellar, and leave you to starve. Oh! I would not be a nun for the whole world; how can you wish it, Fanny?"

Fanny still persisted in her wish, if Isabella would be a nun, too, and she said she would ask her. After some more conversation of the same kind, the young party partook of a slight supper, and soon after departed. Grace gave an account of the evening to her mamma; it had been a pleasant one—nearly all talk. Mrs. Leslie asked how she liked the Duffs at their own home.

"Very much, mamma; Fanny is so odd and amusing, but I cannot quite make out if she is in jest or earnest. Constance does not like some things she says, and all the rest laugh at her; but Constance is sure to be right."

Her mamma said she was glad that Grace liked the Duffs, as well at home as abroad.

"Yes, mamma, I do, I think," returned the young visitor, "though sometimes I was surprised that they were not quite—quite—"

"Quite what?" said her mamma.

"Not quite so good-natured as I expected, I think," continued Grace, "not so good-natured to *each other*, I believe I mean, mamma. I do not mean they were quarrelsome, but they were not more good-natured than some other sisters I have seen, and I thought they would be, because they all seemed so fond of each other, and praised each other so much, whenever I have seen them."

CHAPTER XXXIX

―――――Generous actions meet a base reward.
PARNELL

THE NEXT DAY, Hanson was to call, in her way to a friend's at Hammersmith; and very anxious the two young friends were, to hear how her negotiation with John Edwards, at Spodes', had succeeded. She did not come, however; but sent a message by her brother-in-law instead, saying, her sister's children were ill—they thought of the measles—and she did not like to leave them till they were better, or to come to the house till the danger of infection was past. Grace was disappointed, though she scarcely expected any good news if Hanson had come. Emily had wondered that her mamma had made no inquiries, as she said she would; though as yet, there had not been much opportunity. She fully expected to be questioned in the course of the day; nothing, however, happened concerning the broken cup that day, or the next, which was Sunday. On Monday, the following conversation took place between Mrs. Ward and Mrs. Leslie, which may serve to account for the silence which had surprised Emily. There was always a little space after breakfast; between Mr. Ward's departure for London, and Mrs. Leslie's appointment with her little girl, in her room. Except Mr. Everard or other visitors were in the room, the two ladies were alone, which was the case on this morning. Thomas was removing the breakfast things, and in leaving the room had a narrow escape with the cream jug. This reminded Mrs. Leslie of the broken cup, and she asked if Mrs. Ward had heard any thing more of it.

That lady said she wished to mention it to Mrs. Leslie, "and," continued she, "that is the reason I have not questioned the children, as you shall hear. But did you know that before their grand party, on the sixth, your little girl was very ill?"

"No, indeed," replied Mrs. Leslie, "how could that be? I heard nothing of it; Grace seemed in particularly good spirits, all the evening."

"Yes," answered the other lady, "she managed to get over it very well, but I can assure you it was so. Hanson told Hannah she never saw a child in such a state; she was quite alarmed; and that she lay upon her bed above an hour, trembling to such a degree, as almost to shake the bed."

"Poor Grace!" said her mamma, "she had one of her palpitations!—no, she did not tell me; I wonder what brought it on; do you know, I have never known those palpitations brought on by any thing but excitement, or suffering of mind; you would hardly think it in such a child."

"I was very sorry to hear it," continued Mrs. Ward, "and wished she had sent for some drops of some kind; but Hannah told me that she would not let Miss Emily even come for you, much less tell any one else."

"She never likes me to know when she is ill, but generally sooner or later she alludes to it in some way afterwards," answered Mrs. Leslie; "I rather wonder she has not now, for I remember she seemed quite worn out at night after the party, and I warned her of one of these palpitations—I wonder she did not mention it then."

"Why I cannot help thinking," said Mrs. Ward, "that she might have some reason for it, for Hannah came and told me before breakfast on Saturday, that she had remem-

bered that Miss Emily came down stairs, just before the party, for a cup of coffee, and
that Hanson soon after came in from dressing all the young people, saying that poor
Miss Grace was quite ill, and all the rest I have been telling you. She also said that Emily
was to take her up a cup of coffee, and asked if it was gone, and seemed very anxious
about Grace. She afterwards went up to dress the very last thing; you may remember
Grace was late down that evening, long after all the rest. Now, you know if Grace had
any accident with this cup, it may quite account for her not speaking to you about being
unwell."

"Not at all, I assure you," said Mrs. Leslie, "it is just the thing that would *make* her
speak."

"Oh, indeed," cried the other lady, "you don't know what children are in other
people's houses? she might tell *you* at home, but she might be afraid of me, and very
natural it would be, that she should say nothing about it."

"Indeed," replied Mrs. Leslie, "I should be very sorry to suppose that Grace knew any
thing about the cup.—Besides, do you not remember, that she was in the room when you
were talking about it, and even asked us?—what did she say?"

"I do not know if she spoke; I know Ellen did; but my reason for speaking to
you is, that I would make no farther inquiries, till I had told you this, and asked you
what I should do."

Mrs. Leslie thanked her for this kind consideration, and said, of course she would
question Grace immediately, and hoped Mrs. Ward would do the same by Emily;—for
of course she must know.

"She may know about the illness, but very likely not about the cup," said Mrs. Ward;
"you know Emily was down long before Grace."

Mrs. Leslie was shocked at this insinuation, and a little hurt, and Mrs. Ward, to
support the opinion she had put forward, told Mrs. Leslie, as gradually and gently as
she could, that she had some doubts if Grace practised in a morning, as Mrs. Leslie
believed.

Mrs. Leslie was for a moment startled, but immediately said, "I know she did not for
two mornings, when first she came—she told me. You know, she is at perfect liberty to
do as she pleases any morning, only sometimes I ask her, merely to know how much
sleep she gets, now she is so much later in bed than at home."

Mrs. Ward was quite aware those were the only two mornings she had ever heard of;
perhaps she did not like to acknowledge she was under a mistake, for she went
on—"Surely, you don't expect a child, under such a free permission, to practise every
morning, such weather as this."

"But I expect Grace to tell me the truth," said Mrs. Leslie, "and nothing would
distress me so much as to think there was the slightest error in that respect. I shall
question Grace this instant; I have no more doubt of her than I have of myself, else at
this moment I should be quite miserable."

Mrs. Ward saw that *this* matter would quickly be cleared up, and considered that, in
justice to her own insinuation, her grand charge against Grace should not be passed
over. She believed Grace guilty, therefore she might be quite justified in telling her
mamma her suspicion about naming the Fairy Bower. She accordingly did so by
degrees, giving many proofs, which indeed, one after another, sounded sadly startling.
Poor Mrs. Leslie, on her part, remembered Grace's unusually low spirits that night after

the party, and her downcast manner the next morning; also, she had an impression of being frequently, latterly, puzzled at little things about Grace, which she could not understand. Yet, happy mother! in spite of all this accumulated evidence on every side, she did not doubt her child! such a character may a little girl gain and deserve at the age of ten years. Mrs. Ward did not tell that the last charge against poor Grace had become regularly the talk of the neighbourhood; at both parties they had been at lately, and at two at home, several persons had alluded to it in some way or other. Mrs. Ward might think it would too deeply pain Mrs. Leslie; but it would have been far better, if she thought it right to speak at all, to tell the whole. Mrs. Ward did not know that all the talk of her neighbours originated entirely from her own conversation with Mrs. Mason, above ten days ago.

CHAPTER XL

And if it were possible that he should always do rightly, yet when small numbers are to judge of his conduct, the bad will censure and obstruct him by malevolence, and the good sometimes by mistake.
JOHNSON

. . . Why any secret?
I love not secrets.
WALLENSTEIN

Mrs. LESLIE FOUND that her little daughter had been some time waiting for her; they, therefore, read together, as usual. After which, Mrs. Leslie said, "Grace, my dear, before you leave me, I have a few questions to ask you."

Her mamma's manner was serious, and Grace in a moment thought about the cup; she was not alarmed, as she was at first, about betraying Mary Anne,—she had got Emily's leave to do as she pleased, and she hoped the questions would be about the cup.

"What, mamma?" said she, eagerly and hopefully.

"Why did you not tell me you were ill on the evening of the party?"

This was quite unexpected to Grace—it startled her—and she paused for an answer. At any other time, the one which would have been true *now* would have done, viz., that she never liked to let her mamma know of those palpitations, because they always soon went away; but there was *another* reason, and she felt she could not give this alone; her face of expectation fell, and she was silent.

Mrs. Leslie continued—"Was it, Grace, because you broke the cup?"

"Oh, mamma!" cried Grace, with a voice of joy, "do you know I broke the cup? how glad I am!" and she hid her face against her mamma.

"My dear girl!" exclaimed her mamma, both shocked and amazed, "what can this mean? what could you have been thinking of, Grace, not to say so, when Mrs. Ward was asking about it the other day? and why did you not tell at first? Was that the reason you did not speak of your palpitation?"

"Oh, *no*, mamma!" cried Grace.

"Now, Grace," said her mamma, gravely, "this is a very serious matter; I will explain it to you, and you must answer me quite openly. Mrs. Ward does not *know*, but she *thinks* you broke the cup, and were afraid to say so; she thinks some other things, too, which I shall tell you. You see your character for truth is at stake with her; you are therefore *bound*, my dear child, to clear yourself if you can; at any rate, you can tell *me*. Now, Grace," continued her mamma presently, stroking the fair hair of her child, "you are old enough to act for yourself, and I hope firm enough to tell me exactly the truth, whatever it may be. I will first tell you, that *I* do not believe that you have done any thing very bad, though I must ask you some questions which will make you start."

Grace could only cling round her mother's neck, while her heart beat violently, and presently her tears flowed fast. At last she said, "Mamma, I care for nothing now you say *that*, and now you will know there is something wrong."

Mrs. Leslie said nothing to excite her little girl, but told her to go into the dressing-room and take a little water. "And when you come back, Grace," added she, "you shall explain as much of this mystery as you can." Grace did as she was bid: the water seemed to have a wonderful effect upon her; she felt quite equal to what she had to do, and, what was more, she knew what she meant to do. Since the discovery of the loss of the cup, Grace had foreseen, that most likely her mamma would speak to her, and she had thought much on what to do in that case. She had at last made up her mind; what line she resolved upon taking, will be seen in the following conversation. Grace returned, looking quite calm, and certainly feeling more comfortable than she had done for nearly a fortnight.

"Now, Grace," said her mamma, "tell me first how you broke the cup."

"I did not break it, mamma!"

"My dear child, you really quite puzzle me! what do you mean? you certainly said you did."

"Yes," returned the little girl, "I always *think* I did, because it was quite my fault: it was brought up for me, and I ought to have moved it; but it was Emily who actually broke it. She told me I might tell *you*, but I am not to tell her mamma, only to say that she, Emily, knows all about it."

"But why did not Emily tell?"

"Ah, mamma," said Grace, "there was the fault! I have thought it over and over again, till my head ached, and now I am quite sure *there* was the fault—but it cannot be helped now."

"But, my dear child, it can be helped now, if you tell, though it is indeed a sad pity—why did not Emily tell?"

"Because, mamma, Hanson had promised me to try and get the cup matched, and Emily thought it would be better to wait for the chance of a new cup; she thought her mamma would not be so much vexed."

"And that is all, is it?" asked Mrs. Leslie.

"All about the cup, I think."

"Then now, Grace, about your palpitation—why did it come? and why did you wish me not to know?—for I have heard you did."

"Yes, I did, mamma, and I believe I do now; though you cannot think how I should like to tell you all. I wish I knew what was best! I will tell you all, every bit, if you desire me, but if you do not, I must ask you to do me a very great favour indeed."

"My dear girl," said Mrs. Leslie, "I do not like so much mystery,—I do not think it can be right."

"Indeed, mamma," said Grace, with tears in her eyes, "it is *not right*, but I cannot help it now; the only reason I do not tell you all, is because I do not think you will like it, particularly just *now*; and Mrs. Ward will not like it, and I think you will not know what to do.—Shall I tell you?"

Mrs. Leslie paused for a little time, and then told Grace she would ask her two other questions, which were necessary; meanwhile she would consider over this matter. The first was about practising.

Grace said she had practised every morning an hour, except those she had mentioned before to her mamma,—saying, "Why should I not, mamma? you know I do at home."

The second startled poor Grace excessively on all accounts.—"Did you give the name to the Fairy Bower?"

"Oh, mamma," she cried, "who can think me so wicked! you know I *said* I did, and they drank my health; how could I have sat there, if I had not? or how could I look at you now?"—And she certainly raised eyes on her mamma's face, that must have been hardened in deception to have been any thing but true.—"What made you ask?" continued she.

"Because, my dear, it was observed that you looked pale, and seemed confused. Can you *prove*, Grace," said her mamma, "that you gave the name to the Fairy Bower?"

Grace considered, and said, "Yes, she thought she could." Then she remembered that Emily wished not to be applied to at present, because of Fanny's visit, and she added, "No, mamma, I do not think I could."

"Grace, every thing seems a mystery with you at present," said Mrs. Leslie.

"No, mamma," returned Grace, very despondingly, "only *one* great unfortunate mystery, and now will you say if I shall tell it you?—you know I wish it, but am afraid."

"Grace, are you prepared for the consequences if you do not? Mr. and Mrs. Ward, Emily, and all the rest, may think *doubtfully* of you—of your *truth*,—especially after we are gone; if you tell *me*, I can clear all up."

"Oh, mamma, you do not know half! If I tell you all, though I know you always know what to do, yet I think even *you* will be puzzled; and, indeed, mamma, I think it would be worse to me than all I have gone through, if this unfortunate secret came out through *me;* and I *think* you would not wish it: besides it will not be quite so bad as you fancy,—I have *one* kind friend who knows all."

"Then, my dear child, why does not that friend help you now?—that is the place of a friend."

"Ah, mamma," cried Grace, "there is *my* fault again! I have been full of faults and mistakes,"—and the tears sprung into her eyes—"and that is the reason I have got into such perplexity. At one time I could not do right, but now I think I can just manage to keep right, if you will let me."

"Then on the whole you prefer not telling me,—is that what you mean?"

"I think so, mamma."

Mrs. Leslie paused. She had seen her little girl's struggle between her strong wish of relieving her mind, and a certain feeling of propriety of some sort. She was doubtful if she should allow Grace to sacrifice herself to such a feeling. She saw some one else was in fault, and she naturally guessed Emily, who had already shown a want of straightforwardness. She thought Ellen was Grace's "friend," who had seemed so much more like-minded to Grace than her sister. She approved Grace's feeling, of not betraying Emily, who had been kind to her; and she thought, whatever the mystery was, it must shortly come out. Had Mrs. Ward mentioned the unworthy whisperings and surmises, that were abroad concerning her innocent child, she might have done differently; but Mrs. Leslie had the same generosity of principle as her daughter. Already also she respected Grace's liberty of action, and did not like to force a confession from her. She also believed Grace's judgment, that telling her would only add to the perplexity. She herself did not like to dwell on the alternative that might be presented to her, of betraying Emily to clear her child. Mrs. Ward had frequently laughed at Mrs. Leslie for her constant trust and confidence in others, yet the latter lady continued unchanged, and was now acting on her undoubting principle. Had she, could she ever have, suspected that her hostess entertained such unkindly feelings and thoughts, towards her little inoffensive guest, as to allow herself to be the foundation of a serious charge against her, and to spread it in the neighbourhood, she might *not* have adopted the line, which in the circumstances seemed to her the best, namely, to let matters rest with Grace, where they were, and to trust to Mrs. Ward for believing her and being satisfied for the present, with or without explanation. She therefore continued the conversation with her little girl thus:—"And Grace, you think you can be pretty sure that you will not be uneasy after we are gone, when you think that the family here are not regarding you altogether as you would wish?"

"I am *sure*, mamma, I shall care for nothing, when *you* know there is a secret, for that has been my trouble,—and—and—*this* is my trouble, mamma," continued she, "that I am afraid of every word I speak to you,—but I don't care now."

"Grace, I do not mean that it should always go on so; I do not like such mysteries."

"Do you mean to tell, mamma?" said Grace, looking much alarmed.

"No, I do not, my dear," said Mrs. Leslie; "but I think something must happen before long to bring out the truth."

"The truth, mamma!" cried Grace, thinking her mamma must have the whole matter in her mind.

"Yes, my dear, *the truth*,—you know the truth at present is in the dark."

Grace mused; she wondered how such expressive words could be used by any stranger to all the circumstances.

"Now, Grace," continued Mrs. Leslie, "tell me what was the favour you had to ask of me in case I did not desire to hear all your mystery."

"That you would be so very kind, mamma," said the little girl, "as not to betray me in the least, if you can help it."

Mrs. Leslie agreed to this, and Grace thanked her warmly. Mrs. Leslie asked what she meant to do about the cup.

Grace answered, if her mamma had no objection she would speak to Emily, and would herself immediately go to Mrs. Ward, and tell her how it happened.

Mrs. Leslie gave her leave, if she liked to do so.

"I cannot quite say I *like* it, mamma," said Grace, "for I believe I am a little more afraid of Mrs. Ward than of most people, but I had rather do it."

Grace asked her mamma one question, if she might tell Mrs. Ward properly the reason they did not speak about the cup—that they had hoped to match it. She added, "I did not like to do so, because it seemed as if I wished to. . . ."

"To lessen the fault, I suppose," said her mamma.

Grace assented.

"Well, Grace, it is a pity," returned Mrs. Leslie, "but you must not *refine* too much, (you know the meaning of that word, I think.) Under the circumstances, you had best tell as much of the truth as you can; you know you have by some means or other got into a tangle, and you must not wonder you have to pay for it a little, especially if you think you have not done *quite* right yourself."

Grace carried her mamma's last words away with her, as she often did, and had not done considering them before she had found Emily.

CHAPTER XLI

And mistress of herself, though china fall.
POPE

G RACE DID NOT ask Emily's leave, but told her she was going to tell her mamma her share in the breakage of the cup. "How I wish," she added, "I had broken it myself! Shall I say *you* broke it? or shall I say you know all about it? or will you go and tell your mamma yourself?"

Emily saw Grace was resolved upon going, and was not sorry to be spared, and to have the ice broken for her. She was afraid of her mamma, and had added to that feeling by putting off the evil hour, yet she continued to do the same. This is the way people do who have not firm principle. They act only for the very present moment; then try more to find the most pleasant, or least troublesome, rather than the right way; and to a certain point they succeed. They have often less trouble than others who strive to find the best way; but every now and then they find themselves in terrible straits, and think themselves the most unfortunate people in the whole world. We hope poor Emily will never come to such a pass as this; but she must take heed to herself and make a change, or when she grows up she will be in great danger. She followed the dangerous rule now; she told Grace, if she could not help it, to say, that *"Emily knew all about it."* This would put it off again; Hanson *might* come to-morrow; her mamma *might* be satisfied with Grace's explanation, and not say another word,—so she would be spared all unpleasantness.

Grace found Mrs. Ward alone, else she thought she must have deferred her explanation. She did not give herself time to pause, but at once said, as well as she was able, that the cup and saucer were broken by her fault, and expressed her sorrow for it.

"Then you *did* break it, after all!" said Mrs. Ward

Grace said she did not actually break it herself, but it was through her it was broken, and she considered it all her doing.

Mrs. Ward then asked if any of the servants broke it?—and then, *Who?*

Grace said Emily knew all about it, and would tell her if she wished.

Mrs. Ward then asked Grace why she did not tell her at once, since she was not afraid now.

Grace felt ashamed of answering this question, but said, "There was a chance of getting it matched."

Mrs. Ward assured her that was not likely, and added, "I suppose your mamma sent you here, Grace?"

The little girl said her mamma knew she was come, but did not send her.

Mrs. Ward seemed pleased that she came, but presently said, "How was it, Grace, you did not mention it the other day, when I was asking about it?"

Grace paused for an answer, and at length said, "Because I had promised to say nothing about it."

Mrs. Ward was so kind as not to press Grace farther. She knew now, if she wished it, she could hear all from her own daughter; she therefore only said, "Well, my dear, I am glad you have told me, as mystery about such a thing is unpleasant in a house."

Grace thought Mrs. Ward had never spoken so kindly to her before, and she now ventured to express her sorrow about the accident more strongly, and to allude to her hope that it might be matched.

Mrs. Ward was satisfied by her sorrow, for it seemed sincere, and told her to think no more of it, nor to make herself uneasy about the matching, since she knew it could not be done, even at Spodes'. She added a few more words, making light of the loss, saying it would make the rest more valuable.

Grace thought this very kind, for she had heard how much, and why, Mrs. Ward valued this tea service, and she went away considering what she could do to repair the accident in some way, supposing Hanson was not successful. Mrs. Ward expressed much pleasure to Mrs. Leslie, at her interview with Grace. She said that though Grace could not for some reason explain every point, she was certainly satisfied by her manner. Mrs. Leslie told her hostess that there was some mystery which Grace was not disposed to reveal at present, and that every thing they touched upon seemed to be connected with it; she had no doubt it would come out before long, and, if not, she should take means to discover it; but meanwhile, she begged Mrs. Ward to be so kind as to trust her little girl, for *her sake.*—"And of course," she added, "I need not ask you not to speak to any body of any thing you may have observed in Grace's conduct that appears at present unaccountable; it would be hard, perhaps, to remove a false impression of this kind, once made; and I can most entirely assure you, that in this case it would be *false.*"

In spite of Mrs. Ward's feeling of a sort of general disparagement of Mrs. Leslie's judgment; in particular cases she always found herself compelled to accept it; and this, added to the impression that Grace's manner and conduct had just left on her mind, made her feel somewhat uneasy, on the remembrance of her having unfortunately given vent to her prejudices against the little girl.

Mrs. Ward's interview with her daughter was perplexed, yet, as regarded Grace, satisfactory. Emily told her mamma that she herself broke the cup. Mrs. Ward was not angry, as Emily had expected, and Emily thought how foolish she had been to be so afraid of her mamma; then she thought, perhaps her mamma had been displeased with Grace instead, especially as she implied a question as to Grace's conduct. Emily felt she had been rather cowardly, and now took Grace's part warmly, saying, that Grace had nothing whatever to do with the breakage; that if she had taken *her* advice, it would have been safe now; and that Grace was very anxious the accident should have been mentioned immediately.

Mrs. Ward said that Grace naturally considered she had a share in the accident, since it was for her use the cup was brought up; and she asked her daughter why she did not mention that Grace was so poorly.

"Now, mamma," said Emily, in a more determined manner that she had ever used towards her mother, "I have made up my mind *now* to answer that question, and then you can do as you please. I will tell you all; but if I do, I think it will put an end to Fanny's visit this week."

"Why, Emily," cried Mrs. Ward, "you are full of mysteries! Here is Grace, and Mrs. Leslie, and now *you!* Why cannot you tell me at once, without all this fuss?"

"I am almost sure, mamma, it is all one mystery, and I will tell you at once, for it is exceedingly disagreeable to me to be the only person that knows it;—it is. . . ."

"Stop, Emily," cried her mother, in an authoritative tone. "I cannot at all tell that it is proper for me to hear, and I desire you would not tell it to me or any body else;"—and she was leaving the room.—She returned, however, and asked if Grace knew it; to which Emily answered, "Yes."

Emily felt disappointed that her mamma should not approve of what she was about to do; but she remembered, as a counterpoise, that her mamma had not been displeased, as she had expected, about the cup; and she had some pleasure in the thought that she could triumph to Grace, over the truth of her assertion, that her mamma would care far less for the loss of the cup, than the loss of Fanny Duff's visit to Grosvenor Square.

CHAPTER XLII

He spoke, when instant through the sable glooms
———— ————a flood of radiance came,
Swift as the lightning's flash.
AKENSIDE

T HE LAST EVENING of the young party together need not be particularly described. They had a small party,—the one postponed from the last Friday,—which was added to, and passed very pleasantly.—Perhaps it helped the young people to forget they were to part on the next morning; but Ellen was very full of it, and Grace never had it out of her head for a moment. In spite of every thing, the uncomfortable morning however came. All the family breakfasted, as usual, together. George kept his portion of the table in good spirits, being very absurd about the grief of parting, and crying in different ways for his sisters. "I can't cry for Grace," said he, "because I don't know how she cries, I never saw her! Emily, does Grace ever cry?"

Poor Grace felt very much ashamed, and quite afraid, lest Emily should say any thing uncomfortable to her feelings; for Emily did do so sometimes. Grace however had resolved if she did, to bear it well and good-naturedly, for she had learned in this visit of hers, that her own ways were not every body else's ways. Emily however this time only laughed, and asked George if he thought Grace and she spent their time in their room together, *crying?*

"No! no!" said George, "I know better than that! I know how you spend your time, and talk, as well as if I was there!"

"Well, how?" asked his sister.

"Why first," said he, "you sit over the fire cutting up and quizzing all the people you have been seeing. Emily says, 'How I hate Newton Grey, and all the Thompsons, and indeed all the rest! I think them all monstrous disagreeable,—don't you, Grace?' 'Yes,' says Grace, 'all but your brother George, and I think him more amusing a great deal than any body I ever met before!' Then, presently, up jumps Emily in a great fuss, —'Bless me,' says she, 'we shall be *so* late! I must begin to dress! Grace, dear, let me *do* my hair first!' Then Grace cries, 'Emily, love, only, look! I have got myself into a knot! what shall I do?'—and then Grace falls to crying, though Emily won't tell. 'Never mind,' says Emily; 'there!'—and she breaks the string.—'Now, Grace, dear, come and *do* my frock!' And so you go on till you are both done enough, or very likely quite overdone, like our goose last Michaelmas day."

All this was amusing. George again reverted to Grace's admiration of himself. Grace laughed. "Well," said George, "it's all quite true true, you know, and I have heard you say so once with my own ears."

"If I heard *you* speak of *me*," said Grace, "I am afraid you would not say any thing so pleasant."

"No," replied George, with an odd face, "I dare say I should call you a *prude*."

"Is George calling you a prude, Grace?" said Mr. Ward, who had caught the last words. "Never mind, so much the better! Master George is not the best judge in the world of such things."

This was rather a comfort to Grace, for she had never liked the idea of being a prude, though she hardly knew what it was. She now felt certain that the words she one day heard from George, *did* relate to herself. Meanwhile George was replying to some remark of his sister Emily's, who was pulling at his chain.—"Well," cried he, "I have no objection to show it! I am very proud of it still, and it is more useful to me than any chain I ever had!"

The chain was handed round the table, and its whole history given; in the course of which it was mentioned, that Grace did a great part of it before breakfast, instead of practising. This was not lost on Mrs. Ward. Mr. and Mrs. Ward admired its workmanship, and George was complimented on his good fortune. His papa also added a quaint rebuke to him on the inconsistency of his charge against Grace; and George whispered in a droll manner,—

> "Oh, let's have no feud,
> For George is no prude,
> But George is very rude.

So, Grace, you see, you begin and end with a choriambic."

Mr. Ward was to drive his two guests home in his way to London, so there was not much time for leave takings. Emily and Ellen both promised to write.to Grace, after Isabella's grand party; and Emily assured Grace she would tell her about *every thing*. Mrs. Leslie had also requested that Hanson would call at her house, which was scarcely out of her way, when she went to Hammersmith. Thus all affairs of business and pleasure seemed quite brought to a conclusion. The young people parted in gayer spirits than some of them expected, as Mrs. Ward half promised to bring them over to Cadogan Place, before they dispersed after the holidays.—"I cannot say *when*, Mrs Leslie," added she, "because, you know, this very cold weather Mr. Ward wants the carriage to go to Town; but any morning that is fit for him to go in the gig, I will drive them all over to say 'Good bye' once more to Grace, who, I can assure you, is a great favourite among them."

Mrs. Ward thought this testimony to Grace's popularity quite called for by what had passed that morning; and she kissed Grace, and said "my dear" again, in a way that made Grace observe and remember her kindness; though she was at that moment full of other thoughts towards her younger friends. At last all the farewells, and hopes, and wishes, came to an end, and the trio were closely shut up in the comfortable carriage, on their way towards London. After a little time, Mr. Ward exclaimed, "I have been very remiss, Mrs. Leslie!—it is well I remembered it in time. Yesterday, I sent to Everard, as he had not come down some days, as usual, and asked him to let me drive him home to dinner, since it was your last day. He sent me a note, written in great haste, which you shall see, and he ran in for two minutes just as I was setting off, to say a word on business, and bade me to be sure to remember his message to his little friend, Grace, which you will find in the note. I should be sorry, Grace, you should lose the compliments of such a *great man*, as Mr. Everard."

Mr. Ward handed the note to Mrs. Leslie, which, form the hasty writing, and the motion of the carriage, she was some time reading. On coming to the end, she said, "Here is some Latin, which you must be so good as to translate for us."

Mr. Ward took the note, and read straight through as follows:—

DEAR W.,

Very much obliged for your thought of me. I am engaged to dine with Lord Minorie,—a party I cannot escape from. Pray assure Mrs. Leslie of my most respectful adieux, and give a miniature message of the same kind to the *Grace* (if not the *Queen*) of the Fairy Bower, "Palmam qui meruit ferat," which I suppose you must construe to her, in spite of her classic pretensions.

Ever yours, faithfully,

B. E.

Mr. Ward added, that when Mr. Everard called in the afternoon, he mentioned an idea he had of going to his sister's, at Bath, for the rest of the vacation.—"Quite a sudden notion of his, I fancy," he said.

Mrs. Leslie heard this last remark in quite a mechanical manner. There are moments, be the subject what it may, when the mind seems enlightened all at once to a whole train of events or feelings, though all previously had seemed dark or dead. This was now Mrs. Leslie's case; she had read Mr. Everard's note with no especial understanding, beyond a kind parting with herself and her little daughter. The message to herself she prefectly understood,—and hardly noted Grace's; especially being balked by the few Latin words, almost too ill written for her to decipher as a well known motto. When she heard the note *read* through, and the Latin properly inserted, Mr. Everard's words and manner,—"Do not trust to my words, but do not forget them!—Verbum sapienti,"—and a hundred other coincidences, suddenly rushed to her mind. She felt certain, as by inspiration, that her own little Grace, and not Mary Anne Duff, was the deviser of the Fairy Bower! Here was the grand mystery! This accounted for every thing—for Grace's inconsistencies, perplexities, reserves—her palpitation—the broken cup—the connexion of Fanny's visit with all, of which Mrs. Ward had dropped a hint—her own surprise at detecting Grace's handiwork and ideas—and the wonderment concerning the naming of the Fairy Bower. She had been surprised at the entire cordiality of Grace and Emily, especially at parting.—Now it was clear, Mary Anne, not Emily, was the culprit; *Emily,* not Ellen, was the *"friend."* All this, and a multitude more thoughts, rushed through her mind with the speed of lightning, and she looked at her little girl, the colour on whose cheeks had not yet subsided on Mr. Everard's message. Her mamma read it her own way, as Grace's eyes were fixed on *her;* but Mr. Ward laughed, and complimented Grace on Mr. Everard's fine speeches; saying, they had given her quite a colour. As for Mrs. Leslie, the more she thought of all the events of the last fortnight, the more she was convinced of the truth of her new discovery; and the more she was amazed at what now seemed to her, her unaccountable dulness. Then again she did not wonder; how could she for an instant imagine so young a girl, brought up so carefully too as Mary Anne, could be lost to all right feeling, and such an adept in deceit! and when she looked upon it from this side, she doubted all her former thoughts, and blamed herself severely for allowing such a notion to enter her head. Meanwhile a slight conversation on common topics went on, till Mrs. Leslie and Grace reached their home. Mr. Ward saw them reinstated in their house, and then proceeded on his way to London.

CHAPTER XLIII

Home thou return'st from Thames, whose Naiads long
Have seen thee lingering.
                    COLLINS

GRACE FELT very unsettled, when she came to sit down and try to occupy herself at her home pursuits. Her mamma had said she should not do lessons that morning, since she had not prepared any; but they would begin quite regular the next day. Grace had therefore to set *herself* tasks; she had no difficulty in finding these, but much more in keeping herself steadily to them. She began ruling her ciphering book, which she had left undone for a week before. She wrote half a copy; then she began to learn her lessons, and then practised a little. Between each employment she rose and walked about, and altogether felt restless, and she knew it. It was very irksome to her to set to work heartily, and she felt vexed at not being able to command her mind as she usually could. "Mamma warned me of being unsettled," she thought, "but I am sure it is not the visiting; it is this unfortunate business that has happened, and I do not think any body could help it—there is no use trying;" and she was going on to satisfy herself that her restless state of body and mind was all very proper. Happily her mamma noticed it, and Grace always listened to the slightest remark of her mamma's. However she said, "But mamma, you know this has been such an extraordinary visit, and I have so much to think of."

"My dear," said Mrs. Leslie, "if you live to grow up, you will have many extraordinary things happen to you; most likely much more so than any thing that can occur to you, now that you are but a child. You should therefore take this visit as a trial, a sort of *rehearsal*, Grace, that you may act properly when you are upon the real stage of life."

Grace paused over this, and presently asked, "Mamma, did you ever in your life, when you were quite young, feel unsettled, and thinking of every thing but what you had to do?"

"Yes, my dear, very often; and sometimes when I was old, too.—I am not very far from your state now, Grace," said her mamma, with a smile.

Grace was amazed.—"Why, mamma," cried she, "that is impossible! you have been giving all manner of orders since we came in, and have thought of every thing, and have been nearly an hour reading all that heap of letters, and are now beginning to answer them, quite quietly. You can't have had all the thoughts roaming about your head that I have; I can hardly sit still for a minute."

"You need not tell me that, my dear, for I have seen it some time; and it has got worse and worse, has it not?"

Grace assented; and she knew what her mamma's remark meant to imply. She did not go on arguing as some really good little girls sometimes do; she believed what her mamma said about herself, and wondered at, and admired, her self-command. She therefore asked what her mamma advised her to do.

Mrs. Leslie advised her to sit down and write her French exercise for to-morrow, and not to attempt learning her lessons at present; she could do that in the afternoon.—"By the time your exercise is finished and you have put away this quantity of books, and your desk, and every thing else, Grace," added her mamma, smiling and pointing to the mass of employment with which poor Grace had surrounded herself, "I shall be ready to take a little walk with you, and then it will be dinner time."

Grace put away all the extraneous articles first, and then sat down to her exercise. She did it with a good heart, and presently was surprised to find she was falling quite naturally into her French verbs and genders, and turning as readily as ever to the well known places in her grammar and dictionary. Other thoughts came in between whiles, but not to disturb her or make her restless as before. She was surprised to find nearly an hour had passed in this way, and her mamma was calling her to put on her bonnet, as the sun was shining very invitingly. As she ran up stairs, her thoughts fell, as at home and abroad, on her mamma's goodness and the correctness of her advice.—"Whatever I want," thought she, "mamma can tell me; and whether I think it right or not, or pleasant or unpleasant at the time, it always comes right afterwards." As they went out her mamma gave her a word of praise on the late conquest of her restless spirit. Very sweet it was to Grace's heart, and she pressed her dear mamma's hand as they walked, which was a custom of hers when they went out together.

On the Friday this week, Mrs. Leslie had a note from Mrs. Ward, saying they had so many engagements, she could not bring the young people over the next week, as she had intended. They were engaged at home and abroad the beginning of the week; Wednesday, the 28th, was Isabella's grand party; after which Emily and Ellen were going for a long promised visit for a couple of days to Twickenham. She had therefore arranged to keep Emily and George a day longer from school, and hoped to spend Monday, the 1st of February, with them, in Cadogan Place. She mentioned having taken Fanny Duff to Grosvenor Square the day after they left (which plan had been previously arranged.) There was no more particular news. Mr. Everard was in Bath, but must be back the end of next week. Mrs. Ward went on to say, "The young people miss Grace greatly; I have nothing but lamentations, and George is very funny about it sometimes. Also, *you* have made a great sensation in our world; you, and your singing, are endless topics of conversation."

It gave Grace great pleasure to hear of her young friends, and also to think the day was fixed for seeing them again. All the news in this letter was discussed with her mamma, and Isabella's party was mentioned; Mrs. Leslie asked her little girl, if she had any wish about going, or was disappointed that she did not. Grace said she did not think *really* of going, but she had had rather a wish about it."

"A wish to go?" asked her mamma; "I thought you wished never again to go to a party of this kind, in London."

"Oh, mamma," cried Grace, "Isabella's party could not have been like that; besides, you know, this would have been a different sort of party from any I have ever been at."

"In what respect?" said Mrs. Leslie.

"Why, mamma," answered Grace, rather ashamed, "my reason for wishing to go was, because it was at a nobleman's house; and because I should have seen several little lords and ladies."

"Well, Grace," said Mrs. Leslie, "that is a very fair reason for wishing to go."

"I am glad you do not think it wrong, mamma," said Grace, rather reassured, "for I was glad for the same reason, when Lord Musgrove spoke to me, the other evening, though Lord Musgrove is not like any *old* nobleman—the Earl of Warwick, or the Duke of Northumberland, mamma! It would be next to seeing the King to see the Duke of Northumberland, I think—because of Hotspur."

Mrs. Leslie said, her little girl's feelings were very natural; and she hoped, some day, she would see some of those great people.

"I did not only mean *see*, mamma," said Grace, "when I was speaking just now; I thought of being in the same room with them, and hearing them speak, and perhaps being spoken to by them. Why, you know, mamma, what a thing it would be if the King spoke to me, or the Queen, if we had one! and this would be the same sort of thing."

"Well, my dear," replied Mrs. Leslie, "you would not have met our good King, or even the Duke of Northumberland, at Lord Musgrove's, or any very illustrious people in that way; so you must make that your consolation on this occasion; and happily for us, *good* people are quite as often met with in our rank as in any other. I have often, however, Grace, regretted for you, that it should so be that your youthful days should have fallen upon a time, when, we may say, we have neither King nor Queen. In my young days, our good King was in health, and it was my grandest treat to be taken to see him in processions, and at more private times. Indeed it is a pleasure to me now to look back on those days, and I am sorry you will not have the same."

"But, mamma," said Grace, "I have seen his coach, and the beautiful horses, and the Prince Regent, and that is something near the King himself."

"Yes, my dear, and now we look upon the Prince Regent almost as King; but *I* cannot feel it the same, when I remember his father."

The conversation was here disturbed by the entrance of visitors, and soon after Mrs. Leslie and Grace went out for their walk.

CHAPTER XLIV

I'll read again the Ode that I have writ.
SHAKESPEARE

T HE KIND READER must consent to leave Grace and her mamma a short time, and accompany us to Grosvenor Square, to see what is going on there this very day, just before dinner time. There was a dinner party expected. Isabella not yet being introduced, never joined the company, except at quiet family parties; and she did not much like appearing at all before dinner, from the difficulty of disposing of herself on its announcement. It must be confessed, this ambiguous age is very awkward for young ladies; but Isabella had helped to thrust herself into it two or three years earlier than most of her contemporaries. Besides, had she been older, most likely she would not have been required to appear in any way uncomfortable to herself. She had now retired to the back drawing-room, and was pretty well shaded by the broad back of a capacious chair, on which herself and her friend Fanny Duff were seated. Both were leaning forward on a small table, upon which were pen, ink, and a sheet of paper spread open. Fanny was gazing in a sort of reverie, looking rather puzzled than genius-struck, and presently she laid down her pen, as though giving the matter over for the present. "Gracious me!" cried Isabella, "if mamma does not come down presently, I shall have to receive all the company!—How disagreeable it will be, darling *mignonne!*" added she, in not at all a dissatisfied tone.—"Oh, Fanny!" presently she exclaimed, "we shall have Lord Minorie here presently; how delightful that will be!"

"Who is Lord Minorie?" asked Fanny, with some awe.

"Do you not know Lord Minorie?—Lord Minorie, the poet! Why you might as well not know Lord Byron! He has published volumes upon volumes of poetry, and some people like him better than Lord Byron."

"I should like to see a poet and a Lord," said Fanny, in a tone rather doubtful as to which should have the preeminence.

"Yes, very likely, but that is not what I am thinking of; I should like him to see your verses, *mignonne;* I am sure he will think them very clever, and he could make you quite fashionable, if he chooses. He is such a funny little old man! he always says, 'my dear,' and has such odd manners."

This account rather confused Fanny's notions. She thought a poet was always young and handsome, wore an open collar, and looked very haughty and gloomy; or old and blind, with a long beard, like Homer, or the Welsh bards. She also thought a Lord had always very grand manners, and was tall, and noble in countenance; and her host had helped to establish her ideas. She was amazed to hear Isabella criticise so fearlessly a poet, who had printed volume upon volumes,—and a Lord.

"Here's a carriage!" cried Isabella, "I'm sure it is Lord Minorie, darling *mignonne!* he always comes a long time before any body;" and she went into the other room to receive him.

Fanny changed her place a little, to get a view of the expected guest. In he came presently. His appearance certainly justified Isabella's description; an odd little old man, he certainly was. His young hostess received him with a good deal of air, which he seemed not to appreciate.

"Yes, my dear, yes," said he, in a fidgety manner, "I know I am early; I guessed mamma would not be dressed after her morning's drive.—Well, what have you got here?" continued he, walking to a table, and opening books; "any thing new?—Who's that? eh?" said he, spying Fanny in the next room, and taking up his glass.

Isabella followed him, and attempted a formal introduction, which seemed little heeded.

"What's she about?—writing? let me see,—verses, I declare! why, what's this, my dear? have you got a young poetess hidden here? come, give them to me,—let me read;" and he seated himself at Fanny's side, took out his spectacles with deliberation, and read the following verses. They were in a childish hand-writing, and though ill-written, were not illegible:—

> On living things and dead I call,
> Oh, listen to my verses all,
> And tell me what upon our ball,
>   Is like my friend.
>
> The birds that sing so merrily,
> The moths, and fishes of the sea,
> The skipping lambs, too, full of glee,
>   Are like my friend.
>
> The slow and spouting little stream,
> That runs along but is never seen
> But where it shines high reeds between,
>   Is like my friend.
>
> The red red and the pure white rose,
> That both in summer and winter blows,
> And well would crown her lovely brows,
>   Are like my friend.
>
> The hard and bold and stubborn rock,
> The elm, or deeply planted oak,

> That storms and furious Boreas mock,
>   Are like my friend.
>
> Oh, dearest friend! then come with me,
> Together let us always be,
> Happy in far-off Araby,
>   And let us die!
>
> Or, in a brilliant Fairy Bower,
> Sparkling with light and every flower,
> Where the world and storms have no more power,
>   Do let us die!
>
> Or, in a happy convent's gloom,
> Nuns—shut up in our dismal room,
> Let us our miseries all entomb,
>   And let us die!
>
> Where'er I go, where'er I stray, . . .

Here the MS. broke off. The poet read these lines quickly through to himself.—"Well, done!—very good!—very good indeed, my dear!" said this good-natured gentleman; "I know they are all your own; How old are you?"

"Nearly twelve," answered Fanny, as composedly as she could, for she was naturally elated at so much praise from a poet and a Lord.

"Well," said he, "go on—go on; and by the time you are eighteen you will make a tolerable versifier—perhaps something more by twenty, or so; but you must not soon be satisfied, there's a great deal yet to learn. And now I will criticise your verses, which will be a good lesson for you, for there's a vast deal amiss in them."

Fanny felt disappointed; she thought them *good*, before Lord Minorie appeared, and after his praise, she thought them perfect.

"Now my dear," continued he, "what do you mean by 'our ball?' "

"Our earth," said Fanny.

"Ah, so I suppose; but that won't do at all; and all that stanza is poor—poor indeed!—Moths—moths,—what d'ye mean by that?"

"Butterflies," replied the young poetess, "but it would not come in."

"No," replied Lord Minorie, "nor be a very flattering similitude. Well, *'spouting,'* what is that?"

"Spouting out between the stones," said Fanny.

"Ah! ah" returned the poet, "that won't do! we'll put a mark against *that*. Don't you see something very amiss in this stanza?—oh, for shame!" and he struck out the rhymes *stream* and *seen*; "that will never do! And these lines—

> " 'That runs along and is never seen,'

> " 'Both in summer and winter blows.'

"These do not scan nicely; we must find something better than that. What d'ye mean, my dear, by roses blowing in summer and winter? I never heard of a rose good for any thing that does so."

"Artificial roses," said Fanny.

"No! no!" answered the critic, "never compare a lady to mock flowers,—that won't do at all. Well, I suppose you mean she's as 'firm as a rock,' by this stanza?"

"Yes," replied Fanny.

"Well, we'll make that do," said Lord Minorie, "but it's no compliment, you know, to call a lady bold and stubborn; we must do something with that;" and he put another great stroke across the line. "Boreas—Boreas! Oh, no!" continued he, shaking his head. "Well, the ideas are all fair, very fair. Now we come to a change. Umph! umph! don't be so fond of dying! What's this brilliant fairy bower?"

"It alludes to a bower of my sister's invention," said Fanny

"Well, we'll keep that then! Ah! convent! nuns!—very good! Happy—miseries! that's queer! what were you going on to say, my dear?"

Fanny said, some more verses, but she did not know what.

"You should always have an idea, and don't write too much. Well, we can make something of it—a snug, pretty sonnet, I can see. Here, get me a pen;" and he took out his knife, and deliberately set to mending the pen. "Now for it!"

In a very neat precise hand, very different from his scratches, he inserted his corrections between Fanny's broad lines. When he had got half way, Lady Musgrove came in. "Here I am, my lady," cried he; "coming to you in a moment; but I have found a young Sappho here, and we are busy courting the muses." He then told Fanny to transcribe from his paper what was corrected, while he went and spoke to her Ladyship.

Presently Lord Musgrove entered, and the guests began to arrive. Meanwhile a conversation passed between the poet and his hostess; which, as it relates to one of our friends, we will report.

"I had the great pleasure of meeting and being introduced to your Lordship's friend Mr. Everard, the other day," said the lady.

"Am happy to hear it, but more happy that you call it a pleasure."

"To be sure I do," answered Lady Musgrove, "I think Mr. Everard is one of the most agreeable gentleman-like persons I have seen a long time; and so wonderfully clever and original."

"Yes, yes! enough of that certainly, and unaccountable besides! why now he has taken himself off to Bath—broken all his engagements! no one on earth knows why! But before you use your soft words, your ladyship should see him toss some of his victims; he can do it in grand style, I can tell you."

"There was nothing like that," replied the lady, "it was a juvenile party at Mr. Ward's at Fulham, and he was so pleasant and condescending, entering quite into the amusements of the young people, making extempore odes and speeches,—really most excellent."

"Yes, yes!" said the poet, "he's a good hand enough at all that. I can't do it,—no, not I."

"Besides," said Lady Musgrove, "I had the pleasure of a long conversation with him, and I thought him one of the most sensible men in the world: and his voice,—oh, my Lord! his voice would be the making of him, if he had nothing else in the world. I assure you, his verses and speeches to the children, were as great a treat to us grown people, as a professional reader. They had dressed up what they called a little Fairy Bower, and he took up the notion most happily."

"Ah!" cried the poet, "that reminds me of my business with my young friend there;

your Ladyship will excuse me, and not wait dinner for me if I have not finished, I know."

"Oh, my Lord!" cried his hostess, laughing, "you are a privileged person; you may always do as you please. And he fidgeted into the back drawing-room. He found Fanny and Isabella together had just completed the copy as far as corrected. He then took his pen, and went on. Meanwhile dinner was announced. He nodded to Lady Musgrove's summons as she passed, and said, "Yes, yes, your Ladyship; coming,—coming before your soup's gone round!"

The lady smiled, called him an eccentric being, and the trio were left quite to themselves. The noble poet went on writing very rapidly, soliloquizing criticisms by the way; he mentioned Mr. Everard's name when he came to the Fairy Bower, to Fanny's amazement. He was not long over the three remaining stanzas. "Now," said he, "we will have one more verse and no more;" and he began writing,—But—What's your friend's Christian name?" asked he, quickly.

"Isabella."

"Ah! that will do," replied he, and he wrote off the last verse, as will be presently seen. "There," cried he, "I suppose that's the sort of thing you wished to say! now, young Sappho! write out your own lines fair, and compare them with those I have finished; that will be a good lesson for you; you'll find your ideas were all disjointed, and running one after another. I have put them together and made a whole piece of them. But, remember, it is *not mine!* I have kept to your words, even,—I have only doctored it up a little. Go on, and improve, my dear," said he, rising, and giving her an encouraging pat; "pray who's your friend?"

"Isabella," said Fanny, looking surprised, and signifying Miss Ward.

"Oh!" cried the poet, in a tone not very flattering to either the poetess or the subject of her lay. "Well," said he, "you know it's all your doing;" and he quickly departed for his dinner below; joining the party, as he had promised, "before the soup had gone round."

"He never hears me called any thing but Miss Ward, *mignonne!*" said Isabella as he left the room.

"I wonder he did not guess," said Fanny.

"Oh, he is such an odd old man, darling!" returned her friend. "But now read your verses."

Fanny read as follows:—

> Search Nature's stores for things of worth,
> Of beauty, modesty, and mirth,
> And say what likest most on earth
>   My precious friend.
>
> Like birds that sing so cheerily,
> Like insects in their dance of glee,
> Like bounding lambkins mild and free,
>   My sportive friend.
>
> Like a fair stream that glides unseen,
> Save where it shines tall reeds between,

Yet paints the neighbouring banks with green,
          My modest friend.

Like blushing rose, like rose of white,
Purest and fairest flowers to sight,
Yet frailer than my ladie bright,
          My lovely friend.

Like rooted oak, like deep-set rock,
That stand unmov'd man's fiercest shock,
And twice a thousand tempests mock,
          My constant friend.

Say, dearest! will thou bide with me
In homes of bliss and ecstasy!
Or shall we two more pensively
          Our life's day end!

Shall we in brilliant Fairy Bower,
Sparkling with light and many a flower,
Far, far from man, his pomp and power,
          Our bright days end?

Or shall we, nuns in cloister gloom,
Shut up within our narrow room,
All worldly vanities entomb,
          Our calm days end?

But, precious friend, where'er I dwell,
Or in bright home, or drearier cell,
Still, still with thee, my Isabel,
          My days I'll end!

Isabella was too well satisfied with these verses to repine at what she might have lost in any of Fanny's. Not quite so Fanny: she thought Lord Minorie's version better as a whole, but regretted some favourite lines and ideas of her own, which had been sacrificed. One was in the seond stanza, where she had gathered together birds, beasts, fishes, and insects, (under their representatives, "moths,") as doing homage to her friend. She was sorry to lose any part of the animal creation; and she found her "fishes" had quite disappeared. Then she was sorry to lose the idea of "crowning her lovely brows;" and "Boreas" was also a great friend of hers. But worse than all was the loss of her beloved "far-off Araby," which usually appeared in every composition of hers. If Fanny had followed the kind poet's directions, and copied out her own verses to compare with his, some day, if not now, she might have understood the value of his remarks, and advice. She did not do so at this moment; she only transcribed the remaining verses, thinking the other, if necessary, could be done at any time. Afterwards she got so much more praise for these lines, than for any she had hitherto written, that the idea of so doing quite passed away from her mind. Grace was likely to have written them out at once, merely because she was told to do so by a kind and clever gentleman, who had taken some pains to help her, and staid away from his dinner for the purpose. Fanny did not look upon it in this light, though it would have been much the most proper way of showing her reverence to him as a poet and a Lord.

CHAPTER XLV

What then is taste?————————
————————————a discerning sense
Of decent and sublime, with quick disgust
From things deformed, or disarranged, or gross
In species. This nor gems, nor stores of gold,
Nor purple state, nor culture can bestow.
                                    AKENSIDE

W E MUST PASS ON to the following Friday, which was two days after Isabella's long talked of party. In the evening of that day, the post brought the welcome and expected packet from Fulham. Grace received her portion with joy, and found the promise of a great treat in the quantity it seemed to contain. She opened Emily's naturally first. It ran thus:—

MY DEAR GRACE,

I have got a great many things to tell you; and some very strange, which I will begin with. We went early to Grosvenor Square yesterday, as my aunt had requested, in case we could help Isabella in any thing; for this time she was full of plans, owing to the Fairy Bower; but, you know, she has no taste or management of her own. Well, we got there between five and six, and who do you think we found there? "Why, *Fanny!*" you will say. Yes; but who else?—in her morning dress? she came the day before. You will never guess!—why, Mary Anne! Are you not surprised? Well, guess again, *why* she came.—I am sure you can't. She came to devise something like the Fairy Bower! I assure you when I heard it, I was more angry than I can tell you. But really, angry as I was, I could presently do nothing but laugh. They took us into my aunt's boudoir, a smaller back room, where every thing was prepared to surprise us. All the lights were lit all over the room, and certainly there was a great blaze at first, since the other rooms were not yet lit up. At the end of this room there is a rather deep recess, which generally holds an old fashioned cabinet. This they had removed, and fitted it up (the space, I mean) as a Fairy Bower,—they could not think of any other title. This was the only good idea of the whole; I am sure if *you* had been there, it would have been very pretty indeed; but you never saw such a mixture as it was. There was a great deal more of Isabella's devices than Mary Anne's. Behind was a large transparency, as a big as a door, with—what do you think upon it? The verses of Fanny to Isabella, (which we shall enclose.) It was exceedingly ugly and large. In the middle, from the ceiling, which is very high, hung Isabella's favourite—an immense Chinese lamp; and across the front of the recess, in imitation of the festoons of roses, were suspended rows of coloured lamps, such as they hang out of doors in illuminations, —yellow, red, and blue. Then there was an attempt at flowers and evergreens; but they had not half enough, and it had no effect at all. I stood and laughed till I could hardly stand, and George was more unmerciful still. He said some odd things in jest, about the two Fairy Bowers, and spoke of you. But I felt sure that any one who saw both, must know that the same person did not plan them. Isabella's taste, you know, came in; you remember she wished us to have coloured lamps and transparencies. One thing, I must say, was quite different; and that was Fanny's verses. They seem to me very pretty, really; and all the grown-up people admired them very much indeed. She was quite the "Queen" of the evening, was introduced to a great many grand people, and as much made of her as of Mary Anne, at our party; indeed more, because, you know, Fanny can behave so much better than Mary Anne. She had quite a new frock, which her mamma had got at Madame Fillarie's. My uncle had given her a very handsome long *neligée*, of Venetian beads, which she wore, and looked very well indeed. She was in as good spirits as Mary Anne at our party, but not boisterous, like her. It was rather awkward about the dancing, for they two were the only ones who did not dance; but they were taken into the room with the elder people, and made a great deal of. I think Fanny would have managed to dance, if Mary Anne had not been there. She wished very much to dance with some of the little Lords; there were not a great many, though, and it was not a very pleasant party, though so much better than the London one you were at, that I wished you were there. Ellen has caught a bad cold coming home, and mamma talks of not coming to you on Monday, but some day later; if so, I shall not go to school till the end of the week. Now, good-bye, my dear Grace, and believe me

Yours affectionately,

EMILY WARD.

George desires his love. We have heard nothing of Hanson.

Ellen's letter was as follows:—

MY DEAR GRACE,

I am quite glad I have a cold, because I can write you a long letter; though I am sorry that our visit to Twickenham is put off. Isabella's party last night was very pleasant, but rather dull. Fanny finished her lines the second day she was there. My uncle and aunt were very much pleased with them, and my uncle gave her a beautiful long bead necklace. They were so pleased with them, that they had them printed on large cards, and distributed to every body that came. Some were in letters of gold: we send you one. Isabella and Fanny tried all they could, and at last persuaded my aunt to ask Mary Anne to come and make a Fairy Bower, like ours: so she wrote to aunt Duff, and asked all my cousins to the party, and Mary Anne to come on Monday; and she said she would drive to Winterton on Monday, and bring Mary Anne back, and then all could go home together after the party.

But nobody came but Mary Anne on Monday, and mamma heard to-day the reason. Campbell said he did not like Isabella well enough, and did not want to go; and Constance, you know, *said* she would not go, if they all came to ask her, (you know they *did*—was it not curious?) and it was not worth while sending Charlotte alone; so I believe Mary Anne and Fanny will stay a few days longer. Their Fairy Bower was very showy; but it was not pretty; like the other. They tried to make flowers, but could not; and Isabella sent out quite at last to her mamma's milliner, and got some artificial flowers; but they looked very few and poor, though they were much more beautiful than ours, when you looked close at them, and I believe they cost a great deal. Isabella got her way about the Chinese lamp, and the coloured lamps; but the housemaid came in and made a great fuss, and said she would not have oil in *her* room; and she made Isabella have spirit of wine. There was also a transparency of Fanny's verses behind, which you could have read a long way off, if it had not been for the lamps in front; but it was not pretty. There was one misfortune which I had nearly forgotten: the lights were lit so early, to show us, that all the spirit of wine was burned out, long before the end of the evening. If they could have taken them away, I think it would have been better than at first; but it looked very odd indeed, with these dark balls hanging before the rest: the light behind was not very strong, and none of the lights were well managed.—They wanted you for that, for you understood that part a great deal better than Mary Anne. My sore throat has got worse, instead of better, and I am not to leave my room to-day. I hope you are quite well, and your mamma. I have got her beautiful little scent bag, which she was so kind as to put in my work-box one day, to scent it. I shall now always think of her when I open it, and you too, Grace. I will bring it or send it next week, if they go. I am quite tired of writing.

Believe me, dear Grace,

Yours affectionately,

ELLEN WARD.

Mrs. Leslie had a note from Mrs. Ward, explaining their not coming on Monday. She said Ellen was very poorly, and not likely to be better for a day or two. She had been obliged to put off their visit to Twickenham till Monday. She hoped to come to them, however, on Thursday. She said the party last night was all very well. Mary Anne, however, quite failed in the Fairy Bower, she supposed from Isabella's interference. Fanny got justly great credit for her verses, which were really hers, though Lord Minorie had looked over them and corrected them. She mentioned that Lady Musgrove had told her that Isabella's Fairy Bower was really an expensive affair, though such a poor thing.—With the painting, the transparency, the printing, the flowers, and the lamps, not less than ten pounds.—"A silly piece of business altogether," added Mrs. Ward, "and I was glad that Mary Anne and Fanny had little or nothing to do with these expenses. I refer you to the girls' letters for a fuller account of this grand business."

This completed the account of the party. Grace looked at the dangerous pieces of Emily's letter two or three times, to see if her mamma would make any thing of them. She had known her pass over things much more plain; and whatever they betrayed, she shrunk from concealing any part from her mamma; so, with only a little hesitation, she put the letters into her mamma's hand.

Mrs. Leslie told her to read them to her, if she liked; and said she did not want to hear every word, if there were any "affectionate little sayings," meant for her only.

Grace could not miss any thing with this sort of permission, and read quite through, finding the dangerous passages hardly dangerous at all from their context. Her mamma made no remark about them, but the subjects they afforded furnished conversation for the rest of the evening.

CHAPTER XLVI

Lullaby, lullaby, hush thee, my dear!
Castle Spectre

Monday, THE FIRST OF FEBRUARY, came, but did not bring the hopes with it, it had promised to do; for the visit of the young party was postponed. It was one o'clock: Grace had finished all her lessons early, and was giving herself a treat at her favourite Moravian work, in the space she had gained. She was talking to her mamma of Emily and Ellen's visit to Twickenham, and her mamma had just said she should be glad to know that Ellen's cold was well enough to allow of it, when the door opened, and the servant informed his mistress that there was a person below, named Ann Hanson, waiting to speak to her.

"You may show her in immediately, Richard," said Mrs. Leslie; while poor Grace's needle tried very hard to go on at the same pace as before, and her heart beat alternately with hope and fear.—"Oh," thought she, "it is quite impossible—so I do not expect it at all."

Hanson came in with a smile on her face, which respect could hardly subdue. Grace's intention *not to expect*, was a little shaken; and what could she think of hope when she spied a small neat deal box, half hidden, half exposed, under Hanson's comfortable cloak! Mrs. Leslie asked after the little nieces. They were getting well,—had had the measles very slightly. Poor Grace was obliged to keep quiet, and hear two or three such sentences exchanged, before her extreme eagerness was relieved. It was a good trial; for in life nothing is more common than suspense, and to some tempers nothing more intolerable. Perhaps Grace was of such a frame, for short as the time was, her head ached to a point of intensity, and her heart beat so violently, that she was afraid of speaking. Hanson kept her as short a time as possible. She had been looking smilingly at her all along, which only increased Grace's hopes and fears; and now said, "If you please, ma'am, I have got this box for Miss Grace." Now was it a cup, or something quite different? "It came," continued Hanson, "from Staffordshire only this morning."

Grace had learned to connect Spode and Staffordshire! but she could hardly trust the hope that seemed nearer and nearer. The box luckily had been opened, and was only slightly tied. It was undone. It was full of hay; she displaced it carefully,—and discerned a cup—the very pattern! She sought for the saucer,—found another cup: she looked amazed in Hanson's pleased face, who bade her go on, and she found two saucers.

"Hanson must be a conjurer!" said Mrs. Leslie.

Hanson laughed, and said, "Oh, no, indeed, ma'am."

"Then Hanson's friend!" continued Mrs. Leslie.

"Oh, no, ma'am, indeed, no more than me; only John Edwards is a very clever man, and very good-natured."

Grace had by this time discovered the secret of multiplication. One cup and saucer was new, the other was mended. "Can it really be the broken one!—look, mamma!" cried Grace, "who could ever tell on this side?" She then turned them, and showed two or three rivets, which Hanson said they assured her would bear any wear as well as the new one. "Well, Hanson," said Grace, "how can I ever thank you enough! and John Edwards too! I really had quite given it up."

Hanson said she was quite as pleased to be able to get them, as Miss Grace was to have them; that none of the people at Spodes' could match them, but that a private friend among the workmen could do a great deal. John Edwards came from Staffordshire, and all his family were in Spodes' works: his brother set about matching the cup immediately, and succeeded, she did not know how; also he mended the other. He also sent her word, that if she gave him time, he would at any other time get her as much or as little of the same tea-service, as she wished; there might be a trifle of difference in the pattern or shape, but it would be of no consequence.

Grace had unsprung the lock of the secret drawer of her desk, and asked Hanson what she owed her, not forgetting the mending, and the carriage of the box, which she thought would be very high, coming so far as Staffordshire.

Hanson told her the price of the cup and saucer; but said the box was sent up in one of Spodes' crates, and that James Edwards charged nothing for the mending.

Mrs. Leslie let her little girl pay for the cup and saucer, and herself made a present to Hanson and John Edwards for the trouble they had been at. Hanson was distressed at receiving any thing; but Mrs. Leslie advised her to take it, and perhaps she could spend it on some little thing, for one of her nephews or nieces. Hanson was pacified by this idea, and talked of her little god-son, and a Bible and Prayer-book. She thanked Mrs. Leslie very much, and said that she had had great pleasure in doing any thing for Miss Grace; though she did not think she should have thought so much about it, but for seeing her so ill that evening.

They then talked of Fulham, where Hanson was going to call. They told her she would not see the young ladies, if Ellen was well enough to leave home. Hanson was exceedingly concerned to hear of Ellen's cold.—"Dear! dear!" cried she, "poor dear lamb! she's going to have one of her bad sore throats! I must go and nurse her; nobody knows so much of her as I do." And she began to take her leave that moment. She did not however forget to remark to Grace of her own accord, that she should say nothing of her success at Fulham, except to Miss Emily.

Grace thanked her, and said, certainly she should like to have the pleasure of surprising Mrs. Ward herself with the sight of the cups on Thursday.

"Well, my dear Grace," said Mrs. Leslie, some time after Hanson's departure, "you seem to have forgotten your piece of good fortune; what are you thinking of?"

"I was thinking, mamma," answered the little girl, "how curiously one thing hangs upon another, and how fortunate and unfortunate, things may be at the same time."

Her mamma asked what occasioned these thoughts.

"Why, you know, mamma, the same thing was the cause of the accident, and the cause of its being repaired; because, you know, Hanson pitied me for being ill, as she thought it."

"And I dare say, Grace, if you go on," remarked her mamma, "you could hang a great many more events upon your string."

How Grace would have liked to do so! but instead, she fell into a reverie on the probability of her ever being able to speak openly on this matter to her mamma. We must leave her for the present to her *pros* and her *cons*, and pay a little visit to our friends at Fulham.

The postponement of the Twickenham visit had been equally convenient to both parties concerned. Mrs. Ward engaged, illness not preventing, to send her girls on the Monday, for two days, instead; stating at the same time the possibility of its not being prudent for Ellen to venture out: in that case, little Clara was to go. Monday came. —Ellen, though better, was certainly in no fit state to leave her room. She was disappointed naturally, but pleased that her loss was Clara's gain. She however thought more of her want of a companion, when disabled from her usual pursuits, than of the loss of her expected pleasure among strangers. George was not a very good companion for one sister alone, especially when that sister was not well enough to enter into his high spirits; and George at all times found Emily more suited to him than Ellen. Young people who have high spirits and the power of amusement, should beware of indulging their disposition too much, lest their domestic character should be injured. Many a diverting youth grows into a dull man; and many an entertaining man is acceptable at any place but his own home; where he is always heavy and uninteresting,—perhaps dissatisfied and ill-humoured,—till a stranger calls forth his powers. This looks very like vanity. Accomplishments and lively talents ought in the first instance to be spent on those nearest to us, who usually have the greatest claim on us. We should never forget, that however great or clever a man may be in the world or society, *home* is the element and the trial of a Christian. Ellen was occupied by none of these thoughts, however, but sitting over some work rather dismal, in the day nursery, when the door opened, and Hanson appeared.—"Oh, Hanson!" cried she, "how glad I am I did not go away to day!"

"Oh, Miss Ellen, my poor dear lamb!" cried Hanson, in return, "how grieved I am to see you wrapt up so!—how's your throat?"

Ellen told her she was much better, and was promised to be allowed to come down to breakfast as usual to-morrow.

Hanson said if her mamma would allow it, she certainly would stay till she was down stairs again.

This was very pleasant hearing for Ellen, who was always happy in good Hanson's company. What is more interesting to an affectionate child, than the company of a kind sensible nurse of its younger days? Such a character is invested with the familiarity of childhood and the wisdom of age; and many can bear witness to the maxins of goodness and truth they have learned in a nursery, under such governance. We are glad to leave Ellen and her nurse so well in their situations, and will pass on a few hours.

CHAPTER XLVII

There was an old woman, and what do you think?
She lived upon nothing but victuals and drink;
Victuals and drink were the chief of her diet,
And yet this old woman could never be quiet.
NURSERY RHYME

"MY DEAR," said Mr. Ward, putting in his head at the drawing-room door, as once before he had done at the breakfast-room,—"My dear, Everard came back on Saturday, and I have driven him down; so will you give orders, for I am late?"

Mrs. Ward rang the bell, and did accordingly, for there was a large party to dinner. Several neighbours also came in the evening. Mrs. Mason was among them; and that lady had, as usual, plenty to say, and every body to talk to. Music and singing were going on.—"Ah!" cried she to her next neighbour, "we shall have no such singing to-night, as last time; certainly, whatever one thinks of Mrs. Leslie, she sings like an angel; everyone must confess that."

"And *is* like an angel, I should think," returned the lady, "by all one hears."

"All! not *all!* surely?" remarked Mrs. Mason, "Mrs. Leslie has her enemies, like the rest of us; but for my own part, the worst thing *I* see about her is, that she has really no more sense or management in worldly matters than a child! To think of her playing her cards as she has done! Why the game was in her hands!"—nodding towards Mr. Everard—"and she threw it all up. Though it's no matter of one's own, it really provokes one to see such things."

"Did you want that gentle Mrs. Leslie to marry Mr. Everard?" asked the lady; "I have heard he is a rough man, though so clever."

"Rough! yes, he can be rough! He is rude enough to every body, and sometimes is to me. Why, only the other night, he was about that little Grace!—as rude as a bear!—But never to Mrs. Leslie; when she is by, he is quite a different man, and she could do any thing with him she pleased. I am sure she has no reason to complain of roughness from him: it's quite a treat to hear him speak to her. For my part, I wonder what she can be made of to resist such manners. Besides, you know, he is one of the first lawyers in London! I have heard he has more briefs than any two of his standing put together: and he could live in the very first style if he pleased,—only he's a bachelor, and does not care for show. To think of her letting pass such a catch!"

"But do you know that Everard thought of such a thing, or that Mrs. Leslie refused him?" asked the lady.

"Thought of such a thing! my dear ma'am, to be sure! Why it's notorious, you know, she is an old flame of his; and was he not down here every day, but two or three, all the time she was here! If you had seen his behaviour, you would never doubt. And I am sure if she did not understand, she must either be blind, or more silly and unaccountable than any woman of her age I ever knew."

"But," persisted the other lady, "you know she was not obliged to marry him; perhaps she did not like him."

"Why, what *can* she expect?" returned Mrs. Mason; "here's a man, all the fashion, nobody more sought after, plenty of money, in high practice, astonishingly clever, very much attached to her,—so *constant*, you know; why he might have married all the young ladies in London, *I* know! but he never forgot her. Then he's so handsome and agreeable, if he pleases. For my part, I can't think what she would have! I am sure if I was not married, I should have no objection at all to Mr. Everard, if he took a fancy to me; but Mr. Mason—good man!—is a very kind husband to me. I can only think that Mrs. Leslie has a very cold heart."

The other lady could not but smile at this mode of putting the matter, as she remarked, "You know every body is not obliged to marry again, and perhaps Mrs. Leslie's thoughts are all with her first husband."

This lady did not know or remember that Mrs. Mason had been twice married.

"No, not obliged, of course," said Mrs. Mason, "but when such an offer as this comes, it can be nothing but folly to refuse. Mrs. Leslie married once for love and romance, and all that, and surely she could afford now to marry like the rest of the world. She was a girl then; but now she knows what is what, it is unpardonable; for the sake of her little girl, she ought to consider these things. And Mr. Everard, too, has taken such a vast fancy to Grace; it would have been such a thing for her, poor child!—It's quite absurd to hear the compliments he spends upon that child! Did you hear of the Fairy Bower?"

Just then the other lady was called away to the piano; and in a change of places, Mr. Everard was advanced next to Mrs. Mason. She continued her conversation to him, and he seemed disposed to listen to her more quietly than usual. This encouraged her to go on, and the following discourse took place:—

"Oh, Mr. Everard! we were just speaking of the Fairy Bower, the other night, and your part in that pretty scene: it was, I am sure, very kind of you to amuse us so much, for it was as pleasant to us old people, as to the children; quite a little spectacle!"

Mr. Everard bowed, as an acknowledgement of his share in the compliment. "It is rather sad, however," continued the lady, that it should end as it has;—very unexpected and distressing, I am sure!"

"In what respect, madam?" asked Mr. Everard.

"Why, I mean about poor little Grace Leslie."

"What do you mean?" inquired Mr. Everard, somewhat more hastily.

"Bless me!" cried Mrs. Mason, "have you not heard? I thought every body knew; every body talks of it; only think of your not knowing!"

"What, madam?" said Mr. Everard, somewhat sternly.

Mrs. Mason rather repented her allusion, but under the circumstances she imagined correct, she thought it would be rather a consolation, than otherwise, to Mr. Everard, to hear of any flaws in a quarter he had so much reason to be dissatisfied with. She therefore proceeded,—"Only, that the little girl took more credit than she deserved about the Fairy Bower.—It was very natural, you know, in such a child."

"Not natural, and not true, madam, in Grace Leslie, or any Leslie!" exclaimed Mr. Everard, approaching to his appalling voice; "and by your leave, I will undertake to prove my words."

"Bless my heart, what a man!" thought Mrs. Mason; and she began to wonder less at Mrs. Leslie's conduct. She however replied, "Well, all I can say is, every body believes it, and everybody talks of it."

Mr. Everard scarcely made answer, and as soon as possible, mingled in the crowd. The lady watched him, expecting some formidable outbreak, but he joined the party at the piano, and seemed more agreeable than usual. After a time she gave up repenting any thing, and concluded his words, like some other people's words, meant nothing.

CHAPTER XLVIII

And gave me charms and sigils for defence
Against ill tongues that slander innocence.
DRYDEN

T HE NEXT MORNING Ellen was sufficiently recovered to take her place, according to promise, at the breakfast table. Hanson, however, herself, saw to her wraps, and made her promise not to sit next the door. She was duly congratulated on her return to the world. Mr. Everard had always quaint sayings ready for every occasion, and George called her a Kamschatkan and a monkey. The history of her cold was related to Mr. Everard,—the party in Grosvenor Square talked of,—Fanny's lines,—Lord Minorie, who was there that night,—and the Fairy Bower mentioned. "It was nothing like *ours*, though," said George, triumphantly, "we would not let Isabella have her way here."

"It was a sad failure, certainly," said his mother, "though it cost an absurd sum of money. It was Mary Anne Duff's and Isabella's plan between them."

"Yet they retained Grace Leslie's name of the Fairy Bower?" asked Mr. Everard.

"They had not the *nous* to think of any other," remarked George, "but I am sure there was nothing Fairy or Bowerlike in it. I am sure Grace Leslie would have found a better name; though I don't know if she could, for it was too stupid for her to have any thing to do with!"

"Well," said Ellen, in the slow and mysterious manner which, more or less, usually accompanied her remarks,—"well, do you know, I am exceedingly puzzled about the naming *our* Fairy Bower. Emily does not explain it to me, and I asked Mary Anne the only opportunity I had, but something happened to prevent her answering me, and then I forgot it."

"When did you first hear the name?" asked Mr. Everard.

"On Monday evening, the day before our party," answered Ellen. "George, don't you remember, that when Emily told us all Mary Anne's plan about the ante-room, she ended by calling it the Fairy Bower? and you laughed about it."

"To be sure I did," said George, "I thought it would be great stuff; I said, 'let's have none of your Fairies here."

"Then," continued Ellen, "do you not remember that next morning, before breakfast, Emily told us she was so provoked with poor Grace for coming so late into her room the night before, (Emily was asleep), that she determined to punish her, and not tell her of what we were going to do with the ante-room; and you know how hard we worked to get it done—as we then thought we should—before Grace came in, and how surprised she was!"

George said, he remembered it all, but could not see what she was driving at.

"Why, you know, Grace knew nothing of the Fairy Bower, or ante-room, till she came in, the morning of our party; for she was not with us the evening before, when Emily told us of Mary Anne's plans. I believe, George, she was at work at your chain."

"Well, but what is your puzzle?" said George.

"Oh, George," cried his sister, "do you not see in a minute? How could Grace name the Bower, before she had heard of it? And besides, do you not remember that Emily told us of the whole plan as Mary Anne's?"

"Why then," said George, "you mean to say that either Grace, Emily, or Mary Anne, has told a fib.—Could you not say that at once?"

"Oh, I did not mean to say so!" cried poor Ellen, shocked by such a representation of her perplexity, yet conscious there was some truth in that way of looking upon it.

"I confess," said Mrs. Ward, "I have been in some perplexity about it myself."

"When did you hear the name first *applied*, not *mentioned*?" asked Mr. Everard of Ellen.

"It was not alluded to all through the morning we were at work upon it. I had quite forgotten it; but when George and Emily had lit the lights in the evening, I heard every body calling it the Fairy Bower, and then I remembered Mary Anne had called it so to Emily the evening before."

"You may remember," said Mr. Everard to Mrs. Ward, "that the Queen of the Fairy Bower disclaimed the merit of naming it, in our hearing."

Mrs. Ward assented.

"George, can you throw any light on this mystery?" asked his father.

"No, papa," replied George, "except that I see some one has *fibbed*, and I know who I think most likely."

"We want the witness—Emily Ward," said Mr. Everard, in a professional tone, "I fancy she knows more for certain than all here put together. Why did she not come forward to crown the Queen of the Fairy Bower? Why was she silent so long at supper?"

Mrs. Ward was going to say, "Why was Grace?" when she remembered her engagement with Mrs. Leslie, and was silent.

"When does Emily come back?" asked Mr. Everard.

"To-morrow," replied her mamma.

"And I must be in Kent to-morrow!" continued Mr. Everard; Ward, do you know there are injurious surmises afloat against your late young guest, Grace Leslie?"

"No, indeed, I did not," said Mr. Ward.

"Well, I hear every body is talking it over," returned the other gentleman, "and I doubt not it is, or will be so, considering the quarter whence my information came—Mrs. Mason."

"Oh! I know she has been gossipping," said Mrs. Ward, "and I have tried to stop her; but nobody minds what Mrs. Mason says."

"I do," replied Mr. Everard, "and I am disposed not to lose an hour. Emily is at Twickenham, is she not?"

Mrs. Ward recommended waiting till Emily's return. Mr. Everard repeated that he was engaged for the next week. He said he had had a share in a deception of some sort the evening of the party, that Mrs. Mason had talked to him, and that the little Grace was his god-daughter, and the child of an old and much esteemed friend. *He* therefore was the proper person to unravel the mystery, and he would take it all upon himself.

Mr. Everard spoke when he chose in a manner which made it difficult to oppose him. Mrs. Ward had misgivings; she hardly knew what they were, but Emily's mysterious words, "It would put an end to Fanny's visit," came to her mind; but she could say nothing against Mr. Everard's reasonable intentions. Mr. Ward approved them, and asked what he proposed doing.

Mr. Everard could not exactly say: he should be guided by circumstances. With their permission, he should certainly call on his young friend Emily.

Mr. Ward assented; only begged him not to frighten her out of her wits, for he was her most *terrible* friend.

He promised she should give a good account of his visit, and engaged to let Mr. Ward know next day, in London, the result of his morning's work.

Mr. Everard refused the loan of gig, horse, or any "appliances and means to boot," and, like a true knight errant, sallied forth with nothing but his good cause, good will, and own good—purse, to help him. We think we must follow him to Twickenham, to see how a great man can pay a little lady a visit.

CHAPTER XLIX

Couched like a lion in thy way,
He waits to spring upon his prey.
TICKELL

A very gentle beast, and of a good conscience.
SHAKSPEARE

EMILY WAS amusing herself with her young friends, not long after breakfast, when the servant presented a card to her. She looked at it surprised, and refused it. The maid assured her the gentleman asked particularly for Miss Emily Ward.—"He was a tall gentleman, with spectacles."

Emily again gave a hasty glance at the card, and exclaimed in a terrible fright, "Oh! it's *our* Mr. Everard; what can he want with me?" Then, with a ray of hope, she continued to her young friends, "Does your mamma know Mr. Everard?"

"No, I don't think so, I have never heard his name," was the reply.

"Oh, then," cried Emily, "I am sure she does not; for nobody who has ever seen Mr. Everard once, and heard him speak, forgets him or his name, and I'm sure you would have heard it.—Do you know what he wants me for, Ann?" she said to the servant, who happened to be the upper nurse.

Ann could scarcely help smiling at Miss Emily's terror: she said, "No, but the gentleman seemed glad to hear she was at home, and seemed a pleasant gentleman."—Ann appeared to have some remembrance which occasioned a smile.

"Oh!" cried Emily, "then he is in a good humour! I'll go directly, before he gets out of it."

"Ah! and if you keep him waiting," said Emma, "perhaps he will grow fierce and savage, and eat you up in a mouthful, as the wolf did little Red-Riding-Hood."

"What can he want with me?" cried Emily again, moving towards the door at a pace very unusual with her. "Oh!" she exclaimed, "perhaps Ellen is worse!" and with very different steps she was, without another hesitation, in the drawing-room in a moment. "Is Ellen worse?" cried she, without a thought of her terrible visitor.

"Oh, no, no!" answered Mr. Everard, in a kind tone; "better, a great deal better; I am very sorry, my good young friend, to have alarmed you so; it was very inconsiderate of me; all is well, quite well: come, sit down, and say you graciously accept my apologies."

Poor Emily's fears vanished on one side, to arise on the other; for she could not raise herself high enough to feel Mr. Everard's superior for a moment, so far as to accept his "apologies." She only said she was glad every body was well; and longed to ask what he came for. Mr. Everard spared her the pains: he continued, " 'Then what do you come here for?' you would say. I come by your papa's leave, to ask you one question, which, on the whole, I think you will be very glad to answer. It is concerning your party of the sixth, and relates especially to your Fairy Bower: I believe you know, and I do not think you have any objection to tell, who devised it."

"Grace Leslie!" exclaimed Emily, with more readiness and ease than she ever could have thought possible before her formidable questioner.

"I said *one* question," continued Mr. Everard, "and I am quite satisfied; but if I do not alarm you, I would go on."

He spoke so condescendingly, and smiled so pleasantly, that Emily was amazed at herself, in remembering afterwards that she had told Mr. Everard she was not alarmed, and would answer as many questions as he chose to ask.

"How long have you known it?"

"Since just before the party."

"How did you know it?"

"I found out, and made Grace confess."

"Why did you not tell?"

"Because Grace would not let me, and she made herself ill in entreating me. But I was to speak to—to—." Here Emily made a dead stop.

"What prevented you?" asked the examiner.

"Grace's illness kept me too long,—I could not."

"Why did you not come forward to crown the Queen of the Fairy Bower?"

"Because it should have been Grace."

"Why did you so long hesitate to mention the person who named the Bower?"

"Because I was afraid that Grace would be angry with me."

Mr. Everard complimented Emily on her examination, and said it was a pity it should be lost in a private interview. He also told her that Grace Leslie had been by some people accused of taking to herself the naming the Bower unfairly.

"What a shame!" cried Emily, regardless of Mr. Everard.

"And *that* is the reason, he continued, "that I have made these inquiries of you."

Emily could never have believed beforehand that an interview of this nature with Mr. Everard could be a relief to her:—it *was*. She afterwards considered she had got off very well. She always dreaded *how* this matter would come out, and hoped she should be at school. It was now as good, or perhaps better; for before leaving, Mr. Everard assured her he had taken care she should have no annoyance on the subject. He said he had observed and approved of her conduct, in refusing to take share in any part of what she knew was a deception.

"But Grace!" said Emily, fearlessly, "you do not mean Grace was wrong."

"Grace and you were in different situations; what might be right in the one, might not be so in the other."

Mr. Everard stayed a little longer, and talked of other matters. Emily wondered why she was ever afraid of him. At last he said he would not keep her any longer, thanked her for her frankness, and concluding, as he offered his hand, "And now, my good young friend, you must say I have not frightened you out of your wits."

Emily wondered she had never observed his smile before: it had its effect, for she laughed a little, and said she was frightened at first.

"Ah!" said Mr. Everard, gravely, "that was a sad mistake of mine; I promised your papa I would not frighten you out of your wits."

Emily had forgotten the fear he alluded to, and she answered, "And I am sure you have not; I frightened myself."

"Most gracious maiden!" replied her visitor, with a gallant air, "I beg humbly to accept and acknowledge my pardon;" and with suitable tokens of acknowledgment, he withdrew from the apartment.

Emily had entered into his humour, and enjoyed it. She joined her companions with very different feelings from those she had left them with. She entered laughingly, and in high spirits, for she was relieved from a weight that had occasionally pressed unpleasantly upon her.

What was Mr. Everard's next step? We see him towards the afternoon at Mr. Duff's door, at Winterton. We hear him inquiring for Miss Newmarsh. We presently see them accost. The lady looks surprised: perhaps she is trying to imagine some cause for his visit. The gentleman hopes, nay, is sure, her love of truth will find apologies for him on the liberty he is taking, in intruding himself. She still looks in doubt; and he quickly explains the object of his visit, as follows:—

"I have, madam, to speak of one of your pupils; and I feel it less painful to do so to *you*, than to her mother. What I have to say, concerns your eldest pupil, I think—Mary Anne. It has been my unfortunate duty to discover that Grace Leslie, and not herself, was the deviser of the little toy we all so much admired, under the name of the Fairy Bower. We cannot, madam, call this a trifle."

Miss Newmarsh was thunderstruck; but the certainty of the truth of this discovery reversing the order of nature's laws, flashed upon her like lightning. She could only exclaim, "Is it possible?"

"You will find it too true; and I fear the task I have to perform will be both to herself and to you a painful one. Owing to the unfortunate misrepresentations this young lady has occasioned, Grace Leslie is suspected of unfairness and untruth, and I am thereby driven to require substantial proofs of the truth of my present assertion. I must therefore request the favour of seeing the young lady in question in your presence. I will patiently wait your pleasure here, while you take what measures you think proper, to prepare your pupil for an interview that must be painful. You are perhaps aware, that the little girl on whose behalf I appear, is my god-child."

We will report no more of this distressing scene. Mary Anne must have sunk low enough in the opinion of every reader, and we will spare her the degradation of exhibiting her personally in her well merited exposure. This favour we accord her on account of her age; though certainly that is but a poor excuse: however we avail ourselves of it, as she has time before her to create almost a new character for herself, before she is grown up. As we have it in contenplation to continue her history, as well as that of the other actors in this little tale, at a more advanced period of their lives, we shrink from stigmatizing her, more than our duty as historians positively demands.

CHAPTER L

Virtue has her peculiar set of pains.
YOUNG

WE WILL THEREFORE take our leave of Winterton, and look in upon Mrs. Leslie and her little girl, at about the very same moment this afternoon. A lady, a neighbour, was making a call on Mrs. Leslie. Grace was amusing herself apart, and after a time she left the room. This, though in appearance a natural and voluntary act of Grace's, was the result of habit or good feeling. When Grace was a very little girl, her mamma one day said to her, "Grace, my dear, when ladies and gentlemen are calling on me, and when they have spoken to you, and you do not seem to be wanted, you may go to Hannah's work room." Grace fell into the order very nicely; it seemed no effort and no trial to her; nor did she always leave. Many papas and mammas would quite differ with Mrs. Leslie, on this plan of hers. She knew it had its objections. It was likely to create a timidity and want of ease of mind, if not of manner. Grace certainly had this to a great degree, and it was a severe pain to her as she grew up. This discipline might have occasioned or increased it. If Mrs. Leslie had been aware of this, perhaps still she would have preferred it before the evils of the contrary system. Forward, pert manners; want of reverence to seniors; or where the greatest care is taken, a certain conceit; a readiness to offer opinions unasked; and an almost unconquerable tendency to criticise the feeling and actions of elders, as well as equals; these are the usual unavoidable results of a home education, when children are suffered to mix unreservedly with their parents, and their parents' visitors and friends. Mrs. Leslie was of a temper to feel the objection of the constant presence of other people's children. Whatever was the consequence to her own child, she did not think herself justified to expose her guests and visitors to the same; and she never wished her little Grace to be looked upon as "that little plague always in the way,"—a speech she had heard from many mammas of other friends' children; while at the same time herself might have felt the same remark applicable to the children of those very mammas. On this account it was that Mrs. Leslie gave the order before spoken of to her little girl; and though never alluded to, or re-enforced, it continued to be observed, as in the instance now before us.

"I am glad your little girl has chanced to leave the room," said the lady, when Grace was gone, "not that I do not like her, for you know I think her the nicest child, and the best behaved of all my little acquaintances; but I called to talk to you, of a certain matter, and I could not have done it before her very well."

How many persons have called on their friends to discuss "certain matters," and from the presence of children, being either totally unable, or else driven to do it, at the risk of a breach of confidence, or with the feeling of carrying on unwise and unsafe discussions, before tender and unformed minds. However, this lady called to speak of a matter of fact. Mrs. Leslie answered that she was ready to talk over any matter with such a kind friend as this lady.

"Why," returned the lady, "there is my doubt; I am not quite sure whether you will think it *kind*; but all I can say is, that I am 'doing as I would be done by,' and if you disapprove it, you must pardon me." She then said she had yesterday returned from a visit of a few days at her sister's, at Fulham; that she had heard herself and Grace often mentioned, but that it was of Grace she had to speak.—"Are you aware," she continued, "that some people are thinking of Grace in a very unwarrantable manner?"

"No, indeed!" said Mrs. Leslie, "pray do tell me how."

The lady then told her the evil surmises abroad. She did not mix them up with other gossip she had heard, as that was not to the purpose, but simply stated the charges against Grace. It had become quite a party matter, and people were actually vehement about it. All Mrs. Leslie's supposed virtues and defects were canvassed, and brought to bear upon this subject; as well as those of the little girl. It threatened to make serious breaches, and to leave permanent results; since it scarcely matters what the subject is, if people are disposed to be violent, and array themselves upon opposite sides unscrupulously. This lady, however, we say, did not detail these things; as she saw poor Mrs. Leslie was sufficiently aware of the importance of the communication she had just received.—"My poor dear child!" she exclaimed, "and I have allowed her to sacrifice herself!"

"Then it is not quite new to you," said this lady; "if you know any thing about it, it will perhaps be easier to set things right; and I am sure I shall be ready to do any thing to assist: you know, I may be able to be of some little service, through my sister, Mrs. Wallis; Grace is, with herself, and all her family, a very great favourite, I assure you."

Mrs. Leslie was much obliged to her friend. She sincerely thanked her for taking the pain of telling these things upon herself, and told her she would consider over the matter, and let her know to-morrow what she meant to do. The lady almost immediately took her leave. The day was drawing to a close. Mrs. Leslie and her little girl were soon shut up for the evening, with candles and a comfortable fire. Grace had just placed a music book of her mamma's ready on the piano, as she often was so kind as to sing, at this time, before they quite settled down for their evening. She crept gently to her mamma's side.—"Mamma, I am afraid you are not well," said she.

"Why do you think so, Grace?" asked her mamma.

"You seem so," said Grace; "are you ill, mamma?"

"Why, Grace," said her mamma, "you and I are something alike; I have one of your ailments;" and she raised her little girl's hand, and placed it on her heart.

"Oh, mamma!" cried Grace, looking frightened, "you have a palpitation! what can have happened?"

"*Happened*, my dear!" said her mamma, smiling, "do you think a palpitation cannot come without something having *happened?*"

Poor Grace with conscious feelings dropped her eyes upon the carpet, while the colour rushed to her cheeks.

"I am not ill, my dear girl," continued her mamma cheerfully, and rising for her work-box, "but I have rather a headache, which will go away after a night's rest.

Mrs. Leslie, however, could not shake off her abstraction, while she was considering the best means to take to detect and expose the truth, the concealment of which had so cruelly injured her generous child. Still she could not bear to force the truth from *Grace*, and let it transpire by this means. Her heart and her tongue refused to consent. After divers plans, all of which, for some reason or other, did not please her, she resolved to write to Mr. Ward, and tell him how her little girl was misunderstood in his neighbourhood; and also to mention her own suspicions of the truth of the matter. This satisfied her more than any other idea, and she wondered she had not thought of it before. She had thought of writing to Mrs. Duff, to Miss Newmarsh, and to Mrs. Ward; but rejected all. Mr. Ward seemed quite the proper person; much more so than his wife, who was Mary Anne's own Aunt, and so anxious for the prospects of the family. It would have been a most painful notion to have to insinuate to her, as well as to the other two ladies. Mr. Ward was *her* old friend, and a man of honourable feeling. She felt quite relieved to have settled upon what to do, and was only debating whether or not to write to him that night, before she consulted her kind neighbour, when tea came in, and Grace left the piano. Her mamma desired her to play a little, since she did not want to talk. In the middle of tea, Richard brought up a letter, which he said a tall gentleman in a cloak had left; he did not know the gentleman; it was quite dark, and he did not speak a word, but put the letter in his hand and walked away. Richard seemed to think there was something very mysterious in the stranger. Mrs. Leslie knew at once Mr. Everard's writing, though hurried, and his crest; and from the description, she had no doubt it was himself that left it. She felt rather unwilling to open the letter, though she had not long since written him one, to which she had received no answer. She did, however, open it slowly. It was an envelope, enclosing a folded slip of paper. On the envelope was written merely these words:—

"I will set all right. B. E."

She opened the slip: what was her surprise on reading as follows:—

I confess that I did not invent the Fairy Bower, nor its name, nor any part of it.—Grace Leslie invented it all. I never thought of it, till Grace Leslie put it in my head on Monday evening, January 5. Grace Leslie would not betray me: she might have at any time. I did not know any body knew about it but Grace Leslie. I had no right whatever to be crowned Queen of the Fairy Bower. I beg Grace Leslie's pardon.

Winterton, Feb. 2nd.   MARY ANNE DUFF.

    M. A. Newmarsh, }
    B. Everard,   } Witnesses.

Mrs. Leslie read this singular and unexpected document over two or three times, trying to develope its history. How came Mr. Everard to be at Winterton, and to interfere in it at all? And how did the whole come about? At this moment, too, when she was so engrossed in the subject! She again called to mind Mr. Everard's words to her. She knew his disposition; and the true state of the case passed through her mind. She felt grateful to him for relieving her in her perplexity, and for taking on himself the defence of Grace; for now she thus understood the words, *"I will set all right."* These thoughts occupied but short space. As soon as Mrs. Leslie had mused over the note, she handed it to her little girl, saying, "My dear Grace, this paper concerns you, more than me."

"Me! mamma,"cried Grace, surprised. She took it, and proceeded to read. She was some time gathering the sense of the contents. When she seemed to have done so, Mrs. Leslie asked her if it was true.

"Yes, mamma, indeed it is," cried Grace, in some distress; "I hope you are not angry with me."

"No, not angry at all, my dear child, but very much relieved that somebody has spoken the truth at last."

"But, mamma," returned the little girl, anxiously, "Do you think I ought to have spoken? Have I done right?"

"I hope, my dear, you did right, for I think I should have felt just as you did."

Grace was very much relieved and overcome by this testimony of her mamma's to her conduct; what could satisfy her more? Her next thought was in another direction:—"Oh, poor Mary Anne!" she exclaimed, as she looked at the paper open on the table, "how I wish she could have been spared! Oh, mamma! only think how shocking to have to write that before her governess and Mr. Everard, and for us to see, and her papa and mamma, and all the Wards; and I suppose every body must hear of it, even though we do not mention it. Can we do any thing to prevent it, mamma?"

"Do not forget Grace, the misery you have suffered by a piece of deception, though you could not exactly help it. Let us be thankful, my dear, that the truth has come out without our being concerned in exposing it."

Mrs. Leslie then reminded her little girl of Mrs. Ward's misunderstanding of her conduct all through this sad deceit; and told her, she was not at all sure that Mrs. Ward was satisfied even now. She then, as gently as she could, told Grace, that others too of Mrs. Ward's visitors had the same opinion of her; and that she had been engaged the last few hours in trying to find some way of setting things right. She then showed her Mr. Everard's words on the envelope, saying she had no doubt that her kind godfather alluded to these things by those few words.

Poor Grace was very much affected by hearing all this. She could not think how any grown-up people could think a little girl so wicked. "Such things unhappily are sometimes," said her mamma; and Grace remembered she was condemning Mary Anne. She felt pained at what she had said, and her thoughts again reverted to Mary Anne.

"But, mamma," said she, as she wiped away her last tears, "by what I feel, now I am only suspected, I know how shocking it must be for poor Mary Anne! And you see how sorry she must be, for she has confessed all this, and she asks my pardon: you know she could not do more; she cannot undo all that has happened."

"Your feelings are natural, Grace," replied Mrs. Leslie, "but *we* must do no more; we must let things take their course. Mary Anne cannot undo, it is true; but, you know, it is her own fault that there is any thing to be undone. *You* know, my dear child, better than I can tell you, that if people do wrong, they will suffer, sooner or later, in some way or other. It is a dreadful thing to suffer in such a way, or to be exposed; but, you know," continued Mrs. Leslie, very seriously, "it is better, far better, and really kinder to Mary Anne, that she should be brought to a sense of her error now, be sorry for it, and turn and correct such sad ways, than that she should go on and grow up in them, and perhaps continue in them till the day of her death."

Poor Grace's blood curdled in her veins through all this reflection of her mamma's. She had never so seriously thought of the consequences of encouraging, or not correcting, what is wrong, or, in other words, sin, in others. She was quite silenced: she was always sure her mamma was right in the end, and she submitted. However, the subject furnished conversation for the rest of the evening. "I hope, mamma," said Grace, "you will let me talk a little to you about this, for I wish you to know all,—I always wished you to know all; but there seemed never the right moment to tell you."

"Indeed, my dear child," said Mrs. Leslie, "I wish you could have found the right moment. Why did you not tell me, Grace, the morning of the party?"

"Ah, mamma," replied the little girl, "I know—I am sure now—that that is where I was wrong; and it has made me more unhappy, I think, than all the rest." Poor Grace was obliged to pause for a moment, but presently continued—"I did not forget it, mamma, but every thing was so very unfortunate for me. I tried to speak to you that morning several times, but something always prevented me."

"Tell me how it was, my dear Grace," said Mrs. Leslie, fearing she had been unobservant at the moment of her child's opportunity.

"First, mamma," continued Grace, "I thought I could perhaps speak to you alone, while Emily was asking her mamma about some portfolios of paper; so I followed her, as soon as I could get away from the rest, into the hall. But Mrs. Ward did not leave with Emily, as I thought she would, and Emily was not half a minute—I met her coming out of the dining-room, where you and her mamma were, and while I was thinking whether I ought or ought not to mind Mrs. Ward being with you, Richard passed by me with Mrs. Newton Grey, who, you know, called that morning."

"Did you try again, Grace?" asked Mrs. Leslie.

"Yes, mamma, at luncheon time; but it was very hard indeed to make you understand."

"Was that the day that you lingered behind, Grace?" asked Mrs. Leslie, with feelings as painful as any with which her little daughter had been exercised.

"Yes, mamma," replied Grace, "and you may remember Mrs. Ward made the same remark on my staying away from the rest, as she had done at breakfast that morning, about my being late."

"Yes, my dear, I remember very well," said Mrs. Leslie, recalling with increasing pain the small incidents of the scene; "you had hold of my hand, I bade you go and join your young friends. But was that the morning of the Fairy Bower party?"

"Oh, yes, mamma," replied Grace; "I know it all so well! don't you remember that Miss Newmarsh was at luncheon with us that day, and that she made a remark on my having hold of your hand?"

"Yes, my dear, I remember it all perfectly, now you remind me of that," answered Mrs. Leslie. "And you really meant to tell me, Grace?"

"I meant to ask you what I ought to do—I am sure I did, mamma," replied the little girl; "for I still hoped to do so at dressing time, only my unfortunate palpitation made it quite impossible—you know I did not see you."

"But if you wished it so much, why did you not send for me when you were ill?—you could have done so so very easily."

"Ah, mamma, there I was all wrong again," replied Grace, "and I had not time to think what to do. Emily discovered it all at that moment, and made me confess, and the idea of consulting you went quite out of my head till I was dressed, and had my hand on the lock of your door, and remembered that most likely you were gone down stairs—as you were. I had been trying to persuade Emily to try and speak to Mary Anne, and in doing so, I forgot my first idea of consulting you, till it was too late. Things came on so quick, one after another, and we were so busy working at the Fairy Bower, and preparing, that I seemed to have no time to think all day long."

"My dear girl," said Mrs. Leslie, touched by her child's situation and feelings, and blaming herself infinitely more than she did Grace; "my dear child, I do not blame you; I think almost any thing you had done would have seemed wrong to others afterwards, for some reason or other; for it is often easier to find fault with the conduct of those under difficult circumstances, than to find a better mode of acting. People are apt to forget, or else, perhaps, are quite ignorant of, the minor difficulties, such as you have now described, which often seems to leave but one line of conduct practicable."

"Mamma, you are very kind to say so," answered Grace, the tears now flowing fast, "but I can only think one thing of myself. I know—I feel sure—I was wrong there, and I shall think so all my life. I am sure that any body like Constance would have *made herself* find you out, and speak to you, and I think I should have done so, only all the time I know I was afraid of exposing Mary Anne."

"I hope, my dear child," said Mrs. Leslie, "I shall never try to persuade you improperly out of a conviction of your having done wrong; but I can only say to you, as I should to any one else who blamed you, that I consider myself quite as much in fault, for I now clearly remember how unusual your manner was at that time, and especially at luncheon."

"I am still sure, mamma, that I was wrong," returned Grace, once more, with a mixture of humility and heroism natural only in such characters as hers. "I have thought all along that if the story of the Fairy Bower were written and read, a good many people would say I was wrong, and I should be among the number myself. I *think* I shall say so all my life."

From Grace's continued earnestness of manner, Mrs. Leslie feared this event might prey upon her mind, and she accordingly made a few suitable remarks.

Grace was very grateful for them, but presently added, "To show you, mamma, that I know what I mean, and do not go too far about myself, I will tell you that I do not blame myself for not telling you *after* the night of the Fairy Bower. I became then entangled with Emily, and indeed it turned into quite a different thing. Mrs. Ward, I knew, would be very angry if I had told. The more I thought of speaking to you then, the less it seemed right; though still I wished very much to tell you. It seemed only for my own sake, and to put you into a difficulty instead, because of Fanny's visit. But if I had consulted you the first moment, all these things might have been prevented."

The conversation before long, turned upon other parts of the subject. Grace took up Mary Anne's confession, which seemed very much to have impressed her imagination;

after pondering over it awhile, she remarked that it was not in Mary Anne's own writing. Her mamma said it was Miss Newmarsh's, for she had seen her hand before, and knew it; she showed Grace that her signature was the same, and that Mary Anne's signature was her own writing. She said Mr. Everard most likely had wished Miss Newmarsh to write out Mary Anne's words—for they evidently were Mary Anne's own—for then he had the sanction of her governess's authority; and that neither Miss Newmarsh, nor Mrs. Duff, could refuse to allow such a thing; though extraordinary and most painful; considering that Mary Anne had brought another innocent person into public talk and suspicion.

Poor Grace could not bear to have her share, however unintentional, in the exposure spoken of; but her mamma was right to bring these things before her. Grace was of a susceptible turn, and if her mind were not duly strengthened, she might grow into a meek sentimental character; always ready to blame herself, and take other people's faults upon herself; falling at length into a state of mind most painful to herself, and useless or tiresome to every body about her. This happily, however, Grace was not likely to do; though there was always a tendency in her character to some part of it.

CHAPTER LI

Daily self surpassed.
WORDSWORTH

THE NEXT MORNING Grace awoke with a full remembrance of two things. One, the *exposé* of yesterday; the other, that it was the third day of the month,—the morning of her favourite psalm.—"How singular," thought she, "it should just come to-day." She however read it, as usual, with her mamma; but neither of them made any remark. After her lessons were over, she sat at work rather graver and more silent than usual. Mrs. Leslie inquired what her thoughts were.

"I was thinking, mamma," she said, "what a month this has been to me. It has been more to me, I think, than all my life before. I seem almost a whole year older than I was this day month. I think I have had some *experience,*—have I?"

"Yes, my dear," replied her mamma, "a *little,* but a very little: if you live, you will look back to those scenes as very pleasant and bright; though all does not now seem bright to you; but you will not consider they have done a great deal for you in the way you mean."

"But, mamma," replied Grace, "I *have* learned a few things. You know, when I first went there, every thing looked so bright and new, just like a picture; it was like a dream to me.—I heard them, and looked at them, and wondered at them, and thought them all so very clever; but after a little time, I saw things quite differently.—I did not look on as I had done at first, but I became one of themselves almost; and I then saw a great difference between all of them; and then, mamma, I have learned how much harder it is to do right, among a great many, like myself, than here alone with you; for many things do not seem wrong at first, and other people think differently about them. I believe I think a great many more things wrong, than some of the others, and yet Constance says I am not at all particular. I should like very much, mamma, to be a good deal with Constance."

"Well, my dear, some day perhaps you will, but I have been thinking of something that will please you perhaps quite as well at present: I hope to persuade Mrs. Ward to let Ellen come to us for a week or so, after the holidays are over, and before she goes back to Langham; should you like that?"

"Oh, mamma, to be sure!" cried Grace; "how very kind of you! and I am sure Ellen will like it, for she talks so much of being with you. Do you know, she told me the last Sunday I was there, that she had so longed to ask to come with me to you, every morning, for she thought we read something together; and when I told her what, she said that she read the psalms and some of the lessons every day with her grandmamma, and that she tried to do so alone, now, but found it much harder to do, than when she read them aloud with any one like her grandmamma.—Mrs. Ward seems very clever and very good."

"She is, my dear, I know her very well," said Mrs. Leslie.

"Yes, mamma, I know that; and Ellen has told me a great deal about you, when you used to live there," replied Grace; "I will tell it you all by degrees, when it comes into my head."

Mrs. Leslie had no cause to be alarmed at any report which should travel through Mrs. Ward, of Langham, of the scenes of her youth; she was amused, however, and told Grace she should at any time be glad to hear her own history told by her little daughter.

Grace was to-day full of to-morrow's visit. She made many preparations, remembered all the things she had talked of, and what Emily, Ellen, or George, had particularly expressed a wish to see. She also disposed of the precious cups and saucers, and had them in readiness to present to Mrs. Ward. Many imaginings she had of the mode and the way that Mrs. Ward would see them. She felt some doubt all the time, however, whether she would be much pleased or not.

Mrs. Leslie called this morning on her kind neighbour, and told her, that since their interview, she had found the affair had been taken up by Grace's godfather, and that it was not necessary for her to take any part in what was to follow.

Nothing occurred the next day to disappoint the young people. Very early they arrived, and passed the whole day together. Grace rather dreaded the first meeting: she felt very like the culprit, and wondered if any one would dare mention any of the Duffs. She scarcely thought it possible to allude to the grand circumstances, except with Emily and herself alone. Grace had often found her preconceived notions of other people's doings and sayings very wrong; and though advanced, as she considered, in the knowledge of the world, she had yet a good deal to learn. She had also not taken George sufficiently into her calculations. She soon found she had mistaken. When the young people entered the room, Emily ran up to Grace, greeting her and shaking hands very heartily. Ellen contented herself with less visible manifestations of congratulation; not less perceptible however; while George began, "Why, Grace, here's a pretty go! why, how you have bamboozled us all! making us do homage to Mary Anne, in that '*ridiculous*' way, as she said. Ridiculous, indeed! but then she is always *that*; queen or no queen."

At this moment Grace had to turn away to speak more particularly to Mrs. Ward. This lady kissed Grace, and said something pleasant to her; but she added a wish that this unfortunate affair had never happened, in a way that made Grace feel again how painful and undesirable a part she had acted, in not at once exposing the deception. She felt the remark as a rebuke, and she believed she deserved it. However her discomfort was presently somewhat relieved. Mrs. Ward, who had a very quick eye, caught sight of a small tray on the chiffoneer, on which were placed two coffee cups so like her own, that she exclaimed with surprise. Grace brought them forward and placed them before her: saying, she hoped they would repair her sad accident.

Mrs. Ward was really delighted, and thanked Grace very warmly, not only for the cups, but for the hope she now had of matching her service. Of course she was told the whole history. She said she accepted the cups as a gift from Grace: and that whatever share Grace had in the breakage, was many times over repaid by the return, and by the discovery of a means to match them. Mrs. Ward was quite aware that these cups were costly, and that Grace's little hoard must have been seriously drawn upon.

The young people were now dismissed to their room, in order to enjoy more freedom. As Grace was on her way thither, she considered that this late incident was another instance of a late remark of hers. Certainly Mrs. Ward did not yet seem satisfied about the affair of the Fairy Bower; but the result of the unfortunate accident seemed quite to please her, and Grace hoped it would be the means of restoring her entirely to her good opinion. As soon as the young people were together, Emily began, "Well, Grace, now I can speak to you, and say how glad I am all is come out. I could not up stairs, because, you know, mamma is so vexed about Mary Anne, and the Duffs; but *I* don't care at all. As to Mary Anne, she has got off very well, and it's a great shame she should."

"Oh, Emily!" said Ellen, "you forget she had to confess all before Miss Newmarsh, her papa and mamma, and Mr. Everard; and she had those two papers to write for all of us to see!"

"Nonsense!" cried Emily, "I know Mary Anne better than you do; she would not like it at the time, and I dare say she cried a great deal; but she will not care about it at all, if it is passed over, and all goes on the same;—and it will, because Miss Newmarsh will not punish her, we know, and mamma does not wish to make any talk about it."

"I know," said George, "*I* shall not pass it over; Mary Anne shall never hear the last of it from me."

"*I* mean to give her a good trimming," returned Emily, "but she does not care much for me, and then, ten to one but Constance takes her part when I begin to speak."

"I cannot think how you can both talk in this way about it," said Ellen; "I am sure I could not speak of it to Mary Anne for the whole world!"

"And I dare say Grace could not!" cried George, laughing. "You two tender chickens! why you know it is the best way of making Mary Anne ashamed of herself, and punishing her, and we are bound to do so if her governess will not."

"Oh, George!" said Ellen, "Mary Anne will not care for your way of punishing her; and it would be so very disagreeable too."

"Ha! ha!" cried George, "you have just confessed it! It would be disagreeable to her; and I can tell you, she would dislike my way much more than any body else's way.

—What does she care for Miss Newmarsh and all the rest? Now you shall all see if she does not dislike it; I shall make her cry outright."

Ellen said it would be cruel, and quite unpleasant to them besides.

Emily said she should not be sorry if Mary Anne was punished in some way.—"I am sure she deserves it," added she, "for she has made Grace suffer enough; and Grace is so quiet, nobody thinks of her."

The colour rushed into poor Grace's cheeks at this sudden reference to her.—She wished they would be so kind as not to think of her.

"But indeed, *I* do think of Grace," said George, "I think a great many things of her. First, I think," said he, solemnly, "she is quite as bad as Mary Anne; for she deceived us all."

Grace felt very much distressed, but it did not show to George's eyes.

"Secondly," continued he, "I think she has been, what we call at school, the greatest spooney in the whole world; and I vote that her name should be changed,—very slightly—only two letters, (*c* and *s* are the same.) For the two second letters of her name, *ra* let *oo* be substituted; what do you say to it, Emily?"

"G o o c e, goose!" said Emily, laughing, "Oh, yes! that will do very well!—But you don't understand it, George," she added, fearing, perhaps, Grace might not quite like it.

"But I do," answered her brother, "and I'll prove it to you. Now I should not say that, or any thing like it, to Mary Anne; no! no! trust me! I know better than that. I should talk of Grace's kindness and forbearance, and say it was like nothing Mary Anne would ever meet with again; and that her ingratitude and falsehood were worse than those of the most odious tyrants; and then I will make her give me the worst names from all her histories."

"Oh, George!" cried Emily, "you will spoil all! that will not do; you can do better if you please."

George assured her he would not spoil all, and that she should be satisfied with him.

Grace felt glad there was no chance of her being present.

They then told her that they were to drive over to Winterton the next day: that the Duffs had been all coming to them; but their papa said, most certainly Mary Anne should not for the present enter the house. "Papa is very angry indeed," said Emily; "I am sure I would not have done such a thing, for papa to know, for the world. I had no idea he would be so angry; he says it must be a long time before he allows Mary Anne to come again to us; and if he thought any of the others knew anything about it, he would not let us go there. He said, though, of his own accord, that he was quite sure 'honest Campbell' knew nothing about it."

Grace was glad to hear these little pieces of news, though she still shrunk from discussing the subject herself. She would have been very glad to know that Mr. Ward did not blame her for preventing the disclosure. On this point she was very anxious.

CHAPTER LII

Corruption wins not more than honesty.
SHAKSPEARE

I̲n the evening, Mr. Ward joined the party at dinner. He made a point of noticing Grace very particularly; and as he shook hands with her, he said, "Grace, you have acted very well, and I should be proud if you were a little girl of my own. You have not done as most good girls would have done; but you have the feelings of a little heroine, and I do not judge you by common rules. Mrs. Leslie, you have reason to be satisfied with your daughter."

Poor Grace was very much touched by this approbation: she did not quite understand it all, but she knew it *was* approbation, and Mr. Ward's manner was kind. After dinner, Mr. Ward proposed Grace's health, and again commended her. Her young friends joined in it with great pleasure, and Grace felt much happier than when it was drank before at the grand party. Mrs. Ward had told Mrs. Leslie what Mr. Everard had done, and her husband now finished the relation, as he had seen him that day. Mr. Everard had called on Mrs. Mason himself, and explained the whole affair. He had also shown her the paper, which had been drawn up under his eye. She was all amazement. —"What a sly artful little thing Miss Mary Anne must be after all! Who'd have thought it!—such a fine looking girl too!" She said she would go that moment and put on her bonnet, and tell every one that had been deceived all about it. Mr. Everard left her to do as she pleased; but Mr. Ward assured Mrs. Leslie that he should consider it his duty to see the matter set quite right. He said if it had been a more private matter, perhaps, out of regard to the family, he should not have made a stir; but since the consequences had been so painful and unjust, he did not hesitate for a moment. He then proposed to Mrs. Leslie to come with her little girl the next week, for a day or two, and the young people should not yet return to school, and have a party. He said he had fixed his heart on this plan, and hoped she would consent.

Mrs. Leslie was already doubtful of the effect of all that had passed on Grace's character, and she did not wish any scene for her, attended with so much publicity. Besides this, she felt as delicate as Mrs. Ward herself, on account of the Duff family; and she knew Mrs. Ward would have been glad if all could have been hushed up without any farther exposure. Mrs. Leslie felt Mr. Ward's kindness greatly, but decidedly declined it. She took, however, the opportunity of proposing a visit from Ellen, for a week or a fortnight, before she returned to Langham, as that would be a greater treat to Grace, than any public testimony she could receive.

Mr. Ward soon saw Mrs. Leslie was resolved, and therefore would not press his invitation unduly. He gave his consent, most readily, about Ellen; and before the party departed, it was settled that on the following Monday week Mrs. Ward should bring Ellen over. This was a highly satisfactory termination to all parties. The young people took leave of Grace, hoping they should meet again in the holidays. Emily told Grace, as she put on her bonnet up stairs, that she had never felt so sorry to part with any one: she said she could sit down and cry, and she had never felt the same towards any other companion.—"Why, you know," said she, "I am always as glad as can be to leave them all at school, and there is nobody at home (I do not mean my brothers and sisters) that I care a pin for. I always laugh at the girls who begin whimpering and saying, 'Good bye, dear;' (she gave this in an imitative manner), 'good bye; never mind, dear.'—But really, Grace, I could do almost the same now;" and in spite of her high spirits, as she kissed Grace, the tears fell from her eyes.—"There!" cried she, "I told you so! but I don't mind your seeing them. Now, Grace, will you remember,—I love you really, and that I shall never forget you?"

Grace gave something that did for an answer. She was affected and surprised; she thought Emily must be the strangest girl there ever was in the world: she felt quite sure in her turn she should never forget her.

Whether these young ladies grew up with the same feelings cannot here be told. If the Fairy Bower is fortunate enough to meet with encouragement, it is proposed some day to settle this question, by the relation of facts as they took place. Meanwhile we hasten to the conclusion of this portion of their history. For this purpose, we will beg to pass over to the Monday, at this time fixed for Ellen's much expected visit. Her mamma, as proposed, drove her over. It was nearly the first time Mrs. Ward had been out since she spent the day with them, as she had had a bad cold. It had prevented her accompanying the young people in their leave-takings at both their cousins'. Mrs. Ward brought Mrs. Leslie a letter, giving an account of the doings and feelings at Winterton, upon the detection of Mary Anne's deceit. Mrs. Ward had no objection to *talk* to Mrs. Leslie on the subject, and she freely expressed her opinion upon it, as she did upon most others; but, for the sake of the family, she wished the story to be kept as quiet as possible. —"The letter," said she, "is from Miss Newmarsh; you will like to see how they go on, and can keep it. Miss Newmarsh always writes to me as if I agreed in all she says; it is her way, though she must know how much I often differ. *I* should have been very glad to hear that that deceitful girl, Mary Anne, should have been well punished; instead of being made a sort of heroine in the family, as she is. However, every body has their own way, and I hope Miss Newmarsh's may answer, I am sure; for it is really rather too bad that a whole family is to be disgraced for the misdoings of a little puss like that;—I have no patience with her!"

Mrs. Leslie corrected Mrs. Ward's idea that the whole family must suffer,—every body knew that Mary Anne stood entirely alone in the matter.

"Yes," replied Mrs. Ward, "people *knew* it, but it makes very little difference.—I find, too, in spite of all my endeavours, it has got to Grosvenor Square."

"How could that be?" said Mrs. Leslie, "I thought Mr. Everard had promised he would say nothing; and there seemed no connexion there, except through Lord Minorie."

"The children went to take leave on Saturday week, and they found every body knew.—I believe it was through the servants. I am on my way there now, and indeed must be going," said Mrs. Ward, rising to take leave, which in a few minutes she did.

CHAPTER LIII

So wretched now, so fortunate before!
DRYDEN

Mrs. LESLIE soon after read the letter which had been left her. It was as follows:—

MY DEAR MADAM,

Mrs. Duff is still too much depressed at the late unfortunate event that has taken place in the family, to reply to your kind note herself; she therefore deputes me to send you an account of the state of things among us since the unhappy disclosure took place. She knows you would be anxious to hear more of internals, than the young people would bring home, after their visit on Friday last. She begs me to say how much she was disappointed at not seeing you with them: we all regretted the cause, and sincerely trust that your cold is better. No doubt you had from Mr. Everard a full account of our distressing scene, with my dear, though fallen pupil. Her sorrow indeed was deep and sincere, and I confidently look to it as a pledge of her entire recovery. Her mamma was exceedingly distressed: at which one cannot wonder.—At this moment, too, when we had all been so hopefully looking towards the good which this family might be the happy instrument of effecting, in a quarter where you have so kindly introduced them. It is a bitter disappointment to us all, and should teach us not to lean upon an arm of flesh. Mrs. Duff was much relieved by your kind assurance of Mr. Everard's silence. Mr. Duff was certainly very angry with his daughter; much more so than I had expected from a man of his generally placid temper. He was for adopting very severe measures: at first, he said he would not see his offending child's face for a week; and then insisted on punishment of some kind being administered. He said there were several modes of correction for which she was not too old; and at last proposed, that for three months she should go to bed an hour earlier than her sisters: and that for six, she should not be allowed to join any party of pleasure, except where so doing would make the affair public. If I did not decidedly object to severity, these rules, though practicable under the old system, would not be so under mine. Mr. Duff, however, was very kind in wishing not to disturb my arrangements; but was firmly resolved on some plan of this kind. I talked in vain to him. I showed how unlikely these galling rules would be to touch his daughter's heart; that she would feel his *kindness* very much more, and that then any thing serious he had to say, would come with double weight. But my words went for nothing: I never saw him so decided; and I quite feared the poor girl would fall a sacrifice to a false notion of duty on his part; for the principle on which he acted, was the duty of seeing punishment administered. He is a most excellent man as the head of a family. However, dear Mrs. Duff at last brought all about as we wished, and I am allowed to follow my own plans; for which I am very grateful to both my excellent friends. I have several times talked most seriously and read to Mary Anne, and I have reason to think she lays what she hears to heart. I have enforced the following discipline for three months; not as a punishment, but as a means of recovery.—I have selected at Nisbett's a set of books, suited to my purpose, and I have marked passages in many other books; on these she is to meditate a time beyond her usual exercises of the same nature; and in order to affect this, during the three months, she is to be down stairs every morning a quarter of an hour later than her sisters; also, she is to sit up the same space longer; so that I do trust this most unhappy circumstance will be turned for good to her, and may be the means of bringing her to greater seriousness, than had things gone on in their usual course. I ought to say that the sight of your young people seemed to affect her afterwards greatly, which I thought a good sign. Fanny was very much displeased at first; much more so than I at all expected,—I suppose her new friendship had something to do with it. She has however written to her friend, and is now more reconciled. Charlotte, you know, is of a less sensitive temper than the rest, and she has taken it wonderfully coolly. It has distressed me a good deal; for, though young of her age, she must know enough to be shocked at a thing of this nature; and she must see the trouble it has occasioned us all. However, at first she could hardly be made to comprehend it; and when she did, she made no remark at all; nor has she since; nor has she noticed it in her diary; she goes on exactly as usual, *apparently* more diligent than ever at her studies; since the rest of us have been much disturbed by the excitement that has prevailed. She had however a cold, which settled in her eyes, and this may partly account for what appeared apathetic in her,—poor dear child! but she has never shown the acute feelings of her sisters. Campbell, you know, went to school before the disclosure, and it is thought best not to mention it to him. Constance alone, of our sorrowful group, remains to be noticed.—I reserve her with pleasure to the last, for she certainly is a remarkable girl of her age, and quite a pattern to us all, under any circumstances. Her notices of her sister's unhappy fall, in her diary, are truly edifying, and are worthy a more public view;—but she has her reward. Yet though she feels so deeply her sister's degradation, not a taunt, not a word of reproach, has ever escaped her lips! Those who know her manner, as I do, can see it is constantly in her mind, and a sigh unbidden will sometimes arise; but the only allusion she had made to it was this morning, in their Scripture Realization lesson, which they all take together. I had selected the denial of Peter, and she had prepared a few remarks, very striking and touching: I think they must have had their effect on her sister. I know, my dear madam, I need not apologize for the length of a letter upon a subject so interesting to you; I shall however add nothing extraneous, begging to subscribe myself,

Your respectful and faithful servant,

Feb. 9.

M. A. NEWMARSH.

P.S. Dear Mrs. Newton Grey has been paying us a visit of condolence. She says she knows how to sympathize with us, having so recently suffered with her boy; but she has good hope of his repentance being sincere, and his promises of amendment lasting. She says he was very open about his fault, and that she had every reason to be satisfied with his conduct. I do, however, still wish she would send him, till he goes to college, to Dr. Barker's.

This mention of Mrs. Newton Grey and her son, reminds us that we have to explain not inserting the interview that took place, after that lady had discovered the worst part of her son's conduct. It was of the same character as the former one; but so much more painful, that we willingly spare the reader a sight of it. He professed great frankness and great sorrow, with good resolutions for the future; but we think we may conclude he could not be properly sincere, when the very next day he continued in his old course again. The fact was, he hardly seemed to care about any thing, so that his mother did not hear of his bad ways, and talk to him about them. We hope there are not many such sons; but we fear many youths have something of a tendency to such principles and feelings. Many certainly act very differently and speak very differently, before their parents' faces, and behind their backs. Some do this avowedly, to their companions, and some scarcely acknowledge that they do so, even to their own selves; but in both cases it is *done*; and the youth does not remember he is injuring himself, far more, even, than he is deceiving his parents.

If this account of Newton Grey should meet the eye of any son, who, through weakness, or fear, or any other cause, is conscious of such a tendency, we trust he will be startled by the wickedness of that youth's conduct; and especially observe the pain and anxiety of his mother, when she thinks he has erred in the least. Many a sleepless night did she pass, and many tears did she shed, when such things came before her; as, in spite of all his craft, they would do occasionally. He could, it is true, satisfy her and give her hope, by fair words and religious sayings; but some day, even in this world, the truth was likely to come upon her; and most certainly some day the consequences of his undutifulness and evil doings would come upon him. Mrs. Newton Grey was a woman of much religion; and that is the only comfort we can look forward to for her, under the weight of affliction that seems likely some day to fall on her head. We will now turn away from this painful subject.

CHAPTER LIV

When shall we three meet again?
SHAKSPEARE

EMILY SENT a letter to Grace, through her mamma; it was written from school, and enclosed in a letter home.

Richmond, Feb. 10.

MY DEAR GRACE,

I am writing a note for you to go on Monday, as I think you will like to hear a little of our visit to the Duffs, and Ellen does not know as much of all that has passed, as I do. I told you I should speak to Mary Anne of her behaviour, and so I did. I told her she ought to be ashamed of herself for telling such a story. She asked me what story? and persisted that she had told no more a story than you:

and when I came to think over it, I could not remember that she had actually told a falsehood in *word*, though it was just the same. She said if the people chose to crown her Queen, she could not help it; and it was altogether nonsense, and a thing that none but worldly people would care about; and that nobody but Grace Leslie, who was so grand and sly, would have made such a fuss about. This made me very angry, and I should have had a grand battle with her, and told her what a mean thing we all thought her, and every body else,—only, before I had time, George took her up, and said the same, only much better than I could. He said, "I'll tell you what, Mary Anne, the short and the long of the matter is, that you have disgraced yourself abominably, and that if you were a boy, we should hoot you out of the room; but that being the girl you are, you have no sense of shame, and so are able to look at us all as you do. And as for Grace Leslie, her name should have stuck in your throat and choked you, before you dared to speak of her as you have: she is a great deal too good for *you* to have any thing to do with, and you would not have dared to find fault with her, if she had treated you as you deserve, and had not been so kind." Mary Anne here interrupted him, and said she was sure Grace had not been very kind to *her*, for it was all Grace's fault from beginning to end; for she had made every body believe that herself—that is, Mary Anne—was the inventor of the Fairy Bower. George went on rather more provoked, for he had been quite cool before, "Mary Anne, I wish you were a boy, that you might be punished, for it is no use talking to you; and I will only say, that I here declare, I will not again call you 'my pretty cousin,' or any thing of that sort, till you become a little more like Grace Leslie, both in goodness and prettiness; for I think her the best and the prettiest little girl that I have ever seen." Mary Anne had kept in her vexation, till this, but now could do so no more; she burst out crying, and said we were all very unkind to her; but it was all Grace Leslie's fault, and that George had never been the same to her since Grace came into the house, and that she wished she had never seen or heard of Grace Leslie, and a great deal more. Here Constance came forward, and took her sister's part, who continued sobbing: she said, that certainly if Grace had been straightforward, all that had happened would never have been. She then turned upon *me*, and said I had no right to find fault with Mary Anne; for that, as Mary Anne said, I was as bad myself. (She had said so before, and called me worldly.) I believe you will agree with all Constance said here, so I shall leave Ellen to tell you. I told Mary Anne what papa said of her behaviour, but this was before George spoke. I should not have said as much as I did, (to please you, rather than myself,) only I found she was not punished at all, and all but Fanny behave to her as if she had been very good, instead of very bad; at least they treat her as if she was ill, or had some great trouble. This is very different from the way we are served at school, when we have been naughty; though no girl has been as bad as Mary Anne, since I have been there. Fanny does not fall into the same way, though; she is sharp, and says just what she pleases. She is very proud of her visit in Grosvenor Square, and is always talking of Lord Minorie, &c. &c. They fell out just after we came in. Fanny reproached Mary Anne for breaking off her intimacy with Isabella; and the other answered, that she, of all people, had least to complain of; since Fanny had to thank her for going there at all; and that if Isabella gave her up so easily, it showed that Fanny was not so charming to Isabella as she imagined; and much more of the same sort, which I know you do not like to hear; indeed I am afraid I have told you too much already, and that you will be angry with me. You see I do not forget you yet. I shall think of Ellen going to you on Monday; I should like to be going too,—and it makes school less pleasant even than usual. But did you hear what your mamma said to me about some other holidays? I thought it so very kind of her, for I happened to be feeling very dull in saying good-bye to you, and hearing Ellen's visit planned. I never observed your mamma was so kind before; but now, I remember, she is so very often. Ellen will tell you how strange it was about little Emma and nurse Brown. I never wrote such an odd and such a dull letter in my life, and on two little scraps of paper! I had no idea I had so much to say when I began. Now, good-bye.

> Believe me, my dear Grace,
> Your affectionate
>
> EMILY WARD.

George wished to have his love sent you, and that you should be told that he had made an epigram on Mrs. Mason. He says it is very good, but it is half Latin.

Ellen explained Emily's allusion thus: she said Mary Anne was very much vexed at Emily's rebuking her, and said that she was not fit to to do, since Emily was a great deal worse than she was in some respects; and she called Emily worldly, and alluded to the fault they were all talking of the day of the party. Emily made no answer to this; and Constance spoke, taking Mary Anne's side, and quoting the text about the mote and the beam. Ellen with much hesitation related this. The other part she was called on to explain, was about little Emma and nurse Brown. Little Emma ran the other day to her mamma, Lady Musgrove, crying, "Oh, mamma, I hope you will never let that naughty girl come here again!" "Who do you mean, my dear?" asked Lady Musgrove. "Why Fanny Duff's sister," replied the child. It seemed that good nurse Brown had been telling them in the nursery a story of a naughty little girl, who took away a crown from a good little girl, and pretended it was her own, and wore it, and made herself Queen with it. Nurse told them it was a true story, that they had seen the naughty little girl, and mentioned who it was.—Thus, the tale became known. Emily, thought however, that Isabella would manage to keep up her acquaintance with Fanny, by sacrificing the rest of the family. She had always said she did not care for any of the others. However, at present, all intercourse was *forbidden*.

Mrs. Leslie allowed Grace to read Miss Newmarsh's letter. Her account of Mary Anne was much more promising than Emily's; and being the latest, she was very glad to have seen it, and dwelt on it with pleasure. But all her admiration was expended on Constance. She read the part relating to her two or three times over; and as she closed the letter, she sighed to remember the bar that now stood in the way of her wish, while she thought, "How I wish there was a chance of my knowing Constance better!"

THE END.

3

Tom Brown's School Days

By THOMAS HUGHES

TOM BROWN'S
SCHOOL DAYS

By AN OLD BOY

With Illustrations by Arthur Hughes and Sydney Prior Hall

London

TO

MRS. ARNOLD,

OF FOX HOWE,

THIS BOOK IS (WITHOUT HER PERMISSION)

Dedicated

BY THE AUTHOR,

WHO OWES MORE THAN HE CAN EVER ACKNOWLEDGE

OR FORGET TO HER AND HERS

T HIS IS A FAMOUS BOOK. *Tom Brown's School Days*—never out of print since it was published in 1857—is usually referred to as the perfect Victorian story of a boys' school. It has even inspired an able contemporary novelist, George MacDonald Fraser, to write a series of entertaining stories about the later life of Tom Brown's schoolmate, the bully Harry Flashman.

Thomas Hughes (1822–1896), the author of *Tom Brown's School Days*, attended Rugby School between 1833 and 1842, the last years of the famous reforming headmaster, Thomas Arnold (1795–1842), whom Hughes greatly admired, but whose ideals, somewhat ironically, he failed to grasp completely. Arnold believed that education and religion were inseparable, that "godliness and good learning" were to be pursued together, that intellectual, physical, and moral training must all be emphasized, and that the last was the most important. He did not invent these ideals, which most contemporary religious and educational leaders shared; but at Rugby he strove mightily to put them into effect. He himself preached to the boys from the school pulpit—a practice then most unusual for headmasters (*Tom Brown* includes a famous account of it)—and indelibly impressed his listeners. He preached simply and concentrated upon ethical issues: denouncing sensuality, lying, bullying, disobedience, laziness, and keeping bad company. Yet Tom Brown's Rugby was a hotbed of all these vices. Thoroughly decent in most ways, Tom himself disobeyed the rules, damaged other people's property, and used "cribs" in preparing his lessons, disregarding for most of his schoolboy career the precepts of the headmaster he so greatly revered. Hughes was not deeply troubled by the fact—if indeed he was fully aware of it—that the Rugby he portrayed was not the Rugby the headmaster he admired was striving to create.

The fact is that Thomas Hughes, like his hero Tom Brown, and unlike Thomas Arnold, was an extroverted, outdoors, provincial athlete, preferring the natural beauties of the English countryside to all the art and knowledge of languages that might be gained by foreign travel, a devotee of old-fashioned sports and games, a hearty egalitarian. After his undergraduate years at Oriel College, Oxford, Hughes was called to the Bar in 1848. In the tumultuous social troubles of the late forties and early fifties he fell under the influence of Frederick Denison Maurice (1805–1872), the "Broad Church" leader, who based his religious teachings upon his belief in the infinite love of God for all created beings. Together with Maurice and Charles Kingsley (1819–1875), already a parson and soon to become a well-known novelist, Hughes declared himself a Christian Socialist, an earnest proponent of social justice for the lower classes.

In Hughes and Kingsley, Christian Socialism was combined with "muscular Christianity," a devotion to manly sport and manly behavior. Kingsley cared less than Hughes for games, and was more intellectual and subtle. Hughes was straightforward and simple. It was the manly ideal for which Hughes worked all his life rather than for Arnold's "godliness and good learning." '"In all the new-fangled comprehensive plans" for workmen's schools, Hughes wrote in *Tom Brown*, athletic sports are left out, "and the consequence is, that your great Mechanics' Institutes end in intellectual priggism, and your Christian Young Men's Societies in religious Pharisaism." And in *Tom Brown*, written as his own son, Maurice, was about to go off to school, and—as Hughes later declared—with the "sole object" of preaching to boys, Hughes put the emphasis upon muscular Christian ideals rather than upon those of Thomas Arnold.

Despite the book's praise of Arnold, almost worship of Arnold, then, its doctrines do

353

not echo Arnold's own teachings but embody newer ideas that were to become increas-
ingly fashionable in the years after its publication. This, perhaps, helps to account for
the story's continued popularity: it taught the lessons that, more and more during the
second half of the nineteenth century, young men wanted to learn and older men
wanted to teach them. It popularized the active life, not the contemplative life, a
willingness, even an eagerness, to use one's fists, and a scientific knowledge of the way to
do so—"manliness" above all. Needless to say, those who disapproved—who found that
Tom Brown's and Thomas Hughes's Rugby was not like the Arnoldian Rugby they
remembered—were as sharp in attacking the book as its admirers were in praising it.
The dean of Westminster, A. P. Stanley, and the bishop of Durham, B. F. Westcott, both
Old Rugbeians, protested that Arnold's work had been wholly misrepresented. Charles
Kingsley, on the other hand, praised *Tom Brown* wherever he went, but found that all
the people he talked to had already read it, and thought it "the jolliest book" they had
ever read.

Tom Brown's father, Squire Brown, believes that "a man is to be valued wholly and
solely for that which he is in himself . . . apart from clothes, rank, fortune, and all
externals whatsoever"—a social principle, Hughes conceded, not generally associated
with Tory country gentlemen. So Tom plays with the village boys, who are "full as
manly and honest, and certainly purer, than those in a higher rank; and Tom got more
harm from his equals in his first fortnight at a private school" than he had ever got from
his village friends and social inferiors. The object of a school is "not to ram Latin and
Greek into boys, but to make them good English boys, good future citizens," most of
which must be accomplished after school hours. When the Squire says farewell before
Tom goes off to Rugby, he warns him that "you'll see a great many cruel blackguard
things done, and hear a deal of foul bad talk. But never fear. You tell the truth, keep a
brave and kind heart, and never listen to or say anything you wouldn't have your
mother and sister hear, and you'll never feel ashamed to come home, or we to see you."
Deliberately the Squire has not told Tom to read his Bible and love and serve God: "If
he don't do that for his mother's sake and teaching, he won't for mine." And deliberately he refrains from going into detail about the temptations Tom will meet with,
because it would "never do for an old fellow to go into such things with a boy. He won't
understand me. Do him more harm than good, ten to one." And, since the Squire and
his wife "don't care a straw for Greek," and Tom is going to school to learn to "become a
brave, helpful, truth-telling Englishman, and a gentleman, and a Christian," there is no
mention of book-learning.

This would not have been enough for Arnold. A genuine Arnoldian disciple, such as
E. W. Benson, later archbishop of Canterbury, for example, took quite a different
course. When Benson's diligent and studious beloved elder son went to school in the
seventies, Benson pursued him with detailed harsh criticisms of each school academic
report, continually urging him to work harder at his studies, to cease his inattention, to
do better. Benson, not Hughes, had the true Arnoldian emphasis.

Yet of course Dr. Arnold was aware that there would always be Tom Browns in any
school. And Tom made of Rugby exactly what one would expect of a Hughes hero.
There was drunkenness and bullying, which Tom combatted. There was worse: when
the leading boys were of the wrong sort, it became "a place where a young boy [would]
get more evil than he would if he were turned out to make his way in London streets."

This evil Hughes more directly refers to in his brief mention of the "small friend system," in which "little pretty white-handed, curly-headed boys [were] petted and pampered by some of the big fellows, who wrote their verses for them, taught them to drink and use bad language, and did all they could to spoil them for everything in this world and the next." An Old Rugbeian protested somewhat halfheartedly to this passage, saying that the "small friend system" had not been so bad during the years 1841–1847; Hughes notes the protest but responds that he cannot strike out the passage: "many boys will know why it is left in." And he has Tom say, "Thank goodness, no big fellow ever took to petting me." In the light of Hughes's evident detestation of the corruption and homosexuality inherent in the system, it is worth noting that Dr. Arnold himself entrusts to Tom Brown's care young George Arthur, a little boy in great need of protection, which Tom of course provides with the utmost purity.

Tom's relationship with Arthur turns him into a responsible man. It increases his sensitivity, and it leads him to abandon "cribs" and do his own work. Yet even as a sixth-former, Tom makes mistakes in geography of which Harry and Laura Graham of *Holiday House* would have been ashamed when they were ten years old. Hughes only remarks complacently, "Tom's ethnology and geography were faulty, but sufficient for his needs." Alas, Hughes and Brown were Philistines; Arnold (like his son, Matthew, who invented the word) loathed Philistinism. *Tom Brown* ends with Tom returning to Rugby to visit Arnold's tomb; but at that sacred moment Tom thinks more of Arnold than of God; and, Hughes adds, "young and brave souls ... must win their way through hero-worship" to the worship of God. Hughes intended the passage as profoundly religious, but Arnold himself would have stoutly repudiated it. Paradoxically, then, the novel that for all future generations became the symbol of Arnold's teaching, and of the school he strove to mold in accordance with his ideals, actually embraces wholly different values. But of course it remains a rousing and delightful and realistic story of schoolboy life, the best of its kind.

The text of Tom Brown's School Days, *with illustrations by Arthur Hughes and Sydney Prior Hall, is reprinted from an English edition (London: Macmillan and Co., 1900).*

PREFACE TO THE SIXTH EDITION

I RECEIVED the following letter from an old friend soon after the last edition of this book was published, and resolved, if ever another edition were called for, to print it. For it is clear from this and other like comments, that something more should have been said expressly on the subject of bullying, and how it is to be met.

"MY DEAR——,

"I blame myself for not having earlier suggested whether you could not, in another edition of 'Tom Brown' or another story, denounce more decidedly the evils of *bullying* at schools. You have indeed done so, and in the best way, by making Flashman the bully the most contemptible character; but in that scene of the *tossing*, and similar passages, you hardly suggest that such things should be stopped—and do not suggest any means of putting an end to them.

"This subject has been on my mind for years. It fills me with grief and misery to think what weak and nervous children go through at school—how their health and character for life are destroyed by rough and brutal treatment.

"It was some comfort to be under the old delusion that fear and nervousness can be cured by violence, and that knocking about will turn a timid boy into a bold one. But now we know well enough that is not true. Gradually training a timid child to do bold acts would be most desirable; but *frightening* him and ill-treating him will not make him courageous. Every medical man knows the fatal effects of terror, or agitation, or excitement, to nerves that are over-sensitive. There are different kinds of courage, as you have shown in your character of Arthur.

"A boy may have moral courage, and a finely organized brain and nervous system. Such a boy is calculated, if judiciously educated, to be a great, wise, and useful man; but he may not possess *animal courage;* and one night's *tossing*, or bullying, may produce such an injury to his brain and nerves that his usefulness is spoiled for life. I verily believe that hundreds of noble organizations are thus destroyed every year. Horse-jockeys have learnt to be wiser; they know that a highly nervous horse is utterly destroyed by harshness. A groom who tried to cure a shying horse by roughness and violence would be discharged as a brute and a fool. A man who would regulate his watch with a crowbar would be considered an ass. But the person who thinks a child of delicate and nervous organization can be made bold by bullying is no better.

"He can be made bold by *healthy exercise* and *games* and *sports;* but that is quite a different thing. And even these games and sports should bear some proportion to his strength and capacities.

"I very much doubt whether small children should play with big ones—the rush of a set of great fellows at football, or the speed of a cricket-ball sent by a strong hitter, must be very alarming to a mere child, to a child who might stand up boldly enough among children of his own size and height.

"Look at half a dozen small children playing cricket by themselves; how feeble are their blows, how slowly they bowl. You can measure in that way their capacity.

"Tom Brown and his eleven were bold enough in playing against an eleven of about their own calibre; but I suspect they would have been in a precious funk if they had played against eleven giants, whose bowling bore the same proportion to theirs that theirs does to the small children's above.

"To return to the *tossing*. I must say I think some means might be devised to enable schoolboys to go to bed in quietness and peace—and that some means ought to be devised and enforced. No good, moral or physical, to those who bully or those who are bullied, can ensue from such scenes as take place in the dormitories of schools. I suspect that British wisdom and ingenuity are sufficient to discover a remedy for this evil, if directed in the right direction.

"The fact is, that the condition of a small boy at a large school is one of peculiar hardship and suffering. He is entirely at the mercy of proverbially the roughest things in the universe—great schoolboys; and he is deprived of the protection which the weak have in civilized society: for he may not complain; if he does, he is an outlaw—he has no protector but public opinion, and that a public opinion of the very lowest grade, the opinion of rude and ignorant boys.

"What do schoolboys know of those deep questions of moral and physical philosophy, of the anatomy of mind and body, by which the treatment of a child should be regulated?

"Why should the laws of civilization be suspended for schools? Why should boys be left to herd together with no law but that of force or cunning? What would become of society if it were constituted on the same principles? It would be plunged into anarchy in a week.

"One of our judges, not long ago, refused to extend the protection of the law to a child who had been ill-treated at school. If a party of navvies had given *him* a licking, and he had brought the case before a magistrate, what would he have thought if the magistrate had refused to protect him, on the ground that if such cases were brought before him he might have fifty a day from one town only?

"Now I agree with you that a constant supervision of the master is not desirable or possible—and that telling tales, or constantly referring to the master for protection, would only produce ill-will and worse treatment.

"If I rightly understand your book, it is an effort to improve the condition of schools by improving the tone of morality and public opinion in them. But your book contains the most indubitable proofs that the condition of the younger boys at public schools, except under the rare dictatorship of an old Brooke, is one of great hardship and suffering.

"A timid and nervous boy is from morning till night in a state of bodily fear. He is constantly tormented when trying to learn his lessons. His play-hours are occupied in fagging, in a horrid funk of cricket-balls and foot-balls, and the violent sport of creatures who, to him, are giants. He goes to his bed in fear and trembling,—worse than the reality of the rough treatment to which he is perhaps subjected.

"I believe there is only one complete remedy. It is not in magisterial supervision; nor in telling tales; nor in raising the tone of public opinion among schoolboys— but in the *separation of boys of different ages into different schools*.

"There should be at least *three* different classes of schools,—the first for boys from nine to twelve; the second for boys from twelve to fifteen; the third for those above fifteen. And these schools should be in different localities.

"There ought to be a certain amount of supervision by the master at those times when there are special occasions for bullying, *e.g.* in the long winter evenings, and when the boys are congregated together in the bedrooms. Surely it cannot be an impossibility to keep order and protect the weak at such times. Whatever evils might arise from supervision, they could hardly be greater than those produced by a system which divides boys into despots and slaves.

"Ever yours, very truly,

"F. D."

The question of how to adapt English public school education to nervous and sensitive boys (often the highest and noblest subjects which that education has to deal with) ought to be looked at from every point of view.[1] I therefore add a few extracts from the letter of an old friend and school-fellow, than whom no man in England is better able to speak on the subject.

"What's the use of sorting the boys by ages, unless you do so by strength: and who are often the real bullies? The strong young dog of fourteen, while the victim may be one year or two years older. . . . I deny the fact about the bedrooms: there is trouble at times, and always will be; but so there is in nurseries;—my little girl, who looks like an angel, was bullying the smallest twice to-day.

"Bullying must be fought with in other ways,—by getting not only the Sixth to put it down, but the lower fellows to scorn it, and by eradicating mercilessly the incorrigible; and a master who really cares for his fellows is pretty sure to know instinctively who in his house are likely to be bullied, and, knowing a fellow to be really victimized and harassed, I am sure that he can stop it if he is resolved. There are many kinds of annoyance—sometimes of real cutting persecution for righteousness' sake—that he can't stop; no more could all the ushers in the world; but he can do very much in many ways to make the shafts of the wicked pointless.

"But though, for quite other reasons, I don't like to see very young boys launched at a public school, and though I don't deny (I wish I could) the existence from time to time of bullying, I deny its being a constant condition of school life, and still more, the possibility of meeting it by the means proposed. . . .

"I don't wish to understate the amount of bullying that goes on, but my conviction is that it must be fought, like all school evils, but it more than any, by *dynamics* rather than *mechanics,* by getting the fellows to respect themselves and one another, rather than by sitting by them with a thick stick."

And now, having broken my resolution never to write a Preface, there are just two or three things which I should like to say a word about.

---

[1] For those who believe with me in public school education, the fact stated in the following extract from a note of Mr. G. de Bunsen will be hailed with pleasure, especially now that our alliance with Prussia (the most natural and healthy European alliance for Protestant England) is likely to be so much stronger and deeper than heretofore. Speaking of this book, he says,—"The author is mistaken in saying that public schools, in the English sense, are peculiar to England. Schul Pforte (in the Prussian province of Saxony) is similiar in antiquity and institutions. I like his book all the more for having been there for five years."

Several persons, for whose judgment I have the highest respect, while saying very kind things about this book, have added, that the great fault of it is "too much preaching;" but they hope I shall amend in this matter should I ever write again. Now this I most distinctly decline to do. Why, my whole object in writing at all was to get the chance of preaching! When a man comes to my time of life and has his bread to make, and very little time to spare, is it likely that he will spend almost the whole of his yearly vacation in writing a story just to amuse people? I think not. At any rate, I wouldn't do so myself.

The fact is, that I can scarcely ever call on one of my contemporaries now-a-days without running across a boy already at school, or just ready to go there, whose bright looks and supple limbs remind me of his father, and our first meeting in old times. I can scarcely keep the Latin Grammar out of my own house any longer: and the sight of sons, nephews, and godsons, playing trap-bat-and-ball and reading *Robinson Crusoe*, makes one ask one's self whether there isn't something one would like to say to them before they take their first plunge into the stream of life, away from their own homes, or while they are yet shivering after the first plunge. My sole object in writing was to preach to boys: if ever I write again, it will be to preach to some other age. I can't see that a man has any business to write at all unless he has something which he thoroughly believes and wants to preach about. If he has this, and the chance of delivering himself of it, let him by all means put it in the shape in which it will be most likely to get a hearing; but let him never be so carried away as to forget that preaching is his object.

A black soldier in a West Indian regiment, tied up to receive a couple of dozen for drunkenness, cried out to his captain, who was exhorting him to sobriety in future, "Cap'n, if you preachee, preachee; and if floggee, floggee; but no preachee and floggee too!" to which his captain might have replied, "No, Pompey, I must preach whenever I see a chance of being listened to, which I never did before; so now you must have it altogether; and I hope you may remember some of it."

There is one point which has been made by several of the Reviewers who have noticed this book, and it is one which, as I am writing a Preface, I cannot pass over. They have stated that the Rugby undergraduates they remember at the Universities were "a solemn array," "boys turned into men before their time," "a semi-political, semi-sacerdotal fraternity," &c., giving the idea that Arnold turned out a set of young square-toes who wore long-fingered black gloves and talked with a snuffle. I can only say that their acquaintance must have been limited and exceptional. For I am sure that every one who has had anything like large or continuous knowledge of boys brought up at Rugby, from the times of which this book treats down to this day, will bear me out in saying, that the mark by which you may know them, is, their genial and hearty freshness and youthfulness of character. They lose nothing of the boy that is worth keeping, but build up the man upon it. This is their *differentia* as Rugby boys; and if they never had it, or have lost it, it must be not because they were at Rugby, but in spite of their having been there; the stronger it is in them the more deeply you may be sure have they drunk of the spirit of their school.

But this boyishness in the highest sense is not incompatible with seriousness,—or earnestness, if you like the word better.[1] Quite the contrary. And I can well believe that

---

[1] "To him (Arnold) and his admirers we owe the substitution of the word 'earnest' for its predecessor 'serious.' "—*Edinburgh Review*, No. 217, p. 183.

casual observers, who have never been intimate with Rugby boys of the true stamp, but have met them only in the every-day society of the Universities, at wines, breakfast parties, and the like, may have seen a good deal more of the serious or earnest side of their characters than of any other. For the more the boy was alive in them, the less will they have been able to conceal their thoughts, or their opinion of what was taking place under their noses; and if the greater part of that didn't square with their notions of what was right, very likely they showed pretty clearly that it did not, at whatever risk of being taken for young prigs. They may be open to the charge of having old heads on young shoulders; I think they are, and always were, as long as I can remember; but so long as they have young hearts to keep head and shoulders in order, I, for one, must think this only a gain.

And what gave Rugby boys this character, and has enabled the School, I believe, to keep it to this day? I say fearlessly,—Arnold's teaching and example—above all, that part of it which has been, I will not say sneered at, but certainly not approved—his unwearied zeal in creating "moral thoughtfulness" in every boy with whom he came into personal contact.

He certainly *did* teach us—thank God for it!—that we could not cut our life into slices and say, "In this slice your actions are indifferent, and you needn't trouble your heads about them one way or another; but in this slice mind what you are about, for they are important"—a pretty muddle we should have been in had he done so. He taught us that, in this wonderful world, no boy or man can tell which of his actions is indifferent and which not; that by a thoughtless word or look we may lead astray a brother for whom Christ died. He taught us that life is a whole, made up of actions and thoughts and longings, great and small, noble and ignoble; therefore the only true wisdom for boy or man is to bring the whole life into obedience to Him whose world we live in, and who has purchased us with His blood; and that whether we eat or drink, or whatsoever we do, we are to do all in His name and to His glory; in such teaching, faithfully, as it seems to me, following that of Paul of Tarsus, who was in the habit of meaning what he said, and who laid down this standard for every man and boy in his time. I think it lies with those who say that such teaching will not do for us now, to show why a teacher in the nineteenth century is to preach a lower standard than one in the first.

However, I won't say that the Reviewers have not a certain plausible ground for their dicta. For a short time after a boy has taken up such a life as Arnold would have urged upon him, he has a hard time of it. He finds his judgment often at fault, his body and intellect running away with him into all sorts of pitfalls, and himself coming down with a crash. The more seriously he buckles to his work the oftener these mischances seem to happen; and in the dust of his tumbles and struggles, unless he is a very extraordinary boy, he may often be too severe on his comrades, may think he sees evil in things innocent, may give offence when he never meant it. At this stage of his career, I take it, our Reviewer comes across him, and, not looking below the surface (as a Reviewer ought to do), at once sets the poor boy down for a prig and a Pharisee, when in all likelihood he is one of the humblest and truest and most childlike of the Reviewer's acquaintance.

But let our Reviewer come across him again in a year or two, when the "thoughtful life" has become habitual to him, and fits him as easily as his skin; and, if he be honest, I think he will see cause to reconsider his judgment. For he will find the boy grown into a man, enjoying every-day life, as no man can who has not found out whence comes the capacity for enjoyment, and who is the Giver of the least of the good things of this world—humble, as no man can be who has not proved his own powerlessness to do right in the smallest act which he ever had to do—tolerant, as no man can be who does not live daily and hourly in the knowledge of how Perfect Love is for ever about his path, and bearing with and upholding him.

CHAPTER I

THE BROWN FAMILY

"I'm the Poet of White Horse Vale, Sir,
With liberal notions under my cap."
BALLAD

T HE BROWNS have become illustrious by the pen of Thackeray and the pencil of Doyle, within the memory of the young gentlemen who are now matriculating at the Universities. Notwithstanding the well-merited but late fame which has now fallen upon them, any one at all acquainted with the family must feel, that much has yet to be written and said before the British nation will be properly sensible of how much of its greatness it owes to the Browns. For centuries, in their quiet, dogged, homespun way, they have been subduing the earth in most English counties, and leaving their mark in American forests and Australian uplands. Wherever the fleets and armies of England have won renown, there stalwart sons of the Browns have done yeomen's work. With the yew bow and cloth-yard shaft at Cressy and Agincourt—with the brown bill and pike under the brave Lord Willoughby—with culverin and demi-culverin against Spaniards and Dutchmen—with hand-grenade and sabre, and musket and bayonet, under Rodney and St. Vincent, Wolfe and Moore, Nelson and Wellington, they have carried their lives in their hands; getting hard knocks and hard work in plenty, which was on the whole what they looked for, and the best thing for them; and little praise or pudding, which indeed they, and most of us, are better without. Talbots and Stanleys, St. Maurs, and such-like folk, have led armies and made laws time out of mind; but those noble families would be somewhat astounded—if the accounts ever came to be fairly taken—to find how small their work for England has been by the side of that of the Browns.

These latter, indeed, have until the present generation rarely been sung by poet, or chronicled by sage. They have wanted their "Sacer vates," having been too solid to rise to the top by themselves, and not having been largely gifted with the talent of catching hold of, and holding on tight to, whatever good things happened to be going,—the foundation of the fortunes of so many noble families. But the world goes on its way, and the wheel turns, and the wrongs of the Browns, like other wrongs, seem in a fair way to get righted. And this present writer having for many years of his life been a devout Brown-worshipper, and moreover having the honour of being nearly connected with an eminently respectable branch of the great Brown family, is anxious, so far as in him lies, to help the wheel over, and throw his stone on to the pile.

However, gentle reader, or simple reader, whichever you may be, lest you should be led to waste your precious time upon these pages, I make so bold as at once to tell you the sort of folk you'll have to meet and put up with, if you and I are to jog on comfortably together. You shall hear at once what sort of folk the Browns are, at least my branch of them; and then, if you don't like the sort, why cut the concern at once, and let you and I cry quits before either of us can grumble at the other.

In the first place, the Browns are a fighting family. One may question their wisdom, or wit, or beauty, but about their fight there can be no question. Wherever hard knocks of any kind, visible or invisible, are going, there the Brown who is nearest must shove in his carcase. And these carcases for the most part answer very well to the characteristic propensity; they are a square-headed and snake-necked generation, broad in the shoulder, deep in the chest, and thin in the flank, carrying no lumber. Then for clanship, they are as bad as Highlanders; it is amazing the belief they have in one another. With them there is nothing like the Browns, to the third and fourth generation. "Blood is thicker than water," is one of their pet sayings. They can't be happy unless they are always meeting one another. Never were such people for family gatherings, which, were you a stranger, or sensitive, you might think had better not have been gathered together. For during the whole time of their being together they luxuriate in telling one another their minds on whatever subject turns up; and their minds are wonderfully antagonistic, and all their opinions are downright beliefs. Till you've been among them some time and understand them, you can't think but that they are quarrelling. Not a bit of it: they love and respect one another ten times the more after a good set family arguing bout, and go back, one to his curacy, another to his chambers, and another to his regiment, freshened for work, and more than ever convinced that the Browns are the height of company.

This family training too, combined with their turn for combativeness, makes them eminently quixotic. They can't let anything alone which they think going wrong. They must speak their mind about it, annoying all easy-going folk; and spend their time and money in having a tinker at it, however hopeless the job. It is an impossibility to a Brown to leave the most disreputable lame dog on the other side of a stile. Most other folk get tired of such work. The old Browns, with red faces, white whiskers, and bald heads, go on believing and fighting to a green old age. They have always a crotchet going, till the old man with the scythe reaps and garners them away for troublesome old boys as they are.

And the most provoking thing is, that no failures knock them up, or make them hold their hands, or think you, or me, or other sane people in the right. Failures slide off them like July rain off a duck's back feathers. Jem and his whole family turn out bad, and cheat them one week, and the next they are doing the same thing for Jack; and when he goes to the treadmill, and his wife and children to the workhouse, they will be on the look-out for Bill to take his place.

However, it is time for us to get from the general to the particular; so, leaving the great army of Browns, who are scattered over the whole empire on which the sun never sets, and whose general diffusion I take to be the chief cause of that empire's stability, let us at once fix our attention upon the small nest of Browns in which our hero was hatched, and which dwelt in that portion of the Royal county of Berks which is called the Vale of White Horse.

Most of you have probably travelled down the Great Western Railway as far as Swindon. Those of you who did so with their eyes open, have been aware, soon after leaving the Didcot station, of a fine range of chalk hills running parallel with the railway on the left hand side as you go down, and distant some two or three miles, more or less, from the line. The highest point in the range is the White Horse Hill, which you come in front of just before you stop at the Shrivenham station. If you love English scenery and have a few hours to spare, you can't do better, the next time you pass, than stop at the Farringdon-road or Shrivenham station, and make your way to that highest point. And those who care for the vague old stories that haunt country sides all about England, will not, if they are wise, be content with only a few hours' stay; for, glorious as the view is, the neighbourhood is yet more interesting for its relics of bygone times. I only know two English neighbourhoods thoroughly, and in each, within a circle of five miles, there is enough of interest and beauty to last any reasonable man his life. I believe this to be the case almost throughout the country, but each has a special attraction, and none can be richer than the one I am speaking of and going to introduce you to very particularly; for on this subject I must be prosy; so those that don't care for England in detail may skip the chapter.

Oh young England! young England! You who are born into these racing railroad times, when there's a Great Exhibition, or some monster sight, every year; and you can get over a couple of thousand miles of ground for three pound ten, in a five weeks' holiday; why don't you know more of your own birth-places? You're all in the ends of the earth, it seems to me, as soon as you get your necks out of the educational collar, for Midsummer holidays, long vacations, or what not. Going round Ireland, with a return ticket, in a fortnight; dropping your copies of Tennyson on the tops of Swiss mountains; or pulling down the Danube in Oxford racing-boats. And when you get home for a quiet fortnight, you turn the steam off, and lie on your backs in the paternal garden, surrounded by the last batch of books from Mudie's library, and half bored to death. Well, well! I know it has its good side. You all patter French more or less, and perhaps German; you have seen men and cities, no doubt, and have your opinions, such as they are, about schools of painting, high art, and all that; have seen the pictures at Dresden and the Louvre, and know the taste of sour krout. All I say is, you don't know your own lanes and woods and fields. Though you may be chock-full of science, not one in twenty of you knows where to find the wood-sorrel, or bee-orchis, which grow in the next wood, or on the down three miles off, or what the bog-bean and wood-sage are good for. And as for the country legends, the stories of the old gable-ended farm-houses, the place where the last skirmish was fought in the civil wars, where the parish butts stood, where the last highwayman turned to bay, where the last ghost was laid by the parson, they're gone out of date altogether.

Now, in my time, when we got home by the old coach, which put us down at the cross-roads with our boxes, the first day of the holidays, and had been driven off by the family coachman, singing "Dulce domum" at the top of our voices, there we were, fixtures, till black Monday came round. We had to cut out our own amusements within a walk or a ride of home. And so we got to know all the country folk, and their ways and songs and stories, by heart; and went over the fields, and woods, and hills, again and again, till we made friends of them all. We were Berkshire, or Gloucestershire, or Yorkshire boys; and you're young cosmopolites, belonging to all counties and no countries. No doubt it's all right, I dare say it is. This is the day of large views and glorious humanity, and all that; but I wish back-sword play hadn't gone out in the Vale of White Horse, and that that confounded Great Western hadn't carried away Alfred's Hill to make an embankment.

But to return to the said Vale of White Horse, the country in which the first scenes of this true and interesting story are laid. As I said, the Great Western now runs right through it, and it is a land of large rich pastures, bounded by ox-fences, and covered with fine hedgerow timber, with here and there a nice little gorse or spinney, where abideth poor Charley, having no other cover to which to betake himself for miles and miles, when pushed out some fine November morning by the Old Berkshire. Those who have been there, and well mounted, only know how he and the staunch little pack who dash after him—heads high and sterns low, with a breast-high scent—can consume the ground at such times. There being little plough-land, and few woods, the Vale is only an average sporting country, except for hunting. The villages are straggling, queer, old-fashioned places, the houses being dropped down without the least regularity, in nooks and out-of-the-way corners, by the sides of shadowy lanes and foot-paths, each with its patch of garden. They are built chiefly of good gray stone and thatched; though I see that within the last year or two the red-brick cottages are multiplying, for the Vale is beginning to manufacture largely both brick and tiles. There are lots of waste ground by the side of the roads in every village, amounting often to village greens, where feed the pigs and ganders of the people; and these roads are old-fashioned homely roads, very dirty and badly made, and hardly endurable in winter, but still pleasant jog-trot roads running through the great pasture lands, dotted here and there with little clumps of thorns, where the sleek kine are feeding, with no fence on either side of them, and a

gate at the end of each field, which makes you get out of your gig (if you keep one), and gives you a chance of looking about you every quarter of a mile.

One of the moralists whom we sat under in our youth,—was it the great Richard Swiveller, or Mr. Stiggins?—says, "We are born in a vale, and must take the consequences of being found in such a situation." These consequences I for one am ready to encounter. I pity people who weren't born in a vale. I don't mean a flat country, but a vale: that is, a flat country bounded by hills. The having your hill *always* in view if you choose to turn towards him, that's the essence of a vale. There he is for ever in the distance, your friend and companion; you never lose him as you do in hilly districts.

And then what a hill is the White Horse Hill! There it stands right up above all the rest, nine hundred feet above the sea, and the boldest, bravest shape for a chalk hill that you ever saw. Let us go up to the top of him, and see what is to be found there. Ay, you may well wonder and think it odd you never heard of this before; but wonder or not, as you please, there are hundreds of such things lying about England, which wiser folk than you know nothing of, and care nothing for. Yes, it's a magnificent Roman camp, and no mistake, with gates and ditch and mounds, all as complete as it was twenty years after the strong old rogues left it. Here, right up on the highest point, from which they say you can see eleven counties, they trenched round all the table-land, some twelve or fourteen acres, as was their custom, for they couldn't bear anybody to overlook them, and made their eyrie. The ground falls away rapidly on all sides. Was there ever such turf in the whole world? You sink up to your ankles at every step, and yet the spring of it is delicious. There is always a breeze in the "camp," as it is called; and here it lies, just as the Romans left it, except that cairn on the east side, left by Her Majesty's corps of Sappers and Miners the other day, when they and the Engineer officer had finished their sojourn there, and their surveys for the Ordnance Map of Berkshire. It is altogether a place that you won't forget,—a place to open a man's soul and make him prophesy, as he looks down on that great Vale spread out as the garden of the Lord before him, and wave on wave of the mysterious downs behind; and to the right and left the chalk hills running away into the distance, along which he can trace for miles the old Roman road, "the Ridgeway" ("the Rudge" as the country folk call it), keeping straight along the highest back of the hills;—such a place as Balak brought Balaam to and told him to prophesy against the people in the valley beneath. And he could not, neither shall you, for they are a people of the Lord who abide there.

And now we leave the camp, and descend towards the west, and are on the Ash-down. We are treading on heroes. It is sacred ground for Englishmen, more sacred than all but one or two fields where their bones lie whitening. For this is the actual place where our Alfred won his great battle, the battle of Ashdown ("Æscendum" in the chroniclers), which broke the Danish power, and made England a Christian land. The Danes held the camp and the slope where we are standing—the whole crown of the hill in fact. "The heathen had beforehand seized the higher ground," as old Asser says, having wasted everything behind them from London, and being just ready to burst down on the fair vale, Alfred's own birthplace and heritage. And up the heights came the Saxons, as they did at the Alma. "The Christians led up their line from the lower ground. There stood also on that same spot a single thorn-tree, marvellous stumpy (which we ourselves with our very own eyes have seen)." Bless the old chronicler! does he think nobody ever saw the "single thorn-tree" but himself? Why, there it stands to this very day, just on the edge of the slope, and I saw it not three weeks since; an old single thorn-tree, "marvellous stumpy." At least if it isn't the same tree, it ought to have been, for it's just in the place where the battle must have been won or lost—"around which, as I was saying, the two lines of foemen came together in battle with a huge shout. And in this place, one of the two kings of the heathen and five of his earls fell down and died, and many thousands of the heathen side in the same place."[1] After which crowning mercy, the pious King, that there might never be wanting a sign and a memorial to the country-side, carved out on the northern side of the chalk hill, under the camp, where it is almost precipitous, the great Saxon white horse, which he who will may see from the railway, and which gives its name to the vale, over which it has looked these thousand years and more.

Right down below the White Horse, is a curious deep and broad gully called "the Manger," into one side of which the hills fall with a series of the most lovely sweeping curves, known as "the Giant's Stairs;" they are not a bit like stairs, but I never saw anything like them anywhere else, with their short green turf, and tender blue-bells, and gossamer and thistle-down gleaming in the sun, and the sheep-paths running along their sides like ruled lines.

The other side of the Manger is formed by the Dragon's Hill, a curious little round self-confident fellow, thrown forward from the range, utterly unlike everything round him. On this hill some deliverer of mankind—St. George, the country-folk used to tell me—killed a dragon. Whether it were St. George, I cannot say; but surely a dragon was killed there, for you may see the marks yet where his blood ran down, and more by token the place where it ran down is the easiest way up the hill-side.

Passing along the Ridgeway to the west for about a mile, we come to a little clump of young beech and firs, with a growth of thorn and privet underwood. Here you may find nests of the strong down partridge and peewit, but take care that the keeper isn't down

---

[1]"Pagani editiorem locum præoccupaverant. Christiani ab inferiori loco aciem dirigebant. Erat quoque in eodem loco unica spinosa arbor, brevis admodum (quam nos ipsi nostris propriis oculis vidimus). Circa quam ergo hostiles inter se acies cum ingenti clamore hostiliter conveniunt. Quo in loco alter de duobus Paganorum regibus et quinque comites occisi occubuerunt, et multa millia Paganæ partis in eodem loco. Cecidit illic ergo Bœgsceg Rex, et Sidroc ille senex comes, et Sidroc Junior comes, et Obsbern comes," &c.—*Annales Rerum Gestarum Ælfredi Magni, Auctore Asserio. Recensuit Franciscus Wise.* Oxford, 1722, p. 23.

upon you; and in the middle of it is an old cromlech, a huge flat stone raised on seven or eight others, and led up to by a path, with large single stones set up on each side. This is Wayland Smith's cave, a place of classic fame now; but as Sir Walter has touched it, I may as well let it alone, and refer you to Kenilworth for the legend.

The thick deep wood which you see in the hollow, about a mile off, surrounds Ashdown Park, built by Inigo Jones. Four broad alleys are cut through the wood from circumference to centre, and each leads to one face of the house. The mystery of the downs hangs about house and wood, as they stand there alone, so unlike all around, with the green slopes studded with great stones just about this part, stretching away on all sides. It was a wise Lord Craven, I think, who pitched his tent there.

Passing along the Ridgeway to the east, we soon come to cultivated land. The downs, strictly so called, are no more; Lincolnshire farmers have been imported, and the long fresh slopes are sheep-walks no more, but grow famous turnips and barley. One of these improvers lives over there at the "Seven Barrows" farm, another mystery of the great downs. There are the barrows still, solemn and silent, like ships in the calm sea, the sepulchres of some sons of men. But of whom? It is three miles from the White Horse, too far for the slain of Ashdown to be buried there—who shall say what heroes are waiting there? But we must get down into the vale again, and so away by the Great Western Railway to town, for time and the printer's devil press, and it is a terrible long and slippery descent, and a shocking bad road. At the bottom, however, there is a pleasant public, whereat we must really take a modest quencher, for the down air is provocative of thirst. So we pull up under an old oak which stands before the door.

"What is the name of your hill, landlord?"

"Blawing Stwun Hill, sir, to be sure."

[Reader. *"Sturm?"*

Author. *"Stone,* stupid: the Blowing *Stone."*]

"And of your house? I can't make out the sign."

"Blawing Stwun, sir," says the landlord, pouring out his old ale from a Toby Philpot jug, with a melodious crash, into the long-necked glass.

"What queer names!" say we, sighing at the end of our draught, and holding out the glass to be replenished.

"Bean't queer at all, as I can see, sir," says mine host, handing back our glass, "seeing as this here is the Blawing Stwun, his self," putting his hand on a square lump of stone, some three feet and a half high, perforated with two or three queer holes, like petrified antediluvian rat-holes, which lies there close under the oak, under our very nose. We are more than ever puzzled, and drink our second glass of ale, wondering what will come next. "Like to hear un, sir," says mine host, setting down Toby Philpot on the tray, and resting both hands on the "Stwun." We are ready for anything; and he, without waiting for a reply, applies his mouth to one of the rat-holes. Something must come of it, if he doesn't burst. Good heavens! I hope he has no apoplectic tendencies. Yes, here it comes, sure enough, a grewsome sound between a moan and a roar, and spreads itself away over the valley, and up the hill-side, and into the woods at the back of the house, a ghost-like awful voice. "Um do say, sir," says mine host, rising purple-faced, while the moan is still coming out of the Stwun, "as they used in old times to warn the country-side, by blowing the Stwun when the enemy was a comin'—and as how folks could make un heered then for seven mile round; leastways, so I've heered Lawyer Smith say, and he knows a smart sight about them old times." We can hardly swallow Lawyer Smith's seven miles, but could the blowing of the stone have been a summons, a sort of sending the fiery cross round the neighbourhood in the old times? What old times? Who knows? We pay for our beer, and are thankful.

"And what's the name of the village just below, landlord?"

"Kingstone Lisle, sir."

"Fine plantations you've got here?"

"Yes, sir, the Squire's 'mazing fond of trees and such like."

"No wonder. He's got some real beauties to be fond of. Good day, landlord."

"Good day, sir, and a pleasant ride to 'e."

And now, my boys, you whom I want to get for readers, have you had enough? Will you give in at once, and say you're convinced, and let me begin my story, or will you have more of it? Remember, I've only been over a little bit of the hill-side yet, what you could ride round easily on your ponies in an hour. I'm only just come down into the vale, by Blowing Stone Hill; and if I once begin about the vale, what's to stop me? You'll have to hear all about Wantage, the birthplace of Alfred, and Farringdon, which held out so long for Charles the First (the vale was near Oxford, and dreadfully malignant; full of Throgmortons, Puseys, and Pyes, and such like, and their brawny retainers). Did you ever read Thomas Ingoldsby's "Legend of Hamilton Tighe"? If you haven't, you ought to have. Well, Farringdon is where he lived, before he went to sea; his real name was Hamden Pye, and the Pyes were the great folk at Farringdon. Then there's Pusey. You've heard of the Pusey horn, which King Canute gave to the Puseys of that day, and which the gallant old squire, lately gone to his rest (whom Berkshire freeholders turned out of last Parliament, to their eternal disgrace, for voting according to his conscience), used to bring out on high days, holidays, and bonfire nights. And the splendid old cross church at Uffington, the Uffingas town;—how the whole country-side teems with Saxon names and memories! And the old moated Grange at Compton, nestled close under the hill-side, where twenty Marianas may have lived, with its bright water-lilies in the moat, and its yew walk, "the Cloister walk," and its peerless terraced gardens. There they all are, and twenty things beside, for those who care about them, and have eyes. And these are the sort of things you may find, I believe, every one of you, in any common English country neighbourhood.

Will you look for them under your own noses, or will you not? Well, well; I've done what I can to make you, and if you will go gadding over half Europe now every holidays, I can't help it. I was born and bred a West-countryman, thank God! a Wessex man, a citizen of the noblest Saxon kingdom of Wessex, a regular "Angular Saxon," the very soul of me "adscriptus glebæ." There's nothing like the old country-side for me, and no music like the twang of the real old Saxon tongue, as one gets it fresh from the veritable chaw in the White Horse Vale: and I say with "Gaarge Ridler, the old West-country yeoman,

> "Throo aall the waarld owld Gaarge would bwoast
> Commend me to merry owld England mwoast:
> While vools gwoes prating vur and nigh,
> We stwops at whum, my dog and I."

Here at any rate lived and stopped at home, Squire Brown, J.P. for the county of Berks, in a village near the foot of the White Horse range. And here he dealt out justice and mercy in a rough way, and begat sons and daughters, and hunted the fox, and grumbled at the badness of the roads and the times. And his wife dealt out stockings, and calico shirts, and smock frocks, and comforting drinks to the old folks with the "rheumatiz," and good counsel to all; and kept the coal and clothes clubs going, for yule-tide, when the bands of mummers came round, dressed out in ribbons and coloured paper caps, and stamped round the Squire's kitchen, repeating in true sing-song vernacular the legend of St. George and his fight, and the ten-pound doctor, who plays his part at healing the Saint,—a relic, I believe, of the old Middle-age mysteries. It was the first dramatic representation which greeted the eyes of little Tom, who was brought down into the kitchen by his nurse to witness it, at the mature age of three years. Tom was the eldest child of his parents, and from his earliest babyhood exhibited the family characteristics in great strength. He was a hearty strong boy from the first, given to fighting with and escaping from his nurse, and fraternizing with all the village boys, with whom he made expeditions all round the neighbourhood. And here in the quiet old-fashioned country village, under the shadow of the everlasting hills, Tom Brown was reared, and never left it till he went first to school when nearly eight years of age,—for in those days change of air twice a-year was not thought absolutely necessary for the health of all her Majesty's lieges.

I have been credibly informed, and am inclined to believe, that the various Boards of Directors of Railway Companies, those gigantic jobbers and bribers, while quarrelling about everything else, agreed together some ten years back to buy up the learned profession of Medicine, body and soul. To this end they set apart several millions of money, which they continually distribute judiciously among the Doctors, stipulating only this one thing, that they shall prescribe change of air to every patient who can pay, or borrow money to pay, a railway fare, and see their prescription carried out. If it be not for this, why is it that none of us can be well at home for a year together? It wasn't so twenty years ago,—not a bit of it. The Browns didn't go out of the country once in five years. A visit to Reading or Abingdon twice a-year, at Assizes or Quarter Sessions, which the Squire made on his horse with a pair of saddle-bags containing his wardrobe—a stay of a day or two at some country neighbour's—or an expedition to a county ball or the yeomanry review—made up the sum of the Brown locomotion in most years. A stray Brown from some distant county dropped in every now and then; or from Oxford, on grave nag, an old don, contemporary of the Squire; and were looked upon by the Brown household and the villagers with the same sort of feeling with which we now regard a man who has crossed the Rocky Mountains, or launched a boat on the Great Lake in Central Africa. The White Horse Vale, remember, was traversed by no great road: nothing but country parish roads, and these very bad. Only one coach ran there, and this one only from Wantage to London, so that the western part of the Vale was without regular means of moving on, and certainly didn't seem to want them. There was the canal, by the way, which supplied the country-side with coal, and up and down which continually went the long barges, with the big black men lounging by the side of the horses along the towing-path, and the women in bright-coloured handkerchiefs standing in the sterns steering. Standing I say, but you could never see whether they were standing or sitting, all but their heads and shoulders being out of sight in the cosey

little cabins which occupied some eight feet of the stern, and which Tom Brown pictured to himself as the most desirable of residences. His nurse told him that those good-natured-looking women were in the constant habit of enticing children into the barges and taking them up to London and selling them, which Tom wouldn't believe, and which made him resolve as soon as possible to accept the oft-proffered invitation of these sirens to "young master," to come in and have a ride. But as yet the nurse was too much for Tom.

Yet why should I after all abuse the gadabout propensities of my countrymen? We are a vagabond nation now, that's certain, for better for worse. I am a vagabond; I have been away from home no less than five distinct times in the last year. The Queen sets us the example—we are moving on from top to bottom. Little dirty Jack, who abides in Clement's Inn gateway, and blacks my boots for a penny, takes his month's hop-picking every year as a matter of course. Why shouldn't he? I'm delighted at it. I love vagabonds, only I prefer poor to rich ones;—couriers and ladies' maids, imperials and travelling carriages, are an abomination unto me—I cannot away with them. But for dirty Jack, and every good fellow who, in the words of the capital French song, moves about,

> "Comme le limaçon,
>   Portant tout son bagage,
>   Ses meubles, sa maison,"

on his way back, why, good luck to them, and many a merry road-side adventure, and steaming supper in the chimney corners of road-side inns, Swiss châlets, Hottentot kraals, or wherever else they like to go. So having succeeded in contradicting myself in my first chapter (which gives me great hopes that you will all go on, and think me a good fellow notwithstanding my crotchets), I shall here shut up for the present, and consider my ways; having resolved to "sar' it out," as we say in the Vale, "holus bolus" just as it comes, and then you'll probably get the truth out of me.

CHAPTER II
THE ''VEAST''

"And the King commandeth and forbiddeth, that from henceforth neither fairs nor
markets be kept in Churchyards, for the honour of the Church."
STATUTES: 13 *Edw.I.* Stat. II. cap. vi

As that venerable and learned poet (whose voluminous works we all think it the
correct thing to admire and talk about, but don't read often) most truly says, "The child
is father to the man;" *a fortiori*, therefore, he must be father to the boy. So as we are
going at any rate to see Tom Brown through his boyhood, supposing we never get any
further (which, if you show a proper sense of the value of this history, there is no
knowing but what we may), let us have a look at the life and environments of the child
in the quiet country village to which we were introduced in the last chapter.

Tom, as has been already said, was a robust and combative urchin, and at the age of
four began to struggle against the yoke and authority of his nurse. That functionary was
a good-hearted, tearful, scatter-brained girl, lately taken by Tom's mother, Madam
Brown, as she was called, from the village school to be trained as nurserymaid. Madam
Brown was a rare trainer of servants, and spent herself freely in the profession; for
profession it was, and gave her more trouble by half than many people take to earn a
good income. Her servants were known and sought after for miles round. Almost all the
girls who attained a certain place in the village school were taken by her, one or two at a
time, as housemaids, laundrymaids, nurserymaids, or kitchen-maids, and after a year or
two's drilling were started in life amongst the neighbouring families, with good principles and wardrobes. One of the results of this system was the perpetual despair of Mrs.
Brown's cook and own maid, who no sooner had a notable girl made to their hands than
Missus was sure to find a good place for her and send her off, taking in fresh
importations from the school. Another was, that the house was always full of young
girls, with clean shining faces; who broke plates and scorched linen, but made an
atmosphere of cheerful homely life about the place, good for every one who came
within its influence. Mrs. Brown loved young people, and in fact human creatures in
general, above plates and linen. They were more like a lot of elder children than
servants, and felt to her more as a mother or aunt than as a mistress.

Tom's nurse was one who took in her instruction very slowly,—she seemed to have
two left hands and no head; and so Mrs. Brown kept her on longer than usual, that she
might expend her awkwardness and forgetfulness upon those who would not judge and
punish her too strictly for them.

Charity Lamb was her name. It had been the immemorial habit of the village to
christen children either by Bible names, or by those of the cardinal and other virtues; so
that one was for ever hearing in the village street, or on the green, shrill sounds of
"Prudence! Prudence! thee cum' out o' the gutter;" or, "Mercy! drat the girl, what bist
thee a doin' wi' little Faith?" and there were Ruths, Rachels, Keziahs, in every corner.
The same with the boys; they were Benjamins, Jacobs, Noahs, Enochs. I suppose the
custom has come down from Puritan times—there it is, at any rate, very strong still in
the Vale.

Well, from early morning till dewy eve, when she had it out of him in the cold tub before putting him to bed, Charity and Tom were pitted against one another. Physical power was as yet on the side of Charity, but she hadn't a chance with him wherever head-work was wanted. This war of independence began every morning before breakfast, when Charity escorted her charge to a neighbouring farm-house, which supplied the Browns, and where, by his mother's wish, Master Tom went to drink whey, before breakfast. Tom had no sort of objection to whey, but he had a decided liking for curds, which were forbidden as unwholesome, and there was seldom a morning that he did not manage to secure a handful of hard curds, in defiance of Charity and of the farmer's wife. The latter good soul was a gaunt, angular woman, who, with an old black bonnet on the top of her head, the strings dangling about her shoulders, and her gown tucked through her pocket-holes, went clattering about the dairy, cheese-room, and yard, in high pattens. Charity was some sort of niece of the old lady's, and was consequently free of the farm-house and garden, into which she could not resist going for the purposes of gossip and flirtation with the heir-apparent, who was a dawdling fellow, never out at work as he ought to have been. The moment Charity had found her cousin, or any other occupation, Tom would slip away; and in a minute shrill cries would be heard from the dairy, "Charity, Charity, thee lazy huzzy, where bist?" and Tom would break cover, hands and mouth full of curds, and take refuge on the shaky surface of the great muck reservoir in the middle of the yard, disturbing the repose of the great pigs. Here he was in safety, as no grown person could follow without getting over their knees; and the luckless Charity, while her aunt scolded her from the dairy door, for being "allus hankering about arter our Willum, instead of minding Master Tom," would descend from threats to coaxing, to lure Tom out of the muck, which was rising over his shoes and would soon tell a tale on his stockings, for which she would be sure to catch it from Missus's maid.

Tom had two abettors in the shape of a couple of old boys, Noah and Benjamin by name, who defended him from Charity, and expended much time upon his education. They were both of them retired servants of former generations of the Browns. Noah Crooke was a keen dry old man of almost ninety, but still able to totter about. He talked to Tom quite as if he were one of his own family, and indeed had long completely identified the Browns with himself. In some remote age he had been the attendant of a Miss Brown, and had conveyed her about the country on a pillion. He had a little round picture of the identical gray horse, caparisoned with the identical pillion, before which he used to do a sort of fetish worship, and abuse turnpike-roads and carriages. He wore an old full-bottomed wig, the gift of some dandy old Brown whom he had valeted in the middle of last century, which habiliment Master Tom looked upon with considerable respect, not to say fear; and indeed his whole feeling towards Noah was strongly tainted with awe; and when the old gentleman was gathered to his fathers, Tom's lamentation over him was not unaccompanied by a certain joy at having seen the last of the wig: "Poor old Noah, dead and gone," said he, "Tom Brown so sorry. Put him in the coffin, wig and all."

But old Benjy was young Master's real delight and refuge. He was a youth by the side of Noah, scarce seventy years old. A cheery, humorous, kind-hearted old man, full of sixty years of Vale gossip, and of all sorts of helpful ways for young and old, but above all for children. It was he who bent the first pin with which Tom extracted his first stickleback out of "Pebbly Brook," the little stream which ran through the village. The first stickleback was a splendid fellow, with fabulous red and blue gills. Tom kept him in a small basin till the day of his death, and became a fisherman from that day. Within a month from the taking of the first stickleback, Benjy had carried off our hero to the canal, in defiance of Charity, and between them, after a whole afternoon's popjoying, they had caught three or four small coarse fish and a perch, averaging perhaps two and a half ounces each, which Tom bore home in rapture to his mother as a precious gift, and which she received like a true mother with equal rapture, instructing the cook nevertheless, in a private interview, not to prepare the same for the Squire's dinner. Charity had appealed against old Benjy in the mean time, representing the dangers of the canal banks; but Mrs. Brown, seeing the boy's inaptitude for female guidance, had decided in Benjy's favour, and from thenceforth the old man was Tom's dry nurse. And as they sat by the canal watching their little green and white float, Benjy would instruct him in the doings of deceased Browns. How his grandfather, in the early days of the great war, when there was much distress and crime in the Vale, and the magistrates had been threatened by the mob, had ridden in with a big stick in his hand, and held the Petty Sessions by himself. How his great uncle, the Rector, had encountered and laid the last ghost, who had frightened the old women, male and female, of the parish out of their senses, and who turned out to be the blacksmith's apprentice disguised in drink and a white sheet. It was Benjy too who saddled Tom's first pony and instructed him in the mysteries of horsemanship, teaching him to throw his weight back and keep his hand low; and who stood chuckling outside the door of the girls' school, when Tom rode his little Shetland into the cottage and round the table, where the old dame and her pupils were seated at their work.

Benjy himself was come of a family distinguished in the Vale for their prowess in all athletic games. Some half-dozen of his brothers and kinsmen had gone to the wars, of whom only one had survived to come home, with a small pension, and three bullets in different parts of his body; he had shared Benjy's cottage till his death, and had left him his old dragoon's sword and pistol, which hung over the mantelpiece, flanked by a pair of heavy single sticks with which Benjy himself had won renown long ago as an old gamester, against the picked men of Wiltshire and Somersetshire, in many a good bout at the revels and pastimes of the country-side. For he had been a famous back-sword man in his young days and a good wrestler at elbow and collar.

Back-swording and wrestling were the most serious holiday pursuits of the Vale—those by which men attained fame—and each village had its champion. I suppose that on the whole people were less worked than they are now; at any rate, they seemed to have more time and energy for the old pastimes. The great times for back-swording came round once a year in each village, at the feast. The Vale "veasts" were not the common statute feasts, but much more ancient business. They are literally, so far as one can ascertain, feasts of the dedication, *i. e.* they were first established in the churchyard on the day on which the village church was opened for public worship, which was on the wake or festival of the patron Saint, and have been held on the same day in every year since that time.

There was no longer any remembrance of why the "veast" had been instituted, but nevertheless it had a pleasant and almost sacred character of its own. For it was then that all the children of the village, wherever they were scattered, tried to get home for a holiday to visit their fathers and mothers and friends, bringing with them their wages or some little gift from up the country for the old folk. Perhaps for a day or two before, but at any rate on "veast day" and the day after, in our village, you might see strapping healthy young men and women from all parts of the country going round from house to house in their best clothes, and finishing up with a call on Madam Brown, whom they would consult as to putting out their earnings to the best advantage, or how best to expend the same for the benefit of the old folk. Every household, however poor, managed to raise a "feast-cake" and a bottle of ginger or raisin wine, which stood on the cottage table ready for all comers, and not unlikely to make them remember feast-time, —for feast cake is very solid, and full of huge raisins. Moreover, feast-time was the day of reconciliation for the parish. If Job Higgins and Noah Freeman hadn't spoken for the last six months, their "old women" would be sure to get it patched up by that day. And though there was a good deal of drinking and low vice in the booths of an evening, it was pretty well confined to those who would have been doing the like, "veast or no veast," and on the whole, the effect was humanizing and Christian. In fact, the only reason why this is not the case still, is that gentle-folk and farmers have taken to other amusements, and have, as usual, forgotten the poor. They don't attend the feasts themselves, and call them disreputable, whereupon the steadiest of the poor leave them also, and they become what they are called. Class amusements, be they for dukes or plough-boys, always become nuisances and curses to a country. The true charm of cricket and hunting is, that they are still more or less sociable and universal; there's a place for every man who will come and take his part.

No one in the village enjoyed the approach of "veast day" more than Tom, in the year in which he was taken under old Benjy's tutelage. The feast was held in a large green field at the lower end of the village. The road to Farringdon ran along one side of it, and the brook by the side of the road; and above the brook was another large, gentle, sloping pasture-land, with a footpath running down it from the churchyard; and the old church, the originator of all the mirth, towered up with its gray walls and lancet windows, overlooking and sanctioning the whole, though its own share therein had been forgotten. At the point where the footpath crossed the brook and road, and entered on the field where the feast was held, was a long, low road-side inn, and on the opposite side of the field was a large white thatched farm-house, where dwelt an old sporting farmer, a great promoter of the revels.

Past the old church, and down the footpath, pottered the old man and the child hand in hand early on the afternoon of the day before the feast, and wandered all round the ground, which was already being occupied by the "cheap Jacks," with their green-covered carts and marvellous assortment of wares, and the booths of more legitimate small traders with their tempting arrays of fairings and eatables; and penny peep-shows and other shows, containing pink-eyed ladies, and dwarfs, and boa-constrictors, and wild Indians. But the object of most interest to Benjy, and of course to his pupil also, was the stage of rough planks some four feet high, which was being put up by the village carpenter for the back-swording and wrestling; and after surveying the whole tenderly, old Benjy led his charge away to the roadside inn, where he ordered a glass of ale and a long pipe for himself, and discussed these unwonted luxuries on the bench outside in the soft autumn evening with mine host, another old servant of the Browns, and speculated with him on the likelihood of a good show of old gamesters to contend for the morrow's prizes, and told tales of the gallant bouts of forty years back, to which Tom listened with all his ears and eyes.

But who shall tell the joy of the next morning, when the church bells were ringing a merry peal, and old Benjy appeared in the servants' hall, resplendent in a long blue coat and brass buttons, and a pair of old yellow buckskins and top-boots which he had cleaned for and inherited from Tom's grandfather, a stout thorn stick in his hand, and a nosegay of pinks and lavender in his button-hole, and led away Tom in his best clothes, and two new shillings in his breeches-pockets? Those two, at any rate, look like enjoying the day's revel.

They quicken their pace when they get into the church-yard, for already they see the field thronged with country folk, the men in clean white smocks or velveteen or fustian coats, with rough plush waistcoats of many colours, and the women in the beautiful long scarlet cloak—the usual out-door dress of west-country women in those days, and which often descended in families from mother to daughter—or in new-fashioned stuff shawls, which, if they would but believe it, don't become them half so well. The air resounds with the pipe and tabor, and the drums and trumpets of the showmen shouting at the doors of their caravans, over which tremendous pictures of the wonders to be seen within hang temptingly; while through all rises the shrill "root-too-too-too" of Mr. Punch, and the unceasing pan-pipe of his satellite.

"Lawk a' massey, Mr. Benjamin," cries a stout motherly woman in a red cloak, as they enter the field, "be that you? Well, I never! you do look purely. And how's the Squire, and Madam, and the family?"

Benjy graciously shakes hands with the speaker—who has left our village for some years, but has come over for Veast day on a visit to an old gossip—and gently indicates the heir-apparent of the Browns.

"Bless his little heart! I must gi'un a kiss. Here, Susannah, Susannah!" cries she, raising herself from the embrace, "come and see Mr. Benjamin and young Master Tom. You minds our Sukey, Mr. Benjamin, she be growed a rare slip of a wench since you seen her, though her'll be sixteen come Martinmas. I do aim to take her to see Madam to get her a place."

And Sukey comes bouncing away from a knot of old school-fellows, and drops a curtsey to Mr. Benjamin. And elders come up from all parts to salute Benjy, and girls who have been Madam's pupils to kiss Master Tom. And they carry him off to load him

with fairings; and he returns to Benjy, his hat and coat covered with ribands, and his pockets crammed with wonderful boxes which open upon ever new boxes, and popguns, and trumpets, and apples, and gilt gingerbread from the stall of Angel Heavens, sole vendor thereof, whose booth groans with kings and queens, and elephants and prancing steeds, all gleaming with gold. There was more gold on Angel's cakes, than there is ginger in those of this degenerate age. Skilled diggers might yet make a fortune in the churchyards of the Vale, by carefully washing the dust of the consumers of Angel's gingerbread. Alas! he is with his namesakes, and his receipts have, I fear, died with him.

And then they inspect the penny peep-show, at least Tom does, while old Benjy stands outside and gossips, and walks up the steps, and enters the mysterious doors of the pink-eyed lady and the Irish Giant, who do not by any means come up to their pictures; and the boa will not swallow his rabbit, but there the rabbit is waiting to be swallowed—and what can you expect for tuppence? We are easily pleased in the Vale. Now there is a rush of the crowd, and a tinkling bell is heard, and shouts of laughter; and Master Tom mounts on Benjy's shoulders and beholds a jingling match in all its glory. The games are begun, and this is the opening of them. It is a quaint game, immensely amusing to look at, and as I don't know whether it is used in your counties I had better describe it. A large roped ring is made, into which are introduced a dozen or so of big boys and young men who mean to play; these are carefully blinded and turned loose into the ring, and then a man is introduced not blindfolded, with a bell hung round his neck, and his two hands tied behind him. Of course every time he moves the bell must ring, as he has no hand to hold it, and so the dozen blindfolded men have to catch him. This they cannot always manage if he is a lively fellow, but half of them always rush into the arms of the other half, or drive their heads together, or tumble over; and then the crowd laughs vehemently, and invent nicknames for them on the spur of the moment, and they, if they be choleric, tear off the handkerchiefs which blind them, and not unfrequently pitch into one another, each thinking that the other must have run against him on purpose. It is great fun to look at a jingling match certainly, and Tom shouts and jumps on old Benjy's shoulders at the sight, until the old man feels weary, and shifts him to the strong young shoulders of the groom, who has just got down to the fun.

And now, while they are climbing the pole in another part of the field, and muzzling in a flour-tub in another, the old farmer whose house, as has been said, overlooks the field, and who is master of the revels, gets up the steps on to the stage, and announces to all whom it may concern that a half-sovereign in money will be forthcoming to the old gamester who breaks most heads; to which the Squire and he have added a new hat.

The amount of the prize is sufficient to stimulate the men of the immediate neighbourhood, but not enough to bring any very high talent from a distance; so, after a glance or two round, a tall fellow, who is a down shepherd, chucks his hat on to the stage and climbs up the steps, looking rather sheepish. The crowd of course first cheer, and then chaff as usual, as he picks up his hat and begins handling the sticks to see which will suit him.

"Wooy, Willum Smith, thee canst plaay wi' he arra daay," says his companion to the blacksmith's apprentice, a stout young fellow of nineteen or twenty. Willum's sweetheart is in the "veast" somewhere, and has strictly enjoined him not to get his head broke at back-swording, on pain of her highest displeasure; but as she is not to be seen (the women pretend not to like to see the back-sword play, and keep away from the stage), and as his hat is decidedly getting old, he chucks it on to the stage, and follows himself, hoping that he will only have to break other people's heads, or that after all Rachel won't really mind.

Then follows the greasy cap lined with fur of a half-gipsy, poaching, loafing fellow, who travels the Vale not for much good, I fancy:

"For twenty times was Peter feared
For once that Peter was respected,"

in fact. And then three or four other hats, including the glossy castor of Joe Willis, the self-elected and would-be champion of the neighbourhood, a well-to-do young butcher of twenty-eight or thereabouts, and a great strapping fellow, with his full allowance of bluster. This is a capital show of gamesters, considering the amount of the prize; so while they are picking their sticks and drawing their lots, I think I must tell you, as shortly as I can, how the noble old game of back-sword is played; for it is sadly gone out of late, even in the Vale, and maybe you have never seen it.

The weapon is a good stout ash stick with a large basket handle, heavier and somewhat shorter than a common single-stick. The players are called "old gamesters,"—why I can't tell you,—and their object is simply to break one another's heads: for the moment that blood runs an inch anywhere above the eyebrow, the old gamester to whom it belongs is beaten, and has to stop. A very slight blow with the sticks will fetch blood, so that it is by no means a punishing pastime, if the men don't play on purpose, and savagely, at the body and arms of their adversaries. The old gamester going into action only takes off his hat and coat, and arms himself with a stick: he then loops the fingers of his left hand in a handkerchief or strap which he fastens round his left leg, measuring the length, so that when he draws it tight with his left elbow in the air, that elbow shall just reach as high as his crown. Thus you see, so long as he chooses to keep his left elbow up, regardless of cuts, he has a perfect guard for the left side of his head. Then he advances his right hand above and in front of his head, holding his stick across so that its point projects an inch or two over his left elbow, and thus his whole head is completely guarded, and he faces his man armed in like manner, and they stand some three feet apart, often nearer, and feint, and strike, and return at one another's heads, until one cries "hold," or blood flows; in the first case they are allowed a minute's time, and go on again; in the latter another pair of gamesters are called on. If good men are playing, the quickness of the returns is marvellous; you hear the rattle like that a boy makes drawing his stick along palings, only heavier, and the closeness of the men in action to one another gives it a strange interest, and makes a spell at back-swording a very noble sight.

They are all suited now with sticks, and Joe Willis and the gipsy man have drawn the first lot. So the rest lean against the rails of the stage, and Joe and the dark man meet in the middle, the boards having been strewed with sawdust; Joe's white shirt and spotless drab breeches and boots contrasting with the gipsy's coarse blue shirt and dirty green velveteen breeches and leather gaiters. Joe is evidently turning up his nose at the other, and half insulted at having to break his head.

The gipsy is a tough, active fellow, but not very skilful with his weapon, so that Joe's weight and strength tell in a minute; he is too heavy metal for him: whack, whack, whack, come his blows, breaking down the gipsy's guard, and threatening to reach his head every moment. There it is at last—"Blood, blood!" shout the spectators, as a thin stream oozes out slowly from the roots of his hair, and the umpire calls to them to stop. The gipsy scowls at Joe under his brows in no pleasant manner, while Master Joe swaggers about, and makes attitudes, and thinks himself, and shows that he thinks himself, the greatest man in the field.

Then follow several stout sets-to between the other candidates for the new hat, and at last come the shepherd and Willum Smith. This is the crack set-to of the day. They are both in famous wind, and there is no crying "hold!" The shepherd is an old hand and up to all the dodges; he tries them one after another, and very nearly gets at Willum's head by coming in near, and playing over his guard at the half-stick, but somehow Willum blunders through, catching the stick on his shoulders, neck, sides, every now and then, anywhere but on his head, and his returns are heavy and straight, and he is the youngest gamester and a favourite in the parish, and his gallant stand brings down shouts and cheers, and the knowing ones think he'll win if he keeps steady, and Tom on the groom's shoulder holds his hands together, and can hardly breathe for excitement.

Alas for Willum! his sweetheart getting tired of female companionship has been hunting the booths to see where he can have got to, and now catches sight of him on the stage in full combat. She flushes and turns pale; her old aunt catches hold of her, saying, "Bless 'ee, child, doan't 'ee go a'nigst it;" but she breaks away and runs towards the stage calling his name. Willum keeps up his guard stoutly, but glances for a moment towards the voice. No guard will do it, Willum, without the eye. The shepherd steps round and strikes, and the point of his stick just grazes Willum's forehead, fetching off the skin, and the blood flows, and the umpire cries "Hold," and poor Willum's chance is up for the day. But he takes it very well, and puts on his old hat and coat, and goes down to be scolded by his sweetheart, and led away out of mischief. Tom hears him say coaxingly, as he walks off—

"Now doan't 'ee, Rachel! I wouldn't ha' done it, only I wanted summut to buy 'ee a fairing wi', and I be as vlush o' money as a twod o' veathers."

"Thee mind what I tells 'ee," rejoins Rachel saucily, "and doan't 'ee kep blethering about fairings." Tom resolves in his heart to give Willum the remainder of his two shillings after the back-swording.

Joe Willis has all the luck to-day. His next bout ends in an easy victory, while the

shepherd has a tough job to break his second head; and when Joe and the shepherd meet, and the whole circle expect and hope to see him get a broken crown, the shepherd slips in the first round and falls against the rails, hurting himself so that the old farmer will not let him go on, much as he wishes to try; and that impostor Joe (for he is certainly not the best man) struts and swaggers about the stage the conquering gamester, though he hasn't had five minutes really trying play.

Joe takes the new hat in his hand, and puts the money into it, and then, as if a thought strikes him and he doesn't think his victory quite acknowledged down below, walks to each face of the stage, and looks down, shaking the money, and chaffing, as how he'll stake hat and money and another half-sovereign "agin any gamester as hasn't played already." Cunning Joe! he thus gets rid of Willum and the shepherd, who is quite fresh again.

No one seems to like the offer, and the umpire is just coming down, when a queer old hat, something like a Doctor of Divinity's shovel, is chucked on to the stage, and an elderly quiet man steps out, who has been watching the play, saying he should like to cross a stick wi' the prodigalish young chap.

The crowd cheer, and begin to chaff Joe, who turns up his nose and swaggers across to the sticks. "Imp'dent old wosbird!" says he, "I'll break the bald head on un to the truth."

The old boy is very bald, certainly, and the blood will show fast enough if you can touch him, Joe.

He takes off his long-flapped coat, and stands up in a long-flapped waistcoat, which Sir Roger de Coverley might have worn when it was new, picks out a stick, and is ready for Master Joe, who loses no time, but begins his old game, whack, whack, whack, trying to break down the old man's guard by sheer strength. But it won't do,—he catches every blow close by the basket, and though he is rather stiff in his returns, after a minute walks Joe about the stage, and is clearly a staunch old gamester. Joe now comes in, and making the most of his height, tries to get over the old man's guard at half-stick, by which he takes a smart blow in the ribs and another on the elbow and nothing more. And now he loses wind and begins to puff, and the crowd laugh: "Cry 'hold,' Joe—thee'st met thy match!" Instead of taking good advice and getting his wind, Joe loses his temper, and strikes at the old man's body.

"Blood, blood!" shout the crowd; "Joe's head's broke!"

"Who'd have thought it? How did it come? That body-blow left Joe's head unguarded for a moment, and with one turn of the wrist the old gentleman has picked a neat little bit of skin off the middle of his forehead, and though he won't believe it, and hammers on for three more blows despite of the shouts, is then convinced by the blood trickling into his eye. Poor Joe is sadly crest-fallen, and fumbles in his pocket for the other half-sovereign, but the old gamester won't have it. "Keep thy money, man, and gi's thy hand," says he, and they shake hands; but the old gamester gives the new hat to the shepherd, and, soon after, the half-sovereign to Willum, who thereout decorates his sweetheart with ribbons to his heart's content.

"Who can a be?" "Wur do a cum from?" ask the crowd. And it soon flies about that the old west-country champion, who played a tie with Shaw the Life-guardsman at "Vizes" twenty years before, has broken Joe Willis's crown for him.

How my country fair is spinning out! I see I must skip the wrestling, and the boys jumping in sacks, and rolling wheelbarrows blindfolded; and the donkey-race, and the fight which arose thereout, marring the otherwise peaceful "veast"; and the frightened scurrying away of the female feast-goers, and descent of Squire Brown, summoned by the wife of one of the combatants to stop it; which he wouldn't start to do till he had got on his top-boots. Tom is carried away by old Benjy, dog-tired and surfeited with pleasure, as the evening comes on and the dancing begins in the booths; and though Willum, and Rachel in her new ribbons, and many another good lad and lass don't come away just yet, but have a good step out, and enjoy it, and get no harm thereby, yet we, being sober folk, will just stroll away up through the churchyard, and by the old yew-tree; and get a quiet dish of tea and a parley with our gossips, as the steady ones of our village do, and so to bed.

That's the fair, true sketch, as far as it goes, of one of the larger village feasts in the Vale of Berks, when I was a little boy. They are much altered for the worse, I am told. I haven't been at one these twenty years, but I have been at the statute fairs in some west-country towns, where servants are hired, and greater abominations cannot be found. What village feasts have come to, I fear, in many cases, may be read in the pages of *Yeast* (though I never saw one so bad—thank God!).

Do you want to know why? It is because, as I said before, gentlefolk and farmers have left off joining or taking an interest in them. They don't either subscribe to the prizes, or go down and enjoy the fun.

Is this a good or a bad sign? I hardly know. Bad, sure enough, if it only arises from the further separation of classes consequent on twenty years of buying cheap and selling dear, and its accompanying over-work; or because our sons and daughters have their hearts in London Club-life, or so-called Society, instead of in the old English home-duties; because farmers' sons are apeing fine gentlemen, and farmers' daughters caring more to make bad foreign music than good English cheeses. Good, perhaps, if it be that the time for the old "veast" has gone by, that it is no longer the healthy, sound expression of English country holiday-making; that, in fact, we as a nation have got beyond it, and are in a transition state, feeling for and soon likely to find some better substitute.

Only I have just got this to say before I quit the text. Don't let reformers of any sort think that they are going really to lay hold of the working boys and young men of England by any educational grapnel whatever, which hasn't some *bonâ fide* equivalent for the games of the old country "veast" in it; something to put in the place of the back-swording and wrestling and racing; something to try the muscles of men's bodies, and the endurance of their hearts, to make them rejoice in their strength. In all the new-fangled comprehensive plans which I see, this is all left out: and the consequence is, that your great Mechanics' Institutes end in intellectual priggism, and your Christian Young Men's Societies in religious Pharisaism.

Well, well, we must bide our time. Life isn't all beer and skittles,—but beer and skittles, or something better of the same sort, must form a good part of every Englishman's education. If I could only drive this into the heads of you rising Parliamentary Lords, and young swells who "have your ways made for you," as the saying is,—you, who frequent palaver houses and West-end Clubs, waiting always ready to strap yourselves on to the back of poor dear old John, as soon as the present used-up lot (your fathers and uncles), who sit there on the great Parliamentary-majorities' pack-saddle, and make believe they're guiding him with their red-tape bridle, tumble, or have to be lifted off!

I don't think much of you yet—I wish I could; though you do go talking and lecturing up and down the country to crowded audiences, and are busy with all sorts of philanthropic intellectualism, and circulating libraries and museums, and Heaven only knows what besides, and try to make us think, through newspaper reports, that you are, even as we, of the working classes. But bless your hearts, we "ain't so green," though lots of us of all sorts toady you enough certainly, and try to make you think so.

I'll tell you what to do now: instead of all this trumpeting and fuss, which is only the old Parliamentary-majority dodge over again—just you go, each of you (you've plenty of time for it, if you'll only give up t'other line), and quietly make three or four friends, real friends, among us. You'll find a little trouble in getting at the right sort, because such birds don't come lightly to your lure—but found they may be. Take, say, two out of the professions, lawyer, parson, doctor—which you will; one out of trade, and three or four out of the working classes, tailors, engineers, carpenters, engravers,—there's plenty of choice. Let them be men of your own ages, mind, and ask them to your homes; introduce them to your wives and sisters, and get introduced to theirs: give them good dinners, and talk to them about what is really at the bottom of your hearts, and box, and run, and row with them, when you have a chance. Do all this honestly as man to man, and by the time you come to ride old John, you'll be able to do something more than sit on his back, and may feel his mouth with some stronger bridle than a red-tape one.

Ah, if you only would! But you have got too far out of the right rut, I fear. Too much over-civilization, and the deceitfulness of riches. It is easier for a camel to go through the eye of a needle. More's the pity. I never came across but two of you who could value a man wholly and solely for what was in him; who thought themselves verily and indeed of the same flesh and blood as John Jones and the attorney's clerk, and Bill Smith the coster-monger, and could act as if they thought so.

CHAPTER III
SUNDRY WARS AND ALLIANCES

Poor old Benjy! The "rheumatiz" has much to answer for all through English country sides, but it never played a scurvier trick than in laying thee by the heels, when thou wast yet in a green old age. The enemy, which had long been carrying on a sort of border warfare, and trying his strength against Benjy's on the battle-field of his hands and legs, now, mustering all his forces, began laying siege to the citadel, and overrunning the whole country. Benjy was seized in the back and loins; and though he made strong and brave fight, it was soon clear enough that all which could be beaten of poor old Benjy would have to give in before long.

It was as much as he could do now, with the help of his big stick and frequent stops, to hobble down to the canal with Master Tom, and bait his hook for him, and sit and watch his angling, telling him quaint old country stories, and, when Tom had no sport, and detecting a rat some hundred yards or so off along the bank, would rush off with Toby the turnspit terrier, his other faithful companion, in bootless pursuit, he might have tumbled in and been drowned twenty times over before Benjy could have got near him.

Cheery and unmindful of himself as Benjy was, this loss of locomotive power bothered him greatly. He had got a new object in his old age, and was just beginning to think himself useful again in the world. He feared much too lest Master Tom should fall back again into the hands of Charity and the women. So he tried everything he could think of to get set up. He even went an expedition to the dwelling of one of those queer mortals, who—say what we will, and reason how we will—do cure simple people of diseases of one kind or another without the aid of physic; and so get to themselves the reputation of using charms, and inspire for themselves and their dwellings great respect, not to say fear, amongst a simple folk such as the dwellers in the Vale of White Horse. Where this power, or whatever else it may be, descends upon the shoulders of a man whose ways are not straight, he becomes a nuisance to the neighbourhood; a receiver of stolen goods, giver of love-potions, and deceiver of silly women; the avowed enemy of law and order, of justices of the peace, head-boroughs, and gamekeepers. Such a man in fact as was recently caught tripping, and deservedly dealt with by the Leeds justices, for seducing a girl who had come to him to get back a faithless lover, and had been convicted of bigamy since then. Sometimes, however, they are of quite a different stamp, men who pretend to nothing, and are with difficulty persuaded to exercise their occult arts in the simplest cases.

Of this latter sort was old Farmer Ives, as he was called, the "wise man" to whom Benjy resorted (taking Tom with him as usual), in the early spring of the year next after the feast described in the last chapter. Why he was called "farmer" I cannot say, unless it be that he was the owner of a cow, a pig or two, and some poultry, which he maintained on about an acre of land inclosed from the middle of a wild common, on which probably his father had squatted before lords of manors looked as keenly after their rights as they do now. Here he had lived no one knew how long, a solitary man. It was often rumoured that he was to be turned out and his cottage pulled down, but somehow

it never came to pass; and his pigs and cow went grazing on the common, and his geese hissed at the passing children and at the heels of the horse of my Lord's steward, who often rode by with a covetous eye on the inclosure still unmolested. His dwelling was some miles from our village; so Benjy, who was half ashamed of his errand, and wholly unable to walk there, had to exercise much ingenuity to get the means of transporting himself and Tom thither without exciting suspicion. However, one fine May morning he managed to borrow the old blind pony of our friend the publican, and Tom persuaded Madam Brown to give him a holiday to spend with old Benjy, and to lend them the Squire's light cart, stored with bread and cold meat and a bottle of ale. And so the two in high glee started behind old Dobbin, and jogged along the deep-rutted plashy roads, which had not been mended after their winter's wear, towards the dwelling of the wizard. About noon they passed the gate which opened on to the large common, and old Dobbin toiled slowly up the hill, while Benjy pointed out a little deep dingle on the left, out of which welled a tiny stream. As they crept up the hill the tops of a few birch-trees came in sight, and blue smoke curling up through their delicate light boughs; and then the little white thatched home and inclosed ground of Farmer Ives, lying cradled in the dingle, with the gay gorse common rising behind and on both sides; while in front, after traversing a gentle slope, the eye might travel for miles and miles over the rich vale. They now left the main road and struck into a green track over the common marked lightly with wheel and horse-shoe, which led down into the dingle and stopped at the rough gate of Farmer Ives. Here they found the farmer, an iron-gray old man, with a bushy eyebrow and strong aquiline nose, busied in one of his vocations. He was a horse and cow doctor, and was tending a sick beast which had been sent up to be cured. Benjy hailed him as an old friend, and he returned the greeting cordially enough, looking however hard for a moment both at Benjy and Tom, to see whether there was more in their visit than appeared at first sight. It was a work of some difficulty and danger for Benjy to reach the ground, which however he managed to do without mishap; and then he devoted himself to unharnessing Dobbin and turning him out for a graze ("a run" one could not say of that virtuous steed) on the common. This done, he extricated the cold provisions from the cart, and they entered the farmer's wicket; and he, shutting up the knife with which he was taking maggots out of the cow's back and sides, accompanied them towards the cottage. A big old lurcher got up slowly from the door-stone, stretching first one hind leg and then the other, and taking Tom's caresses and the presence of Toby, who kept however at a respectful distance, with equal indifference.

"Us be cum to pay 'ee a visit. I've a been long minded to do't for old sake's sake, only I vinds I dwon't get about now as I'd used to't. I be so plaguy bad wi' th' rumatiz in my back." Benjy paused, in hopes of drawing the farmer at once on the subject of his ailments without further direct application.

"Ah, I see as you bean't quite so lissom as you was," replied the farmer with a grim smile, as he lifted the latch of his door; "we bean't so young as we was, nother on us, wuss luck."

The farmer's cottage was very like those of the better class of peasantry in general. A snug chimney corner with two seats, and a small carpet on the hearth, an old flint gun and a pair of spurs over the fire-place, a dresser with shelves on which some bright pewter plates and crockeryware were arranged, an old walnut table, a few chairs and settles, some framed samplers, and an old print or two, and a bookcase with some dozen volumes on the walls, a rack with flitches of bacon, and other stores fastened to the ceiling, and you have the best part of the furniture. No sign of occult art is to be seen, unless the bundles of dried herbs hanging to the rack and in the ingle and the row of labelled phials on one of the shelves betoken it.

Tom played about with some kittens who occupied the hearth, and with a goat who walked demurely in at the open door, while their host and Benjy spread the table for dinner—and was soon engaged in conflict with the cold meat, to which he did much honour. The two old men's talk was of old comrades and their deeds, mute inglorious Miltons of the Vale, and of the doings thirty years back—which didn't interest him much, except when they spoke of the making of the canal, and then indeed he began to listen with all his ears; and learned to his no small wonder that his dear and wonderful canal had not been there always—was not in fact so old as Benjy or Farmer Ives, which caused a strange commotion in his small brain.

After dinner Benjy called attention to a wart which Tom had on the knuckles of his hand, and which the family doctor had been trying his skill on without success, and begged the farmer to charm it away. Farmer Ives looked at it, muttered something or another over it, and cut some notches in a short stick, which he handed to Benjy, giving him instructions for cutting it down on certain days, and cautioning Tom not to meddle with the wart for a fortnight. And then they strolled out and sat on a bench in the sun with their pipes, and the pigs came up and grunted sociably and let Tom scratch them; and the farmer, seeing how he liked animals, stood up and held his arms in the air and gave a call, which brought a flock of pigeons wheeling and dashing through the birch-trees. They settled down in clusters on the farmer's arms and shoulders, making love to him and scrambling over one another's backs to get to his face; and then he threw them all off, and they fluttered about close by, and lighted on him again and again when he held up his arms. All the creatures about the place were clean and fearless, quite unlike their relations elsewhere; and Tom begged to be taught how to make all the pigs and cows and poultry in our village tame, at which the farmer only gave one of his grim chuckles.

It wasn't till they were just ready to go, and old Dobbin was harnessed, that Benjy broached the subject of his rheumatism again, detailing his symptoms one by one. Poor old boy! He hoped the farmer could charm it away as easily as he could Tom's wart, and was ready with equal faith to put another notched stick into his other pocket, for the cure of his own ailments. The physician shook his head, but nevertheless produced a bottle and handed it to Benjy with instructions for use. "Not as 't'll do 'ee much good—leastways I be afeared not," shading his eyes with his hand and looking up at them in the cart: "there's only one thing as I knows on as'll cure old folks like you and I o' th' rhumatis."

"Wot be that then, farmer?" inquired Benjy.

"Churchyard mould," said the old iron-gray man with another chuckle. And so they said their good-byes and went their ways home. Tom's wart was gone in a fortnight, but not so Benjy's rheumatism, which laid him by the heels more and more. And though Tom still spent many an hour with him, as he sat on a bench in the sunshine, or by the chimney corner when it was cold, he soon had to seek elsewhere for his regular companions.

Tom had been accustomed often to accompany his mother in her visits to the cottages, and had thereby made acquaintance with many of the village boys of his own age. There was Job Rudkin, son of widow Rudkin, the most bustling woman in the parish. How she could ever have had such a stolid boy as Job for a child must always remain a mystery. The first time Tom went to their cottage with his mother, Job was not indoors, but he entered soon after, and stood with both hands in his pockets staring at Tom. Widow Rudkin, who would have had to cross Madam to get at young Hopeful—a breach of good manners of which she was wholly incapable—began a series of pantomime signs, which only puzzled him, and at last, unable to contain herself longer, burst out with, "Job! Job! where's thy cap?"

"What! beant 'ee on ma' head, mother?" replied Job, slowly extricating one hand from a pocket and feeling for the article in question; which he found on his head sure enough, and left there, to his mother's horror and Tom's great delight.

Then there was poor Jacob Dodson the half-witted boy, who ambled about cheerfully, undertaking messages and little helpful odds and ends for every one, which, however, poor Jacob managed always hopelessly to embrangle. Everything came to pieces in his hands, and nothing would stop in his head. They nicknamed him Jacob Doodle-calf.

But above all there was Harry Winburn, the quickest and best boy in the parish. He might be a year older than Tom, but was very little bigger, and he was the Crichton of our village boys. He could wrestle and climb and run better than all the rest, and learned all that the schoolmaster could teach him faster than that worthy at all liked. He was a boy to be proud of, with his curly brown hair, keen gray eye, straight active figure, and little ears and hands and feet, "as fine as a lord's," as Charity remarked to Tom one day, talking as usual great nonsense. Lords' hands and ears and feet are just as ugly as other folks' when they are children, as any one may convince himself if he likes to look. Tight boots and gloves, and doing nothing with them, I allow make a difference by the time they are twenty.

Now that Benjy was laid on the shelf, and his young brothers were still under petticoat government, Tom, in search of companions, began to cultivate the village boys generally more and more. Squire Brown, be it said, was a true blue Tory to the backbone, and believed honestly that the powers which be were ordained of God, and that loyalty and steadfast obedience were men's first duties. Whether it were in consequence or in spite of his political creed I do not mean to give an opinion, though I have one; but certain it is, that he held therewith divers social principles not generally supposed to be true blue in colour. Foremost of these, and the one which the Squire loved to propound above all others, was the belief that a man is to be valued wholly and solely for that which he is in himself, for that which stands up in the four fleshly walls of him, apart from clothes, rank, fortune, and all externals whatsoever. Which belief I take to be a wholesome corrective of all political opinions, and, if held sincerely, to make all opinions equally harmless, whether they be blue, red, or green. As a necessary corollary to this belief, Squire Brown held further that it didn't matter a straw whether his son associated with lords' sons or ploughmen's sons, provided they were brave and honest. He himself had played football and gone birds'-nesting with the farmers whom he met at vestry and the labourers who tilled their fields, and so had his father and grandfather with their progenitors. So he encouraged Tom in his intimacy with the boys of the village, and forwarded it by all means in his power, and gave them the run of a close for a playground, and provided bats and balls and a football for their sports.

Our village was blessed amongst other things with a well-endowed school. The building stood by itself, apart from the master's house, on an angle of ground where three roads met; an old gray stone building with a steep roof and mullioned windows. On one of the opposite angles stood Squire Brown's stables and kennel, with their backs to the road, over which towered a great elm-tree; on the third stood the village carpenter and wheelwright's large open shop, and his house and the schoolmaster's, with long low eaves, under which the swallows built by scores.

The moment Tom's lessons were over, he would now get him down to this corner by the stables, and watch till the boys came out of school. He prevailed on the groom to cut notches for him in the bark of the elm, so that he could climb into the lower branches, and there he would sit watching the school door, and speculating on the possibility of turning the elm into a dwelling-place for himself and friends after the manner of the Swiss Family Robinson. But the school hours were long and Tom's patience short, so that soon he began to descend into the street, and go and peep in at the school door and the wheelwright's shop, and look out for something to while away the time. Now the wheelwright was a choleric man, and, one fine afternoon, returning from a short absence, found Tom occupied with one of his pet adzes, the edge of which was fast vanishing under our hero's care. A speedy flight saved Tom from all but one sound cuff on the ears, but he resented this unjustifiable interruption of his first essays at carpentering, and still more the further proceedings of the wheelwright, who cut a switch and hung it over the door of his workshop, threatening to use it upon Tom if he came within twenty yards of his gate. So Tom, to retaliate, commenced a war upon the swallows who dwelt under the wheelwright's eaves, whom he harassed with sticks and stones; and being fleeter of foot than his enemy, escaped all punishment, and kept him

in perpetual anger. Moreover his presence about the school door began to incense the master, as the boys in that neighbourhood neglected their lessons in consequence; and more than once he issued into the porch, rod in hand, just as Tom beat a hasty retreat. And he and the wheelwright, laying their heads together, resolved to acquaint the Squire with Tom's afternoon occupations; but in order to do it with effect, determined to take him captive and lead him away to judgment fresh from his evil doings. This they would have found some difficulty in doing, had Tom continued the war single-handed, or rather single-footed, for he would have taken to the deepest part of Pebbly Brook to escape them; but, like other active powers, he was ruined by his alliances. Poor Jacob Doodle-calf could not go to the school with the other boys, and one fine afternoon, about three o'clock (the school broke up at four), Tom found him ambling about the street, and pressed him into a visit to the school-porch. Jacob, always ready to do what he was asked, consented, and the two stole down to the school together. Tom first reconnoitred the wheelwright's shop, and seeing no signs of activity, thought all safe in that quarter and ordered at once an advance of all his troops upon the school-porch. The door of the school was ajar, and the boys seated on the nearest bench at once recognized and' opened a correspondence with the invaders. Tom waxing bold, kept putting his head into the school and making faces at the master when his back was turned. Poor Jacob, not in the least comprehending the situation, and in high glee at finding himself so near the school, which he had never been allowed to enter, suddenly, in a fit of enthusiasm, pushed by Tom, and ambling three steps into the school, stood there, looking round him and nodding with a self-approving smile. The master, who was stooping over a boy's slate, with his back to the door, became aware of something unusual, and turned quickly round. Tom rushed at Jacob, and began dragging him back by his smock-frock, and the master made at them, scattering forms and boys in his career. Even now they might have escaped, but that in the porch, barring retreat,

appeared the crafty wheelwright, who had been watching all their proceedings. So they were seized, the school dismissed, and Tom and Jacob led away to Squire Brown as lawful prize, the boys following to the gate in groups, and speculating on the result.

The Squire was very angry at first, but the interview, by Tom's pleading, ended in a compromise. Tom was not to go near the school till three o'clock, and only then if he had done his own lessons well, in which case he was to be the bearer of a note to the master from Squire Brown, and the master agreed in such case to release ten or twelve of the best boys an hour before the time of breaking up, to go off and play in the close. The wheelwright's adzes and swallows were to be for ever respected; and that hero and the master withdrew to the servants' hall to drink the Squire's health, well satisfied with their day's work.

The second act of Tom's life may now be said to have begun. The war of independence had been over for some time: none of the women now, not even his mother's maid, dared offer to help him in dressing or washing. Between ourselves, he had often at first to run to Benjy in an unfinished state of toilet; Charity and the rest of them seemed to take a delight in putting impossible buttons and ties in the middle of his back; but he would have gone without nether integuments altogether, sooner than have had recourse to female valeting. He had a room to himself, and his father gave him sixpence a week pocket-money. All this he had achieved by Benjy's advice and assistance. But now he had conquered another step in life, the step which all real boys so long to make; he had got amongst his equals in age and strength, and could measure himself with other boys; he lived with those whose pursuits and wishes and ways were the same in kind as his own.

The little governess who had lately been installed in the house found her work grow wondrously easy, for Tom slaved at his lessons in order to make sure of his note to the schoolmaster. So there were very few days in the week in which Tom and the village boys were not playing in their close by three o'clock. Prisoner's base, rounders, high-cock-a-lorum, cricket, football, he was soon initiated into the delights of them all; and though most of the boys were older than himself, he managed to hold his own very well. He was naturally active and strong, and quick of eye and hand, and had the advantage of light shoes and well-fitting dress, so that in a short time he could run and jump and climb with any of them.

They generally finished their regular games half an hour or so before tea-time, and then began trials of skill and strength in many ways. Some of them would catch the Shetland pony who was turned out in the field, and get two or three together on his back, and the little rogue, enjoying the fun, would gallop off for fifty yards and then turn round, or stop short and shoot them on to the turf, and then graze quietly on till he felt another load; others played at peg-top or marbles, while a few of the bigger ones stood up for a bout at wrestling. Tom at first only looked on at this pastime, but it had peculiar attractions for him, and he could not long keep out of it. Elbow and collar wrestling as practised in the western counties was, next to back-swording, the way to fame for the youth of the Vale; and all the boys knew the rules of it, and were more or less expert. But Job Rudkin and Harry Winburn were the stars, the former stiff and sturdy, with legs like small towers, the latter pliant as india-rubber and quick as lightning. Day after day they stood foot to foot, and offered first one hand and then the other, and grappled and closed and swayed and strained, till a well-aimed crook of the heel or thrust of the loin took effect, and a fair back-fall ended the matter. And Tom watched with all his eyes, and first challenged one of the less scientific, and threw him; and so one by one wrestled his way up to the leaders.

Then indeed for months he had a poor time of it; it was not long indeed before he could manage to keep his legs against Job, for that hero was slow of offence, and gained his victories chiefly by allowing others to throw themselves against his immovable legs and loins. But Harry Winburn was undeniably his master; from the first clutch of hands when they stood up, down to the last trip which sent him on to his back on the turf, he felt that Harry knew more and could do more than he. Luckily Harry's bright unconsciousness, and Tom's natural good temper, kept them from ever quarrelling; and so Tom worked on and on, and trod more and more nearly on Harry's heels, and at last mastered all the dodges and falls except one. This one was Harry's own particular invention and pet; he scarcely ever used it except when hard pressed, but then out it came, and as sure as it did, over went poor Tom. He thought about that fall at his meals, in his walks, when he lay awake in bed, in his dreams—but all to no purpose; until Harry one day in his open way suggested to him how he thought it should be met, and in a week from that time the boys were equal, save only the slight difference of strength in Harry's favour, which some extra ten months of age gave. Tom had often afterwards reason to be thankful for that early drilling, and above all for having mastered Harry Winburn's fall.

Besides their home games, on Saturdays the boys would wander all over the neighbourhood; sometimes to the downs, or up to the camp, where they cut their initials out in the springy turf, and watched the hawks soaring, and the "peert" bird, as Harry Winburn called the gray plover, gorgeous in his wedding feathers; and so home, racing down the Manger with many a roll among the thistles, or through Uffington-wood to watch the fox cubs playing in the green rides; sometimes to Rosy Brook, to cut long whispering reeds which grew there, to make pan-pipes of; sometimes to Moor Mills, where was a piece of old forest land, with short browsed turf and tufted brambly thickets stretching under the oaks, amongst which rumour declared that a raven, last of his race, still lingered; or to the sand-hills, in vain quest of rabbits; and birds'-nesting in the season, anywhere and everywhere.

The few neighbours of the Squire's own rank every now and then would shrug their shoulders as they drove or rode by a party of boys with Tom in the middle, carrying along bulrushes or whispering reeds, or great bundles of cowslip and meadow-sweet, or young starlings or magpies, or other spoil of wood, brook, or meadow; and Lawyer Red-tape might mutter to Squire Straightback at the Board that no good would come of the young Browns, if they were let run wild with all the dirty village boys, whom the best farmers' sons even would not play with. And the Squire might reply with a shake of his head that *his* sons only mixed with their equals, and never went into the village without the governess or a footman. But, luckily, Squire Brown was full as stiff-backed as his neighbours, and so went on his own way; and Tom and his younger brothers, as they grew up, went on playing with the village boys, without the idea of equality or inequality (except in wrestling, running, and climbing,) ever entering their heads, as it doesn't till it's put there by Jack Nastys or fine ladies' maids.

I don't mean to say it would be the case in all villages, but it certainly was so in this one; the village boys were full as manly and honest, and certainly purer, than those in a higher rank; and Tom got more harm from his equals in his first fortnight at a private school, where he went when he was nine years old, than he had from his village friends from the day he left Charity's apron-strings.

Great was the grief amongst the village school-boys when Tom drove off with the Squire, one August morning, to meet the coach on his way to school. Each of them had given him some little present of the best that he had, and his small private box was full of peg-tops, white marbles (called "alley-taws" in the Vale), screws, birds'-eggs, whip-cord, jews-harps, and other miscellaneous boys' wealth. Poor Jacob Doodle-calf, in floods of tears, had pressed upon him with spluttering earnestness his lame pet hedge-hog (he had always some poor broken-down beast or bird by him); but this Tom had been obliged to refuse by the Squire's order. He had given them all a great tea under the big elm in their playground, for which Madam Brown had supplied the biggest cake ever seen in our village; and Tom was really as sorry to leave them as they to lose him, but his sorrow was not unmixed with the pride and excitement of making a new step in life.

And this feeling carried him through his first parting with his mother better than could have been expected. Their love was as fair and whole as human love can be, perfect self-sacrifice on the one side meeting a young and true heart on the other. It is not within the scope of my book, however, to speak of family relations, or I should have much to say on the subject of English mothers,—ay, and of English fathers, and sisters, and brothers too.

Neither have I room to speak of our private schools: what I have to say is about public schools, those much abused and much belauded institutions peculiar to England. So we must hurry through Master Tom's year at a private school as fast as we can.

It was a fair average specimen, kept by a gentleman, with another gentleman as second master; but it was little enough of the real work they did—merely coming into school when lessons were prepared and all ready to be heard. The whole discipline of the school out of lesson hours was in the hands of the two ushers, one of whom was always with the boys in their playground, in the school, at meals—in fact at all times and everywhere, till they were fairly in bed at night.

Now the theory of private schools is (or was) constant supervision out of school; therein differing fundamentally from that of public schools.

It may be right or wrong: but if right, this supervision surely ought to be the especial work of the head-master, the responsible person. The object of all schools is not to ram Latin and Greek into boys, but to make them good English boys, good future citizens; and by far the most important part of that work must be done, or not done, out of school hours. To leave it, therefore, in the hands of inferior men, is just giving up the highest and hardest part of the work of education. Were I a private school-master, I should say, let who will hear the boys their lessons, but let me live with them when they are at play and rest.

The two ushers at Tom's first school were not gentlemen, and very poorly educated, and were only driving their poor trade of usher to get such living as they could out of it. They were not bad men, but had little heart for their work, and of course were bent on making it as easy as possible. One of the methods by which they endeavoured to accomplish this was by encouraging tale-bearing, which had become a frightfully common vice in the school in consequence, and had sapped all the foundations of school morality. Another was, by favouring grossly the biggest boys, who alone could have given them much trouble; whereby those young gentlemen became most abominable tyrants, oppressing the little boys in all the small mean ways which prevail in private schools.

Poor little Tom was made dreadfully unhappy in his first week, by a catastrophe which happened to his first letter home. With huge labour he had, on the very evening of his arrival, managed to fill two sides of a sheet of letter-paper with assurances of his love for dear mamma, his happiness at school, and his resolves to do all she would wish.

This missive, with the help of the boy who sat at the desk next him, also a new arrival, he managed to fold successfully; but this done, they were sadly put to it for means of sealing. Envelopes were then unknown, they had no wax and dared not disturb the stillness of the evening school-room by getting up and going to ask the usher for some. At length Tom's friend, being of an ingenious turn of mind, suggested sealing with ink, and the letter was accordingly stuck down with a blob of ink, and duly handed by Tom, on his way to bed, to the housekeeper to be posted. It was not till four days afterwards that the good dame sent for him, and produced the precious letter and some wax, saying, "Oh, Master Brown, I forgot to tell you before, but your letter isn't sealed." Poor Tom took the wax in silence and sealed his letter, with a huge lump rising in his throat during the process, and then ran away to a quiet corner of the playground, and burst into an agony of tears. The idea of his mother waiting day after day for the letter he had promised her at once, and perhaps thinking him forgetful of her, when he had done all in his power to make good his promise, was as bitter a grief as any which he had to undergo for many a long year. His wrath then was proportionately violent when he was aware of two boys, who stopped close by him, and one of whom, a fat gaby of a fellow, pointed at him and called him "Young mammy-sick!" Whereupon Tom arose, and giving vent thus to his grief and shame and rage, smote his derider on the nose, and made it bleed—which sent that young worthy howling to the usher, who reported Tom for violent and unprovoked assault and battery. Hitting in the face was a felony punishable with flogging, other hitting only a misdemeanour—a distinction not altogether clear in principle. Tom however escaped the penalty by pleading "primum tempus"; and having written a second letter to his mother, inclosing some forget-me-nots, which he picked on their first half-holiday walk, felt quite happy again, and began to enjoy vastly a good deal of his new life.

These half-holiday walks were the great events of the week. The whole fifty boys started after dinner with one of the ushers for Hazeldown, which was distant some mile or so from the school. Hazeldown measured some three miles round, and in the neighbourhood were several woods full of all manner of birds and butterflies. The usher walked slowly round the down with such boys as liked to accompany him; the rest scattered in all directions, being only bound to appear again when the usher had completed his round, and accompany him home. They were forbidden, however, to go anywhere except on the down and into the woods, the village had been especially prohibited, where huge bulls'-eyes and unctuous toffy might be procured in exchange for coin of the realm.

Various were the amusements to which the boys then betook themselves. At the entrance of the down, there was a steep hillock, like the barrows of Tom's own downs. This mound was the weekly scene of terrific combats, at a game called by the queer name of "mud-patties." The boys who played divided into sides under different leaders, and one side occupied the mound. Then, all parties having provided themselves with many sods of turf, cut with their bread-and-cheese knives, the side which remained at the bottom proceeded to assault the mound, advancing up on all sides under cover of a heavy fire of turfs, and then struggling for victory with the occupants, which was theirs as soon as they could, even for a moment, clear the summit, when they in turn became the besieged. It was a good, rough, dirty game, and of great use in counteracting the sneaking tendencies of the school. Then others of the boys spread over the downs, looking for the holes of humble-bees and mice, which they dug up without mercy, often (I regret to say) killing and skinning the unlucky mice, and (I do not regret to say) getting well stung by the humble-bees. Others went after butterflies and birds'-eggs in their seasons; and Tom found on Hazeldown, for the first time, the beautiful little blue butterfly with golden spots on his wings, which he had never seen on his own downs, and dug out his first sand-martin's nest. This latter achievement resulted in a flogging, for the sand-martins built in a high bank close to the village, consequently out of bounds; but one of the bolder spirits of the school, who never could be happy unless he was doing something to which risk was attached, easily persuaded Tom to break bounds and visit the martin's bank. From whence it being only a step to the toffy shop, what could be more simple than to go on there and fill their pockets; or what more certain than that on their return, a distribution of treasure having been made, the usher should shortly detect the forbidden smell of bulls'-eyes, and, a search ensuing, discover the state of the breeches-pockets of Tom and his ally?

This ally of Tom's was indeed a desperate hero in the sight of the boys, and feared as one who dealt in magic, or something approaching thereto. Which reputation came to him in this wise. The boys went to bed at eight, and of course consequently lay awake in the dark for an hour or two, telling ghost-stories by turns. One night when it came to his turn, and he had dried up their souls by his story, he suddenly declared that he would make a fiery hand appear on the door; and to the astonishment and terror of the boys in his room, a hand, or something like it, in pale light, did then and there appear. The fame of this exploit having spread to the other rooms, and being discredited there, the young necromancer declared that the same wonder would appear in all the rooms in turn, which it accordingly did; and the whole circumstances having been privately reported to one of the ushers as usual, that functionary, after listening about at the doors of the rooms, by a sudden descent caught the performer in his night-shirt, with a box of phosphorus in his guilty hand. Lucifer-matches and all the present facilities for getting acquainted with fire were then unknown; the very name of phosphorus had something diabolic in it to the boy-mind; so Tom's ally, at the cost of a sound flogging, earned what many older folk covet much—the very decided fear of most of his companions.

He was a remarkable boy, and by no means a bad one. Tom stuck to him till he left, and got into many scrapes by so doing. But he was the great opponent of the tale-bearing habits of the school, and the open enemy of the ushers; and so worthy of all support.

Tom imbibed a fair amount of Latin and Greek at the school, but somehow on the whole it didn't suit him, or he it, and in the holidays he was constantly working the Squire to send him at once to a public school. Great was his joy then, when in the middle of his third half-year, in October, 183–, a fever broke out in the village, and the master having himself slightly sickened of it, the whole of the boys were sent off at a day's notice to their respective homes.

The Squire was not quite so pleased as Master Tom to see that young gentleman's brown, merry face appear at home, some two months before the proper time, for the Christmas holidays; and so, after putting on his thinking cap, he retired to his study and wrote several letters, the result of which was, that one morning at the breakfast-table, about a fortnight after Tom's return, he addressed his wife with—"My dear, I have arranged that Tom shall go to Rugby at once, for the last six weeks of this half year, instead of wasting them, in riding and loitering about home. It is very kind of the Doctor to allow it. Will you see that his things are all ready by Friday, when I shall take him up to town, and send him down the next day by himself.

Mrs. Brown was prepared for the announcement, and merely suggested a doubt whether Tom were yet old enough to travel by himself. However, finding both father and son against her on this point, she gave in, like a wise woman, and proceeded to prepare Tom's kit for his launch into a public school.

CHAPTER IV
THE STAGE COACH

"Let the steam-pot hiss till it's hot,
Give me the speed of the Tantivy trot."
Coaching Song, BY R. E. E. WARBURTON, ESQ.

Now, sir, time to get up, if you please. Tally-ho coach for Leicester'll be round in half-an-hour, and don't wait for nobody." So spake the Boots of the Peacock Inn, Islington, at half-past two o'clock on the morning of a day in the early part of November

183–, giving Tom at the same time a shake by the shoulder, and then putting down a candle and carrying off his shoes to clean.

Tom and his father arrived in town from Berkshire the day before, and finding, on inquiry, that the Birmingham coaches which ran from the city did not pass through Rugby, but deposited their passengers at Dunchurch, a village three miles distant on the main road, where said passengers had to wait for the Oxford and Leicester coach in the evening, or to take a post-chaise—had resolved that Tom should travel down by the Tally-ho, which diverged from the main road and passed through Rugby itself. And as the Tally-ho was an early coach, they had driven out to the Peacock to be on the road.

Tom had never been in London, and would have liked to have stopped at the Belle Savage, where they had been put down by the Star, just at dusk, that he might have gone roving about those endless, mysterious, gas-lit streets, which, with their glare and hum and moving crowds, excited him so that he couldn't talk even. But as soon as he found that the Peacock arrangement would get him to Rugby by twelve o'clock in the day, whereas otherwise he wouldn't be there till the evening, all other plans melted away; his one absorbing aim being to become a public school-boy as fast as possible, and six hours sooner or later seeming to him of the most alarming importance.

Tom and his father had alighted at the Peacock at about seven in the evening; and having heard with unfeigned joy the paternal order, at the bar, of steaks and oyster sauce for supper in half an hour, and seen his father seated cosily by the bright fire in the coffee-room with the paper in his hand—Tom had run out to see about him, had wondered at all the vehicles passing and repassing, and had fraternized with the Boots and ostler, from whom he ascertained that the Tally-ho was a tip-top goer, ten miles an hour including stoppages, and so punctual that all the road set their clocks by her.

Then being summoned to supper, he had regaled himself in one of the bright little boxes of the Peacock coffee-room, on the beef-steak and unlimited oyster-sauce and brown stout (tasted then for the first time—a day to be marked for ever by Tom with a white stone); had at first attended to the excellent advice which his father was bestowing on him from over his glass of steaming brandy-and-water, and then begun nodding, from the united effects of the stout, the fire, and the lecture; till the Squire, observing Tom's state, and remembering that it was nearly nine o'clock, and that the Tally-ho left at three, sent the little fellow off to the chambermaid, with a shake of the hand (Tom having stipulated in the morning before starting, that kissing should now cease between them), and a few parting words.

"And now, Tom, my boy," said the Squire, "remember you are going, at your own earnest request, to be chucked into this great school, like a young bear, with all your troubles before you—earlier than we should have sent you perhaps. If schools are what they were in my time, you'll see a great many cruel blackguard things done, and hear a deal of foul bad talk. But never fear. You tell the truth, keep a brave and kind heart, and never listen to or say anything you wouldn't have your mother and sister hear, and you'll never feel ashamed to come home, or we to see you."

The allusion to his mother made Tom feel rather chokey, and he would have liked to have hugged his father well, if it hadn't been for the recent stipulation.

As it was, he only squeezed his father's hand, and looked bravely up and said, "I'll try, father."

"I know you will, my boy. Is your money all safe?"

"Yes," said Tom, diving into one pocket to make sure.

"And your keys?" said the Squire.

"All right," said Tom, diving into the other pocket.

"Well then, good night. God bless you! I'll tell Boots to call you, and be up to see you off."

Tom was carried off by the chambermaid in a brown study, from which he was roused in a clean little attic, by that buxom person calling him a little darling and kissing him as she left the room; which indignity he was too much surprised to resent. And still thinking of his father's last words, and the look with which they were spoken, he knelt down and prayed, that, come what might, he might never bring shame or sorrow on the dear folk at home.

Indeed, the Squire's last words deserved to have their effect, for they had been the result of much anxious thought. All the way up to London he had pondered what he should say to Tom by way of parting advice; something that the boy could keep in his head ready for use. By way of assisting meditation, he had even gone the length of taking out his flint and steel and tinder, and hammering away for a quarter of an hour till he had manufactured a light for a long Trichinopoli cheroot, which he silently puffed; to the no small wonder of Coachee, who was an old friend, and an institution on the Bath road, and who always expected a talk on the prospects and doings, agricultural and social, of the whole county when he carried the Squire.

To condense the Squire's meditation, it was somewhat as follows: "I won't tell him to read his Bible, and love and serve God; if he don't do that for his mother's sake and teaching, he won't for mine. Shall I go into the sort of temptations he'll meet with? No, I can't do that. Never do for an old fellow to go into such things with a boy. He won't understand me. Do him more harm than good, ten to one. Shall I tell him to mind his work, and say he's sent to school to make himself a good scholar? Well, but he isn't sent to school for that—at any rate, not for that mainly. I don't care a straw for Greek particles, or the digamma; no more does his mother. What is he sent to school for? Well, partly because he wanted so to go. If he'll only turn out a brave, helpful, truth-telling Englishman, and a gentleman, and a Christian, that's all I want," thought the Squire; and upon this view of the case he framed his last words of advice to Tom, which were well enough suited to his purpose.

For they were Tom's first thoughts as he tumbled out of bed at the summons of

Boots, and proceeded rapidly to wash and dress himself. At ten minutes to three he was down in the coffee-room in his stockings, carrying his hat-box, coat, and comforter in his hand; and there he found his father nursing a bright fire, and a cup of hot coffee and a hard biscuit on the table.

"Now then, Tom, give us your things here, and drink this; there's nothing like starting warm, old fellow."

Tom addressed himself to the coffee, and prattled away while he worked himself into his shoes and his great coat, well warmed through; a Petersham coat with velvet collar, made tight after the abominable fashion of those days. And just as he is swallowing his last mouthful, winding his comforter round his throat, and tucking the ends into the breast of his coat, the horn sounds, Boots looks in and says, "Tally-ho, sir"; and they hear the ring and the rattle of the four fast trotters and the town-made drag, as it dashes up to the Peacock.

"Anything for us, Bob?" says the burly guard, dropping down from behind, and slapping himself across the chest.

"Young genl'm'n, Rugby; three parcels, Leicester; hamper o' game, Rugby," answers Ostler.

"Tell young gent to look alive," says Guard, opening the hind-boot and shooting in the parcels after examining them by the lamps. "Here, shove the portmanteau up a-top—I'll fasten him presently. Now then, sir, jump up behind."

"Good-bye, father—my love at home." A last shake of the hand. Up goes Tom, the guard catching his hat-box and holding on with one hand, while with the other he claps the horn to his mouth. Toot, toot, toot! the ostlers let go their heads, the four bays plunge at the collar, and away goes the Tally-ho into the darkness, forty-five seconds from the time they pulled up; Ostler, Boots, and the Squire stand looking after them under the Peacock lamp.

"Sharp work!" says the Squire, and goes in again to his bed, the coach being well out of sight and hearing.

Tom stands up on the coach and looks back at his father's figure as long as he can see it, and then the guard having disposed of his luggage comes to an anchor, and finishes his buttonings and other preparations for facing the three hours before dawn; no joke for those who minded cold, on a fast coach in November, in the reign of his late majesty.

I sometimes think that you boys of this generation are a deal tenderer fellows than we used to be. At any rate you're much more comfortable travellers, for I see every one of you with his rug or plaid, and other dodges for preserving the caloric, and most of you going in those fuzzy, dusty, padded first-class carriages. It was another affair altogether, a dark ride on the top of the Tally-ho, I can tell you, in a tight Petersham coat, and your feet dangling six inches from the floor. Then you knew what cold was, and what it was to be without legs, for not a bit of feeling had you in them after the first half-hour. But it had its pleasures, the old dark ride. First there was the consciousness of silent endurance, so dear to every Englishman,—of standing out against something, and not giving in. Then there was the music of the rattling harness, and the ring of the horses' feet on the hard road, and the glare of the two bright lamps through the steaming hoar frost, over the leaders' ears, into the darkness; and the cheery toot of the guard's horn, to warn some drowsy pikeman or the ostler at the next change; and the looking forward to daylight—and last, but not least, the delight of returning sensation in your toes.

Then the break of dawn and the sunrise, where can they be ever seen in perfection but from a coach roof? You want motion and change and music to see them in their glory; not the music of singing men and singing women, but good, silent music, which sets itself in your own head, the accompaniment of work and getting over the ground.

The Tally-ho is past St. Alban's, and Tom is enjoying the ride, though half-frozen. The guard, who is alone with him on the back of the coach, is silent, but has muffled Tom's feet up in straw, and put the end of an oat-sack over his knees. The darkness has driven him inwards, and he has gone over his little past life, and thought of all his doings and promises, and of his mother and sister, and his father's last words; and has made fifty good resolutions, and means to bear himself like a brave Brown as he is, though a young one. Then he has been forward into the mysterious boy-future, speculating as to what sort of place Rugby is, and what they do there, and calling up all the stories of public schools which he has heard from big boys in the holidays. He is chock full of hope and life, notwithstanding the cold, and kicks his heels against the back-board, and would like to sing, only he doesn't know how his friend the silent guard might take it.

And now the dawn breaks at the end of the fourth stage, and the coach pulls up at a little road-side inn with huge stables behind. There is a bright fire gleaming through the red curtains of the bar window, and the door is open. The coachman catches his whip into a double thong, and throws it to the ostler; the steam of the horses rises straight up into the air. He has put them along over the last two miles, and is two minutes before his time; he rolls down from the box and into the inn. The guard rolls off behind. "Now, sir," says he to Tom, "you just jump down, and I'll give you a drop of something to keep the cold out."

Tom finds a difficulty in jumping, or indeed in finding the top of the wheel with his feet, which may be in the next world for all he feels; so the guard picks him off the coach top, and sets him on his legs, and they stump off into the bar, and join the coachman and the other outside passengers.

Here a fresh-looking barmaid serves them each with a glass of early purl as they stand before the fire, coachman and guard exchanging business remarks. The purl warms the cockles of Tom's heart, and makes him cough.

"Rare tackle that, sir, of a cold morning," says the coachman, smiling. "Time's up." They are out again and up; Coachee the last, gathering the reins into his hands and talking to Jem the ostler about the mare's shoulder, and then swinging himself up on to the box—the horses dashing off in a canter before he falls into his seat. Toot-toot-tootle-too goes the horn, and away they are again, five-and-thirty miles on their road (nearly half way to Rugby, thinks Tom), and the prospect of breakfast at the end of the stage.

And now they begin to see, and the early life of the country-side comes out; a market cart or two, men in smock-frocks going to their work pipe in mouth, a whiff of which is no bad smell this bright morning. The sun gets up, and the mist shines like silver gauze. They pass the hounds jogging along to a distant meet, at the heels of the huntsman's hack, whose face is about the colour of the tails of his old pink, as he exchanges greetings with coachman and guard. Now they pull up at a lodge and take on board a well muffled-up sportsman, with his gun-case and carpet-bag. An early up-coach meets them, and the coachmen gather up their horses, and pass one another with the accustomed lift of the elbow, each team doing eleven miles an hour, with a mile to spare behind if necessary. And here comes breakfast.

"Twenty minutes here, gentlemen," says the coachman, as they pull up at half-past seven at the inn-door.

Have we not endured nobly this morning, and is not this a worthy reward for much endurance? There is the low dark wainscoted room hung with sporting prints; the hat-stand (with a whip or two standing up in it belonging to bagmen who are still snug in bed) by the door; the blazing fire, with the quaint old glass over the mantelpiece, in which is stuck a large card with the list of the meets for the week of the county hounds. The table covered with the whitest of cloths and of china, and bearing a pigeon-pie, ham, round of cold boiled beef cut from a mammoth ox, and the great loaf of household bread on a wooden trencher. And here comes in the stout head waiter, puffing under a tray of hot viands; kidneys and a steak, transparent rashers and poached eggs, buttered toast and muffins, coffee and tea, all smoking hot. The table can never hold it all; the cold meats are removed to the sideboard, they were only put on for show and to give us an appetite. And now fall on, gentlemen all. It is a well-known sporting-house, and the breakfasts are famous. Two or three men in pink, on their way to the meet, drop in, and are very jovial and sharp-set, as indeed we all are.

"Tea or coffee, sir?" says head waiter, coming round to Tom.

"Coffee, please," says Tom, with his mouth full of muffin and kidney; coffee is a treat to him, tea is not.

Our coachman, I perceive, who breakfasts with us, is a cold beef man. He also eschews hot potations, and addicts himself to a tankard of ale, which is brought him by the barmaid. Sportsman looks on approvingly, and orders a ditto for himself.

Tom has eaten kidney and pigeon-pie, and imbibed coffee, till his little skin is as tight as a drum; and then has the further pleasure of paying head waiter out of his own purse in a dignified manner, and walks out before the inn-door to see the horses put to. This is done leisurely and in a highly-finished manner by the ostlers, as if they enjoyed the not being hurried. Coachman comes out with his waybill and puffing a fat cigar which the sportsman has given him. Guard emerges from the tap, where he prefers breakfasting, licking round a tough-looking doubtful cheroot, which you might tie round your finger, and three whiffs of which would knock any one else out of time.

The pinks stand about the inn-door lighting cigars and waiting to see us start, while their hacks are led up and down the market-place, on which the inn looks. They all know our sportsman, and we feel a reflected credit when we see him chatting and laughing with them.

"Now, sir, please," says the coachman; all the rest of the passengers are up; the guard is locking up the hind boot.

"A good run to you!" says the sportsman to the pinks, and is by the coachman's side in no time.

"Let 'em go, Dick!" The ostlers fly back, drawing off the cloths from their glossy loins, and away we go through the market-place and down the High Street, looking in at the first-floor windows, and seeing several worthy burgesses shaving thereat; while all the shop-boys who are cleaning the windows, and housemaids who are doing the steps, stop and look pleased as we rattle past, as if we were a part of their legitimate morning's amusement. We clear the town, and are well out between the hedgerows again as the town clock strikes eight.

The sun shines almost warmly, and breakfast has oiled all springs and loosened all tongues. Tom is encouraged by a remark or two of the guard's between the puffs of his oily cheroot, and besides is getting tired of not talking. He is too full of his destination to talk about anything else; and so asks the guard if he knows Rugby.

"Goes through it every day of my life. Twenty minutes afore twelve down—ten o'clock up."

"What sort of place is it, please?" says Tom.

Guard looks at him with a comical expression. "Werry out-o'-the-way place, sir; no paving streets, nor no lighting. 'Mazin' big horse and cattle fair in autumn—lasts a week—just over now. Takes town a week to get clean after it. Fairish hunting country. But slow place, sir, slow place: off the main road, you see—only three coaches a day, and one on 'em a two-oss wan, more like a hearse nor a coach—Regulator—comes from Oxford. Young genl'm'n at school calls her Pig and Whistle, and goes up to college by her (six miles an hour) when they goes to enter. Belong to school, sir?"

"Yes," says Tom, not unwilling for a moment that the guard should think him an old boy. But then having some qualms as to the truth of the assertion, and seeing that if he were to assume the character of an old boy he couldn't go on asking the questions he wanted, added—"that is to say, I'm on my way there. I'm a new boy."

The guard looked as if he knew this quite as well as Tom.

"You're werry late, sir," says the guard; "only six weeks to-day to the end of the half." Tom assented. "We takes up fine loads this day six weeks, and Monday and Tuesday arter. Hopes we shall have the pleasure of carrying you back."

Tom said he hoped they would; but he thought within himself that his fate would probably be the Pig and Whistle.

"It pays uncommon cert'nly," continues the guard. "Werry free with their cash is the young genl'm'n. But, Lor', bless you, we gets into such rows all 'long the road, what wi' their pea-shooters, and long whips, and hollering, and upsetting every one as comes by; I'd a sight sooner carry one or two on 'em, sir, as I may be a carryin' of you now, than a coach-load."

"What do they do with the pea-shooters?" inquires Tom.

"Do wi' 'em! Why, peppers every one's faces as we comes near, 'cept the young gals, and breaks windows wi' them too, some on 'em shoots so hard. Now 'twas just here last June, as we was a driving up the first-day boys, they was mendin' a quarter-mile of road, and there was a lot of Irish chaps, reg'lar roughs, a breaking stones. As we comes up, 'Now, boys,' says young gent on the box (smart young fellow and desper't reckless), 'here's fun! let the Pats have it about the ears.' 'God's sake, sir!' says Bob (that's my mate the coachman), 'don't go for to shoot at 'em, they'll knock us off the coach.' 'Damme, Coachee,' says young my lord, 'you ain't afraid; hoora, boys! let 'em have it.' 'Hoora!' sings out the others, and fill their mouths chock full of peas to last the whole line. Bob seeing as 'twas to come, knocks his hat over his eyes, hollers to his 'osses, and shakes 'em up, and away we goes up to the line on 'em, twenty miles an hour. The Pats begin to hoora too, thinking it was a runaway, and first lot on 'em stands grinnin' and wavin' their old hats as we comes abreast on 'em; and then you'd ha' laughed to see how took aback and choking savage they looked, when they gets the peas a stinging all over 'em.

But bless you, the laugh weren't all of our side, sir, by a long way. We was going so fast, and they was so took aback, that they didn't take what was up till we was half-way up the line. Then 'twas, 'look out all,' surely. They howls all down the line fit to frighten you, some on 'em runs arter us and tries to clamber up behind, only we hits 'em over the fingers and pulls their hands off; one as had had it very sharp act'ly runs right at the leaders, as though he'd ketch 'em by the heads, only luck'ly for him he misses his tip, and comes over a heap o' stones first. The rest picks up stones, and gives it us right away till we gets out of shot, the young gents holding out werry manful with the pea-shooters and such stones as lodged on us, and a pretty many there was too. Then Bob picks hisself up again, and looks at young gent on box werry solemn. Bob'd had a rum un in the ribs, which'd like to ha' knocked him off the box, or made him drop the reins. Young gent on box picks hisself up, and so does we all, and looks round to count damage. Box's head cut open and his hat gone; 'nother young gent's hat gone; mine knocked in at the side, and not one on us as wasn't black and blue somewheres or another, most on 'em all over. Two pound ten to pay for damage to paint, which they subscribed for there and then, and give Bob and me a extra half-sovereign each; but I wouldn't go down that line again not for twenty half-sovereigns." And the guard shook his head slowly, and got up and blew a clear, brisk toot-toot.

"What fun!" said Tom, who could scarcely contain his pride at this exploit of his future school-fellows. He longed already for the end of the half that he might join them.

" 'Taint such good fun though, sir, for the folk as meets the coach, nor for we who has to go back with it next day. Them Irishers last summer had all got stones ready for us, and was all but letting drive, and we'd got two reverend gents aboard too. We pulled up at the beginning of the line, and pacified them, and we're never going to carry no more pea-shooters, unless they promises not to fire where there's a line of Irish chaps a stone-breaking." The guard stopped and pulled away at his cheroot, regarding Tom benignantly the while.

"Oh, don't stop! tell us something more about the pea-shooting."

"Well, there'd like to have been a pretty piece of work over it at Bicester, a while back. We was six mile from the town, when we meets an old square-headed gray-haired yeoman chap, a jogging along quite quiet. He looks up at the coach, and just then a pea hits him on the nose, and some catches his cob behind and makes him dance up on his hind legs. I see'd the old boy's face flush and look plaguy awkward, and I thought we was in for somethin' nasty.

"He turns his cob's head, and rides quietly after us just out of shot. How that 'ere cob did step! we never shook him off not a dozen yards in the six miles. At first the young gents was werry lively on him; but afore we got in, seeing how steady the old chap come on, they was quite quiet, and laid their heads together what they should do. Some was for fighting, some for axing his pardon. He rides into the town close after us, comes up when we stops, and says the two as shot at him must come before a magistrate; and a great crowd comes round, and we couldn't get the osses to. But the young 'uns they all stand by one another, and says all or none must go, and as how they'd fight it out, and have to be carried. Just as 'twas gettin' serious, and the old boy and the mob was going to pull 'em off the coach, one little fellow jumps up and says, 'Here,—I'll stay—I'm only going three miles further. My father's name's Davis; he's known about here, and I'll go before the magistrate with this gentleman.' 'What! be thee parson Davis's son?' says the old boy. 'Yes,' says the young 'un. 'Well, I be mortal sorry to meet thee in such company, but for thy father's sake and thine (for thee bi'st a brave young chap) I'll say no more about it.' Didn't the boys cheer him, and the mob cheered the young chap—and then one of the biggest gets down, and begs his pardon werry gentlemanly for all the rest, saying as they all had been plaguy vexed from the first, but didn't like to ax his pardon till then, 'cause they felt they hadn't ought to shirk the consequences of their joke. And then they all got down, and shook hands with the old boy, and asked him to all parts of the country, to their homes, and we drives off twenty minutes behind time, with cheering and hollering as if we was county members. But, Lor' bless you, sir," says the guard, smacking his hand down on his knee and looking full into Tom's face, "ten minutes arter they was all as bad as ever."

Tom showed such undisguised and open-mouthed interest in his narrations, that the old guard rubbed up his memory, and launched out into a graphic history of all the performances of the boys on the roads for the last twenty years. Off the road he couldn't go; the exploit must have been connected with horses or vehicles to hang in the old fellow's head. Tom tried him off his own ground once or twice, but found he knew nothing beyond, and so let him have his head, and the rest of the road bowled easily away; for old Blow-hard (as the boys called him) was a dry old file, with much kindness and humour, and a capital spinner of a yarn when he had broken the neck of his day's work, and got plenty of ale under his belt.

What struck Tom's youthful imagination most was the desperate and lawless character of most of the stories. Was the guard hoaxing him? He couldn't help hoping that they were true. It's very odd how almost all English boys love danger; you can get ten to join a game, or climb a tree, or swim a stream, when there's a chance of breaking their limbs or getting drowned, for one who'll stay on level ground, or in his depth, or play quoits or bowls.

The guard had just finished an account of a desperate fight which had happened at one of the fairs between the drovers and the farmers with their whips, and the boys with cricket-bats and wickets, which arose out of a playful but objectionable practice of the boys going round to the public-houses and taking the linch-pins out of the wheels of the gigs, and was moralizing upon the way in which the Doctor, "a terrible stern man he'd heard tell," had come down upon several of the performers, "sending three on 'em off next morning in a po-shay with a parish constable," when they turned a corner and neared the milestone, the third from Rugby. By the stone two boys stood, their jackets buttoned tight, waiting for the coach.

"Look here, sir," says the guard, after giving a sharp toot-toot, "there's two on 'em, out and out runners they be. They comes out about twice or three times a week, and spirts a mile alongside of us."

And as they came up, sure enough, away went two boys along the foot-path, keeping up with the horses; the first a light clean-made fellow going on springs, the other stout and round-shouldered, labouring in his pace, but going as dogged as a bull-terrier.

Old Blow-hard looked on admiringly. "See how beautiful that there un holds hisself together, and goes from his hips, sir," said he; "he's a 'mazin' fine runner. Now many coachmen as drives a first-rate team'd put it on, and try and pass 'em. But Bob, sir, bless you, he's tender-hearted; he'd sooner pull in a bit if he see'd 'em a gettin' beat. I do b'lieve too as that there un'd sooner break his heart than let us go by him afore next milestone."

At the second milestone the boys pulled up short, and waved their hats to the guard, who had his watch out and shouted "4.56," thereby indicating that the mile had been done in four seconds under the five minutes. They passed several more parties of boys, all of them objects of the deepest interest to Tom, and came in sight of the town at ten minutes before twelve. Tom fetched a long breath, and thought he had never spent a pleasanter day. Before he went to bed he had quite settled that it must be the greatest day he should ever spend, and didn't alter his opinion for many a long year—if he has yet.

CHAPTER V

RUGBY AND FOOTBALL

"————Foot and eye opposed
In dubious strife."
SCOTT

"AND SO HERE'S RUGBY, sir, at last, and you'll be in plenty of time for dinner at the School-house, as I tell'd you," said the old guard, pulling his horn out of its case, and tootle-tooing away; while the coachman shook up his horses, and carried them along the side of the school close, round Deadman's corner, past the school gates, and down the High Street to the Spread Eagle; the wheelers in a spanking trot, and leaders cantering, in a style which would not have disgraced "Cherry Bob," "ramping, stamping, tearing, swearing Billy Harwood," or any other of the old coaching heroes.

Tom's heart beat quick as he passed the great school-field or close, with its noble elms, in which several games at football were going on, and tried to take in at once the long line of gray buildings, beginning with the chapel, and ending with the school-house, the residence of the head-master, where the great flag was lazily waving from the highest round tower. And he began already to be proud of being a Rugby boy, as he passed the school-gates, with the oriel-window above, and saw the boys standing there, looking as if the town belonged to them, and nodding in a familiar manner to the coachman, as if any one of them would be quite equal to getting on the box, and working the team down street as well as he.

One of the young heroes, however, ran out from the rest, and scrambled up behind; where, having righted himself, and nodded to the guard, with "How do, Jem?" he turned short round to Tom, and, after looking him over for a minute, began—

"I say, you fellow, is your name Brown?"

"Yes," said Tom, in considerable astonishment, glad however to have lighted on some one already who seemed to know him.

"Ah, I thought so: you know my old aunt, Miss East, she lives somewhere down your way in Berkshire. She wrote to me that you were coming to-day, and asked me to give you a lift."

Tom was somewhat inclined to resent the patronizing air of his new friend, a boy of just about his own height and age, but gifted with the most transcendent coolness and assurance, which Tom felt to be aggravating and hard to bear, but couldn't for the life of him help admiring and envying—especially when young my lord begins hectoring two or three long loafing fellows, half porter, half stableman, with a strong touch of the blackguard; and in the end arranges with one of them, nicknamed Cooey, to carry Tom's luggage up to the School-house for sixpence.

"And hark 'ee, Cooey, it must be up in ten minutes, or no more jobs from me. Come along, Brown." And away swaggers the young potentate, with his hands in his pockets, and Tom at his side.

"All right, sir," says Cooey, touching his hat, with a leer and a wink at his companions.

"Hullo tho'," says East, pulling up, and taking another look at Tom, "this'll never do—haven't you got a hat?—we never wear caps here. Only the louts wear caps. Bless you, if you were to go into the quadrangle with that thing on, I——don't know what'd happen." The very idea was quite beyond young Master East, and he looked unutterable things.

Tom thought his cap a very knowing affair, but confessed that he had a hat in his hat-box; which was accordingly at once extracted from the hind boot, and Tom equipped in his go-to-meeting roof, as his new friend called it. But this didn't quite suit his fastidious taste in another minute, being too shiny; so, as they walk up the town, they dive into Nixon's the hatter's, and Tom is arrayed, to his utter astonishment, and without paying for it, in a regulation cat-skin at seven-and-sixpence: Nixon undertaking to send the best hat up to the matron's room, School-house, in half an hour.

"You can send in a note for a tile on Monday, and make it all right, you know," said Mentor; "we're allowed two seven-and-sixers a half, besides what we bring from home."

Tom by this time began to be conscious of his new social position and dignities, and to luxuriate in the realized ambition of being a public school-boy at last, with a vested right of spoiling two seven-and-sixers in half a year.

"You see," said his friend, as they strolled up towards the school-gates, in explanation of his conduct, "a great deal depends on how a fellow cuts up at first. If he's got nothing odd about him, and answers straightforward, and holds his head up, he gets on. Now you'll do very well as to rig, all but that cap. You see I'm doing the handsome thing by you, because my father knows yours; besides, I want to please the old lady. She gave me half-a-sov. this half, and perhaps'll double it next, if I keep in her good books."

There's nothing like candour for a lower-school boy, and East was a genuine specimen—frank, hearty, and good-natured, well satisfied with himself and his position, and chock full of life and spirits, and all the Rugby prejudices and traditions which he had been able to get together, in the long course of one half year during which he had been at the School-house.

And Tom, notwithstanding his bumptiousness, felt friends with him at once, and began sucking in all his ways and prejudices, as fast as he could understand them.

East was great in the character of cicerone; he carried Tom through the great gates, where were only two or three boys. These satisfied themselves with the stock questions, —"You fellow, what's your name? Where do you come from? How old are you? Where do you board? and, What form are you in?"—and so they passed on through the quadrangle and a small courtyard, upon which looked down a lot of little windows (belonging, as his guide informed him, to some of the School-house studies), into the matron's room, where East introduced Tom to that dignitary; made him give up the key of his trunk, that the matron might unpack his linen, and told the story of the hat and of his own presence of mind: upon the relation whereof the matron laughingly scolded him, for the coolest new boy in the house; and East, indignant at the accusation of newness, marched Tom off into the quadrangle, and began showing him the schools, and examining him as to his literary attainments; the result of which was a prophecy that they would be in the same form, and could do their lessons together.

"And now come in and see my study; we shall have just time before dinner; and afterwards, before calling over, we'll do the close."

Tom followed his guide through the School-house hall, which opens into the quadrangle. It is a great room thirty feet long and eighteen high, or thereabouts, with two great tables running the whole length, and two large fire-places at the side, with blazing fires

in them, at one of which some dozen boys were standing and lounging, some of whom shouted to East to stop; but he shot through with his convoy, and landed him in the long dark passages, with a large fire at the end of each, upon which the studies opened. Into one of these, in the bottom passage, East bolted with our hero, slamming and bolting the door behind them, in case of pursuit from the hall, and Tom was for the first time in a Rugby boy's citadel.

He hadn't been prepared for separate studies, and was not a little astonished and delighted with the palace in question.

It wasn't very large certainly, being about six feet long by four broad. It couldn't be called light, as there were bars and a grating to the window; which little precautions were necessary in the studies on the ground-floor looking out into the close, to prevent the exit of small boys after locking up, and the entrance of contraband articles. But it was uncommonly comfortable to look at, Tom thought. The space under the window at the further end was occupied by a square table covered with a reasonably clean and whole red and blue check tablecloth; a hard-seated sofa covered with red stuff occupied one side, running up to the end, and making a seat for one, or by sitting close, for two, at the table; and a good stout wooden chair afforded a seat to another boy, so that three could sit and work together. The walls were wainscoted half-way up, the wainscot being covered with green baize, the remainder with a bright-patterned paper, on which hung three or four prints of dogs' heads, Grimaldi winning the Aylesbury steeple-chase, Amy Robsart, the reigning Waverley beauty of the day, and Tom Crib in a posture of defence, which did no credit to the science of that hero, if truly represented. Over the door were a row of hat-pegs, and on each side bookcases with cupboards at the bottom; shelves and cupboards being filled indiscriminately with school-books, a cup or two, a mousetrap and candlesticks, leather straps, a fustian bag, and some curious-looking articles, which puzzled Tom not a little, until his friend explained that they were climbing-irons, and showed their use. A cricket-bat and small fishing-rod stood up in one corner.

This was the residence of East and another boy in the same form, and had more interest for Tom than Windsor Castle, or any other residence in the British Isles. For was he not about to become the joint owner of a similar home, the first place he could call his own? One's own—what a charm there is in the words. How long it takes boy and man to find out their worth! how fast most of us hold on to them! faster and more jealously, the nearer we are to that general home into which we can take nothing, but must go naked as we came into the world. When shall we learn that he who multiplieth possessions multiplieth troubles, and that the one single use of things which we call our own is that they may be his who hath need of them?

"And shall I have a study like this, too?" said Tom.

"Yes, of course, you'll be chummed with some fellow on Monday, and you can sit here till then."

"What nice places!"

"They're well enough," answered East, patronizingly, "only uncommon cold at nights sometimes. Gower—that's my chum—and I make a fire with paper on the floor after supper generally, only that makes it so smoky."

"But there's a big fire out in the passage," said Tom.

"Precious little we get out of that though," said East; "Jones the præpostor has the study at the fire end, and he has rigged up an iron rod and green baize curtain across the passage, which he draws at night, and sits there with his door open; so he gets all the fire, and hears if we come out of our studies after eight, or make a noise. However, he's taken to sitting in the fifth-form room lately, so we do get a bit of fire now sometimes; only to keep a sharp look-out that he don't catch you behind his curtain when he comes down—that's all.

A quarter-past one now struck, and the bell began tolling for dinner, so they went into the hall and took their places, Tom at the very bottom of the second table, next to the præpostor (who sat at the end to keep order there), and East a few paces higher. And now Tom for the first time saw his future schoolfellows in a body. In they came, some hot and ruddy from football or long walks, some pale and chilly from hard reading in their studies, some from loitering over the fire at the pastrycook's, dainty mortals, bringing with them pickles and sauce-bottles to help them with their dinners. And a great big-bearded man, whom Tom took for a master, began calling over the names, while the great joints were being rapidly carved on the third table in the corner by the old verger and the housekeeper. Tom's turn came last, and meanwhile he was all eyes, looking first with awe at the great man, who sat close to him, and was helped first, and who read a hard-looking book all the time he was eating; and when he got up and walked off to the fire, at the small boys round him, some of whom were reading, and the rest talking in whispers to one another, or stealing one another's bread, or shooting pellets, or digging their forks through the tablecloth. However, notwithstanding his curiosity, he managed to make a capital dinner by the time the big man called "Stand up!" and said grace.

As soon as dinner was over, and Tom had been questioned by such of his neighbours as were curious as to his birth, parentage, education, and other like matters, East, who evidently enjoyed his new dignity of patron and Mentor, proposed having a look at the close, which Tom, athirst for knowledge, gladly assented to, and they went out through the quadrangle and past the big fives' court, into the great playground.

"That's the chapel, you see," said East, "and there just behind it is the place for fights; you see it's most out of the way of the masters, who all live on the other side and don't come by here after first lesson or callings-over. That's when the fights come off. And all this part where we are is the little side-ground, right up to the trees, and on the other side of the trees is the big side-ground, where the great matches are played. And there's the island in the furthest corner; you'll know that well enough next half, when there's island fagging. I say, it's horrid cold, let's have a run across," and away went East, Tom close behind him. East was evidently putting his best foot foremost, and Tom, who was mighty proud of his running, and not a little anxious to show his friend that although a new boy he was no milksop, laid himself down to work in his very best style. Right across the close they went, each doing all he knew, and there wasn't a yard between them when they pulled up at the island moat.

"I say," said East, as soon as he got his wind, looking with much increased respect at Tom, "you ain't a bad scud, not by no means. Well, I'm as warm as a toast now."

"But why do you wear white trousers in November?" said Tom. He had been struck by this peculiarity in the costume of almost all the School-house boys.

"Why, bless us, don't you know?—No, I forgot. Why, to-day's the School-house match. Our house plays the whole of the School at football. And we all wear white trousers, to show 'em we don't care for hacks. You're in luck to come to-day. You just will see a match; and Brooke's going to let me play in quarters. That's more than he'll do for any other lower-school boy, except James, and he's fourteen."

"Who's Brooke?"

"Why, that big fellow who called over at dinner, to be sure. He's cock of the school, and head of the School-house side, and the best kick and charger in Rugby."

"Oh, but do show me where they play. And tell me about it. I love football so, and have played all my life. Won't Brooke let me play?"

"Not he," said East, with some indignation; "why, you don't know the rules—you'll be a month learning them. And then it's no joke playing-up in a match, I can tell you. Quite another thing from your private school games. Why, there's been two collar-bones broken this half, and a dozen fellows lamed. And last year a fellow had his leg broken."

Tom listened with the profoundest respect to this chapter of accidents, and followed East across the level ground till they came to a sort of gigantic gallows of two poles eighteen feet high, fixed upright in the ground some fourteen feet apart, with a cross bar running from one to the other at the height of ten feet or thereabouts.

"This is one of the goals," said East, "and you see the other, across there, right opposite, under the Doctor's wall. Well, the match is for the best of three goals; whichever side kicks two goals wins: and it won't do, you see, just to kick the ball through these posts, it must go over the cross bar; any height'll do, so long as it's between the posts. You'll have to stay in goal to touch the ball when it rolls behind the posts, because if the other side touch it they have a try at goal. Then we fellows in quarters, we play just about in front of goal here, and have to turn the ball and kick it back before the big fellows on the other side can follow it up. And in front of us all the big fellows play, and that's where the scrummages are mostly."

Tom's respect increased as he struggled to make out his friend's technicalities, and the other set to work to explain the mysteries of "off your side," "drop-kicks," "punts," "places," and the other intricacies of the great science of football.

"But how do you keep the ball between the goals?" said he; "I can't see why it mightn't go right down to the chapel."

"Why, that's out of play," answered East. "You see this gravel-walk running down all along this side of the playing-ground, and the line of elms opposite on the other? Well, they're the bounds. As soon as the ball gets past them, it's in touch, and out of play. And then whoever first touches it has to knock it straight out amongst the players-up, who make two lines with a space between them, every fellow going on his own side. Ain't there just fine scrummages then! and the three trees you see there which come out into the play, that's a tremendous place when the ball hangs there, for you get thrown against the trees, and that's worse than any hack."

Tom wondered within himself as they strolled back again towards the fives' court, whether the matches were really such break-neck affairs as East represented, and whether, if they were, he should ever get to like them and play-up well.

He hadn't long to wonder, however, for next minute East cried out, "Hurra! here's the punt-about,—come along and try your hand at a kick." The punt-about is the practice-ball, which is just brought out and kicked about anyhow from one boy to another before callings-over and dinner, and at other odd times. They joined the boys who had brought it out, all small School-house fellows, friends of East; and Tom had the pleasure of trying his skill, and performed very creditably, after first driving his foot three inches into the ground, and then nearly kicking his leg into the air, in vigorous efforts to accomplish a drop-kick after the manner of East.

Presently more boys and bigger came out, and boys from other houses on their way to calling-over, and more balls were sent for. The crowd thickened as three o'clock approached; and when the hour struck, one hundred and fifty boys were hard at work. Then the balls were held, the master of the week came down in cap and gown to calling-over, and the whole school of three hundred boys swept into the big school to answer to their names.

"I may come in, mayn't I?" said Tom, catching East by the arm and longing to feel one of them.

"Yes, come along, nobody'll say anything. You won't be so eager to get into calling-over after a month," replied his friend; and they marched into the big school together, and up to the further end where that illustrious form, the lower fourth, which had the honour of East's patronage for the time being, stood.

The master mounted into the high desk by the door, and one of the præpostors of the week stood by him on the steps, the other three marching up and down the middle of the school with their canes, calling out "Silence, silence!" The sixth form stood close by the door on the left, some thirty in number, mostly great big grown men, as Tom thought, surveying them from a distance with awe; the fifth form behind them, twice their number, and not quite so big. These on the left; and on the right the lower fifth, shell, and all the junior forms in order: while up the middle marched the three præpostors.

Then the præpostor who stands by the master calls out the names, beginning with the sixth form; and as he calls, each boy answers "here" to his name, and walks out. Some of the sixth stop at the door to turn the whole string of boys into the close; it is a great match-day, and every boy in the school, will-he, nill-he, must be there. The rest of the sixth go forwards into the close, to see that no one escapes by any of the side gates.

To-day, however, being the School-house match, none of the School-house præpostors stay by the door to watch for truants of their side; there is *carte blanche* to the School-house fags to go where they like: "They trust to our honour," as East proudly informs Tom; "they know very well that no School-house boy would cut the match. If he did, we'd very soon cut him, I can tell you."

The master of the week being short-sighted, and the præpostors of the week small and not well up to their work, the lower school boys employ the ten minutes which elapse before their names are called in pelting one another vigorously with acorns, which fly about in all directions. The small præpostors dash in every now and then, and generally chastise some quiet, timid boy who is equally afraid of acorns and canes, while the principal performers get dexterously out of the way; and so calling-over rolls on somehow, much like the big world, punishments lighting on wrong shoulders, and matters going generally in a queer, cross-grained way, but the end coming somehow, which is after all the great point. And now the master of the week has finished, and locked up the big school; and the præpostors of the week come out, sweeping the last remnant of the school fags—who had been loafing about the corners by the fives' court, in hopes of a chance of bolting—before them into the close.

"Hold the punt-about!" "To the goals!" are the cries, and all stray balls are impounded by the authorities; and the whole mass of boys moves up towards the two goals, dividing as they go into three bodies. That little band on the left, consisting of from fifteen to twenty boys, Tom amongst them, who are making for the goal under the School-house wall, are the School-house boys who are not to play-up, and have to stay in goal. The larger body moving to the island goal are the School boys in a like predicament. The great mass in the middle are the players-up, both sides mingled together; they are hanging their jackets, and all who mean real work, their hats, waistcoats, neck-handkerchiefs, and braces, on the railings round the small trees; and there they go by twos and threes up to their respective grounds. There is none of the colour and tastiness of get-up, you will perceive, which lends such a life to the present game at Rugby, making the dullest and worst-fought match a pretty sight. Now each house has its own uniform of cap and jersey, of some lively colour: but at the time we are speaking of plush caps have not yet come in, or uniforms of any sort, except the School-house white trousers, which are abominably cold to-day: let us get to work, bare-headed, and girded with our plain leather straps—but we mean business, gentlemen.

And now that the two sides have fairly sundered, and each occupies its own ground, and we get a good look at them, what absurdity is this? You don't mean to say that those fifty or sixty boys in white trousers, many of them quite small, are going to play that huge mass opposite? Indeed I do, gentlemen; they're going to try at any rate, and won't make such a bad fight of it either, mark my word; for hasn't old Brooke won the toss, with his lucky halfpenny, and got choice of goals and kick-off? The new ball you may see lie there quite by itself, in the middle, pointing towards the School or island goal; in another minute it will be well on its way there. Use that minute in remarking how the School-house side is drilled. You will see in the first place, that the sixth-form boy, who has the charge of goal, has spread his force (the goal-keepers) so as to occupy the whole space behind the goal-posts, at distances of about five yards apart; a safe and well-kept goal is the foundation of all good play. Old Brooke is talking to the captain of quarters; and now he moves away. See how that youngster spreads his men (the light brigade) carefully over the ground, half-way between their own goal and the body of their own players-up (the heavy brigade). These again play in several bodies; there is young Brooke and the bull-dogs—mark them well—they are the "fighting brigade," the "die-hards," larking about at leap-frog to keep themselves warm, and playing tricks on one another. And on each side of old Brooke, who is now standing in the middle of the ground and just going to kick-off, you see a separate wing of players-up, each with a boy of acknowledged prowess to look to—here Warner, and there Hedge; but over all is old Brooke, absolute as he of Russia, but wisely and bravely ruling over willing and worshipping subjects, a true football king. His face is earnest and careful as he glances a last time over his array, but full of pluck and hope, the sort of look I hope to see in my general when I go out to fight.

The School side is not organized in the same way. The goal-keepers are all in lumps, any-how and no-how; you can't distinguish between the players-up and the boys in quarters, and there is divided leadership; but with such odds in strength and weight it must take more than that to hinder them from winning; and so their leaders seem to think, for they let the players-up manage themselves.

But now look, there is a slight move forward of the School-house wings; a shout of "Are you ready?" and loud affirmative reply. Old Brooke takes half-a-dozen quick steps, and away goes the ball spinning towards the School goal,—seventy yards before it touches ground, and at no point above twelve or fifteen feet high, a model kick-off; and the School-house cheer and rush on; the ball is returned, and they meet it and drive it back amongst the masses of the School already in motion. Then the two sides close, and you can see nothing for minutes but a swaying crowd of boys, at one point violently agitated. That is where the ball is, and there are the keen players to be met, and the glory and the hard knocks to be got: you hear the dull thud thud of the ball, and the shouts of "Off your side," "Down with him," "Put him over," "Bravo." This is what we call "a scrummage," gentlemen, and the first scrummage in a School-house match was no joke in the consulship of Plancus.

But see! it has broken; the ball is driven out on the School-house side, and a rush of the School carries it past the School-house players-up. "Look out in quarters," Brooke's and twenty other voices ring out; no need to call though: the School-house captain of quarters has caught it on the bound, dodges the foremost School boys, who are heading the rush, and sends it back with a good drop-kick well into the enemy's country. And then follows rush upon rush, and scrummage upon scrummage, the ball now driven through into the School-house quarters, and now into the School goal; for the School-house have not lost the advantage which the kick-off and a slight wind gave them at the outset, and are slightly "penning" their adversaries. You say, you don't see much in it all; nothing but a struggling mass of boys, and a leather ball which seems to excite them all to great fury, as a red rag does a bull. My dear sir, a battle would look much the same to you, except that the boys would be men, and the balls iron; but a battle would be worth your looking at for all that, and so is a football match. You can't be expected to appreciate the delicate strokes of play, the turns by which a game is lost and won,—it takes an old player to do that, but the broad philosophy of football you can understand if you will. Come along with me a little nearer, and let us consider it together.

The ball has just fallen again where the two sides are thickest, and they close rapidly around it in a scrummage; it must be driven through now by force or skill, till it flies out on one side or the other. Look how differently the boys face it! Here come two of the bull-dogs, bursting through the outsiders; in they go, straight to the heart of the scrummage, bent on driving that ball out on the opposite side. That is what they mean to do. My sons, my sons! you are too hot; you have gone past the ball, and must struggle now right through the scrummage, and get round and back again to your own side, before you can be of any further use. Here comes young Brooke; he goes in as straight as you, but keeps his head, and backs and bends, holding himself still behind the ball, and driving it furiously when he gets the chance. Take a leaf out of his book, you young chargers. Here comes Speedicut, and Flashman the School-house bully with shouts and great action. Won't you two come up to young Brooke, after locking-up, by the School-house fire, with "Old fellow, wasn't that just a splendid scrummage by the three trees?" But he knows you, and so do we. You don't really want to drive that ball through that scrummage, chancing all hurt for the glory of the School-house—but to make us think that's what you want—a vastly different thing; and fellows of your kidney will never go through more than the skirts of a scrummage, where it's all push and no kicking. We respect boys who keep out of it, and don't sham going in; but you—we had rather not say what we think of you.

Then the boys who are bending and watching on the outside, mark them—they are most useful players, the dodgers; who seize on the ball the moment it rolls out from amongst the chargers, and away with it across to the opposite goal: they seldom go into the scrummage, but must have more coolness than the chargers: as endless as are boys' characters, so are their ways of facing or not facing a scrummage at football.

Three-quarters of an hour are gone; first winds are failing, and weight and numbers beginning to tell. Yard by yard the School-house have been driven back, contesting every inch of ground. The bull-dogs are the colour of mother earth from shoulder to ankle, except young Brooke, who has a marvellous knack of keeping his legs. The School-house are being penned in their turn, and now the ball is behind their goal, under the Doctor's wall. The Doctor and some of his family are there looking on, and seem as anxious as any boy for the success of the School-house. We get a minute's breathing time before old Brooke kicks out, and he gives the word to play strongly for touch, by the three trees. Away goes the ball, and the bull-dogs after it, and in another minute there is shout of "In touch!" "Our ball!" Now's your time, old Brooke, while your men are still fresh. He stands with the ball in his hand, while the two sides form in deep lines opposite one another: he must strike it straight out between them. The lines are thickest close to him, but young Brooke and two or three of his men are shifting up further, where the opposite line is weak. Old Brooke strikes it out straight and strong, and it falls opposite his brother. Hurra! that rush has taken it right through the School line, and away past the three trees, far into their quarters, and young Brooke and the bull-dogs are close upon it. The School leaders rush back, shouting "Look out in goal," and strain every nerve to catch him, but they are after the fleetest foot in Rugby. There they go straight for the School goal-posts, quarters scattering before them. One after another the bull-dogs go down, but young Brooke holds on. "He is down." No! a long stagger, but the danger is past; that was the shock of Crew, the most dangerous of dodgers. And now he is close to the School goal, the ball not three yards before him. There is a hurried rush of the School fags to the spot, but no one throws himself on the ball, the only chance, and young Brooke has touched it right under the School goal-posts.

The School leaders come up furious, and administer toco to the wretched fags nearest at hand; they may well be angry, for it is all Lombard-street to a china orange that the School-house kick a goal with the ball touched in such a good place. Old Brooke of course will kick it out, but who shall catch and place it? Call Crab Jones. Here he comes, sauntering along with a straw in his mouth, the queerest, coolest fish in Rugby: if he were tumbled into the moon this minute, he would just pick himself up without taking his hands out of his pockets or turning a hair. But it is a moment when the boldest charger's heart beats quick. Old Brooke stands with the ball under his arm motioning the School back; he will not kick-out till they are all in goal, behind the posts; they are all edging forwards, inch by inch, to get nearer for the rush at Crab Jones, who stands there in front of old Brooke to catch the ball. If they can reach and destroy him before he catches, the danger is over; and with one and the same rush they will carry it right away to the School-house goal. Fond hope! it is kicked out and caught beautifully. Crab strikes his heel into the ground, to mark the spot where the ball was caught, beyond which the School line may not advance; but there they stand, five deep, ready to rush the moment the ball touches the ground. Take plenty of room! don't give the rush a chance of reaching you! place it true and steady! Trust Crab Jones—he has made a small hole with his heel for the ball to lie on, by which he is resting on one knee, with his eye on old Brooke. "Now!" Crab places the ball at the word, old Brooke kicks, and it rises slowly and truly as the School rush forward.

Then a moment's pause, while both sides look up at the spinning ball. There it flies, straight between the two posts, some five feet above the cross-bar, an unquestioned goal; and a shout of real genuine joy rings out from the School-house players-up, and a faint echo of it comes over the close from the goal-keepers under the Doctor's wall. A goal in the first hour—such a thing hasn't been done in the School-house match these five years.

"Over!" is the cry: the two sides change goals, and the School-house goal-keepers come threading their way across through the masses of the School; the most openly triumphant of them, amongst whom is Tom, a School-house boy of two hours' standing, getting their ears boxed in the transit. Tom indeed is excited beyond measure, and it is all the sixth-form boy, kindest and safest of goal-keepers, has been able to do, to keep him from rushing out whenever the ball has been near their goal. So he holds him by his side, and instructs him in the science of touching.

At this moment Griffith, the itinerant vendor of oranges from Hill Morton, enters the close with his heavy baskets; there is a rush of small boys upon the little pale-faced man, the two sides mingling together, subdued by the great Goddess Thirst, like the English and French by the streams in the Pyrenees. The leaders are past oranges and apples, but some of them visit their coats, and apply innocent-looking ginger-beer bottles to

their mouths. It is no ginger-beer though, I fear, and will do you no good. One short
mad rush, and then a stitch in the side, and no more honest play; that's what comes of
those bottles.

But now Griffith's baskets are empty, the ball is placed again midway, and the School
are going to kick off. Their leaders have sent their lumber into goal, and rated the rest
soundly, and one hundred and twenty picked players-up are there, bent on retrieving
the game. They are to keep the ball in front of the School-house goal, and then to drive
it in by sheer strength and weight. They mean heavy play and no mistake, and so old
Brooke sees; and places Crab Jones in quarters just before the goal, with four or five
picked players, who are to keep the ball away to the sides, where a try at goal, if
obtained, will be less dangerous than in front. He himself, and Warner and Hedge,
who have saved themselves till now, will lead the charges.

"Are you ready?" "Yes." And away comes the ball kicked high in the air, to give the
School time to rush on and catch it as it falls. And here they are amongst us. Meet them
like Englishmen, you School-house boys, and charge them home. Now is the time to
show what mettle is in you—and there shall be a warm seat by the hall fire, and honour,
and lots of bottled beer to-night, for him who does his duty in the next half-hour. And
they are well met. Again and again the cloud of their players-up gathers before our
goal, and comes threatening on, and Warner or Hedge, with young Brooke and the
relics of the bull-dogs, break through and carry the ball back; and old Brooke ranges
the field like Job's war-horse: the thickest scrummage parts asunder before his rush, like
the waves before a clipper's bows; his cheery voice rings over the field, and his eye is
everywhere. And if these miss the ball, and it rolls dangerously in front of our goal,
Crab Jones and his men have seized it and sent it away towards the sides with the
unerring drop-kick. This is worth living for; the whole sum of school-boy existence
gathered up into one straining, struggling half-hour, a half-hour worth a year of
common life.

The quarter to five has struck, and the play slackens for a minute before goal; but
there is Crew, the artful dodger, driving the ball in behind our goal, on the island side,
where our quarters are weakest. Is there no one to meet him? Yes! look at little East! the
ball is just at equal distances between the two, and they rush together, the young man of
seventeen and the boy of twelve, and kick it at the same moment. Crew passes on without
a stagger; East is hurled forward by the shock, and plunges on his shoulder, as if he

would bury himself in the ground; but the ball rises straight into the air, and falls behind Crew's back, while the "bravos" of the School-house attest the pluckiest charge of all that hard-fought day. Warner picks East up lame and half stunned, and he hobbles back into goal, conscious of having played the man.

And now the last minutes are come, and the School gather for their last rush, every boy of the hundred and twenty who has a run left in him. Reckless of the defence of their own goal, on they come across the level big-side ground, the ball well down amongst them, straight for our goal, like the column of the Old Guard up the slope at Waterloo. All former charges have been child's play to this. Warner and Hedge have met them, but still on they come. The bull-dogs rush in for the last time; they are hurled over or carried back, striving hand, foot, and eyelids. Old Brooke comes sweeping round the skirts of the play, and turning short round picks out the very heart of the scrummage, and plunges in. It wavers for a moment—he has the ball! No, it has passed him, and his voice rings out clear over the advancing tide, "Look out in goal." Crab Jones catches it for a moment; but before he can kick, the rush is upon him and passes over him; and he picks himself up behind them with his straw in his mouth, a little dirtier, but as cool as ever.

The ball rolls slowly in behind the School-house goal not three yards in front of a dozen of the biggest School players-up.

There stands the School-house præpostor, safest of goal-keepers, and Tom Brown by his side, who has learned his trade by this time. Now is your time, Tom. The blood of all the Browns is up, and the two rush in together, and throw themselves on the ball, under the very feet of the advancing column; the præpostor on his hands and knees arching his back, and Tom all along on his face. Over them topple the leaders of the rush, shooting over the back of the præpostor, but falling flat on Tom, and knocking all the wind out of his small carcase. "Our ball," says the præpostor, rising with his prize; "but get up there, there's a little fellow under you." They are hauled and roll off him, and Tom is discovered a motionless body.

Old Brooke picks him up. "Stand back, give him air," he says; and then feeling his limbs, adds, "No bones broken. How do you feel, young un?"

"Hah-hah," gasps Tom as his wind comes back, "pretty well, thank you—all right."

"Who is he?" says Brooke. "Oh, it's Brown, he's a new boy; I know him," says East, coming up.

"Well, he is a plucky youngster, and will make a player," says Brooke.

And five o'clock strikes. "No side" is called, and the first day of the School-house match is over.

CHAPTER VI
AFTER THE MATCH

"————Some food we had."
SHAKSPERE

ἡς ποτος ἁδυς
THEOCR. ID.

As the boys scattered away from the ground, and East, leaning on Tom's arm, and limping along, was beginning to consider what luxury they should go and buy for tea to celebrate that glorious victory, the two Brookes came striding by. Old Brooke caught sight of East, and stopped; put his hand kindly on his shoulder and said, "Bravo, youngster, you played famously; not much the matter, I hope?"

"No, nothing at all," said East, "only a little twist from that charge."

"Well, mind and get all right for next Saturday;" and the leader passed on, leaving East better for those few words than all the opodeldoc in England would have made him, and Tom ready to give one of his ears for as much notice. Ah! light words of those whom we love and honour, what a power ye are, and how carelessly wielded by those who can use you! Surely for these things also God will ask an account.

"Tea's directly after locking-up, you see," said East, hobbling along as fast as he could, "so you come along down to Sally Harrowell's; that's our School-house tuckshop—she bakes such stunning murphies, we'll have a penn'orth each for tea; come along, or they'll all be gone."

Tom's new purse and money burnt in his pocket; he wondered, as they toddled through the quadrangle and along the street, whether East would be insulted if he suggested further extravagance, as he had not sufficient faith in a pennyworth of potatoes. At last he blurted out,—

"I say, East, can't we get something else besides potatoes? I've got lots of money, you know."

"Bless us, yes, I forgot," said East, "you've only just come. You see all my tin's been gone this twelve weeks, it hardly ever lasts beyond the first fortnight; and our allowances were all stopped this morning for broken windows, so I haven't got a penny. I've got a tick at Sally's, of course; but then I hate running it high, you see, towards the end of the half, 'cause one has to shell out for it all directly one comes back, and that's a bore."

Tom didn't understand much of this talk, but seized on the fact that East had no money, and was denying himself some little pet luxury in consequence. "Well, what shall I buy?" said he; "I'm uncommon hungry."

"I say," said East, stopping to look at him and rest his leg, "you're a trump, Brown. I'll do the same by you next half. Let's have a pound of sausages then; that's the best grub for tea I know of."

"Very well," said Tom, as pleased as possible; "where do they sell them?"

"Oh, over here, just opposite;" and they crossed the street and walked into the cleanest little front room of a small house, half parlour, half shop, and bought a pound

of most particular sausages; East talking pleasantly to Mrs. Porter while she put them in paper, and Tom doing the paying part.

From Porter's they adjourned to Sally Harrowell's, where they found a lot of school-house boys waiting for the roast potatoes, and relating their own exploits in the day's match at the top of their voices. The street opened at once into Sally's kitchen, a low brick-floored room, with large recess for fire, and chimney-corner seats. Poor little Sally, the most good-natured and much-enduring of womankind, was bustling about, with a napkin in her hand, from her own oven to those of the neighbours' cottages up the yard at the back of the house. Stumps, her husband, a short easy-going shoemaker, with a beery humorous eye and ponderous calves, who lived mostly on his wife's earnings, stood in a corner of the room, exchanging shots of the roughest description of repartee with every boy in turn. "Stumps, you lout, you've had too much beer again to-day." " 'Twasn't of your paying for, then."—"Stumps's calves are running down into his ankles, they want to get to grass." "Better be doing that, than gone altogether like yours," &c. &c. Very poor stuff it was, but it served to make time pass; and every now and then Sally arrived in the middle with a smoking tin of potatoes, which was cleared off in a few seconds, each boy as he seized his lot running off to the house with "Put me down two-penn'orth, Sally;" "Put down three-penn'orth between me and Davis," &c. How she ever kept the accounts so straight as she did, in her head and on her slate, was a perfect wonder.

East and Tom got served at last, and started back for the School-house, just as the locking-up bell began to ring; East on the way recounting the life and adventures of Stumps, who was a character. Amongst his other small avocations, he was the hind carrier of a sedan-chair, the last of its race, in which the Rugby ladies still went out to tea, and in which, when he was fairly harnessed and carrying a load, it was the delight of small and mischievous boys to follow him and whip his calves. This was too much for the temper even of Stumps, and he would pursue his tormentors in a vindictive and apoplectic manner when released, but was easily pacified by twopence to buy beer with.

The lower schoolboys of the School-house, some fifteen in number, had tea in the lower-fifth school, and were presided over by the old verger or head-porter. Each boy had a quarter of a loaf of bread and pat of butter, and as much tea as he pleased; and there was scarcely one who didn't add to this some further luxury, such as baked potatoes, a herring, sprats, or something of the sort; but few, at this period of the half-year, could live up to a pound of Porter's sausages, and East was in great magnificence upon the strength of theirs. He had produced a toasting-fork from his study, and set Tom to toast the sausages, while he mounted guard over their butter and potatoes; " 'cause," as he explained, "you're a new boy, and they'll play you some trick and get our butter, but you can toast just as well as I." So Tom, in the midst of three or four more urchins similarly employed, toasted his face and the sausages at the same time before the huge fire, till the latter cracked; when East from his watch-tower shouted that they were done, and then the feast proceeded, and the festive cups of tea were filled and emptied, and Tom imparted of the sausages in small bits to many neighbours, and thought he had never tasted such good potatoes or seen such jolly boys. They on their parts waived all ceremony, and pegged away at the sausages and potatoes, and remembering Tom's performance in goal, voted East's new crony a brick. After tea, and while the things were being cleared away, they gathered round the fire, and the talk on the match still went on; and those who had them to show pulled up their trousers and showed the hacks they had received in the good cause.

They were soon, however, all turned out of the school, and East conducted Tom up to his bedroom, that he might get on clean things and wash himself before singing.

"What's singing?" said Tom, taking his head out of his basin, where he had been plunging it in cold water.

"Well, you are jolly green," answered his friend from a neighbouring basin. "Why, the last six Saturdays of every half we sing of course; and this is the first of them. No first lesson to do, you know, and lie in bed to-morrow morning."

"But who sings?"

"Why everybody, of course; you'll see soon enough. We begin directly after supper, and sing till bed-time. It ain't such good fun now though as in the summer half, 'cause then we sing in the little fives' court, under the library, you know. We take out tables, and the big boys sit round and drink beer; double allowance on Saturday nights; and we cut about the quadrangle between the songs, and it looks like a lot of robbers in a cave. And the louts come and pound at the great gates, and we pound back again, and shout at them. But this half we only sing in the hall. Come along down to my study."

Their principal employment in the study was to clear out East's table, removing the drawers and ornaments and tablecloth; for he lived in the bottom passage, and his table was in requisition for the singing.

Supper came in due course at seven o'clock, consisting of bread and cheese and beer, which was all saved for the singing; and directly afterwards the fags went to work to prepare the hall. The School-house hall, as has been said, is a great long high room, with two large fires on one side, and two large iron-bound tables, one running down the middle, and the other along the wall opposite the fireplaces. Around the upper fire the fags placed the tables in the form of a horse-shoe, and upon them the jugs with the Saturday night's allowance of beer. Then the big boys used to drop in and take their seats, bringing with them bottled beer and song-books; for although they all knew the songs by heart, it was the thing to have an old manuscript book descended from some departed hero, in which they were all carefully written out.

The sixth-form boys had not yet appeared; so to fill up the gap an interesting and time-honoured ceremony was gone through. Each new boy was placed on the table in turn and made to sing a solo, under the penalty of drinking a large mug of salt and water if he resisted or broke down. However, the new boys all sing like nightingales to-night, and the salt water is not in requisition; Tom, as his part, performing the old west-country song of "The Leather Bottèl" with considerable applause. And at the half-hour down came the sixth and fifth form boys, and take their places at the tables, which are filled up by the next biggest boys, the rest, for whom there is no room at the table, standing round outside.

The glasses and mugs are filled, and then the fugleman strikes up the old sea-song—

> "A wet sheet and a flowing sea,
> And a wind that follows fast," &c.

which is the invariable first song in the School-house, and all the seventy voices join in, not mindful of harmony, but bent on noise, which they attain decidedly, but the general effect isn't bad. And then follow "The British Grenadiers," "Billy Taylor," "The Siege of Seringapatam," "Three Jolly Postboys," and other vociferous songs in rapid succession, including "The Chesapeake and Shannon," a song lately introduced in honour of old Brooke; and when they come to the words—

> "Brave Broke he waved his sword, crying, Now, my lads, aboard,
> And we'll stop their playing Yankee-doodle-dandy oh!"

you expect the roof to come down. The sixth and fifth know that "brave Broke" of the *Shannon* was no sort of relation to our old Brooke. The fourth form are uncertain in their belief, but for the most part hold that old Brooke *was* a midshipman then on board his uncle's ship. And the lower school never doubt for a moment that it was our old Brooke who led the boarders, in what capacity they care not a straw. During the pauses the bottled-beer corks fly rapidly, and the talk is fast and merry, and the big boys, at least all of them who have a fellow-feeling for dry throats, hand their mugs over their shoulders to be emptied by the small ones who stand round behind.

Then Warner, the head of the house, gets up and wants to speak, but he can't, for every boy knows what's coming; and the big boys who sit at the tables pound them and cheer; and the small boys who stand behind pound one another, and cheer, and rush about the hall cheering. Then silence being made, Warner reminds them of the old School-house custom of drinking the healths, on the first night of singing, of those who are going to leave at the end of the half. "He sees that they know what he is going to say already—(loud cheers)—and so won't keep them, but only ask them to treat the toast as it deserves. It is the head of the eleven, the head of big-side football, their leader on this glorious day—Pater Brooke!"

And away goes the pounding and cheering again, becoming deafening when old Brooke gets on his legs: till, a table having broken down, and a gallon or so of beer been upset, and all throats getting dry, silence ensues, and the hero speaks, leaning his hands on the table, and bending a little forwards. No action, no tricks of oratory; plain, strong, and straight, like his play.

"Gentlemen of the School-house! I am very proud of the way in which you have received my name, and I wish I could say all I should like in return. But I know I shan't. However, I'll do the best I can to say what seems to me ought to be said by a fellow who's just going to leave, and who has spent a good slice of his life here. Eight years it is, and eight such years as I can never hope to have again. So now I hope you'll all listen to me—(loud cheers of 'that we will')—for I'm going to talk seriously. You're bound to listen to me, for what's the use of calling me 'pater,' and all that, if you don't mind what I say? And I'm going to talk seriously, because I feel so. It's a jolly time, too, getting to the end of the half, and a goal kicked by us first day—(tremendous applause)—after one of the hardest and fiercest day's play I can remember in eight years—(frantic shoutings). The School played splendidly, too, I will say, and kept it up to the last. That last charge of theirs would have carried away a house. I never thought to see anything again of old Crab there, except little pieces, when I saw him tumbled over by it—(laughter and shouting, and great slapping on the back of Jones by the boys nearest him). Well, but we beat 'em—(cheers). Ay, but why did we beat 'em? Answer me that—(shouts of 'your play'). Nonsense! 'Twasn't the wind and kick-off either—that wouldn't do it. 'Twasn't because we've half-a-dozen of the best players in the school, as we have. I wouldn't change Warner, and Hedge, and Crab, and the young un, for any six on their side—(violent cheers). But half-a-dozen fellows can't keep it up for two hours against two hundred. Why is it, then? I'll tell you what I think. It's because we've more reliance on one another, more of a house feeling, more fellowship than the School can have. Each of us knows and can depend on his next-hand man better—that's why we beat 'em to-day. We've union, they've division—there's the secret—(cheers). But how's this to be kept up? How's it to be improved? That's the question. For I take it we're all in earnest about beating the School, whatever else we care about. I know I'd sooner win two School-house matches running than get the Balliol scholarship any day—(frantic cheers).

"Now, I'm as proud of the house as any one. I believe it's the best house in the school, out-and-out—(cheers). But it's a long way from what I want to see it. First, there's a deal of bullying going on. I know it well. I don't pry about and interfere; that only makes it more underhand, and encourages the small boys to come to us with their fingers in their eyes telling tales, and so we should be worse off than ever. It's very little kindness for the sixth to meddle generally—you youngsters, mind that. You'll be all the better football players for learning to stand it, and to take your own parts, and fight it through. But depend on it, there's nothing breaks up a house like bullying. Bullies are cowards, and one coward makes many; so good-bye to the School-house match if bullying gets ahead here. (Loud applause from the small boys, who look meaningly at Flashman and other boys at the tables.) Then there's fuddling about in the public-house, and drinking bad spirits, and punch, and such rot-gut stuff. That won't make good drop-kicks or chargers of you, take my word for it. You get plenty of good beer here, and that's enough for you; and drinking isn't fine or manly, whatever some of you may think of it.

"One other thing I must have a word about. A lot of you think and say, for I've heard you, 'There's this new doctor hasn't been here so long as some of us, and he's changing all the old customs. Rugby, and the School-house especially, are going to the dogs. Stand up for the good old ways, and down with the Doctor!' Now I'm as fond of old Rugby customs and ways as any of you, and I've been here longer than any of you, and I'll give you a word of advice in time, for I shouldn't like to see any of you getting sacked. 'Down with the Doctor's' easier said than done. You'll find him pretty tight on his perch, I take it, and an awkwardish customer to handle in that line. Besides now, what customs has he put down? There was the good old custom of taking the linchpins out of the farmers' and bagmen's gigs at the fairs, and a cowardly blackguard custom it was. We all know what came of it, and no wonder the Doctor objected to it. But come now, any of you, name a custom that he has put down."

"The hounds," calls out a fifth-form boy, clad in a green cutaway with brass buttons and cord trousers, the leader of the sporting interest, and reputed a great rider and keen hand generally.

"Well, we had six or seven mangey harriers and beagles belonging to the house, I'll allow, and had had them for years, and that the Doctor put them down. But what good ever came of them? Only rows with all the keepers for ten miles round; and big-side Hare and Hounds is better fun ten times over. What else?"

No answer.

"Well, I won't go on. Think it over for yourselves: you'll find, I believe, that he don't meddle with any one that's worth keeping. And mind now, I say again, look out for squalls, if you will go your own way, and that way ain't the Doctor's, for it'll lead to grief. You all know that I'm not the fellow to back a master through thick and thin. If I saw him stopping football, or cricket, or bathing, or sparring, I'd be as ready as any fellow to stand up about it. But he don't—he encourages them; didn't you see him out to-day for half-an-hour watching us?—(loud cheers for the Doctor)—and he's a strong, true man, and a wise one too, and a public-school man too—(cheers)—and so let's stick to him, and talk no more rot, and drink his health as the head of the house—(loud cheers). And now I've done blowing up, and very glad I am to have done. But it's a solemn thing to be thinking of leaving a place which one has lived in and loved for eight years; and if one can say a word for the good of the old house at such a time, why, it should be said, whether bitter or sweet. If I hadn't been proud of the house and you—ay, no one knows how proud—I shouldn't be blowing you up. And now let's get to singing. But before I sit down, I must give you a toast to be drunk with three-times-three and all the honours. It's a toast which I hope every one of us, wherever he may go hereafter, will never fail to drink when he thinks of the brave bright days of his boyhood. It's a toast which should bind us all together, and to those who've gone before and who'll come after us here. It is the dear old School-house—the best house of the best school in England!"

My dear boys, old and young, you who have belonged, or do belong, to other schools and other houses, don't begin throwing my poor little book about the room, and abusing me and it, and vowing you'll read no more when you get to this point. I allow you've provocation for it. But come now—would you, any of you, give a fig for a fellow who didn't believe in, and stand up for, his own house and his own school? You know you wouldn't. Then don't object to me cracking up the old School-house, Rugby. Haven't I a right to do it, when I'm taking all the trouble of writing this true history for all of your benefits? If you ain't satisfied, go and write the history of your own houses in your own times, and say all you know for your own schools and houses, provided it's true, and I'll read it without abusing you.

The last few words hit the audience in their weakest place; they had been not altogether enthusiastic at several parts of old Brooke's speech; but "the best house of the best school in England" was too much for them all, and carried even the sporting and drinking interests off their legs into rapturous applause, and (it is to be hoped) resolutions to lead a new life and remember old Brooke's words: which however they didn't altogether do, as will appear hereafter.

But it required all old Brooke's popularity to carry down parts of his speech; especially that relating to the Doctor. For there are no such bigoted holders by established forms and customs, be they never so foolish or meaningless, as English school-boys, at least as the school-boys of our generation. We magnified into heroes every boy who had left, and looked upon him with awe and reverence when he revisited the place a year or so afterwards, on his way to or from Oxford or Cambridge; and happy was the boy who remembered him, and sure of an audience as he expounded what he used to do and say, though it were sad enough stuff to make angels, not to say head-masters, weep.

We looked upon every trumpery little custom and habit which had obtained in the School as though it had been a law of the Medes and Persians, and regarded the infringement or variation of it as a sort of sacrilege. And the Doctor, than whom no man or boy had a stronger liking for old school customs which were good and sensible, had, as has already been hinted, come into most decided collision with several which were neither the one nor the other. And as old Brooke had said, when he came into collision with boys or customs, there was nothing for them but to give in or take themselves off; because what he said had to be done, and no mistake about it. And this was beginning to be pretty clearly understood; the boys felt that there was a strong man over them, who would have things his own way; and hadn't yet learned that he was a wise and loving man also. His personal character and influence had not had time to make itself felt, except by a very few of the bigger boys with whom he came more directly into contact; and he was looked upon with great fear and dislike by the great majority even of his own house. For he had found School, and School-house, in a state of monstrous licence and misrule, and was still employed in the necessary but unpopular work of setting up order with a strong hand.

However, as has been said, old Brooke triumphed, and the boys cheered him and then the Doctor. And then more songs came, and the healths of the other boys about to leave, who each made a speech, one flowery, another maudlin, a third prosy, and so on, which are not necessary to be here recorded.

Half-past nine struck in the middle of the performance of "Auld Lang Syne," a most obstreperous proceeding; during which there was an immense amount of standing with one foot on the table, knocking mugs together and shaking hands, without which accompaniments it seems impossible for the youth of Britain to take part in that famous old song. The under-porter of the School-house entered during the performance, bearing five or six long wooden candlesticks with lighted dips in them, which he proceeded to stick into their holes in such part of the great tables as he could get at; and then stood outside the ring till the end of the song, when he was hailed with shouts.

"Bill, you old muff, the half-hour hasn't struck." "Here, Bill, drink some cocktail." "Sing us a song, old boy." "Don't you wish you may get the table?" Bill drank the proffered cocktail not unwillingly, and putting down the empty glass, remonstrated, "Now, gentlemen, there's only ten minutes to prayers, and we must get the hall straight."

Shouts of "No, no!" and a violent effort to strike up "Billy Taylor" for the third time. Bill looked appealingly to old Brooke, who got up and stopped the noise. "Now then, lend a hand, you youngsters, and get the tables back, clear away the jugs and glasses. Bill's right. Open the windows, Warner." The boy addressed, who sat by the long ropes, proceeded to pull up the great windows, and let in a clear fresh rush of night air, which made the candles flicker and gutter, and the fires roar. The circle broke up, each collaring his own jug, glass, and song-book; Bill pounced on the big table, and began to rattle it away to its place outside the buttery-door. The lower-passage boys carried off their small tables, aided by their friends; while above all, standing on the great hall-

table, a knot of untiring sons of harmony made night doleful by a prolonged performance of "God save the King." His Majesty King William IV. then reigned over us, a
monarch deservedly popular amongst the boys addicted to melody, to whom he was
chiefly known from the beginning of that excellent, if slightly vulgar, song in which they
much delighted—

> "Come, neighbours all, both great and small,
>   Perform your duties here,
> And loudly sing 'live Billy our king,'
>   For bating the tax upon beer."

Others of the more learned in songs also celebrated his praises in a sort of ballad, which
I take to have been written by some Irish loyalist. I have forgotten all but the chorus,
which ran—

> "God save our good King William, be his name for ever blest,
>   He's the father of all his people, and the guardian of all the rest."

In troth we were loyal subjects in those days, in a rough way. I trust that our successors
make as much of her present Majesty, and, having regard to the greater refinement of
the times, have adopted or written other songs equally hearty, but more civilized, in her
honour.

Then the quarter to ten struck, and the prayer-bell rang. The sixth and fifth form
boys ranged themselves in their school order along the wall, on either side of the great
fires, the middle-fifth and upper school boys round the long table in the middle of the
hall, and the lower-school boys round the upper part of the second long table, which
ran down the side of the hall furthest from the fires. Here Tom found himself at the
bottom of all in a state of mind and body not at all fit for prayers, as he thought; and so
tried hard to make himself serious, but couldn't, for the life of him, do anything but
repeat in his head the choruses of some of the songs, and stare at all the boys opposite,
wondering at the brilliancy of their waistcoats, and speculating what sort of fellows they
were. The steps of the head-porter are heard on the stairs, and a light gleams at the
door. "Hush!" from the fifth-form boys who stand there, and then in strides the Doctor,
cap on head, book in one hand, and gathering up his gown in the other. He walks up
the middle, and takes his post by Warner, who begins calling over the names. The
Doctor takes no notice of anything, but quietly turns over his book and finds the place,
and then stands, cap in hand and finger in book, looking straight before his nose. He
knows better than any one when to look, and when to see nothing; to-night is singing
night, and there's been lots of noise and no harm done; nothing but beer drunk, and
nobody the worse for it; though some of them do look hot and excited. So the Doctor
sees nothing, but fascinates Tom in a horrible manner as he stands there, and reads out
the Psalm, in that deep, ringing, searching voice of his. Prayers are over, and Tom still
stares open-mouthed after the Doctor's retiring figure, when he feels a pull at his sleeve,
and turning round, sees East.

"I say, were you ever tossed in a blanket?"

"No," said Tom; "why?"

" 'Cause there'll be tossing to-night, most likely, before the sixth come up to bed. So if you funk, you just come along and hide, or else they'll catch you and toss you."

"Were you ever tossed? Does it hurt?" inquired Tom.

"Oh yes, bless you, a dozen times," said East, as he hobbled along by Tom's side up-stairs. "It don't hurt unless you fall on the floor. But most fellows don't like it."

They stopped at the fireplace in the top passage, where were a crowd of small boys whispering together, and evidently unwilling to go up into the bedrooms. In a minute, however, a study door opened, and a sixth-form boy came out, and off they all scuttled up the stairs, and then noiselessly dispersed to their different rooms. Tom's heart beat rather quick as he and East reached their room, but he had made up his mind. "I shan't hide, East," said he.

"Very well, old fellow," replied East, evidently pleased; "no more shall I—they'll be here for us directly."

The room was a great big one with a dozen beds in it, but not a boy that Tom could see except East and himself. East pulled off his coat and waistcoat, and then sat on the bottom of his bed whistling and pulling off his boots; Tom followed his example.

A noise and steps are heard in the passage, the door opens, and in rush four or five great fifth-form boys, headed by Flashman in his glory.

Tom and East slept in the further corner of the room, and were not seen at first.

"Gone to ground, eh?" roared Flashman; "push 'em out then, boys! look under the beds:" and he pulled up the little white curtain of the one nearest him. "Who-o-op," he roared, pulling away at the leg of a small boy, who held on tight to the leg of the bed, and sung out lustily for mercy.

"Here, lend a hand, one of you, and help me pull out this young howling brute. Hold your tongue, sir, or I'll kill you."

"Oh, please, Flashman, please, Walker, don't toss me! I'll fag for you, I'll do anything, only don't toss me."

"You be hanged," said Flashman, lugging the wretched boy along, " 'twon't hurt you,——you! Come along, boys, here he is."

"I say, Flashey," sung out another of the big boys, "drop that; you heard what old Pater Brooke said to-night. I'll be hanged if we'll toss any one against their will—no more bullying. Let him go, I say."

Flashman, with an oath and a kick, released his prey, who rushed headlong under his bed again, for fear they should change their minds, and crept along underneath the other beds, till he got under that of the sixth-form boy, which he knew they daren't disturb.

There's plenty of youngsters don't care about it," said Walker. "Here, here's Scud East—you'll be tossed, won't you, young un?" Scud was East's nickname, or Black, as we called it, gained by his fleetness of foot.

"Yes," said East, "if you like, only mind my foot."

"And here's another who didn't hide. Hullo! new boy; what's your name, sir?"

"Brown."

"Well, Whitey Brown, you don't mind being tossed?"

"No," said Tom, setting his teeth.

"Come along then, boys," sung out Walker, and away they all went, carrying along Tom and East, to the intense relief of four or five other small boys, who crept out from under the beds and behind them.

"What a trump Scud is!" said one. "They won't come back here now."

"And that new boy, too; he must be a good plucked one."

"Ah! wait till he has been tossed on to the floor; see how he'll like it then!"

Meantime the procession went down the passage to Number 7, the largest room, and the scene of the tossing, in the middle of which was a great open space. Here they joined other parties of the bigger boys, each with a captive or two, some willing to be tossed, some sullen, and some frightened to death. At Walker's suggestion all who were afraid were let off, in honour of Pater Brooke's speech.

Then a dozen big boys seized hold of a blanket, dragged from one of the beds. "In with Scud! quick, there's no time to lose." East was chucked into the blanket. "Once, twice, thrice, and away!" up he went like a shuttlecock, but not quite up to the ceiling.

"Now, boys, with a will," cried Walker, "once, twice, thrice, and away!" This time he went clean up, and kept himself from touching the ceiling with his hand, and so again a third time, when he was turned out, and up went another boy. And then came Tom's turn. He lay quite still, by East's advice, and didn't dislike the "once, twice, thrice"; but the "away" wasn't so pleasant. They were in good wind now, and sent him slap up to the ceiling first time, against which his knees came rather sharply. But the moment's pause before descending was the rub, the feeling of utter helplessness and of leaving his whole inside behind him sticking to the ceiling. Tom was very near shouting to be set down, when he found himself back in the blanket, but thought of East, and didn't; and so took his three tosses without a kick or a cry, and was called a young trump for his pains.

He and East, having earned it, stood now looking on. No catastrophe happened, as all the captives were cool hands, and didn't struggle. This didn't suit Flashman. What your real bully likes in tossing, is when the boys kick and struggle, or hold on to one side of the blanket, and so get pitched bodily on to the floor; it's no fun to him when no one is hurt or frightened.

"Let's toss two of them together, Walker," suggested he.

"What a cursed bully you are, Flashey!" rejoined the other. "Up with another one."

And so no two boys were tossed together, the peculiar hardship of which is, that it's too much for human nature to lie still then and share troubles; and so the wretched pair of small boys struggle in the air which shall fall a-top in the descent, to the no small risk of both falling out of the blanket, and the huge delight of brutes like Flashman.

But now there's a cry that the præposter of the room is coming; so the tossing stops, and all scatter to their different rooms; and Tom is left to turn in, with the first day's experience of a public school to meditate upon.

CHAPTER VII
SETTLING TO THE COLLAR

"Says Giles, ' 'Tis mortal hard to go,
    But if so be's I must:
I means to follow arter he
    As goes hisself the fust.' "
BALLAD

Everybody, i suppose, knows the dreamy delicious state in which one lies, half asleep, half awake, while consciousness begins to return after a sound night's rest in a new place which we are glad to be in, following upon a day of unwonted excitement and exertion. There are few pleasanter pieces of life. The worst of it is that they last such a short time; for nurse them as you will, by lying perfectly passive in mind and body, you can't make more than five minutes or so of them. After which time the stupid, obtrusive, wakeful entity which we call "I," as impatient as he is stiff-necked, spite of our teeth will force himself back again, and take possession of us down to our very toes.

It was in this state that Master Tom lay at half-past seven on the morning following the day of his arrival, and from his clean little white bed watched the movements of

Bogle (the generic name by which the successive shoeblacks of the School-house were known), as he marched round from bed to bed, collecting the dirty shoes and boots, and depositing clean ones in their places.

There he lay, half-doubtful as to where exactly in the universe he was, but conscious that he had made a step in life which he had been anxious to make. It was only just light as he looked lazily out of the wide windows, and saw the tops of the great elms, and the rooks circling about, and cawing remonstrances to the lazy ones of their commonwealth before starting in a body for the neighbouring ploughed fields. The noise of the room-door closing behind Bogle, as he made his exit with the shoe-basket under his arm, roused him thoroughly, and he sat up in bed and looked round the room. What in the world could be the matter with his shoulders and loins? He felt as if he had been severely beaten all down his back, the natural results of his performances at his first match. He drew up his knees and rested his chin on them, and went over all the events of yesterday, rejoicing in his new life, what he had seen of it, and all that was to come.

Presently one or two of the other boys roused themselves, and began to sit up and talk to one another in low tones. Then East, after a roll or two, came to an anchor also, and, nodding to Tom, began examining his ankle.

"What a pull," said he, "that it's lie-in-bed, for I shall be as lame as a tree, I think."

It was Sunday morning, and Sunday lectures had not yet been established; so that nothing but breakfast intervened between bed and eleven o'clock chapel—a gap by no means easy to fill up: in fact, though received with the correct amount of grumbling, the first lecture instituted by the Doctor shortly afterwards was a great boon to the School. It was lie-in-bed, and no one was in a hurry to get up, especially in rooms where the sixth-form boy was a good-tempered fellow, as was the case in Tom's room, and allowed the small boys to talk and laugh and do pretty much what they pleased, so long as they didn't disturb him. His bed was a bigger one than the rest, standing in the corner by the fire-place, with a washing-stand and large basin by the side, where he lay in state with his white curtains tucked in so as to form a retiring place: an awful subject of contemplation to Tom, who slept nearly opposite, and watched the great man rouse himself and take a book from under his pillow, and begin reading, leaning his head on his hand, and turning his back to the room. Soon, however, a noise of striving urchins arose, and muttered encouragements from the neighbouring boys, of "Go it, Tadpole!" "Now, young Green!" "Haul away his blanket!" "Slipper him on the hands!" Young Green and little Hall, commonly called Tadpole, from his great black head and thin legs, slept side by side far away by the door, and were for ever playing one another tricks, which usually ended, as on this morning, in open and violent collision; and now, unmindful of all order and authority, there they were, each hauling away at the other's bedclothes with one hand, and with the other, armed with a slipper, belabouring whatever portion of the body of his adversary came within reach.

"Hold that noise up in the corner," called out the præpostor, sitting up and looking round his curtains; and the Tadpole and young Green sank down into their disordered beds; and then, looking at his watch, added, "Hullo, past eight!—whose turn for hot water?"

(Where the præpostor was particular in his ablutions, the fags in his room had to descend in turn to the kitchen, and beg or steal hot water for him; and often the custom extended further, and two boys went down every morning to get a supply for the whole room.)

"East's and Tadpole's," answered the senior fag, who kept the rota.

"I can't go," said East, "I'm dead lame."

"Well, be quick some of you, that's all," said the great man, as he turned out of bed, and putting on his slippers, went out into the great passage, which runs the whole length of the bedrooms, to get his Sunday habiliments out of his portmanteau.

"Let me go for you," said Tom to East, "I should like it."

"Well, thank'ee, that's a good fellow. Just pull on your trousers, and take your jug and mine, Tadpole will show you the way."

And so Tom and the Tadpole, in nightshirts and trousers, started off down-stairs, and through "Thos's hole," as the little buttery, where candles and beer and bread and cheese were served out at night, was called, across the School-house court, down a long passage, and into the kitchen; where, after some parley with the stalwart, handsome cook, who declared that she had filled a dozen jugs already, they got their hot water, and returned with all speed and great caution. As it was, they narrowly escaped capture by some privateers from the fifth-form rooms, who were on the look-out for the hot-water convoys, and pursued them up to the very door of their room, making them spill half their load in the passage. "Better than going down again tho'," as Tadpole remarked, "as we should have had to do if those beggars had caught us."

By the time that the calling-over bell rang, Tom and his new comrades were all down, dressed in their best clothes, and he had the satisfaction of answering "here" to his name for the first time, the præpostor of the week having put it in at the bottom of his list. And then came breakfast and a saunter about the close and town with East, whose lameness only became severe when any fagging had to be done. And so they whiled away the time until morning chapel.

It was a fine November morning, and the close soon became alive with boys of all ages, who sauntered about on the grass, or walked round the gravel walk, in parties of two or three. East, still doing the cicerone, pointed out all the remarkable characters to Tom as they passed: Osbert, who could throw a cricket-ball from the little side-ground over the rook trees to the Doctor's wall; Gray, who had got the Balliol scholarship, and, what East evidently thought of much more importance, a half-holiday for the School by his success; Thorne, who had run ten miles in two minutes over the hour; Black, who had held his own against the cock of the town in the last row with the louts; and many more heroes, who then and there walked about and were worshipped, all trace of whom has long since vanished from the scene of their fame; and the fourth-form boy who reads their names rudely cut out on the old hall tables, or painted upon the big side-cupboard (if hall tables, and big side-cupboards still exist), wonders what manner of boys they were. It will be the same with you who wonder, my sons, whatever your prowess may be in cricket, or scholarship, or football. Two or three years, more or less, and then the steadily advancing, blessed wave will pass over your names as it has passed over ours. Nevertheless, play your games and do your work manfully—see only that that be done, and let the remembrance of it take care of itself.

The chapel-bell began to ring at a quarter to eleven, and Tom got in early and took his place in the lowest row, and watched all the other boys come in and take their places, filling row after row; and tried to construe the Greek text which was inscribed over the door with the slightest possible success, and wondered which of the masters, who walked down the chapel and took their seats in the exalted boxes at the end, would be his lord. And then came the closing of the doors, and the Doctor in his robes, and the service, which, however, didn't impress him much, for his feeling of wonder and curiosity was too strong. And the boy on one side of him was scratching his name on the oak panelling in front, and he couldn't help watching to see what the name was, and whether it was well scratched: and the boy on the other side went to sleep and kept falling against him; and on the whole, though many boys even in that part of the school were serious and attentive, the general atmosphere was by no means devotional; and when he got out into the close again, he didn't feel at all comfortable, or as if he had been to church.

But at afternoon chapel it was quite another thing. He had spent the time after dinner in writing home to his mother, and so was in a better frame of mind; and his first curiosity was over, and he could attend more to the service. As the hymn after the prayers was being sung, and the chapel was getting a little dark, he was beginning to feel that he had been really worshipping. And then came that great event in his, as in every Rugby boy's life of that day—the first sermon from the Doctor.

More worthy pens than mine have described that scene. The oak pulpit standing out by itself above the School seats. The tall, gallant form, the kindling eye, the voice, now soft as the low notes of a flute, now clear and stirring as the call of the light infantry bugle, of him who stood there Sunday after Sunday, witnessing and pleading for his Lord, the King of righteousness and love and glory, with whose Spirit he was filled, and in whose power he spoke. The long lines of young faces, rising tier above tier down the whole length of the chapel, from the little boy's who had just left his mother to the young man's who was going out next week into the great world rejoicing in his strength. It was a great and solemn sight, and never more so than at this time of year, when the only lights in the chapel were in the pulpit and at the seats of the præpostors of the week, and the soft twilight stole over the rest of the chapel, deepening into darkness in the high gallery behind the organ.

But what was it after all which seized and held these three hundred boys, dragging them out of themselves, willing or unwilling, for twenty minutes, on Sunday afternoons? True, there always were boys scattered up and down the School, who in heart and head were worthy to hear and able to carry away the deepest and wisest words there spoken. But these were a minority always, generally a very small one, often so small a one as to be countable on the fingers of your hand. What was it that moved and held us, the rest of the three hundred reckless, childish boys, who feared the Doctor with all our hearts, and very little besides in heaven or earth; who thought more of our sets in the School than of the Church of Christ, and put the traditions of Rugby and the public opinion of boys in our daily life above the laws of God? We couldn't enter into half that we heard; we hadn't the knowledge of our own hearts or the knowledge of one another; and little enough of the faith, hope, and love needed to that end. But we listened, as all boys in their better moods will listen (ay, and men too for the matter of that), to a man whom we felt to be, with all his heart and soul and strength, striving against whatever was mean and unmanly and unrighteous in our little world. It was not the cold clear voice of one giving advice and warning from serene heights to those who were struggling and sinning below, but the warm living voice of one who was fighting for us and by our sides, and calling on us to help him and ourselves and one another. And so, wearily and little by little, but surely and steadily on the whole, was brought home to the young boy, for the first time, the meaning of his life: that it was no fool's or sluggard's paradise into which he had wandered by chance, but a battle-field ordained from of old, where there are no spectators, but the youngest must take his side, and the stakes are life and death. And he who roused this consciousness in them, showed them at the same time, by every word he spoke in the pulpit, and by his whole daily life, how that battle was to be fought; and stood there before them their fellow-soldier and the captain of their band. The true sort of captain, too, for a boy's army, one who had no misgivings, and gave no uncertain word of command, and, let who would yield or make truce, would fight the fight out (so every boy felt) to the last gasp and the last drop of blood. Other sides of his character might take hold of and influence boys here and there, but it was this thoroughness and undaunted courage which more than anything else won his way to the hearts of the great mass of those on whom he left his mark, and made them believe first in him, and then in his Master.

It was this quality above all others which moved such boys as our hero, who had nothing whatever remarkable about him except excess of boyishness: by which I mean animal life in its fullest measure, good nature and honest impulses, hatred of injustice and meanness, and thoughtlessness enough to sink a three-decker. And so, during the next two years, in which it was more than doubtful whether he would get good or evil from the School, and before any steady purpose or principle grew up in him, whatever his week's sins and shortcomings might have been, he hardly ever left the chapel on Sunday evenings without a serious resolve to stand by and follow the Doctor, and a feeling that it was only cowardice (the incarnation of all other sins in such a boy's mind) which hindered him from doing so with all his heart.

The next day Tom was duly placed in the third form, and began his lessons in a corner of the big School. He found the work very easy, as he had been well grounded and knew his grammar by heart; and, as he had no intimate companions to make him idle (East and his other School-house friends being in the lower-fourth, the form above him), soon gained golden opinions from his master, who said he was placed too low, and should be put out at the end of the half-year. So all went well with him in School, and he wrote the most flourishing letters home to his mother, full of his own success and the unspeakable delights of a public school.

In the house, too, all went well. The end of the half-year was drawing near, which kept everybody in a good humour, and the house was ruled well and strongly by Warner and Brooke. True, the general system was rough and hard, and there was bullying in nooks and corners, bad signs for the future; but it never got further, or dared show itself openly, stalking about the passages and hall and bedrooms, and making the life of the small boys a continual fear.

Tom, as a new boy, was of right excused fagging for the first month, but in his enthusiasm for his new life this privilege hardly pleased him; and East and others of his young friends discovering this, kindly allowed him to indulge his fancy, and take their turns at night fagging and cleaning studies. These were the principal duties of the fags in the house. From supper until nine o'clock three fags taken in order stood in the passages, and answered any præpostor who called "Fag," racing to the door, the last comer having to do the work. This consisted generally of going to the buttery for beer

and bread and cheese (for the great men did not sup with the rest, but had each his own allowance in his study or the fifth-form room), cleaning candlesticks and putting in new candles, toasting cheese, bottling beer, and carrying messages about the house; and Tom, in the first blush of his hero-worship, felt it a high privilege to receive orders from, and be the bearer of the supper of Old Brooke. And besides this night-work, each præpostor had three or four fags specially allotted to him, of whom he was supposed to be the guide, philosopher, and friend, and who in return for these good offices had to clean out his study every morning by turns, directly after first lesson and before he returned from breakfast. And the pleasure of seeing the great men's studies, and looking at their pictures, and peeping into their books, made Tom a ready substitute for any boy who was too lazy to do his own work. And so he soon gained the character of a good-natured, willing fellow, who was ready to do a turn for any one.

In all the games too he joined with all his heart, and soon became well versed in all the mysteries of football, by continual practice at the School-house little-side, which played daily.

The only incident worth recording here, however, was his first run at Hare-and-hounds. On the last Tuesday but one of the half-year he was passing through the hall after dinner, when he was hailed with shouts from Tadpole, and several other fags seated at one of the long tables, the chorus of which was, "Come and help us tear up scent."

Tom approached the table in obedience to the mysterious summons, always ready to help, and found the party engaged in tearing up old newspapers, copy-books, and magazines, into small pieces, with which they were filling four large canvas bags.

"It's the turn of our house to find scent for Big-side Hare-and-hounds," exclaimed Tadpole; "tear away, there's no time to lose before calling-over."

"I think it's a great shame," said another small boy, "to have such a hard run for the last day."

"Which run is it?" said Tadpole.

"Oh, the Barby run, I hear," answered the other; "nine miles at least, and hard ground; no chance of getting in at the finish, unless you're a first-rate scud."

"Well, I'm going to have a try," said Tadpole; "it's the last run of the half, and if a fellow gets in at the end, Big-side stands ale and bread and cheese and a bowl of punch; and the Cock's such a famous place for ale."

"I should like to try too," said Tom.

"Well then, leave your waistcoat behind, and listen at the door, after calling-over, and you'll hear where the meet is."

After calling-over, sure enough, there were two boys at the door, calling out, "Big-side Hare-and-hounds meet at White Hall;" and Tom, having girded himself with leather strap, and left all superfluous clothing behind, set off for White Hall, an old gable-ended house some quarter of a mile from the town, with East, whom he had persuaded to join, notwithstanding his prophecy that they could never get in, as it was the hardest run of the year.

At the meet they found some forty or fifty boys, and Tom felt sure, from having seen many of them run at football, that he and East were more likely to get in than they.

After a few minutes' waiting, two well-known runners, chosen for the hares, buckled on the four bags filled with scent, compared their watches with those of young Brooke and Thorne, and started off at a long, slinging trot across the fields in the direction of Barby.

Then the hounds clustered round Thorne, who explained shortly, "They're to have six minutes' law. We run into the Cock, and every one who comes in within a quarter of an hour of the hares 'll be counted, if he has been round Barby church." Then came a minute's pause or so, and then the watches are pocketed, and the pack is led through the gateway into the field which the hares had first crossed. Here they break into a trot, scattering over the field to find the first traces of the scent which the hares throw out as they go along. The old hounds make straight for the likely points, and in a minute a cry of "forward" comes from one of them, and the whole pack quickening their pace make for the spot, while the boy who hit the scent first, and the two or three nearest to him, are over the first fence, and making play along the hedgerow in the long grass-field beyond. The rest of the pack rush at the gap already made, and scramble through, jostling one another. "Forward" again, before they are half through; the pace quickens into a sharp run, the tail hounds all straining to get up to the lucky leaders. They are gallant hares, and the scent lies thick right across another meadow and into a ploughed field, where the pace begins to tell; then over a good wattle with a ditch on the other side, and down a large pasture studded with old thorns, which slopes down to the first brook; the great Leicestershire sheep charge away across the field as the pack comes racing down the slope. The brook is a small one, and the scent lies right ahead up the opposite slope, and as thick as ever; not a turn or a check to favour the tail hounds, who strain on, now trailing in a long line, many a youngster beginning to drag his legs heavily, and feel his heart beat like a hammer, and the bad plucked ones thinking that after all it isn't worth while to keep it up.

Tom, East, and the Tadpole had a good start, and are well up for such young hands, and after rising the slope and crossing the next field, find themselves up with the leading hounds, who have over-run the scent and are trying back; they have come a mile and a half in about eleven minutes, a pace which shows that it is the last day. About twenty-five of the original starters only show here, the rest having already given in; the leaders are busy making casts into the fields on the left and right, and the others get their second winds.

Then comes the cry of "Forward" again, from young Brooke, from the extreme left, and the pack settles down to work again steadily and doggedly, the whole keeping pretty well together. The scent, though still good, is not so thick; there is no need of that, for in this part of the run every one knows the line which must be taken, and so there are no casts to be made, but good downright running and fencing to be done. All who are now up mean coming in, and they come to the foot of Barby Hill without losing more than two or three more of the pack. This last straight two miles and a half is always a vantage ground for the hounds, and the hares know it well; they are generally viewed on the side of Barby Hill, and all eyes are on the look-out for them to-day. But not a sign of them appears, so now will be the hard work for the hounds, and there is nothing for it but to cast about for the scent, for it is now the hares' turn, and they may baffle the pack dreadfully in the next two miles.

Ill fares it now with our youngsters that they are School-house boys, and so follow young Brooke, for he takes the wide casts round to the left, conscious of his own powers, and loving the hard work. For if you would consider for a moment, you small boys, you would remember that the Cock, where the run ends and the good ale will be going, lies far out to the right on the Dunchurch road, so that every cast you take to the left is so much extra work. And at this stage of the run, when the evening is closing in already, no one remarks whether you run a little cunning or not; so you should stick to those crafty hounds who keep edging away to the right, and not follow a prodigal like young Brooke, whose legs are twice as long as yours and of cast-iron, wholly indifferent to one or two miles more or less. However, they struggle after him, sobbing and plunging along, Tom and East pretty close, and Tadpole, whose big head begins to pull him down, some thirty yards behind.

Now comes a brook, with stiff clay banks, from which they can hardly drag their legs, and they hear faint cries for help from the wretched Tadpole, who has fairly stuck fast. But they have too little run left in themselves to pull up for their own brothers. Three fields more, and another check, and then "forward" called away to the extreme right.

The two boys' souls die within them; they can never do it. Young Brooke thinks so too, and says kindly, "You'll cross a lane after next field, keep down it, and you'll hit the Dunchurch road below the Cock," and then steams away for the run in, in which he's sure to be first, as if he were just starting. They struggle on across the next field, the "forwards" getting fainter and fainter, and then ceasing. The whole hunt is out of ear-shot, and all hope of coming in is over.

"Hang it all!" broke out East, as soon as he had got wind enough, pulling off his hat and mopping at his face, all spattered with dirt and lined with sweat, from which went up a thick stream into the still cold air. "I told you how it would be. What a thick I was to come! Here we are, dead beat, and yet I know we're close to the run in, if we knew the country."

"Well," said Tom, mopping away, and gulping down his disappointment, "it can't be

helped. We did our best, anyhow. Hadn't we better find this lane and go down it, as young Brooke told us?"

"I suppose so—nothing else for it," grunted East. "If ever I go out last day again," growl—growl—growl.

So they tried back slowly and sorrowfully, and found the lane, and went limping down it, plashing in the cold puddly ruts, and beginning to feel how the run had taken it out of them. The evening closed in fast, and clouded over, dark, cold, and dreary.

"I say, it must be locking-up, I should think," remarked East, breaking the silence; "it's so dark."

"What if we're late?" said Tom.

"No tea, and sent up to the Doctor," answered East.

The thought didn't add to their cheerfulness. Presently a faint halloo was heard from an adjoining field. They answered it and stopped, hoping for some competent rustic to guide them, when over a gate some twenty yards ahead crawled the wretched Tadpole, in a state of collapse; he had lost a shoe in the brook, and had been groping after it up to his elbows in the stiff wet clay, and a more miserable creature in the shape of boy seldom has been seen.

The sight of him, notwithstanding, cheered them, for he was some degrees more wretched than they. They also cheered him, as he was no longer under the dread of passing his night alone in the fields. And so, in better heart, the three plashed painfully down the never-ending lane. At last it widened, just as utter darkness set in, and they came out on a turnpike-road, and there paused, bewildered, for they had lost all bearings, and knew not whether to turn to the right or left.

Luckily for them they had not to decide, for lumbering along the road, with one lamp lighted and two spavined horses in the shafts, came a heavy coach, which after a moment's suspense they recognized as the Oxford coach, the redoubtable Pig and Whistle.

It lumbered slowly up, and the boys mustering their last run, caught it as it passed, and began clambering up behind, in which exploit East missed his footing and fell flat on his nose along the road. Then the others hailed the old scarecrow of a coachman, who pulled up and agreed to take them in for a shilling; so there they sat on the back seat, drubbing with their heels, and their teeth chattering with cold, and jogged into Rugby some forty minutes after locking-up.

Five minutes afterwards three small, limping, shivering figures steal along through the Doctor's garden, and into the house by the servants' entrance (all the other gates have been closed long since), where the first thing they light upon in the passage is old Thomas, ambling along, candle in one hand and keys in the other.

He stops and examines their condition with a grim smile. "Ah! East, Hall, and Brown, late for locking-up. Must go up to the Doctor's study at once."

"Well but, Thomas, mayn't we go and wash first? You can put down the time, you know."

"Doctor's study d'rectly you come in—that's the orders," replied old Thomas, motioning towards the stairs at the end of the passage which led up into the Doctor's house; and the boys turned ruefully down it, not cheered by the old verger's muttered remark, "What a pickle they boys be in!" Thomas referred to their faces and habiliments, but they construed it as indicating the Doctor's state of mind. Upon the short flight of stairs they paused to hold counsel.

"Who'll go in first?" inquires Tadpole.

"You—you're the senior," answered East.

"Catch me—look at the state I'm in," rejoined Hall, showing the arms of his jacket. "I must get behind you two."

"Well, but look at me," said East, indicating the mass of clay behind which he was standing; "I'm worse than you, two to one; you might grow cabbages on my trousers."

"That's all down below, and you can keep your legs behind the sofa," said Hall. "Here, Brown, you're the show-figure—you must lead."

"But my face is all muddy," argued Tom.

"Oh, we're all in one boat for that matter; but come on, we're only making it worse, dawdling here."

"Well, just give us a brush then," said Tom; and they began trying to rub off the superfluous dirt from each other's jackets, but it was not dry enough, and the rubbing made them worse; so in despair they pushed through the swing-door at the head of the stairs, and found themselves in the Doctor's hall.

"That's the library door," said East in a whisper, pushing Tom forwards. The sound of merry voices and laughter came from within, and his first hesitating knock was unanswered. But at the second, the Doctor's voice said "Come in," and Tom turned the handle, and he, with the others behind him, sidled into the room.

The Doctor looked up from his task; he was working away with a great chisel at the bottom of a boy's sailing boat, the lines of which he was no doubt fashioning on the model of one of Nicias' galleys. Round him stood three or four children; the candles burnt brightly on a large table at the further end, covered with books and papers, and a great fire threw a ruddy glow over the rest of the room. All looked so kindly, and

homely, and comfortable, that the boys took heart in a moment, and Tom advanced from behind the shelter of the great sofa. The Doctor nodded to the children, who went out, casting curious and amused glances at the three young scarecrows.

"Well, my little fellows," began the Doctor, drawing himself up with his back to the fire, the chisel in one hand and his coat-tails in the other, and his eyes twinkling as he looked them over; "what makes you so late?"

"Please, sir, we've been out Big-side Hare-and-hounds, and lost our way."

"Hah! you couldn't keep up, I suppose?"

"Well, sir," said East, stepping out, and not liking that the Doctor should think lightly of his running powers, "we got round Barby all right, but then—"

"Why, what a state you're in, my boy!" interrupted the Doctor, as the pitiful condition of East's garments was fully revealed to him.

"That's the fall I got, sir, in the road," said East, looking down at himself; "the Old Pig came by—"

"The what?" said the Doctor.

"The Oxford coach, sir," explained Hall.

"Hah! yes, the Regulator," said the Doctor.

"And I tumbled on my face, trying to get up behind," went on East.

"You're not hurt, I hope?" said the Doctor.

"Oh no, sir."

"Well now, run up-stairs, all three of you, and get clean things on, and then tell the housekeeper to give you some tea. You're too young to try such long runs. Let Warner know I've seen you. Good-night."

"Good-night, sir." And away scuttled the three boys in high glee.

"What a brick, not to give us even twenty lines to learn!" said the Tadpole, as they reached their bedroom; and in half an hour afterwards they were sitting by the fire in the housekeeper's room at a sumptuous tea, with cold meat, "twice as good a grub as we should have got in the hall," as the Tadpole remarked with a grin, his mouth full of buttered toast. All their grievances were forgotten, and they were resolving to go out the first Big-side next half, and thinking Hare-and-hounds the most delightful of games.

A day or two afterwards the great passage outside the bedrooms was cleared of the boxes and portmanteaus, which went down to be packed by the matron, and great

games of chariot-racing, and cock-fighting, and bolstering went on in the vacant space, the sure sign of a closing half-year.

Then came the making up of parties for the journey home, and Tom joined a party who were to hire a coach, and post with four horses to Oxford.

Then the last Saturday on which the Doctor came round to each form to give out the prizes, and hear the masters' last reports of how they and their charges had been conducting themselves; and Tom, to his huge delight, was praised, and got his remove into the lower-fourth, in which all his School-house friends were.

On the next Tuesday morning at four o'clock hot coffee was going on in the housekeeper's and matron's rooms; boys wrapped in great-coats and mufflers were swallowing hasty mouthfuls, rushing about, tumbling over luggage, and asking questions all at once of the matron; outside the School-gates were drawn up several chaises and the four-horse coach which Tom's party had chartered, the post-boys in their best jackets and breeches, and a cornopean-player, hired for the occasion, blowing away "A southerly wind and a cloudy sky," waking all peaceful inhabitants half-way down the High Street.

Every minute the bustle and hubbub increased: porters staggered about with boxes and bags, the cornopean played louder. Old Thomas sat in his den with a great yellow bag by his side, out of which he was paying journey-money to each boy, comparing by the light of a solitary dip the dirty, crabbed little list is his own handwriting, with the Doctor's list and the amount of his cash; his head was on one side, his mouth screwed up, and his spectacles dim from early toil. He had prudently locked the door, and carried on his operations solely through the window, or he would have been driven wild and lost all his money.

"Thomas, do be quick, we shall never catch the High-flyer at Dunchurch."

"That's your money, all right, Green."

"Hullo, Thomas, the Doctor said I was to have two-pound-ten; you've only given me two pound."—(I fear that Master Green is not confining himself strictly to truth.) Thomas turns his head more on one side than ever, and spells away at the dirty list. Green is forced away from the window.

"Here, Thomas, never mind him, mine's thirty shillings." "And mine too," "and mine," shouted others.

One way or another, the party to which Tom belonged all got packed and paid, and

sallied out to the gates, the cornopean playing frantically "Drops of Brandy," in allusion, probably, to the slight potations in which the musician and postboys had been already indulging. All luggage was carefully stowed away inside the coach and in the front and hind boots, so that not a hat-box was visible outside. Five or six small boys, with pea-shooters, and the cornopean-player, got up behind; in front the big boys, mostly smoking, not for pleasure, but because they are now gentlemen at large—and this is the most correct public method of notifying the fact.

"Robinson's coach will be down the road in a minute, it has gone up to Bird's to pick up,—we'll wait till they're close, and make a race of it," says the leader. "Now, boys, half-a-sovereign apiece if you beat 'em into Dunchurch by one hundred yards."

"All right, sir," shouted the grinning postboys.

Down comes Robinson's coach in a minute or two, with a rival cornopean, and away go the two vehicles, horses galloping, boys cheering, horns playing loud. There is a special providence over schoolboys as well as sailors, or they must have upset twenty times in the first five miles; sometimes actually abreast of one another, and the boys on the roofs exchanging volleys of peas, now nearly running over a post-chaise which had started before them, now half-way up a bank, now with a wheel-and-a-half over a yawning ditch; and all this in a dark morning, with nothing but their own lamps to guide them. However, it's all over at last, and they have run over nothing but an old pig in Southam Street; the last peas are distributed in the Corn Market at Oxford, where they arrive between eleven and twelve, and sit down to a sumptuous breakfast at the Angel, which they are made to pay for accordingly. Here the party breaks up, all going now different ways; and Tom orders out a chaise and pair as grand as a lord, though he has scarcely five shillings left in his pocket and more than twenty miles to get home.

"Where to, sir?"

"Red Lion, Farringdon," says Tom, giving ostler a shilling.

"All right, sir. Red Lion, Jem," to the postboy, and Tom rattles away towards home. At Farringdon, being known to the innkeeper, he gets that worthy to pay for the Oxford horses and forward him in another chaise at once; and so the gorgeous young gentleman arrives at the paternal mansion, and Squire Brown looks rather blue at having to pay two pound ten shillings for the posting expenses from Oxford. But the boy's intense joy at getting home, and the wonderful health he is in, and the good character he brings, and the brave stories he tells of Rugby, its doings and delights, soon mollify the Squire, and three happier people didn't sit down to dinner that day in England (it is the boy's first dinner at six o'clock at home, great promotion already) than the Squire and his wife and Tom Brown, at the end of his first half year at Rugby.

CHAPTER VIII

THE WAR OF INDEPENDENCE

"They are slaves who will not choose
Hatred, scoffing, and abuse,
Rather than in silence shrink
From the truth they needs must think:
They are slaves who dare not be
In the right with two or three."
(LOWELL, *Stanzas on Freedom*)

T HE LOWER-FOURTH FORM, in which Tom found himself at the beginning of the next half-year, was the largest form in the Lower school, and numbered upwards of forty boys. Young gentlemen of all ages from nine to fifteen were to be found there, who expended such part of their energies as was devoted to Latin and Greek upon a book of Livy, the Bucolics of Virgil, and the Hecuba of Euripides, which were ground out in small daily portions. The driving of this unlucky lower-fourth must have been grievous work to the unfortunate master, for it was the most unhappily constituted of any in the school. Here stuck the great stupid boys, who for the life of them could never master the accidence; the objects alternately of mirth and terror to the youngsters, who were daily taking them up and laughing at them in lesson, and getting kicked by them for so doing in play-hours. There were no less than three unhappy fellows in tail coats, with incipient down on their chins, whom the Doctor and the master of the form were always endeavouring to hoist into the Upper school, but whose parsing and construing resisted the most well-meant shoves. Then came the mass of the form, boys of eleven and twelve, the most mischievous and reckless age of British youth, of whom East and Tom Brown were fair specimens. As full of tricks as monkeys, and of excuses as Irish women, making fun of their master, one another, and their lessons, Argus himself would have been puzzled to keep an eye on them; and as for making them steady or serious for half an hour together, it was simply hopeless. The remainder of the form consisted of young prodigies of nine and ten, who were going up the school at the rate of a form a half-year, all boys' hands and wits being against them in their progress. It would have been one man's work to see that the precocious youngsters had fair play; and as the master had a good deal besides to do, they hadn't, and were for ever being shoved down three or four places, their verses stolen, their books inked, their jackets whitened, and their lives otherwise made a burden to them.

The lower-fourth, and all the forms below it, were heard in the great school, and were not trusted to prepare their lessons before coming in, but were whipped into school three-quarters of an hour before the lesson began by their respective masters, and there, scattered about on the benches, with dictionary and grammar, hammered out their twenty lines of Virgil and Euripides in the midst of Babel. The masters of the Lower school walked up and down the great school together during this three-quarters of an hour, or sat in their desks reading or looking over copies, and keeping such order as was possible. But the lower-fourth was just now an overgrown form, too large for any one man to attend to properly, and consequently the elysium or ideal form of the young scapegraces who formed the staple of it.

Tom, as has been said, had come up from the third with a good character, but the temptations of the lower-fourth soon proved too strong for him, and he rapidly fell away, and became as unmanageable as the rest. For some weeks, indeed, he succeeded in maintaining the appearance of steadiness, and was looked upon favourably by his new master, whose eyes were first opened by the following little incident.

Besides the desk which the master himself occupied, there was another large unoccupied desk in the corner of the great school, which was untenanted. To rush and seize upon this desk, which was ascended by three steps and held four boys, was the great object of ambition of the lower fourthers; and the contentions for the occupation of it bred such disorder, that at last the master forbade its use altogether. This of course was a challenge to the more adventurous spirits to occupy it, and as it was capacious enough for two boys to lie hid there completely, it was seldom that it remained empty, notwithstanding the veto. Small holes were cut in the front, through which the occupants watched the masters as they walked up and down, and as lesson time approached, one boy at a time stole out and down the steps, as the masters' backs were turned, and mingled with the general crowd on the forms below. Tom and East had successfully occupied the desk some half-dozen times, and were grown so reckless that they were in the habit of playing small games with fives'-balls inside when the masters were at the other end of the big school. One day, as ill-luck would have it, the game became more exciting than usual, and the ball slipped through East's fingers, and rolled slowly down the steps and out into the middle of the school, just as the masters turned in their walk and faced round upon the desk. The young delinquents watched their master, through the look-out holes, march slowly down the school straight upon their retreat, while all the boys in the neighbourhood of course stopped their work to look on: and not only were they ignominiously drawn out, and caned over the hand then and there, but their characters for steadiness were gone from that time. However, as they only shared the fate of some three-fourths of the rest of the form, this did not weigh heavily upon them.

In fact the only occasions on which they cared about the matter were the monthly examinations, when the Doctor came round to examine their form, for one long awful hour, in the work which they had done in the preceding month. The second monthly examination came round soon after Tom's fall, and it was with anything but lively anticipations that he and the other lower-fourth boys came in to prayers on the morning of the examination day.

Prayers and calling-over seemed twice as short as usual, and before they could get construes of a tithe of the hard passages marked in the margin of their books, they were all seated round, and the Doctor was standing in the middle, talking in whispers to the master. Tom couldn't hear a word which passed, and never lifted his eyes from his book; but he knew by a sort of magnetic instinct that the Doctor's under-lip was coming out, and his eye beginning to burn, and his gown getting gathered up more and more tightly in his left hand. The suspense was agonizing, and Tom knew that he was sure on such occasions to make an example of the School-house boys. "If he would only begin," thought Tom, "I shouldn't mind."

At last the whispering ceased, and the name which was called out was not Brown. He looked up for a moment, but the Doctor's face was too awful; Tom wouldn't have met his eye for all he was worth, and buried himself in his book again.

The boy who was called up first was a clever, merry School-house boy, one of their set: he was some connection of the Doctor's, and a great favourite, and ran in and out of his house as he liked, and so was selected for the first victim.

"Triste lupus stabulis," began the luckless youngster, and stammered through some eight or ten lines.

"There, that will do," said the Doctor; "now construe."

On common occasions, the boy could have construed the passage well enough probably, but now his head was gone.

"Triste lupus, the sorrowful wolf," he began.

A shudder ran through the whole form, and the Doctor's wrath fairly boiled over; he made three steps up to the construer and gave him a good box on the ear. The blow was not a hard one, but the boy was so taken by surprise that he started back; the form caught the back of his knees, and over he went on to the floor behind. There was a dead silence over the whole school; never before and never again while Tom was at school did the Doctor strike a boy in lesson. The provocation must have been great. However, the victim had saved his form for that occasion, for the Doctor turned to the top bench, and put on the best boys for the rest of the hour; and though, at the end of the lesson, he gave them all such a rating as they did not forget, this terrible field-day passed over without any severe visitations in the shape of punishments or floggings. Forty young scapegraces expressed their thanks to the "sorrowful wolf" in their different ways before second lesson.

But a character for steadiness once gone is not easily recovered, as Tom found, and for years afterwards he went up the school without it, and the masters' hands were against him, and his against them. And he regarded them, as a matter of course, as his natural enemies.

Matters were not so comfortable either in the house as they had been, for old Brooke left at Christmas, and one or two others of the sixth-form boys at the following Easter. Their rule had been rough, but strong and just in the main, and a higher standard was beginning to be set up; in fact, there had been a short foretaste of the good time which followed some years later. Just now, however, all threatened to return into darkness and chaos again. For the new præpostors were either small young boys, whose cleverness had carried them up to the top of the school, while in strength of body and character they were not yet fit for a share in the government; or else big fellows of the wrong sort, boys whose friendships and tastes had a downward tendency, who had not caught the meaning of their position and work, and felt none of its responsibilities. So under this no-government the School-house began to see bad times. The big fifth-form boys, who were a sporting and drinking set, soon began to usurp power, and to fag the little boys as if they were præpostors, and to bully and oppress any who showed signs of resistance. The bigger sort of sixth-form boys just described soon made common cause with the fifth, while the smaller sort, hampered by their colleagues' desertion to the enemy, could not make head against them. So the fags were without their lawful masters and protectors, and ridden over rough-shod by a set of boys whom they were not bound to obey, and whose only right over them stood in their bodily powers; and, as old Brooke had prophesied, the house by degrees broke up into small sets and parties, and lost the strong feeling of fellowship which he set so much store by, and with it much of the prowess in games and the lead in all school matters which he had done so much to keep up.

In no place in the world has individual character more weight than at a public school. Remember this, I beseech you, all you boys who are getting into the upper forms. Now is the time in all your lives, probably, when you may have more wide influence for good or evil on the society you live in than you ever can have again. Quit yourselves like men, then; speak up, and strike out if necessary, for whatsoever is true, and manly, and lovely, and of good report; never try to be popular, but only to do your duty and help others to do theirs, and you may leave the tone of feeling in the school higher than you found it, and so be doing good which no living soul can measure to generations of your countrymen yet unborn. For boys follow one another in herds like sheep, for good or evil; they hate thinking, and have rarely any settled principles. Every school, indeed, has its own traditionary standard of right and wrong, which cannot be transgressed with impunity, marking certain things as low and blackguard, and certain others as lawful and right. This standard is ever varying, though it changes only slowly and little by little; and subject only to such standard, it is the leading boys for the time being who give the tone to all the rest, and make the School either a noble institution for the training of Christian Englishmen, or a place where a young boy will get more evil than he would if he were turned out to make his way in London streets, or anything between these two extremes.

The change for the worse in the School-house, however, didn't press very heavily on our youngsters for some time; they were in a good bedroom, where slept the only præpostor left who was able to keep thorough order, and their study was in his passage; so though they were fagged more or less, and occasionally kicked or cuffed by the bullies, they were on the whole well off, and the fresh, brave school-life, so full of games, adventures, and good-fellowship, so ready at forgetting, so capacious at enjoying, so bright at forecasting, outweighed a thousand-fold their troubles with the master of their form, and the occasional ill-usage of the big boys in the house. It wasn't till some year or so after the events recorded above that the præpostor of their room and passage left. None of the other sixth-form boys would move into their passage, and, to the disgust and indignation of Tom and East, one morning after breakfast they were seized upon by Flashman, and made to carry down his books and furniture into the unoccupied study which he had taken. From this time they began to feel the weight of the tyranny of Flashman and his friends, and, now that trouble had come home to their own doors, began to look out for sympathizers and partners amongst the rest of the fags; and meetings of the oppressed began to be held, and murmurs to arise, and plots to be laid as to how they should free themselves and be avenged on their enemies.

While matters were in this state, East and Tom were one evening sitting in their study. They had done their work for first lesson, and Tom was in a brown study, brooding, like a young William Tell, upon the wrongs of fags in general, and his own in particular.

"I say, Scud," said he at last, rousing himself to snuff the candle, "what right have the fifth-form boys to fag us as they do?"

"No more right than you have to fag them," answered East, without looking up from an early number of Pickwick, which was just coming out, and which he was luxuriously devouring, stretched on his back on the sofa.

Tom relapsed into his brown study, and East went on reading and chuckling. The contrast of the boys' faces would have given infinite amusement to a looker-on, the one so solemn and big with mighty purpose, the other radiant and bubbling over with fun.

"Do you know, old fellow, I've been thinking it over a good deal," began Tom again.

"Oh yes, I know, fagging you are thinking of. Hang it all,—but listen here, Tom— here's fun. Mr. Winkle's horse—"

"And I've made up my mind," broke in Tom, "that I won't fag except for the sixth."

"Quite right too, my boy," cried East, putting his finger on the place and looking up; "but a pretty peck of troubles you'll get into, if you're going to play that game. However, I'm all for a strike myself, if we can get others to join—it's getting too bad."

"Can't we get some sixth-form fellow to take it up?" asked Tom.

"Well, perhaps we might; Morgan would interfere, I think. Only," added East, after a moment's pause, "you see, we should have to tell him about it, and that's against School principles. Don't you remember what old Brooke said about learning to take our own parts?"

"Ah, I wish old Brooke were back again—it was all right in his time."

"Why, yes, you see, then the strongest and best fellows were in the sixth, and the fifth-form fellows were afraid of them, and they kept good order; but now our sixth-form fellows are too small, and the fifth don't care for them, and do what they like in the house."

"And so we get a double set of masters," cried Tom, indignantly; "the lawful ones, who are responsible to the Doctor at any rate, and the unlawful—the tyrants, who are responsible to nobody."

"Down with the tyrants!" cried East; "I'm all for law and order, and hurra for a revolution."

"I shouldn't mind if it were only for young Brooke now," said Tom, "he's such a good-hearted, gentlemanly fellow, and ought to be in the sixth—I'd do anything for him. But that blackguard Flashman, who never speaks to one without a kick or an oath—"

"The cowardly brute," broke in East, "how I hate him! And he knows it too, he knows that you and I think him a coward. What a bore that he's got a study in this passage! Don't you hear them now at supper in his den? Brandy punch going, I'll bet. I wish the Doctor would come out and catch him. We must change our study as soon as we can."

"Change or no change, I'll never fag for him again," said Tom, thumping the table.

"Fa-a-a-ag!" sounded along the passage from Flashman's study. The two boys looked at one another in silence. It had struck nine, so the regular night-fags had left duty, and they were the nearest to the supper-party. East sat up, and began to look comical, as he always did under difficulties.

"Fa-a-a-ag!" again. No answer.

"Here, Brown! East! you cursed young skulks," roared out Flashman, coming to his open door, "I know you're in—no shirking."

Tom stole to their door, and drew the bolts as noiselessly as he could; East blew out the candle.

"Barricade the first," whispered he. "Now, Tom, mind, no surrender."

"Trust me for that," said Tom between his teeth.

In another minute they heard the supper-party turn out and come down the passage to their door. They held their breaths, and heard whispering, of which they only made out Flashman's words, "I know the young brutes are in."

Then came summonses to open, which being unanswered, the assault commenced: luckily the door was a good strong oak one, and resisted the united weight of Flashman's party. A pause followed, and they heard a besieger remark, "They're in safe enough—don't you see how the door holds at top and bottom? so the bolts must be drawn. We should have forced the lock long ago." East gave Tom a nudge, to call attention to this scientific remark.

Then came attacks on particular panels, one of which at last gave way to the repeated kicks; but it broke inwards, and the broken pieces got jammed across, the door being lined with green baize, and couldn't easily be removed from outside: and the besieged, scorning further concealment, strengthened their defences by pressing the end of their sofa against the door. So, after one or two more ineffectual efforts, Flashman and Co. retired, vowing vengeance in no mild terms.

The first danger over, it only remained for the besieged to effect a safe retreat, as it was now near bed-time. They listened intently and heard the supper-party resettle themselves, and then gently drew back first one bolt and then the other. Presently the convivial noises began again steadily. "Now then, stand by for a run," said East, throwing the door wide open and rushing into the passage, closely followed by Tom. They were too quick to be caught, but Flashman was on the look-out, and sent an empty pickle-jar whizzing after them, which narrowly missed Tom's head, and broke into twenty pieces at the end of the passage. "He wouldn't mind killing one, if he wasn't caught," said East, as they turned the corner.

There was no pursuit, so the two turned into the hall, where they found a knot of small boys round the fire. Their story was told—the war of independence had broken out—who would join the revolutionary forces? Several others present bound themselves not to fag for the fifth form at once. One or two only edged off, and left the rebels. What else could they do? "I've a good mind to go to the doctor straight," said Tom.

"That'll never do—don't you remember the levy of the school last half?" put in another.

In fact, the solemn assembly, a levy of the school, had been held, at which the captain of the school had got up, and, after premising that several instances had occurred of matters having been reported to the masters; that this was against public morality and School tradition; that a levy of the sixth had been held on the subject, and they had resolved that the practice must be stopped at once; and given out that any boy, in whatever form, who should thenceforth appeal to a master, without having first gone to some præpostor and laid the case before him, should be thrashed publicly, and sent to Coventry.

"Well, then, let's try the sixth. Try Morgan," suggested another. "No use"—"Blabbing won't do," was the general feeling.

"I'll give you fellows a piece of advice," said a voice from the end of the hall. They all turned round with a start, and the speaker got up from a bench on which he had been lying unobserved, and gave himself a shake; he was a big loose-made fellow, with huge limbs which had grown too far through his jacket and trousers. "Don't you go to anybody at all—you just stand out; say you won't fag—they'll soon get tired of licking you. I've tried it on years ago with their forerunners."

"No! did you? Tell us how it was?" cried a chorus of voices, as they clustered round him.

"Well, just as it is with you. The fifth form would fag us, and I and some more struck, and we beat 'em. The good fellows left off directly, and the bullies who kept on soon got afraid."

"Was Flashman here then?"

"Yes! and a dirty little snivelling, sneaking fellow he was too. He never dared join us, and used to toady the bullies by offering to fag for them, and peaching against the rest of us."

"Why wasn't he cut then?" said East.

"Oh, toadies never get cut, they're too useful. Besides, he has no end of great hampers from home, with wine and game in them; so he toadied and fed himself into favour."

The quarter-to-ten bell now rang, and the small boys went off up-stairs, still consulting together, and praising their new counsellor, who stretched himself out on the bench before the hall fire again. There he lay, a very queer specimen of boyhood, by name Diggs, and familiarly called "the Mucker." He was young for his size, and a very clever fellow, nearly at the top of the fifth. His friends at home, having regard, I suppose, to his age, and not to his size and place in the school, hadn't put him into tails; and even his jackets were always too small; and he had a talent for destroying clothes and making himself look shabby. He wasn't on terms with Flashman's set, who sneered at his dress and ways behind his back; which he knew, and revenged himself by asking Flashman the most disagreeable questions, and treating him familiarly whenever a crowd of boys were round him. Neither was he intimate with any of the other bigger boys, who were warned off by his oddnesses, for he was a very queer fellow; besides, amongst other failings, he had that of impecuniosity in a remarkable degree. He brought as much money as other boys to school, but got rid of it in no time, no one knew how. And then, being also reckless, borrowed from any one, and when his debts accumulated and creditors pressed, would have an auction in the Hall of everything he possessed in the world, selling even his school-books, candlestick, and study table. For weeks after one of these auctions, having rendered his study uninhabitable, he would live about in the fifth-form room and Hall, doing his verses on old letter-backs and odd scraps of paper, and learning his lessons no one knew how. He never meddled with any little boy, and was popular with them, though they all looked on him with a sort of compassion, and called him "Poor Diggs," not being able to resist appearances, or to disregard wholly even the sneers of their enemy Flashman. However, he seemed equally indifferent to the sneers of big boys and the pity of small ones, and lived his own queer life with much apparent enjoyment to himself. It is necessary to introduce Diggs thus particularly, as he not only did Tom and East good service in their present warfare, as is about to be told, but soon afterwards, when he got into the sixth, chose them for his fags, and excused them from study-fagging, thereby earning unto himself eternal gratitude from them, and all who are interested in their history.

And seldom had small boys more need of a friend, for the morning after the siege the storm burst upon the rebels in all its violence. Flashman laid wait, and caught Tom before second lesson, and receiving a point blank "No" when told to fetch his hat, seized him and twisted his arm, and went through the other methods of torture in use: "He couldn't make me cry though," as Tom said triumphantly to the rest of the rebels, "and I kicked his shins well, I know." And soon it crept out that a lot of the fags were in league, and Flashman excited his associates to join him in bringing the young vagabonds to their senses; and the house was filled with constant chasings, and sieges, and lickings of all sorts; and in return, the bullies' beds were pulled to pieces and drenched with water, and their names written up on the walls with every insulting epithet which the fag invention could furnish. The war in short raged fiercely; but soon, as Diggs had told them, all the better fellows in the fifth gave up trying to fag them, and public feeling began to set against Flashman and his two or three intimates, and they were obliged to keep their doings more secret, but being thorough bad fellows, missed no opportunity of torturing in private. Flashman was an adept in all ways, but above all in the power of saying cutting and cruel things, and could often bring tears to the eyes of boys in this way, which all the thrashings in the world wouldn't have wrung from them.

And as his operations were being cut short in other directions, he now devoted himself chiefly to Tom and East, who lived at his own door, and would force himself into their study whenever he found a chance, and sit there, sometimes alone, and sometimes with a companion, interrupting all their work, and exulting in the evident pain which every now and then he could see he was inflicting on one or the other.

The storm had cleared the air for the rest of the house, and a better state of things now began than there had been since old Brooke had left; but an angry dark spot of thunder-cloud still hung over the end of the passage where Flashman's study and that of East and Tom lay.

He felt that they had been the first rebels, and that the rebellion had been to a great extent successful; but what above all stirred the hatred and bitterness of his heart against them was, that in the frequent collisions which there had been of late, they had openly called him coward and sneak,—the taunts were too true to be forgiven. While he was in the act of thrashing them, they would roar out instances of his funking at football, or shirking some encounter with a lout of half his own size. These things were all well enough known in the house, but to have his own disgrace shouted out by small boys, to feel that they despised him, to be unable to silence them by any amount of torture, and to see the open laugh and sneer of his own associates (who were looking on, and took no trouble to hide their scorn from him, though they neither interfered with his bullying or lived a bit the less intimately with him), made him beside himself. Come what might, he would make those boys' lives miserable. So the strife settled down into a personal affair between Flashman and our youngsters; a war to the knife, to be fought out in the little cockpit at the end of the bottom passage.

Flashman, be it said, was about seventeen years old, and big and strong of his age. He played well at all games where pluck wasn't much wanted, and managed generally to keep up appearances where it was; and having a bluff, off-hand manner, which passed for heartiness, and considerable powers of being pleasant when he liked, went down with the school in general for a good fellow enough. Even in the School-house, by dint of his command of money, the constant supply of good things which he kept up, and his adroit toadyism, he had managed to make himself not only tolerated, but rather popular amongst his own contemporaries; although young Brooke scarcely spoke to him, and one or two others of the right sort showed their opinions of him whenever a chance offered. But the wrong sort happened to be in the ascendant just now, and so Flashman was a formidable enemy for small boys. This soon became plain enough. Flashman left no slander unspoken, and no deed undone, which could in any way hurt his victims, or isolate them from the rest of the house. One by one most of the other rebels fell away from them, while Flashman's cause prospered, and several other fifth-form boys began to look black at them and ill-treat them as they passed about the house. By keeping out of bounds, or at all events out of the house and quadrangle, all day, and carefully barring themselves in at night, East and Tom managed to hold on without feeling very miserable; but it was as much as they could do. Greatly were they drawn then towards old Diggs, who, in an uncouth way, began to take a good deal of notice of them, and once or twice came to their study when Flashman was there, who immediately decamped in consequence. The boys thought that Diggs must have been watching.

When therefore, about this time, an auction was one night announced to take place in the Hall, at which, amongst the superfluities of other boys, all Diggs' Penates for the time being were going to the hammer, East and Tom laid their heads together, and resolved to devote their ready cash (some four shillings sterling) to redeem such articles as that sum would cover. Accordingly, they duly attended to bid, and Tom became the owner of two lots of Diggs' things:—lot 1, price one-and-three-pence, consisting (as the auctioneer remarked) of a "valuable assortment of old metals," in the shape of a mouse-trap, a cheese-toaster without a handle, and a saucepan: lot 2, of a villainous dirty table-cloth and green-baize curtain; while East, for one-and-sixpence, purchased a leather paper-case, with a lock but no key, once handsome, but now much the worse for wear. But they had still the point to settle of how to get Diggs to take the things without hurting his feelings. This they solved by leaving them in his study, which was never locked when he was out. Diggs, who had attended the auction, remembered who had bought the lots, and came to their study soon after, and sat silent for some time, cracking his great red finger-joints. Then he laid hold of their verses, and began looking over and altering them, and at last got up, and turning his back to them, said, "You're uncommon good-hearted little beggars, you two—I value that paper-case, my sister gave it to me last holidays—I won't forget;" and so tumbled out into the passage, leaving them somewhat embarrassed, but not sorry that he knew what they had done.

The next morning was Saturday, the day on which the allowances of one shilling a-week were paid, an important event to spendthrift youngsters; and great was the disgust amongst the small fry to hear that all the allowances had been impounded for the Derby lottery. That great event in the English year, the Derby, was celebrated at Rugby in those days by many lotteries. It was not an improving custom, I own, gentle reader, and led to making books, and betting, and other objectionable results; but when our great Houses of Palaver think it right to stop the nation's business on that day, and many of the members bet heavily themselves, can you blame us boys for following the example of our betters?—at any rate we did follow it. First there was the great School lottery, where the first prize was six or seven pounds; then each house had one or more separate lotteries. These were all nominally voluntary, no boy being compelled to put in his shilling who didn't choose to do so; but besides Flashman, there were three or four other fast sporting young gentlemen in the School-house, who considered subscription a matter of duty and necessity, and so, to make their duty come easy to the small boys, quietly secured the allowances in a lump when given out for distribution, and kept them. It was no use grumbling,—so many fewer tartlets and apples were eaten and fives'-balls bought on that Saturday; and after locking-up, when the money would otherwise have been spent, consolation was carried to many a small boy by the sound of the night-fags shouting along the passages, "Gentlemen sportsmen of the School-house, the lottery's going to be drawn in the Hall." It was pleasant to be called a gentleman sportsman—also to have a chance of drawing a favourite horse.

The Hall was full of boys, and at the head of one of the long tables stood the sporting interest, with a hat before them, in which were the tickets folded up. One of them then began calling out the list of the house; each boy as his name was called drew a ticket from the hat and opened it; and most of the bigger boys, after drawing, left the Hall directly to go back to their studies or the fifth-form room. The sporting interest had all drawn blanks, and they were sulky accordingly; neither of the favourites had yet been drawn, and it had come down to the upper-fourth. So now, as each small boy came up and drew his ticket, it was seized and opened by Flashman, or some other of the standers-by. But no great favourite is drawn until it comes to the Tadpole's turn, and he shuffles up and draws, and tries to make off, but is caught, and his ticket is opened like the rest.

"Here you are! Wanderer! the third favourite," shouts the opener.

"I say, just give me my ticket, please," remonstrates Tadpole.

"Hullo, don't be in a hurry," breaks in Flashman; "what'll you sell Wanderer for now?"

"I don't want to sell," rejoins Tadpole.

"Oh, don't you! Now listen, you young fool—you don't know anything about it; the horse is no use to you. He won't win, but I want him as a hedge. Now, I'll give you half-a-crown for him." Tadpole holds out, but between threats and cajoleries at length sells half for one shilling and sixpence, about a fifth of its fair market value; however, he is glad to realize anything, and, as he wisely remarks, "Wanderer mayn't win, and the tizzy is safe anyhow."

East presently comes up and draws a blank. Soon after comes Tom's turn; his ticket, like the others, is seized and opened. "Here you are then," shouts the opener, holding it up, "Harkaway! By Jove, Flashey, your young friend's in luck."

"Give me the ticket," says Flashman with an oath, leaning across the table with open hand, and his face black with rage.

"Wouldn't you like it?" replies the opener, not a bad fellow at the bottom, and no admirer of Flashman. "Here, Brown, catch hold," and he hands the ticket to Tom, who pockets it; whereupon Flashman makes for the door at once, that Tom and the ticket may not escape, and there keeps watch until the drawing is over and all the boys are gone, except the sporting set of five or six, who stay to compare books, make bets, and so on, Tom, who doesn't choose to move while Flashman is at the door, and East, who stays by his friend anticipating trouble. The sporting set now gathered round Tom. Public opinion wouldn't allow them actually to rob him of his ticket, but any humbug or intimidation by which he could be driven to sell the whole or part at an under-value was lawful.

"Now, young Brown, come, what'll you sell me Harkaway for? I hear he isn't going to start. I'll give you five shillings for him," begins the boy who had opened the ticket. Tom, remembering his good deed, and moreover in his forlorn state wishing to make a friend, is about to accept the offer, when another cries out, "I'll give you seven shillings." Tom hesitated, and looked from one to the other.

"No, no!" said Flashman, pushing in, "leave me to deal with him; we'll draw lots for it afterwards. Now, sir, you know me—you'll sell Harkaway to us for five shillings, or you'll repent it."

"I won't sell a bit of him," answered Tom, shortly.

"You hear that now!" said Flashman, turning to the others. "He's the coxiest young blackguard in the house—I always told you so. We're to have all the trouble and risk of getting up the lotteries for the benefit of such fellows as he."

Flashman forgets to explain what risk they ran, but he speaks to willing ears. Gambling makes boys selfish and cruel as well as men.

"That's true,—we always draw blanks," cried one. "Now, sir, you shall sell half, at any rate."

"I won't," said Tom, flushing up to his hair, and lumping them all in his mind with his sworn enemy.

"Very well then, let's roast him," cried Flashman, and catches hold of Tom by the collar: one or two boys hesitate, but the rest join in. East seizes Tom's arm and tries to pull him away, but is knocked back by one of the boys, and Tom is dragged along struggling. His shoulders are pushed against the mantelpiece, and he is held by main

force before the fire, Flashman drawing his trousers tight by way of extra torture. Poor East, in more pain even than Tom, suddenly thinks of Diggs, and darts off to find him. "Will you sell now for ten shillings?" says one boy who is relenting.

Tom only answers by groans and struggles.

"I say, Flashey, he has had enough," says the same boy, dropping the arm he holds.

"No, no, another turn'll do it," answers Flashman. But poor Tom is done already, turns deadly pale, and his head falls forward on his breast, just as Diggs, in frantic excitement, rushes into the Hall with East at his heels.

"You cowardly brutes!" is all he can say, as he catches Tom from them and supports him to the Hall table. "Good God! he's dying. Here, get some cold water—run for the housekeeper."

Flashman and one or two others slink away; the rest, ashamed and sorry, bend over Tom or run for water, while East darts off for the housekeeper. Water comes, and they throw it on his hands and face, and he begins to come to. "Mother!"—the words came feebly and slowly—"it's very cold to-night." Poor old Diggs is blubbering like a child. "Where am I?" goes on Tom, opening his eyes. "Ah! I remember now;" and he shut his eyes again and groaned.

"I say," is whispered, "we can't do any good, and the housekeeper will be here in a minute;" and all but one steal away; he stays with Diggs, silent and sorrowful, and fans Tom's face.

The housekeeper comes in with strong salts, and Tom soon recovers enough to sit up. There is a smell of burning; she examines his clothes, and looks up inquiringly. The boys are silent.

"How did he come so?" No answer.

"There's been some bad work here," she adds, looking very serious, "and I shall speak to the Doctor about it." Still no answer.

"Hadn't we better carry him to the sick-room?" suggests Diggs.

"Oh, I can walk now," says Tom; and, supported by East and the housekeeper, goes to the sick-room. The boy who held his ground is soon amongst the rest, who are all in fear of their lives. "Did he peach?" "Does she know about it?"

"Not a word—he's a staunch little fellow." And pausing a moment he adds, "I'm sick of this work; what brutes we've been!"

Meantime Tom is stretched on the sofa in the house-keeper's room, with East by his side, while she gets wine and water and other restoratives.

"Are you much hurt, dear old boy?" whispers East.

"Only the back of my legs," answers Tom. They are indeed badly scorched, and part of his trousers burnt through. But soon he is in bed with cold bandages. At first he feels broken, and thinks of writing home and getting taken away; and the verse of a hymn he had learned years ago sings through his head, and he goes to sleep, murmuring—

> "Where the wicked cease from troubling,
> And the weary are at rest."

But after a sound night's rest, the old boy-spirit comes back again. East comes in reporting that the whole house is with him, and he forgets everything, except their old resolve never to be beaten by that bully Flashman.

Not a word could the housekeeper extract from either of them, and though the Doctor knew all that she knew that morning, he never knew any more.

I trust and believe that such scenes are not possible now at school, and that lotteries and betting-books have gone out; but I am writing of schools as they were in our time, and must give the evil with the good.

CHAPTER IX
A CHAPTER OF ACCIDENTS

"Wherein I [speak] of most disastrous chances,
Of moving accidents by flood and field,
Of hair-breadth 'scapes."
SHAKSPEARE

WHEN TOM CAME BACK into school after a couple of days in the sick-room, he found matters much changed for the better, as East had led him to expect. Flashman's brutality had disgusted most even of his intimate friends, and his cowardice had once more been made plain to the house; for Diggs had encountered him on the morning after the lottery, and after high words on both sides had struck him, and the blow was not returned. However, Flashey was not unused to this sort of thing, and had lived through as awkward affairs before, and, as Diggs had said, fed and toadied himself back into favour again. Two or three of the boys who had helped to roast Tom came up and begged his pardon, and thanked him for not telling anything. Morgan sent for him, and was inclined to take the matter up warmly, but Tom begged him not to do it; to which he agreed, on Tom's promising to come to him at once in future—a promise which I regret to say he didn't keep. Tom kept Harkaway all to himself, and won the second prize in the lottery, some thirty shillings, which he and East contrived to spend in about three days in the purchase of pictures for their study, two new bats and a cricket-ball, all the best that could be got, and a supper of sausages, kidneys, and beef-steak pies to all the rebels. Light come, light go; they wouldn't have been comfortable with money in their pockets in the middle of the half.

The embers of Flashman's wrath, however, were still smouldering, and burst out every now and then in sly blows and taunts, and they both felt that they hadn't quite done with him yet. It wasn't long, however, before the last act of that drama came, and with it the end of bullying for Tom and East at Rugby. They now often stole out into the hall at nights, incited thereto, partly by the hope of finding Diggs there and having a talk with him, partly by the excitement of doing something which was against rules: for, sad to say, both of our youngsters, since their loss of character for steadiness in their form, had got into the habit of doing things which were forbidden, as a matter of adventure; just in the same way, I should fancy, as men fall into smuggling, and for the same sort of reasons. Thoughtlessness in the first place. It never occurred to them to consider why such and such rules were laid down, the reason was nothing to them, and they only looked upon rules as a sort of challenge from the rule-makers, which it would be rather bad pluck in them not to accept; and then again, in the lower parts of the school they hadn't enough to do. The work of the form they could manage to get through pretty easily, keeping a good enough place to get their regular yearly remove; and not having much ambition beyond this, their whole superfluous steam was available for games and scrapes. Now, one rule of the house which it was a daily pleasure of all such boys to break, was that after supper all fags, except the three on duty in the passages, should remain in their own studies until nine o'clock; and if caught about the passages or hall, or in one another's studies, they were liable to punishments or caning.

The rule was stricter than its observance; for most of the sixth spent their evening in the fifth-form room, where the library was, and the lessons were learnt in common. Every now and then, however, a præpostor would be seized with a fit of district visiting, and would make a tour of the passages and hall, and the fags' studies. Then, if the owner were entertaining a friend or two, the first kick at the door and ominous "Open here" had the effect of the shadow of a hawk over a chicken-yard; every one cut to cover—one small boy diving under the sofa, another under the table, while the owner would hastily pull down a book or two and open them, and cry out in a meek voice, "Hullo, who's there?" casting an anxious eye round, to see that no protruding leg or elbow could betray the hidden boys. "Open, sir, directly; it's Snooks." "Oh, I'm very sorry; I didn't know it was you, Snooks;" and then with well-feigned zeal the door would be opened, young hopeful praying that that beast Snooks mightn't have heard the scuffle caused by his coming. If a study was empty, Snooks proceeded to draw the passages and hall to find the truants.

Well, one evening, in forbidden hours, Tom and East were in the hall. They occupied the seats before the fire nearest the door, while Diggs sprawled as usual before the further fire. He was busy with a copy of verses, and East and Tom were chatting together in whispers by the light of the fire, and splicing a favourite old fives'-bat which had sprung. Presently a step came down the bottom passage; they listened a moment, assured themselves that it wasn't a præpostor, and then went on with their work, and the door swung open, and in walked Flashman. He didn't see Diggs, and thought it a good chance to keep his hand in; and as the boys didn't move for him, struck one of them, to make them get out of his way.

"What's that for?" growled the assaulted one.

"Because I choose. You've no business here; go to your study."

"You can't send us."

"Can't I? Then I'll thrash you if you stay," said Flashman, savagely.

"I say, you two," said Diggs from the end of the hall, rousing up and resting himself on his elbow, "you'll never get rid of that fellow till you lick him. Go in at him, both of you—I'll see fair play."

Flashman was taken aback, and retreated two steps. East looked at Tom. "Shall we try!" said he. "Yes," said Tom, desperately. So the two advanced on Flashman, with clenched fists and beating hearts. They were about up to his shoulder, but tough boys of their age, and in perfect training; while he, though strong and big, was in poor condition from his monstrous habit of stuffing and want of exercise. Coward as he was, however, Flashman couldn't swallow such an insult as this; besides, he was confident of having easy work, and so faced the boys, saying, "You impudent young blackguards!"—Before he could finish his abuse, they rushed in on him, and began pummelling at all of him which they could reach. He hit out wildly and savagely, but the full force of his blows didn't tell, they were too near to him. It was long odds, though, in point of strength, and in another minute Tom went spinning backwards over a form, and Flashman turned to demolish East with a savage grin. But now Diggs jumped down from the table on which he had seated himself. "Stop there," shouted he, "the round's over—half-minute time allowed."

"What the——is it to you?" faltered Flashman, who began to lose heart.

"I'm going to see fair, I tell you," said Diggs with a grin, and snapping his great red

fingers; " 'taint fair for you to be fighting one of them at a time. Are you ready, Brown? Time's up."

The small boys rushed in again. Closing they saw was their best chance, and Flashman was wilder and more flurried than ever: he caught East by the throat, and tried to force him back on the iron-bound table; Tom grasped his waist, and, remembering the old throw he had learned in the Vale from Harry Winburn, crooked his leg inside Flashman's, and threw his whole weight forward. The three tottered for a moment, and then over they went on to the floor, Flashman striking his head against a form in the hall.

The two youngsters sprang to their legs, but he lay there still. They began to be frightened. Tom stooped down, and then cried out, scared out of his wits, "He's bleeding awfully; come here, East! Diggs,—he's dying!"

"Not he," said Diggs, getting leisurely off the table; "it's all sham—he's only afraid to fight it out."

East was as frightened as Tom. Diggs lifted Flashman's head, and he groaned.

"What's the matter?" shouted Diggs.

"My skull's fractured," sobbed Flashman.

"Oh, let me run for the housekeeper," cried Tom. "What shall we do?"

"Fiddlesticks! it's nothing but the skin broken," said the relentless Diggs, feeling his head. "Cold water and a bit of rag's all he'll want."

"Let me go," said Flashman, surlily, sitting up; "I don't want your help."

"We're really very sorry," began East.

"Hang your sorrow," answered Flashman, holding his handkerchief to the place; "you shall pay for this, I can tell you, both of you." And he walked out of the hall.

"He can't be very bad," said Tom with a deep sigh, much relieved to see his enemy march so well.

"Not he," said Diggs, "and you'll see you won't be troubled with him any more. But, I say, your head's broken too—your collar is covered with blood."

"Is it though?" said Tom, putting up his hand; "I didn't know it."

"Well, mop it up, or you'll have your jacket spoilt. And you have got a nasty eye, Scud; you'd better go and bathe it well in cold water."

"Cheap enough too, if we're done with our old friend Flashey," said East, as they made off up-stairs to bathe their wounds.

They had done with Flashman in one sense, for he never laid finger on either of them again; but whatever harm a spiteful heart and venomous tongue could do them, he took care should be done. Only throw dirt enough, and some of it is sure to stick; and so it was with the fifth form and the bigger boys in general, with whom he associated more or less, and they not at all. Flashman managed to get Tom and East into disfavour, which did not wear off for some time after the author of it had disappeared from the School world. This event, much prayed for by the small fry in general, took place a few months after the above encounter. One fine summer evening Flashman had been regaling himself on gin-punch, at Brownsover; and having exceeded his usual limits, started home uproarious. He fell in with a friend or two coming back from bathing, proposed a glass of beer, to which they assented, the weather being hot, and they thirsty souls, and unaware of the quantity of drink which Flashman had already on board. The short result was, that Flashey became beastly drunk: they tried to get him along, but couldn't; so they chartered a hurdle and two men to carry him. One of the masters came upon them, and they naturally enough fled. The flight of the rest raised the master's suspicions, and the good angel of the fags incited him to examine the freight, and, after examination, to convoy the hurdle himself up to the School-house; and the Doctor, who had long had his eye on Flashman, arranged for his withdrawal next morning.

The evil that men, and boys too, do, lives after them: Flashman was gone, but our boys, as hinted above, still felt the effects of his hate. Besides, they had been the movers of the strike against unlawful fagging. The cause was righteous—the result had been triumphant to a great extent; but the best of the fifth, even those who had never fagged the small boys, or had given up the practice cheerfully, couldn't help feeling a small grudge against the first rebels. After all, their form had been defied—on just grounds, no doubt; so just, indeed, that they had at once acknowledged the wrong, and remained passive in the strife: had they sided with Flashman and his set, the rebels must have given way at once. They couldn't help, on the whole, being glad that they had so acted, and that the resistance had been successful against such of their own form as had shown fight; they felt that law and order had gained thereby, but the ringleaders they couldn't quite pardon at once. "Confoundedly coxy those young rascals will get, if we don't mind," was the general feeling.

So it is, and must be always, my dear boys. If the angel Gabriel were to come down from heaven, and head a successful rise against the most abominable and unrighteous vested interest which this poor old world groans under, he would most certainly lose his character for many years, probably for centuries, not only with the upholders of said vested interest, but with the respectable mass of the people whom he had delivered. They wouldn't ask him to dinner, or let their names appear with his in the papers; they would be very careful how they spoke of him in the Palaver, or at their clubs. What can we expect, then, when we have only poor gallant blundering men like Kossuth, Garibaldi, Mazzini, and righteous causes which do not triumph in their hands; men who have holes enough in their armour, God knows, easy to be hit by respectabilities sitting in their lounging chairs, and having large balances at their bankers'? But you are brave gallant boys, who hate easy-chairs, and have no balances or bankers. You only want to have your heads set straight to take the right side; so bear in mind that majorities, especially respectable ones, are nine times out of ten in the wrong; and that if you see a man or boy striving earnestly on the weak side, however wrong-headed or blundering he may be, you are not to go and join the cry against him. If you can't join him and help him, and make him wiser, at any rate remember that he has found something in the world which he will fight and suffer for, which is just what you have got to do for yourselves; and so think and speak of him tenderly.

So East and Tom, the Tadpole, and one or two more, became a sort of young Ishmaelites, their hands against every one, and every one's hand against them. It has been already told how they got to war with the masters and the fifth form, and with the sixth it was much the same. They saw the præpostors cowed by or joining with the fifth and shirking their own duties; so they didn't respect them, and rendered no willing obedience. It had been one thing to clean out studies for sons of heroes like old Brooke, but was quite another to do the like for Snooks and Green, who had never faced a good scrummage at football, and couldn't keep the passages in order at night. So they only slurred through their fagging just well enough to escape a licking, and not always that, and got the character of sulky, unwilling fags. In the fifth-form room, after supper, when such matters were often discussed and arranged, their names were for ever coming up.

"I say, Green," Snooks began one night, "isn't that new boy, Harrison, your fag?"

"Yes; why?"

"Oh, I know something of him at home, and should like to excuse him. Will you swop?"

"Who will you give me?"

"Well, let's see, there's Willis, Johnson—No, that won't do. Yes, I have it—there's young East, I'll give you him."

"Don't you wish you may get it?" replied Green. "I'll give you two for Willis, if you like."

"Who then?" asked Snooks.

"Hall and Brown."

"Wouldn't have 'em at a gift."

"Better than East, though; for they ain't quite so sharp," said Green, getting up and leaning his back against the mantel-piece—he wasn't a bad fellow, and couldn't help not being able to put down the unruly fifth form. His eye twinkled as he went on, "Did I ever tell you how the young vagabond sold me last half?"

"No—how?"

"Well, he never half cleaned my study out, only just stuck the candlesticks in the cupboard, and swept the crumbs on to the floor. So at last I was mortal angry, and had him up, and made him go through the whole performance under my eyes: the dust the young scamp made nearly choked me, and showed that he hadn't swept the carpet before. Well, when it was all finished, 'Now, young gentleman,' says I, 'mind, I expect this to be done every morning, floor swept, table-cloth taken off and shaken, and everything dusted.' 'Very well,' grunts he. Not a bit of it though—I was quite sure in a day or two that he never took the table-cloth off even. So I laid a trap for him: I tore up some paper and put half-a-dozen bits on my table one night, and the cloth over them, as usual. Next morning after breakfast up I came, pulled off the cloth, and sure enough there was the paper, which fluttered down on to the floor. I was in a towering rage. 'I've got you now,' thought I, and sent for him while I got out my cane. Up he came as cool as you please, with his hands in his pockets. 'Didn't I tell you to shake my table-cloth every morning?' roared I. 'Yes,' says he. 'Did you do it this morning?' 'Yes.' 'You young liar! I put these pieces of paper on the table last night, and if you'd taken the table-cloth off you'd have seen them, so I'm going to give you a good licking.' Then my youngster takes one hand out of his pocket, and just stoops down and picks up two of the bits of paper, and holds them out to me. There was written on each, in great round text, 'Harry East, his mark.' The young rogue had found my trap out, taken away my paper, and put some of his there, every bit ear-marked. I'd a great mind to lick him for his impudence; but, after all, one has no right to be laying traps, so I didn't. Of course I was at his mercy till the end of the half, and, in his weeks, my study was so frowsy, I couldn't sit in it."

"They spoil one's things so, too," chimed in a third boy. "Hall and Brown were night-fags last week: I called fag, and gave them my candlesticks to clean; away they went, and didn't appear again. When they'd had time enough to clean them three times over, I went out to look after them. They weren't in the passages, so down I went into the hall, where I heard music, and there I found them sitting on the table, listening to Johnson who was playing the flute, and my candlesticks stuck between the bars well into the fire, red-hot, clean spoiled; they've never stood straight since, and I must get some more. However, I gave them a good licking, that's one comfort."

Such were the sort of scrapes they were always getting into: and so, partly by their own faults, partly from circumstances, partly from the faults of others, they found themselves outlaws, ticket-of-leave men, or what you will in that line: in short, danger-ous parties, and lived the sort of hand-to-mouth, wild, reckless life which such parties generally have to put up with. Nevertheless, they never quite lost favour with young Brooke, who was now the cock of the house, and just getting into the sixth, and Diggs stuck to them like a man, and gave them store of good advice, by which they never in the least profited.

And even after the house mended, and law and order had been restored, which soon happened after young Brooke and Diggs got into the sixth, they couldn't easily or at once return into the paths of steadiness, and many of the old wild out-of-bounds habits stuck to them as firmly as ever. While they had been quite little boys, the scrapes they got into in the School hadn't much mattered to any one; but now they were in the upper school, all wrong-doers from which were sent up straight to the Doctor at once: so they began to come under his notice; and as they were a sort of leaders in a small way amongst their own contemporaries, his eye, which was everywhere, was upon them.

It was a toss-up whether they turned out well or ill, and so they were just the boys who caused most anxiety to such a master. You have been told of the first occasion on which they were sent up to the Doctor, and the remembrance of it was so pleasant that they had much less fear of him than most boys of their standing had. "It's all his look," Tom used to say to East, "that frightens fellows: don't you remember, he never said anything to us my first half-year, for being an hour late for locking up?"

The next time that Tom came before him, however, the interview was of a very different kind. It happened just about the time at which we have now arrived, and was the first of a series of scrapes into which our hero managed now to tumble.

The river Avon at Rugby is a slow and not very clear stream, in which chub, dace, roach, and other coarse fish are (or were) plentiful enough, together with a fair sprinkling of small jack, but no fish worth sixpence either for sport or food. It is, however, a capital river for bathing, as it has many nice small pools and several good reaches for swimming, all within about a mile of one another, and at an easy twenty minutes' walk from the school. This mile of water is rented, or used to be rented, for bathing purposes by the Trustees of the School, for the boys. The footpath to Brownsover crosses the river by "the Planks," a curious old single-plank bridge running for fifty or sixty yards into the flat meadows on each side of the river,—for in the winter there are frequent floods. Above the Planks were the bathing-places for the smaller boys; Sleath's, the first bathing-place, where all new boys had to begin, until they had proved to the bathing men (three steady individuals, who were paid to attend daily through the summer to prevent accidents) that they could swim pretty decently, when they were allowed to go on to Anstey's, about one hundred and fifty yards below. Here there was a hole about six feet deep and twelve feet across, over which the puffing urchins struggled to the opposite side, and thought no small beer of themselves for having been out of their depths. Below the Planks came larger and deeper holes, the first of which was Wratislaw's, and the last Swift's, a famous hole, ten or twelve feet deep in parts, and thirty yards across, from which there was a fine swimming reach right down to the Mill. Swift's was reserved for the sixth and fifth forms, and had a spring board and two sets of steps: the others had one set of steps each, and were used indifferently by all the lower boys, though each house addicted itself more to one hole than to another. The School-house at this time affected Wratislaw's hole, and Tom and East, who had learnt to swim like fishes, were to be found there as regular as the clock through the summer, always twice, and often three times a day.

Now the boys either had, or fancied they had, a right also to fish at their pleasure over the whole of this part of the river, and would not understand that the right (if any) only extended to the Rugby side. As ill luck would have it, the gentleman who owned the opposite bank, after allowing it for some time without interference, had ordered his keepers not to let the boys fish on his side; the consequence of which had been, that there had been first wranglings and then fights between the keepers and boys; and so keen had the quarrel become, that the landlord and his keepers, after a ducking had been inflicted on one of the latter, and a fierce fight ensued thereon, had been up to the great school at calling-over to identify the delinquents, and it was all the Doctor himself and five or six masters could do to keep the peace. Not even his authority could prevent the hissing; and so strong was the feeling, that the four præpostors of the week walked up the school with their canes, shouting S-s-s-s-i-lenc-c-c-c-e at the top of their voices. However, the chief offenders for the time were flogged and kept in bounds, but the victorious party had brought a nice hornet's nest about their ears. The landlord was hissed at the School-gates as he rode past, and when he charged his horse at the mob of boys, and tried to thrash them with his whip, was driven back by cricket-bats and wickets, and pursued with pebbles and fives'-balls; while the wretched keepers' lives were a burthen to them, from having to watch the waters so closely.

The School-house boys of Tom's standing, one and all, as a protest against this tyranny and cutting short of their lawful amusements, took to fishing in all ways, and especially by means of night-lines. The little tackle-maker at the bottom of the town would soon have made his fortune had the rage lasted, and several of the barbers began to lay in fishing-tackle. The boys had this great advantage over their enemies, that they spent a large portion of the day in nature's garb by the river side, and so, when tired of swimming, would get out on the other side and fish, or set night-lines, till the keepers hove in sight, and then plunge in and swim back and mix with the other bathers, and the keepers were too wise to follow across the stream.

While things were in this state, one day, Tom and three or four others were bathing at Wratislaw's, and had, as a matter of course, been taking up and re-setting night-lines. They had all left the water, and were sitting or standing about at their toilets, in all costumes from a shirt upwards, when they were aware of a man in a velveteen shooting-coat approaching from the other side. He was a new keeper, so they didn't recognize or notice him, till he pulled up right opposite, and began:—

"I see'd some of you young gentlemen over this side a fishing just now."

"Hullo, who are you? what business is that of yours, old Velveteens?"

"I'm the new under-keeper, and master's told me to keep a sharp look-out on all o' you young chaps. And I tells'ee I means business, and you'd better keep on your own side, or we shall fall out."

"Well, that's right, Velveteens—speak out, and let's know your mind at once."

"Look, here, old boy," cried East, holding up a miserable coarse fish or two and a small jack, "would you like to smell 'em and see which bank they lived under?"

"I'll give you a bit of advice, keeper," shouted Tom, who was sitting in his shirt paddling with his feet in the river; "you'd better go down there to Swift's, where the big boys are; they're beggars at setting lines, and'll put you up to a wrinkle or two for catching the five-pounders." Tom was nearest to the keeper, and that officer, who was getting angry at the chaff, fixed his eyes on our hero, as if to take a note of him for future use. Tom returned his gaze with a steady stare, and then broke into a laugh, and struck into the middle of a favourite School-house song—

> As I and my companions
>   Were sitting of a snare,
> The gamekeeper was watching us;
>   For him we did not care:
> For we can wrestle and fight, my boys,
>   And jump out anywhere.
>   For it's my delight of a likely night,
>   In the season of the year.

The chorus was taken up by the other boys with shouts of laughter, and the keeper turned away with a grunt, but evidently bent on mischief. The boys thought no more of the matter.

But now came on the may-fly season; the soft hazy summer weather lay sleepily along the rich meadows by Avon side, and the green and gray flies flickered with their graceful lazy up and down flight over the reeds and the water and the meadows, in myriads upon myriads. The may-flies must surely be the lotus-eaters of the ephemeræ; the happiest, laziest, carelessest fly that dances and dreams out his few hours of sunshiny life by English rivers.

Every little pitiful coarse fish in the Avon was on the alert for the flies, and gorging his wretched carcase with hundreds daily, the gluttonous rogues! and every lover of the gentle craft was out to avenge the poor may-flies.

So one fine Thursday afternoon, Tom having borrowed East's new rod, started by himself to the river. He fished for some time with small success: not a fish would rise at

him; but as he prowled along the bank, he was presently aware of mighty ones feeding in a pool on the opposite side, under the shade of a huge willow-tree. The stream was deep here, but some fifty yards below was a shallow, for which he made off hot-foot; and forgetting landlords, keepers, solemn prohibitions of the Doctor, and everything else, pulled up his trousers, plunged across, and in three minutes was creeping along on all fours towards the clump of willows.

It isn't often that great chub, or any other coarse fish, are in earnest about anything, but just then they were thoroughly bent on feeding, and in half an hour Master Tom had deposited three thumping fellows at the foot of the giant willow. As he was baiting for a fourth pounder, and just going to throw in again, he became aware of a man coming up the bank not one hundred yards off. Another look told him that it was the under-keeper. Could he reach the shallow before him? No, not carrying his rod. Nothing for it but the tree; so Tom laid his bones to it, shinning up as fast as he could, and dragging up his rod after him. He had just time to reach and crouch along upon a huge branch some ten feet up, which stretched out over the river, when the keeper arrived at the clump. Tom's heart beat fast as he came under the tree; two steps more and he would have passed, when, as ill-luck would have it, the gleam on the scales of the dead fish caught his eye, and he made a dead point at the foot of the tree. He picked up the fish one by one; his eye and touch told him that they had been alive and feeding within the hour. Tom crouched lower along the branch, and heard the keeper beating the clump. "If I could only get the rod hidden," thought he, and began gently shifting it to get it alongside of him; "willow-trees don't throw out straight hickory shoots twelve feet long, with no leaves, worse luck." Alas! the keeper catches the rustle, and then a sight of the rod, and then of Tom's hand and arm.

"Oh, be up ther' be 'ee?" says he, running under the tree. "Now you come down this minute."

"Tree'd at last," thinks Tom, making no answer, and keeping as close as possible, but working away at the rod, which he takes to pieces: "I'm in for it, unless I can starve him out." And then he begins to meditate getting along the branch for a plunge, and scramble to the other side; but the small branches are so thick, and the opposite bank so difficult, that the keeper will have lots of time to get round by the ford before he can get out, so he gives that up. And now he hears the keeper beginning to scramble up the trunk. That will never do; so he scrambles himself back to where his branch joins the trunk, and stands with lifted rod.

"Hullo, Velveteens, mind your fingers if you come any higher."

The keeper stops and looks up, and then with a grin says, "Oh! be you, be it, young measter? Well, here's luck. Now I tells 'ee to come down at once, and 't'll be best for 'ee."

"Thank 'ee, Velveteens, I'm very comfortable," said Tom, shortening the rod in his hand, and preparing for battle.

"Werry well, please yourself," says the keeper, descending however to the ground again, and taking his seat on the bank; "I bean't in no hurry, so you may take your time. I'll larn 'ee to gee honest folk names afore I've done with 'ee."

"My luck as usual," thinks Tom; "what a fool I was to give him a black. If I'd called him 'keeper' now I might get off. The return match is all his way."

The keeper quietly proceeded to take out his pipe, fill, and light it, keeping an eye on Tom, who now sat disconsolately across the branch, looking at keeper—a pitiful sight for men and fishes. The more he thought of it the less he liked it. "It must be getting near second calling-over," thinks he. Keeper smokes on stolidly. "If he takes me up, I shall be flogged safe enough. I can't sit here all night. Wonder if he'll rise at silver."

"I say, keeper," said he meekly, "let me go for two bob?"

"Not for twenty neither," grunts his persecutor.

And so they sat on till long past second calling-over, and the sun came slanting in through the willow-branches, and telling of locking-up near at hand.

"I'm coming down, keeper," said Tom at last, with a sigh, fairly tired out. "Now what are you going to do?"

"Walk 'ee up to School, and give 'ee over to the Doctor, them's my orders," says Velveteens, knocking the ashes out of his fourth pipe, and standing up and shaking himself.

"Very good," said Tom; "but hands off, you know. I'll go with you quietly, so no collaring or that sort of thing."

Keeper looked at him a minute—"Werry good," said he at last; and so Tom descended, and wended his way drearily by the side of the keeper, up to the School-house, where they arrived just at locking-up. As they passed the School-gates, the Tadpole and several others who were standing there caught the state of things, and rushed out, crying, "Rescue!" but Tom shook his head, so they only followed to the Doctor's gate, and went back sorely puzzled.

How changed and stern the Doctor seemed from the last time that Tom was up there, as the keeper told the story, not omitting to state how Tom had called him blackguard names. "Indeed, sir," broke in the culprit, "it was only Velveteens." The Doctor only asked one question.

"You know the rule about the banks, Brown?"

"Yes, sir."

"Then wait for me to-morrow, after first lesson."

"I thought so," muttered Tom.

"And about the rod, sir?" went on the keeper. "Master's told we as we might have all the rods—"

"Oh, please, sir," broke in Tom, "the rod isn't mine." The Doctor looked puzzled; but the keeper, who was a good-hearted fellow, and melted at Tom's evident distress, gave up his claim. Tom was flogged next morning, and a few days afterwards met Velveteens, and presented him with half-a-crown for giving up the rod claim, and they became sworn friends; and I regret to say that Tom had many more fish from under the willow that may-fly season, and was never caught again by Velveteens.

It wasn't three weeks before Tom, and now East by his side, were again in the awful presence. This time, however, the Doctor was not so terrible. A few days before, they had been fagged at fives to fetch the balls that went off the Court. While standing watching the game, they saw five or six nearly new balls hit on the top of the School. "I say, Tom," said East, when they were dismissed, "couldn't we get those balls somehow?"

"Let's try, anyhow."

So they reconnoitred the walls carefully, borrowed a coal-hammer from old Stumps, bought some big nails, and after one or two attempts, scaled the Schools, and possessed themselves of huge quantities of fives'-balls. The place pleased them so much that they spent all their spare time there, scratching and cutting their names on the top of every tower; and at last, having exhausted all other places, finished up with inscribing H. EAST, T. BROWN, on the minute-hand of the great clock; in the doing of which, they held the minute-hand, and disturbed the clock's economy. So next morning, when masters and boys came trooping down to prayers, and entered the quadrangle, the injured minute-hand was indicating three minutes to the hour. They all pulled up, and took their time. When the hour struck, doors were closed, and half the school late. Thomas being set to make inquiry, discovers their names on the minute-hand, and reports accordingly; and they are sent for, a knot of their friends making derisive and panto-mimic allusions to what their fate will be as they walk off.

But the Doctor, after hearing their story, doesn't make much of it, and only gives them thirty lines of Homer to learn by heart, and a lecture on the likelihood of such exploits ending in broken bones.

Alas! almost the next day was one of the great fairs in the town; and as several rows and other disagreeable accidents had of late taken place on these occasions, the Doctor gives out, after prayers in the morning, that no boy is to go down into the town. Wherefore East and Tom, for no earthly pleasure except that of doing what they are told not to do, start away, after second lesson, and making a short circuit through the fields, strike a back lane which leads into the town, go down it, and run plump upon one of the masters as they emerge into the High Street. The master in question, though a very clever, is not a righteous man; he has already caught several of his own pupils, and gives them lines to learn, while he sends East and Tom, who are not his pupils, up to the Doctor; who, on learning that they had been at prayers in the morning, flogs them soundly.

The flogging did them no good at the time, for the injustice of their captor was rankling in their minds; but it was just the end of the half, and on the next evening but one Thomas knocks at their door, and says the Doctor wants to see them. They look at one another in silent dismay. What can it be now? Which of their countless wrong-doings can he have heard of officially? However, it's no use delaying, so up they go to the study. There they find the Doctor, not angry, but very grave. "He has sent for them to speak very seriously before they go home. They have each been flogged several times in the half-year for direct and wilful breaches of rules. This cannot go on. They are doing no good to themselves or others, and now they are getting up in the School, and have influence. They seem to think that rules are made capriciously, and for the pleasure of the masters; but this is not so, they are made for the good of the whole School, and must and shall be obeyed. Those who thoughtlessly or wilfully break them will not be allowed to stay at the School. He should be sorry if they had to leave, as the School might do them both much good, and wishes them to think very seriously in the holidays over what he has said. Good-night."

And so the two hurry off horribly scared; the idea of having to leave has never crossed their minds and is quite unbearable.

As they go out, they meet at the door old Holmes, a sturdy cheery præpostor of another house, who goes in to the Doctor; and they hear his genial hearty greeting of the new-comer, so different to their own reception, as the door closes, and return to their study with heavy hearts, and tremendous resolves to break no more rules.

Five minutes afterwards the master of their form, a late arrival and a model young master, knocks at the Doctor's study-door. "Come in!" and as he enters the Doctor goes on, to Holmes—"you see, I do not know anything of the case officially, and if I take any notice of it at all, I must publicly expel the boy. I don't wish to do that, for I think there is some good in him. There's nothing for it but a good sound thrashing," he paused to shake hands with the master, which Holmes does also, and then prepares to leave.

"I understand. Good-night, sir."

"Good-night, Holmes. And remember," added the Doctor, emphasizing the words, "a good sound thrashing before the whole house."

The door closed on Holmes; and the Doctor, in answer to the puzzled look of his lieutenant, explained shortly. "A gross case of bullying. Wharton, the head of the house, is a very good fellow, but slight and weak, and severe physical pain is the only way to deal with such a case; so I have asked Holmes to take it up. He is very careful and trustworthy, and has plenty of strength. I wish all the sixth had as much. We must have it here, if we are to keep order at all."

Now I don't want any wiseacres to read this book; but if they should, of course they will prick up their long ears, and howl, or rather bray, at the above story. Very good, I don't object; but what I have to add for you boys is this, that Holmes called a levy of his house after breakfast next morning, made them a speech on the case of bullying in question, and then gave the bully a "good sound thrashing;" and that years afterwards, that boy sought out Holmes, and thanked him, saying it had been the kindest act which had ever been done upon him, and the turning-point in his character; and a very good fellow he became, and a credit to his School.

After some other talk between them, the Doctor said, "I want to speak to you about two boys in your form, East and Brown: I have just been speaking to them. What do you think of them?"

"Well, they are not hard workers, and very thoughtless and full of spirits—but I can't help liking them. I think they are sound good fellows at the bottom."

"I'm glad of it. I think so too. But they make me very uneasy. They are taking the lead a good deal amongst the fags in my house, for they are very active, bold fellows. I should be sorry to lose them, but I shan't let them stay if I don't see them gaining character and manliness. In another year they may do great harm to all the younger boys."

"Oh, I hope you won't send them away," pleaded their master.

"Not if I can help it. But now I never feel sure, after any half-holiday, that I shan't have to flog one of them next morning, for some foolish, thoughtless scrape. I quite dread seeing either of them."

They were both silent for a minute. Presently the Doctor began again:—

"They don't feel that they have any duty or work to do in the School, and how is one to make them feel it?"

"I think if either of them had some little boy to take care of, it would steady them. Brown is the most reckless of the two, I should say; East wouldn't get into so many scrapes without him."

"Well," said the Doctor, with something like a sigh, "I'll think of it." And they went on to talk of other subjects.

Part II

"I [hold] it truth, with him who sings
    To one clear harp in divers tones,
    That men may rise on stepping-stones
Of their dead selves to higher things."
        TENNYSON

CHAPTER I
HOW THE TIDE TURNED

"Once to every man and nation, comes the moment to decide,
In the strife of Truth with Falsehood, for the good or evil side: . . .

Then it is the brave man chooses, while the coward stands aside,
Doubting in his abject spirit, till his Lord is crucified."
        LOWELL

THE TURNING-POINT in our hero's school career had now come, and the manner of it was as follows. On the evening of the first day of the next half-year, Tom, East, and another School-house boy, who had just been dropped at the Spread Eagle by the old

Regulator, rushed into the matron's room in high spirits, such as all real boys are in when they first get back, however fond they may be of home.

"Well, Mrs. Wixie," shouted one, seizing on the methodical, active little dark-eyed woman, who was busy stowing away the linen of the boys who had already arrived into their several pigeon-holes, "here we are again, you see, as jolly as ever. Let us help you put the things away."

"And, Mary," cried another (she was called indifferently by either name), "who's come back? Has the Doctor made old Jones leave? How many new boys are there?"

"Am I and East to have Gray's study? You know you promised to get it for us if you could," shouted Tom.

"And am I to sleep in Number 4?" roared East.

"How's old Sam, and Bogle, and Sally?"

"Bless the boys!" cries Mary, at last getting in a word, "why, you'll shake me to death. There, now do go away up to the housekeeper's room and get your suppers; you know I haven't time to talk—you'll find plenty more in the house. Now, Master East, do let those things alone—you're mixing up three new boys' things." And she rushed at East, who escaped round the open trunks holding up a prize.

"Hullo, look here, Tommy," shouted he, "here's fun!" and he brandished above his head some pretty little night-caps, beautifully made and marked, the work of loving fingers in some distant country home. The kind mother and sisters, who sewed that delicate stitching with aching hearts, little thought of the trouble they might be bringing on the young head for which they were meant. The little matron was wiser, and snatched the caps from East before he could look at the name on them.

"Now, Master East, I shall be very angry if you don't go," said she; "there's some capital cold beef and pickles up-stairs, and I won't have you old boys in my room first night."

"Hurrah for the pickles! Come along, Tommy; come along, Smith. We shall find out who the young Count is, I'll be bound: I hope he'll sleep in my room. Mary's always vicious first week."

As the boys turned to leave the room, the matron touched Tom's arm, and said, "Master Brown, please stop a minute, I want to speak to you."

"Very well, Mary. I'll come in a minute, East; don't finish the pickles—"

"Oh, Master Brown," went on the little matron, when the rest had gone, "you're to have Gray's study, Mrs. Arnold says. And she wants you to take in this young gentleman. He's a new boy, and thirteen years old, though he don't look it. He's very delicate, and has never been from home before. And I told Mrs. Arnold I thought you'd be kind to him, and see that they don't bully him at first. He's put into your form, and I've given him the bed next to yours in Number 4; so East can't sleep there this half."

Tom was rather put about by this speech. He had got the double study which he coveted, but here were conditions attached which greatly moderated his joy. He looked across the room, and in the far corner of the sofa was aware of a slight pale boy, with large blue eyes and light fair hair, who seemed ready to shrink through the floor. He saw at a glance that the little stranger was just the boy whose first half-year at a public school would be misery to himself if he were left alone, or constant anxiety to any one who meant to see him through his troubles. Tom was too honest to take in the youngster and then let him shift for himself; and if he took him as his chum instead of East, where

were all his pet plans of having a bottled-beer cellar under his window, and making night-lines and slings, and plotting expeditions to Brownsover Mills and Caldecott's Spinney? East and he had made up their minds to get this study, and then every night from locking-up till ten they would be together to talk about fishing, drink bottled-beer, read Marryat's novels, and sort birds' eggs. And this new boy would most likely never go out of the close, and would be afraid of wet feet, and always getting laughed at, and called Molly, or Jenny, or some derogatory feminine nickname.

The matron watched him for a moment, and saw what was passing in his mind, and so, like a wise negotiator, threw in an appeal to his warm heart. "Poor little fellow," said she in almost a whisper, "his father's dead, and he's got no brothers. And his mamma, such a kind sweet lady, almost broke her heart at leaving him this morning; and she said one of his sisters was like to die of decline, and so——"

"Well, well," burst in Tom, with something like a sigh at the effort, "I suppose I must give up East. Come along, young 'un. What's your name? We'll go and have some supper, and then I'll show you our study."

"His name's George Arthur," said the matron, walking up to him with Tom, who grasped his little delicate hand as the proper preliminary to making a chum of him, and felt as if he could have blown him away. "I've had his books and things put into the study, which his mamma has had new papered, and the sofa covered, and new green-baize curtains over the door" (the diplomatic matron threw this in, to show that the new boy was contributing largely to the partnership comforts). "And Mrs. Arnold told me to say," she added, "that she should like you both to come up to tea with her. You know the way, Master Brown, and the things are just gone up I know."

Here was an announcement for Master Tom! He was to go up to tea the first night, just as if he were a sixth or fifth-form boy, and of importance in the school world, instead of the most reckless young scapegrace amongst the fags. He felt himself lifted on to a higher social and moral platform at once. Nevertheless he couldn't give up without a sigh the idea of the jolly supper in the housekeeper's room with East and the rest, and a rush round to all the studies of his friends afterwards, to pour out the deeds and wonders of the holidays, to plot fifty plans for the coming half-year, and to gather news of who had left and what new boys had come, who had got who's study, and where the new præpostors slept. However, Tom consoled himself with thinking that he couldn't have done all this with the new boy at his heels, and so marched off along the passages to the Doctor's private house with his young charge in tow, in monstrous good humour with himself and all the world.

It is needless, and would be impertinent, to tell how the two young boys were received in that drawing-room. The lady who presided there is still living, and has carried with her to her peaceful home in the North the respect and love of all those who ever felt and shared that gentle and high-bred hospitality. Ay, many is the brave heart, now doing its work and bearing its load in country curacies, London chambers, under the Indian sun, and in Australian towns and clearings, which looks back with fond and grateful memory to that School-house drawing-room, and dates much of its highest and best training to the lessons learnt there.

Besides Mrs. Arnold and one or two of the elder children, there were one of the younger masters, young Brooke, who was now in the sixth, and had succeeded to his brother's position and influence, and another sixth-form boy, talking together before the fire. The master and young Brooke, now a great strapping fellow six feet high, eighteen years old, and powerful as a coal-heaver, nodded kindly to Tom, to his intense glory, and then went on talking; the other did not notice them. The hostess, after a few kind words, which led the boys at once and insensibly to feel at their ease and to begin talking to one another, left them with her own children while she finished a letter. The young ones got on fast and well, Tom holding forth about a prodigious pony he had been riding out hunting, and hearing stories of the winter glories of the lakes, when tea came in, and immediately after the Doctor himself.

How frank, and kind, and manly was his greeting to the party by the fire! It did Tom's heart good to see him and young Brooke shake hands, and look one another in the face; and he didn't fail to remark that Brooke was nearly as tall and quite as broad as the Doctor. And his cup was full, when in another moment his master turned to him with another warm shake of the hand, and, seemingly oblivious of all the late scrapes which he had been getting into, said, "Ah, Brown, you here! I hope you left your father and all well at home?"

"Yes, sir, quite well."

"And this is the little fellow who is to share your study. Well, he doesn't look as we should like to see him. He wants some Rugby air, and cricket. And you must take him some good long walks, to Bilton Grange, and Caldecott's Spinney, and show him what a little pretty country we have about here."

Tom wondered if the Doctor knew that his visits to Bilton Grange were for the purpose of taking rooks' nests (a proceeding strongly discountenanced by the owner thereof), and those to Caldecott's Spinney were prompted chiefly by the conveniences for setting night-lines. What didn't the Doctor know? And what a noble use he always made of it! He almost resolved to abjure rook-pies and night-lines for ever. The tea went merrily off, the Doctor now talking of holiday doings, and then of the prospects of the half-year, what chance there was for the Balliol scholarship, whether the eleven would be a good one. Everybody was at his ease, and everybody felt that he, young as he might be, was of some use in the little School world, and had a work to do there.

Soon after tea the doctor went off to his study, and the young boys a few minutes afterwards took their leave, and went out of the private door which led from the Doctor's house into the middle passage.

At the fire, at the further end of the passage, was a crowd of boys in loud talk and laughter. There was a sudden pause when the door opened, and then a great shout of greeting, as Tom was recognized marching down the passage.

"Hullo, Brown, where do you come from?"

"Oh, I've been to tea with the Doctor," says Tom, with great dignity.

"My eye!" cried East. "Oh! so that's why Mary called you back, and you didn't come to supper. You lost something—that beef and pickles was no end good."

"I say, young fellow," cried Hall, detecting Arthur, and catching him by the collar, "what's your name? Where do you come from? How old are you?"

Tom saw Arthur shrink back and look scared as all the group turned to him, but thought it best to let him answer, just standing by his side to support in case of need.

"Arthur, sir. I come from Devonshire."

"Don't call me 'sir,' you young muff. How old are you?"

"Thirteen."

"Can you sing?"

The poor boy was trembling and hesitating. Tom struck in—"You be hanged, Tadpole. He'll have to sing, whether he can or not, Saturday twelve weeks, and that's long enough off yet."

"Do you know him at home, Brown?"

"No; but he's my chum in Gray's old study, and it's near prayer time, and I haven't had a look at it yet. Come along, Arthur."

Away went the two, Tom longing to get his charge safe under cover, where he might advise him on his deportment.

"What a queer chum for Tom Brown," was the comment at the fire; and it must be confessed so thought Tom himself, as he lighted his candle, and surveyed the new green-baize curtains and the carpet and sofa with much satisfaction.

"I say, Arthur, what a brick your mother is to make us so cosy. But look here now, you must answer straight up when the fellows speak to you, and don't be afraid. If you're afraid, you'll get bullied. And don't you say you can sing; and don't you ever talk about home, or your mother and sisters."

Poor little Arthur looked ready to cry.

"But please," said he, "mayn't I talk about—about home to you?"

"Oh yes, I like it. But don't talk to boys you don't know, or they'll call you home-sick, or mamma's darling, or some such stuff. What a jolly desk! Is that yours? And what stunning binding! why your school-books look like novels."

And Tom was soon deep in Arthur's goods and chattels, all new, and good enough for a fifth-form boy, and hardly thought of his friends outside till the prayer-bell rang.

I have already described the School-house prayers; they were the same on the first night as on the other nights, save for the gaps caused by the absence of those boys who came late, and the line of new boys who stood all together at the further table—of all sorts and sizes, like young bears with all their troubles to come, as Tom's father had said to him when he was in the same position. He thought of it as he looked at the line, and poor little slight Arthur standing with them, and as he was leading him up-stairs to Number 4, directly after prayers, and showing him his bed. It was a huge, high, airy room, with two large windows looking on to the School close. There were twelve beds in the room. The one in the furthest corner by the fireplace, occupied by the sixth-form boy, who was responsible for the discipline of the room, and the rest by boys in the lower-fifth and other junior forms, all fags (for the fifth-form boys, as has been said, slept in rooms by themselves). Being fags, the eldest of them was not more than about sixteen years old, and were all bound to be up and in bed by ten; the sixth-form boys came to bed from ten to a quarter-past (at which time the old verger came round to put the candles out), except when they sat up to read.

Within a few minutes therefore of their entry, all the other boys who slept in Number 4 had come up. The little fellows went quietly to their own beds, and began undressing, and talking to each other in whispers; while the elder, amongst whom was Tom, sat chatting about on one another's beds, with their jackets and waistcoats off. Poor little Arthur was overwhelmed with the novelty of his position. The idea of sleeping in the room with strange boys had clearly never crossed his mind before, and was as painful as it was strange to him. He could hardly bear to take his jacket off; however, presently, with an effort, off it came, and then he paused and looked at Tom, who was sitting at the bottom of his bed talking and laughing.

"Please, Brown," he whispered, "may I wash my face and hands?"

"Of course, if you like," said Tom, staring; "that's your washhand-stand, under the window, second from your bed. You'll have to go down for more water in the morning if you use it all." And on he went with his talk, while Arthur stole timidly from between the beds out to his washing-stand, and began his ablutions, thereby drawing for a moment on himself the attention of the room.

On went the talk and laughter. Arthur finished his washing and undressing, and put on his night-gown. He then looked round more nervously than ever. Two or three of the little boys were already in bed, sitting up with their chins on their knees. The light burned clear, the noise went on. It was a trying moment for the poor little lonely boy; however, this time he didn't ask Tom what he might or might not do, but dropped on his knees by his bedside, as he had done every day from his childhood, to open his heart to Him who heareth the cry and beareth the sorrows of the tender child, and the strong man in agony.

Tom was sitting at the bottom of his bed unlacing his boots, so that his back was towards Arthur, and he didn't see what had happened, and looked up in wonder at the sudden silence. Then two or three boys laughed and sneered, and a big brutal fellow who was standing in the middle of the room, picked up a slipper, and shied it at the kneeling boy, calling him a snivelling young shaver. Then Tom saw the whole, and the next moment the boot he had just pulled off flew straight at the head of the bully, who had just time to throw up his arm and catch it on his elbow.

"Confound you, Brown, what's that for?" roared he, stamping with pain.

"Never mind what I mean," said Tom, stepping on to the floor, every drop of blood in his body tingling; "if any fellow wants the other boot, he knows how to get it."

What would have been the result is doubtful, for at this moment the sixth-form boy

came in, and not another word could be said. Tom and the rest rushed into bed
and finished their unrobing there, and the old verger, as punctual as the clock, had
put out the candle in another minute, and toddled on to the next room, shutting their
door with his usual "Good-night, gen'l'm'n."

There were many boys in the room by whom that little scene was taken to heart
before they slept. But sleep seemed to have deserted the pillow of poor Tom. For some
time his excitement, and the flood of memories which chased one another through his
brain, kept him from thinking or resolving. His head throbbed, his heart leapt, and he
could hardly keep himself from springing out of bed and rushing about the room. Then
the thought of his own mother came across him, and the promise he had made at her
knee, years ago, never to forget to kneel by his bedside, and give himself up to his
Father, before he laid his head on the pillow, from which it might never rise; and he lay
down gently, and cried as if his heart would break. He was only fourteen years old.

It was no light act of courage in those days, my dear boys, for a little fellow to say his
prayers publicly, even at Rugby. A few years later, when Arnold's manly piety had
begun to leaven the School, the table's turned; before he died, in the School-house at
least, and I believe in the other house, the rule was the other way. But poor Tom had
come to school in other times. The first few nights after he came he did not kneel down
because of the noise, but sat up in bed till the candle was out, and then stole out and
said his prayers, in fear lest some one should find him out. So did many another poor
little fellow. Then he began to think that he might just as well say his prayers in bed,
and then that it didn't matter whether he was kneeling, or sitting, or lying down. And so
it had come to pass with Tom, as with all who will not confess their Lord before men;
and for the last year he had probably not said his prayers in earnest a dozen times.

Poor Tom! the first and bitterest feeling which was like to break his heart was the
sense of his own cowardice. The vice of all others which he loathed was brought in and
burned in on his own soul. He had lied to his mother, to his conscience, to his God. How
could he bear it? And then the poor little weak boy, whom he had pitied and almost
scorned for his weakness, had done that which he, braggart as he was, dared not do.
The first dawn of comfort came to him in swearing to himself that he would stand by
that boy through thick and thin, and cheer him, and help him, and bear his burdens,
for the good deed done that night. Then he resolved to write home next day and tell his
mother all, and what a coward her son had been. And then peace came to him as he

resolved, lastly, to bear his testimony next morning. The morning would be harder than the night to begin with, but he felt that he could not afford to let one chance slip. Several times he faltered, for the devil showed him first all his old friends calling him "Saint" and "Square-toes," and a dozen hard names, and whispered to him that his motives would be misunderstood, and he would only be left alone with the new boy; whereas it was his duty to keep all means of influence, that he might do good to the largest number. And then came the more subtle temptation, "Shall I not be showing myself braver than others by doing this? Have I any right to begin it now? Ought I not rather to pray in my own study, letting other boys know that I do so, and trying to lead them to it, while in public at least I should go on as I have done?" However, his good angel was too strong that night, and he turned on his side and slept, tired of trying to reason, but resolved to follow the impulse which had been so strong, and in which he had found peace.

Next morning he was up and washed and dressed, all but his jacket and waistcoat, just as the ten minutes' bell began to ring, and then in the face of the whole room knelt down to pray. Not five words could he say—the bell mocked him; he was listening for every whisper in the room—what were they all thinking of him? He was ashamed to go on kneeling, ashamed to rise from his knees. At last, as it were from his inmost heart, a still small voice seemed to breathe forth the words of the publican, "God be merciful to me a sinner!" He repeated them over and over, clinging to them as for his life, and rose from his knees comforted and humbled, and ready to face the whole world. It was not needed: two other boys besides Arthur had already followed his example, and he went down to the great School with a glimmering of another lesson in his heart—the lesson that he who has conquered his own coward spirit has conquered the whole outward world; and that other one which the old prophet learnt in the cave in Mount Horeb, when he hid his face, and the still small voice asked, "What doest thou here, Elijah?" that however we may fancy ourselves alone on the side of good, the King and Lord of men is nowhere without His witnesses; for in every society, however seemingly corrupt and godless, there are those who have not bowed the knee to Baal.

He found too how greatly he had exaggerated the effect to be produced by his act. For a few nights there was a sneer or a laugh when he knelt down, but this passed off soon, and one by one all the other boys but three or four followed the lead. I fear that this was in some measure owing to the fact that Tom could probably have thrashed any boy in the room except the præpostor; at any rate, every boy knew that he would try upon very slight provocation, and didn't choose to run the risk of a hard fight because Tom Brown had taken a fancy to say his prayers. Some of the small boys of Number 4 communicated the new state of things to their chums, and in several other rooms the poor little fellows tried it on; in one instance or so, where the præpostor heard of it and interfered very decidedly, with partial success; but in the rest, after a short struggle, the confessors were bullied or laughed down, and the old state of things went on for some time longer. Before either Tom Brown or Arthur left the School-house, there was no room in which it had not become the regular custom. I trust it is so still, and that the old heathen state of things has gone out for ever.

CHAPTER II

THE NEW BOY

"And Heaven's rich instincts in him grew,
As effortless as woodland nooks
Send violets up and paint them blue."
LOWELL

I DO NOT MEAN to recount all the little troubles and annoyances which thronged upon Tom at the beginning of this half-year, in his new character of bear-leader to a gentle little boy straight from home. He seemed to himself to have become a new boy again, without any of the long-suffering and meekness indispensable for supporting that character with moderate success. From morning till night he had the feeling of responsibility on his mind, and even if he left Arthur in their study or in the close for an hour, was never at ease till he had him in sight again. He waited for him at the doors of the school after every lesson and every calling-over; watched that no tricks were played him, and none but the regulation questions asked; kept his eye on his plate at dinner and breakfast, to see that no unfair depredations were made upon his viands; in short, as East remarked, cackled after him like a hen with one chick.

Arthur took a long time thawing, too, which made it all the harder work; was sadly timid; scarcely ever spoke unless Tom spoke to him first, and worst of all, would agree with him in everything, the hardest thing in the world for a Brown to bear. He got quite angry sometimes, as they sat together of a night in their study, at this provoking habit of agreement, and was on the point of breaking out a dozen times with a lecture upon the propriety of a fellow having a will of his own and speaking out; but managed to restrain himself by the thought that he might only frighten Arthur, and the remembrance of the lesson he had learnt from him on his first night at Number 4. Then he would resolve to sit still and not say a word till Arthur began; but he was always beat at that game, and had presently to begin talking in despair, fearing lest Arthur might think he was vexed at something if he didn't, and dog-tired of sitting tongue-tied.

It was hard work! But Tom had taken it up, and meant to stick to it, and go through with it so as to satisfy himself; in which resolution he was much assisted by the chaffing of East and his other old friends who began to call him "dry-nurse," and otherwise to break their small wit on him. But when they took other ground, as they did every now and then, Tom was sorely puzzled.

"Tell you what, Tommy," East would say, "you'll spoil young Hopeful with too much coddling. Why can't you let him go about by himself and find his own level? He'll never be worth a button, if you go on keeping him under your skirts."

"Well, but he ain't fit to fight his own way yet; I'm trying to get him to it every day—but he's very odd. Poor little beggar! I can't make him out a bit. He ain't a bit like anything I've ever seen or heard of—he seems all over nerves; anything you say seems to hurt him like a cut or a blow."

"That sort of boy's no use here," said East, "he'll only spoil. Now I'll tell you what to do, Tommy. Go and get a nice large band-box made, and put him in with plenty of cotton-wool and a pap-bottle, labelled 'With care—this side up,' and send him back to mamma."

"I think I shall make a hand of him though," said Tom, smiling, "say what you will. There's something about him, every now and then, which shows me he's got pluck somewhere in him. That's the only thing after all that'll wash, ain't it, old Scud? But how to get at it and bring it out?"

Tom took one hand out of his breeches-pocket and stuck it in his back hair for a scratch, giving his hat a tilt over his nose, his one method of invoking wisdom. He stared at the ground with a ludicrously puzzled look, and presently looked up and met East's eyes. That young gentleman slapped him on the back and then put his arm round his shoulder, as they strolled through the quadrangle together. "Tom," said he, "blest if you ain't the best old fellow ever was—I do like to see you go into a thing. Hang it, I wish I could take things as you do—but I never can get higher than a joke. Everything's a joke. If I was going to be flogged next minute, I should be in a blue funk, but I couldn't help laughing at it for the life of me."

"Brown and East, you go and fag for Jones on the great fives'-court."

"Hullo, though, that's past a joke," broke out East, springing at the young gentleman who addressed them, and catching him by the collar. "Here, Tommy, catch hold of him t'other side before he can holla."

The youth was seized, and dragged struggling out of the quadrangle into the School-house hall. He was one of the miserable little pretty white-handed, curly-headed boys, petted and pampered by some of the big fellows, who wrote their verses for them, taught them to drink and use bad language, and did all they could to spoil them for everything[1] in this world and the next. One of the avocations in which these young gentlemen took particular delight was in going about and getting fags for their protectors, when those heroes were playing any game. They carried about pencil and paper with them, putting down the names of all the boys they sent, always sending five times as many as were wanted, and getting all those thrashed who didn't go. The present youth belonged to a house which was very jealous of the School-house, and always picked out School-house fags when he could find them. However, this time he'd got the wrong sow by the ear. His captors slammed the great door of the hall, and East put his back against it, while Tom gave the prisoner a shake-up, took away his list, and stood him up on the floor, while he proceeded leisurely to examine that document.

"Let me out, let me go!" screamed the boy in a furious passion. "I'll go and tell Jones this minute, and he'll give you both the——thrashing you ever had."

"Pretty little dear," said East, patting the top of his hat; "hark how he swears, Tom. Nicely brought-up young man, ain't he, I don't think."

"Let me alone,——you," roared the boy, foaming with rage, and kicking at East, who quietly tripped him up, and deposited him on the floor in a place of safety.

"Gently, young fellow," said he; " 'tain't improving for little whippersnappers like you to be indulging in blasphemy; so you stop that, or you'll get something you won't like."

"I'll have you both licked when I get out, that I will," rejoined the boy, beginning to snivel.

"Two can play at that game, mind you," said Tom, who had finished his examination of the list. "Now you just listen here. We've just come across the fives'-court, and Jones has four fags there already, two more than he wants. If he'd wanted us to change, he'd have stopped us himself. And here, you little blackguard, you've got seven names down on your list besides ours, and five of them School-house." Tom walked up to him, and jerked him on to his legs; he was by this time whining like a whipped puppy.

"Now just listen to me. We ain't going to fag for Jones. If you tell him you've sent us, we'll each of us give you such a thrashing as you'll remember." And Tom tore up the list and threw the pieces into the fire.

"And mind you, too," said East, "don't let me catch you again sneaking about the School-house, and picking up our fags. You haven't got the sort of hide to take a sound licking kindly;" and he opened the door and sent the young gentleman flying into the quadrangle with a parting kick.

"Nice boy, Tommy," said East, shoving his hands in his pockets, and strolling to the fire.

"Worst sort we breed," responded Tom, following his example. "Thank goodness, no big fellow ever took to petting me."

"You'd never have been like that," said East. "I should like to have put him in a museum:—Christian young gentleman, nineteenth century, highly educated. Stir him up with a long pole, Jack, and hear him swear like a drunken sailor! He'd make a respectable public open its eyes, I think."

"Think he'll tell Jones?" said Tom.

---

[1]A kind and wise critic, an old Rugbœan, notes here in the margin: "The small friend system was not so utterly bad from 1841–1847." Before that, too, there were many noble friendships between big and little boys, but I can't strike out the passage; many boys will know why it is left in.

"No," said East. "Don't care if he does."

"Nor I," said Tom. And they went back to talk about Arthur.

The young gentleman had brains enough not to tell Jones, reasoning that East and Brown, who were noted as some of the toughest fags in the School, wouldn't care three straws for any licking Jones might give them, and would be likely to keep their words as to passing it on with interest.

After the above conversation, East came a good deal to their study, and took notice of Arthur; and soon allowed to Tom that he was a thorough little gentleman, and would get over his shyness all in good time; which much comforted our hero. He felt every day, too, the value of having an object in his life, something that drew him out of himself; and it being the dull time of the year, and no games going about for which he much cared, was happier than he had ever yet been at school, which was saying a great deal.

The time which Tom allowed himself away from his charge was from locking up till supper time. During this hour or hour and a half he used to take his fling, going round to the studies of all his acquaintance, sparring or gossiping in the hall, now jumping the old iron-bound tables, or carving a bit of his name on them, then joining in some chorus of merry voices; in fact, blowing off his steam, as we should now call it.

This process was so congenial to his temper, and Arthur showed himself so pleased at the arrangement, that it was several weeks before Tom was ever in their study before supper. One evening, however, he rushed in to look for an old chisel, or some corks, or other article essential to his pursuit for the time being, and while rummaging about in the cupboards, looked up for a moment, and was caught at once by the figure of poor little Arthur. The boy was sitting with his elbows on the table, and his head leaning on his hands, and before him an open book, on which his tears were falling fast. Tom shut the door at once, and sat down on the sofa by Arthur, putting his arm round his neck.

"Why, young'un! what's the matter?" said he kindly; "you ain't unhappy, are you?"

"Oh no, Brown," said the little boy, looking up with the great tears in his eyes; "you are so kind to me, I'm very happy."

"Why don't you call me Tom? lots of boys do that I don't like half so much as you. What are you reading, then? Hang it, you must come about with me, and not mope yourself," and Tom cast down his eyes on the book, and saw it was the Bible. He was silent for a minute, and thought to himself, "Lesson Number 2, Tom Brown;" and then said gently—

"I'm very glad to see this, Arthur, and ashamed that I don't read the Bible more myself. Do you read it every night before supper while I'm out?"

"Yes."

"Well, I wish you'd wait till afterwards, and then we'd read together. But, Arthur, why does it make you cry?"

"Oh, it isn't that I'm unhappy. But at home, while my father was alive, we always read the lessons after tea; and I love to read them over now, and try to remember what he said about them. I can't remember all, and I think I scarcely understand a great deal of what I do remember. But it all comes back to me so fresh, that I can't help crying sometimes to think I shall never read them again with him."

Arthur had never spoken of his home before, and Tom hadn't encouraged him to do so, as his blundering school-boy reasoning made him think that Arthur would be softened and less manly for thinking of home. But now he was fairly interested, and forgot all about chisels and bottled beer; while with very little encouragement Arthur launched into his home history, and the prayer-bell put them both out sadly when it rang to call them to the hall.

From this time Arthur constantly spoke of his home, and above all, of his father, who had been dead about a year, and whose memory Tom soon got to love and reverence almost as much as his own son did.

Arthur's father had been the clergyman of a parish in the Midland Counties, which had risen into a large town during the war, and upon which the hard years which followed had fallen with fearful weight. The trade had been half ruined: and then came the old sad story, of masters reducing their establishments, men turned off and wandering about, hungry and wan in body, and fierce in soul, from the thought of wives and children starving at home, and the last sticks of furniture going to the pawn-shop. Children taken from school, and lounging about the dirty streets and courts, too listless almost to play, and squalid in rags and misery. And then the fearful struggle between the employers and men; lowerings of wages, strikes, and the long course of oft-repeated crime, ending every now and then with a riot, a fire, and the county yeomanry. There is no need here to dwell upon such tales; the Englishman into whose soul they have not sunk deep is not worthy the name; you English boys for whom this book is meant (God bless your bright faces and kind hearts!) will learn it all soon enough.

Into such a parish and state of society Arthur's father had been thrown at the age of twenty-five, a young married parson, full of faith, hope, and love. He had battled with it like a man, and had lots of fine Utopian ideas about the perfectibility of mankind, glorious humanity, and such-like, knocked out of his head; and a real wholesome Christian love for the poor struggling, sinning men, of whom he felt himself one, and with and for whom he spent fortune, and strength, and life, driven into his heart. He had battled like a man, and gotten a man's reward. No silver teapots or salvers, with flowery inscriptions setting forth his virtues and the appreciation of a genteel parish; no fat living or stall, for which he never looked, and didn't care; no sighs and praises of comfortable dowagers and well got-up young women, who worked him slippers, sugared his tea, and adored him as "a devoted man;" but a manly respect, wrung from the unwilling souls of men who fancied his order their natural enemies; the fear and hatred of every one who was false or unjust in the district, were he master or man; and the blessed sight of women and children daily becoming more human and more homely, a comfort to themselves and to their husbands and fathers.

These things of course took time, and had to be fought for with toil and sweat of brain and heart, and with the life-blood poured out. All that, Arthur had laid his account to give, and took as a matter of course; neither pitying himself, nor looking on himself as a martyr, when he felt the wear and tear making him feel old before his time, and the stifling air of fever-dens telling on his health. His wife seconded him in everything. She had been rather fond of society, and much admired and run after before her marriage: and the London world to which she had belonged pitied poor Fanny Evelyn when she married the young clergyman, and went to settle in that smoky hole Turley, a very nest of Chartism and Atheism, in a part of the country which all the decent families had had to leave for years. However, somehow or other she didn't seem to care. If her husband's living had been amongst green fields and near pleasant neighbours she would have liked it better, that she never pretended to deny. But there they were: the air wasn't bad after all; the people were very good sort of people, civil to you if you were civil to them, after the first brush; and they didn't expect to work miracles, and convert them all off-hand into model Christians. So he and she went quietly among the folk, talking to and treating them just as they would have done people of their own rank. They didn't feel that they were doing anything out of the common way, and so were perfectly natural, and had none of that condescension or conciseness of manner which so outrages the independent poor. And thus they gradually won respect and confidence; and after sixteen years he was looked up to by the whole neighbourhood as *the* just man, *the* man to whom masters and men could go in their strikes, and in all their quarrels and difficulties, and by whom the right and true word would be said without fear or favour. And the women had come round to take her advice, and go to her as a friend in all their troubles; while the children all worshipped the very ground she trod on.

They had three children, two daughters and a son, little Arthur, who came between his sisters. He had been a very delicate boy from his childhood; they thought he had a tendency to consumption, and so he had been kept at home and taught by his father, who had made a companion of him, and from whom he had gained good scholarship, and a knowledge of and interest in many subjects which boys in general never come across till they are many years older.

Just as he reached his thirteenth year, and his father had settled that he was strong enough to go to school, and, after much debating with himself, had resolved to send him there, a desperate typhus fever broke out in the town: most of the other clergy, and almost all the doctors, ran away; the work fell with tenfold weight on those who stood to their work. Arthur and his wife both caught the fever, of which he died in a few days, and she recovered, having been able to nurse him to the end, and store up his last words. He was sensible to the last, and calm and happy, leaving his wife and children with fearless trust for a few years in the hands of the Lord and Friend who had lived and died for him, and for whom he, to the best of his power, had lived and died. His widow's mourning was deep and gentle; she was more affected by the request of the Committee of a Freethinking Club, established in the town by some of the factory hands (which he had striven against with might and main, and nearly suppressed), that some of their number might be allowed to help bear the coffin, than by anything else. Two of them were chosen, who, with six other labouring men, his own fellow-workmen and friends, bore him to his grave—a man who had fought the Lord's fight even unto the death. The shops were closed and the factories shut that day in the parish, yet no master stopped the day's wages; but for many a year afterwards the townsfolk felt the want of that brave, hopeful, loving parson and his wife, who had lived to teach them mutual forbearance and helpfulness, and had *almost* at last given them a glimpse of what this old world would be if people would live for God and each other instead of for themselves.

What has all this to do with our story? Well, my dear boys, let a fellow go on his own way, or you won't get anything out of him worth having. I must show you what sort of a man it was who had begotten and trained little Arthur, or else you won't believe in him, which I am resolved you shall do; and you won't see how he, the timid weak boy, had points in him from which the bravest and strongest recoiled, and made his presence and example felt from the first on all sides, unconsciously to himself, and without the least attempt at proselytizing. The spirit of his father was in him, and the friend to whom his father had left him did not neglect the trust.

After supper that night, and almost nightly for years afterwards, Tom and Arthur, and by degrees East occasionally, and sometimes one, sometimes another of their friends, read a chapter of the Bible together and talked it over afterwards. Tom was at first utterly astonished, and almost shocked, at the sort of way in which Arthur read the book and talked about the men and women whose lives were there told. The first night they happened to fall on the chapters about the famine in Egypt, and Arthur began talking about Joseph as if he were a living statesman; just as he might have talked about Lord Grey and the Reform Bill; only that they were much more living realities to him. The book was to him, Tom saw, the most vivid and delightful history of real people, who might do right or wrong, just like any one who was walking about in Rugby—the Doctor, or the masters, or the sixth-form boys. But the astonishment soon passed off, the scales seemed to drop from his eyes, and the book became at once and for ever to him the great human and divine book, and the men and women, whom he had looked upon as something quite different from himself, became his friends and counsellors.

For our purposes, however, the history of one night's reading will be sufficient, which must be told here, now we are on the subject, though it didn't happen till a year afterwards, and long after the events recorded in the next chapter of our story.

Arthur, Tom, and East were together one night, and read the story of Naaman coming to Elisha to be cured of his leprosy. When the chapter was finished, Tom shut his Bible with a slap.

"I can't stand that fellow Naaman," said he, "after what he'd seen and felt, going back and bowing himself down in the house of Rimmon, because his effeminate scoundrel of a master did it. I wonder Elisha took the trouble to heal him. How he must have despised him."

"Yes, there you go off as usual, with a shell on your head," struck in East, who always took the opposite side to Tom; half from love of argument, half from conviction. "How do you know he didn't think better of it? how do you know his master was a scoundrel? His letter don't look like it, and the book don't say so."

"I don't care," rejoined Tom; "why did Naaman talk about bowing down, then, if he didn't mean to do it? He wasn't likely to get more in earnest when he got back to Court, and away from the Prophet."

"Well, but, Tom," said Arthur, "look what Elisha says to him, 'Go in peace.' He wouldn't have said that if Naaman had been in the wrong."

"I don't see that that means more than saying, 'You're not the man I took you for.'"

"No, no, that won't do at all," said East; "read the words fairly, and take men as you find them. I like Naaman, and think he was a very fine fellow."

"I don't," said Tom, positively.

"Well, I think East is right," said Arthur; "I can't see but what it's right to do the best you can, though it mayn't be the best absolutely. Every man isn't born to be a martyr."

"Of course, of course," said East; "but he's on one of his pet hobbies. How often have I told you, Tom, that you must drive a nail where it'll go."

"And how often have I told you," rejoined Tom, "that it'll always go where you want, if you only stick to it and hit hard enough. I hate half-measures and compromises."

"Yes, he's a whole-hog man, is Tom. Must have the whole animal, hair and teeth, claws and tail," laughed East. "Sooner have no bread any day than half the loaf."

"I don't know," said Arthur, "it's rather puzzling; but ain't most right things got by proper compromises, I mean where the principle isn't given up?"

"That's just the point," said Tom; "I don't object to a compromise, where you don't give up your principle."

"Not you," said East laughingly. "I know him of old, Arthur, and you'll find him out some day. There isn't such a reasonable fellow in the world, to hear him talk. He never wants anything but what's right and fair; only when you come to settle what's right and fair, it's everything that he wants, and nothing that you want. And that's his idea of a compromise. Give me the Brown compromise when I'm on his side."

"Now, Harry," said Tom, "no more chaff—I'm serious. Look here—this is what makes my blood tingle;" and he turned over the pages of his Bible and read, "Shadrach, Meshach, and Abednego answered and said to the king, O Nebuchadnezzar, we are not careful to answer thee in this matter. If it *be* so, our God whom we serve is able to deliver us from the burning fiery furnace, and He will deliver us out of thine hand, O king. But *if not*, be it known unto thee, O king, that we will *not* serve thy gods, nor worship the golden image which thou hast set up." He read the last verse twice, emphasizing the nots, and dwelling on them as if they gave him actual pleasure, and were hard to part with.

They were silent a minute, and then Arthur said, "Yes, that's a glorious story, but it don't prove your point, Tom, I think. There are times when there is only one way, and that the highest, and then the men are found to stand in the breach."

"There's always a highest way, and it's always the right one," said Tom. "How many times has the Doctor told us that in his sermons in the last year, I should like to know!"

"Well, you ain't going to convince us—is he, Arthur? No Brown compromise to-night," said East, looking at his watch. "But it's past eight, and we must go to first lesson. What a bore!"

So they took down their books and fell to work; but Arthur didn't forget, and thought long and often over the conversation.

CHAPTER III

ARTHUR MAKES A FRIEND

"Let Nature be your teacher:
Sweet is the lore which Nature brings;
Our meddling intellect
Mis-shapes the beauteous forms of things.
We murder to dissect—
Enough of Science and of Art;
Close up those barren leaves;
Come forth, and bring with you a heart
That watches and receives."
WORDSWORTH

About six weeks after the beginning of the half, as Tom and Arthur were sitting one night before supper beginning their verses, Arthur suddenly stopped, and looked up, and said, "Tom, do you know anything of Martin?"

"Yes," said Tom, taking his hand out of his back hair, and delighted to throw his Gradus ad Parnassum on to the sofa; "I know him pretty well. He's a very good fellow, but as mad as a hatter. He's called Madman, you know. And never was such a fellow for getting all sorts of rum things about him. He tamed two snakes last half, and used to carry them about in his pocket, and I'll be bound he's got some hedgehogs and rats in his cupboard now, and no one knows what besides."

"I should like very much to know him," said Arthur; "he was next to me in the form to-day, and he'd lost his book and looked over mine, and he seemed so kind and gentle, that I liked him very much."

"Ah, poor old Madman, he's always losing his books," said Tom, "and getting called up and floored because he hasn't got them."

"I like him all the better," said Arthur.

"Well, he's great fun, I can tell you," said Tom, throwing himself back on the sofa, and chuckling at the remembrance. "We had such a game with him one day last half. He had been kicking up horrid stinks for some time in his study, till I suppose some fellow told Mary, and she told the doctor. Anyhow, one day a little before dinner, when he came down from the library, the Doctor, instead of going home, came striding into the hall. East and I and five or six other fellows were at the fire, and preciously we stared, for he don't come in like that once a year, unless it is a wet day and there's a fight in the hall. 'East,' says he, 'just come and show me Martin's study.' 'Oh, here's a game,' whispered the rest of us, and we all cut up-stairs after the Doctor, East leading. As we got into the New Row, which was hardly wide enough to hold the Doctor and his gown, click, click, click, we heard in the old Madman's den. Then that stopped all of a sudden, and the bolts went to like fun; the Madman knew East's step, and thought there was going to be a siege.

" 'It's the Doctor, Martin. He's here and wants to see you,' sings out East.

"Then the bolts went back slowly, and the door opened, and there was the old Madman standing, looking precious scared; his jacket off, his shirt-sleeves up to his elbows, and his long skinny arms all covered with anchors and arrows and letters, tattooed in with gun-powder like a sailor-boy's, and a stink fit to knock you down coming out. 'Twas all the Doctor could do to stand his ground, and East and I, who were looking in under his arms, held our noses tight. The old magpie was standing on the window-sill, all his feathers drooping, and looking disgusted and half-poisoned.

" 'What can you be about, Martin?' says the Doctor; 'you really mustn't go on in this way—you're a nuisance to the whole passage.'

" 'Please, sir, I was only mixing up this powder, there isn't any harm in it;' and the Madman seized nervously on his pestle-and-mortar, to show the Doctor the harmlessness of his pursuits, and went on pounding; click, click, click; he hadn't given six clicks before, puff! up went the whole into a great blaze, away went the pestle-and-mortar across the study, and back we tumbled into the passage. The magpie fluttered down into the court, swearing, and the Madman danced out, howling, with his fingers in his mouth. The Doctor caught hold of him, and called to us to fetch some water. 'There, you silly fellow,' said he, quite pleased though to find he wasn't much hurt, 'you see you don't know the least what you're doing with all these things; and now, mind, you must give up practising chemistry by yourself.' Then he took hold of his arm and looked at it, and I saw he had to bite his lip, and his eyes twinkled; but he said, quite grave, 'Here, you see, you've been making all these foolish marks on yourself, which you can never get out, and you'll be very sorry for it in a year or two: now come down to the housekeeper's room, and let us see if you are hurt.' And away went the two, and we all stayed and had a regular turn-out of the den, till Martin came back with his hand

bandaged and turned us out. However, I'll go and see what he's after, and tell him to come in after prayers to supper." And away went Tom to find the boy in question, who dwelt in a little study by himself, in New Row.

The aforesaid Martin, whom Arthur had taken such a fancy for, was one of those unfortunates who were at that time of day (and are, I fear, still) quite out of their places at a public school. If we knew how to use our boys, Martin would have been seized upon and educated as a natural philosopher. He had a passion for birds, beasts, and insects, and knew more of them and their habits than any one in Rugby; except perhaps the Doctor, who knew everything. He was also an experimental chemist on a small scale, and had made unto himself an electric machine, from which it was his greatest pleasure and glory to administer small shocks to any small boys who were rash enough to venture into his study. And this was by no means an adventure free from excitement; for, besides the probability of a snake dropping on to your head or twining lovingly up your leg, or a rat getting into your breeches-pocket in search of food, there was the animal and chemical odour to be faced, which always hung about the den, and the chance of being blown up in some of the many experiments which Martin was always trying, with the most wondrous results in the shape of explosions and smells that mortal boy ever heard of. Of course, poor Martin, in consequence of his pursuits, had become an Ishmaelite in the house. In the first place, he half-poisoned all his neighbours, and they in turn were always on the lookout to pounce upon any of his numerous live-stock, and drive him frantic by enticing his pet old magpie out of his window into a neighbouring study, and making the disreputable old bird drunk on toast soaked in beer and sugar. Then Martin, for his sins, inhabited a study looking into a small court some ten feet across, the window of which was completely commanded by those of the studies opposite in the Sick-room Row, these latter being at a slightly higher elevation. East, and another boy of an equally tormenting and ingenious turn of mind, now lived exactly opposite, and had expended huge pains and time in the preparation of instruments of annoyance for the behoof of Martin and his live colony. One morning an old basket made its appearance, suspended by a short cord outside Martin's window, in which were deposited an amateur nest containing four young hungry jackdaws, the pride and glory of Martin's life for the time being, and which he was currently asserted to have hatched upon his own person. Early in the morning and late at night he was to be seen half out of window, administering to the varied wants of his callow brood. After deep cogitation, East and his chum had spliced a knife on to the end of a fishing-rod; and having watched Martin out, had, after half an hour's severe sawing, cut the string by which the basket was suspended, and tumbled it on to the pavement below, with hideous remonstrance from the occupants. Poor Martin, returning from his short absence, collected the fragments and replaced his brood (except one whose neck had been broken in the descent) in their old location, suspending them this time by string and wire twisted together, defiant of any sharp instrument which his persecutors could command. But, like the Russian engineers at Sebastopol, East and his chum had an answer for every move of the adversary; and the next day had mounted a gun in the shape of a pea-shooter upon the ledge of their window, trained so as to bear exactly upon the spot which Martin had to occupy while tending his nurslings. The moment he began to feed they began to shoot; in vain did the enemy himself invest in a pea-shooter, and endeavour to answer the fire while he fed the young birds with his other hand; his attention was divided, and his shots flew wild, while every one of theirs told on his face and hands, and drove him into howlings and imprecations. He had been driven to ensconce the nest in a corner of his already too well-filled den.

His door was barricaded by a set of ingenious bolts of his own invention, for the sieges were frequent by the neighbours when any unusually ambrosial odour spread itself from the den to the neighbouring studies. The door panels were in a normal state of smash, but the frame of the door resisted all besiegers, and behind it the owner carried on his varied pursuits; much in the same state of mind, I should fancy, as a border-farmer lived in, in the days of the moss-troopers, when his hold might be summoned or his cattle carried off at any minute of night or day.

"Open, Martin, old boy—it's only I, Tom Brown."

"Oh, very well, stop a moment." One bolt went back. "You're sure East isn't there?"

"No, no; hang it, open." Tom gave a kick, the other bolt creaked, and he entered the den.

Den indeed it was, about five feet six inches long by five wide, and seven feet high. About six tattered school-books, and a few chemical books, Taxidermy, Stanley on Birds, and an odd volume of Bewick, the latter in much better preservation, occupied the top shelves. The other shelves, where they had not been cut away and used by the owner for other purposes, were fitted up for the abiding places of birds, beasts, and reptiles. There was no attempt at carpet or curtain. The table was entirely occupied by the great work of Martin, the electric machine, which was covered carefully with the remains of his table-cloth. The jackdaw cage occupied one wall; and the other was adorned by a small hatchet, a pair of climbing irons, and his tin candle-box, in which he was for the time being endeavouring to raise a hopeful young family of field-mice. As nothing should be let to lie useless, it was well that the candle-box was thus occupied, for candles Martin never had. A pound was issued to him weekly, as to the other boys, but as candles were available capital, and easily exchangeable for birds'-eggs or young birds, Martin's pound invariably found its way in a few hours to Howlett's the bird-fancier's, in the Bilton road, who would give a hawk's or nightingale's egg or young linnet in exchange. Martin's ingenuity was therefore for ever on the rack to supply himself with a light; just now he had hit upon a grand invention, and the den was lighted by a flaring cotton-wick issuing from a ginger-beer bottle full of some doleful composition. When light altogether failed him, Martin would loaf about by the fires in the passages or Hall, after the manner of Diggs, and try to do his verses or learn his lines by the fire-light.

"Well, old boy, you haven't got any sweeter in the den this half. How that stuff in the bottle stinks. Never mind, I ain't going to stop, but you come up after prayers to our study; you know young Arthur; we've got Gray's study. We'll have a good supper and talk about birds'-nesting."

Martin was evidently highly pleased at the invitation, and promised to be up without fail.

As soon as prayers were over, and the sixth and fifth-form boys had withdrawn to the aristocratic seclusion of their own room, and the rest, or democracy, had sat down to their supper in the hall, Tom and Arthur, having secured their allowances of bread and cheese, started on their feet to catch the eye of the præpostor of the week, who remained in charge during supper, walking up and down the hall. He happened to be an easy-going fellow, so they got a pleasant nod to their "Please may I go out?" and away they scrambled to prepare for Martin a sumptuous banquet. This Tom had insisted on, for he was in great delight on the occasion; the reason of which delight must be expounded. The fact was that this was the first attempt at a friendship of his own which Arthur had made, and Tom hailed it as a grand step. The ease with which he himself became hail-fellow-well-met with anybody, and blundered into and out of twenty friend-ships a half-year, made him sometimes sorry and sometimes angry at Arthur's reserve and loneliness. True, Arthur was always pleasant, and even jolly, with any boys who came with Tom to their study; but Tom felt that it was only through him, as it were, that his chum associated with others, and that but for him Arthur would have been dwelling in a wilderness. This increased his consciousness of responsibility; and though he hadn't reasoned it out and made it clear to himself, yet somehow he knew that this responsibility, this trust which he had taken on him without thinking about it, head-over-heels in fact, was the centre and turning-point of his school-life, that which was to make him or mar him; his appointed work and trial for the time being. And Tom was becoming a new boy, though with frequent tumbles in the dirt and perpetual hard battle with himself, and was daily growing in manfulness and thoughtfulness, as every high-couraged and well-principled boy must, when he finds himself for the first time consciously at grips with self and the devil. Already he could turn almost without a sigh from the school-gates, from which had just scampered off East and three or four others of his own particular set, bound for some jolly lark not quite according to law, and involving probably a row with louts, keepers, or farm-labourers, the skipping dinner or calling-over, some of Phœbe Jennings' beer, and a very possible flogging at the end of all as a relish. He had quite got over the stage in which he would grumble to himself. "Well, hang it, it's very hard of the Doctor to have saddled me with Arthur. Why couldn't he have chummed him with Fogey, or Thomkin, or any of the fellows who never do anything but walk round the close, and finish their copies the first day they're set?" But although all this was past, he longed and felt that he was right in longing for more time for the legitimate pastimes of cricket, fives, bathing, and fishing, within bounds, in which Arthur could not yet be his companion; and he felt that when the young'un (as he now generally called him) had found a pursuit and some other friend for himself, he should be able to give more time to the education of his own body with a clear conscience.

And now what he so wished for had come to pass; he almost hailed it as a special providence (as indeed it was, but not for the reasons he gave for it—what providences are?) that Arthur should have singled out Martin of all fellows for a friend. "The old Madman is the very fellow," thought he; "he will take him scrambling over half the country after birds' eggs and flowers, make him run and swim and climb like an Indian, and not teach him a word of anything bad, or keep him from his lessons. What luck!" And so, with more than his usual heartiness, he dived into his cupboard, and hauled out an old knuckle-bone of ham, and two or three bottles of beer, together with the solemn pewter only used on state occasions; while Arthur, equally elated at the easy accomplishment of his first act of volition in the joint establishment, produced from his side a bottle of pickles and a pot of jam, and cleared the table. In a minute or two the noise of the boys coming up from supper was heard, and Martin knocked and was admitted, bearing his bread and cheese, and the three fell to with hearty good will upon the viands, talking faster than they ate, for all shyness disappeared in a moment before Tom's bottled-beer and hospitable ways. "Here's Arthur, a regular young town-mouse, with a natural taste for the woods, Martin, longing to break his neck climbing trees, and with a passion for young snakes."

"Well, I say," sputtered out Martin eagerly, "will you come to-morrow, both of you, to Caldecott's Spinney, then, for I know of a kestrel's nest, up a fir-tree?—I can't get at it without help; and, Brown, you can climb against any one."

"Oh yes, do let us go," said Arthur; "I never saw a hawk's nest, nor a hawk's egg."

"You just come down to my study then, and I'll show you five sorts," said Martin.

"Ay, the old Madman has got the best collection in the house, out-and-out," said Tom; and then Martin, warming with unaccustomed good cheer and the chance of a convert, launched out into a proposed birds'-nesting campaign, betraying all manner of important secrets; a golden-crested wren's nest near Butlin's Mound, a moor-hen who was sitting on nine eggs in a pond down the Barby-road, and a kingfisher's nest in a corner of the old canal above Brownsover Mill. He had heard, he said, that no one had ever got a kingfisher's nest out perfect, and that the British Museum, or the Government, or somebody, had offered £100 to any one who could bring them a nest and eggs not damaged. In the middle of which astounding announcement, to which the others were listening with open ears, and already considering the application of the £100, a knock came to the door, and East's voice was heard craving admittance.

"There's Harry," said Tom; "we'll let him in—I'll keep him steady, Martin. I thought the old boy would smell out the supper."

The fact was, that Tom's heart had already smitten him for not asking his "fidus Achates" to the feast, although only an extempore affair; and though prudence and the desire to get Martin and Arthur together alone at first had overcome his scruples, he was now heartily glad to open the door, broach another bottle of beer, and hand over the old ham-knuckle to the searching of his old friend's pocket-knife.

"Ah, you greedy vagabonds," said East, with his mouth full, "I knew there was something going on when I saw you cut off out of hall so quick with your suppers. What a stunning tap, Tom! You are a wunner for bottling the swipes."

"I've had practice enough for the sixth in my time, and it's hard if I haven't picked up a wrinkle or two for my own benefit."

"Well, old Madman, and how goes the birds'-nesting campaign? How's Howlett? I expect the young rooks'll be out in another fortnight, and then my turn comes."

"There'll be no young rooks fit for pies for a month yet; shows how much you know about it," rejoined Martin, who, though very good friends with East, regarded him with considerable suspicion for his propensity to practical jokes.

"Scud knows nothing and cares for nothing but grub and mischief," said Tom; "but young rook pie, specially when you've had to climb for them, is very pretty eating. However, I say, Scud, we're all going after a hawk's nest to-morrow, in Caldecott's Spinney; and if you'll come and behave yourself, we'll have a stunning climb."

"And a bathe in Aganippe. Hooray! I'm your man."

"No, no; no bathing in Aganippe; that's where our betters go."

"Well, well, never mind. I'm for the hawk's nest, and anything that turns up."

And the bottled-beer being finished, and his hunger appeased, East departed to his study, "that sneak Jones," as he informed them, who had just got into the sixth and occupied the next study, having instituted a nightly visitation upon East and his chum, to their no small discomfort.

When he was gone, Martin rose to follow, but Tom stopped him. "No one goes near New Row," said he, "so you may just as well stop here and do your verses, and then we'll have some more talk. We'll be no end quiet; besides, no præpostor comes here now—we haven't been visited once this half."

So the table was cleared, the cloth restored, and the three fell to work with Gradus and dictionary upon the morning's vulgus.

They were three very fair examples of the way in which such tasks were done at Rugby, in the consulship of Plancus. And doubtless the method is little changed, for there is nothing new under the sun, especially at schools.

Now be it known unto all you boys who are at schools which do not rejoice in the time-honoured institution of the Vulgus (commonly supposed to have been established by Willian of Wykeham at Winchester, and imported to Rugby by Arnold more for the sake of the lines which were learnt by heart with it than for its own intrinsic value, as I've always understood), that it is a short exercise in Greek or Latin verse, on a given subject, the minimum number of lines being fixed for each form.

The master of the form gave out at fourth lesson on the previous day the subject for next morning's vulgus, and at first lesson each boy had to bring his vulgus ready to be looked over; and with the vulgus, a certain number of lines from one of the Latin or Greek poets then being construed in the form had to be got by heart. The master at first lesson called up each boy in the form in order, and put him on in the lines. If he couldn't say them, or seem to say them, by reading them off the master's or some other boy's book who stood near, he was sent back, and went below all the boys who did so say or seem to say them; but in either case his vulgus was looked over by the master, who gave and entered in his book, to the credit or discredit of the boy, so many marks as the composition merited. At Rugby vulgus and lines were the first lesson every other day in the week, on Tuesdays, Thursdays, and Saturdays; and as there were thirty-eight weeks in the school year, it is obvious to the meanest capacity that the master of each form had to set one hundred and fourteen subjects every year, two hundred and twenty-eight every two years, and so on. Now, to persons of moderate invention this was a considerable task, and human nature being prone to repeat itself, it will not be wondered that the masters gave the same subjects sometimes over again after a certain lapse of time. To meet and rebuke this bad habit of the masters, the schoolboy mind, with its accustomed ingenuity, had invented an elaborate system of tradition. Almost every boy kept his own vulgus written out in a book, and these books were duly handed down from boy to boy, till (if the tradition has gone on till now) I suppose the popular boys, in whose hands bequeathed vulgus-books have accumulated, are prepared with three or four vulguses on any subject in heaven or earth, or in "more worlds than one," which an unfortunate master can pitch upon. At any rate, such lucky fellows had generally one for themselves and one for a friend in my time. The only objection to the traditionary method of doing your vulguses was, the risk that the successions might have become confused, and so that you and another follower of traditions should show up the same identical vulgus some fine morning; in which case, when it happened, considerable grief was the result—but when did such risk hinder boys or men from short cuts and pleasant paths?

Now in the study that night, Tom was the upholder of the traditionary method of vulgus doing. He carefully produced two large vulgus-books, and began diving into them, and picking out a line here, and an ending there (tags as they were vulgarly called), till he had gotten all that he thought he could make fit. He then proceeded to patch his tags together with the help of his Gradus, producing an incongruous and feeble result of eight elegiac lines, the minimum quantity for his form, and finishing up with two highly moral lines extra, making ten in all, which he cribbed entire from one of his books, beginning "O genus humanum," and which he himself must have used a dozen times before, whenever an unfortunate or wicked hero, of whatever nation or language under the sun, was the subject. Indeed he began to have great doubts whether the master wouldn't remember them, and so only threw them in as extra lines, because in any case they would call off attention from the other tags, and if detected, being extra lines, he wouldn't be sent back to do two more in their place, while if they pass muster again he would get marks for them.

The second method, pursued by Martin, may be called the dogged, or prosaic method. He, no more than Tom, took any pleasure in the task, but having no old vulgus-books of his own, or any one's else, could not follow the traditionary method, for which too, as Tom remarked, he hadn't the genius. Martin then proceeded to write down eight lines in English, of the most matter-of-fact kind, the first that came into his head; and to convert these, line by line, by main force of Gradus and dictionary, into Latin that would scan. This was all he cared for, to produce eight lines with no false quantities or concords: whether the words were apt, or what the sense was, mattered nothing; and as the article was all new, not a line beyond the minimum did the followers of the dogged method ever produce.

The third, or artistic method, was Arthur's. He considered first what point in the character or event which was the subject could most neatly be brought out within the limits of a vulgus, trying always to get his idea into the eight lines, but not binding himself to ten or even twelve lines if he couldn't do this. He then set to work, as much as possible without Gradus or other help, to clothe his idea in appropriate Latin or Greek, and would not be satisfied till he had polished it well up with the aptest and most poetic words and phrases he could get at.

A fourth method indeed was used in the school, but of too simple a kind to require a comment. It may be called the vicarious method, obtained amongst big boys of lazy or bullying habits, and consisted simply in making clever boys whom they could thrash do their whole vulgus for them, and construe it to them afterwards; which latter is a method not to be encouraged, and which I strongly advise you all not to practise. Of the others, you will find the traditionary most troublesome, unless you can steal your vulguses whole (*experto crede*), and that the artistic method pays the best both in marks and other ways.

The vulguses being finished by nine o'clock, and Martin having rejoiced above measure in the abundance of light, and of Gradus and dictionary, and other conveniences almost unknown to him for getting through the work, and having been pressed by Arthur to come and do his verses there whenever he liked, the three boys went down to Martin's den, and Arthur was initiated into the lore of birds'-eggs, to his great delight. The exquisite colouring and forms astonished and charmed him, who had scarcely ever seen any but a hen's egg or an ostrich's, and by the time he was lugged away to bed he had learned the names of at least twenty sorts, and dreamt of the glorious perils of tree-climbing, and that he had found a roc's egg in the island as big as Sinbad's, and clouded like a tit-lark's, in blowing which Martin and he had nearly been drowned in the yolk.

CHAPTER IV
THE BIRD-FANCIERS

"I have found out a gift for my fair,
  I have found where the wood-pigeons breed:
But let me the plunder forbear,
  She would say 'twas a barbarous deed."
ROWE

"And now, my lad, take them five shilling,
  And on my advice in future think;
So Billy pouched them all so willing,
  And got that night disguised in drink."
MS. BALLAD

T HE NEXT MORNING at first lesson Tom was turned back in his lines, and so had to wait till the second round, while Martin and Arthur said theirs all right and got out of school at once. When Tom got out and ran down to breakfast at Harrowell's they were missing, and Stumps informed him that they had swallowed down their breakfasts and gone off together, where, he couldn't say. Tom hurried over his own breakfast, and went first to Martin's study and then to his own, but no signs of the missing boys were to be found. He felt half angry and jealous of Martin—where could they be gone?

He learnt second lesson with East and the rest in no very good temper, and then went out into the quadrangle. About ten minutes before school Martin and Arthur arrived in the quadrangle breathless; and, catching sight of him, Arthur rushed up, all excitement, and with a bright glow on his face.

"Oh, Tom, look here!" cried he, holding out three moor-hen's eggs; "we've been down the Barby-road to the pool Martin told us of last night, and just see what we've got."

Tom wouldn't be pleased, and only looked out for something to find fault with.

"Why, young 'un," said he, "what have you been after? You don't mean to say you've been wading?"

The tone of reproach made poor little Arthur shrink up in a moment and look piteous, and Tom with a shrug of his shoulders turned his anger on Martin.

"Well, I didn't think, Madman, that you'd have been such a muff as to let him be getting wet through at this time of day. You might have done the wading yourself."

"So I did, of course, only he would come in too, to see the nest. We left six eggs in; they'll be hatched in a day or two."

"Hang the eggs!" said Tom; "a fellow can't turn his back for a moment but all his work's undone. He'll be laid up for a week for this precious lark, I'll be bound."

"Indeed, Tom, now," pleaded Arthur, "my feet ain't wet, for Martin made me take off my shoes and stockings and trousers."

"But they are wet, and dirty too—can't I see?" answered Tom; "and you'll be called up and floored when the master sees what a state you're in. You haven't looked at second lesson, you know." Oh, Tom, you old humbug! you to be upbraiding any one with not learning their lessons. If you hadn't been floored yourself now at first lesson, do you mean to say you wouldn't have been with them? and you've taken away all poor little Arthur's joy and pride in his first birds' eggs, and he goes and puts them down in the study, and takes down his books with a sigh, thinking he has done something horribly wrong, whereas he has learnt on in advance much more than will be done at second lesson.

But the old Madman hasn't, and gets called up and makes some frightful shots, losing about ten places, and all but getting floored. This somewhat appeases Tom's wrath, and by the end of the lesson he has regained his temper. And afterwards in their study he begins to get right again, as he watches Arthur's intense joy at seeing Martin blowing the eggs and glueing them carefully on to bits of card-board, and notes the anxious loving looks which the little fellow casts sidelong at him. And then he thinks, "What an ill-tempered beast I am! Here's just what I was wishing for last night come about, and I'm spoiling it all," and in another five minutes has swallowed the last mouthful of his bile, and is repaid by seeing his little sensitive plant expand again and sun itself in his smiles.

After dinner the Madman is busy with the preparations for their expedition, fitting new straps on to his climbing-irons, filling large pill-boxes with cotton-wool, and sharpening East's small axe. They carry all their munitions into calling-over, and directly afterwards, having dodged such præpostors as are on the look-out for fags at cricket, the four set off at a smart trot down the Lawford footpath straight for Caldecott's Spinney and the hawk's nest.

Martin leads the way in high feather; it is quite a new sensation to him, getting companions, and he finds it very pleasant, and means to show them all manner of proofs of his science and skill. Brown and East may be better at cricket and football and games, thinks he, but out in the fields and woods see if I can't teach them something. He has taken the leadership already, and strides away in front with his climbing-irons strapped under one arm, his pecking-bag under the other, and his pockets and hat full of pill-boxes, cotton-wool, and other etceteras. Each of the others carries a pecking-bag, and East his hatchet.

When they had crossed three or four fields without a check, Arthur began to lag; and Tom seeing this shouted to Martin to pull up a bit: "We ain't out Hare-and-hounds— what's the good of grinding on at this rate?"

"There's the Spinney," said Martin, pulling up on the brow of a slope at the bottom of which lay Lawford brook, and pointing to the top of the opposite slope; "the nest is in one of those high fir-trees at this end. And down by the brook there I know of a sedge-bird's nest; we'll go and look at it coming back."

"Oh, come on, don't let us stop," said Arthur, who was getting excited at the sight of the wood; so they broke into a trot again, and were soon across the brook, up the slope, and into the Spinney. Here they advanced as noiselessly as possible, lest keepers or other enemies should be about, and stopped at the foot of a tall fir, at the top of which Martin pointed out with pride the kestrel's nest, the object of their quest.

"Oh, where! which is it?" asks Arthur, gaping up in the air, and having the most vague idea of what it would be like.

"There, don't you see?" said East, pointing to a lump of mistletoe in the next tree, which was a beech: he saw that Martin and Tom were busy with the climbing-irons, and couldn't resist the temptation of hoaxing. Arthur stared and wondered more than ever.

"Well, how curious! it doesn't look a bit like what I expected," said he.

"Very odd birds, kestrels," said East, looking waggishly at his victim, who was still star-gazing.

"But I thought it was in a fir-tree?" objected Arthur.

"Ah, don't you know? that's a new sort of fir which old Caldecott brought from the Himalayas."

"Really!" said Arthur; "I'm glad I know that—how unlike our firs they are! They do very well too here, don't they? The Spinney's full of them."

"What's that humbug he's telling you?" cried Tom, looking up, having caught the word Himalayas, and suspecting what East was after.

"Only about this fir," said Arthur, putting his hand on the stem of the beech.

"Fir!" shouted Tom, "why, you don't mean to say, young 'un, you don't know a beech when you see one?"

Poor little Arthur looked terribly ashamed, and East exploded in laughter which made the wood ring.

"I've hardly ever seen any trees," faltered Arthur.

"What a shame to hoax him, Scud!" cried Martin. "Never mind, Arthur, you shall know more about trees than he does in a week or two."

"And isn't that the kestrel's nest then?" asked Arthur.

"That! why, that's a piece of mistletoe. There's the nest, that lump of sticks up this fir."

"Don't believe him, Arthur," struck in the incorrigible East; "I just saw an old magpie go out of it."

Martin did not deign to reply to this sally, except by a grunt, as he buckled the last buckle of his climbing-irons; and Arthur looked reproachfully at East without speaking.

But now came the tug of war. It was a very difficult tree to climb until the branches were reached, the first of which was some fourteen feet up, for the trunk was too large at the bottom to be swarmed; in fact, neither of the boys could reach more than half round it with their arms. Martin and Tom, both of whom had irons on, tried it without success at first; the fir bark broke away where they stuck the irons in as soon as they leant any weight on their feet, and the grip of their arms wasn't enough to keep them up; so, after getting up three or four feet, down they came slithering to the ground, barking their arms and faces. They were furious, and East sat by laughing and shouting at each failure, "Two to one on the old magpie!"

"We must try a pyramid," said Tom at last. "Now, Scud, you lazy rascal, stick yourself against the tree!"

"I dare say! and have you standing on my shoulders with the irons on: what do you think my skin's made of?" However, up he got, and leant against the tree, putting his head down and clasping it with his arms as far as he could.

"Now then, Madman," said Tom, "you next."

"No, I'm lighter than you; you go next." So Tom got on East's shoulders, and grasped the tree above, and then Martin scrambled up on to Tom's shoulders, amidst the totterings and groanings of the pyramid, and, with a spring which sent his supporters howling to the ground, clasped the stem some ten feet up, and remained clinging. For a moment or two they thought he couldn't get up, but then holding on with arms and teeth, he worked first one iron, then the other, firmly into the bark, got another grip with his arms, and in another minute had hold of the lowest branch.

"All up with the old magpie now," said East; and, after a minute's rest, up went Martin, hand over hand, watched by Arthur with fearful eagerness.

"Isn't it very dangerous?" said he.

"Not a bit," answered Tom; "you can't hurt if you only get good hand-hold. Try every branch with a good pull before you trust it, and then up you go."

Martin was now amongst the small branches close to the nest, and away dashed the old bird, and soared up above the trees, watching the intruder.

"All right—four eggs!" shouted he.

"Take 'em all!" shouted East; "that'll be one a-piece."

"No, no! leave one, and then she won't care," said Tom.

We boys had an idea that birds couldn't count, and were quite content as long as you left one egg. I hope it is so.

Martin carefully put one egg into each of his boxes and the third into his mouth, the only other place of safety, and came down like a lamplighter. All went well till he was within ten feet of the ground, when, as the trunk enlarged, his hold got less and less firm, and at last down he came with a run, tumbling on to his back on the turf, spluttering and spitting out the remains of the great egg, which had broken by the jar of his fall.

"Ugh, ugh! something to drink—ugh! it was addled," spluttered he, while the wood rang again with the merry laughter of East and Tom.

Then they examined the prizes, gathered up their things, and went off to the brook, where Martin swallowed huge draughts of water to get rid of the taste; and they visited the sedge-bird's nest, and from thence struck across the country in high glee, beating the hedges and brakes as they went along; and Arthur at last, to his intense delight, was allowed to climb a small hedgerow oak for a magpie's nest with Tom, who kept all round him like a mother, and showed him where to hold and how to throw his weight;

and though he was in a great fright, didn't show it; and was applauded by all for his lissomness.

They crossed a road soon afterwards, and there close to them lay a great heap of charming pebbles.

"Look here," shouted East, "here's luck! I've been longing for some good honest pecking this half-hour. Let's fill the bags, and have no more of this foozling birds'-nesting."

No one objected, so each boy filled the fustian bag he carried full of stones: they crossed into the next field, Tom and East taking one side of the hedges, and the other two the other side. Noise enough they made certainly, but it was too early in the season for the young birds, and the old birds were too strong on the wing for our young marksmen, and flew out of shot after the first discharge. But it was great fun, rushing along the hedgerows, and discharging stone after stone at blackbirds and chaffinches, though no result in the shape of slaughtered birds was obtained; and Arthur soon entered into it, and rushed to head back the birds, and shouted, and threw, and tumbled into ditches, and over and through hedges, as wild as the Madman himself.

Presently the party, in full cry after an old blackbird (who was evidently used to the thing and enjoyed the fun, for he would wait till they came close to him and then fly on for forty yards or so, and, with an impudent flicker of his tail, dart into the depths of the quickset), came beating down a high double hedge, two on each side.

"There he is again," "Head him," "Let drive," "I had him there," "Take care where you're throwing, Madman," the shouts might have been heard a quarter of a mile off. They were heard some two hundred yards off by a farmer and two of his shepherds, who were doctoring sheep in a fold in the next field.

Now, the farmer in question rented a house and yard situate at the end of the field in which the young bird-fanciers had arrived, which house and yard he didn't occupy or keep any one else in. Nevertheless, like a brainless and unreasoning Briton, he persisted in maintaining on the premises a large stock of cocks, hens, and other poultry. Of course, all sorts of depredators visited the place from time to time: foxes and gipsies wrought havoc in the night; while in the day time, I regret to have to confess that visits from the Rugby boys, and consequent disappearances of ancient and respectable fowls, were not unfrequent. Tom and East had during the period of their outlawry visited the barn in question for felonious purposes, and on one occasion had conquered and slain a duck there, and borne away the carcase triumphantly, hidden in their handkerchiefs. However, they were sickened of the practice by the trouble and anxiety which the wretched duck's body caused them. They carried it to Sally Harrowell's, in hopes of a good supper; but she, after examining it, made a long face, and refused to dress or have anything to do with it. Then they took it into their study, and began plucking it themselves; but what to do with the feathers, where to hide them?

"Good gracious, Tom, what a lot of feathers a duck has!" groaned East, holding a bagful in his hand, and looking disconsolately at the carcase, not yet half plucked.

"And I do think he's getting high too, already," said Tom, smelling at him cautiously, "so we must finish him up soon."

"Yes, all very well, but how are we to cook him? I'm sure I ain't going to try it on in the hall or passages; we can't afford to be roasting ducks about, our character's too bad."

"I wish we were rid of the brute," said Tom, throwing him on the table in disgust. And after a day or two more it became clear that got rid of he must be; so they packed

him and sealed him up in brown paper, and put him in the cupboard of an unoccupied study, where he was found in the holidays by the matron, a grewsome body.

They had never been duck-hunting there since, but others had, and the bold yeoman was very sore on the subject, and bent on making an example of the first boys he could catch. So he and his shepherds crouched behind the hurdles, and watched the party, who were approaching all unconscious.

Why should that old guinea-fowl be lying out in the hedge just at this particular moment of all the year? Who can say? Guinea-fowls always are—so are all other things, animals, and persons, requisite for getting one into scrapes, always ready when any mischief can come of them. At any rate, just under East's nose popped out the old guinea-hen, scuttling along and shrieking, "Come back, come back," at the top of her voice. Either of the other three might perhaps have withstood the temptation, but East first lets drive the stone he has in his hand at her, and then rushes to turn her into the hedge again. He succeeds, and then they are all at it for dear life, up and down the hedge in full cry, the "Come back, come back," getting shriller and fainter every minute.

Meantime, the farmer and his men steal over the hurdles and creep down the hedge towards the scene of action. They are almost within a stone's throw of Martin, who is pressing the unlucky chase hard, when Tom catches sight of them, and sings out, "Louts, 'ware louts, your side! Madman, look ahead!" and then catching hold of Arthur, hurries him away across the field towards Rugby as hard as they can tear. Had he been by himself, he would have stayed to see it out with the others, but now his heart sinks and all his pluck goes. The idea of being led up to the Doctor with Arthur for bagging fowls quite unmans and takes half the run out of him.

However, no boys are more able to take care of themselves than East and Martin; they dodge the pursuers, slip through a gap, and come pelting after Tom and Arthur, whom they catch up in no time; the farmer and his men are making good running about a field behind. Tom wishes to himself that they had made off in any other direction, but now they are all in for it together, and must see it out.

"You won't leave the young 'un, will you?" says he, as they haul poor little Arthur, already losing wind from the fright, through the next hedge. "Not we," is the answer from both. The next hedge is a stiff one; the pursuers gain horribly on them, and they only just pull Arthur through, with two great rents in his trousers, as the foremost shepherd comes up on the other side. As they start into the next field, they are aware of

two figures walking down the footpath in the middle of it, and recognizes Holmes and Diggs taking a constitutional. Those good-natured fellows immediately shout, "On." "Let's go to them and surrender," pants Tom.—Agreed.—And in another minute the four boys, to the great astonishment of those worthies, rush breathless up to Holmes and Diggs, who pull up to see what is the matter; and then the whole is explained by the appearance of the farmer and his men, who unite their forces and bear down on the knot of boys.

There is no time to explain, and Tom's heart beats frightfully quick, as he ponders, "Will they stand by us?"

The farmer makes a rush at East and collars him; and that young gentleman, with unusual discretion, instead of kicking his shins, looks appealingly at Holmes, and stands still.

"Hullo there, not so fast," says Holmes, who is bound to stand up for them till they are proved in the wrong. "Now what's all this about?"

"I've got the young varmint at last, have I," pants the farmer; "why, they've been a skulking about my yard and stealing my fowls, that's where 'tis; and if I doan't have they flogged for it, every one on 'em, my name ain't Thompson."

Holmes looks grave and Diggs's face falls. They are quite ready to fight, no boys in the school more so; but they are præpostors, and understand their office, and can't uphold unrighteous causes.

"I haven't been near his old barn this half," cries East. "Nor I," "Nor I," chime in Tom and Martin.

"Now, Willum, didn't you see 'em there last week?"

"Ees, I seen 'em sure enough," says Willum, grasping a prong he carried, and preparing for action.

The boys deny stoutly, and Willum is driven to admit that, "if it worn't they 'twas chaps as like 'em as two peas'n;" and "leastways he'll swear he see'd them two in the yard last Martinmas," indicating East and Tom.

Holmes has had time to meditate. "Now, sir," says he to Willum, "you see you can't remember what you have seen, and I believe the boys."

"I doan't care," blusters the farmer; "they was arter my fowls to-day, that's enough for I. Willum, you catch hold o' t'other chap. They've been a sneaking about this two hours,

I tells 'ee," shouted he, as Holmes stands between Martin and Willum, "and have druv a matter of a dozen young pullets pretty nigh to death."

"Oh, there's a wacker!" cried East; "we haven't been within a hundred yards of his barn; we haven't been up here above ten minutes, and we've seen nothing but a tough old guinea-hen, who ran like a greyhound."

"Indeed, that's all true, Holmes, upon my honour," added Tom; "we weren't after his fowls; guinea-hen ran out of the hedge under our feet, and we've seen nothing else."

"Drat their talk. Thee catch hold o' t'other, Willum, and come along wi' 'un."

"Farmer Thompson," said Holmes, warning off Willum and the prong with his stick, while Diggs faced the other shepherd, cracking his fingers like pistol shots, "now listen to reason—the boys haven't been after your fowls, that's plain."

"Tells 'ee I seed 'em. Who be you, I should like to know?"

"Never you mind, Farmer," answered Holmes. "And now I'll just tell you what it is—you ought to be ashamed of yourself for leaving all that poultry about, with no one to watch it, so near the School. You deserve to have it all stolen. So if you choose to come up to the Doctor with them, I shall go with you, and tell him what I think of it."

The farmer began to take Holmes for a master; besides, he wanted to get back to his flock. Corporal punishment was out of the question, the odds were too great; so he began to hint at paying for the damage. Arthur jumped at this, offering to pay anything, and the farmer immediately valued the guinea-hen at half-a-sovereign.

"Half-a-sovereign!" cried East, now released from the farmer's grip; "well, that is a good one! the old hen ain't hurt a bit, and she's seven years old, I know, and as tough as whipcord; she couldn't lay another egg to save her life."

It was at last settled that they should pay the farmer two shillings, and his man one shilling, and so the matter ended, to the unspeakable relief of Tom, who hadn't been able to say a word, being sick at heart at the idea of what the Doctor would think of him: and now the whole party of boys marched off down the foot-path towards Rugby. Holmes, who was one of the best boys in the School, began to improve the occasion. "Now, you youngsters," said he, as he marched along in the middle of them, "mind this; you're very well out of this scrape. Don't you go near Thompson's barn again, do you hear?"

Profuse promises from all, especially East.

"Mind, I don't ask questions," went on Mentor, "but I rather think some of you have been there before this after his chickens. Now, knocking over other people's chickens, and running off with them, is stealing. It's a nasty word, but that's the plain English of it. If the chickens were dead and lying in a shop, you wouldn't take them, I know that, any more than you would apples out of Griffith's basket; but there's no real difference between chickens running about and apples on a tree, and the same articles in a shop. I wish our morals were sounder in such matters. There's nothing so mischievous as these school distinctions, which jumble up right and wrong, and justify things in us for which poor boys would be sent to prison." And good old Holmes delivered his soul on the walk home of many wise sayings, and, as the song says—

> "Gee'd 'em a sight of good advice"

which same sermon sank into them all, more or less, and very penitent they were for several hours. But truth compels me to admit that East at any rate forgot it all in a week, but remembered the insult which had been put upon him by Farmer Thompson, and with the Tadpole and other hair-brained youngsters, committed a raid on the barn soon afterwards, in which they were caught by the shepherds and severely handled, besides having to pay eight shillings, all the money they had in the world, to escape being taken up to the Doctor.

Martin became a constant inmate in the joint study from this time, and Arthur took to him so kindly that Tom couldn't resist slight fits of jealousy, which however he managed to keep to himself. The kestrel's eggs had been broken, strange to say, and formed the nucleus of Arthur's collection, at which Martin worked heart and soul; and introduced Arthur to Howlett the bird-fancier, and instructed him in the rudiments of the art of stuffing. In token of his gratitude, Arthur allowed Martin to tattoo a small anchor on one of his wrists, which decoration, however, he carefully concealed from Tom. Before the end of the half-year he had trained into a bold climber and good runner, and, as Martin had foretold, knew twice as much about trees, birds, flowers, and many other things, as our good-hearted and facetious young friend Harry East.

CHAPTER V

THE FIGHT

"Surgebat Macnevisius
Et mox jactabat ultro,
Pugnabo tuâ gratiâ
Feroci hoc Mactwoltro."
ETONIAN

THERE IS A certain sort of fellow, we who are used to studying boys all know him well enough, of whom you can predicate with almost positive certainty, after he has been a month at school, that he is sure to have a fight, and with almost equal certainty that he will have but one. Tom Brown was one of these; and as it is our well-weighed intention to give a full, true, and correct account of Tom's only single combat with a school-fellow in the manner of our old friend *Bell's Life*, let those young persons whose stomachs are not strong, or who think a good set-to with the weapons which God has given us all, an uncivilized, unchristian, or ungentlemanly affair, just skip this chapter at once, for it won't be to their taste.

It was not at all usual in those days for two School-house boys to have a fight. Of course there were exceptions, when some cross-grained, hard-headed fellow came up who would never be happy unless he was quarrelling with his nearest neighbours, or when there was some class-dispute, between the fifth-form and the fags, for instance, which required blood-letting; and a champion was picked out on each side tacitly, who settled the matter by a good hearty mill. But for the most part, the constant use of those surest keepers of the peace, the boxing-gloves, kept the School-house boys from fighting one another. Two or three nights in every week the gloves were brought out, either in the hall or fifth-form room; and every boy who was ever likely to fight at all knew all his neighbours' prowess perfectly well, and could tell to a nicety what chance he would have in a stand-up fight with any other boy in the house. But of course no such experience could be gotten as regarded boys in other houses; and as most of the other houses were more or less jealous of the School-house, collisions were frequent.

After all, what would life be without fighting, I should like to know? From the cradle to the grave, fighting, rightly understood, is the business, the real highest, honestest business of every son of man. Every one who is worth his salt has his enemies, who must be beaten, be they evil thoughts and habits in himself, or spiritual wickednesses in high places, or Russians, or Border-ruffians, or Bill, Tom, or Harry, who will not let him live his life in quiet till he has thrashed them.

It is no good for Quakers, or any other body of men, to uplift their voices against fighting. Human nature is too strong for them, and they don't follow their own precepts. Every soul of them is doing his own piece of fighting, somehow and somewhere. The world might be a better world without fighting, for anything I know, but it wouldn't be our world; and therefore I am dead against crying peace when there is no peace, and isn't meant to be. I am as sorry as any man to see folk fighting the wrong people and the wrong things, but I'd a deal sooner see them doing that, than that they should have no fight in them. So having recorded, and being about to record, my hero's fights of all sorts, with all sorts of enemies, I shall now proceed to give an account of his passage-at-arms with the only one of his school-fellows whom he ever had to encounter in this manner.

It was drawing towards the close of Arthur's first half-year, and the May evenings were lengthening out. Locking-up was not till eight o'clock, and everybody was beginning to talk about what he would do in the holidays. The shell, in which form all our *dramatis personæ* now are, were reading amongst other things the last book of Homer's Iliad, and had worked through it as far as the speeches of the women over Hector's body. It is a whole school-day, and four or five of the School-house boys (amongst whom are Arthur, Tom, and East) are preparing third lesson together. They have finished the regulation forty lines, and are for the most part getting very tired, notwithstanding the exquisite pathos of Helen's lamentation. And now several long four-syllabled words come together, and the boy with the dictionary strikes work.

"I am not going to look out any more words," says he; "we've done the quantity. Ten to one we shan't get so far. Let's go out into the close."

"Come along, boys," cries East, always ready to leave "the grind," as he called it; "our old coach is laid up, you know, and we shall have one of the new masters, who's sure to go slow and let us down easy."

So an adjournment to the close was carried *nem. con.*, little Arthur not daring to uplift his voice; but, being deeply interested in what they were reading, stayed quietly behind, and learnt on for his own pleasure.

As East had said, the regular master of the form was unwell, and they were to be heard by one of the new masters, quite a young man, who had only just left the University. Certainly it would be hard lines, if, by dawdling as much as possible in coming in and taking their places, entering into long-winded explanations of what was the usual course of the regular master of the form, and others of the stock contrivances of boys for wasting time in school, they could not spin out the lesson so that he should not work them through more than the forty lines; as to which quantity there was a perpetual fight going on between the master and his form, the latter insisting, and enforcing by passive resistance, that it was the prescribed quantity of Homer for a shell lesson, the former that there was no fixed quantity, but that they must always be ready to go on to fifty or sixty lines if there were time within the hour. However, notwithstanding all their efforts, the new master got on horribly quick; he seemed to have the bad taste to be really interested in the lesson, and to be trying to work them up into something like appreciation of it, giving them good spirited English words, instead of the wretched bald stuff into which they rendered poor old Homer; and construing over each piece himself to them, after each boy, to show them how it should be done.

Now the clock strikes the three-quarters; there is only a quarter of an hour more; but the forty lines are all but done. So the boys, one after another, who are called up, stick more and more, and make balder and ever more bald work of it. The poor young master is pretty near beat by this time, and feels ready to knock his head against the wall, or his fingers against somebody else's head. So he gives up altogether the lower and middle parts of the form, and looks round in despair at the boys on the top bench, to see if there is one out of whom he can strike a spark or two, and who will be too chivalrous to murder the most beautiful utterances of the most beautiful woman of the old world. His eye rests on Arthur, and he calls him up to finish construing Helen's speech. Whereupon all the other boys draw long breaths, and begin to stare about and take it easy. They are all safe; Arthur is the head of the form, and sure to be able to construe, and that will tide on safely till the hour strikes.

Arthur proceeds to read out the passage in Greek before construing it, as the custom is. Tom, who isn't paying much attention, is suddenly caught by the falter in his voice as he reads the two lines—

ἀλλὰ σὺ τόν γ' ἐπέεσσι παραιφάμενος κατέρυκες,
Σῇ τ' ἀγανοφροσύνῃ καὶ σοῖς ἀγανοῖς ἐπέεσσιν.

He looks up at Arthur. "Why, bless us," thinks he, "what can be the matter with the young'un? He's never going to get floored. He's sure to have learnt to the end." Next moment he is re-assured by the spirited tone in which Arthur begins construing, and betakes himself to drawing dogs' heads in his note-book, while the master, evidently enjoying the change, turns his back on the middle bench and stands before Arthur, beating a sort of time with his hand and foot, and saying, "Yes, yes," "very well," as Arthur goes on.

But as he nears the fatal two lines, Tom catches that falter and again looks up. He sees that there is something the matter, Arthur can hardly get on at all. What can it be?

Suddenly at this point Arthur breaks down altogether, and fairly bursts out crying, and dashes the cuff of his jacket across his eyes, blushing up to the roots of his hair, and feeling as if he should like to go down suddenly through the floor. The whole form are taken aback; most of them stare stupidly at him, while those who are gifted with presence of mind find their places and look steadily at their books, in hopes of not catching the master's eye and getting called up in Arthur's place.

The master looks puzzled for a moment, and then seeing, as the fact is, that the boy is really affected to tears by the most touching thing in Homer, perhaps in all profane poetry put together, steps up to him and lays his hand kindly on his shoulder, saying, "Never mind, my little man, you've construed very well. Stop a minute, there's no hurry."

Now, as luck would have it, there sat next above Tom on that day, in the middle bench of the form, a big boy, by name Williams, generally supposed to be the cock of the shell, therefore of all the school below the fifths. The small boys, who are great speculators on the prowess of their elders, used to hold forth to one another about Williams' great strength, and to discuss whether East or Brown would take a licking from him. He was called Slogger Williams, from the force with which it was supposed he could hit. In the main, he was a rough good-natured fellow enough, but very much alive to his own dignity. He reckoned himself the king of the form, and kept up his position with the strong hand, especially in the matter of forcing boys not to construe more than the legitimate forty lines. He had already grunted and grumbled to himself, when Arthur went on reading beyond the forty lines. But now that he had broken down just in the middle of all the long words, the Slogger's wrath was fairly roused.

"Sneaking little brute," muttered he, regardless of prudence, "clapping on the water-works just in the hardest place; see if I don't punch his head after fourth lesson."

"Whose?" said Tom, to whom the remark seemed to be addressed.

"Why, that little sneak, Arthur's," replied Williams.

"No, you shan't," said Tom.

"Hullo!" exclaimed Williams, looking at Tom with great surprise for a moment, and then giving him a sudden dig in the ribs with his elbow, which sent Tom's books flying on to the floor, and called the attention of the master, who turned suddenly round, and seeing the state of things, said—

"Williams, go down three places, and then go on."

The Slogger found his legs very slowly, and proceeded to go below Tom and two other boys with great disgust, and then, turning round and facing the master, said, "I haven't learnt any more, sir; our lesson is only forty lines."

"Is that so?" said the master, appealing generally to the top bench. No answer.

"Who is the head boy of the form?" said he, waxing wroth.

"Arthur, sir," answered three or four boys, indicating our friend.

"Oh, your name's Arthur. Well now, what is the length of your regular lesson?"

Arthur hesitated a moment, and then said, "We call it only forty lines, sir."

"How do you mean, you call it?"

"Well, sir, Mr. Graham says we ain't to stop there, when there's time to construe more."

"I understand," said the master. "Williams, go down three more places, and write me out the lesson in Greek and English. And now, Arthur, finish construing."

"Oh! would I be in Arthur's shoes after fourth lesson?" said the little boys to one another; but Arthur finished Helen's speech without any further catastrophe, and the clock struck four, which ended third lesson.

Another hour was occupied in preparing and saying fourth lesson, during which Williams was bottling up his wrath; and when five struck, and the lessons for the day were over, he prepared to take summary vengeance on the innocent cause of his misfortune.

Tom was detained in school a few minutes after the rest, and on coming out into the quadrangle, the first thing he saw was a small ring of boys, applauding Williams, who was holding Arthur by the collar.

"There, you young sneak," said he, giving Arthur a cuff on the head with his other hand, "what made you say that—"

"Hullo!" said Tom, shouldering into the crowd, "you drop that, Williams; you shan't touch him."

"Who'll stop me?" said the Slogger, raising his hand again.

"I," said Tom; and suiting the action to the word, he struck the arm which held Arthur's arm so sharply, that the Slogger dropped it with a start, and turned the full current of his wrath on Tom.

"Will you fight?"

"Yes, of course."

"Huzza, there's going to be a fight between Slogger Williams and Tom Brown!"

The news ran like wildfire about, and many boys who were on their way to tea at their several houses turned back, and sought the back of the chapel, where the fights come off.

"Just run and tell East to come and back me," said Tom to a small School-house boy, who was off like a rocket to Harrowell's, just stopping for a moment to poke his head into the School-house hall, where the lower boys were already at tea, and sing out, "Fight! Tom Brown and Slogger Williams."

Up start half the boys at once, leaving bread, eggs, butter, sprats, and all the rest to take care of themselves. The greater part of the remainder follow in a minute, after swallowing their tea, carrying their food in their hands to consume as they go. Three or four only remain, who steal the butter of the more impetuous, and make to themselves an unctuous feast.

In another minute East and Martin tear through the quadrangle, carrying a sponge, and arrive at the scene of action just as the combatants are beginning to strip.

Tom felt he had got his work cut out for him, as he stripped off his jacket, waistcoat, and braces. East tied his handkerchief round his waist, and rolled up his shirt-sleeves for him: "Now, old boy, don't you open your mouth to say a word, or try to help yourself a bit,—we'll do all that; you keep all your breath and strength for the Slogger." Martin meanwhile folded the clothes, and put them under the chapel rails; and now Tom, with East to handle him, and Martin to give him a knee, steps out on the turf, and is ready for all that may come: and here is the Slogger too, all stripped, and thirsting for the fray.

It doesn't look a fair match at first glance: Williams is nearly two inches taller, and probably a long year older than his opponent, and he is very strongly made about the arms and shoulders,—"peels well," as the little knot of big fifth-form boys, the amateurs, say; who stand outside the ring of little boys, looking complacently on, but taking no active part in the proceedings. But down below he is not so good by any means; no spring from the loins, and feeblish, not to say shipwrecky about the knees. Tom, on the contrary, though not half so strong in the arms, is good all over, straight, hard, and springy, from neck to ankle, better perhaps in his legs than anywhere. Besides, you can see by the clear white of his eye, and fresh bright look of his skin, that he is in tip-top training, able to do all he knows; while the Slogger looks rather sodden, as if he didn't take much exercise and ate too much tuck. The time-keeper is chosen, a large ring made, and the two stand up opposite one another for a moment, giving us time just to make our little observations.

"If Tom'll only condescend to fight with his head and heels," as East mutters to Martin, "we shall do."

But seemingly he won't, for there he goes in, making play with both hands. Hard all, is the word; the two stand to one another like men; rally follows rally in quick succession, each fighting as if he thought to finish the whole thing out of hand. "Can't last at this rate," say the knowing ones, while the partisans of each make the air ring with their shouts and counter-shouts, of encouragement, approval, and defiance.

"Take it easy, take it easy—keep away, let him come after you," implores East, as he wipes Tom's face after the first round with a wet sponge, while he sits back on Martin's knee, supported by the Madman's long arms, which tremble a little from excitement.

"Time's up," calls the time-keeper.

"There he goes again, hang it all!" growls East, as his man is at it again, as hard as ever. A very severe round follows, in which Tom gets out and out the worst of it, and is at last hit clean off his legs, and deposited on the grass by a right-hander from the Slogger.

Loud shouts rise from the boys of Slogger's house, and the School-house are silent and vicious, ready to pick quarrels anywhere.

"Two to one in half-crowns on the big 'un," says Rattle, one of the amateurs, a tall fellow, in thunder-and-lightning waistcoat, and puffy good-natured face.

"Done!" says Groove, another amateur of quieter look, taking out his note-book to enter it, for our friend Rattle sometimes forgets these little things.

Meantime East is freshing up Tom with the sponges for next round, and has set two other boys to rub his hands.

"Tom, old boy," whispers he, "this may be fun for you, but it's death to me. He'll hit all the fight out of you in another five minutes, and then I shall go and drown myself in the island ditch. Feint him—use your legs! draw him about! he'll lose his wind then in no time, and you can go into him. Hit at his body too; we'll take care of his frontispiece by and by."

Tom felt the wisdom of the counsel, and saw already that he couldn't go in and finish the Slogger off at mere hammer and tongs, so changed his tactics completely in the third round. He now fights cautiously, getting away from and parrying the Slogger's lunging hits, instead of trying to counter, and leading his enemy a dance all round the ring after him. "He's funking; go in, Williams," "Catch him up," "Finish him off," scream the small boys of the Slogger party.

"Just what we want," thinks East, chuckling to himself, as he sees Williams, excited by these shouts, and thinking the game in his own hands, blowing himself in his exertions to get to close quarters again, while Tom is keeping away with perfect ease.

They quarter over the ground again and again, Tom always on the defensive.

The Slogger pulls up at last for a moment, fairly blown.

"Now then, Tom," sings out East, dancing with delight. Tom goes in in a twinkling, and hits two heavy body blows, and gets away again before the Slogger can catch his wind, which when he does he rushes with blind fury at Tom, and being skilfully parried and avoided, overreaches himself and falls on his face, amidst terrific cheers from the School-house boys.

"Double your two to one?" says Groove to Rattle, notebook in hand.

"Stop a bit," says that hero, looking uncomfortably at Williams, who is puffing away on his second's knee, winded enough, but little the worse in any other way.

After another round the Slogger too seems to see that he can't go in and win right off, and has met his match or thereabouts. So he too begins to use his head, and tries to make Tom lose his patience, and come in before his time. And so the fight sways on, now one, and now the other getting a trifling pull.

Tom's face begins to look very one-sided—there are little queer bumps on his forehead, and his mouth is bleeding; but East keeps the wet sponge going so scientifically, that he comes up looking as fresh and bright as ever. Williams is only slightly marked in the face, but by the nervous movement of his elbows you can see that Tom's body blows are telling. In fact, half the vice of the Slogger's hitting is neutralized, for he daren't lunge out freely for fear of exposing his sides. It is too interesting by this time for much shouting, and the whole ring is very quiet.

"All right, Tommy," whispers East; "hold on's the horse that's to win. We've got the last. Keep your head, old boy."

But where is Arthur all this time? Words cannot paint the poor little fellow's distress. He couldn't muster courage to come up to the ring, but wandered up and down from the great fives'-court to the corner of the chapel rails, now trying to make up his mind to throw himself between them, and try to stop them; then thinking of running in and telling his friend Mary, who he knew would instantly report to the Doctor. The stories he had heard of men being killed in prize-fights rose up horribly before him.

Once only, when the shouts of "Well done, Brown!" "Huzza for the School-house!" rose higher than ever, he ventured up to the ring, thinking the victory was won. Catching sight of Tom's face in the state I have described, all fear of consequences vanishing out of his mind, he rushed straight off to the matron's room, beseeching her to get the fight stopped, or he should die.

But it's time for us to get back to the close. What is this fierce tumult and confusion? The ring is broken, and high and angry words are being bandied about; "It's all fair,"—"It isn't,"—"No hugging!" the fight is stopped. The combatants, however, sit there quietly, tended by their seconds, while their adherents wrangle in the middle. East can't help shouting challenges to two or three of the other side, though he never leaves Tom for a moment, and plies the sponges as fast as ever.

The fact is, that at the end of the last round, Tom, seeing a good opening, had closed with his opponent, and after a moment's struggle, had thrown him heavily, by help of the fall he had learnt from his village rival in the vale of White Horse. Williams hadn't the ghost of a chance with Tom at wrestling; and the conviction broke at once on the Slogger faction, that if this were allowed their man must be licked. There was a strong feeling in the School against catching hold and throwing, though it was generally ruled all fair within limits; so the ring was broken and the fight stopped.

The School-house are over-ruled—the fight is on again, but there is to be no throwing; and East in high wrath threatens to take his man away after next round (which he don't mean to do, by the way), when suddenly young Brooke comes through the small gate at the end of the chapel. The School-house faction rush to him. "Oh, hurra! now we shall get fair play."

"Please, Brooke, come up, they won't let Tom Brown throw him."

"Throw whom?" says Brooke, coming up to the ring. "Oh! Williams, I see. Nonsense! of course he may throw him, if he catches him fairly above the waist."

Now, young Brooke, you're in the sixth, you know, and you ought to stop all fights. He looks hard at both boys. "Anything wrong?" says he to East, nodding at Tom.

"Not a bit."

"Not beat at all?"

"Bless you, no! Heaps of fight in him. Ain't there, Tom?"

Tom looks at Brooke and grins.

"How's he?" nodding at Williams.

"So, so; rather done, I think, since his last fall. He won't stand above two more."

"Time's up!" The boys rise again and face one another. Brooke can't find it in his heart to stop them just yet, so the round goes on, the Slogger waiting for Tom, and reserving all his strength to hit him out should he come in for the wrestling dodge again, for he feels that that must be stopped, or his sponge will soon go up in the air.

And now another new-comer appears on the field, to wit, the under-porter, with his long brush and great wooden receptacle for dust under his arm. He has been sweeping out the schools.

"You'd better stop, gentlemen," he says; "the Doctor knows that Brown's fighting—he'll be out in a minute."

"You go to Bath, Bill," is all that that excellent servitor gets by his advice. And being a man of his hands, and a staunch upholder of the School-house, can't help stopping to look on for a bit, and see Tom Brown, their pet craftsman, fight a round.

It is grim earnest now, and no mistake. Both boys feel this, and summon every power of head, hand, and eye to their aid. A piece of luck on either side, a foot slipping, a blow getting well home, or another fall, may decide it. Tom works slowly round for an opening; he has all the legs, and can choose his own time; the Slogger waits for the attack, and hopes to finish it by some heavy right-handed blow. As they quarter slowly over the ground, the evening sun comes out from behind a cloud and falls full on Williams's face. Tom darts in; the heavy right-hand is delivered, but only grazes his head. A short rally at close quarters, and they close; in another moment the Slogger is thrown again heavily for the third time.

"I'll give you three or two on the little one in half-crowns," said Groove to Rattle.

"No, thank'ee," answers the other, diving his hands further into his coat-tails.

Just at this stage of the proceedings, the door of the turret which leads to the Doctor's library suddenly opens, and he steps into the close, and makes straight for the ring, in which Brown and the Slogger are both seated on their seconds' knees for the last time.

"The Doctor! the Doctor!" shouts some small boy who catches sight of him, and the ring melts away in a few seconds, the small boys tearing off, Tom collaring his jacket and waistcoat, and slipping through the little gate by the chapel, and round the corner to Harrowell's with his backers, as lively as need be; Williams and his backers making off not quite so fast across the close; Groove, Rattle, and the other bigger fellows trying to combine dignity and prudence in a comical manner, and walking off fast enough, they hope, not to be recognized, and not fast enough to look like running away.

Young Brooke alone remains on the ground by the time the Doctor gets there, and touches his hat, not without a slight inward qualm.

"Hah! Brooke. I am surprised to see you here. Don't you know that I expect the sixth to stop fighting?"

Brooke felt much more uncomfortable than he had expected, but he was rather a favourite with the Doctor for his openness and plainness of speech; so blurted out, as he walked by the Doctor's side, who had already turned back—

"Yes, sir, generally. But I thought you wished us to exercise a discretion in the matter too—not to interfere too soon."

"But they have been fighting this half-hour and more," said the Doctor.

"Yes, sir; but neither was hurt. And they're the sort of boys who'll be all the better friends now, which they wouldn't have been if they had been stopped any earlier—before it was so equal."

"Who was fighting with Brown?" said the Doctor.

"Williams, sir, of Thompson's. He is bigger than Brown, and had the best of it at first, but not when you came up, sir. There's a good deal of jealousy between our house and Thompson's, and there would have been more fights if this hadn't been let go on, or if either of them had had much the worst of it."

"Well but, Brooke," said the Doctor, "doesn't this look a little as if you exercised your discretion by only stopping a fight when the School-house boy is getting the worst of it?"

Brooke, it must be confessed, felt rather gravelled.

"Now remember," added the Doctor, as he stopped at the turret-door, "this fight is not to go on—you'll see to that. And I expect you to stop all fights in future at once."

"Very well, sir," said young Brooke, touching his hat, and not sorry to see the turret-door close behind the Doctor's back.

Meantime Tom and the staunchest of his adherents had reached Harrowell's, and Sally was bustling about to get them a late tea, while Stumps had been sent off to Tew, the butcher, to get a piece of raw beef for Tom's eye, which was to be healed off-hand, so that he might show well in the morning. He was not a bit the worse, except a slight difficulty in his vision, a singing in his ears, and a sprained thumb, which he kept in a cold-water bandage, while he drank lots of tea, and listened to the Babel of voices talking and speculating of nothing but the fight, and how Williams would have given in after another fall (which he didn't in the least believe), and how on earth the Doctor could have got to know of it,—such bad luck! He couldn't help thinking to himself that he was glad he hadn't won; he liked it better as it was, and felt very friendly to the Slogger. And then poor little Arthur crept in and sat down quietly near him, and kept looking at him and the raw beef with such plaintive looks that Tom at last burst out laughing.

"Don't make such eyes, young 'un," said he, "there's nothing the matter."

"Oh, but, Tom, are you much hurt? I can't bear thinking it was all for me."

"Not a bit of it, don't flatter yourself. We were sure to have had it out sooner or later."

"Well, but you won't go on, will you? You'll promise me you won't go on?"

"Can't tell about that—all depends on the houses. We're in the hands of our countrymen, you know. Must fight for the School-house fag, if so be."

However, the lovers of the science were doomed to disappointment this time. Directly after locking-up one of the night fags knocked at Tom's door.

"Brown, young Brooke wants you in the sixth-form room."

Up went Tom to the summons, and found the magnates sitting at their supper.

"Well, Brown," said young Brooke, nodding to him, "how do you feel?"

"Oh, very well, thank you, only I've sprained my thumb, I think."

"Sure to do that in a fight. Well, you hadn't the worst of it, I could see. Where did you learn that throw?"

"Down in the country when I was a boy."

"Hullo! why, what are you now? Well, never mind, you're a plucky fellow. Sit down and have some supper."

Tom obeyed, by no means loth. And the fifth-form boy next him filled him a tumbler of bottled beer, and he ate and drank, listening to the pleasant talk, and wondering how soon he should be in the fifth, and one of that much-envied society.

As he got up to leave, Brooke said, "You must shake hands to-morrow morning; I shall come and see that done after first lesson."

And so he did. And Tom and the Slogger shook hands with great satisfaction and mutual respect. And for the next year or two, whenever fights were being talked of, the small boys who had been present shook their heads wisely, saying, "Ah! but you should just have seen the fight between Slogger Williams and Tom Brown!"

And now, boys all, three words before we quit the subject. I have put in this chapter on fighting of malice prepense, partly because I want to give you a true picture of what every-day school life was in my time, and not a kid-glove and go-to-meeting-coat picture; and partly because of the cant and twaddle that's talked of boxing and fighting with fists now-a-days. Even Thackeray has given in to it; and only a few weeks ago there was some rampant stuff in the *Times* on the subject, in an article on field-sports.

Boys will quarrel, and when they quarrel will sometimes fight. Fighting with fists is the natural and English way for English boys to settle their quarrels. What substitute for it is there, or ever was there, amongst any nation under the sun? What would you like to see take its place?

Learn to box, then, as you learn to play cricket and football. Not one of you will be the worse, but very much the better, for learning to box well. Should you never have to use it in earnest, there's no exercise in the world so good for the temper and for the muscles of the back and legs.

As to fighting, keep out of it if you can, by all means. When the time comes, if it ever should, that you have to say "Yes" or "No" to a challenge to fight, say "No" if you can—only take care you make it clear to yourselves why you say "No." It's a proof of the highest courage, if done from true Christian motives. It's quite right and justifiable, if done from a simple aversion to physical pain and danger. But don't say "No" because you fear a licking, and say or think it's because you fear God, for that's neither Christian nor honest. And if you do fight, fight it out; and don't give in while you can stand and see.

CHAPTER VI

FEVER IN THE SCHOOL

"This our hope for all that's mortal,
And we too shall burst the bond;
Death keeps watch beside the portal,
But 'tis life that dwells beyond."
JOHN STERLING

T WO YEARS HAVE PASSED since the events recorded in the last chapter, and the end of the summer half-year is again drawing on. Martin has left and gone on a cruise in the South Pacific, in one of his uncle's ships; the old magpie, as disreputable as ever, his last bequest to Arthur, lives in the joint study. Arthur is nearly sixteen, and at the head of the twenty, having gone up the school at the rate of a form a half-year. East and Tom have been much more deliberate in their progress, and are only a little way up the fifth form. Great strapping boys they are, but still thorough boys, filling about the same place in the house that young Brooke filled when they were new boys, and much the same sort of fellows. Constant intercourse with Arthur has done much for both of them, especially for Tom; but much remains yet to be done, if they are to get all the good out of Rugby which is to be got there in these times. Arthur is still frail and delicate, with more spirit than body; but, thanks to his intimacy with them and Martin, has learned to swim, and run, and play cricket, and has never hurt himself by too much reading.

One evening, as they were all sitting down to supper in the fifth-form room, some one started a report that a fever had broken out at one of the boarding-houses; "they say," he added, "that Thompson is very ill, and that Dr. Robertson has been sent for from Northampton."

"Then we shall all be sent home," cried another. "Hurrah! five weeks' extra holidays, and no fifth-form examination!"

"I hope not," said Tom; "there'll be no Marylebone match then at the end of the half."

Some thought one thing, some another, many didn't believe the report; but the next day, Tuesday, Dr. Robertson arrived, and stayed all day, and had long conferences with the Doctor.

On Wednesday morning, after prayers, the Doctor addressed the whole school. There were several cases of fever in different houses, he said; but Dr. Robertson, after the most careful examination, had assured him that it was not infectious, and that if proper care were taken, there could be no reason for stopping the school-work at present. The examinations were just coming on, and it would be very unadvisable to break-up now. However, any boys who chose to do so were at liberty to write home, and, if their parents wished it, to leave at once. He should send the whole school home if the fever spread.

The next day Arthur sickened, but there was no other case. Before the end of the week thirty or forty boys had gone, but the rest stayed on. There was a general wish to please the Doctor, and a feeling that it was cowardly to run away.

On the Saturday Thompson died, in the bright afternoon, while the cricket-match was going on as usual on the big-side ground: the Doctor coming from his death-bed, passed along the gravel-walk at the side of the close, but no one knew what had happened till the next day. At morning lecture it began to be rumoured, and by afternoon chapel was known generally; and a feeling of seriousness and awe at the actual presence of death among them came over the whole school. In all the long years of his ministry the Doctor perhaps never spoke words which sank deeper than some of those in that day's sermon.

"When I came yesterday from visiting all but the very death-bed of him who has been taken from us, and looked around upon all the familiar objects and scenes within our own ground, where your common amusements were going on with your common cheerfulness and activity, I felt there was nothing painful in witnessing that; it did not seem in any way shocking or out of tune with those feelings which the sight of a dying Christian must be supposed to awaken. The unsuitableness in point of natural feeling between scenes of mourning and scenes of liveliness did not at all present itself. But I did feel that if at that moment any of those faults had been brought before me which sometimes occur amongst us; had I heard that any of you had been guilty of falsehood, or of drunkennness, or of any other such sin; had I heard from any quarter the language of profaneness, or of unkindness, or of indecency; had I heard or seen any signs of that wretched folly which courts the laugh of fools by affecting not to dread evil and not to care for good, then the unsuitableness of any of these things with the scene I had just quitted would indeed have been most intensely painful. And why? Not because such things would really have been worse than at any other time, but because at such a moment the eyes are opened really to know good and evil, because we then feel what it is so to live as that death becomes an infinite blessing, and what it is so to live also, that it were good for us if we had never been born."

Tom had gone into chapel in sickening anxiety about Arthur, but he came out cheered and strengthened by those grand words, and walked up alone to their study. And when he sat down and looked round, and saw Arthur's straw-hat and cricket-jacket hanging on their pegs, and marked all his little neat arrangements, not one of which had been disturbed, the tears indeed rolled down his cheeks; but they were calm and blessed tears, and he repeated to himself, "Yes, Geordie's eyes are opened—he knows what it is so to live as that death becomes an infinite blessing. But do I? Oh, God, can I bear to lose him?"

The week passed mournfully away. No more boys sickened, but Arthur was reported worse each day, and his mother arrived early in the week. Tom made many appeals to be allowed to see him, and several times tried to get up to the sick-room; but the housekeeper was always in the way, and at last spoke to the Doctor, who kindly but peremptorily forbade him.

Thompson was buried on the Tuesday, and the burial service, so soothing and grand always, but beyond all words solemn when read over a boy's grave to his companions, brought him much comfort, and many strange new thoughts and longings. He went back to his regular life, and played cricket and bathed as usual: it seemed to him that this was the right thing to do, and the new thoughts and longings became more brave and healthy for the effort. The crisis came on Saturday, the day week that Thompson had died; and during that long afternoon Tom sat in his study reading his Bible, and going every half-hour to the house-keeper's room, expecting each time to hear that the gentle and brave little spirit had gone home. But God had work for Arthur to do: the crisis passed—on Sunday evening he was declared out of danger; on Monday he sent a message to Tom that he was almost well, had changed his room, and was to be allowed to see him the next day.

It was evening when the housekeeper summoned him to the sick-room. Arthur was lying on the sofa by the open window, through which the rays of the western sun stole gently, lighting up his white face and golden hair. Tom remembered a German picture of an angel which he knew; often had he thought how transparent and golden and spirit-like it was; and he shuddered to think how like it Arthur looked, and felt a shock as if his blood had all stopped short, as he realized how near the other world his friend must have been to look like that. Never till that moment had he felt how his little chum had twined himself round his heart-strings; and as he stole gently across the room and knelt down, and put his arm round Arthur's head on the pillow, felt ashamed and half angry at his own red and brown face, and the bounding sense of health and power which filled every fibre of his body, and made every movement of mere living a joy to

him. He needn't have troubled himself; it was this very strength and power so different from his own which drew Arthur so to him.

Arthur laid his thin white hand, on which the blue veins stood out so plainly, on Tom's great brown fist, and smiled at him; and then looked out of the window again, as if he couldn't bear to lose a moment of the sunset, into the tops of the great feathery elms, round which the rooks were circling and clanging, returning in flocks from their evening's foraging parties. The elms rustled, the sparrows in the ivy just outside the window chirped and fluttered about, quarrelling, and making it up again; the rooks young and old talked in chorus, and the merry shouts of the boys and the sweet click of the cricket-bats came up cheerily from below.

"Dear George," said Tom, "I am so glad to be let up to see you at last. I've tried hard to come so often, but they wouldn't let me before."

"Oh, I know, Tom; Mary has told me every day about you, and how she was obliged to make the Doctor speak to you to keep you away. I'm very glad you didn't get up, for you might have caught it; and you couldn't stand being ill, with all the matches going on. And you're in the eleven, too, I hear—I'm so glad."

"Yes, ain't it jolly?" said Tom proudly; "I'm ninth too. I made forty at the last pie-match, and caught three fellows out. So I was put in above Jones and Tucker. Tucker's so savage, for he was head of the twenty-two."

"Well, I think you ought to be higher yet," said Arthur, who was as jealous for the renown of Tom in games, as Tom was for his as a scholar.

"Never mind, I don't care about cricket or anything now you're getting well, Geordie; and I shouldn't have hurt, I know, if they'd have let me come up,—nothing hurts me. But you'll get about now directly, won't you? You won't believe how clean I've kept the study. All your things are just as you left them; and I feed the old magpie just when you used, though I have to come in from big-side for him, the old rip. He won't look pleased all I can do, and sticks his head first on one side and then on the other, and blinks at me before he'll begin to eat, till I'm half inclined to box his ears. And whenever East comes in, you should see him hop off to the window, dot and go one, though Harry wouldn't touch a feather of him now."

Arthur laughed. "Old Gravey has a good memory; he can't forget the sieges of poor Martin's den in old times." He paused a moment, and then went on: "You can't think how often I've been thinking of old Martin since I've been ill; I suppose one's mind gets restless, and likes to wander off to strange unknown places. I wonder what queer new pets the old boy has got; how he must be revelling in the thousand new birds, beasts, and fishes!"

Tom felt a pang of jealousy, but kicked it out in a moment. "Fancy him on a South-Sea Island, with the Cherokees or Patagonians, or some such wild niggers!" (Tom's ethnology and geography were faulty, but sufficient for his needs); "they'll make the old Madman cock medicine-man and tattoo him all over. Perhaps he's cutting about now all blue, and has a squaw and a wigwam. He'll improve their boomerangs, and be able to throw them too, without having old Thomas sent after him by the Doctor to take them away."

Arthur laughed at the remembrance of the boomerang story, but then looked grave again, and said, "He'll convert all the island, I know."

"Yes, if he don't blow it up first."

"Do you remember, Tom, how you and East used to laugh at him and chaff him, because he said he was sure the rooks all had calling-over or prayers, or something of the sort, when the locking-up bell rang? Well, I declare," said Arthur, looking up seriously into Tom's laughing eyes, "I do think he was right. Since I've been lying here, I've watched them every night; and, do you know, they really do come and perch, all of them, just about locking-up time; and then first there's a regular chorus of caws, and then they stop a bit, and one old fellow, or perhaps two or three in different trees, caw solos, and then off they all go again, fluttering about and cawing anyhow till they roost."

"I wonder if the old blackies do talk," said Tom, looking up at them. "How they must abuse me and East, and pray for the Doctor for stopping the slinging!"

"There! look, look!" cried Arthur, "don't you see the old fellow without a tail coming up? Martin used to call him the 'clerk.' He can't steer himself. You never saw such fun as he is in a high wind, when he can't steer himself home, and gets carried right past the trees, and has to bear up again and again before he can perch."

The locking-up bell began to toll, and the two boys were silent, and listened to it. The sound soon carried Tom off to the river and the woods, and he began to go over in his mind the many occasions on which he had heard that toll coming faintly down the breeze, and had to pack his rod in a hurry and make a run for it, to get in before the gates were shut. He was roused with a start from his memories by Arthur's voice, gentle and weak from his late illness.

"Tom, will you be angry if I talk to you very seriously?"

"No, dear old boy, not I. But ain't you faint, Arthur, or ill? What can I get you? Don't say anything to hurt yourself now—you are very weak; let me come up again."

"No, no, I shan't hurt myself: I'd sooner speak to you now, if you don't mind. I've asked Mary to tell the Doctor that you are with me, so you needn't go down to calling-over; and I mayn't have another chance, for I shall most likely have to go home for change of air to get well, and mayn't come back this half."

"Oh, do you think you must go away before the end of the half? I'm so sorry. It's more than five weeks yet to the holidays, and all the fifth-form examination and half the cricket-matches to come yet. And what shall I do all that time alone in our study? Why, Arthur, it will be more than twelve weeks before I see you again. Oh, hang it, I can't stand that! Besides, who's to keep me up to working at the examination books? I shall come out bottom of the form, as sure as eggs is eggs."

Tom was rattling on, half in joke, half in earnest, for he wanted to get Arthur out of his serious vein, thinking it would do him harm; but Arthur broke in—

"Oh, please, Tom, stop, or you'll drive all I had to say out of my head. And I'm already horribly afraid I'm going to make you angry."

"Don't gammon, young 'un," rejoined Tom (the use of the old name, dear to him from old recollections, made Arthur start and smile, and feel quite happy); "you know you ain't afraid, and you've never made me angry since the first month we chummed together. Now I'm going to be quite sober for a quarter of an hour, which is more than I am once in a year; so make the most of it; heave ahead, and pitch into me right and left."

"Dear Tom, I ain't going to pitch into you," said Arthur, piteously; "and it seems so cocky in me to be advising you, who've been my backbone ever since I've been at Rugby, and have made the school a paradise to me. Ah, I see I shall never do it, unless I go head-over-heels at once, as you said when you taught me to swim. Tom, I want you to give up using vulgus-books and cribs."

Arthur sank back on to his pillow with a sigh, as if the effort had been great; but the worst was now over, and he looked straight at Tom, who was evidently taken aback. He leant his elbows on his knees, and stuck his hands into his hair, whistled a verse of "Billy Taylor," and then was quite silent for another minute. Not a shade crossed his face, but he was clearly puzzled. At last he looked up, and caught Arthur's anxious look, took his hand, and said simply—

"Why, young 'un?"

"Because you're the honestest boy in Rugby, and that ain't honest."

"I don't see that."

"What were you sent to Rugby for?"

"Well, I don't know exactly—nobody ever told me. I suppose because all boys are sent to a public school in England."

"But what do you think yourself? What do you want to do here, and to carry away?"

Tom thought a minute. "I want to be A 1 at cricket and football, and all the other games, and to make my hands keep my head against any fellow, lout or gentleman. I want to get into the sixth before I leave, and to please the Doctor; and I want to carry away just as much Latin and Greek as will take me through Oxford respectably. There now, young 'un, I never thought of it before, but that's pretty much about my figure. Ain't it all on the square? What have you got to say to that?"

"Why, that you are pretty sure to do all that you want, then."

"Well, I hope so. But you've forgot one thing, what I want to leave behind me. I want to leave behind me," said Tom, speaking slow, and looking much moved, "the name of a fellow who never bullied a little boy, or turned his back on a big one."

Arthur pressed his hand, and after a moment's silence went on: "You say, Tom, you want to please the Doctor. Now, do you want to please him by what he thinks you do, or by what you really do?"

"By what I really do, of course."

"Does he think you use cribs and vulgus-books?"

Tom felt at once that his flank was turned, but he couldn't give in. "He was at Winchester himself," said he; "he knows all about it."

"Yes, but does he think *you* use them? Do you think he approves of it?"

"You young villain!" said Tom, shaking his fist at Arthur, half vexed and half pleased, "I never think about it. Hang it—there, perhaps he don't. Well, I suppose he don't."

Arthur saw that he had got his point; he knew his friend well, and was wise in silence as in speech. He only said, "I would sooner have the doctor's good opinion of me as I really am, than any man's in the world."

After another minute, Tom began again: "Look here, young 'un, how on earth am I to get time to play the matches this half, if I give up cribs? We're in the middle of that long crabbed chorus in the Agamemnon; I can only just make head or tail of it with the crib. Then there's Pericles's speech coming on in Thucydides, and 'The Birds' to get up for the examination, besides the Tacitus." Tom groaned at the thought of his accumulated labours. "I say, young 'un, there's only five weeks or so left to holidays; mayn't I go on as usual for this half? I'll tell the Doctor about it some day, or you may."

Arthur looked out of the window; the twilight had come on, and all was silent. He repeated in a low voice, "In this thing the Lord pardon thy servant, that when my master goeth into the house of Rimmon to worship there, and he leaneth on my hand, and I bow down myself in the house of Rimmon, when I bow down myself in the house of Rimmon, the Lord pardon thy servant in this thing."

Not a word more was said on the subject, and the boys were again silent—one of those blessed, short silences, in which the resolves which colour a life are so often taken.

Tom was the first to break it. "You've been very ill indeed, haven't you, Geordie?" said he, with a mixture of awe and curiosity, feeling as if his friend had been in some strange place or scene, of which he could form no idea, and full of the memory of his own thoughts during the last week.

"Yes, very. I'm sure the Doctor thought I was going to die. He gave me the Sacrament last Sunday, and you can't think what he is when one is ill. He said such brave, and tender, and gentle things to me, I felt quite light and strong after it, and never had any more fear. My mother brought our old medical man, who attended me when I was a poor sickly child; he said my constitution was quite changed, and that I'm fit for anything now. If it hadn't, I couldn't have stood three days of this illness. That's all thanks to you, and the games you've made me fond of."

"More thanks to old Martin," said Tom; "he's been your real friend."

"Nonsense, Tom; he never could have done for me what you have."

"Well, I don't know; I did little enough. Did they tell you—you won't mind hearing it now, I know—that poor Thompson died last week? The other three boys are getting quite round, like you."

"Oh, yes, I heard of it."

Then Tom, who was quite full of it, told Arthur of the burial-service in the chapel, and how it had impressed him and, he believed, all the other boys. "And though the

Doctor never said a word about it," said he, "and it was a half-holiday and match day, there wasn't a game played in the close all the afternoon, and the boys all went about as if it were Sunday."

"I'm very glad of it," said Arthur. "But, Tom, I've had such strange thoughts about death lately. I've never told a soul of them, not even my mother. Sometimes I think they're wrong, but, do you know, I don't think in my heart I could be sorry at the death of any of my friends."

Tom was taken quite aback. "What in the world is the young 'un after now?" thought he; "I've swallowed a good many of his crotchets, but this altogether beats me. He can't be quite right in his head." He didn't want to say a word, and shifted about uneasily in the dark; however, Arthur seemed to be waiting for an answer, so at last he said, "I don't think I quite see what you mean, Geordie. One's told so often to think about death, that I've tried it on sometimes, especially this last week. But we won't talk of it now. I'd better go—you're getting tired, and I shall do you harm."

"No, no, indeed I ain't, Tom; you must stop till nine, there's only twenty minutes. I've settled you shall stop till nine. And oh! do let me talk to you—I must talk to you. I see it's just as I feared. You think I'm half mad—don't you now?"

"Well, I did think it odd what you said, Geordie, as you ask me."

Arthur paused a moment, and then said quickly, "I'll tell you how it all happened. At first, when I was sent to the sick-room, and found I had really got the fever, I was terribly frightened. I thought I should die, and I could not face it for a moment. I don't think it was sheer cowardice at first, but I thought how hard it was to be taken away from my mother and sisters, and you all, just as I was beginning to see my way to many things, and to feel that I might be a man and do a man's work. To die without having fought, and worked, and given one's life away, was too hard to bear. I got terribly impatient, and accused God of injustice, and strove to justify myself; and the harder I strove the deeper I sank. Then the image of my dear father often came across me, but I turned from it. Whenever it came, a heavy numbing throb seemed to take hold of my heart, and say, 'Dead—dead—dead.' And I cried out, 'The living, the living shall praise Thee, O God; the dead cannot praise Thee. There is no work in the grave; in the night no man can work. But I can work. I can do great things. I *will* do great things. Why wilt Thou slay me?' And so I struggled and plunged, deeper and deeper, and went down into a living black tomb. I was alone there, with no power to stir or think; alone with myself; beyond the reach of all human fellowship; beyond Christ's reach, I thought, in my nightmare. You, who are brave and bright and strong, can have no idea of that agony. Pray to God you never may. Pray as for your life."

Arthur stopped—from exhaustion, Tom thought; but what between his fear lest Arthur should hurt himself, his awe, and longing for him to go on, he couldn't ask, or stir to help him.

Presently he went on, but quite calm and slow. "I don't know how long I was in that state. For more than a day, I know; for I was quite conscious, and lived my outer life all the time, and took my medicines, and spoke to my mother, and heard what they said. But I didn't take much note of time; I thought time was over for me, and that that tomb was what was beyond. Well, on last Sunday morning, as I seemed to lie in that tomb, alone, as I thought, for ever and ever, the black dead wall was cleft in two, and I was caught up and borne through into the light by some great power, some living mighty spirit. Tom, do you remember the living creatures and the wheels in Ezekiel? It was just like that; 'when they went I heard the noise of their wings, like the noise of great waters, as the voice of the Almighty, the voice of speech, as the noise of an host; when they stood they let down their wings'—'and they went every one straight forward; whither the spirit was to go they went, and they turned not when they went.' And we rushed through the bright air, which was full of myriads of living creatures, and paused on the brink of a great river. And the power held me up, and I knew that that great river was the grave, and death dwelt there; but not the death I had met in the black tomb—that I felt was gone for ever. For on the other bank of the great river I saw men and women and children rising up pure and bright, and the tears were wiped from their eyes, and they put on glory and strength, and all weariness and pain fell away. And beyond were a multitude which no man could number, and they worked at some great work; and they who rose from the river went on and joined in the work. They all worked, and each worked in a different way, but all at the same work. And I saw there my father, and the men in the old town whom I knew when I was child; many a hard stern man, who never came to church, and whom they called atheist and infidel. There they were, side by side with my father, whom I had seen toil and die for them, and women and little children, and the seal was on the foreheads of all. And I longed to see what the work was, and could not; so I tried to plunge in the river, for I thought I would join them, but I could not. Then I looked about to see how they got into the river. And this I could not see, but I saw myriads on this side, and they too worked, and I knew that it was the same work; and the same seal was on their foreheads. And though I saw that there was toil and anguish in the work of these, and that most that were working were blind and feeble, yet I longed no more to plunge into the river, but more and more to know what the work was. And as I looked I saw my mother and my sisters, and I saw the Doctor, and you, Tom, and hundreds more whom I knew; and at last I saw myself too, and I was toiling and doing ever so little a piece of the great work. Then it all melted away, and the power left me, and as it left me I thought I heard a voice say, 'The vision is for an appointed time; though it tarry, wait for it, for in the end it shall speak and not lie, it shall surely come, it shall not tarry.' It was early morning I know, then, it was so quiet and cool, and my mother was fast asleep in the chair by my bedside; but it wasn't only a dream of mine. I know it wasn't a dream. Then I fell into a deep sleep, and only woke after afternoon chapel; and the Doctor came and gave me the Sacrament, as I told you. I told him and my mother I should get well—I knew I should; but I couldn't tell them why. Tom," said Arthur, gently, after another minute, "do you see why I could not grieve now to see my dearest friend die? It can't be—it isn't, all fever or illness. God would never have let me see it so clear if it wasn't true. I don't understand it all yet—it will take me my life and longer to do that—to find out what the work is."

When Arthur stopped there was a long pause. Tom could not speak, he was almost afraid to breathe, lest he should break the train of Arthur's thoughts. He longed to hear more, and to ask questions. In another minute nine o'clock struck, and a gentle tap at the door called them both back into the world again. They did not answer, however, for a moment, and so the door opened and a lady came in carrying a candle.

She went straight to the sofa, and took hold of Arthur's hand, and then stooped down and kissed him.

"My dearest boy, you feel a little feverish again. Why didn't you have lights? You've talked too much, and excited yourself in the dark."

"Oh, no, mother, you can't think how well I feel. I shall start with you to-morrow for Devonshire. But, mother, here's my friend; here's Tom Brown—you know him?"

"Yes, indeed, I've known him for years," she said, and held out her hand to Tom, who was now standing up behind the sofa. This was Arthur's mother: tall and slight and fair, with masses of golden hair drawn back from the broad white forehead, and the calm blue eye meeting his so deep and open—the eye that he knew so well, for it was his friend's over again, and the lovely tender mouth that trembled while he looked—she stood there, a woman of thirty-eight, old enough to be his mother, and one whose face showed the lines which must be written on the faces of good men's wives and widows —but he thought he had never seen anything so beautiful. He couldn't help wondering if Arthur's sisters were like her.

Tom held her hand, and looked on straight in her face; he could neither let it go nor speak.

"Now, Tom," said Arthur, laughing, "where are your manners? you'll stare my mother out of countenance." Tom dropped the little hand with a sigh. "There, sit down, both of you. Here, dearest mother, there's room here;" and he made a place on the sofa for her. "Tom, you needn't go; I'm sure you won't be called up at first lesson." Tom felt that he would risk being floored at every lesson for the rest of his natural school-life sooner than go; so sat down. "And now," said Arthur, "I have realized one of the dearest wishes of my life—to see you two together."

And then he led away the talk to their home in Devonshire, and the red bright earth, and the deep green combes, and the peat streams like cairngorm pebbles, and the wild moor with its high cloudy Tors for a giant background to the picture—till Tom got jealous and stood up for the clear chalk streams, and the emerald water meadows and great elms and willows of the dear old Royal county, as he gloried to call it. And the mother sat on quiet and loving, rejoicing in their life. The quarter-to-ten struck, and the bell rang for bed, before they had well begun their talk, as it seemed.

Then Tom rose with a sigh to go.

"Shall I see you in the morning, Geordie?" said he, as he shook his friend's hand. "Never mind though; you'll be back next half, and I shan't forget the house of Rimmon."

Arthur's mother got up and walked with him to the door, and there gave him her hand again, and again his eyes met that deep loving look, which was like a spell upon him. Her voice trembled slightly as she said, "Good night—you are one who knows what our Father has promised to the friend of the widow and the fatherless. May He deal with you as you have dealt with me and mine!"

Tom was quite upset; he mumbled something about owing everything good in him to Geordie—looked in her face again, pressed her hand to his lips, and rushed downstairs to his study, where he sat till old Thomas came kicking at the door, to tell him his allowance would be stopped if he didn't go off to bed. (It would have been stopped anyhow, but that he was a great favourite with the old gentleman, who loved to come out in the afternoons into the close to Tom's wicket, and bowl slow twisters to him, and talk of the glories of bygone Surrey heroes, with whom he had played former generations.) So Tom roused himself, and took up his candle to go to bed; and then for the first time was aware of a beautiful new fishing-rod, with old Eton's mark on it, and a splendidly bound Bible, which lay on his table, on the title-page of which was written—"TOM BROWN, from his affectionate and grateful friends, Frances Jane Arthur; George Arthur."

I leave you all to guess how he slept, and what he dreamt of.

CHAPTER VII
HARRY EAST'S DILEMMAS AND DELIVERANCES

"The Holy Supper is kept indeed,
In whatso we share with another's need—
Not that which we give, but what we share
For the gift without the giver is bare:
Who bestows himself with his alms feeds three,
Himself, his hungering neighbour, and Me."
LOWELL, *The Vision of Sir Launfal*, p. 11.

T HE NEXT MORNING, after breakfast, Tom, East, and Gower met as usual to learn their second lesson together. Tom had been considering how to break his proposal of giving up the crib to the others, and having found no better way (as indeed none better can ever be found by man or boy), told them simply what had happened; how he had been to see Arthur, who had talked to him upon the subject, and what he had said, and for his part he had made up his mind, and wasn't going to use cribs any more: and not being quite sure of his ground, took the high and pathetic tone, and was proceeding to say, "how that having learnt his lessons with them for so many years, it would grieve him much to put an end to the arrangement, and he hoped at any rate that if they wouldn't go on with him, they should still be just as good friends, and respect one another's motives—but——"

Here the other boys, who had been listening with open eyes and ears, burst in—

"Stuff and nonsense!" cried Gower. "Here, East, get down the crib and find the place."

"Oh, Tommy, Tommy!" said East, proceeding to do as he was bidden, "that it should ever have come to this! I knew Arthur'd be the ruin of you some day, and you of me. And now the time's come,"—and he made a doleful face.

"I don't know about ruin," answered Tom; "I know that you and I would have had the sack long ago, if it hadn't been for him. And you know it as well as I."

"Well, we were in a baddish way before he came, I own; but this new crotchet of his is past a joke."

"Let's give it a trial, Harry; come—you know how often he has been right and we wrong."

"Now, don't you two be jawing away about young Square-toes," struck in Gower. "He's no end of a sucking wiseacre, I dare say; but we've no time to lose, and I've got the fives'-court at half-past nine."

"I say, Gower," said Tom, appealingly, "be a good fellow, and let's try if we can't get on without the crib."

"What! in this chorus? Why, we shan't get through ten lines."

"I say, Tom," cried East, having hit on a new idea, "don't you remember, when we were in the upper fourth, and old Momus caught me construing off the leaf of a crib which I'd torn out and put in my book, and which would float out on to the floor; he sent me up to be flogged for it?"

"Yes, I remember it very well."

"Well, the Doctor, after he'd flogged me, told me himself that he didn't flog me for using a translation, but for taking it in to lesson, and using it there when I hadn't learnt a word before I came in. He said there was no harm in using a translation to get a clue to hard passages, if you tried all you could first to make them out without."

"Did he, though?" said Tom; "then Arthur must be wrong."

"Of course he is," said Gower, "the little prig. We'll only use the crib when we can't construe without it. Go ahead, East."

And on this agreement they started: Tom, satisfied with having made his confession, and not sorry to have a *locus pænitentiæ*, and not to be deprived altogether of the use of his old and faithful friend.

The boys went on as usual, each taking a sentence in turn, and the crib being handed to the one whose turn it was to construe. Of course Tom couldn't object to this, as, was it not simply lying there to be appealed to in case the sentence should prove too hard altogether for the construer? But it must be owned that Gower and East did not make very tremendous exertions to conquer their sentences before having recourse to its help. Tom, however, with the most heroic virtue and gallantry rushed into his sentence, searching in a high-minded manner for nominative and verb, and turning over his dictionary frantically for the first hard word that stopped him. But in the meantime Gower, who was bent on getting to fives, would peep quietly into the crib, and then suggest, "Don't you think this is the meaning?" "I think you must take it this way, Brown;" and as Tom didn't see his way to not profiting by these suggestions, the lesson went on about as quickly as usual, and Gower was able to start for the fives'-court within five minutes of the half-hour.

When Tom and East were left face to face, they looked at one another for a minute, Tom puzzled, and East chock-full of fun, and then burst into a roar of laughter.

"Well, Tom," said East, recovering himself, "I don't see any objection to the new way. It's about as good as the old one, I think; besides the advantage it gives one of feeling virtuous, and looking down on one's neighbours."

Tom shoved his hand into his back hair. "I ain't so sure," said he; "you two fellows carried me off my legs: I don't think we really tried one sentence fairly. Are you sure you remember what the Doctor said to you?"

"Yes. And I'll swear I couldn't make out one of my sentences to-day. No, nor ever could. I really don't remember," said East, speaking slowly and impressively, "to have come across one Latin or Greek sentence this half that I could go and construe by the light of nature. Whereby I am sure Providence intended cribs to be used."

"The thing to find out," said Tom, meditatively, "is how long one ought to grind at a sentence without looking at the crib. Now I think if one fairly looks out all the words one don't know, and then can't hit it, that's enough."

"To be sure, Tommy," said East demurely, but with a merry twinkle in his eye. "Your new doctrine too, old fellow," added he, "when one comes to think of it, is a cutting at the root of all school morality. You'll take away mutual help, brotherly love, or, in the vulgar tongue, giving construes, which I hold to be one of our highest virtues. For how can you distinguish between getting a construe from another boy, and using a crib? Hang it, Tom, if you're going to deprive all our school-fellows of the chance of exercising Christian benevolence and being good Samaritans, I shall cut the concern."

"I wish you wouldn't joke about it, Harry; it's hard enough to see one's way, a precious sight harder than I thought last night. But I suppose there's a use and an abuse of both, and one'll get straight enough somehow. But you can't make out anyhow that one has a right to use old vulgus-books and copy-books."

"Hullo, more heresy! How fast a fellow goes downhill when he once gets his head before his legs. Listen to me, Tom. Not use old vulgus-books?—why, you Goth! ain't we to take the benefit of the wisdom, and admire and use the work and past generations? Not use old copy-books! W hy you might as well say we ought to pull down Westminster Abbey, and put up a go-to-meeting-shop with churchwarden windows; or never read Shakespere, but only Sheridan Knowles. Think of all the work and labour that our predecessors have bestowed on these very books; and are we to make their work of no value?"

"I say, Harry, please don't chaff; I'm really serious."

"And then, is it not our duty to consult the pleasure of others rather than our own, and above all that of our masters? Fancy then the difference to them in looking over a vulgus which has been carefully touched and retouched by themselves and others, and which must bring them a sort of dreamy pleasure, as if they'd met the thought or expression of it somewhere or another—before they were born perhaps; and that of cutting up, and making picture-frames round all your and my false quantities, and other monstrosities. Why, Tom, you wouldn't be so cruel as never to let old Momus hum over the 'O genus humanum' again, and then look up doubtingly through his spectacles, and end by smiling and giving three extra marks for it: just for old sake's sake, I suppose."

"Well," said Tom, getting up in something as like a huff as he was capable of, "it's deuced hard that when a fellow's really trying to do what he ought, his best friends'll do nothing but chaff him and try to put him down." And he stuck his books under his arm and his hat on his head, preparatory to rushing out into the quadrangle, to testify with his own soul of the faithlessness of friendships.

"Now don't be an ass, Tom," said East, catching hold of him, "you know me well enough by this time; my bark's worse than my bite. You can't expect to ride your new crotchet without anybody's trying to stick a nettle under his tail and make him kick you off: especially as we shall all have to go on foot still. But now sit down, and let's go over it again. I'll be as serious as a judge."

Then Tom sat himself down on the table, and waxed eloquent about all the righteousnessess and advantages of the new plan, as was his wont whenever he took up anything; going into it as if his life depended upon it, and sparing no abuse which he could think of, the opposite method, which he denounced as ungentlemanly, cowardly, mean, lying, and no one knows what besides. "Very cool of Tom," as East thought, but didn't say, "seeing as how he only came out of Egypt himself last night at bed-time."

"Well, Tom," said he at last, "you see, when you and I came to school there were none of these sort of notions. You may be right—I dare say you are. Only what one has always felt about the masters is, that it's a fair trial of skill and last between us and them—like a match at football, or a battle. We're natural enemies in school, that's the fact. We've got to learn so much Latin and Greek and do so many verses, and they've got to see that we do it. If we can slip the collar and do so much less without getting caught, that's one to us. If they can get more out of us, or catch us shirking, that's one to them. All's fair in war but lying. If I run my luck against theirs, and go into school without looking at my lessons and don't get called up, why am I a snob or a sneak? I don't tell the master I've learnt it. He's got to find out whether I have or not; what's he paid for? If he calls me up and I get floored, he makes me write it out in Greek and English. Very good; he's caught me, and I don't grumble. I grant you, if I go and snivel to him, and tell him I've really tried to learn it, but found it so hard without a translation, or say I've had a tooth-ache or any humbug of that kind, I'm a snob. That's my school morality; it's served me, and you too, Tom, for the matter of that, these five years. And it's all clear and fair, no mistake about it. We understand it, and they understand it, and I don't know what we're to come to with any other."

Tom looked at him pleased, and a little puzzled. He had never heard East speak his mind seriously before, and couldn't help feeling how completely he had hit his own theory and practice up to that time.

"Thank you, old fellow," said he. "You're a good old brick to be serious, and not put out with me. I said more than I meant, I dare say, only you see I know I'm right: whatever you and Gower and the rest do, I shall hold on—I must. And as it's all new and an uphill game, you see, one must hit hard and hold on tight at first."

"Very good," said East; "hold on and hit away, only don't hit under the line."

"But I must bring you over, Harry, or I shan't be comfortable. Now, I'll allow all you've said. We've always been honourable enemies with the masters. We found a state of war when we came, and went into it of course. Only don't you think things are altered a good deal? I don't feel as I used to the masters. They seem to me to treat one quite differently."

"Yes, perhaps they do," said East; "there's a new set you see, mostly, who don't feel sure of themselves yet. They don't want to fight till they know the ground."

"I don't think it's only that," said Tom. "And then the Doctor, he does treat one so openly, and like a gentleman, and as if one was working with him."

"Well, so he does," said East; "he's a splendid fellow, and when I get into the sixth I shall act accordingly. Only you know he has nothing to do with our lessons now, except examining us. I say, though," looking at his watch, "it's just the quarter. Come along."

As they walked out they got a message, to say "that Arthur was just starting, and would like to say good-bye;" so they went down to the private entrance of the School-house, and found an open carriage, with Arthur propped up with pillows in it, looking already better, Tom thought.

They jumped up on to the steps to shake hands with him, and Tom mumbled thanks for the presents he had found in his study, and looked round anxiously for Arthur's mother.

East, who had fallen back into his usual humour, looked quaintly at Arthur, and said—

"So you've been at it again, through that hot-headed convert of yours there. He's been making our lives a burden to us all the morning about using cribs. I shall get floored to a certainty at second lesson, if I'm called up."

Arthur blushed and looked down. Tom struck in—

"Oh, it's all right. He's converted already; he always comes through the mud after us, grumbling and sputtering."

The clock struck, and they had to go off to school, wishing Arthur a pleasant holiday; Tom lingering behind a moment to send his thanks and love to Arthur's mother.

Tom renewed the discussion after second lesson, and succeeded so far as to get East to promise to give the new plan a fair trial.

Encouraged by his success, in the evening, when they were sitting alone in the large study, where East lived now almost, "*vice* Arthur on leave," after examining the new fishing-rod, which both pronounced to be the genuine article ("play enough to throw a midge tied on a single hair against the wind, and strength enough to hold a grampus"), they naturally began talking about Arthur. Tom, who was still bubbling over with last night's scene and all the thoughts of the last week, and wanting to clinch and fix the whole in his own mind, which he could never do without first going through the process of belabouring somebody else with it all, suddenly rushed into the subject of Arthur's illness, and what he had said about death.

East had given him the desired opening; after a serio-comic grumble, "that life wasn't worth having now they were tied to a young beggar who was always 'raising his standard'; and that he, East, was like a prophet's donkey, who was obliged to struggle on after the donkeyman who went after the prophet; that he had none of the pleasure of starting the new crotchets, and didn't half understand them, but had to take the kicks and carry the luggage as if he had all the fun,"—he threw his legs up on to the sofa, and put his hands behind his head, and said—

"Well, after all, he's the most wonderful little fellow I ever came across. There ain't such a meek, humble boy in the school. Hanged if I don't think now, really, Tom, that he believes himself a much worse fellow than you or I, and that he don't think he has more influence in the house than Dot Bowles, who came last quarter and isn't ten yet. But he turns you and me round his little finger, old boy—there's no mistake about that." And East nodded at Tom sagaciously.

"Now or never!" thought Tom; so shutting his eyes and hardening his heart, he went straight at it, repeating all that Arthur had said, as near as he could remember it, in the very words, and all he had himself thought. The life seemed to ooze out of it as he went on, and several times he felt inclined to stop, give it all up, and change the subject. But somehow he was borne on, he had a necessity upon him to speak it all out, and did so. At the end he looked at East with some anxiety, and was delighted to see that that young gentleman was thoughtful and attentive. The fact is, that in the stage of his inner life at which Tom had lately arrived, his intimacy with and friendship for East could not have lasted if he had not made him aware of, and a sharer in, the thoughts that were beginning to exercise him. Nor indeed could the friendship have lasted if East had shown no sympathy with these thoughts; so that it was a great relief to have unbosomed himself, and to have found that his friend could listen.

Tom had always had a sort of instinct that East's levity was only skin-deep; and this instinct was a true one. East had no want of reverence for anything he felt to be real; but his was one of those natures that burst into what is generally called recklessness and impiety the moment they feel that anything is being poured upon them for their good which does not come home to their inborn sense of right, or which appeals to anything like self-interest in them. Daring and honest by nature, and out-spoken to an extent which alarmed all respectabilities, with a constant fund of animal health and spirits which he did not feel bound to curb in any way, he had gained for himself with the steady part of the school (including as well those who wished to appear steady as those who really were so) the character of a boy with whom it would be dangerous to be intimate; while his own hatred of everything cruel, or underhand, or false, and his hearty respect for what he could see to be good and true, kept off the rest.

Tom, besides being very like East in many points of character, had largely developed in his composition the capacity for taking the weakest side. This is not putting it strongly enough; it was a necessity with him, he couldn't help it any more than he could eating or drinking. He could never play on the strongest side with any heart at football or cricket, and was sure to make friends with any boy who was unpopular, or down on his luck.

Now, though East was not what is generally called unpopular, Tom felt more and more every day, as their characters developed, that he stood alone, and did not make friends among their contemporaries; and therefore sought him out. Tom was himself much more popular, for his power of detecting humbug was much less acute, and his instincts were much more sociable. He was at this period of his life, too, largely given to taking people for what they gave themselves out to be; but his singleness of heart, fearlessness, and honesty were just what East appreciated, and thus the two had been drawn into great intimacy.

This intimacy had not been interrupted by Tom's guardianship of Arthur.

East had often, as has been said, joined them in reading the Bible; but their discussions had almost always turned upon the characters of the men and women of whom they read, and not become personal to themselves. In fact, the two had shrunk from personal religious discussion, not knowing how it might end; and fearful of risking a friendship very dear to both, and which they felt somehow, without quite knowing why, would never be the same, but either tenfold stronger or sapped at its foundation after such a communing together.

What a bother all this explaining is! I wish we could get on without it. But we can't. However, you'll all find, if you haven't found it out already, that a time comes in every human friendship when you must go down into the depths of yourself, and lay bare what is there to your friend, and wait in fear for his answer. A few moments may do it; and it may be (most likely will be, as you are English boys) that you will never do it but once. But done it must be, if the friendship is to be worth the name. You must find what is there, at the very root and bottom of one another's hearts; and if you are at one there, nothing on earth can, or at least ought to sunder you.

East had remained lying down until Tom finished speaking, as if fearing to interrupt him; he now sat up at the table, and leant his head on one hand, taking up a pencil with the other, and working little holes with it in the table-cover. After a bit he looked up, stopped the pencil, and said, "Thank you very much, old fellow; there's no other boy in the house would have done it for me but you or Arthur. I can see well enough," he went on after a pause, "all the best big fellows look on me with suspicion; they think I'm a devil-may-care, reckless young scamp. So I am—eleven hours out of twelve, but not the twelfth. Then all of our contemporaries worth knowing follow suit, of course; we're very good friends at games and all that, but not a soul of them but you and Arthur ever tried to break through the crust, and see whether there was anything at the bottom of me; and then the bad ones I won't stand, and they know that."

"Don't you think that's half fancy, Harry?"

"Not a bit of it," said East bitterly, pegging away with his pencil. "I see it all plain

enough. Bless you, you think everybody's as straightforward and kind-hearted as you are."

"Well, but what's the reason of it? There must be a reason. You can play all the games as well as any one, and sing the best song, and are the best company in the house. You fancy you're not liked, Harry. It's all fancy."

"I only wish it was, Tom. I know I could be popular enough with all the bad ones, but that I won't have, and the good ones won't have me."

"Why not?" persisted Tom; "you don't drink or swear, or get out at night; you never bully, or cheat at lessons. If you only showed you liked it, you'd have all the best fellows in the house running after you."

"Not I," said East. Then with an effort he went on, "I'll tell you what it is. I never stop the Sacrament. I can see, from the Doctor downwards, how that tells against me."

"Yes, I've seen that," said Tom, "and I've been very sorry for it, and Arthur and I have talked about it. I've often thought of speaking to you, but it's so hard to begin on such subjects. I'm very glad you've opened it. Now, why don't you?"

"I've never been confirmed," said East.

"Not been confirmed!" said Tom, in astonishment. "I never thought of that. Why weren't you confirmed with the rest of us nearly three years ago? I always thought you'd been confirmed at home."

"No," answered East sorrowfully; "you see this was how it happened. Last Confirmation was soon after Arthur came, and you were so taken up with him, I hardly saw either of you. Well, when the Doctor sent round for us about it, I was living mostly with Green's set—you know the sort. They all went in—I dare say it was all right, and they got good by it; I don't want to judge them. Only all I could see of their reasons drove me just the other way. 'Twas 'because the Doctor liked it;' 'no boy got on who didn't stay the Sacrament:' it was the 'correct thing,' in fact, like having a good hat to wear on

Sundays. I couldn't stand it. I didn't feel that I wanted to lead a different life, I was very well content as I was, and I wasn't going to sham religious to curry favour with the Doctor, or any one else."

East stopped speaking, and pegged away more diligently than ever with his pencil. Tom was ready to cry. He felt half sorry at first that he had been confirmed himself. He seemed to have deserted his earliest friend, to have left him by himself at his worst need for those long years. He got up and went and sat by East and put his arm over his shoulder.

"Dear old boy," he said, "how careless and selfish I've been. But why didn't you come and talk to Arthur and me?"

"I wish to heaven I had," said East, "but I was a fool. It's too late talking of it now."

"Why too late? You want to be confirmed now, don't you?"

"I think so," said East. "I've thought about it a good deal: only often I fancy I must be changing, because I see it's to do me good here, just what stopped me last time. And then I go back again."

"I'll tell you now how 'twas with me," said Tom warmly. "If it hadn't been for Arthur, I should have done just as you did. I hope I should. I honour you for it. But then he made it out just as if it was taking the weak side before all the world—going in once for all against everything that's strong and rich and proud and respectable, a little band of brothers against the whole world. And the Doctor seemed to say so too, only he said a great deal more."

"Ah!" groaned East, "but there again, that's just another of my difficulties whenever I think about the matter. I don't want to be one of your saints, one of your elect, whatever the right phrase is. My sympathies are all the other way; with the many, the poor devils who run about the streets and don't go to church. Don't stare, Tom; mind, I'm telling you all that's in my heart—as far as I know it—but it's all a muddle. You must be gentle with me if you want to land me. Now I've seen a deal of this sort of religion, I was bred up in it, and I can't stand it. If nineteen-twentieths of the world are to be left to uncovenanted mercies, and that sort of thing, which means in plain English to go to hell, and the other twentieth are to rejoice at it all, why—"

"Oh! but, Harry, they ain't, they don't," broke in Tom, really shocked. "Oh, how I wish Arthur hadn't gone! I'm such a fool about these things. But it's all you want too, East; it is indeed. It cuts both ways somehow, being confirmed and taking the Sacrament. It makes you feel on the side of all the good and all the bad too, of everybody in the world. Only there's some great dark strong power, which is crushing you and everybody else. That's what Christ conquered, and we've got to fight. What a fool I am! I can't explain. If Arthur were only here!"

"I begin to get a glimmering of what you mean," said East.

"I say now," said Tom, eagerly, "do you remember how we both hated Flashman?"

"Of course I do," said East; "I hate him still. What then?"

"Well, when I came to take the Sacrament, I had a great struggle about that. I tried to put him out of my head; and when I couldn't do that, I tried to think of him as evil, as something that the Lord who was loving me hated, and which I might hate too. But it wouldn't do. I broke down; I believe Christ Himself broke me down; and when the Doctor gave me the bread and wine, and leant over me praying, I prayed for poor Flashman, as if it had been you or Arthur."

East buried his face in his hands on the table. Tom could feel the table tremble. At last he looked up. "Thank you again, Tom," said he; "you don't know what you may have done for me to-night. I think I see now how the right sort of sympathy with poor devils is got at."

"And you'll stop the Sacrament next time, won't you?" said Tom.

"Can I, before I'm confirmed?"

"Go and ask the Doctor."

"I will."

That very night, after prayers, East followed the Doctor and the old Verger bearing the candle, up-stairs. Tom watched, and saw the Doctor turn round when he heard footsteps following him closer than usual, and say, "Hah, East! Do you want to speak to me, my man?"

"If you please, sir;" and the private door closed, and Tom went to his study in a state of great trouble of mind.

It was almost an hour before East came back: then he rushed in breathless.

"Well, it's all right," he shouted, seizing Tom by the hand. "I feel as if a ton weight were off my mind."

"Hurra," said Tom. "I knew it would be; but tell us all about it."

"Well, I just told him all about it. You can't think how kind and gentle he was, the great grim man, whom I've feared more than anybody on earth. When I stuck, he lifted me, just as if I'd been a little child. And he seemed to know all I'd felt, and to have gone through it all. And I burst out crying—more than I've done this five years, and he sat down by me, and stroked my head; and I went blundering on, and told him all; much worse things than I've told you. And he wasn't shocked a bit, and didn't snub me, or tell me I was a fool, and it was all nothing but pride or wickedness, though I dare say it was. And he didn't tell me not to follow out my thoughts, and he didn't give me any cut-and-dried explanation. But when I'd done he just talked a bit—I can hardly remember what he said, yet; but it seemed to spread round me like healing, and strength, and light; and to bear me up, and plant me on a rock, where I could hold my footing, and fight for myself. I don't know what to do, I feel so happy. And it's all owing to you, dear old boy!" and he seized Tom's hand again.

"And you're to come to the Communion?" said Tom.

"Yes, and to be confirmed in the holidays."

Tom's delight was as great as his friend's. But he hadn't yet had out all his own talk, and was bent on improving the occasion: so he proceeded to propound Arthur's theory about not being sorry for his friends' deaths, which he had hitherto kept in the background, and by which he was much exercised; for he didn't feel it honest to take what pleased him and throw over the rest, and was trying vigorously to persuade himself that he should like all his best friends to die off-hand.

But East's powers of remaining serious were exhausted, and in five minutes he was saying the most ridiculous things he could think of, till Tom was almost getting angry again.

Despite of himself, however, he couldn't help laughing and giving it up, when East appealed to him with, "Well, Tom, you ain't going to punch my head, I hope, because I insist upon being sorry when you got to earth?"

And so their talk finished for that time, and they tried to learn first lesson; with very poor success, as appeared next morning, when they were called up and narrowly escaped being floored, which ill-luck, however, did not sit heavily on either of their souls.

CHAPTER VIII

TOM BROWN'S LAST MATCH

"Heaven grant the manlier heart, that timely, ere
Youth fly, with life's real tempest would be coping;
The fruit of dreamy hoping
Is, waking, blank despair."
CLOUGH. *Ambarvalia*

THE CURTAIN NOW RISES upon the last act of our little drama—for hard-hearted publishers warn me that a single volume must of necessity have an end. Well, well! the pleasantest things must come to an end. I little thought last long vacation, when I began these pages to help while away some spare time at a watering-place, how vividly many an old scene which had lain hid away for years in some dusty old corner of my brain, would come back again, and stand before me as clear and bright as if it had happened yesterday. The book has been a most grateful task to me, and I only hope that all you, my dear young friends who read it (friends assuredly you must be, if you get as far as this), will be half as sorry to come to the last stage as I am.

Not but what there has been a solemn and a sad side to it. As the old scenes became living, and the actors in them became living too, many a grave in the Crimea and distant India, as well as in the quiet churchyards of our dear old country, seemed to open and send forth their dead, and their voices and looks and ways were again in one's ears and eyes, as in the old School-days. But this was not sad; how should it be, if we believe as our Lord has taught us? How should it be, when one more turn of the wheel, and we shall be by their sides again, learning from them again, perhaps, as we did when we were new boys.

Then there were others of the old faces so dear to us once, who had somehow or another just gone clean out of sight—are they dead or living? We know not, but the thought of them brings no sadness with it. Wherever they are, we can well believe they are doing God's work and getting His wages.

But are there not some, whom we still see sometimes in the streets, whose haunts and homes we know, whom we could probably find almost any day in the week if we were set to do it, yet from whom we are really farther than we are from the dead, and from those who have gone out of our ken? Yes, there are and must be such; and therein lies the sadness of old School memories. Yet of these our old comrades, from whom more than time and space separate us, there are some, by whose sides we can feel sure that we shall stand again when time shall be no more. We may think of one another now as dangerous fanatics or narrow bigots, with whom no truce is possible, from whom we shall only sever more and more to the end of our lives, whom it would be our respective duties to imprison or hang, if we had the power. We must go our way, and they theirs, as long as flesh and spirit hold together: but let our own Rugby poet speak words of healing for this trial:—

"To veer how vain! on, onward strain,
  Brave barks! in light, in darkness too;
Through winds and tides one compass guides,—
To that, and your own selves, be true.

"But, O blithe breeze! and O great seas,
  Though ne'er that earliest parting past,
On your wide plain they join again,
  Together lead them home at last.

"One port, methought, alike they sought,
  One purpose hold where'er they fare.
O bounding breeze, O rushing seas!
  At last, at last, unite them there!"[1]

This is not mere longing, it is prophecy. So over these too, our old friends, who are friends no more, we sorrow not as men without hope. It is only for those who seem to us to have lost compass and purpose, and to be driven helplessly on rocks and quicksands; whose lives are spent in the service of the world, the flesh, and the devil; for self alone,

---

[1] CLOUGH, *Ambarvalia,*

and not for their fellow-men, their country, or their God, that we must mourn and pray without sure hope and without light; trusting only that He, in whose hands they as well as we are, who has died for them as well as for us, who sees all His creatures

> "With larger other eyes than ours,
> To make allowance for us all,"

will, in His own way and at His own time, lead them also home.

*   *   *   *   *

Another two years have passed, and it is again the end of the summer half-year at Rugby; in fact, the School has broken up. The fifth-form examinations were over last week, and upon them have followed the speeches, and the sixth-form examinations for exhibitions; and they too are over now. The boys have gone to all the winds of heaven, except the town boys and the eleven, and the few enthusiasts besides who have asked leave to stay in their houses to see the result of the cricket matches. For this year the Wellesburn return match and the Marylebone match was played at Rugby, to the great delight of the town and neighbourhood, and the sorrow of those aspiring young cricketers who have been reckoning for the last three months on showing off at Lords' ground.

The Doctor started for the Lakes yesterday morning, after an interview with the Captain of the eleven, in the presence of Thomas, at which he arranged in what school the cricket dinners were to be, and all other matters necessary for the satisfactory carrying out of the festivities; and warned them as to keeping all spirituous liquors out of the close, and having the gates closed by nine o'clock.

The Wellesburn match was played out with great success yesterday, the School winning by three wickets; and to-day the great event of the cricketing year, the Marylebone match, is being played. What a match it has been! The London eleven came down by an afternoon train yesterday, in time to see the end of the Wellesburn match; and as soon as it was over, their leading men and umpire inspected the ground, criticizing it rather unmercifully. The Captain of the School eleven, and one or two others, who had played the Lords' match before, and knew old Mr. Aislabie and several of the Lords' men, accompanied them: while the rest of the eleven looked on from under the Three Trees with admiring eyes, and asked one another the names of the illustrious strangers, and recounted how many runs each of them had made in the late matches in *Bell's Life*. They looked such hard-bitten, wiry, whiskered fellows, that their young adversaries felt rather desponding as to the result of the morrow's match. The ground was at last chosen, and two men set to work upon it to water and roll; and then, there being yet some half-hour of daylight, some one had suggested a dance on the turf. The close was half full of citizens and their families, and the idea was hailed with enthusiasm. The cornopean-player was still on the ground; in five minutes the eleven and half-a-dozen of the Wellesburn and Marylebone men got partners somehow or another, and a merry country-dance was going on, to which every one flocked, and new couples joined in every minute, till there were a hundred of them going down the middle and up again—and the long line of school buildings looked gravely down on them, every window glowing with the last rays of the western sun, and the rooks clanged about in the tops of the old elms, greatly excited, and resolved on having their country-dance too, and the great flag flapped lazily in the gentle western breeze. Altogether it was a

sight which would have made glad the heart of our brave old founder, Lawrence Sheriff, if he were half as good a fellow as I take him to have been. It was a cheerful sight to see; but what made it so valuable in the sight of the Captain of the School eleven was, that he there saw his young hands shaking off their shyness and awe of the Lords' men, as they crossed hands and capered about on the grass together; for the strangers entered into it all, and threw away their cigars, and danced and shouted like boys; while old Mr. Aislabie stood by looking on in his white hat, leaning on a bat, in benevolent enjoyment. "This hop will be worth thirty runs to us to-morrow, and will be the making of Raggles and Johnson," thinks the young leader, as he revolves many things in his mind, standing by the side of Mr. Aislabie, whom he will not leave for a minute, for he feels that the character of the School for courtesy is resting on his shoulders.

But when a quarter to nine struck, and he saw old Thomas beginning to fidget about with the keys in his hand, he thought of the Doctor's parting monition, and stopped the cornopean at once, notwithstanding the loud-voiced remonstrances from all sides; and the crowd scattered away from the close, the eleven all going into the School-house, where supper and beds were provided for them by the Doctor's orders.

Deep had been the consultations at supper as to the order of going in, who should bowl the first over, whether it would be best to play steady or freely; and the youngest hands declared that they shouldn't be a bit nervous, and praised their opponents as the jolliest fellows in the world, except perhaps their old friends the Wellesburn men. How far a little good-nature from their elders will go with the right sort of boys!

The morning had dawned bright and warm, to the intense relief of many an anxious youngster, up betimes to mark the signs of the weather. The eleven went down in a body before breakfast, for a plunge in the cold bath in a corner of the close. The ground was in splendid order, and soon after ten o'clock, before spectators had arrived, all was ready, and two of the Lords' men took their places at the wickets; the School, with the usual liberality of young hands, having put their adversaries in first. Old Bailey stepped up to the wicket, and called play, and the match has begun.

* * * * *

"Oh, well bowled! well bowled, Johnson!" cries the Captain, catching up the ball and sending it high above the rook trees, while the third Marylebone man walks away from the wicket, and old Bailey gravely sets up the middle stump again and puts the bails on.

"How many runs?" away scamper three boys to the scoring-table, and are back again in a minute amongst the rest of the eleven, who are collected together in a knot between wicket. "Only eighteen runs, and three wickets down!" "Huzza for old Rugby!" sings out Jack Raggles, the long-stop, toughest and burliest of boys, commonly called "Swiper Jack"; and forthwith stands on his head, and brandishes his legs in the air in triumph, till the next boy catches hold of his heels, and throws him over on to his back.

"Steady there, don't be such an ass, Jack," says the Captain; "we haven't got the best wicket yet. Ah, look out now at cover-point," adds he, as he sees a long-armed, bare-headed, slashing-looking player coming to the wicket. "And, Jack, mind your hits; he steals more runs than any man in England."

And they all find that they have got their work to do now; the new-comer's off-hitting is tremendous, and his running like a flash of lightning. He is never in his ground except when his wicket is down. Nothing in the whole game so trying to boys; he has stolen three byes in the first ten minutes, and Jack Raggles is furious, and begins throwing over savagely to the further wicket, until he is sternly stopped by the Captain. It is all that young gentleman can do to keep his team steady, but he knows that everything depends on it, and faces his work bravely. The score creeps up to fifty, the boys begin to look blank, and the spectators, who are now mustering strong, are very silent. The ball flies off his bat to all parts of the field, and he gives no rest and no catches to any one. But cricket is full of glorious chances, and the goddess who presides over it loves to bring down the most skilful players. Johnson the young bowler is getting wild, and bowls a ball almost wide to the off; the batter steps out and cuts it beautifully to where cover-point is standing very deep, in fact almost off the ground. The ball comes skimming and twisting along about three feet from the ground; he rushes at it, and it sticks somehow or other in the fingers of his left hand, to the utter astonishment of himself and the whole field. Such a catch hasn't been made in the close for years, and the cheering is maddening. "Pretty cricket," says the Captain, throwing himself on the ground by the deserted wicket with a long breath: he feels that a crisis has passed.

I wish I had space to describe the match; how the Captain stumped the next man off a leg-shooter, and bowled small cobs to old Mr. Aislabie, who came in for the last wicket. How the Lords' men were out by half-past twelve o'clock for ninety-eight runs. How the Captain of the School eleven went in first to give his men pluck, and scored twenty-five in beautiful style; how Rugby was only four behind in the first innings. What a glorious dinner they had in the fourth-form school, and how the cover-point hitter sang the most topping comic songs, and old Mr. Aislabie made the best speeches that ever were heard, afterwards. But I haven't space, that's the fact, and so you must fancy it all, and carry yourselves on to half-past seven o'clock, when the School are again in, with five wickets down, and only thirty-two runs to make to win. The Marylebone men played carelessly in their second innings, but they are working like horses now to save the match.

There is much healthy, hearty, happy life scattered up and down the close; but the group to which I beg to call your especial attention is there, on the slope of the island, which looks towards the cricket-ground. It consists of three figures; two are seated on a bench, and one on the ground at their feet. The first, a tall, slight, and rather gaunt man, with a bushy eyebrow, and a dry humorous smile, is evidently a clergyman. He is carelessly dressed, and looks rather used up, which isn't much to be wondered at, seeing that he has just finished six weeks of examination work; but there he basks, and spreads himself out in the evening sun, bent on enjoying life, though he doesn't quite know what to do with his arms and legs. Surely it is our friend the young Master, whom we have had glimpses of before, but his face has gained a great deal since we last came across him.

And by his side, in white flannel shirt and trousers, straw hat, the Captain's belt, and the untanned yellow cricket shoes which all the eleven wear, sits a strapping figure, near six feet high, with ruddy tanned face and whiskers, curly brown hair and a laughing dancing eye. He is leaning forward with his elbows resting on his knees, and dandling his favourite bat, with which he has made thirty or forty runs to-day, in his strong brown hands. It is Tom Brown, grown into a young man nineteen years old, a præpostor and Captain of the eleven, spending his last day as a Rugby boy, and let us hope as much wiser as he is bigger, since we last had the pleasure of coming across him.

And at their feet on the warm dry ground, similarly dressed, sits Arthur, Turkish fashion, with his bat across his knees. He too is no longer a boy, less of a boy in fact than Tom, if one may judge from the thoughtfulness of his face, which is somewhat paler too than one could wish; but his figure, though slight, is well knit and active, and all his old timidity has disappeared, and is replaced by silent quaint fun, with which his face twinkles all over, as he listens to the broken talk between the other two, in which he joins every now and then.

All three are watching the game eagerly, and joining in the cheering which follows every good hit. It is pleasing to see the easy friendly footing which the pupils are on with their master, perfectly respectful, yet with no reserve and nothing forced in their intercourse. Tom has clearly abandoned the old theory of "natural enemies" in this case at any rate.

But it is time to listen to what they are saying, and see what we can gather out of it.

"I don't object to your theory," says the master, "and I allow you have made a fair case for yourself. But now, in such books as Aristophanes, for instance, you've been reading a play this half with the Doctor, haven't you?"

"Yes, the Knights," answered Tom.

"Well, I'm sure you would have enjoyed the wonderful humour of it twice as much if you had taken more pains with your scholarship."

"Well, sir, I don't believe any boy in the form enjoyed the sets-to between Cleon and the Sausage-seller more than I did—eh, Arthur?" said Tom, giving him a stir with his foot.

"Yes, I must say he did," said Arthur. "I think, sir, you've hit upon the wrong book there."

"Not a bit of it," said the master. "Why, in those very passages of arms, how can you thoroughly appreciate them unless you are master of the weapons? and the weapons are the language, which you, Brown, have never half worked at; and so, as I say, you must have lost all the delicate shades of meaning which make the best part of the fun."

"Oh! well played—bravo, Johnson!" shouted Arthur, dropping his bat and clapping furiously, and Tom joined in with a "bravo, Johnson!" which might have been heard at the chapel.

"Eh! what was it? I didn't see," inquired the master; "they only got one run, I thought?"

"No, but such a ball, three-quarters length and coming straight for his leg bail.

Nothing but that turn of the wrist could have saved him, and he drew it away to leg for a safe one. Bravo, Johnson!"

"How well they are bowling, though," said Arthur; "they don't mean to be beat, I can see."

"There now," struck in the master, "you see that's just what I have been preaching this half-hour. The delicate play is the true thing. I don't understand cricket, so I don't enjoy those fine draws which you tell me are the best play, though when you or Raggles hit a ball hard away for six I am as delighted as any one. Don't you see the analogy?"

"Yes, sir," answered Tom, looking up roguishly, "I see; only the question remains whether I should have got most good by understanding Greek particles or cricket thoroughly. I'm such a thick, I never should have had time for both."

"I see you are an incorrigible," said the master with a chuckle; "but I refute you by an example. Arthur there has taken in Greek and cricket too."

"Yes, but no thanks to him; Greek came natural to him. Why, when he first came I remember he used to read Herodotus for pleasure as I did Don Quixote, and couldn't have made a false concord if he'd tried ever so hard—and then I looked after his cricket."

"Out! Bailey has given him out—do you see, Tom?" cries Arthur. "How foolish of them to run so hard."

"Well, it can't be helped, he has played very well. Whose turn is it to go in?"

"I don't know; they've got your list in the tent."

"Let's go and see," said Tom, rising; but at this moment Jack Raggles and two or three more came running to the island moat.

"Oh, Brown, mayn't I go in next?" shouts the Swiper.

"Whose name is next on the list?" says the Captain.

"Winter's, and then Arthur's," answers the boy who carries it: "but there are only twenty-six runs to get, and no time to lose. I heard Mr. Aislabie say that the stumps must be drawn at a quarter past eight exactly."

"Oh, do let the Swiper go in," chorus the boys; so Tom yields against his better judgment.

"I dare say now I've lost the match by this nonsense," he says, as he sits down again; "they'll be sure to get Jack's wicket in three or four minutes; however, you'll have the chance, sir, of seeing a hard hit or two," adds he, smiling, and turning to the master.

"Come, none of your irony, Brown," answers the master. "I'm beginning to understand the game scientifically. What a noble game it is, too!"

"Isn't it? But it's more than a game. It's an institution," said Tom.

"Yes," said Arthur, "the birthright of British boys old and young, as *habeas corpus* and trial by jury are of British men."

"The discipline and reliance on one another which it teaches is so valuable, I think," went on the master, "it ought to be such an unselfish game. It merges the individual in the eleven; he doesn't play that he may win, but that his side may."

"That's very true," said Tom, "and that's why football and cricket, now one comes to think of it, are such much better games than fives' or hare-and-hounds, or any others where the object is to come in first or to win for oneself, and not that one's side may win."

"And then the Captain of the eleven!" said the master, "what a post is his in our School-world! almost as hard as the Doctor's; requiring skill and gentleness and firmness, and I know not what other rare qualities."

"Which don't he may wish he may get!" said Tom, laughing; "at any rate he hasn't got them yet, or he wouldn't have been such a flat to-night as to let Jack Raggles go in out of his turn."

"Ah, the Doctor never would have done that," said Arthur, demurely. "Tom, you've a great deal to learn yet in the art of ruling."

"Well, I wish you'd tell the Doctor so then, and get him to let me stop till I'm twenty. I don't want to leave, I'm sure."

"What a sight it is," broke in the master, "the Doctor as a ruler! Perhaps ours is the only little corner of the British Empire which is thoroughly, wisely, and strongly ruled just now. I'm more and more thankful every day of my life that I came here to be under him."

"So am I, I'm sure," said Tom; "and more and more sorry that I've got to leave."

"Every place and thing one sees here reminds one of some wise act of his," went on the master. "This island now—you remember the time, Brown, when it was laid out in small gardens, and cultivated by frost-bitten fags in February and March?"

"Of course I do," said Tom; "didn't I hate spending two hours in the afternoon grubbing in the tough dirt with the stump of a fives'-bat? But turf-cart was good fun enough."

"I dare say it was, but it was always leading to fights with the townspeople; and then the stealing flowers out of all the gardens in Rugby for the Easter show was abominable."

"Well, so it was," said Tom, looking down, "but we fags couldn't help ourselves. But what has that to do with the Doctor's ruling?"

"A great deal, I think," said the master; "what brought island-fagging to an end?"

"Why, the Easter Speeches were put off till Mid-summer," said Tom, "and the sixth had the gymnastic poles put up here."

"Well, and who changed the time of the Speeches, and put the idea of gymnastic poles into the heads of their worships the sixth form?" said the master.

"The Doctor, I suppose," said Tom. "I never thought of that."

"Of course you didn't," said the master, "or else, fag as you were, you would have shouted with the whole school against putting down old customs. And that's the way that all the Doctor's reforms have been carried out when he has been left to himself—quietly and naturally, putting a good thing in the place of a bad, and letting the bad die out; no wavering, and no hurry—the best thing that could be done for the time being, and patience for the rest."

"Just Tom's own way," chimed in Arthur, nudging Tom with his elbow, "driving a nail where it will go;" to which allusion Tom answered by a sly kick.

"Exactly so," said the master, innocent of the allusion and by-play.

Meantime Jack Raggles, with his sleeves tucked up above his great brown elbows, scorning pads and gloves, has presented himself at the wicket; and having run one for a forward drive of Johnson's, is about to receive his first ball. There are only twenty-four runs to make, and four wickets to go down; a winning match if they play decently steady. The ball is a very swift one, and rises fast, catching Jack on the outside of the thigh, and bounding away as if from india-rubber, while they run two for a leg-bye amidst great applause, and shouts from Jack's many admirers. The next ball is a beautifully-pitched ball for the outer stump, which the reckless and unfeeling Jack catches hold of, and hits right round to leg for five, while the applause becomes deafening: only seventeen runs to get with four wickets—the game is all but ours!

It is over now, and Jack walks swaggering about his wicket, with his bat over his shoulder, while Mr. Aislabie holds a short parley with his men. Then the cover-point hitter, that cunning man, goes on to bowl slow twisters. Jack waves his hand triumphantly towards the tent, as much as to say, "See if I don't finish it all off now in three hits."

Alas, my son Jack! the enemy is too old for thee. The first ball of the over Jack steps out and meets, swiping with all his force. If he had only allowed for the twist! but he hasn't, and so the ball goes spinning up straight in the air, as if it would never come down again. Away runs Jack, shouting and trusting to the chapter of accidents, but the bowler runs steadily under it, judging every spin, and calling out "I have it," catches it, and playfully pitches it on to the back of the stalwart Jack, who is departing with a rueful countenance.

"I knew how it would be," says Tom, rising. "Come along, the game's getting very serious."

So they leave the island and go to the tent, and after deep consultation Arthur is sent in, and goes off to the wicket with a last exhortation from Tom to play steady and keep his bat straight. To the suggestions that Winter is the best bat left, Tom only replies, "Arthur is the steadiest, and Johnson will make the runs if the wicket is only kept up."

"I am surprised to see Arthur in the eleven," said the master, as they stood together in front of the dense crowd, which was now closing in round the ground.

"Well, I'm not quite sure that he ought to be in for his play," said Tom, "but I couldn't help putting him in. It will do him so much good, and you can't think what I owe him."

The master smiled. The clock strikes eight, and the whole field becomes fevered with excitement. Arthur, after two narrow escapes, scores one; and Johnson gets the ball. The bowling and fielding are superb, and Johnson's batting worthy the occasion. He makes here a two, and there a one, managing to keep the ball to himself, and Arthur backs up and runs perfectly: only eleven runs to make now, and the crowd scarcely breathe. At last Arthur gets the ball again, and actually drives it forward for two, and feels prouder than when he got the three best prizes, at hearing Tom's shout of joy, "Well played, well played, young un!"

But the next ball is too much for the young hand, and his bails fly different ways. Nine runs to make, and two wickets to go down—it is too much for human nerves.

Before Winter can get in, the omnibus which is to take the Lords' men to the train pulls up at the side of the close, and Mr. Aislabie and Tom consult, and give out that the stumps will be drawn after the next over. And so ends the great match. Winter and Johnson carry out their bats, and, it being a one day's match, the Lords' men are declared the winners, they having scored the most in the first innings.

But such a defeat is a victory: so think Tom and all the School eleven, as they accompany their conquerors to the omnibus, and send them off with three ringing cheers, after Mr. Aislabie has shaken hands all round, saying to Tom, "I must compliment you, sir, on your eleven, and I hope we shall have you for a member if you come up to town."

As Tom and the rest of the eleven were turning back into the close, and everybody was beginning to cry out for another country-dance, encouraged by the success of the night before, the young master, who was just leaving the close, stopped him, and asked him to come up to tea at half-past eight, adding, "I won't keep you more than half an hour, and ask Arthur to come up too."

"I'll come up with you directly, if you'll let me," said Tom, "for I feel rather melancholy, and not quite up to the country-dance and supper with the rest!"

"Do, by all means," said the master; "I'll wait here for you."

So Tom went off to get his boots and things from the tent, to tell Arthur of the invitation, and to speak to his second in command about stopping the dancing and shutting up the close as soon as it grew dusk. Arthur promised to follow as soon as he had had a dance. So Tom handed his things over to the man in charge of the tent, and walked quietly away to the gate where the master was waiting, and the two took their way together up the Hillmorton road.

Of course they found the master's house locked up, and all the servants away in the close, about this time no doubt footing it away on the grass, with extreme delight to themselves, and in utter oblivion of the unfortunate bachelor their master, whose one enjoyment in the shape of meals was his "dish of tea" (as our grandmothers called it) in the evening; and the phrase was apt in his case, for he always poured his out into the saucer before drinking. Great was the good man's horror at finding himself shut out of his own house. Had he been alone, he would have treated it as a matter of course, and would have strolled contentedly up and down his gravel-walk until some one came home; but he was hurt at the stain on his character of host, especially as the guest was a pupil. However, the guest seemed to think it a great joke, and presently, as they poked about round the house, mounted a wall, from which he could reach a passage window: the window, as it turned out, was not bolted, so in another minute Tom was in the house and down at the front door, which he opened from inside. The master chuckled grimly at this burglarious entry, and insisted on leaving the hall-door and two of the front windows open, to frighten the truants on their return; and then the two set about foraging for tea, in which operation the master was much at fault, having the faintest possible idea of where to find anything, and being moreover wondrously short-sighted; but Tom by a sort of instinct knew the right cupboards in the kitchen and pantry, and soon managed to place on the snuggery table better materials for a meal than had appeared there probably during the reign of his tutor, who was then and there initiated, amongst other things, into the excellence of that mysterious condiment, a dripping-cake. The cake was newly baked, and all rich and flaky; Tom had found it reposing in the cook's private cupboard, awaiting her return; and as a warning to her, they finished it to the last crumb. The kettle sang away merrily on the hob of the snuggery, for, notwithstanding the time of year, they lighted a fire, throwing both the windows wide open at the same time; the heaps of books and papers were pushed away to the other end of the table, and the great solitary engraving of King's College Chapel over the mantelpiece looked less stiff than usual, as they settled themselves down in the twilight to the serious drinking of tea.

After some talk on the match, and other indifferent subjects, the conversation came naturally back to Tom's approaching departure, over which he began again to make his moan.

"Well, we shall all miss you quite as much as you will miss us," said the master. "You are the Nestor of the School now, are you not?"

"Yes, ever since East left," answered Tom.

"By the bye, have you heard from him?"

"Yes, I had a letter in February, just before he started for India to join his regiment."

"He will make a capital officer."

"Ay, won't he!" said Tom, brightening; "no fellow could handle boys better, and I suppose soldiers are very like boys. And he'll never tell them to go where he won't go himself. No mistake about that—a braver fellow never walked."

"His year in the sixth will have taught him a good deal that will be useful to him now."

"So it will," said Tom, staring into the fire. "Poor dear Harry," he went on, "how well I remember the day we were put out of the twenty. How he rose to the situation, and burnt his cigar-cases, and gave away his pistols, and pondered on the constitutional authority of the sixth, and his new duties to the Doctor, and the fifth form, and the fags. Ay, and no fellow ever acted up to them better, though he was always a people's man—for the fags, and against constituted authorities. He couldn't help that, you know. I'm sure the Doctor must have liked him?" said Tom, looking up inquiringly.

"The Doctor sees the good in every one, and appreciates it," said the master, dogmatically; "but I hope East will get a good colonel. He won't do if he can't respect those above him. How long it took him, even here, to learn the lesson of obeying."

"Well, I wish I were alongside of him," said Tom. "If I can't be at Rugby, I want to be at work in the world, and not dawdling away three years at Oxford."

"What do you mean by 'at work in the world'?" said the master, pausing with his lips close to his saucerful of tea, and peering at Tom over it.

"Well, I mean real work; one's profession; whatever one will have really to do, and make one's living by. I want to be doing some real good, feeling that I am not only at play in the world," answered Tom, rather puzzled to find out himself what he really did mean.

"You are mixing up two very different things in your head, I think, Brown," said the master, putting down the empty saucer, "and you ought to get clear about them. You talk of 'working to get your living,' and 'doing some real good in the world,' in the same breath. Now, you may be getting a very good living in a profession, and yet doing no good at all in the world, but quite the contrary, at the same time. Keep the latter before you as your one object, and you will be right, whether you make a living or not; but if you dwell on the other, you'll very likely drop into mere money-making, and let the world take care of itself for good or evil. Don't be in a hurry about finding your work in the world for yourself; you are not old enough to judge for yourself yet, but just look about you in the place you find yourself in, and try to make things a little better and honester there. You'll find plenty to keep your hand in at Oxford, or wherever else you go. And don't be led away to think this part of the world important and that unimportant. Every corner of the world is important. No man knows whether this part or that is most so, but every man may do some honest work in his own corner." And then the good man went on to talk wisely to Tom of the sort of work which he might take up as an undergraduate; and warned him of the prevalent University sins, and explained to him the many and great differences between University and School life; till the twilight changed into darkness, and they heard the truant servants stealing in by the back entrance.

"I wonder where Arthur can be," said Tom at last, looking at his watch; "why, it's nearly half-past nine already."

"Oh, he is comfortably at supper with the eleven, forgetful of his oldest friends," said the master. "Nothing has given me greater pleasure," he went on, "than your friendship for him; it has been the making of you both."

"Of me, at any rate," answered Tom; "I should never have been here now but for him. It was the luckiest chance in the world that sent him to Rugby, and made him my chum."

"Why do you talk of lucky chances?" said the master; "I don't know that there are any such things in the world; at any rate, there was neither luck nor chance in that matter."

Tom looked at him inquiringly, and he went on. "Do you remember when the Doctor lectured you and East at the end of one half-year, when you were in the shell, and had been getting into all sorts of scrapes?"

"Yes, well enough," said Tom, "it was the half-year before Arthur came."

"Exactly so," answered the master. "Now, I was with him a few minutes afterwards, and he was in great distress about you two. And, after some talk, we both agreed that you in particular wanted some object in the school beyond games and mischief; for it was quite clear that you never would make the regular school work your first object. And so the Doctor, at the beginning of the next half-year, looked out the best of the new boys, and separated you and East, and put the young boy into your study, in the hope that when you had somebody to lean on you, you would begin to stand a little steadier yourself, and get manliness and thoughtfulness. And I can assure you he has watched the experiment ever since with great satisfaction. Ah! not one of you boys will ever know the anxiety you have given him, or the care with which he has watched over every step in your school lives."

Up to this time, Tom had never wholly given in to, or understood the Doctor. At first he had thoroughly feared him. For some years, as I have tried to show, he had learnt to regard him with love and respect, and to think him a very great and wise and good man. But, as regarded his own position in the School, of which he was no little proud, Tom had no idea of giving any one credit for it but himself; and, truth to tell, was a very self-conceited young gentleman on the subject. He was wont to boast that he had fought his own way fairly up the School, and had never made up to, or been taken up by any big fellow or master, and that it was now quite a different place from what it was when he first came. And, indeed, though he didn't actually boast of it, yet in his secret soul he did to a great extent believe, that the great reform in the School had been owing quite as much to himself as to any one else. Arthur, he acknowledged, had done him good, and taught him a good deal, so had other boys in different ways, but they had not had the same means of influence on the School in general; and as for the Doctor, why, he was a splendid master, but every one knew that masters could do very little out of school hours. In short, he felt on terms of equality with his chief, so far as the social state of the School was concerned, and thought that the Doctor would find it no easy matter to get on without him. Moreover, his School Toryism was still strong, and he looked still with some jealousy on the Doctor, as somewhat of a fanatic in the matter of change; and thought it very desirable for the School that he should have some wise person (such as himself) to look sharply after vested School-rights, and see that nothing was done to the injury of the republic without due protest.

It was a new light to him to find, that, besides teaching the sixth, and governing and guiding the whole School, editing classics, and writing histories, the great Headmaster had found time in those busy years to watch over the career, even of him, Tom Brown, and his particular friends,—and, no doubt, of fifty other boys at the same time; and all this without taking the least credit to himself, or seeming to know, or let any one else know, that he ever thought particularly of any boy at all.

However, the Doctor's victory was complete from that moment over Tom Brown at any rate. He gave way at all points, and the enemy marched right over him, cavalry, infantry, and artillery, and the land transport corps, and the camp followers. It had taken eight long years to do it, but now it was done thoroughly, and there wasn't a corner of him left which didn't believe in the Doctor. Had he returned to School again, and the Doctor begun the half-year by abolishing fagging, and football, and the Saturday half-holiday, or all or any of the most cherished School institutions, Tom would have supported him with the blindest faith. And so, after a half confession of his previous shortcomings, and sorrowful adieus to his tutor, from whom he received two beautifully bound volumes of the Doctor's Sermons, as a parting present, he marched down to the School-house, a hero-worshipper, who would have satisfied the soul of Thomas Carlyle himself.

There he found the eleven at high jinks after supper, Jack Raggles shouting comic songs, and performing feats of strength; and was greeted by a chorus of mingled remonstrance at his desertion, and joy at his reappearance. And falling in with the humour of the evening, he was soon as great a boy as all the rest; and at ten o'clock was chaired round the quadrangle, on one of the hall benches borne aloft by the eleven, shouting in chorus, "For he's a jolly good fellow," while old Thomas, in a melting mood, and the other School-house servants, stood looking on.

And the next morning after breakfast he squared up all the cricketing accounts, went round to his tradesmen and other acquaintance, and said his hearty good-byes; and by twelve o'clock was in the train, and away for London, no longer a school-boy, and divided in his thoughts between hero-worship, honest regrets over the long stage of his life which was now slipping out of sight behind him, and hopes and resolves for the next stage upon which he was entering with all the confidence of a young traveller.

CHAPTER IX

FINIS

"Strange friend, past, present, and to be;
Loved deeplier, darklier understood;
Behold, I dream a dream of good,
And mingle all the world with thee."
TENNYSON

IN THE SUMMER OF 1842, our hero stopped once again at the well-known station; and, leaving his bag and fishing-rod with a porter, walked slowly and sadly up towards the town. It was now July. He had rushed away from Oxford the moment that term was over, for a fishing ramble in Scotland with two college friends, and had been for three weeks living on oatcake, mutton-hams, and whiskey, in the wildest parts of Skye. They had descended one sultry evening on the little inn at Kyle Rhea ferry; and while Tom and another of the party put their tackle together and began exploring the stream for a sea-trout for supper, the third strolled into the house to arrange for their entertainment. Presently he came out in a loose blouse and slippers, a short pipe in his mouth, and an old newspaper in his hand, and threw himself on the heathery scrub which met the shingle, within easy hail of the fishermen. There he lay, the picture of free-and-easy, loafing, hand-to-mouth young England, "improving his mind," as he shouted to them, by the perusal of the fortnight-old weekly paper, soiled with the marks of toddy-glasses and tobacco-ashes, the legacy of the last traveller, which he had hunted out from the kitchen of the little hostelry, and, being a youth of a communicative turn of mind, began imparting the contents to the fishermen as he went on.

"What a bother they are making about these wretched Corn-laws; here's three or four columns full of nothing but sliding-scales and fixed duties—Hang this tobacco, it's always going out!—Ah, here's something better—a splendid match between Kent and England, Brown! Kent winning by three wickets. Felix fifty-six runs without a chance, and not out!"

Tom, intent on a fish which had risen at him twice, answered only with a grunt.

"Anything about the Goodwood?" called out the third man.

"Rory O'More drawn. Butterfly colt amiss," shouted the student.

"Just my luck," grumbled the inquirer, jerking his flies off the water, and throwing again with a heavy sullen splash, and frightening Tom's fish.

"I say, can't you throw lighter over there? we ain 't fishing for grampuses," shouted Tom across the stream.

"Hullo, Brown! here's something for you," called out the reading man next moment. "Why, your old master, Arnold of Rugby, is dead."

Tom's hand stopped half-way in his cast, and his line and flies went all tangling round and round his rod; you might have knocked him over with a feather. Neither of his companions took any notice of him, luckily; and with a violent effort he set to work mechanically to disentangle his line. He felt completely carried off his moral and intellectual legs, as if he had lost his standing-point in the invisible world. Besides which, the deep loving loyalty which he felt for his old leader made the shock intensely painful. It was the first great wrench of his life, the first gap which the angel Death had made in his circle, and he felt numbed, and beaten down, and spiritless. Well, well! I believe it was good for him and for many others in like case; who had to learn by that loss, that the soul of man cannot stand or lean upon any human prop, however strong, and wise, and good; but that He upon whom alone it can stand and lean will knock away all such props in His own wise and merciful way, until there is no ground or stay left but Himself, the Rock of Ages, upon whom alone a sure foundation for every soul of man is laid.

As he wearily laboured at his line, the thought struck him, "It may be all false, a mere newspaper lie," and he strode up to the recumbent smoker.

"Let me look at the paper," said he.

"Nothing else in it," answered the other, handing it up to him listlessly. "Hullo, Brown! what's the matter, old fellow—ain't you well?"

"Where is it?" said Tom, turning over the leaves, his hands trembling, and his eyes swimming, so that he could not read.

"What? What are you looking for?" said his friend, jumping up and looking over his shoulder.

"That—about Arnold," said Tom.

"Oh, here," said the other, putting his finger on the paragraph. Tom read it over and over again; there could be no mistake of identity, though the account was short enough.

"Thank you," said he at last, dropping the paper. "I shall go for a walk: don't you and

Herbert wait supper for me." And away he strode, up over the moor at the back of the house, to be alone, and master his grief if possible.

His friend looked after him, sympathizing and wondering, and, knocking the ashes out of his pipe, walked over to Herbert. After a short parley, they walked together up to the house.

"I'm afraid that confounded newspaper has spoiled Brown's fun for this trip."

"How odd that he should be so fond of his old master," said Herbert. Yet they also were both public-school men.

The two, however, notwithstanding Tom's prohibition, waited supper for him, and had everything ready when he came back some half an hour afterwards. But he could not join in their cheerful talk, and the party was soon silent, notwithstanding the efforts of all three. One thing only had Tom resolved, and that was, that he couldn't stay in Scotland any longer; he felt an irresistible longing to get to Rugby, and then home, and soon broke it to the others, who had too much tact to oppose.

So by daylight the next morning he was marching through Ross-shire, and in the evening hit the Caledonian canal, took the next steamer, and travelled as fast as boat and railway could carry him to the Rugby station.

As he walked up to the town, he felt shy and afraid of being seen, and took the back streets; why, he didn't know, but he followed his instinct. At the School-gates he made a dead pause; there was not a soul in the quadrangle—all was lonely, and silent, and sad. So with another effort he strode through the quadrangle, and into the School-house offices.

He found the little matron in her room in deep mourning; shook her hand, tried to talk, and moved nervously about; she was evidently thinking of the same subject as he, but he couldn't begin talking.

"Where shall I find Thomas?" said he at last, getting desperate.

"In the servants' hall, I think, sir. But won't you take anything?" said the matron, looking rather disappointed.

"No, thank you," said he, and strode off again to find the old Verger, who was sitting in his little den as of old puzzling over hieroglyphics.

He looked up through his spectacles, as Tom seized his hand and wrung it.

"Ah! you've heard all about it, sir, I see," said he.

Tom nodded, and then sat down on the shoe-board, while the old man told his tale, and wiped his spectacles, and fairly flowed over with quaint, homely, honest sorrow.

By the time he had done, Tom felt much better.

"Where is he buried, Thomas?" said he at last.

"Under the altar in the chapel, sir," answered Thomas. "You'd like to have the key, I dare say."

"Thank you, Thomas—yes, I should very much." And the old man fumbled among his bunch, and then got up, as though he would go with him; but after a few steps stopped short, and said, "Perhaps you'd like to go by yourself, sir?"

Tom nodded, and the bunch of keys were handed to him, with an injunction to be sure and lock the door after him, and bring them back before eight o'clock.

He walked quickly through the quadrangle and out into the close. The longing which had been upon him and driven him thus far, like the gad-fly in the Greek legends, giving him no rest in mind or body, seemed all of a sudden not to be satisfied, but to shrivel up, and pall. "Why should I go on? It's no use," he thought, and threw himself at full length on the turf, and looked vaguely and listlessly at all the well-known objects. There were a few of the town boys playing cricket, their wicket pitched on the best piece in the middle of the big-side ground, a sin about equal to sacrilege in the eyes of a captain of the eleven. He was very nearly getting up to go and send them off. "Pshaw! they won't remember me. They've more right there than I," he muttered. And the thought that his sceptre had departed, and his mark was wearing out, came home to him for the first time, and bitterly enough. He was lying on the very spot where the fights came off; where he himself had fought six years ago his first and last battle. He conjured up the scene till he could almost hear the shouts of the ring, and East's whisper in his ear; and looking across the close to the Doctor's private door, half expected to see it open, and the tall figure in cap and gown come striding under the elm-trees towards him.

No, no! that sight could never be seen again. There was no flag flying on the round tower; the School-house windows were all shuttered up; and when the flag went up again, and the shutters came down, it would be to welcome a stranger. All that was left on earth of him whom he had honoured, was lying cold and still under the chapel floor. He would go in and see the place once more, and then leave it once for all. New men and new methods might do for other people; let those who would, worship the rising star; he at least would be faithful to the sun which had set. And so he got up, and walked to the chapel-door and unlocked it, fancying himself the only mourner in all the broad land, and feeding on his own selfish sorrow.

He passed through the vestibule, and then paused for a moment to glance over the empty benches. His heart was still proud and high, and he walked up to the seat which he had last occupied as a sixth-form boy, and sat himself down there to collect his thoughts.

And, truth to tell, they needed collecting and setting in order not a little. The memories of eight years were all dancing through his brain, and carrying him about whither they would; while, beneath them all, his heart was throbbing with the dull sense of a loss that could never be made up to him. The rays of the evening sun came solemnly through the painted windows above his head, and fell in gorgeous colours on the opposite wall, and the perfect stillness soothed his spirit by little and little. And he turned to the pulpit, and looked at it, and then, leaning forward with his head on his hands, groaned aloud. "If he could only have seen the Doctor again for one five minutes,—have told him all that was in his heart, what he owed to him, how he loved and reverenced him, and would by God's help follow his steps in life and death,—he could have borne it all without a murmur. But that he should have gone away for ever without knowing it all, was too much to bear."——"But am I sure that he does not know it all?"—the thought made him start—"May he not even now be near me, in this very chapel? If he be, am I sorrowing as he would have me sorrow—as I should wish to have sorrowed when I shall meet him again?"

He raised himself up and looked round; and after a minute rose and walked humbly down to the lowest bench, and sat down on the very seat which he had occupied on his first Sunday at Rugby. And then the old memories rushed back again, but softened and subdued, and soothing him as he let himself be carried away by them. And he looked up at the great painted window above the altar, and remembered how when a little boy he

used to try not to look through it at the elm-trees and the rooks, before the painted glass came—and the subscription for the painted glass, and the letter he wrote home for money to give to it. And there, down below, was the very name of the boy who sat on his right hand on that first day, scratched rudely in the oak panelling.

And then came the thought of all his old school-fellows; and form after form of boys, nobler, and braver, and purer than he, rose up and seemed to rebuke him. Could he not think of them, and what they had felt and were feeling, they who had honoured and loved from the first, the man whom he had taken years to know and love? Could he not think of those yet dearer to him who was gone, who bore his name and shared his blood, and were now without a husband or a father? Then the grief which he began to share with others became gentle and holy, and he rose up once more, and walked up the steps to the altar; and while the tears flowed freely down his cheeks, knelt down humbly and hopefully, to lay down there his share of a burden which had proved itself too heavy for him to bear in his own strength.

Here let us leave him—where better could we leave him, than at the altar, before which he had first caught a glimpse of the glory of his birthright, and felt the drawing of the bond which links all living souls together in one brotherhood—at the grave beneath the altar of him who had opened his eyes to see that glory, and softened his heart till it could feel that bond?

And let us not be hard on him, if at that moment his soul is fuller of the tomb and him who lies there, than of the altar and Him of whom it speaks. Such stages have to be gone through, I believe, by all young and brave souls, who must win their way through hero-worship, to the worship of Him who is the King and Lord of heroes. For it is only through our mysterious human relationships,—through the love and tenderness and purity of mothers, and sisters, and wives,—through the strength and courage and wisdom of fathers, and brothers, and teachers,—that we can come to the knowledge of Him, in whom alone the love, and the tenderness, and the purity, and the strength, and the courage, and the wisdom of all these dwell for ever and ever in perfect fulness.

THE END